Oxford Elementary Learner's Dictionary

SECOND EDITION

Edited by Angela Crawley

Phonetics Editor
Michael Ashby

DOMINVS ILLVMINATIO MEA

Oxford University Press

OXFORD
UNIVERSITY PRESS

Great Clarendon Street, Oxford OX2 6DP

Oxford University Press is a department of the University of
Oxford. It furthers the University's objective of excellence in
research, scholarship, and education by publishing worldwide in

Oxford New York

Athens Auckland Bangkok Bogotá Buenos Aires
Cape Town Chennai Dar es Salaam Delhi Florence
Hong Kong Istanbul Karachi Kolkata Kuala Lumpur Madrid
Melbourne Mexico City Mumbai Nairobi Paris São Paulo
Shanghai Singapore Taipei Tokyo Toronto Warsaw

with associated companies in Berlin Ibadan

Oxford is a registered trade mark of Oxford University Press
in the UK and in certain other countries

© Oxford University Press, 1994
First published 1994
Thirteenth impression 2001

ISBN 0 19 431275 5

Acknowledgements
Editorial team
Editor: Angela Crawley

Assistant Editor: Felicity Brooks

Phonetics Editor: Michael Ashby

Compilers: Evadne Adrian-Vallance
Alice Deignan, Gary Dexter
Fiona MacKenzie

Designers
Herb Bowes, Phil Hall

Illustrators
Anna Brookes, Martin Cox, Angelika Elsebach, Gay Galsworthy, Hardlines, Margaret Heath, Richard Lewington, Vanessa Luff,
Coral Mula, Oxford Illustrators, Martin Shovel, Harry Venning, Margaret Wellbank, Michael Woods

We would like to thank the large team who made the production of this dictionary possible once the text was complete.
Thanks are also due to all the teachers and students who contributed comments and advice
at various stages throughout the project

Typeset in Great Britain by Tradespools Ltd, Frome, Somerset
Printed in China

Contents

DICTIONARY QUIZ

This quiz shows how the **Oxford Elementary Learner's Dictionary** can help you. You will find the answers to all these questions in the dictionary.

---

1 On which part of your body do you wear **wellingtons**?

2 When is **Boxing Day**?

Meanings
The dictionary explains the meanings of words in simple language. The example sentences also help you to understand words and use them correctly. For more about this, look at page 264.

---

3 What is a young **goat** called?

4 What is the opposite of **wide**?

5 *I bought this book in the library.*
In this sentence, the word **library** is wrong. What is the right word?

Vocabulary
There are many notes (shown by ☻) that give useful extra vocabulary or show the differences between words.

The dictionary has a lot of pictures that help you understand words and that give extra vocabulary. As well as the pictures in the main part of the dictionary, there are special pages (with blue edges) that have pictures showing things like The Human Body and Shapes and Sizes.

6 What is the name of the thick part of a **tree**, that grows up from the ground?

7 What is the name of this shape?

8 Is the word **lung** a noun, a verb or an adjective?

Grammar

You can check if a new word is a noun, a verb, an adjective, etc by looking in the dictionary.

9 Is it correct to say: Can you give me some **information**s?

The dictionary tells you about nouns. For example, it gives irregular and difficult noun plurals and tells you if a word cannot be used in the plural.

10 What is the past tense of the verb **break**?

The important verb forms are listed for each verb, and there is a list of irregular verbs with their past tenses and past participles on page 421.

11 What is the *-ing* form of the verb **hit**?

Spelling

You can use the dictionary to check how to spell a word, and it also shows small changes in the spelling of other forms of the word, for example the plurals of nouns and the *-ing* forms of verbs.

12 How do you spell the plural of **party**?

13 Do the words **peace** and **piece** have the same sound?

Pronunciation

The dictionary gives the pronunciation of words, and at the bottom of every page and on page 428 you will find help with reading the symbols.

14 How do you <u>say</u> this **date**: 4 July 2010?

Extra information

The special pages (with blue edges) also give useful information on topics like Dates, Numbers and Time.

15 What is the word for a person who comes from **Germany**?

At the back of the dictionary there is a list of geographical names.

Answers

1 your feet 2 26 December 3 a kid 4 narrow 5 bookshop 6 the trunk 7 a cylinder 8 a noun 9 No. ('The word 'information' does not have a plural form.) 10 broke 11 hitting 12 parties 13 yes 14 the fourth of July (or July the fourth), two thousand and ten 15 a German

Aa

a /ə/, /eɪ/ *article*
1 one or any: *Would you like a drink?* ◇ *A dog has four legs.* ◇ *He's a teacher.*
2 each, or for each: *She phones her mother three times a week.* ◇ *This wine costs £4 a bottle.*

---

a or an?

Before a word that starts with the sound of a, e, i, o or u, you use **an**, not **a**. Be careful! It is the sound that is important, not the spelling:

a box	**an** apple
a singer	**an** hour
a university	**an** MP

---

abandon /ə'bændən/ *verb* (**abandons, abandoning, abandoned** /ə'bændənd/)
1 leave somebody or something completely: *He abandoned his car in the snow.*
2 stop doing something before it is finished: *When the rain started, we abandoned our game.*

abbey /'æbi/ *noun* (*plural* **abbeys**)
a building where religious men or women (called **monks** and **nuns**) live or lived

abbreviate /ə'briːvieɪt/ *verb* (**abbreviates, abbreviating, abbreviated**)
make a word shorter by not saying or writing some of the letters: *The word 'telephone' is often abbreviated to 'phone'.*
abbreviation /ə'briːvieɪʃn/ *noun*
a short form of a word: *TV is an abbreviation for 'television'.*

ability /ə'bɪləti/ *noun* (*plural* **abilities**)
the power and knowledge to do something: *She has the ability to pass the exam, but she must work harder.*

able /'eɪbl/ *adjective*
be able to have the power and knowledge to do something: *Will you be able to come to the party?* ◇ *Is Simon able to swim?* ☞ Look at **can**.

aboard /ə'bɔːd/ *adverb, preposition*
on or onto a ship, train, bus or an aeroplane: *Are all the passengers aboard the ship?* ◇ *We went aboard the plane.*

abolish /ə'bɒlɪʃ/ *verb* (**abolishes, abolishing, abolished** /ə'bɒlɪʃt/)
stop or end something by law: *The Americans abolished slavery in 1863.*
abolition /ˌæbə'lɪʃn/ *noun* (no plural)
the abolition of hunting

about /ə'baʊt/ *preposition, adverb*
1 a little more or less than; a little before or after: *She's about 50 years old.* ◇ *I arrived at about two o'clock.*
2 of; on the subject of: *a book about cats* ◇ *We talked about the problem.* ◇ *What are you thinking about?*
3 in or to different places or in different directions: *The children were running about in the garden.* ◇ *There were books lying about on the floor.*
4 almost: *Dinner is about ready.*
5 in a place; here: *Is your mother about? I want to speak to her.*
be about to be going to do something very soon: *The film is about to start.*

above /ə'bʌv/ *preposition, adverb*
1 in or to a higher place; higher than somebody or something: *I looked up at the sky above.* ◇ *My bedroom is above the kitchen.* ◇ *There is a picture on the wall above the fireplace.* ☞ picture on page 125
2 more than a number or price: *children aged ten and above*
above all more than any other thing; what is most important: *He's handsome and intelligent and, above all, he's kind!*

abroad /ə'brɔːd/ *adverb*
in or to another country: *Are you going abroad this summer?* ◇ *She lives abroad.*

absence /'æbsəns/ *noun* (no plural)
a time when a person or thing is not there: *I am doing Julie's job in her absence.*

absent /'æbsənt/ *adjective*
not there; away: *He was absent from work yesterday because he was ill.*

absolute /'æbsəluːt/ *adjective*
complete: *I've never played chess before. I'm an absolute beginner.*
absolutely *adverb*
completely: *You're absolutely right.*

---

absorb /əb'sɔːb/ *verb* (**absorbs, absorbing, absorbed** /əb'sɔːbd/)
take in something like liquid or heat, and hold it: *The dry ground absorbed all the rain.*

abstract /'æbstrækt/ *adjective*
1 about an idea, not a real thing: *abstract thought*
2 not like a real thing: *an abstract painting*

absurd /əb'sɜːd/ *adjective*
so silly that it makes you laugh: *You look absurd in that hat!* ◇ *Don't be absurd! Of course I can't learn Japanese in three days!*

abuse /ə'bjuːz/ *verb* (**abuses, abusing, abused** /ə'bjuːzd/)
1 use something in a wrong or bad way: *The manager often abuses her power.*
2 be cruel or unkind to somebody: *The children were abused by their father.*
3 say rude things to somebody

abuse /ə'bjuːs/ *noun* (no plural)
1 using something in a wrong or bad way: *drug abuse*
2 being cruel or unkind to somebody: *child abuse*
3 rude words: *The lorry driver shouted abuse at the cyclist.*

accent /'æksent/ *noun*
1 the way a person from a certain place or country speaks a language: *She speaks English with an American accent.*
2 saying one word or part of a word more strongly than another: *In the word 'because', the accent is on the second part of the word.*

accept /ək'sept/ *verb* (**accepts, accepting, accepted**)
1 say 'yes' when somebody asks you to have or do something: *I accepted the invitation to his party.* ◇ *Please accept this present.*
2 believe that something is true: *She can't accept that her son is dead.*

acceptable /ək'septəbl/ *adjective*
allowed by most people; good enough: *It's not acceptable to make so many mistakes.*

access /'ækses/ *noun* (no plural)
a way to go into a place or to use something: *We don't have access to the garden from our flat.* ◇ *Do you have access to a computer at home?*

accident /'æksɪdənt/ *noun*
something, often bad, that happens by chance: *I had an accident when I was driving to work – my car hit a tree.* ◇ *I'm sorry I broke your watch – it was an accident.*

by accident by chance; not because you have planned it: *I took Jane's book by accident. I thought it was mine.*

accidental /ˌæksɪ'dentl/ *adjective*
If something is accidental, it happens by chance: *accidental death*

accidentally /ˌæksɪ'dentəli/ *adverb*
He accidentally broke the window.

accommodation /əˌkɒmə'deɪʃn/ *noun* (no plural)
a place to stay or live: *It's difficult to find cheap accommodation in London.*

accompany /ə'kʌmpəni/ *verb* (**accompanies, accompanying, accompanied** /ə'kʌmpənid/)
1 go with somebody to a place: *Four teachers accompanied the class on their skiing holiday.*
2 happen at the same time as something else: *Thunder is usually accompanied by lightning.*
3 play music while somebody sings or plays another instrument: *You sing and I'll accompany you on the guitar.*

accord /ə'kɔːd/ *noun* (no plural)
of your own accord because you want to, not because somebody has asked you: *She left the job of her own accord.*

according to /ə'kɔːdɪŋ tə/ *preposition*
as somebody or something says: *According to Mike, this film is really good.* ◇ *The church was built in 1395, according to this book.*

account /ə'kaʊnt/ *noun*
1 words that somebody says or writes about something that happened: *He gave the police an account of the car accident.*
2 an amount of money that you keep in a bank: *I paid the money into my bank account.*
3 accounts (plural) lists of all the money that a person or business receives and pays: *Who keeps (= does) the accounts for your business?*

on no account, not on any account not for any reason: *On no account must you open this door.*

take account of something, take something into account remember something when you are thinking about other things: *John is always last, but you must take his age into account — he is much younger than the other children.*

accountant /ə'kaʊntənt/ *noun*
a person whose job is to make lists of all the money that people or businesses receive and pay: *Kitty is an accountant.*

accurate /'ækjərət/ *adjective*
exactly right, with no mistakes: *He gave an accurate description of the thief.* ✪ opposite: **inaccurate**
accurately *adverb*
The map was accurately drawn.

accuse /ə'kju:z/ *verb* (**accuses, accusing, accused** /ə'kju:zd/)
say that somebody has done something wrong: *The police accused the woman of stealing.* ◇ *He was accused of murder.*
accusation /,ækju'zeɪʃn/ *noun*
The accusations were not true.

ace /eɪs/ *noun*
a playing-card which has only one shape on it: *the ace of hearts*

ache /eɪk/ *verb* (**aches, aching, ached** /eɪkt/)
give you pain: *My legs ached after the long walk.*
ache *noun*
a pain that lasts for a long time: *I've got a headache.* ◇ *She's got toothache.* ◇ *stomach-ache* ◇ *earache*

achieve /ə'tʃi:v/ *verb* (**achieves, achieving, achieved** /ə'tʃi:vd/)
do or finish something well after trying hard: *He worked hard and achieved his aim of becoming a doctor.*
achievement /ə'tʃi:vmənt/ *noun*
something that somebody has done after trying hard: *Climbing Mount Everest was his greatest achievement.*

acid /'æsɪd/ *noun*
a liquid that can burn things
acid rain /,æsɪd 'reɪn/ *noun* (no plural)
rain that has chemicals in it from factories, for example. It can damage trees, rivers and buildings.

acknowledge /ək'nɒlɪdʒ/ *verb* (**acknowledges, acknowledging, acknowledged** /ək'nɒlɪdʒd/)
1 agree that something is true: *He acknowledged that he had made a mistake.*
2 say or write that you have received something: *She never acknowledged my letter.*

acorn /'eɪkɔ:n/ *noun*
a small nut that is the fruit of an oak tree

acquaintance /ə'kweɪntəns/ *noun*
a person that you know a little

acquire /ə'kwaɪə(r)/ *verb* (**acquires, acquiring, acquired** /ə'kwaɪəd/)
get or buy something: *He acquired some English from listening to pop songs.*

acre /'eɪkə(r)/ *noun*
a measure of land (= 0.405 of a hectare): *a farm of 40 acres*

acrobat /'ækrəbæt/ *noun*
a person who does difficult movements of the body, for example in a **circus**

across /ə'krɒs/ *adverb, preposition*
1 from one side to the other side of something: *We walked across the field.* ☞ picture on page 128
2 on the other side of something: *There is a bank across the road.*
3 from side to side: *The river is two kilometres across.*

act¹ /ækt/ *verb* (**acts, acting, acted**)
1 do something, or behave in a certain way: *Doctors acted quickly to save the boy's life after the accident.* ◇ *Stop acting like a child!*
2 pretend to be somebody else in a play, film or television programme
act as something do the job of another person, usually for a short time: *He acted as manager while his boss was ill.*

act² /ækt/ *noun*
1 something that you do: *an act of kindness*
2 one part of a play: *This play has five acts.*
3 a law that a government makes
in the act of while doing something wrong: *I caught him in the act of stealing the money.*

acting /'æktɪŋ/ *noun* (no plural)
being in plays or films: *Have you ever done any acting?*

action /'ækʃn/ *noun*
1 (no plural) doing things: *Now is the time for action!* ◇ *I like films with a lot of action in them.*
2 (*plural* **actions**) something that you do: *The little girl copied her mother's actions.*
in action doing something; working: *We watched the machine in action.*

p	b	t	d	k	g	tʃ	dʒ	f	v	θ	ð
pen	bad	tea	did	cat	got	chain	jam	fall	van	thin	this

active /'æktɪv/ *adjective*
If you are active, you are always busy and able to do a lot of things: *My grandmother is 75 but she's still very active.*
in the active where the person or thing doing the action is the subject of a sentence or verb: *In the sentence 'A girl broke the window', the verb is in the active.*
✪ opposite: **passive**

activity /æk'tɪvəti/ *noun*
1 (no plural) a lot of things happening and people doing things: *On the day of the festival there was a lot of activity in the streets.*
2 (*plural* **activities**) something that you do: *Watching TV is one of his favourite activities.*

actor /'æktə(r)/ *noun*
a person who acts in plays, films or television programmes

actress /'æktrəs/ *noun* (*plural* **actresses**)
a woman who acts in plays, films or television programmes

actual /'æktʃuəl/ *adjective*
that really happened; real: *He said the price of the holiday would be £300, but the actual cost was more.*

actually /'æktʃuəli/ *adverb*
1 really; in fact: *We thought it was going to rain, but actually it was sunny all day.*
2 a word that you use to disagree politely or when you say something new: *'Let's go by bus.' 'Actually, I think it would be quicker to go by train.'* ◇ *I don't agree. I thought the film was very good, actually.*

ad /æd/ *short for* **advertisement**

AD /ˌeɪ 'diː/
'AD' in a date shows that it was after Christ was born: *AD 1066* ☞ Look at **BC**.

adapt /ə'dæpt/ *verb* (**adapts, adapting, adapted**)
1 change the way that you do things because you are in a new situation: *He has adapted very well to being at a new school.*
2 change something so that you can use it in a different way: *The car was adapted for use as a taxi.*

add /æd/ *verb* (**adds, adding, added**)
1 put something with something else: *Mix the flour with the milk and then add the eggs.* ◇ *Add your name to the list.*
2 put numbers together: *If you add 2 and*

5 *together, you get 7.* ✪ opposite: **subtract**
3 say something more: *'Go away – and don't come back again,' she added.*

addict /'ædɪkt/ *noun*
a person who cannot stop wanting something that is very bad for him/her: *a drug addict*

addicted /ə'dɪktɪd/ *adjective*
not able to stop wanting something that is bad for you: *He is addicted to heroin.*

addition /ə'dɪʃn/ *noun*
1 (no plural) putting numbers together: *We learnt addition and subtraction at primary school.*
2 (*plural* **additions**) a thing or person that you add to other things or people: *They have a new addition to their family (= a new baby).*
in addition also: *She plays the guitar, and in addition she writes her own songs.*
in addition to something as well as something: *He speaks five languages in addition to English.*

address /ə'dres/ *noun* (*plural* **addresses**)
the number of the house and the name of the street and town where somebody lives or works: *My address is 18 Wilton Street, London NW10.* ◇ *Are you still living at that address?* ☞ picture on page 299
address *verb* (**addresses, addressing, addressed** /ə'drest/)
write on a letter or parcel the name and address of the person you are sending it to: *The letter was addressed to James Philips.*

adequate /'ædɪkwət/ *adjective*
enough for what you need: *They are very poor and do not have adequate food or clothing.* ✪ opposite: **inadequate**

adjective /'ædʒɪktɪv/ *noun*
a word that you use with a noun, that tells you more about it: *In the sentence 'This soup is hot', 'hot' is an adjective.*

adjust /ə'dʒʌst/ *verb* (**adjusts, adjusting, adjusted**)
make a small change to something, to make it better: *You can adjust the height of this chair.*

administration /əd,mɪnɪ'streɪʃn/ *noun* (no plural)
controlling or managing something, for example a business, an office or a school

s	z	ʃ	ʒ	h	m	n	ŋ	l	r	j	w
so	**zoo**	**shoe**	**vision**	**hat**	**man**	**no**	**sing**	**leg**	**red**	**yes**	**wet**

admiral /'ædmərəl/ *noun*
a very important officer in the navy

admire /əd'maɪə(r)/ *verb* (**admires, admiring, admired** /əd'maɪəd/)
think or say that somebody or something is very good: *I really admire you for doing such a difficult job.* ◇ *They were admiring the view from the top of the tower.*
admiration /ˌædmə'reɪʃn/ *noun* (no plural)
I have great admiration for her work.

admission /əd'mɪʃn/ *noun* (no plural)
1 letting somebody go into a place: *There is no admission to the park after 8 p.m.*
2 the money that you pay to go into a place: *Admission to the zoo is £4.*

admit /əd'mɪt/ *verb* (**admits, admitting, admitted**)
1 say that you have done something wrong: *He admitted stealing the money.* ◇ *I admit that I made a mistake.* ◌ opposite: **deny**
2 let somebody or something go into a place: *This ticket admits one person to the museum.*

adopt /ə'dɒpt/ *verb* (**adopts, adopting, adopted**)
take the child of another person into your family to become your own child: *They adopted Stephen after his parents died.*

adore /ə'dɔː(r)/ *verb* (**adores, adoring, adored** /ə'dɔːd/)
love somebody or something very much: *She adores her grandchildren.*

adult /'ædʌlt/ *noun*
a person or an animal that has grown to the full size; not a child: *Adults as well as children will enjoy this film.*
adult *adjective*
an adult ticket

advance /əd'vɑːns/ *noun* (no plural)
in advance before something happens: *We paid for the tickets in advance.*

advanced /əd'vɑːnst/ *adjective*
of or for somebody who is already good at something; difficult: *an advanced English class*

advantage /əd'vɑːntɪdʒ/ *noun*
something that helps you or that is useful: *When you're travelling in South America,*
it's a great advantage if you speak Spanish. ◇ *One advantage of camping is that it's cheap.* ◌ opposite: **disadvantage**
take advantage of something use something to help yourself: *Buy now and take advantage of these special prices!*

adventure /əd'ventʃə(r)/ *noun*
something exciting that you do or that happens to you: *She wrote a book about her adventures in Africa.*

adventurous /əd'ventʃərəs/ *adjective*
An adventurous person likes to do exciting, dangerous things.

adverb /'ædvɜːb/ *noun*
a word that tells you how, when or where something happens: *In the sentence 'Please speak slowly', 'slowly' is an adverb.*

advertise /'ædvətaɪz/ *verb* (**advertises, advertising, advertised** /'ædvətaɪzd/)
give people information on posters, in newspapers or on television about jobs, things to buy or events to go to: *I saw those trainers advertised on TV.* ◇ *We sold our car by advertising it in the newspaper.*

advertisement /əd'vɜːtɪsmənt/ *noun*
information on a poster, in a newspaper or on television that tells you about a job, something to buy or an event to go to: *I saw an advertisement on TV for a new kind of chocolate bar.* ◌ The short form is **advert** /'ædvɜːt/ or **ad**.

advertising /'ædvətaɪzɪŋ/ *noun* (no plural)
telling people about things to buy. *He works in advertising.* ◇ *The magazine gets a lot of money from advertising.*

advice /əd'vaɪs/ *noun* (no plural)
words that you say to help somebody decide what to do: *He will give you advice about where to go.*
take somebody's advice do what somebody says you should do: *I took the doctor's advice and stayed in bed.*
◌ Be careful! You cannot say 'an advice'. You can say 'some advice' or 'a piece of advice': *I need some advice.* ◇ *Let me give you a piece of advice.*

advise /əd'vaɪz/ *verb* (**advises, advising, advised** /əd'vaɪzd/)
tell somebody what you think they should

i:	i	ɪ	e	æ	ɑ:	ɒ	ɔ:	ʊ	u	u:
see	happy	sit	ten	cat	father	got	saw	put	situation	too

do: *The doctor advised him to stop smoking.*

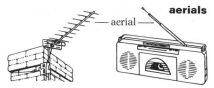

aerials

— aerial —

aerial /ˈeərɪəl/ *noun*
a wire that receives radio or television signals

aeroplane

aeroplane /ˈeərəpleɪn/ *noun*
a machine that has wings and can fly
✪ An aeroplane (or **plane**) **lands** and **takes off** at an **airport**.

aerosol /ˈeərəsɒl/ *noun*
a can with liquid in it. You press a button to make the liquid come out in a lot of very small drops.

affair /əˈfeə(r)/ *noun*
1 something that happens; an event: *The wedding was a very quiet affair.*
2 something that you need to do or think about; business: *Don't worry about that – it's not your affair.* ◇ *foreign affairs*

affect /əˈfekt/ *verb* (**affects, affecting, affected**)
make something different: *Smoking can affect your health.*

affection /əˈfekʃn/ *noun* (no plural)
the feeling of loving or liking somebody: *She has great affection for her aunt.*
affectionate /əˈfekʃənət/ *adjective*
that feels or shows love: *She gave him an affectionate kiss.*
affectionately *adverb*
He smiled at his son affectionately.

afford /əˈfɔːd/ *verb*
can afford something If you can af-

ford something, you have enough money to pay for it: *I can't afford a holiday.*

afraid /əˈfreɪd/ *adjective*
If you are afraid of something, it makes you feel fear: *Some people are afraid of snakes.*
◇ *I was afraid to open the door.*
I'm afraid ... a polite way of saying that you are sorry: *I'm afraid I've broken your calculator.* ◇ *I'm afraid that I can't come to your party.*

after[1] /ˈɑːftə(r)/ *preposition*
1 later than somebody or something: *Jane arrived after dinner.* ◇ *After doing my homework, I went out.*
2 behind or following somebody or something: *Ten comes after nine.* ◇ *Close the door after you.*
3 trying to get or catch somebody or something: *The police officer ran after her.*
after all 1 when you thought something different would happen: *I was worried about the exam, but it wasn't difficult after all.* **2** do not forget: *She doesn't understand. After all, she's only two.*

after[2] /ˈɑːftə(r)/ *conjunction, adverb*
at a time later than somebody or something: *We arrived after the film had started.* ◇ *Jane left at ten o'clock and I left soon after.*

afternoon /ˌɑːftəˈnuːn/ *noun*
the part of a day between midday and the evening: *We had lunch and in the afternoon we went for a walk.* ◇ *I saw Jane this afternoon.* ◇ *Yesterday afternoon I went shopping.* ◇ *I'll see you on Monday afternoon.*

afterwards /ˈɑːftəwədz/ *adverb*
later: *We had dinner and went to see a film afterwards.*

again /əˈgen/ *adverb*
1 one more time; once more: *Could you say that again, please?* ◇ *I will never see him again.*
2 in the way that somebody or something was before: *You'll soon feel well again.*
again and again many times: *I've told you again and again not to do that!*

against /əˈgenst/ *preposition*
1 on the other side in a game, fight, etc: *They played against a football team from another village.*

ʌ	ɜː	ə	eɪ	əʊ	aɪ	aʊ	ɔɪ	ɪə	eə	ʊə
cup	bird	about	say	go	five	now	boy	near	hair	pure

2 If you are against something, you do not like it: *Many people are against the plan.*
3 next to and touching somebody or something: *Put the cupboard against the wall.* ☞ picture on page 125
4 to stop something: *Have you had an injection against the disease?*

age /eɪdʒ/ *noun*
1 (*plural* **ages**) the amount of time that somebody or something has been in the world: *She is seven years of age.* ◇ *I started work at the age of 16.* ☻ When you want to ask about somebody's age, you usually say 'How old are you?'
2 (no plural) being old: *Her hair was grey with age.*
3 (*plural* **ages**) a certain time in history: *the Stone Age* (= when people used stone tools)
4 **ages** (plural) a very long time: *We waited ages for a bus.* ◇ *She's lived here for ages.*

aged /eɪdʒd/ *adjective*
at the age of: *They have two children, aged three and five.*

agency /'eɪdʒənsi/ *noun* (*plural* **agencies**)
the work or office of somebody who does business for others: *A travel agency plans holidays for people.*

agent /'eɪdʒənt/ *noun*
a person who does business for another person or for a company: *An actor's agent tries to find work for actors and actresses.* ◇ *a travel agent.*

aggressive /ə'gresɪv/ *adjective*
If you are aggressive, you are ready to argue or fight: *He often gets aggressive after drinking alcohol.*

ago /ə'gəʊ/ *adverb*
before now; in the past: *His wife died five years ago.* ◇ *I learned to drive a long time ago.*
long ago a very long time in the past: *Long ago there were no cars or aeroplanes.*

agony /'ægəni/ *noun* (*plural* **agonies**)
very great pain: *He screamed in agony.*

agree /ə'griː/ *verb* (**agrees, agreeing, agreed** /ə'griːd/)
1 have the same idea as another person about something: *Martin thinks we*
should go by train but I don't agree. ◇ *I agree with you.* ☻ opposite: **disagree**
2 say 'yes' when somebody asks you to do something: *Amy agreed to pay me.*
3 decide something with another person: *We agreed to meet on March 3rd.* ◇ *Liz and I agreed on a plan.*

agreement /ə'griːmənt/ *noun*
1 (*plural* **agreements**) a plan or decision that two or more people or countries have made together: *There is a trade agreement between the two countries* (= they have agreed to buy things from and sell things to each other).
2 (no plural) having the same ideas as somebody or something: *We talked about which film we wanted to see, but there was not much agreement.* ☻ opposite: **disagreement**

agriculture /'ægrɪkʌltʃə(r)/ *noun* (no plural)
keeping animals and growing plants for food; farming
agricultural /ˌægrɪ'kʌltʃərəl/ *adjective*
agricultural workers

ahead /ə'hed/ *adverb*
1 in front of somebody or something: *We could see a light ahead of us.*
2 into the future: *We must look ahead and make a plan.*
3 doing better than other people: *Fiona is ahead of the other students in her class.*
go ahead do something that you want to do; start to do something: *'Can I borrow your bicycle?' 'Yes, go ahead.'*

aid /eɪd/ *noun* (no plural)
help, or something that gives help: *He walks with the aid of a stick.* ◇ *The government sent aid to the children of Ethiopia.* ◇ *a hearing aid* (= a small thing that you put in your ear so you can hear better)
in aid of somebody or **something** to get money for somebody or something: *There was a concert in aid of the new hospital.*

AIDS /eɪdz/ *noun* (no plural)
a serious illness that stops the body protecting itself against diseases

aim /eɪm/ *verb* (**aims, aiming, aimed** /eɪmd/)
1 point something, for example a gun, at

						tʃ	dʒ	f	v	θ	ð
p	b	t	d	k	g	ch**ain**	**j**am	**f**all	**v**an	**th**in	**th**is
pen	**b**ad	**t**ea	**d**id	**c**at	**g**ot						

somebody or something that you want to hit: *The farmer aimed his gun at the rabbit.*
2 want or plan to do something: *He's aiming to leave at nine o'clock.*
3 plan something for a certain person or group: *This book is aimed at teenagers.*
aim *noun*
something that you want and plan to do: *Kate's aim is to find a good job.*

air /eə(r)/ *noun* (no plural)
1 what you take in through your nose and mouth when you breathe
2 the space around and above things: *He threw the ball up in the air.*
by air in an aircraft: *It's more expensive to travel by air than by train.*

air-conditioning /'eə kən,dıʃnıŋ/ *noun* (no plural)
a way of keeping the air in a building dry and not too hot
air-conditioned /'eə kən,dıʃnd/ *adjective*
with air-conditioning: *an air-conditioned office*

aircraft /'eəkrɑːft/ *noun* (plural **aircraft**)
a machine that can fly, for example an aeroplane or a helicopter

air force /'eə fɔːs/ *noun*
the aircraft that a country uses for fighting, and the people who fly them

air-hostess /'eə həʊstəs/ *noun* (plural **air-hostesses**)
a woman whose job is to look after people on an aeroplane: *Alison is an air-hostess.*

airline /'eəlaın/ *noun*
a company with aeroplanes that carry people or goods: *Lufthansa is a German airline.*

airmail /'eəmeıl/ *noun* (no plural)
a way of sending letters and parcels by aeroplane: *an airmail letter*

airplane /'eərpleın/ *American English for* **aeroplane**

airport /'eəpɔːt/ *noun*
a place where people get on and off aeroplanes, with buildings where passengers can wait: *I'll meet you at the airport.*

aisle /aıl/ *noun*
a way between lines of seats, for example in a church or theatre

alarm¹ /ə'lɑːm/ *noun*
1 (no plural) a sudden feeling of fear: *He heard a noise, and jumped out of bed in alarm.*
2 (*plural* **alarms**) something that tells you about danger, for example by making a loud noise: *Does your car have an alarm?*
3 an alarm clock

alarm² /ə'lɑːm/ *verb* (**alarms, alarming, alarmed** /ə'lɑːmd/)
make somebody or something suddenly feel afraid or worried: *The noise alarmed the bird and it flew away.* ◇ *She was alarmed to hear that Peter was ill.*

alarm clock /ə'lɑːm klɒk/ *noun*
a clock that makes a noise to wake you up

alarm clock

album /'ælbəm/ *noun*
1 a cassette, compact disc or record with about 50 minutes of music on it: *Have you heard this album?* Look at **single**.
2 a book with empty pages where you can put photographs or stamps, for example: *a photograph album*

alcohol /'ælkəhɒl/ *noun* (no plural)
1 the liquid in drinks, for example wine, beer or whisky, that can make people feel drunk
2 drinks like wine, beer or whisky
alcoholic /,ælkə'hɒlık/ *adjective*
an alcoholic drink

ale /eıl/ *noun* (no plural)
beer ✿ **Beer** is the word that we usually use.

alert¹ /ə'lɜːt/ *adjective*
awake and ready to do things: *A good driver is always alert.*

alert² /ə'lɜːt/ *noun*
a warning of danger: *There was a bomb alert at the station.*

A level /'eı levl/ *noun*
an examination in one subject that children at schools in England, Wales and Northern Ireland take when they are 18 ✿ 'A level' is short for **Advanced level**.

alien /'eıliən/ *noun*
a person or an animal that comes from another planet in space

s	z	ʃ	ʒ	h	m	n	ŋ	l	r	j	w
so	**zoo**	**sh**oe	vi**si**on	**h**at	**m**an	**no**	si**ng**	**l**eg	**r**ed	**y**es	**w**et

alight /ə'laɪt/ adjective
on fire; burning: *A fire started in the kitchen and soon the whole house was alight.*
set something alight make something start to burn: *The petrol was set alight by a cigarette.*

alike /ə'laɪk/ adjective
almost the same; not different: *The two sisters are very alike.*
alike adverb
in the same way: *The twins always dress alike* (= wear the same clothes).

alive /ə'laɪv/ adjective
living; not dead: *Are your grandparents alive?*

all¹ /ɔːl/ adjective, pronoun
1 every one of a group: *All cats are animals but not all animals are cats.* ◇ *I invited thirty people to the party, but not all of them came.* ◇ *Are you all listening?*
2 every part of something; the whole of something: *She's eaten all the bread.* ◇ *It rained all day.*

all² /ɔːl/ adverb
completely: *She lives all alone.* ◇ *He was dressed all in black.*
all along from the beginning: *I knew all along that she was lying.*

alley /'æli/ noun (plural **alleys**)
a narrow path between two buildings

alliance /ə'laɪəns/ noun
an agreement between countries or people to work together and help each other

alligator /'ælɪɡeɪtə(r)/ noun
a big long animal with sharp teeth. Alligators live in and near rivers in hot parts of the world.

allow /ə'laʊ/ verb (**allows, allowing, allowed** /ə'laʊd/)
say that somebody can have or do something: *My parents allow me to stay out late at weekends.* ◇ *Smoking is not allowed in most cinemas.* ◇ *You're not allowed to park your car here.*

all right /ˌɔːl 'raɪt/ adjective
1 good or good enough: *Is everything all right?*
2 well; not hurt: *I was ill, but I'm all right now.*
3 yes, I agree: *'Let's go home.' 'All right.'*

ally /'ælaɪ/ noun (plural **allies**)
a person or country that agrees to help an-

other person or country, for example in a war

almond /'ɑːmənd/ noun
a nut that you can eat

almost /'ɔːlməʊst/ adverb
nearly; not quite: *It's almost three o'clock.* ◇ *I almost fell into the river!*

alone /ə'ləʊn/ adverb
1 without any other person: *I don't like being alone in the house.* ◇ *My grandmother lives alone.*
2 only: *You alone can help me.*

along¹ /ə'lɒŋ/ preposition
1 from one end of something towards the other end: *We walked along the road.*
☞ picture on page 128
2 in a line next to something long: *There are trees along the river bank.*

along² /ə'lɒŋ/ adverb
1 forward: *He drove along very slowly.*
2 with me, you, etc: *We're going to the cinema. Why don't you come along too?*

alongside /ə'lɒŋsaɪd/ preposition
next to something: *Put your bike alongside mine.*

aloud /ə'laʊd/ adverb
speaking so that other people can hear: *I read the story aloud to my sister.*

alphabet /'ælfəbet/ noun
all the letters of a language: *The English alphabet starts with A and ends with Z.*
alphabetical /ˌælfə'betɪkl/ adjective
in the order of the alphabet: *Put these words in alphabetical order* (= with words beginning with A first, then B, then C, etc).

already /ɔːl'redi/ adverb
before now or before then: *'Would you like something to eat.' 'No, thank you – I've already eaten.'* ◇ *We ran to the station but the train had already left.*

already and **yet**

Yet means the same as **already**, but you only use it in negative sentences and in questions:

*I have finished this book **already**.*

*I haven't finished this book **yet**.*

*Have you finished this book **yet**?*

alright /ˌɔːl'raɪt/ = **all right**

also /'ɔːlsəʊ/ *adverb*
as well; too: *She speaks French and she is also learning Spanish.*

alter /'ɔːltə(r)/ *verb* (**alters, altering, altered** /'ɔːltəd/)
1 become different; change
2 make something different; change something: *These trousers are too long – I'm going to alter them* (= make them shorter by sewing).
alteration /ˌɔːltə'reɪʃn/ *noun*
a small change

alternate /ɔːl'tɜːnət/ *adjective*
first one and then the other: *At school we have English and German lessons on alternate days* (= English on Mondays, German on Tuesdays, English again on Wednesdays, etc).

alternative¹ /ɔːl'tɜːnətɪv/ *adjective*
different; other: *The theatre has no tickets for the first of June – can you choose an alternative date?*

alternative² /ɔːl'tɜːnətɪv/ *noun*
a thing that you can do instead of another thing: *We could go by train – the alternative is to take the car.*

although /ɔːl'ðəʊ/ *conjunction*
1 in spite of something; though: *Although she was ill, she went to work.* ◇ *I bought the shoes although they were expensive.*
2 but: *I think he's from Sweden, although I'm not sure.*

altogether /ˌɔːltə'geðə(r)/ *adverb*
1 counting everything or everybody: *Chris gave me £3 and Simon gave me £4, so I've got £7 altogether.*
2 completely: *I don't altogether agree with you.*

aluminium /ˌæljə'mɪniəm/ *noun* (no plural)
a light metal

aluminum /ə'luːmɪnəm/ *American English for* **aluminium**

always /'ɔːlweɪz/ *adverb*
1 at all times; every time: *I have always lived in London.* ◇ *The train is always late.*
2 for ever: *I will always remember that day.*
3 again and again: *My sister is always borrowing my clothes!*

am *form of* **be**

a.m. /ˌeɪ 'em/
You use 'a.m.' after a time to show that it is between midnight and midday: *I start work at 9 a.m.* ✿ We use **p.m.** for times between midday and midnight.

amateur /'æmətə(r)/ *noun*
a person who does something because he/she enjoys it, but does not get money for it
amateur *adjective*
an amateur photographer
☞ Look at **professional**.

amaze /ə'meɪz/ *verb* (**amazes, amazing, amazed** /ə'meɪzd/)
make somebody very surprised: *Matthew amazed me by remembering my birthday.*
amazed *adjective*
If you are amazed, you are very surprised: *I was amazed to see John – I thought he was in Canada.*
amazement /ə'meɪzmənt/ *noun* (no plural)
great surprise: *She looked at me in amazement.*
amazing *adjective*
If something is amazing, it surprises you very much: *She told us an amazing story.*
amazingly *adverb*
Jo plays the violin amazingly well.

ambassador /æm'bæsədə(r)/ *noun*
an important person who goes to another country and works there for the government of his/her own country: *the British Ambassador to Germany* ✿ An ambassador works in an **embassy**.

ambition /æm'bɪʃn/ *noun*
1 (no plural) a very strong wish to do well: *Louise is intelligent, but she has no ambition.*
2 something that you want to do: *My ambition is to become a doctor.*
ambitious /æm'bɪʃəs/ *adjective*
A person who is ambitious wants to do well.

ambulance /'æmbjələns/ *noun*
a special van that takes people who are ill or hurt to hospital

ammunition /ˌæmjə'nɪʃn/ *noun* (no plural)
things that you fire from a gun or throw to hurt or damage people or things: *The plane was carrying ammunition to the soldiers.*

ʌ	ɜː	ə	eɪ	əʊ	aɪ	aʊ	ɔɪ	ɪə	eə	ʊə
cup	bird	about	say	go	five	now	boy	near	hair	pure

among /ə'mʌŋ/, **amongst** /ə'mʌŋst/ *preposition*
1 in the middle of: *The house stands among the trees.* ☞ picture on page 125
2 for or by more than two things or people: *He divided the money amongst his six children.*

---

among or **between**?

We use **among** and **amongst** when we are talking about more than two people or things. If there are only two people or things, we use **between**:

Sarah and I divided the cake between us.

I was standing between Alice and Kathy.

---

amount[1] /ə'maʊnt/ *noun*
how much there is of something: *He spent a large amount of money.*

amount[2] /ə'maʊnt/ *verb* (**amounts, amounting, amounted**)
amount to something make a certain amount when you put everything together: *The cost of the repairs amounted to £500.*

amp /æmp/ *noun*
a measure of electricity

amplifier /'æmplɪfaɪə(r)/ *noun*
an electrical machine that makes sounds louder

amuse /ə'mjuːz/ *verb* (**amuses, amusing, amused** /ə'mjuːzd/)
1 make somebody smile or laugh: *Rick's joke did not amuse his mother.*
2 keep somebody happy and busy: *We played games to amuse ourselves on the long journey.*

amusement /ə'mjuːzmənt/ *noun* (no plural)
the feeling that you have when you think something is funny: *We watched in amusement as the dog chased its tail.*

amusing /ə'mjuːzɪŋ/ *adjective*
Something that is amusing makes you smile or laugh: *an amusing story*

an /ən/, /æn/ *article*
1 one or any: *I ate an apple.*
2 each, or for each: *It costs £2 an hour to park your car here.*
☞ Note at **a**

anaesthetic /ˌænəs'θetɪk/ *noun*
something that a doctor gives you so that you will not feel pain in an **operation**

ancestor /'ænsestə(r)/ *noun*
Your ancestors are the people in your family who lived a long time before you: *My ancestors came from Norway.*

anchor /'æŋkə(r)/ *noun*
a heavy metal thing that you drop into the water from a boat to stop the boat moving away

ancient /'eɪnʃənt/ *adjective*
very old; from a time long ago: *ancient buildings*

and /ənd/, /ænd/ *conjunction*
a word that joins words or parts of sentences together: *fish and chips* ◇ *They sang and danced all evening.* ◇ *The cat was black and white.*

anesthetic American English for **anaesthetic**

angel /'eɪndʒl/ *noun*
a messenger that comes from God. In pictures, angels usually have wings.

anger /'æŋgə(r)/ *noun* (no plural)
the strong feeling that you have when you are not pleased about something: *He was filled with anger when he saw the boy trying to steal his car.*

angle /'æŋgl/ *noun*
the space between two lines that meet: *an angle of 40°* ☞ picture on page 161

angry /'æŋgri/ *adjective* (**angrier, angriest**)
If you are angry, you feel or show anger: *My father was angry with me when I got home late.*
angrily /'æŋgrəli/ *adverb*
'Somebody has taken my book!' she shouted angrily.

animal /'ænɪml/ *noun*
1 any living thing that is not a plant
2 any living thing that is not a bird, fish, insect, reptile or human: *Cats, horses and rats are animals.*

ankle /'æŋkl/ *noun*
the part of your leg where it joins your foot ☞ picture on page 126

anniversary /ˌænɪ'vɜːsəri/ *noun* (**plural anniversaries**)
a day when you remember something

---

p	b	t	d	k	g	tʃ	dʒ	f	v	θ	ð
pen	**bad**	**tea**	**did**	**cat**	**got**	**chain**	**jam**	**fall**	**van**	**thin**	**this**

special that happened on the same day in another year: *Today is their 25th wedding anniversary.*

announce /ə'naʊns/ *verb* (**announces, announcing, announced** /ə'naʊnst/)
tell a lot of people about something important: *The teacher announced the winner of the competition.* ◇ *She announced that she was going to have a baby.*
announcement /ə'naʊnsmənt/ *noun*
telling people about something: *I have an important announcement to make.*

announcer /ə'naʊnsə(r)/ *noun*
a person whose job is to tell us about programmes on radio or television

annoy /ə'nɔɪ/ *verb* (**annoys, annoying, annoyed** /ə'nɔɪd/)
make somebody a little angry: *My brother annoys me when he leaves his clothes all over the floor.*
annoyance /ə'nɔɪəns/ *noun* (no plural)
the feeling of being a little angry: *She could not hide her annoyance when I arrived late.*
annoyed *adjective*
a little angry: *I was annoyed when he forgot to phone me.* ◇ *My dad is annoyed with me.*
annoying *adjective*
If a person or thing is annoying, he/she/it makes you a little angry: *It's annoying when people don't listen to you.*

annual /'ænjuəl/ *adjective*
1 that happens or comes once every year: *There is an annual meeting in June.*
2 for one year: *What is your annual income?* (= How much money do you get for one year's work?)
annually /'ænjuəli/ *adverb*
The company makes 50 000 cars annually.

anonymous /ə'nɒnɪməs/ *adjective*
1 If a person is anonymous, other people do not know his/her name: *An anonymous caller told the police about the bomb.*
2 If something is anonymous, you do not know who did, gave or made it: *She received an anonymous letter.*

anorak /'ænəræk/ *noun*
a short coat with a part (called a **hood**) that covers your head

another /ə'nʌðə(r)/ *adjective, pronoun*
1 one more thing or person: *Would you*

like another drink? ◇ *I like these cakes – can I have another one?*
2 a different thing or person: *I can't see you tomorrow – can we meet another day?* ◇ *I've read this book. Do you have another?*

answer¹ /'ɑːnsə(r)/ *verb* (**answers, answering, answered** /'ɑːnsəd/)
1 say or write something when somebody has asked a question: *I asked him if he was hungry but he didn't answer.* ◇ *I couldn't answer all the exam questions.*
2 write a letter to somebody who has written to you: *She didn't answer my letter.*
answer the door open the door when somebody knocks or rings: *Can you answer the door, please?*
answer the telephone pick up the telephone when it rings, and speak

answer² /'ɑːnsə(r)/ *noun*
1 something that you say or write when you answer somebody: *I asked Lucy a question but she didn't give me an answer.* ◇ *Have you had an answer to your letter?*
2 a way of stopping a problem: *If you are tired, the answer is to go to bed early!*

answerphone /'ɑːnsəfəʊn/, **answering machine** /'ɑːnsərɪŋ məʃiːn/ *noun*
a machine that answers the telephone for you and keeps messages so that you can listen to them later: *He wasn't at home, so I left a message on his answerphone.*

ant /ænt/ *noun*
a very small insect that lives in big groups

antelope /'æntɪləʊp/ *noun*
a wild animal with horns and long thin legs, that can run fast

anti- /'ænti/ *prefix*
anti- at the beginning of a word often means 'against':
an anti-smoking campaign

anticipate /æn'tɪsɪpeɪt/ *verb* (**anticipates, anticipating, anticipated**)
think that something will happen and be ready for it: *We didn't anticipate so many problems.*

anticlockwise /ˌænti'klɒkwaɪz/ *adjective, adverb*
When something moves anticlockwise, it

s	z	ʃ	ʒ	h	m	n	ŋ	l	r	j	w
so	**zoo**	**shoe**	vision	**hat**	**man**	**no**	sing	**leg**	**red**	**yes**	**wet**

moves in the opposite direction to the hands of a clock.

antique /æn'ti:k/ noun
an old thing that is worth a lot of money: *These chairs are antiques.*
antique *adjective*
an antique vase

anxiety /æŋ'zaɪəti/ noun (plural **anxieties**)
a feeling of worry and fear

anxious /'æŋkʃəs/ adjective
1 worried and afraid: *She's anxious because her daughter hasn't arrived yet.*
2 If you are anxious to do something, you want to do it very much: *My family are anxious to meet you.*
anxiously *adverb*
We waited anxiously.

any /'eni/ adjective, pronoun
1 a word that you use in questions and after 'not' and 'if'; some: *Have you got any money?* ◇ *I don't speak any Spanish.* ◇ *She asked if I had any milk.* ◇ *I want some chocolate but there isn't any.*
2 no special one: *Come any day next week.* ◇ *Take any book you want.*
any *adverb*
a little: *I can't walk any faster.*

anybody /'enibɒdi/, **anyone** /'eniwʌn/ pronoun
1 any person: *There wasn't anybody there.* ◇ *Did you see anyone you know?*
2 no special person: *Anybody* (= all people) *can play this game.*

anything /'eniθɪŋ/ pronoun
1 a thing of any kind: *Is there anything in that box?* ◇ *I can't see anything.*
2 no special thing: *'What would you like to drink?' 'Oh, anything. I don't mind.'*
anything else something more: *'Would you like anything else?' asked the waitress.*
anything like the same as somebody or something in any way: *She isn't anything like her sister.*

anyway /'eniweɪ/, **anyhow** /'enihaʊ/ adverb
1 a word that you use when you give a second reason for something: *I don't want to see the film and anyhow I haven't got any money.*
2 no matter what is true; however: *It was very expensive but she bought it anyway.*
3 a word that you use when you start to

talk about something different: *That's what John said. Anyway, how are you?*

anywhere /'eniweə(r)/ adverb
1 at, in or to any place: *Are you going anywhere this summer?* ◇ *I can't find my pen anywhere.*
2 no special place: *'Where shall I sit?' 'Oh, anywhere – it doesn't matter.'*

apart /ə'pɑ:t/ adverb
1 away from the others; away from each other: *The two houses are 500 metres apart.* ◇ *My mother and father live apart.*
2 into parts: *He took my radio apart to repair it.*
apart from somebody or **something** if you do not count somebody or something: *There were ten people in the room, apart from me.* ◇ *I like all vegetables apart from carrots.*

apartment /ə'pɑ:tmənt/ American English for **flat**[1]

ape /eɪp/ noun
an animal like a big monkey with no tail: *Gorillas and chimpanzees are apes.*

apologize /ə'pɒlədʒaɪz/ verb (**apologizes, apologizing, apologized** /ə'pɒlədʒaɪzd/)
say that you are sorry about something that you have done: *I apologized to John for losing his book.*

apology /ə'pɒlədʒi/ noun (plural **apologies**)
words that you say or write to show that you are sorry about something you have done: *Please accept my apologies.*

apostrophe /ə'pɒstrəfi/ noun
the sign (') that you use in writing. You use it to show that you have left a letter out of a word, for example in 'I'm' (I am). You also use it to show that something belongs to somebody or something, for example in 'the boy's room'.

appalling /ə'pɔ:lɪŋ/ adjective
very bad; terrible: *appalling cruelty*

apparent /ə'pærənt/ adjective
easy to see or understand; clear: *It was apparent that she didn't like him.*
apparently *adverb*
1 You use 'apparently' to talk about what

iː	i	ɪ	e	æ	ɑː	ɒ	ɔː	ʊ	u	uː
see	happy	sit	ten	cat	father	got	saw	put	situation	too

another person said, when you do not know if it is true: *Apparently, she has a big house and three cars.*
2 it seems: *He went to school today, so he's apparently feeling better.*

appeal¹ /ə'piːl/ *verb* (**appeals, appealing, appealed** /ə'piːld/)
ask in a serious way for something that you want very much: *They appealed for food and clothing.*
appeal to somebody please or interest somebody: *Living in a big city doesn't appeal to me.*

appeal² /ə'piːl/ *noun*
asking for something in a serious way: *They made an appeal for help.*

appear /ə'pɪə(r)/ *verb* (**appears, appearing, appeared** /ə'pɪəd/)
1 come and be seen: *The sun suddenly appeared from behind a cloud.* ◇ *We waited for an hour but he didn't appear.*
2 seem: *It appears that I was wrong.*

appearance /ə'pɪərəns/ *noun*
1 the coming of somebody or something; when somebody or something is seen: *Jane's appearance at the party surprised everybody.* ◇ *Is this your first appearance on television?*
2 what somebody or something looks like: *Her new glasses change her appearance.*

appetite /'æpɪtaɪt/ *noun*
the feeling that you want to eat: *Swimming always gives me an appetite* (= makes me hungry).

applaud /ə'plɔːd/ *verb* (**applauds, applauding, applauded**)
make a noise by hitting your hands together to show that you like something: *We all applauded loudly at the end of the song.*

applause /ə'plɔːz/ *noun* (no plural)
when a lot of people hit their hands together to show that they like something: *loud applause*

apple /'æpl/ *noun*
a hard round fruit

appliance
/ə'plaɪəns/ *noun*
a useful machine for doing something in the house: *Washing-machines and irons are electrical appliances.*

apple

applicant /'æplɪkənt/ *noun*
a person who asks for a job or a place at a university, for example: *There were six applicants for the job.*

application /ˌæplɪ'keɪʃn/ *noun*
writing to ask for something, for example a job

application form /ˌæplɪ'keɪʃn fɔːm/ *noun*
a special piece of paper that you write on when you are trying to get something, for example a job

apply /ə'plaɪ/ *verb* (**applies, applying, applied** /ə'plaɪd/)
1 write to ask for something: *Simon has applied for a place at university.*
2 be about or be important to somebody or something: *This notice applies to all children over the age of twelve.*

appoint /ə'pɔɪnt/ *verb* (**appoints, appointing, appointed**)
choose somebody for a job: *The bank has appointed a new manager.*

appointment /ə'pɔɪntmənt/ *noun*
1 a time that you have fixed to meet somebody: *I've got an appointment with the doctor at ten o'clock.* ◇ *You can telephone to make an appointment.*
2 a job **۞ Job** is the word that we usually use.

appreciate /ə'priːʃieɪt/ *verb* (**appreciates, appreciating, appreciated**)
1 understand and enjoy something: *Van Gogh's paintings were only appreciated after his death.*
2 understand something: *I appreciate your problem, but I can't help you.*
3 be pleased about something that somebody has done for you: *Thank you for your help. I appreciate it.*

appreciation /əˌpriːʃi'eɪʃn/ *noun* (no plural)
We gave her some flowers to show our appreciation for her hard work.

apprentice /ə'prentɪs/ *noun*
a young person who is learning to do a job

approach¹ /ə'prəʊtʃ/ *verb*
(**approaches, approaching, approached** /ə'prəʊtʃt/)
come near or nearer to somebody or something: *When you approach the village, you will see a big house on your right.* ◇ *I was approached by an old lady.* ◇ *The exams were approaching.*

approach² /ə'prəʊtʃ/ *noun*
1 (no plural) coming nearer to somebody or something: *the approach of winter*
2 (*plural* **approaches**) a way of doing something: *This is a new approach to learning languages.*

appropriate /ə'prəʊpriət/ *adjective*
right for that time or place; suitable: *Jeans and T-shirts aren't appropriate for an interview.* ✪ opposite: **inappropriate**

approval /ə'pru:vl/ *noun* (no plural)
showing or saying that somebody or something is good or right: *Tania's parents gave the marriage their approval.*

approve /ə'pru:v/ *verb* (**approves, approving, approved** /ə'pru:vd/)
think or say that something or somebody is good or right: *My parents don't approve of my friends.* ◇ *She doesn't approve of smoking.* ✪ opposite: **disapprove**

approximate /ə'prɒksɪmət/ *adjective*
almost correct but not exact: *The approximate time of arrival is three o'clock.*
approximately *adverb*
about; not exactly: *I live approximately two kilometres from the station.*

apricot /'eɪprɪkɒt/ *noun*
a small soft yellow fruit

April /'eɪprəl/ *noun*
the fourth month of the year

apron /'eɪprən/ *noun*
a thing that you wear over the front of your clothes to keep them clean, for example when you are cooking

arch /ɑ:tʃ/ *noun*
(*plural* **arches**)
a part of a bridge, building or wall that is in the shape of a half circle

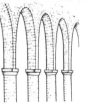
arch

archaeology
/,ɑ:ki'ɒlədʒi/ *noun*
(no plural)
the study of very old things like buildings and objects that are found in the ground
archaeologist /,ɑ:ki'ɒlədʒɪst/ *noun*
a person who studies or knows a lot about archaeology

archbishop /,ɑ:tʃ'bɪʃəp/ *noun*
a very important priest in the Christian church: *the Archbishop of Canterbury*

archeologist, archeology *American English for* **archaeologist, archaeology**

architect /'ɑ:kɪtekt/ *noun*
a person whose job is to plan buildings

architecture /'ɑ:kɪtektʃə(r)/ *noun* (no plural)
1 planning and making buildings
2 the shape of buildings: *Do you like modern architecture?*

are *form of* **be**

area /'eəriə/ *noun*
1 a part of a town, country or the world: *Do you live in this area?* ◇ *the desert areas of North Africa*
2 the size of a flat place. If a room is three metres wide and four metres long, it has an area of twelve square metres.
3 a space that you use for something special: *The restaurant has a non-smoking area* (= a part where you must not smoke).

arena /ə'ri:nə/ *noun* (*plural* **arenas**)
a place with seats around it where you can watch things like sports matches and concerts

aren't /ɑ:nt/ = **are not**

argue /'ɑ:gju:/ *verb* (**argues, arguing, argued** /'ɑ:gju:d/)
1 talk angrily with somebody because you do not agree: *My parents argue a lot.* ◇ *I often argue with my brother about music.*
2 say why you think something is right or wrong: *Helen argued that we shouldn't eat meat.*

argument /'ɑ:gjəmənt/ *noun*
an angry talk between people with different ideas: *They had an argument about where to go on holiday.* ◇ *I had an argument with my father.*

arithmetic /ə'rɪθmətɪk/ *noun* (no plural)
working with numbers to find an answer

arm /ɑ:m/ *noun*
the part of your body from your shoulder to your hand: *Put your arms in the air.* ◇ *He was carrying a book under his arm.* ☞ picture on page 126
arm in arm with your arm holding another person's arm: *The two friends walked arm in arm.*

p	b	t	d	k	g	tʃ	dʒ	f	v	θ	ð
pen	**b**ad	**t**ea	**d**id	**c**at	**g**ot	**ch**ain	**j**am	**f**all	**v**an	**th**in	**th**is

armchair

armchair /ˈɑːmtʃeə(r)/ *noun*
a soft chair with parts where you can put your arms: *She was asleep in an armchair.*

armed /ɑːmd/ *adjective*
with a weapon, for example a gun: *an armed robber* ◇ *Are the police armed in your country?*
the armed forces /ði ˌɑːmd ˈfɔːsɪz/ *noun*
the army, air force and navy

armor *American English for* **armour**

armour /ˈɑːmə(r)/ *noun* (no plural)
metal clothes that men wore long ago to cover their bodies when they were fighting: *a suit of armour*

arms /ɑːmz/ *noun* (plural)
guns, bombs and other weapons for fighting

army /ˈɑːmi/ *noun* (*plural* **armies**)
a large group of soldiers who fight on land in a war: *He joined the army when he was 17.* ◇ *the Swiss Army*

around /əˈraʊnd/ *preposition, adverb*
1 in or to different places or in different directions: *We walked around for an hour looking for a restaurant.* ◇ *The children were running around the house.* ◇ *Her clothes were lying around the room.*
2 on or to all sides of something, often in a circle: *We sat around the table.* ◇ *He ran around the track.* ◇ *There is a wall around the garden.*
3 in the opposite direction or in another direction: *Turn around and go back the way you came.*
4 a little more or less than; a little before or after: *We met at around seven o'clock.*
5 in a place; near here: *Is there a bank around here?* ◇ *Is Helen around? I want to speak to her.*

arrange /əˈreɪndʒ/ *verb* (**arranges**, **arranging**, **arranged** /əˈreɪndʒd/)
1 make a plan for the future: *I have arranged to meet Tim at six o'clock.* ◇ *We*

arranged a big party for Debbie's birthday.
2 put things in a certain order or place: *Arrange the chairs in a circle.*

arrangement /əˈreɪndʒmənt/ *noun*
1 something that you plan or agree for the future: *They are making the arrangements for their wedding.*
2 a group of things put together so that they look nice: *a flower arrangement*

arrest /əˈrest/ *verb* (**arrests**, **arresting**, **arrested**)
When the police arrest somebody, they make that person a prisoner because they think that he/she has done something wrong: *The thief was arrested yesterday.*
arrest *noun*
arresting somebody: *The police made five arrests.*
be under arrest be a prisoner of the police

arrival /əˈraɪvl/ *noun*
coming to a place: *My brother met me at the airport on my arrival.* ☞ Look at **departure**.

arrive /əˈraɪv/ *verb* (**arrives**, **arriving**, **arrived** /əˈraɪvd/)
1 come to a place: *What time does the train arrive in Paris?* ◇ *Has my letter arrived?*
2 come or happen: *Summer has arrived!*

arrogant /ˈærəɡənt/ *adjective*
A person who is arrogant thinks that he/she is better or more important than other people.

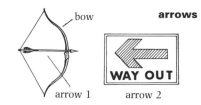

bow   **arrows**

WAY OUT

arrow 1   arrow 2

arrow /ˈærəʊ/ *noun*
1 a long thin piece of wood or metal with a point at one end. You shoot an arrow from a **bow**.
2 a sign in the shape of an arrow, that shows where something is or where you should go

art /ɑːt/ *noun*
1 (no plural) making beautiful things, like

paintings and drawings: *He's studying art at college.*
2 (no plural) beautiful things like paintings and drawings that somebody has made: *modern art*
3 the arts (plural) things like films, plays and literature: *How much money does the government spend on the arts?*

article /'ɑːtɪkl/ *noun*
1 a piece of writing in a newspaper or magazine: *Did you read the article about Spain in yesterday's newspaper?*
2 a thing: *Many of the articles in the shop are half-price.* ◇ *articles of clothing* (= things like skirts, coats and trousers)
3 The words 'a', 'an' and 'the' are called articles.

artificial /ˌɑːtɪ'fɪʃl/ *adjective*
made by people; not natural: *artificial flowers*

artist /'ɑːtɪst/ *noun*
a person who paints or draws pictures: *Monet was a famous French artist.*

artistic /ɑː'tɪstɪk/ *adjective*
good at painting, drawing or making beautiful things: *He's very artistic.*

as /əz/, /æz/ *conjunction, preposition*
1 while; at the same time that something is happening: *As I was going out, the telephone rang.*
2 because: *She didn't go to school as she was ill.*
3 in the same way; like: *Please do as I tell you!*
4 in the job of: *She works as a secretary for a big company.*
as ... as words that you use to compare people or things; the same amount: *Paul is as tall as his father.* ◇ *I haven't got as many clothes as you have.*

ash /æʃ/ *noun* (*plural* **ash** or **ashes**)
the grey stuff that you see after something has burned: *cigarette ash*

ashamed /ə'ʃeɪmd/ *adjective*
sorry and unhappy about something that you have done, or unhappy because you are not as good as other people in some way: *I was ashamed about lying to my parents.* ◇ *She was ashamed of her old clothes.*

ashore /ə'ʃɔː(r)/ *adverb*
onto the land: *We left the boat and went ashore.*

ashtray /'æʃtreɪ/ *noun*
a small dish for cigarette ash and the ends of cigarettes

aside /ə'saɪd/ *adverb*
on or to one side; away: *He put the letter aside while he did his homework.*

ask /ɑːsk/ *verb* (**asks**, **asking**, **asked** /ɑːskt/)
1 try to get an answer by using a question: *I asked him what the time was.* ◇ *'What's your name?' she asked.* ◇ *Liz asked the teacher a question.* ◇ *I asked if I could go home early.*
2 say that you would like somebody to do something for you: *I asked Sara to drive me to the station.*
3 invite somebody: *Mark has asked me to a party on Saturday.*
ask for somebody say that you want to speak to somebody: *Phone this number and ask for Mrs Green.*
ask for something say that you want somebody to give you something: *He asked his parents for a computer.*

asleep /ə'sliːp/ *adjective*
sleeping: *The baby is asleep in the bedroom.* ✪ opposite: **awake**
fall asleep start sleeping: *He fell asleep in front of the fire.*

aspect /'æspekt/ *noun*
one part of a problem, idea, etc: *Spelling is one of the most difficult aspects of learning English.*

aspirin /'æsprɪn/ *noun*
a medicine that stops pain: *I took two aspirins* (= two tablets of aspirin) *for my headache.*

assassinate /ə'sæsɪneɪt/ *verb* (**assassinates**, **assassinating**, **assassinated**)
kill an important or famous person: *John F Kennedy was assassinated in 1963.*
assassination /əˌsæsɪ'neɪʃn/ *noun*
killing an important or famous person

assault /ə'sɔːlt/ *verb* (**assaults**, **assaulting**, **assaulted**)
suddenly start fighting or hurting somebody: *He assaulted a policeman.*
assault *noun*
an assault on an old lady

assembly /ə'sembli/ *noun* (*plural* **assemblies**)
a meeting of a big group of people for a

special reason: *Our school assembly* (= a meeting of all the students and teachers in the school) *is at 9.30 in the morning.*

assist /ə'sɪst/ *verb* (**assists, assisting, assisted**)
help somebody: *The driver assisted her with her suitcases.*

assistance /ə'sɪstəns/ *noun* (no plural)
help: *I can't move this piano without your assistance.*
✪ Help is the word that we usually use.

assistant /ə'sɪstənt/ *noun*
a person who helps: *Ms Dixon is not here today. Would you like to speak to her assistant?* ☞ Look also at **shop assistant.**

associate /ə'səʊʃieɪt/ *verb* (**associates, associating, associated**)
put two ideas together in your mind: *We usually associate Austria with snow and skiing.*

association /ə,səʊsi'eɪʃn/ *noun*
a group of people who join or work together for a special reason: *the Football Association*

assume /ə'sjuːm/ *verb* (**assumes, assuming, assumed** /ə'sjuːmd/)
think that something is true when you are not completely sure: *Jo is not here today, so I assume that she is ill.*

assure /ə'ʃʊə(r)/ *verb* (**assures, assuring, assured** /ə'ʃʊəd/)
tell somebody what is true or certain so that they feel less worried: *I assure you that the dog isn't dangerous.*

astonish /ə'stɒnɪʃ/ *verb* (**astonishes, astonishing, astonished** /ə'stɒnɪʃt/)
surprise somebody very much: *The news astonished everyone.*
astonished *adjective*
If you are astonished, you are very surprised: *I was astonished when I heard that Louise was getting married.*
astonishing *adjective*
If something is astonishing, it surprises you very much: *astonishing news*
astonishment /ə'stɒnɪʃmənt/ *noun* (no plural)
great surprise: *He looked at me in astonishment when I told him the news.*

astronaut /'æstrənɔːt/ *noun*
a person who travels in a spaceship

astronomy /ə'strɒnəmi/ *noun* (no plural)
the study of the sun, moon, planets and stars
astronomer /ə'strɒnəmə(r)/ *noun*
a person who studies or knows a lot about astronomy

at /ət/, /æt/ *preposition*
1 a word that shows where: *They are at school.* ◇ *Jane is at home.* ◇ *The answer is at the back of the book.*
2 a word that shows when: *I go to bed at eleven o'clock.* ◇ *At night you can see the stars.* ☞ Look at page 297.
3 towards somebody or something: *Look at the picture.* ◇ *I smiled at her.* ◇ *Somebody threw an egg at the President.*
4 a word that shows what somebody is doing or what is happening: *The two countries are at war.*
5 a word that shows how much, how fast, etc: *I bought two lemons at 20 pence each.*
6 a word that shows how well somebody or something does something: *I'm not very good at maths.*
7 because of something: *We laughed at his jokes.*

ate *form of* **eat**

athlete /'æθliːt/ *noun*
a person who is good at sports like running, jumping or throwing: *Athletes from all over the world go to the Olympic Games.*

athletics /æθ'letɪks/ *noun* (plural)
sports like running, jumping or throwing

atlas /'ætləs/ *noun* (*plural* **atlases**)
a book of maps: *an atlas of the world*

atmosphere /'ætməsfɪə(r)/ *noun*
1 (no plural) all the gases around the earth
2 (no plural) the air in a place: *a smoky atmosphere*
3 (*plural* **atmospheres**) the feeling that places or people give you: *The atmosphere in the office was very friendly.*

atom /'ætəm/ *noun*
one of the very small things that everything is made of: *Water is made of atoms of hydrogen and oxygen.*
atomic /ə'tɒmɪk/ *adjective*
1 of or about atoms: *atomic physics*
2 using the great power that is made by

ʌ	ɜː	ə	eɪ	əʊ	aɪ	aʊ	ɔɪ	ɪə	eə	ʊə
c**u**p	b**ir**d	**a**bout	s**ay**	g**o**	f**i**ve	n**ow**	b**oy**	n**ear**	h**air**	p**ure**

breaking atoms: *an atomic bomb*
◇ *atomic energy*

attach /ə'tætʃ/ *verb* (**attaches, attaching, attached** /ə'tætʃt/)
join or fix one thing to another thing: *I attached the photo to the letter.*
be attached to somebody or **something** like somebody or something very much: *He's very attached to you.*

attack /ə'tæk/ *verb* (**attacks, attacking, attacked** /ə'tækt/)
start fighting or hurting somebody or something: *The army attacked the town.*
◇ *The old man was attacked and his money was stolen.*
attack *noun*
1 trying to hurt somebody or something: *There was an attack on the President.*
2 a time when you are ill: *an attack of flu*

attempt /ə'tempt/ *verb* (**attempts, attempting, attempted**)
try to do something: *He attempted to swim from England to France.* ◐ **Try** is the word that we usually use.
attempt *noun*
She made no attempt to help me.

attend /ə'tend/ *verb* (**attends, attending, attended**)
go to or be at a place where something is happening: *Did you attend the meeting?*

attention /ə'tenʃn/ *noun* (no plural)
looking or listening carefully and with interest: *Can I have your attention, please?* (= please listen to me)
pay attention look or listen carefully: *Please pay attention to what I'm saying.*

attic /'ætɪk/ *noun*
the room or space under the roof of a house: *My old clothes are in a box in the attic.*

attitude /'ætɪtjuːd/ *noun*
the way you think or feel about something: *What's your attitude to marriage?*

attorney /ə'tɜːni/ *American English for* **lawyer**

attract /ə'trækt/ *verb* (**attracts, attracting, attracted**)
1 make somebody or something come nearer: *Magnets attract metal.* ◇ *The birds were attracted by the smell of fish.*
2 make somebody like somebody or something: *He was attracted to her.*

attraction /ə'trækʃn/ *noun*
1 (*plural* **attractions**) something that people like and feel interested in: *London has a lot of tourist attractions, like Big Ben and Buckingham Palace.*
2 (no plural) liking somebody or something very much; being liked very much: *I can't understand his attraction to her.*

attractive /ə'træktɪv/ *adjective*
1 A person who is attractive is nice to look at: *He's very attractive.*
2 Something that is attractive pleases you or interests you: *That's an attractive idea.*
◐ opposite: **unattractive**

auction /'ɔːkʃn/ *noun*
a sale where each thing is sold to the person who will give the most money for it
auction *verb* (**auctions, auctioning, auctioned** /'ɔːkʃnd/)
sell something at an auction

audience /'ɔːdiəns/ *noun*
all the people who are watching or listening to a film, play, concert or the television

August /'ɔːɡəst/ *noun*
the eighth month of the year

aunt /ɑːnt/ *noun*
the sister of your mother or father, or the wife of your uncle: *Aunt Mary* ☞ picture on page 127

auntie /'ɑːnti/ *noun*
aunt

au pair /ˌəʊ 'peə(r)/ *noun*
a young person from another country who stays with a family for a short time to learn a language. An au pair helps in the house and looks after the children.

authentic /ɔː'θentɪk/ *adjective*
real and true: *That's not an authentic Van Gogh painting – it's just a copy.*

author /'ɔːθə(r)/ *noun*
a person who writes books or stories: *Who is your favourite author?*

authority /ɔː'θɒrəti/ *noun*
1 (no plural) the power to tell people what they must do: *The police have the authority to stop cars.*
2 (*plural* **authorities**) a group of people that tell other people what they must do: *the city authorities*

autobiography /ˌɔːtəbaɪ'ɒɡrəfi/ *noun* (*plural* **autobiographies**)
a book that a person has written about his/her life

p	b	t	d	k	ɡ	tʃ	dʒ	f	v	θ	ð
pen	**bad**	**tea**	**did**	**cat**	**got**	**chain**	**jam**	**fall**	**van**	**thin**	**this**

autograph /'ɔ:təɡrɑ:f/ *noun*
a famous person's name, that he/she has written: *He asked Madonna for her autograph.*

automatic /ˌɔ:tə'mætɪk/ *adjective*
1 If a machine is automatic, it can work by itself, without people controlling it: *an automatic washing-machine*
2 that you do without thinking: *Breathing is automatic.*
automatically /ˌɔ:tə'mætɪkli/ *adverb*
This light comes on automatically at five o'clock.

automobile /'ɔ:təməbi:l/ *American English for* **car**

autumn /'ɔ:təm/ *noun*
the part of the year between summer and winter: *In autumn, the leaves begin to fall from the trees.*

available /ə'veɪləbl/ *adjective*
ready for you to use, have or see: *I phoned the hotel to ask if there were any rooms available.* ◇ *I'm sorry – the doctor is not available this afternoon.*

avenue /'ævənju:/ *noun*
a wide road or street: *I live in Connaught Avenue.* ○ The short way of writing 'Avenue' in addresses is **Ave**: *Burnham Ave*

average /'ævərɪdʒ/ *noun*
1 (*plural* **averages**) a word that you use when you work with numbers: *The average of 2, 3 and 7 is 4 ($2 + 3 + 7 = 12$, and $12 \div 3 = 4$).*
2 (no plural) what is ordinary or usual: *Tom's work at school is above average (= better than the average).*
average *adjective*
The average age of the students is 19.

avoid /ə'vɔɪd/ *verb* (**avoids**, **avoiding**, **avoided**)
1 stay away or go away from somebody or something: *We crossed the road to avoid our teacher.*
2 stop something from happening; try not to do something: *You should avoid eating too much chocolate.*

awake /ə'weɪk/ *adjective*
not sleeping: *The children are still awake.*
○ opposite: **asleep**

award /ə'wɔ:d/ *noun*
a prize or money that you give to somebody who has done something very well: *She won the award for best actress.*
award *verb* (**awards**, **awarding**, **awarded**)
give a prize or money to somebody: *He was awarded first prize in the writing competition.*

aware /ə'weə(r)/ *adjective*
If you are aware of something, you know about it: *I was aware that somebody was watching me.* ◇ *He's not aware of the problem.* ○ opposite: **unaware**

away /ə'weɪ/ *adverb*
1 to or in another place: *She ran away.* ◇ *He put his books away.*
2 from a place: *The sea is two kilometres away.*
3 not here: *Tim is away from school today because he is ill.*
4 in the future: *Our holiday is only three weeks away.*

awful /'ɔ:fl/ *adjective*
very bad: *The pain was awful.* ◇ *What awful weather!*

awfully /'ɔ:fli/ *adverb*
very: *It was awfully hot.* ◇ *I'm awfully sorry!*

awkward /'ɔ:kwəd/ *adjective*
1 difficult to do or use, for example: *This big box will be awkward to carry.*
2 not comfortable: *I felt awkward at the party because I didn't know anybody.*
3 difficult to please: *My son is very awkward. He never likes the food I give him.*
4 not able to move your body in an easy way: *He's very awkward when he dances.*

ax *American English for* **axe**

axe /æks/ *noun*
a tool for cutting wood: *He chopped down the tree with an axe.*

s	z	ʃ	ʒ	h	m	n	ŋ	l	r	j	w
so	**zoo**	**shoe**	**vision**	**hat**	**man**	**no**	**sing**	**leg**	**red**	**yes**	**wet**

Bb

baby /'beɪbi/ noun
(plural **babies**)
a very young child:
She's going to have
a baby.

baby

babysit /'beɪbɪsɪt/
verb (**babysits**,
babysitting,
babysat /'beɪbɪsæt/,
has **babysat**)
look after a child for a short time when the
parents are not there
babysitter noun
a person who babysits

bachelor /'bætʃələ(r)/ noun
1 a man who has never married
2 a person who has finished studying at a
university or college and who has a first
degree: a Bachelor of Science

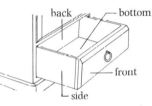

back¹ /bæk/ noun
1 the part that is behind or farthest from
the front: The answers are at the back of
the book. ◇ Write your address on the
back of the cheque. ◇ We sat in the back
of the car.
2 the part of a person or an animal between the neck and the bottom: He lay on
his back and looked up at the sky. ☞ picture on page 126
back to front
with the back part
in front
**behind some-
body's back**
when somebody is
not there, so that
he/she does not
know about it:
Don't talk about
Kate behind her
back.

back to front

back² /bæk/ adjective
away from the front: the back door

back³ /bæk/ adverb
1 away from the front: I looked back to see
if she was coming.
2 in or to the place where somebody or
something was before: I'll be back (= I will
return) at six o'clock. ◇ Give the book
back to me when you've read it. ◇ We
walked to the shops and back.
3 as a way of returning or answering
something: He paid me the money back.
◇ I wrote her a letter, but she didn't write
back. ◇ I was out when she phoned, so I
phoned her back.
back and forth first one way and then
the other, many times: She travels back
and forth between London and Glasgow.

back⁴ /bæk/ verb (**backs**, **backing**,
backed /bækt/)
1 move backwards or make something
move backwards: She backed the car out of
the garage.
2 say that you think that somebody or
something is right or the best: They're
backing their school team.
back away move away backwards:
Sally backed away from the big dog.
back out not do something that you
promised or agreed to do: Paul backed out
of the game, so we only had ten players.

backbone /'bækbəʊn/ noun
the line of bones down the back of your
body

background /'bækgraʊnd/ noun
the things at the back in a picture: This is a
photo of my house with the mountains in
the background. ✪ opposite: **foreground**

backpack /'bækpæk/ noun
a bag that you carry on your back, for example when you are walking or climbing

backstroke /'bækstrəʊk/ noun (no
plural)
a way of swimming on your back

backward /'bækwəd/ adjective
1 towards the back: a backward step
2 slow to learn or change: They live in a
backward part of the country, where there
is no electricity.

i:	i	ɪ	e	æ	ɑː	ɒ	ɔː	ʊ	u	uː
see	happy	sit	ten	cat	father	got	saw	put	situation	too

backwards /'bækwədz/, **backward**
/'bækwəd/ adverb
1 away from the front; towards the back:
He fell backwards and hit the back of his
head.
2 with the back or the end first: If you say
the alphabet backwards, you start with
'Z'.
backwards and forwards first one
way and then the other way, many times:
The dog ran backwards and forwards.

bacon /'beɪkən/ noun (no plural)
thin pieces of meat from a pig, that is prepared using salt or smoke: We had bacon
and eggs for breakfast. ☞ Note at **pig**

bacteria /bæk'tɪəriə/ noun (plural)
very small things that live in air, water,
earth, plants and animals. Some bacteria
can make us ill.

bad /bæd/ adjective (**worse**, **worst**)
1 not good or nice: The weather was very
bad. ◇ He's had some bad news – his
uncle has died. ◇ a bad smell
2 serious: She had a bad accident.
3 not done or made well: bad driving
4 not able to work or do something well:
My eyesight is bad. ◇ He's a bad teacher.
5 too old to eat; not fresh: bad eggs
bad at something If you are bad at
something, you cannot do it well: I'm very
bad at sports.
bad for you If something is bad for you,
it can make you ill: Smoking is bad for
you.
go bad become too old to eat: This fish
has gone bad.
not bad quite good: 'What was the film
like?' 'Not bad.'
too bad words that you use to say that
you cannot change something: 'I want to
go out.' 'Too bad – you can't!'

badge /bædʒ/ noun
a small thing made of metal, plastic or
cloth that you wear on your clothes. A
badge can show that you belong to a
school or club, for example, or it can have
words or a picture on it: His jacket had a
school badge on the pocket.

badly /'bædli/ adverb (**worse**, **worst**)
1 in a bad way; not well: She played
badly. ◇ These clothes are badly made.
2 very much: He was badly hurt in the accident. ◇ I badly need a holiday.

badminton /'bædmɪntən/ noun (no
plural)
a game for two or four players who try to
hit a kind of light ball with feathers on it
(called a **shuttlecock**) over a high net,
using **rackets**: Do you want to play
badminton?

bad-tempered /,bæd 'tempəd/ adjective
often angry: He's bad-tempered in the
mornings.

bag /bæg/ noun
a thing made of cloth, paper, leather, etc,
for holding and carrying things: He put
the apples in a paper bag. ◇ a plastic
shopping bag ☞ Look also at **carrier bag**
and **handbag** and at the picture at
container.

baggage /'bægɪdʒ/ noun (no plural)
bags and suitcases that you take with you
when you travel: We put all our baggage
in the car.

baggy /'bægi/ adjective
If clothes are baggy, they are big and loose:
He was wearing baggy trousers.

bagpipes /'bægpaɪps/ noun (plural)
a musical instrument that is often played
in Scotland

bake /beɪk/ verb (**bakes**, **baking**, **baked**
/beɪkt/)
cook food in an oven: My brother baked a
cake for my birthday. ◇ baked potatoes

baked beans /,beɪkt 'biːnz/ noun
(plural)
beans cooked in tomato sauce, that you
buy in a tin

baker /'beɪkə(r)/ noun
a person who makes and sells bread and
cakes ◯ A shop that sells bread and cakes
is called a **baker's** or a **bakery**.

balance¹ /'bæləns/ verb (**balances**,
balancing, **balanced** /'bælənst/)
make yourself or something stay without
falling to one side or the other: He balanced
the bag on his head. ◇ She balanced on
one leg.

balance² /'bæləns/ noun
1 (no plural) when two sides are the same,
so that something will not fall
2 (no plural) when two things are the
same, so that one is not bigger or more im-

portant, for example: *You need a balance between work and play.* ✪ opposite: **imbalance**
3 (*plural* **balances**) how much money you have or must pay after you have spent or paid some: *The jacket costs £100. You can pay £10 now and the balance* (= £90) *next week.*
keep your balance stay steady without falling: *He tried to keep his balance on the ice.*
lose your balance become unsteady; fall: *She lost her balance and fell off her bike.*

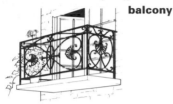
balcony

balcony /ˈbælkəni/ *noun* (*plural* **balconies**)
a small place on the outside wall of a building, above the ground, where you can stand or sit.

bald /bɔːld/ *adjective*
with no hair or not much hair: *My dad is going* (= becoming) *bald.* ☞ picture at **hair**

ball /bɔːl/ *noun*
1 a round thing that you use in games and sports: *Throw the ball to me.* ◇ *a football* ◇ *a tennis-ball*
2 any round thing: *a ball of string* ◇ *a snowball* ☞ picture on page 261
3 a big formal party where people dance

ballerina /ˌbæləˈriːnə/ *noun*
a woman who dances in ballets

ballet /ˈbæleɪ/ *noun*
a kind of dancing that tells a story with music but no words: *I went to see a ballet.* ◇ *Do you like ballet?*
ballet dancer /ˈbæleɪ dɑːnsə(r)/ *noun*
a person who dances in ballets

balloon /bəˈluːn/ *noun*
1 a small thing like a bag made of coloured rubber. You fill it with air or gas to make it big and round: *We are going to hang balloons around the room for the party.*
2 a very big bag that you fill with gas or air so that it can fly. People ride in a basket under it: *I would like to go up in a balloon.*

ballot /ˈbælət/ *noun*
when people choose somebody or something by writing secretly on a piece of paper: *We held a ballot to choose a new president.*

ball-point /ˈbɔːl pɔɪnt/ *noun*
a pen that has a very small ball at the end

ban /bæn/ *verb* (**bans**, **banning**, **banned** /bænd/)
say that something must stop or must not happen: *The film was banned* (= people were not allowed to see it).
ban *noun*
There is a ban on smoking in petrol stations.

banana /bəˈnɑːnə/ *noun*
a long yellow fruit

banana

band /bænd/ *noun*
1 a group of people who play music together: *a rock band* ◇ *a jazz band*
2 a thin flat piece of material that you put around something: *I put a rubber band round the letters to keep them together.* ◇ *The hat had a red band round it.*

bandage /ˈbændɪdʒ/ *noun*
a long piece of white cloth that you put around a part of the body that is hurt
bandage *verb* (**bandages**, **bandaging**, **bandaged** /ˈbændɪdʒd/)
put a bandage around a part of the body: *The doctor bandaged my foot.*

bandit /ˈbændɪt/ *noun*
a person who attacks and robs people who are travelling: *They were killed by bandits in the mountains.*

bang¹ /bæŋ/ *noun*
1 a sudden very loud noise: *He shut the door with a bang.*
2 hitting somebody or something hard; being hit hard: *He fell and got a bang on the head.*
3 *American English for* **fringe 1**

bang² /bæŋ/ *verb* (**bangs**, **banging**, **banged** /bæŋd/)
make a loud noise by hitting something hard or by closing something: *He banged his head on the ceiling.* ◇ *Don't bang the door!*

banisters /ˈbænɪstəz/ *noun* (plural)
a thing like a fence at the side of stairs that you hold on to when you go up or down

p	b	t	d	k	g	tʃ	dʒ	f	v	θ	ð
pen	**b**ad	**t**ea	**d**id	**c**at	**g**ot	**ch**ain	**j**am	**f**all	**v**an	**th**in	**th**is

bank /bæŋk/ *noun*
1 a place that keeps money safe for people: *I've got £300 in the bank.*

○ If you have a bank **account**, you can **save** money, **pay** money **in** (or **deposit** it), or **draw** it **out** (or **withdraw** it). At a bank, you can also **exchange** the money of one country for the money of another. If you want to **borrow** money, a bank may **lend** it to you.

2 the land along the side of a river: *I climbed out of the boat onto the bank.*

bank holiday /ˌbæŋk ˈhɒlədeɪ/ *noun*
a day when the banks are closed and everybody in Britain has a holiday

banknote /ˈbæŋknəʊt/ *noun*
a piece of paper money: *These are German banknotes.*

bankrupt /ˈbæŋkrʌpt/ *adjective*
not able to pay the money that you should pay to people: *His business went* (= became) *bankrupt.*

banner /ˈbænə(r)/ *noun*
a long piece of cloth with words on it. People carry banners to show what they think: *The banner said 'Stop the war'.*

baptize /bæpˈtaɪz/ *verb* (**baptizes**, **baptizing**, **baptized** /bæpˈtaɪzd/)
put water on somebody or put somebody in water, and give them a name, to show that they belong to the Christian Church
baptism /ˈbæptɪzm/ *noun*
a special time when somebody is baptized

bar¹ /bɑː(r)/ *noun*
1 a place where people can buy and have drinks and sometimes food: *There's a bar in the hotel.* ◇ *a coffee bar*
2 a long table where you buy drinks in a bar or pub: *We stood at the bar.*
3 a long piece of metal: *an iron bar*
4 a piece of something hard: *a bar of soap* ◇ *a bar of chocolate* ☞ picture on page 261

bar² /bɑː(r)/ *verb* (**bars**, **barring**, **barred** /bɑːd/)
put something across a place so that people cannot pass: *A line of police barred the road.*

barbecue /ˈbɑːbɪkjuː/ *noun*
a party where you cook food on a fire outside: *We had a barbecue on the beach.*

barbed wire /ˌbɑːbd ˈwaɪə(r)/ *noun* (no plural)
wire with a lot of sharp points on it. Some fences are made of barbed wire.

barber /ˈbɑːbə(r)/ *noun*
a person whose job is to cut men's hair: *I went to the barber's* (= the barber's shop) *to have my hair cut.*

bare /beə(r)/ *adjective*
1 with no clothes or anything else covering it: *He had bare feet* (= he wasn't wearing shoes or socks). ◇ *The walls were bare* (= with no pictures on them).
2 empty: *The garden always looks very bare in winter.*

barefoot /ˈbeəfʊt/ *adjective, adverb*
with no shoes or socks on your feet: *The children ran barefoot along the beach.*

barely /ˈbeəli/ *adverb*
almost not; only just: *She barely ate anything.*

bargain¹ /ˈbɑːgən/ *noun*
something that is cheaper than usual: *This dress was a bargain – it only cost £10.*

bargain² /ˈbɑːgən/ *verb* (**bargains**, **bargaining**, **bargained** /ˈbɑːgənd/)
talk with somebody about the right price for something: *I think she'll sell the car for less if you bargain with her.*

barge /bɑːdʒ/ *noun*
a long boat with a flat bottom for carrying things or people on rivers or canals

bark¹ /bɑːk/ *noun* (no plural)
the stuff that covers the outside of a tree

bark² /bɑːk/ *noun*
the short loud noise that a dog makes
bark *verb* (**barks**, **barking**, **barked** /bɑːkt/)
make this noise: *The dog always barks at people it doesn't know.*

barley /ˈbɑːli/ *noun* (no plural)
a plant that we use for food and for making beer and some other drinks

barmaid /ˈbɑːmeɪd/ *noun*
a woman who sells drinks in a bar or pub

barman /ˈbɑːmən/ *noun* (*plural* **barmen** /ˈbɑːmən/)
a man who sells drinks in a bar or pub

barn /bɑːn/ *noun*
a large building on a farm where you keep crops or animals

s	z	ʃ	ʒ	h	m	n	ŋ	l	r	j	w
so	**zoo**	**shoe**	**vision**	**hat**	**man**	**no**	**sing**	**leg**	**red**	**yes**	**wet**

barometer /bəˈrɒmɪtə(r)/ *noun*
an instrument that helps us to know what the weather will be

barracks /ˈbærəks/ *noun* (plural)
a building or group of buildings where soldiers live: *an army barracks*

barrel /ˈbærəl/ *noun*
1 a big container for liquids, with round sides and flat ends: *a beer barrel* ◇ *a barrel of oil*
2 the long metal part of a gun that a bullet goes through

barricade /ˌbærɪˈkeɪd/ *noun*
a wall of things that people build quickly to stop other people going somewhere: *There was a barricade of lorries across the road.*
barricade *verb* (**barricades, barricading, barricaded**)
stop people going somewhere by building a barricade: *He barricaded the door to keep the police out.*

barrier /ˈbæriə(r)/ *noun*
a fence or gate that stops you going somewhere: *You must show your ticket at the barrier before you get on the train.*

barrow /ˈbærəʊ/ *noun*
a small cart that you can push or pull by hand

base¹ /beɪs/ *noun*
1 the bottom part of something; the part that something stands on: *The lamp has a flat base.*
2 the place that you start from and go back to: *She travels all over the world but London is her base* (= the place where she lives). ◇ *an army base*

base² /beɪs/ *verb* (**bases, basing, based** /beɪst/)
base something on something
make something, using another thing as an important part: *The film is based on a true story.*

baseball /ˈbeɪsbɔːl/ *noun*
1 (no plural) an American game for two teams of nine players who try to hit a ball with a **bat** on a large field: *We played baseball in the park.*
2 (*plural* **baseballs**) a ball for playing this game

basement /ˈbeɪsmənt/ *noun*
the part of a building that is under the ground

bases *plural of* **basis**

bash /bæʃ/ *verb* (**bashes, bashing, bashed** /bæʃt/)
hit somebody or something very hard: *I fell and bashed my knee.*

basic /ˈbeɪsɪk/ *adjective*
most important and necessary; simple: *A person's basic needs are food, clothes and a place to live.*
basically /ˈbeɪsɪkli/ *adverb*
mostly; mainly: *Basically I like her, but I don't always agree with what she says.*

basin /ˈbeɪsn/ *noun*
a round bowl for cooking or mixing food ☞ Look also at **wash-basin**.

basis /ˈbeɪsɪs/ *noun* (*plural* **bases** /ˈbeɪsiːz/)
the most important part or idea, from which something grows: *Her notes formed the basis of a book.*

basket

basket /ˈbɑːskɪt/ *noun*
a container made of thin sticks or thin pieces of plastic or metal, that you use for holding or carrying things: *a shopping basket* ◇ *a bread basket* ☞ Look also at **waste-paper basket**.

basketball

basketball /ˈbɑːskɪtbɔːl/ *noun*
1 (no plural) a game for two teams of five players who try to throw a ball into a high net

2 (*plural* **basketballs**) a ball for playing this game

bass /beɪs/ *adjective*
with a deep sound: *She plays the bass guitar.* ◇ *a bass drum*

bat /bæt/ *noun*
1 an animal like a mouse with wings. Bats come out and fly at night.
2 a piece of wood for hitting the ball in a game like cricket or table tennis: *a baseball bat*

batch /bætʃ/ *noun* (*plural* **batches**)
a group of things: *She made a batch of cakes.*

bath /bɑːθ/ *noun* (*plural* **baths** /bɑːðz/)
1 a large thing that you fill with water and sit in to wash your body
2 washing your body in a bath: *I had a bath this morning.*

bathe /beɪð/ *verb* (**bathes**, **bathing**, **bathed** /beɪðd/)
1 wash a part of your body carefully: *He bathed the cut on his finger.*
2 swim in the sea or in a lake or river: *On hot days we often bathe in the lake.* ✪ It is more usual to say **go swimming**.

bathroom /ˈbɑːθruːm/ *noun*
a room where you can wash and have a bath or shower ✪ In American English, a **bathroom** is also a room with a toilet in it.

battery /ˈbætri/
noun (*plural*
batteries)
a thing that gives
electricity. You put
batteries inside
things like torches
and radios to make
them work: *The car needs a new battery.*

batteries

battle /ˈbætl/ *noun*
1 a fight between armies in a war: *Who won the battle?*
2 trying very hard to do something difficult: *a battle against the illness*
battle *verb* (**battles**, **battling**, **battled** /ˈbætld/)
try very hard to do something difficult: *The doctors battled to save her life.*

bay /beɪ/ *noun* (*plural* **bays**)
a place where the land goes inwards and the sea fills the space: *There was a ship in the bay.* ◇ *the Bay of Biscay*

bazaar /bəˈzɑː(r)/ *noun*
a market in Asia or Africa

BC /ˌbiː ˈsiː/
'BC' in a date shows it was before Christ was born: *Julius Caesar died in 44 BC.* ☞ Look at **AD**.

be /bi/, /biː/ *verb*
1 a word that you use when you name or describe somebody or something: *I'm* (= I am) *Ben.* ◇ *Grass is green.* ◇ *Are you hot?* ◇ *Lucy is a doctor.* ◇ *Where were you yesterday?* ◇ *It is six o'clock.*
2 happen: *Her birthday was in May.*
3 a word that you use with another verb: *'What are you doing?' 'I am reading.'*
4 a word that you use with part of another verb to show that something happens to somebody or something: *This cheese is made in France.* ◇ *The house was built in 1910.*
5 a word that shows that something must or will happen: *You are to go to bed immediately!*

beach /biːtʃ/ *noun* (*plural* **beaches**)
a piece of land next to the sea that is covered with sand or stones: *a sandy beach* ◇ *We lay on the beach in the sun.*

bead /biːd/ *noun*
a small ball of wood, glass or plastic with a hole in the middle. Beads are put on a string to make a necklace.

beak /biːk/ *noun*
the hard pointed part of a bird's mouth ☞ picture at **bird**

beam /biːm/ *noun*
1 a long heavy piece of wood that holds up a roof or ceiling
2 a line of light: *sunbeams*

bean /biːn/ *noun*
the long thin part of
some plants, or the
seeds inside it, that
we use as food:
green beans
◇ *coffee beans*

bean

bear[1] /beə(r)/ *noun*
a big wild animal with thick fur ☞ Look also at **teddy bear**.

bear[2] /beə(r)/ *verb* (**bears**, **bearing**, **bore** /bɔː(r)/, **has borne** /bɔːn/)

be

present tense		short forms	negative short forms
I	**am** /æm/	I**'m**	I**'m not**
you	**are** /ɑː(r)/	you**'re**	you **aren't**
he/she/it	**is** /ɪz/	he**'s**/she**'s**/it**'s**	he/she/it **isn't**
we	**are**	we**'re**	we **aren't**
you	**are**	you**'re**	you **aren't**
they	**are**	they**'re**	they **aren't**

past tense		
I	**was** /wɒz/	*present participle* **being**
you	**were** /wɜː(r)/	*past participle* **been**
he/she/it	**was**	
we	**were**	
you	**were**	
they	**were**	

1 have pain or problems without complaining: *The pain was difficult to bear.*
2 hold somebody or something up so that they do not fall: *The ice is too thin to bear your weight.*
can't bear something hate something: *I can't bear this music.* ◇ *He can't bear having nothing to do.*

beard /bɪəd/ *noun*
the hair on a man's chin and cheeks: *He has got a beard.*
bearded *adjective*
with a beard: *a bearded man*

– beard

beast /biːst/ *noun*
1 a big animal
✪ **Animal** is the word that we usually use.
2 an unkind or cruel person

beat¹ /biːt/ *noun*
a sound that comes again and again: *We heard the beat of the drums.* ◇ *Can you feel her heartbeat?*

beat² /biːt/ *verb* (**beats, beating, beat, has beaten** /'biːtn/)
1 win a fight or game against a person or group of people: *Daniel always beats me at tennis.* ◇ *Our team was beaten.*
2 hit somebody or something very hard many times: *She beats her dog with a stick.* ◇ *The rain was beating on the roof.*
3 make the same sound or movement many times: *His heart was beating fast.*
4 mix food quickly with a fork, for example: *Beat the eggs and sugar together.*

beautiful /'bjuːtəfl/ *adjective*
very nice to see, hear or smell; lovely: *Those flowers are beautiful.* ◇ *What a beautiful song!* ◇ *a beautiful woman*
✪ When we talk about people, we usually use **beautiful** and **pretty** for women and girls, and **handsome** and **good-looking** for men and boys.

beautifully /'bjuːtəfli/ *adverb*
Louis sang beautifully.

beauty /'bjuːti/ *noun* (no plural)
being beautiful: *She was a woman of great beauty.* ◇ *the beauty of the mountains*

because /bɪ'kɒz/ *conjunction*
for the reason that: *He was angry because I was late.*
because of something as a result of something: *We stayed at home because of the rain.*

become /bɪ'kʌm/ *verb* (**becomes, becoming, became** /bɪ'keɪm/, **has become**)
grow or change and begin to be something: *She became a doctor in 1982.* ◇ *The weather is becoming colder.*
become of somebody or **something** happen to somebody or something: *What became of David? I haven't seen him for years.*

p	b	t	d	k	g	tʃ	dʒ	f	v	θ	ð
pen	**b**ad	**t**ea	**d**id	**c**at	**g**ot	**ch**ain	**j**am	**f**all	**v**an	**th**in	**th**is

bed /bed/ *noun*
1 a thing that you sleep on: *I was tired, so I went to bed.* ◇ *The children are in bed.*
2 the bottom of a river or the sea
bed and breakfast a small hotel or a house where you can sleep and have breakfast: *I stayed in a bed and breakfast.*
make the bed put the covers on a bed so that it is tidy and ready for somebody to sleep in it

bedclothes /'bedkləʊðz/ *noun* (plural) all the covers (for example **sheets, blankets** or **duvets**) that you put on a bed

bedroom /'bedruːm/ *noun* a room where you sleep

bedsit /'bedsɪt/, **bedsitter** /ˌbed'sɪtə(r)/ *noun* one room that you live and sleep in

bee /biː/ *noun* a small insect that flies and makes honey

beef /biːf/ *noun* (no plural) meat from a cow: *roast beef* ☞ Note at **cow**

beefburger /'biːfbɜːɡə(r)/ *noun* beef cut into very small pieces and made into a flat round shape

beehive /'biːhaɪv/ *noun* a box where bees live

been
1 *form of* **be**
2 *form of* **go**[1]
have been to have gone to a place and come back: *Have you ever been to Scotland?* ☞ Note at **go**

beer /bɪə(r)/ *noun*
1 (no plural) an alcoholic drink made from grain: *a pint of beer*
2 (plural **beers**) a glass, bottle or can of beer: *Three beers, please.*

beetle /'biːtl/ *noun* an insect with hard wings and a shiny body

beetroot /'biːtruːt/ *noun* a round dark-red vegetable that you cook before you eat it

before[1] /bɪ'fɔː(r)/ *preposition*
1 earlier than somebody or something: *He arrived before me.* ◇ *I lived in America before coming to England.*
2 in front of somebody or something: *B comes before C in the alphabet.*

before[2] /bɪ'fɔː(r)/ *adverb* at an earlier time; in the past: *I've never met them before.* ◇ *I've seen this film before.*

before[3] /bɪ'fɔː(r)/ *conjunction* earlier than the time that: *I said goodbye before I left.*

beforehand /bɪ'fɔːhænd/ *adverb* at an earlier time than something: *Tell me beforehand if you are going to be late.*

beg /beɡ/ *verb* (**begs, begging, begged** /beɡd/)
1 ask for money or food because you are very poor: *There are a lot of people begging in the streets.*
2 ask somebody for something in a very strong way: *She begged me to stay with her.* ◇ *He begged for help.*
I beg your pardon 1 I am sorry: *'You've taken my seat.' 'Oh, I beg your pardon.'* **2** What did you say?

beggar /'beɡə(r)/ *noun* a person who asks other people for money or food

begin /bɪ'ɡɪn/ *verb* (**begins, beginning, began** /bɪ'ɡæn/, **has begun** /bɪ'ɡʌn/) start to do something or start to happen: *The film begins at 7.30.* ◇ *The baby began crying.* ◇ *I'm beginning to feel cold.* ◇ *The name John begins with a 'J'.*
to begin with at first; at the beginning: *To begin with he was afraid of the water, but he soon learned to swim.*

beginner /bɪ'ɡɪnə(r)/ *noun* a person who is starting to do or learn something

beginning /bɪ'ɡɪnɪŋ/ *noun* the time or place where something starts; the first part of something: *I didn't see the beginning of the film.*

begun *form of* **begin**

behalf /bɪ'hɑːf/ *noun*
on behalf of somebody, on somebody's behalf for somebody; in the place of somebody: *Mr Smith is away, so I am writing to you on his behalf.*

behave /bɪ'heɪv/ *verb* (**behaves, behaving, behaved** /bɪ'heɪvd/) do and say things in a certain way when you are with other people: *They behaved very kindly towards me.* ◇ *The children behaved badly all day.*
behave yourself be good; do and say

s	z	ʃ	ʒ	h	m	n	ŋ	l	r	j	w
so	**zoo**	**shoe**	**vision**	**hat**	**man**	**no**	**sing**	**leg**	**red**	**yes**	**wet**

the right things: *Did the children behave themselves?*

behavior *American English for* **behaviour**

behaviour /bɪ'heɪvjə(r)/ *noun* (no plural)
the way you are; the way that you do and say things when you are with other people: *The teacher was pleased with the children's good behaviour.*

behind /bɪ'haɪnd/ *preposition, adverb*
1 at or to the back of somebody or something: *I hid behind the wall.* ◇ *I went in front and Jim followed behind.* ☞ picture on page 125
2 slower or less good than somebody or something; slower or less good than you should be: *She is behind with her work because she has been ill.*
3 in the place where you were before: *I got off the train and left my suitcase behind (= on the train).*

being¹ *form of* **be**

being² /'biːɪŋ/ *noun*
a person or living thing: *a being from another planet*

belief /bɪ'liːf/ *noun*
a sure feeling that something is true or real: *his belief in God*

believe /bɪ'liːv/ *verb* (**believes, believing, believed** /bɪ'liːvd/)
feel sure that something is true or right; feel sure that what somebody says is true: *She says she didn't take the money. Do you believe her?* ◇ *Long ago, people believed that the earth was flat.*
believe in somebody or **something** feel sure that somebody or something is real: *Do you believe in ghosts?*

bell /bel/ *noun*
a metal thing that makes a sound when something hits or touches it: *The church bells were ringing.* ◇ *I rang the bell and he answered the door.*

bell

belly /'beli/ *noun* (*plural* **bellies**)
the part of your body between your chest and your legs; your stomach

belong /bɪ'lɒŋ/ *verb* (**belongs, belonging, belonged** /bɪ'lɒŋd/)
have its right or usual place: *That chair belongs in my room.*
belong to somebody be somebody's: *'Who does this pen belong to?' 'It belongs to me.'*
belong to something be in a group, club, etc: *She belongs to the tennis club.*

belongings /bɪ'lɒŋɪŋz/ *noun* (plural)
the things that you own: *They lost all their belongings in the fire.*

below /bɪ'ləʊ/ *preposition, adverb*
1 in or to a lower place than somebody or something: *From the plane we could see the mountains below.* ◇ *Your mouth is below your nose.* ◇ *Do not write below this line.* ☞ picture on page 125
2 less than a number or price: *The temperature was below zero.*

belt /belt/ *noun*
a long piece of cloth or leather that you wear around the middle of your body ☞ picture at **suit**. Look also at **safety-belt** and **seat-belt**.

bench

bench /bentʃ/ *noun* (*plural* **benches**)
1 a long seat made of wood or metal, usually outside
2 a long table where somebody, for example a carpenter, works

bend¹ /bend/ *verb* (**bends, bending, bent** /bent/, **has bent**)
become curved; make something that was straight into a curved shape:

He is **bending** down.

Bend your legs! ◇ *She couldn't bend the metal bar.*
bend down, bend over move your body forward and down: *She bent down to put on her shoes.*

bend² /bend/ *noun*
a part of a road or river that is not straight: *Drive slowly – there's a bend in the road.*

iː	i	ɪ	e	æ	ɑː		ɒ	ɔː	ʊ	u	uː
see	happy	sit	ten	cat	father		got	saw	put	situation	too

beneath /bɪ'niːθ/ preposition, adverb
in or to a lower place than somebody or
something: *From the tower, they looked
down on the city beneath.* ✪ **Under** and
below are the words that we usually use.

benefit /'benɪfɪt/ verb (**benefits**, **bene-
fiting**, **benefited**)
be good or helpful in some way: *The new
law will benefit families with children.*
benefit from something get something good or useful from something: *She
will benefit from a holiday.*
benefit noun
something that is good or helpful: *What
are the benefits of having a computer?* ◇ *I
did it for your benefit* (= to help you).

bent form of **bend**[1]

berry /'beri/ noun (plural **berries**)
a small soft fruit with seeds in it: *a strawberry* ◇ *a blackberry* ◇ *raspberries*

beside /bɪ'saɪd/ preposition
at the side of somebody or something; next
to somebody or something: *Come and sit
beside me.* ☞ picture on page 125

besides[1] /bɪ'saɪdz/ preposition
as well as somebody or something; if you
do not count somebody or something:
*There were four people in the room, be-
sides me and Jim.*

besides[2] /bɪ'saɪdz/ adverb
also: *I don't like this shirt. Besides, it's too
expensive.*

best[1] /best/ adjective (**good**, **better**,
best)
most good: *This is the best ice-cream I
have ever eaten!* ◇ *Tom is my best friend.*

best[2] /best/ adverb
1 most well: *I work best in the morning.*
2 more than all others; most: *Which picture do you like best?*

best[3] /best/ noun (no plural)
the most good person or thing: *Mike and
Ian are good at tennis but Paul is the best.*
all the best words that you use when
you say goodbye to somebody, to wish
them success
do your best do all that you can: *I don't
know if I can finish the work today, but I'll
do my best.*

best man /ˌbest 'mæn/ noun
a man at a wedding who helps the man
who is getting married

bet /bet/ verb (**bets**, **betting**, **bet** or **betted**, **has bet** or **has betted**)
say what you think will happen. If you are
right, you win money, but if you are
wrong, you lose money: *I bet you £5 that
our team will win.*
I bet I am sure: *I bet it will rain tomorrow.* ◇ *I bet you can't climb that tree.*
bet noun
I lost the bet.

betray /bɪ'treɪ/ verb (**betrays**, **betray-
ing**, **betrayed** /bɪ'treɪd/)
do something that harms somebody who
was your friend: *The guards betrayed the
King and let the enemy into the castle.*

better /'betə(r)/ adjective (**good**, **better**,
best)
1 more good: *This book is better than that
one.*
2 less ill: *I was ill yesterday, but I feel better now.*
better adverb
more well: *You speak French better than I
do.*
better off happier, richer, etc: *You look
ill – you would be better off in bed.* ◇ *I'm
better off now that I've got a new job.*
had better ought to; should: *You'd better go now if you want to catch the train.*

between /bɪ'twiːn/ preposition
1 in the space in the middle of two things
or people: *The letter B comes between A
and C.* ◇ *I sat between Sylvie and
Bruno.* ☞ picture on page 125
2 to and from two places: *The boat sails
between Dover and Calais.*
3 more than one thing but less than another thing: *The meal will cost between
£10 and £15.*
4 after one time and before the next time:
I'll meet you between 4 and 4.30.
5 for or by two or more people or things:
We shared the cake between us (= each of
us had some cake).
6 a word that you use when you compare
two people or things: *What is the difference between the two hotels?*
☞ Note at **among**
in between in the middle of two things,
people, times, etc: *I found my shoe in between two rocks.*

beware /bɪ'weə(r)/ verb
beware of somebody or **something**
be careful because somebody or something

ʌ	ɜː	ə	eɪ	əʊ	aɪ	aʊ	ɔɪ	ɪə	eə	ʊə
cup	**bird**	**about**	**say**	**go**	**five**	**now**	**boy**	**near**	**hair**	**pure**

is dangerous: *Beware of the dog!* (words written on a sign)

bewildered /bɪ'wɪldəd/ *adjective*
If you are bewildered, you do not understand something or you do not know what to do: *He was bewildered by all the noises of the big city.*

beyond /bɪ'jɒnd/ *preposition, adverb*
on the other side of something; further than something: *The road continues beyond Birmingham.* ◇ *We could see the lake and the mountains beyond.*

bib /bɪb/ *noun*
a piece of cloth or plastic that a baby wears under its chin when it is eating

Bible /'baɪbl/ *noun*
the holy book of the Christian and Jewish religions

saddle handlebars **bicycle**
tyre
pedal
chain

bicycle /'baɪsɪk(ə)l/ *noun*
a machine with two wheels. You sit on a bicycle and move your legs to make the wheels turn: *Can you ride a bicycle?* ❍ The short form of 'bicycle' is **bike**. **Cycle** means to travel by bicycle.

bid /bɪd/ *verb* (**bids, bidding, bid, has bid**)
offer some money because you want to buy something: *He bid £10 000 for the painting.*
bid *noun*
an offer of money for something that you want to buy: *She made a bid of £250 for the vase.*

big /bɪg/ *adjective* (**bigger, biggest**)
1 not small; large: *Milan is a big city.* ◇ *This shirt is too big for me.* ◇ *How big is your flat?* ☞ picture on page 262
2 great or important: *a big problem*
3 older: *Amy is my big sister.*

bike /baɪk/ *noun*
a bicycle or a motorcycle

bill /bɪl/ *noun*
1 a piece of paper that shows how much money you must pay for something: *Can I have the bill, please?* (in a restaurant)
2 *American English for* **note**[1] **3**: *a ten-dollar bill*

billion /'bɪliən/ *number*
1 000 000 000; one thousand million: *five billion pounds* ◇ *There are billions of people in the world.*

bin /bɪn/ *noun*
1 a thing that you put rubbish in: *I threw the empty bag in the bin.* ☞ Look also at **dustbin**.
2 a thing with a lid that you keep things in: *a bread bin*

bind /baɪnd/ *verb* (**binds, binding, bound** /baʊnd/, **has bound**)
tie string or rope round something to hold it firmly: *They bound the prisoner's arms and legs together.*

bingo /'bɪŋgəʊ/ *noun* (no plural)
a game where each player has a card with numbers on it. When the person who controls the game says all the numbers on your card, you win the game.

binoculars /bɪ'nɒkjələz/ *noun* (plural)
special glasses that you use to see things that are far away

biography /baɪ'ɒɡrəfi/ *noun* (*plural* **biographies**)
the story of a person's life, that another person writes: *Have you read the biography of Nelson Mandela?*

biology /baɪ'ɒlədʒi/ *noun* (no plural)
the study of the life of animals and plants: *Biology is my favourite subject at school.*
biologist /baɪ'ɒlədʒɪst/ *noun*
a person who studies or knows a lot about biology

wing **bird**
beak

bird /bɜːd/ *noun*
an animal with feathers and wings: *Gulls and sparrows are birds.*

❍ Most birds can **fly** and **sing**. They build **nests** and **lay eggs**.

bird of prey /ˌbɜːd əv ˈpreɪ/ *noun*
a bird that catches and eats small birds and animals: *Eagles are birds of prey.*

Biro /ˈbaɪərəʊ/ *noun* (*plural* **Biros**)
a pen that has a very small ball at the end
✪ Biro is a trade mark.

birth /bɜːθ/ *noun*
the time when a baby comes out of its mother; being born: *the birth of a baby* ◇ *What's your date of birth?* (= the date when you were born)
give birth have a baby: *My sister gave birth to her second child last week.*

birthday /ˈbɜːθdeɪ/ *noun* (*plural* **birthdays**)
the day each year that is the same as the date when you were born: *My birthday is on May 2nd.* ◇ *a birthday present*
✪ When it is a person's birthday, we say **Happy Birthday!** or **Many happy returns!**

biscuit /ˈbɪskɪt/ *noun*
a kind of small thin dry cake: *a packet of biscuits* ◇ *a chocolate biscuit*

biscuits

bishop /ˈbɪʃəp/ *noun*
an important priest in the Christian church, who looks after all the churches in a large area

bit /bɪt/ *noun*
a small piece or amount of something: *Would you like a bit of cake?* ◇ *Some bits of the film were very funny.*
a bit **1** a little: *You look a bit tired.* **2** a short time: *Let's wait a bit.*
a bit of a rather a: *It's a bit of a long way to the station.*
bit by bit slowly or a little at a time: *Bit by bit, I started to feel better.*
come to bits, fall to bits break into small pieces: *The cake fell to bits when I tried to cut it.*

bite¹ /baɪt/ *verb* (**bites**, **biting**, **bit** /bɪt/, **has bitten** /ˈbɪtn/)
1 cut something with your teeth: *That dog bit my leg!*
2 If an insect or snake bites you, it hurts you by pushing a small sharp part into your skin: *I've been bitten by mosquitoes.*

bite² /baɪt/ *noun*
1 a piece of food that you can put in your mouth: *He took a bite of his sandwich.*
2 a painful place on your skin made by an insect or dog, for example: *a snake bite*

bitter¹ /ˈbɪtə(r)/ *adjective*
1 with a sharp unpleasant taste, like very strong coffee; not sweet
2 angry and sad about something that has happened: *He felt very bitter about losing his job.*
3 very cold: *a bitter wind*

bitter² /ˈbɪtə(r)/ *noun* (no plural)
a dark beer: *A pint of bitter, please.*

black /blæk/ *adjective* (**blacker**, **blackest**)
1 with the colour of the sky at night: *a black dog*
2 with dark skin: *Martin Luther King was a famous black leader.*
3 without milk: *black coffee*
black *noun*
1 the colour of the sky at night: *She was dressed in black.*
2 a person with dark skin
black and white with the colours black, white and grey only: *We watched a black and white film on TV.*

blackberry /ˈblækbəri/ *noun* (*plural* **blackberries**)
a small soft black fruit that grows on a bush

blackbird /ˈblækbɜːd/ *noun*
a bird with black feathers

blackboard /ˈblækbɔːd/ *noun*
a dark board that a teacher writes on with chalk: *Look at the blackboard.*

blackcurrant /ˌblækˈkʌrənt/ *noun*
a small round black fruit that grows on a bush

blackmail /ˈblækmeɪl/ *noun* (no plural)
saying that you will tell something bad about somebody if they do not give you money or do something for you

blade /bleɪd/ *noun*
1 the flat sharp part of a knife, sword or another thing that cuts
2 a long thin leaf of grass or wheat: *a blade of grass*

blame /bleɪm/ *verb* (**blames**, **blaming**, **blamed** /bleɪmd/)
say that a certain person or thing made

something bad happen: *The other driver blamed me for the accident.*
blame *noun* (no plural)
take the blame say that you are the person who did something wrong: *Eve took the blame for the mistake.*

blank /blæŋk/ *adjective*
1 with no writing, pictures or anything else on it: *a blank piece of paper*
2 If your face is blank, it shows no feelings or understanding: *I asked her a question, but she just gave me a blank look.*

blanket /'blæŋkɪt/ *noun*
a thick cover that you put on a bed

blast¹ /blɑːst/ *noun*
1 when a bomb explodes: *Two people were killed in the blast.*
2 a sudden movement of air: *a blast of cold air*
3 a loud sound made by a musical instrument like a trumpet
blast-off /'blɑːst ɒf/ *noun*
the time when a spacecraft leaves the ground

blast² /blɑːst/ *verb* (**blasts, blasting, blasted**)
make a hole in something with an explosion: *They blasted through the mountain to make a tunnel.*

blaze /bleɪz/ *noun*
a large strong fire: *The firemen put out the blaze.*
blaze *verb* (**blazes, blazing, blazed** /bleɪzd/)
burn strongly and brightly: *a blazing fire*

blazer /'bleɪzə(r)/ *noun*
a jacket. Blazers sometimes show which school or club you belong to.

bleak /bliːk/ *adjective* (**bleaker, bleakest**)
cold and grey: *It was a bleak winter's day.*

bleed /bliːd/ *verb* (**bleeds, bleeding, bled** /bled/, **has bled**)
lose blood: *I have cut my hand and it's bleeding.*

blend /blend/ *verb* (**blends, blending, blended**)
1 mix: *Blend the sugar and the butter together.*
2 look or sound good together: *These colours blend very well.*

blend *noun*
a mixture of things: *This is a blend of two different kinds of coffee.*

bless /bles/ *verb* (**blesses, blessing, blessed** /blest/)
ask for God's help for somebody or something: *The priest blessed the young couple.*
Bless you! words that you say to somebody when they sneeze

blew *form of* **blow¹**

blind¹ /blaɪnd/ *adjective*
not able to see: *The blind man had a dog to help him.* ◇ *My cat is going* (= becoming) *blind.*
the blind *noun* (plural)
people who are blind
blindness /'blaɪndnəs/ *noun* (no plural)
being blind

blind² /blaɪnd/ *noun*
a piece of cloth or other material that you pull down to cover a window

blind

blindfold /'blaɪndfəʊld/ *noun*
a piece of cloth that you put over somebody's eyes so that they cannot see
blindfold *verb* (**blindfolds, blindfolding, blindfolded**)
put a piece of cloth over somebody's eyes so that they cannot see

blink /blɪŋk/ *verb* (**blinks, blinking, blinked** /blɪŋkt/)
shut and open your eyes very quickly

blister /'blɪstə(r)/ *noun*
a small painful place on your skin, that is full of liquid. Rubbing or burning can cause blisters: *My new shoes gave me blisters.*

blizzard /'blɪzəd/ *noun*
a very bad storm with snow and strong winds

blob /blɒb/ *noun*
a small piece of a thick liquid: *There are blobs of paint on the floor.*

block¹ /blɒk/ *noun*
1 a big heavy piece of something, with flat sides: *a block of wood* ◇ *The bridge is made of concrete blocks.*
2 a big building with a lot of offices or flats inside: *an office block* ◇ *a block of flats*

3 a group of buildings with streets all round it: *We drove round the block looking for the hotel.*
4 a thing that stops somebody or something from moving forward: *The police have put road blocks around the town.*

block² /blɒk/ *verb* (**blocks, blocking, blocked** /blɒkt/)
stop somebody or something from moving forward: *A fallen tree blocked the road.*

blond /blɒnd/ *adjective*
with light-coloured hair: *He's got blond hair.* ✿ The spelling **blonde** is used for women: *She is tall and blonde.*
blonde *noun*
a woman who has blond hair

blood /blʌd/ *noun* (no plural)
the red liquid inside your body

bloody¹ /'blʌdi/ *adjective* (**bloodier, bloodiest**)
1 covered with blood: *a bloody nose*
2 with a lot of killing: *It was a bloody war.*

bloody² /'blʌdi/ *adjective, adverb*
a rude word that you use to make what you say stronger, often because you are angry: *The bloody train was late again!*

bloom /bluːm/ *verb* (**blooms, blooming, bloomed** /bluːmd/)
have flowers: *Roses bloom in the summer.*

blossom /'blɒsəm/ *noun* (no plural)
the flowers on a tree or bush: *The apple trees are covered in blossom.*
blossom *verb* (**blossoms, blossoming, blossomed** /'blɒsəmd/)
have flowers: *The cherry trees are blossoming.*

blouse /blaʊz/ *noun*
a piece of clothing like a shirt that a woman or girl wears on the top part of her body

blow¹ /bləʊ/ *verb* (**blows, blowing, blew** /bluː/, **has blown** /bləʊn/)
1 When air or wind blows, it moves: *The wind was blowing from the sea.*
2 move something through the air: *The wind blew my hat off.*
3 send air out from your mouth
4 send air out from your mouth into a musical instrument, for example, to make a noise: *The referee blew his whistle.*
blow up 1 explode; make something explode, for example with a bomb: *The plane*

blew up. ◇ *They blew up the station.*
2 fill something with air: *We blew up some balloons for the party.*

blow² /bləʊ/ *noun*
1 hitting somebody or something hard; being hit hard: *He felt a blow on the back of his head and he fell.*
2 something that happens suddenly and that makes you very unhappy: *Her father's death was a terrible blow to her.*

blue /bluː/ *adjective* (**bluer, bluest**)
with the colour of a clear sky on a sunny day: *He wore a blue shirt.* ◇ *dark-blue carpet* ◇ *Her eyes are bright blue.*
blue *noun*
She was dressed in blue.

blunt /blʌnt/ *adjective*
1 with an edge or point that is not sharp: *This pencil is blunt.*
2 If you are blunt, you say what you think in a way that is not polite: *She was very blunt and told me that she didn't like my plan.*

blur /blɜː(r)/ *verb* (**blurs, blurring, blurred** /blɜːd/)
make something less clear: *If you move while you are taking the photo, it will be blurred.*

blush /blʌʃ/ *verb* (**blushes, blushing, blushed** /blʌʃt/)
If you blush, your face suddenly becomes red because you are shy, for example: *She blushed when he looked at her.*

boar /bɔː(r)/ *noun*
1 a male pig
2 a wild pig

board¹ /bɔːd/ *noun*
1 a long thin flat piece of wood: *I nailed a board across the broken window.* ◇ *floorboards*
2 a flat piece of wood, for example, that you use for a special purpose: *There is a list of names on the notice-board.* ◇ *a chess-board* ◇ *an ironing-board* ☞ Look also at **blackboard**.
3 a group of people who have a special job, for example controlling a company: *the board of directors*
on board on a ship or an aeroplane: *How many passengers are on board?*

board² /bɔːd/ *verb* (**boards, boarding, boarded**)
get on a ship, bus, train or an aeroplane:

We boarded the plane at Gatwick.
◇ *Flight BA 193 to Paris is now boarding* (= is ready for passengers to get on).
boarding card /'bɔ:dɪŋ kɑ:d/ *noun*
a card that you must show when you get on an aeroplane or a ship

boarding-school /'bɔ:dɪŋ sku:l/ *noun*
a school where the pupils live

boast /bəʊst/ *verb* (**boasts, boasting, boasted**)
talk in a way that shows you are too proud of something that you have or something that you can do: *He boasted that he was the fastest runner in the school.*

boats

boat /bəʊt/ *noun*
a small ship for travelling on water: *a fishing boat* ◇ *We travelled by boat.*

body /'bɒdi/ *noun* (*plural* **bodies**)
1 all of a person or an animal, but not the mind: *Arms, legs, hands and feet are all parts of the body.* ◇ *the human body*
2 all of a person or animal, but not the legs, arms or head
3 a dead person: *The police found a body in the river.*

bodyguard /'bɒdigɑ:d/ *noun*
a person or group of people whose job is to keep an important person safe: *The President's bodyguards all carry guns.*

boil /bɔɪl/ *verb* (**boils, boiling, boiled** /bɔɪld/)
1 When a liquid boils, it becomes very hot and makes steam and bubbles: *Water boils at 100° C.*
2 heat a liquid until it boils: *I boiled some water for the pasta.*
3 cook something in very hot water: *Boil the rice in a pan.* ◇ *a boiled egg*
boil over boil and flow over the sides of a pan: *Don't let the milk boil over.*

boiler /'bɔɪlə(r)/ *noun*
a big metal container that heats water for a building

boiling /'bɔɪlɪŋ/ *adjective*
very hot: *Open the window – I'm boiling.*

bold /bəʊld/ *adjective* (**bolder, boldest**)
brave and not afraid: *It was very bold of you to ask for more money.*
boldly *adverb*
He boldly said that he disagreed.

bolt /bəʊlt/ *noun*
1 a piece of metal that you move across to lock a door
2 a thick metal pin that you use with another piece of metal (called a **nut**) to fix things together
bolt *verb* (**bolts, bolting, bolted**)
lock a door by putting a bolt across it

bomb /bɒm/ *noun*
a thing that explodes and hurts or damages people or things: *Aircraft dropped bombs on the city.* ◇ *A bomb went off* (= exploded) *at the station.*
bomb *verb* (**bombs, bombing, bombed** /bɒmd/)
attack people or a place with bombs: *The city was bombed in the war.*

bone /bəʊn/ *noun*
one of the hard white parts inside the body of a person or an animal: *She broke a bone in her foot.* ◇ *This fish has a lot of bones in it.*

bonfire /'bɒnfaɪə(r)/ *noun*
a big fire that you make outside
Bonfire Night /'bɒnfaɪə naɪt/ *another word for* **Guy Fawkes Night** ☞ Note at **guy**

bonnet /'bɒnɪt/ *noun*
1 the front part of a car that covers the engine ☞ picture at **car**
2 a soft hat that you tie under your chin

book¹ /bʊk/ *noun*
a thing that you read or write in, that has a lot of pieces of paper joined together inside a cover: *I'm reading a book by George Orwell.* ◇ *an exercise book*

book² /bʊk/ *verb* (**books, booking, booked** /bʊkt/)
ask somebody to keep something for you so that you can use it later: *We booked a table*

for six at the restaurant. ◇ *The hotel is fully booked* (= all the rooms are full).

book in tell the person at the desk in a hotel that you have arrived

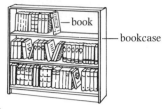
— book
— bookcase

bookcase /'bʊk keɪs/ *noun*
a piece of furniture that you put books in

booking /'bʊkɪŋ/ *noun*
asking somebody to keep something for you so that you can use it later: *When did you make your booking?*

booking-office /'bʊkɪŋ ɒfɪs/ *noun*
a place where you buy tickets

booklet /'bʊklət/ *noun*
a small thin book

bookshop /'bʊkʃɒp/ *noun*
a shop that sells books

boom /buːm/ *verb* (**booms**, **booming**, **boomed** /buːmd/)
make a loud deep sound: *We heard the guns booming in the distance.*

boots

boot /buːt/ *noun*
1 a shoe that covers your foot and ankle and sometimes part of your leg
2 the part of a car where you can put bags and boxes, usually at the back ☞ picture at **car**

border /'bɔːdə(r)/ *noun*
1 a line between two countries: *You need a passport to cross the border.*
2 a line along the edge of something: *a white tablecloth with a blue border*

bore¹ *form of* **bear**²

bore² /bɔː(r)/ *verb* (**bores**, **boring**, **bored** /bɔːd/)
If something bores you, it makes you feel

tired because it is not interesting: *He bores everyone with his long stories.*

bored *adjective*
not interested; unhappy because you have nothing interesting to do: *I'm bored with this book.* ◇ *I'm bored. What can I do?*

boredom /'bɔːdəm/ *noun* (no plural)
being bored

boring *adjective*
not interesting: *That lesson was boring!*

bore³ /bɔː(r)/ *verb* (**bores**, **boring**, **bored** /bɔːd/)
make a thin round hole in something: *These insects bore holes in wood.*

born /bɔːn/ *adjective*
be born start your life: *I was born in 1980.* ◇ *Where were you born?*

borne *form of* **bear**²

borrow or lend?

She is **lending** her son some money.

He is **borrowing** some money from his mother.

borrow /'bɒrəʊ/ *verb* (**borrows**, **borrowing**, **borrowed** /'bɒrəʊd/)
take and use something that you will give back after a short time: *I borrowed some books from the library.* ◇ *He borrowed £10 from his father.*

boss /bɒs/ *noun* (*plural* **bosses**)
a person who controls a place where people work and tells people what they must do: *I asked my boss for a holiday.*

bossy /'bɒsi/ *adjective* (**bossier**, **bossiest**)
A bossy person likes to tell other people what to do: *My sister is very bossy.*

both /bəʊθ/ *adjective, pronoun*
the two; not only one but also the other: *Hold it in both hands.* ◇ *Both her brothers are doctors.* ◇ *Both of us like skiing.* ◇ *We both like skiing.*

both *adverb*
both ... and not only ... but also: *She is both rich and intelligent.*

bother /ˈbɒðə(r)/ *verb* (**bothers, bothering, bothered** /ˈbɒðəd/)
1 do something that gives you extra work or that takes extra time: *Don't bother to do the washing-up – I'll do it later.*
2 worry somebody; stop somebody from doing something, for example thinking, working or sleeping: *Don't bother me now – I'm busy!* ◇ *Is this music bothering you?* ◇ *I'm sorry to bother you, but could you tell me the way to the station?*
bother *noun* (no plural)
trouble or difficulty: *'Thanks for your help!' 'It was no bother.'*
bothered *adjective*
worried
can't be bothered If you can't be bothered to do something, you do not want to do it because it is too much work: *I can't be bothered to do my homework now.*

bottle /ˈbɒtl/ *noun*
a tall round glass or plastic container for liquids, with a thin part at the top: *a beer bottle* ◇ *They drank two bottles of water.*

bottle

bottom /ˈbɒtəm/ *noun*
1 the lowest part of something: *They live at the bottom of the hill.* ◇ *The book was at the bottom of my bag.* ◇ *Look at the picture at the bottom of the page.* ✪ opposite: **top** ☞ picture at **back**
2 the last part of something; the end: *The bank is at the bottom of the road.* ✪ opposite: **top**
3 the part of your body that you sit on: *She fell on her bottom.* ☞ picture on page 126
bottom *adjective*
lowest: *Put the book on the bottom shelf.*
✪ opposite: **top**

bought *form of* **buy**

boulder /ˈbəʊldə(r)/ *noun*
a very big rock

bounce /baʊns/ *verb* (**bounces, bouncing, bounced** /ˈbaʊnst/)
1 When a ball bounces, it moves away quickly after it hits something hard: *The ball bounced off the wall.*

2 make a ball do this: *The boy was bouncing a basketball.*
3 jump up and down a lot: *The children were bouncing on their beds.*

bound¹ *form of* **bind**

bound² /baʊnd/ *adjective*
bound to certain to do something: *She works very hard, so she is bound to pass the exam.*

bound³ /baʊnd/ *adjective*
bound for going to a place: *This ship is bound for New York.*

bound⁴ /baʊnd/ *verb* (**bounds, bounding, bounded**)
jump, or run with small jumps: *The dog bounded up the steps.*

boundary /ˈbaʊndri/ *noun* (*plural* **boundaries**)
a line between two places: *This fence is the boundary between the two gardens.*

bouquet /buˈkeɪ/ *noun*
a group of flowers that you give or get as a present: *She gave me a bouquet of roses.*

bow¹ /baʊ/ *verb* (**bows, bowing, bowed** /baʊd/)
bend your head or body forward to show respect: *The actors bowed at the end of the play.*
bow *noun*
He gave a bow and left the room.

bow²

bow² /bəʊ/ *noun*
a kind of knot with two round parts, that you use when you are tying shoes, ribbons, etc

bow³ /bəʊ/ *noun*
1 a curved piece of wood with a string between the two ends. You use a bow to send **arrows** through the air. ☞ picture at **arrow**
2 a long thin piece of wood with strong

strings along it. You use it to play a **violin** or another musical instrument that has strings. ☞ picture at **violin**

bowl¹ /bəʊl/ noun
a deep round dish or container: *a sugar bowl* ◇ *a bowl of soup*

bowl

bowl² /bəʊl/ verb (**bowls**, **bowling**, **bowled** /bəʊld/) throw a ball so that somebody can hit it in a game of cricket

box¹ /bɒks/ noun (plural **boxes**)
a container with straight sides. A box often has a lid: *Put the books in a cardboard box.* ◇ *a box of chocolates* ◇ *a box of matches* ☞ picture at **container**

box² /bɒks/ verb (**boxes**, **boxing**, **boxed** /bɒkst/)
fight with your hands, wearing thick gloves, as a sport

boxer noun
a person who boxes as a sport: *Muhammad Ali was a famous boxer.*

boxing noun (no plural)
the sport of fighting with your hands, wearing thick gloves

Boxing Day /'bɒksɪŋ deɪ/ noun
the day after Christmas Day; 26 December ✪ In England and Wales, Boxing Day is a holiday.

box office /'bɒks ɒfɪs/ noun
a place where you buy tickets in a theatre or cinema

boy /bɔɪ/ noun (plural **boys**)
a male child; a young man

boyfriend /'bɔɪfrend/ noun
a boy or man who is somebody's special friend: *She has had a lot of boyfriends.*

Boy Scout /,bɔɪ 'skaʊt/ noun
a member of a special club for boys

bra /brɑː/ noun (plural **bras**)
a thing that a woman wears under her other clothes to cover and support her breasts

bracelet /'breɪslət/ noun
a pretty piece of metal, wood or plastic that you wear around your arm

brackets /'brækɪts/ noun (plural)
marks like these ( ) that you use in writing: (*This sentence is written in brackets.*)

braid /breɪd/ American English for **plait**

bracelet

brain /breɪn/ noun
the part inside the head of a person or an animal that thinks and feels: *The brain controls the rest of the body.*

brake /breɪk/ noun
a thing that you move to make a car, bicycle, etc go slower or stop: *I put my foot on the brake.*

brake verb (**brakes**, **braking**, **braked** /breɪkt/)
use a brake: *A child ran into the road and the driver braked suddenly.*

branch /brɑːntʃ/ noun (plural **branches**)
1 one of the parts of a tree that grow out from the **trunk** ☞ picture at **tree**
2 an office or a shop that is part of a big company: *This bank has branches all over the country.*

brand /brænd/ noun
the name of a thing you buy that a certain company makes: *'Nescafé' is a famous brand of coffee.*

brand-new /,brænd 'njuː/ adjective
completely new: *a brand-new car*

brandy /'brændi/ noun
1 (no plural) a strong alcoholic drink
2 (plural **brandies**) a glass of brandy

brass /brɑːs/ noun (no plural)
a yellow metal

brave /breɪv/ adjective (**braver**, **bravest**)
ready to do dangerous or difficult things without fear: *It was brave of her to go into the burning building.*

bravely adverb
He fought bravely in the war.

bravery /'breɪvəri/ noun (no plural)
being brave

bread /bred/ noun (no plural)
food made from flour and baked in an oven: *I bought a loaf of bread.* ◇ *a slice of bread and butter*

breadth /bredθ/ noun
how far it is from one side of something to the other ✪ The adjective is **broad**.

ʌ	ɜː	ə	eɪ	əʊ	aɪ	aʊ	ɔɪ	ɪə	eə	ʊə
cup	bird	about	say	go	five	now	boy	near	hair	pure

bread

a loaf of bread

slice

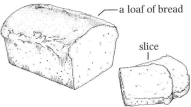

break¹ /breɪk/ verb (**breaks, breaking, broke** /brəʊk/, **has broken** /'brəʊkən/)
1 make something go into smaller pieces by dropping it or hitting it, for example: *He broke the window.* ◇ *She has broken her arm.*
2 go into smaller pieces by falling or hitting, for example: *I dropped the cup and it broke.*
3 stop working; damage a machine so that it stops working: *The TV is broken.* ◇ *You've broken my watch.*
break down, 1 If a machine or car breaks down, it stops working: *We were late because our car broke down.* **2** If a person breaks down, he/she starts to cry: *He broke down when he heard the bad news.*
break in, break into something go into a place by breaking a door or window so that you can steal something: *Thieves broke into the house. They broke in through a window.*
break off take away a piece of something by breaking it: *He broke off a piece of chocolate for me.*
break out 1 start suddenly: *A fire broke out last night.* **2** get free from a place like a prison: *Four prisoners broke out of the jail last night.*
break up start the school holidays: *We break up at the end of July.*
break up with somebody stop being with somebody, for example a husband or wife, boyfriend or girlfriend: *Susy broke up with her boyfriend last week.*

break² /breɪk/ noun
1 a short time when you stop doing something: *We worked all day without a break.*
2 a place where something opens or has broken: *The sun shone through a break in the clouds.*

breakdown /'breɪkdaʊn/ noun
a time when a machine, car, etc stops working: *We* (= our car) *had a breakdown on the motorway.*

breakfast /'brekfəst/ noun
the first meal of the day: *I had breakfast at seven o'clock.*

breast /brest/ noun
1 one of the two soft round parts of a woman's body that can give milk
2 the front part of a bird's body

breast-stroke /'brest strəʊk/ noun (no plural)
a way of swimming on your front

breath /breθ/ noun
taking in or letting out air through your nose and mouth: *Take a deep breath.*
hold your breath stop breathing for a short time
out of breath breathing very quickly: *She was out of breath after climbing the stairs.*

breathe /briːð/ verb (**breathes, breathing, breathed** /briːðd/)
take in and let out air through your nose and mouth: *The doctor told me to breathe in and then breathe out again slowly.*

breathless /'breθləs/ adjective
If you are breathless, you are breathing quickly or with difficulty.

breed¹ /briːd/ verb (**breeds, breeding, bred** /bred/, **has bred**)
1 make young animals: *Birds breed in the spring.*
2 keep animals to make young ones: *They breed horses on their farm.*

breed² /briːd/ noun
a kind of animal: *There are many different breeds of dog.*

breeze /briːz/ noun
a light wind

brewery /'bruːəri/ noun (plural **breweries**)
a place where beer is made

bribe /braɪb/ noun
money or a present that you give to somebody to make them do something
bribe verb (**bribes, bribing, bribed** /braɪbd/)
give a bribe to somebody: *The prisoner bribed the guard to let him go free.*

brick /brɪk/ noun
a small block made of hard clay, with two

p	b	t	d	k	g	tʃ	dʒ	f	v	θ	ð
pen	**b**ad	**t**ea	**d**id	**c**at	**g**ot	**ch**ain	**j**am	**f**all	**v**an	**th**in	**th**is

long sides and two short sides. Bricks are used for building: *a brick wall*

bricklayer /ˈbrɪkleɪə(r)/ *noun*
a person whose job is to build things with bricks

bride /braɪd/ *noun*
a woman on the day of her wedding

bridegroom /ˈbraɪdɡruːm/ *noun*
a man on the day of his wedding

bridesmaid /ˈbraɪdzmeɪd/ *noun*
a girl or woman who helps a bride at her wedding

bridge

bridge /brɪdʒ/ *noun*
a thing that is built over a road, railway or river so that people, trains or cars can cross it: *We walked over the bridge.*

brief /briːf/ *adjective* (**briefer**, **briefest**)
short or quick: *a brief telephone call*
in brief in a few words: *Here is the news in brief.* (words said on a radio or television programme)
briefly *adverb*
We stopped work briefly for a drink.

briefcase

briefcase /ˈbriːfkeɪs/ *noun*
a flat case for carrying papers in

bright /braɪt/ *adjective* (**brighter**, **brightest**)
1 with a lot of light: *It was a bright sunny day.* ◇ *That lamp is very bright.*
2 with a strong colour: *a bright-yellow shirt*
3 clever: *She is the brightest child in the class.*
brightly *adverb*
brightly coloured clothes

brightness /ˈbraɪtnəs/ *noun* (no plural)
the brightness of the sun

brighten /ˈbraɪtn/, **brighten up** *verb* (**brightens**, **brightening**, **brightened** /ˈbraɪtnd/)
become brighter or happier; make something brighter: *These flowers will brighten the room up.* ◇ *Her face brightened when she heard the good news.*

brilliant /ˈbrɪliənt/ *adjective*
1 with a lot of light; very bright: *brilliant sunshine*
2 very intelligent: *a brilliant student*
3 very good; excellent: *The film was brilliant!*
brilliance /ˈbrɪliəns/ *noun* (no plural)
the brilliance of the light
brilliantly *adverb*
She played brilliantly.

brim /brɪm/ *noun*
1 the edge around the top of something like a cup, bowl or glass
2 the wide part around the bottom of a hat

bring /brɪŋ/ *verb* (**brings**, **bringing**, **brought** /brɔːt/, **has brought**)
1 come to a place with somebody or something: *Can you bring me a glass of water?* ◇ *Can I bring a friend to the party?*
2 make something happen: *Money doesn't always bring happiness.*
bring back **1** return something: *I have brought back the book you lent me.*
2 make you remember something: *These old photographs bring back a lot of happy memories.*
bring somebody up look after a child until he/she is grown up: *He was brought up by his aunt after his parents died.*
bring something up **1** be sick, so that food comes up from your stomach and out of your mouth **2** start to talk about something: *Can you bring up this problem at the next meeting?*

brisk /brɪsk/ *adjective* (**brisker**, **briskest**)
quick and using a lot of energy: *We went for a brisk walk.*

bristle /ˈbrɪsl/ *noun*
a short thick hair like the hair on a brush

brittle /ˈbrɪtl/ *adjective*
Something that is brittle is hard but breaks easily: *This glass is very brittle.*

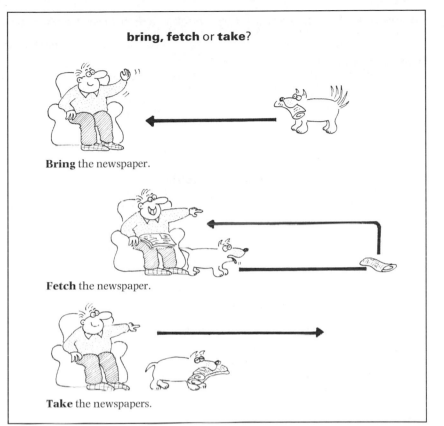

bring, fetch or **take?**

Bring the newspaper.

Fetch the newspaper.

Take the newspapers.

broad /brɔ:d/ *adjective* (**broader, broadest**)
large from one side to the other; wide: *a broad river* ✿ The noun is **breadth**.
✿ opposite: **narrow**

broadcast /'brɔ:dkɑ:st/ *verb* (**broadcasts, broadcasting, broadcast, has broadcast**)
send out sound or pictures by radio or television: *The BBC broadcasts the news at 9 p.m.*
broadcast *noun*
something that is sent out by radio or television: *a news broadcast*
broadcaster *noun*
a person whose job is to talk on radio or television

brochure /'brəʊʃə(r)/ *noun*
a thin book with pictures of things you can buy or places you can go on holiday: *a travel brochure*

broke, broken *forms of* **break**[1]

broken /'brəʊkən/ *adjective*
in pieces or not working: *a broken window* ◇ *'What's the time?' 'I don't know – my watch is broken.'*

bronze /brɒnz/ *noun* (no plural)
a brown metal made from copper and tin: *a bronze medal*

brooch /brəʊtʃ/ *noun* (*plural* **brooches**)
a pretty thing with a pin at the back that you wear on your clothes

broom /bru:m/ *noun*
a brush with a long handle that you use for sweeping

brother /'brʌðə(r)/ *noun*
Your brother is a man or boy who has the

i:	i	ɪ	e	æ	ɑ:	ɒ	ɔ:	ʊ	u	u:
s**ee**	h**a**pp**y**	s**i**t	t**e**n	c**a**t	f**a**ther	g**o**t	s**a**w	p**u**t	sit**u**ation	t**oo**

same parents as you: *My younger brother is called Tim.* ◇ *Gavin and Nick are brothers.* ☞ picture on page 127

brother-in-law /ˈbrʌðər ɪn lɔ:/ *noun*
(*plural* **brothers-in-law**)
1 the brother of your wife or husband
2 the husband of your sister
☞ picture on page 127

brought *form of* **bring**

brow /braʊ/ *noun*
the part of your face above your eyes

brown /braʊn/ *adjective* (**browner, brownest**)
with the colour of coffee: *brown eyes* ◇ *She is brown* (= she has brown skin) *because she has been in the sun.*
brown *noun*
the colour of coffee

bruise /bru:z/ *noun*
a dark mark on your skin that comes after something hits it
bruise *verb* (**bruises, bruising, bruised** /bru:zd/)
He fell and bruised his leg.

brush /brʌʃ/ *noun*
(*plural* **brushes**)
a thing that you use for sweeping, cleaning, painting or making your hair tidy: *She swept the snow off the path with a brush.*
☞ Look also at **hairbrush, paintbrush** and **toothbrush.**

brushes

brush *verb* (**brushes, brushing, brushed** /brʌʃt/)
use a brush to do something: *I brush my teeth twice a day.* ◇ *Brush your hair!*

Brussels sprout /ˌbrʌslz ˈspraʊt/ *noun*
a round green vegetable like a very small cabbage

brutal /ˈbru:tl/ *adjective*
very cruel: *a brutal murder*
brutally /ˈbru:təli/ *adverb*
She was brutally attacked.

bubble /ˈbʌbl/ *noun*
a small ball of air or gas inside a liquid: *You can see bubbles in a glass of champagne.*

bubble *verb* (**bubbles, bubbling, bubbled** /ˈbʌbld/)
make a lot of bubbles: *When water boils, it bubbles.*

bucket /ˈbʌkɪt/ *noun*
a round metal or plastic container with a handle. You use a bucket for carrying water, for example

bucket

buckle /ˈbʌkl/ *noun*
a metal or plastic thing on the end of a belt or strap that you use for joining it to the other end

bud /bʌd/ *noun*
a leaf or flower before it opens: *There are buds on the trees in spring.* ☞ picture at **plant**

Buddhist /ˈbʊdɪst/ *noun*
a person who follows the religion of **Buddhism,** started in India by Buddha
Buddhist *adjective*
a Buddhist temple

budge /bʌdʒ/ *verb* (**budges, budging, budged** /bʌdʒd/)
move a little or make something move a little: *I'm trying to move this rock but it won't budge.*

budgerigar /ˈbʌdʒərɪgɑ:(r)/, **budgie** /ˈbʌdʒi/ *noun*
a small blue or green bird that people often keep as a pet

budget /ˈbʌdʒɪt/ *noun*
a plan of how much money you will have and how you will spend it: *We have a weekly budget for food.*
budget *verb* (**budgets, budgeting, budgeted**)
plan how much money you will have and how you will spend it: *I am budgeting carefully because I want to buy a new car.*

buffet /ˈbʊfeɪ/ *noun*
1 a place on a train or at a station where you can buy food and drinks
2 a meal when all the food is on a big table and you take what you want

bug /bʌg/ *noun*
1 a small insect

ʌ	ɜ:	ə	eɪ	əʊ	aɪ	aʊ	ɔɪ	ɪə	eə	ʊə
cup	bird	about	say	go	five	now	boy	near	hair	pure

2 an illness that is not serious: *I've caught a bug.*

build /bɪld/ *verb* (**builds, building, built** /bɪlt/, **has built**)
make something by putting parts together: *He built a wall in front of the house.* ◇ *The bridge is built of stone.*

builder /'bɪldə(r)/ *noun*
a person whose job is to make buildings

building /'bɪldɪŋ/ *noun*
a thing with a roof and walls. Houses, schools, churches and shops are all buildings.

building society /'bɪldɪŋ səsaɪətɪ/ *noun* (*plural* **building societies**)
a kind of bank that lends you money when you want to buy a house or flat

built *form of* **build**

bulb /bʌlb/ *noun*
1 the glass part of an electric lamp that gives light
2 a round thing that some plants grow from: *a tulip bulb*

bulge /bʌldʒ/ *verb* (**bulges, bulging, bulged** /bʌldʒd/)
become bigger than usual; go out in a round shape from something that is usually flat: *My stomach is bulging – I have eaten too much.*
bulge *noun*
a round part that goes out from something that is usually flat: *a bulge in the wall*

bulky /'bʌlkɪ/ *adjective* (**bulkier, bulkiest**)
big, heavy and difficult to carry

bull /bʊl/ *noun*
the male of the cow and of some other animals ☞ Note and picture at **cow**

bulldozer /'bʊldəʊzə(r)/ *noun*
a big heavy machine that moves earth and makes land flat

bullet /'bʊlɪt/ *noun*
a small piece of metal that shoots out of a gun: *The bullet hit him in the leg.*

bulletin-board /'bʊlətɪn bɔːd/ *American English for* **notice-board**

bully /'bʊlɪ/ *noun* (*plural* **bullies**)
a person who hurts or frightens a weaker person

bully *verb* (**bullies, bullying, bullied** /'bʊlɪd/)
hurt or frighten a weaker person: *She was bullied by the older girls at school.*

bum /bʌm/ *noun*
the part of your body that you sit on ☉ Be careful! Some people think this word is quite rude. **Bottom** is the more usual word.

bump¹ /bʌmp/ *verb* (**bumps, bumping, bumped** /bʌmpt/)
1 hit somebody or something when you are moving: *She bumped into a chair.*
2 hit a part of your body against something hard: *I bumped my head on the ceiling.*
bump into somebody meet somebody by chance: *I bumped into David today.*

bump² /bʌmp/ *noun*
1 when something hits another thing; the sound that this makes: *He fell and hit the ground with a bump.*
2 a small round fat place on your body where you have hit it: *I've got a bump on my head.*
3 a small part on something flat that is higher than the rest: *The car hit a bump in the road.*

bumper /'bʌmpə(r)/ *noun*
a bar on the front and back of a car, lorry, etc. It helps to protect the car if it hits something.

bumpy /'bʌmpɪ/ *adjective* (**bumpier, bumpiest**)
1 with a lot of bumps: *a bumpy road*
2 that shakes you: *We had a very bumpy journey in an old bus.*

bun /bʌn/ *noun*
a small round cake or piece of bread

bunch /bʌntʃ/ *noun* (*plural* **bunches**)
a group of things that grow together or that you tie or hold together: *a bunch of grapes* ◇ *a bunch of flowers* ☞ picture on page 261

bundle /'bʌndl/ *noun*
a group of things that you tie or wrap together: *a bundle of old newspapers* ☞ picture on page 261

bungalow /'bʌŋgələʊ/ *noun*
a house that has only one floor, with no upstairs rooms

p	b	t	d	k	g	tʃ	dʒ	f	v	θ	ð
pen	**bad**	**tea**	**did**	**cat**	**got**	**ch**ain	**jam**	**fall**	**van**	**thin**	**this**

bunk /bʌŋk/ *noun*
a narrow bed that is fixed to a wall, on a ship or train, for example

bunny /'bʌni/ *noun* (*plural* **bunnies**)
a child's word for **rabbit**

buoy /bɔɪ/ *noun* (*plural* **buoys**)
a thing that floats in the sea to show ships where there are dangerous places

burger /'bɜ:gə(r)/ *noun*
meat cut into very small pieces and made into a flat round shape, that you eat between two pieces of bread: *a beefburger*

burglar /'bɜ:glə(r)/ *noun*
a person who goes into a building to steal things
burglary /'bɜ:gləri/ *noun* (*plural* **burglaries**)
going into a house to steal things: *There were two burglaries in this street last week.*
burgle /'bɜ:gl/ *verb* (**burgles**, **burgling**, **burgled** /'bɜ:gld/)
go into a building to steal things: *Our house was burgled.*

burial /'beriəl/ *noun*
the time when a dead body is put in the ground ✪ The verb is **bury**.

buried, buries *forms of* **bury**

burn[1] /bɜ:n/ *verb* (**burns**, **burning**, **burnt** /bɜ:nt/ or **burned** /bɜ:nd/, **has burnt** or **has burned**)
1 make flames and heat; be on fire: *Paper burns easily.* ◇ *She escaped from the burning building.*
2 harm or destroy somebody or something with fire or heat: *I burned my fingers on a match.* ◇ *We burned the wood on the fire.*
burn down burn, or make a building burn, until there is nothing left: *Their house burned down.*

burn[2] /bɜ:n/ *noun*
a place on your body where fire or heat has hurt it: *I've got a burn on my arm from the cooker.*

burp /bɜ:p/ *verb* (**burps**, **burping**, **burped** /bɜ:pt/)
make a noise from your mouth when air suddenly comes up from your stomach: *He burped loudly.*
burp *noun*
I heard a loud burp.

burrow /'bʌrəʊ/ *noun*
a hole in the ground where some animals, for example rabbits, live

burst[1] /bɜ:st/ *verb* (**bursts**, **bursting**, **burst**, **has burst**)
1 break open suddenly because there is too much inside; make something break open suddenly: *The bag was so full that it burst.* ◇ *The balloon burst.*
2 go or come suddenly: *Steve burst into the room.*
burst into something start doing something suddenly: *He read the letter and burst into tears* (= started to cry). ◇ *The car burst into flames* (= started to burn).
burst out laughing suddenly start to laugh: *When she saw my hat, she burst out laughing.*

burst[2] /bɜ:st/ *noun*
something that happens suddenly and quickly: *a burst of laughter*

bury /'beri/ *verb* (**buries**, **burying**, **buried** /'berid/, **has buried**)
1 put a dead body in the ground ✪ The noun is **burial**.
2 put something in the ground or under something: *The dog buried a bone in the garden.*

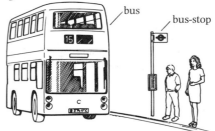
bus
bus-stop

bus /bʌs/ *noun* (*plural* **buses**)
a thing like a big car, that carries a lot of people: *We went to town by bus.* ◇ *Where do you get off the bus?*
bus-stop /'bʌs stɒp/ *noun*
a place where buses stop and people get on and off

bush /bʊʃ/ *noun*
1 (*plural* **bushes**) a plant like a small tree with a lot of branches: *a rose bush*
2 **the bush** (no plural) wild country with a lot of small trees in Africa or Australia

business /'bɪznəs/ *noun*
1 (no plural) buying and selling things: *I*

want to go into business when I leave school. ◇ Business is not very good this year.
2 (plural **businesses**) a place where people sell or make things, for example a shop or factory
it's none of your business, mind your own business words that you use when you do not want to tell somebody about something that is private: 'Where are you going?' 'Mind your own business!'
on business because of your work: John is in Germany on business.

businessman /ˈbɪznəsmən/ noun (plural **businessmen**)
a man who works in an office and whose job is about buying and selling things

businesswoman /ˈbɪznəswʊmən/ noun (plural **businesswomen**)
a woman who works in an office and whose job is about buying and selling things

busy /ˈbɪzi/ adjective (**busier**, **busiest**)
1 with a lot of things that you must do; working or not free: Mr Jones can't see you now – he's busy.
2 with a lot of things happening: I had a busy morning. ◇ The shops are always busy at Christmas.
busily /ˈbɪzɪli/ adverb
He was busily writing a letter.

but¹ /bət/, /bʌt/ conjunction
a word that you use to show something different: My sister speaks French but I don't. ◇ He worked hard but he didn't pass the exam. ◇ The weather was sunny but cold.

but² /bət/, /bʌt/ preposition
except: She eats nothing but chocolate.

butcher /ˈbʊtʃə(r)/ noun
a person who cuts and sells meat **⊘** A shop that sells meat is called a **butcher's**.

butter /ˈbʌtə(r)/ noun (no plural)
soft yellow food that is made from milk. You put it on bread or use it in cooking: She spread butter on the bread.
butter verb (**butters**, **buttering**, **buttered** /ˈbʌtəd/)
put butter on bread: I buttered the toast.

butterfly /ˈbʌtəflaɪ/ noun (plural **butterflies**)
an insect with big coloured wings

butterfly

button /ˈbʌtn/ noun
1 a small round thing on clothes. You push it through a small hole (a **buttonhole**) to hold clothes together.
2 a small thing on a machine, that you push: Press this button to ring the bell.

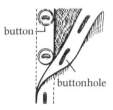
button
buttonhole

buy /baɪ/ verb (**buys**, **buying**, **bought** /bɔːt/, **has bought**)
give money to get something: I bought a new watch. ◇ He bought the car from a friend. ☞ Look at **sell**.

buzz /bʌz/ verb (**buzzes**, **buzzing**, **buzzed** /bʌzd/)
make a sound like bees
buzz noun (plural **buzzes**)
the buzz of insects

by¹ /baɪ/ preposition
1 very near: The telephone is by the door. ◇ They live by the sea.
2 from one side of somebody or something to the other; past: He walked by me without speaking.
3 not later than: I must finish this work by six o'clock.
4 a word that shows who or what did something: a painting by Matisse ◇ She was caught by the police.
5 using something: I go to work by train. ◇ He paid by cheque.
6 a word that shows how: You turn the computer on by pressing this button.
7 a word that shows how you measure something: We buy material by the metre.
8 a word that shows which part: She took me by the hand.

by[2] /baɪ/ *adverb*
past: *She drove by without stopping.*

bye /baɪ/, **bye-bye** /ˌbaɪ 'baɪ/
goodbye

Cc

C *short way of writing* **Celsius, centigrade**

cab /kæb/ *noun*
1 *another word for* **taxi**
2 the part of a lorry, train or bus where the driver sits

cabbage /'kæbɪdʒ/ *noun*
a large round vegetable with thick green leaves

cabin /'kæbɪn/ *noun*
1 a small bedroom on a ship
2 a part of an aircraft: *the passengers in the first-class cabin*
3 a small simple house made of wood: *a log cabin at the edge of the lake*

cabinet /'kæbɪnət/ *noun*
1 (*plural* **cabinets**) a piece of furniture that you can keep things in: *a bathroom cabinet* ◇ *a filing cabinet* (= one that you use in an office to keep files in)
2 **the Cabinet** (no plural) a group of the most important people in the government

cable /'keɪbl/ *noun*
1 a wire that carries electricity or messages
2 a very strong thick rope or wire
cable television /ˌkeɪbl 'telɪvɪʒn/ *noun*
(no plural)
a way of sending pictures and sound along wires

cactus /'kæktəs/ *noun* (*plural* **cactuses** or **cacti** /'kæktaɪ/)
a plant with a lot of sharp points that grows in hot dry places

café /'kæfeɪ/ *noun*
a place where you can have a drink and something to eat

cage /keɪdʒ/ *noun*
a place with bars round it where animals or birds are kept so that they cannot escape

cage

cake /keɪk/ *noun*
sweet food that you make from flour, eggs, sugar and butter and bake in the oven: *a chocolate cake* ◇ *Would you like a piece of cake?*

calculate /'kælkjuleɪt/ *verb* (**calculates, calculating, calculated**)
find the answer by using mathematics: *Can you calculate how much the holiday will cost?*

calculator /'kælkjuleɪtə(r)/ *noun*
an electronic instrument that adds, subtracts, multiplies and divides

calendar /'kæləndə(r)/ *noun*
a list of the days, weeks and months of one year: *Look at the calendar and tell me what day of the week December 2nd is this year.*

calf[1] /kɑːf/ *noun* (*plural* **calves** /kɑːvz/)
a young cow ☞ Note and picture at **cow**

calf[2] /kɑːf/ *noun* (*plural* **calves** /kɑːvz/)
the back of your leg, below your knee ☞ picture on page 126

call[1] /kɔːl/ *noun*
1 a loud cry or shout: *a call for help*
2 using the telephone: *I had a call from James.* ◇ *I haven't got time to talk now – I'll give you a call later.*
3 a short visit to somebody: *We paid a call on Katie.*

call[2] /kɔːl/ *verb* (**calls, calling, called** /kɔːld/)
1 speak loudly and clearly so that somebody who is far away can hear you:

ʌ	ɜː	ə	eɪ	əʊ	aɪ	aʊ	ɔɪ	ɪə	eə	ʊə
cup	bird	about	say	go	five	now	boy	near	hair	pure

'*Breakfast is ready,*' *she called.* ◇ *She called out the names of the winners.*
2 ask somebody to come: *He was so ill that we had to call the doctor.*
3 give a name to somebody or something: *They called the baby Sophie.*
4 telephone somebody: *I'll call you later.*
◇ *Who's calling, please?*
be called have as a name: '*What is your teacher called?*' '*She's called Mrs Gray.*'
call somebody back telephone somebody again: *I can't talk now – I'll call you back later.*
call collect *American English for* **reverse the charges**
call for somebody go to somebody's house on your way to a place so that they can come with you: *Rosie usually calls for me in the morning and we walk to school together.*
call in make a short visit: *I'll call in to see you this evening.*
call off say that something that you have planned will not happen: *We called off the race because it was raining.*

call-box /'kɔːl bɒks/ *noun* (*plural* **callboxes**)
a kind of small building in the street or in a public place that has a telephone in it

calm¹ /kɑːm/ *adjective* (**calmer, calmest**)
1 quiet, and not excited or afraid: *Try to keep calm – there's no danger.*
2 without much wind: *calm weather*
3 without big waves: *calm sea*
calmly *adverb*
He spoke calmly about the accident.

calm² /kɑːm/ *verb* (**calms, calming, calmed** /kɑːmd/)
calm down become less afraid or excited; make somebody less afraid or excited: *Calm down and tell me what happened.*

calorie /'kæləri/ *noun*
Food that has a lot of calories in it can make you fat.

calves *plural of* **calf**

came *form of* **come**

camel /'kæml/ *noun*
a large animal with one or two round parts (called **humps**) on its back. Camels carry people and things in the desert.

camera /'kæmərə/ *noun*
a thing that you use for taking photographs or moving pictures: *I need a new film for my camera.*

camp /kæmp/ *noun*
a place where people live in tents for a short time
camp *verb* (**camps, camping, camped** /kæmpt/)
live in a tent for a short time: *Ask the farmer if we can camp in his field.* ◐ It is more usual to say **go camping** when you mean that you are living in a tent on holiday: *We went camping last summer.*
camping *noun* (no plural)
living in a tent for a short time: *Camping isn't much fun when it rains.*
camp-site /'kæmp saɪt/ *noun*
a place where you can camp

campaign /kæm'peɪn/ *noun*
a plan to get a special result: *a campaign to stop people smoking*

can¹ /kən/, /kæn/ *modal verb*
1 be able to; be strong enough, clever enough, etc: *She can speak three languages.* ◇ *Can you ski?*
2 be allowed to: *You can go now.* ◇ *Can I have some more soup, please?* ◇ *The doctor says she can't go back to school yet.*
3 a word that you use when you ask somebody to do something: *Can you tell me the time, please?*
4 be possible or likely: *It can be very cold in the mountains in winter.*
5 a word that you use with verbs like 'see', 'hear', 'smell' and 'taste': *I can smell something burning.* ◇ '*What's that noise?*' '*I can't hear anything.*'

◐ The negative form of 'can' is **cannot** /'kænɒt/ or the short form **can't** /kɑːnt/:

She can't swim.

The past tense of 'can' is **could**. You use **be able to**, not **can**, to make the future and perfect tenses:

*I **can** see it.*

*You **will be able to** see it if you stand on this chair.*

☞ Look at the Note on page 227 to find out more about **modal verbs**.

---

p	b	t	d	k	g	tʃ	dʒ	f	v	θ	ð
pen	**bad**	**tea**	**did**	**cat**	**got**	**chain**	**jam**	**fall**	**van**	**thin**	**this**

can² /kæn/ *noun*
a metal container for food or drink that keeps it fresh: *a can of lemonade* ☞ picture at **container**

canal /kə'næl/ *noun*
a path that is made through the land and filled with water so that boats can travel on it: *the Suez Canal*

canary /kə'neəri/ *noun* (*plural* **canaries**)
a small yellow bird that people often keep as a pet

cancel /'kænsl/ *verb* (**cancels, cancelling, cancelled** /'kænsld/)
say that something that you have planned will not happen: *The singer was ill, so the concert was cancelled.* ✪ In American English the spellings are **canceling** and **canceled**.
cancellation /ˌkænsə'leɪʃn/ *noun*
the cancellation of the President's visit

cancer /'kænsə(r)/ *noun*
a very dangerous illness that makes some **cells** (very small parts in the body) grow too fast: *Smoking can cause cancer.*

candidate /'kændɪdət/ *noun*
1 a person who wants to be chosen for something: *When the director leaves, there will be a lot of candidates for her job.*
2 a person who takes an examination

candle /'kændl/ *noun*
a long round piece of wax with a string in the middle that burns to give light
candlestick /'kændlstɪk/ *noun*
a thing that holds a candle

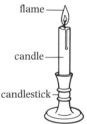
flame
candle
candlestick

candy /'kændi/
American English for **sweet² 1**

cane /keɪn/ *noun*
the hollow stem of some plants: *sugar cane*

canned /kænd/ *adjective*
in a can: *canned drinks*

cannibal /'kænɪbl/ *noun*
a person who eats other people

cannot /'kænɒt/ = **can not**

canoe /kə'nu:/ *noun*
a light narrow boat that you use on rivers. You move it through the water with a piece of wood (called a **paddle**). ✪ When you talk about using a canoe, you often say **go canoeing**: *We went canoeing on the river.*

can't /kɑ:nt/ = **can not**

canteen /kæn'ti:n/ *noun*
the place where people eat when they are at school or work

canvas /'kænvəs/ *noun* (no plural)
strong heavy cloth. Tents and sails are often made of canvas, and it is also used for painting pictures on.

cap /kæp/ *noun*
1 a soft hat: *a baseball cap*
2 a thing that covers the top of a bottle or tube: *Put the cap back on the bottle.*

cap

capable /'keɪpəbl/ *adjective*
1 able to do something: *You are capable of passing the exam if you work harder.*
2 able to do things well: *a capable student*
✪ opposite: **incapable**

capacity /kə'pæsəti/ *noun* (*plural* **capacities**)
how much a container can hold: *a tank with a capacity of 1000 litres*

cape /keɪp/ *noun*
1 a piece of clothing like a coat without sleeves
2 a high part of the land that goes out into the sea: *Cape Horn*

capital /'kæpɪtl/ *noun*
1 the most important city in a country, where the government is: *Rome is the capital of Italy.*
2 (*also* **capital letter**) a big letter of the alphabet: *A, B and C are capitals, a, b and c are not.* ◇ *Names of people and places begin with a capital letter.*

capsize /kæp'saɪz/ *verb* (**capsizes, capsizing, capsized** /kæp'saɪzd/)
turn over in the water: *During the storm, the boat capsized.*

captain /'kæptɪn/ *noun*
1 the person who is in charge of a ship or an aircraft: *The captain sent a message by radio for help.*
2 the leader of a group of people: *He's the captain of the school football team.*

s	z	ʃ	ʒ	h	m	n	ŋ	l	r	j	w
so	**zoo**	**shoe**	vision	**hat**	**man**	**no**	sing	**leg**	**red**	**yes**	**wet**

caption /'kæpʃn/ *noun*
the words above or below a picture in a book or newspaper, that tell you about it

captive /'kæptɪv/ *noun*
a person who is not free; a prisoner

captivity /kæp'tɪvəti/ *noun* (no plural)
in captivity kept in a place that you cannot leave: *Wild animals are often unhappy in captivity* (= in a zoo, for example).

capture /'kæptʃə(r)/ *verb* (**captures, capturing, captured** /'kæptʃəd/)
catch somebody and keep them somewhere so that they cannot leave: *The police captured the robbers.*
capture *noun* (no plural)
the capture of the escaped prisoners

car /kɑː(r)/ *noun*
1 a vehicle with four wheels, usually with enough space for four or five people: *She travels to work by car.*
2 *American English for* **carriage**
car park /'kɑː pɑːk/ *noun*
a piece of land or a building where you can put your car for a time

caravan /'kærəvæn/ *noun*
a small house on wheels, that a car or a horse can pull

carbon /'kɑːbən/ *noun* (no plural)
the chemical that coal and diamonds are made of and that is in all living things

card /kɑːd/ *noun*
1 a piece of thick stiff paper with writing or pictures on it: *We send Christmas cards, birthday cards and postcards to our friends.* ☞ Look also at **credit card** and **phonecard**.
2 a playing-card; one of a set of 52 cards called a **pack of cards** that you use to play games. A pack has four groups of thirteen cards: **hearts**, **clubs**, **diamonds** and **spades**: *Let's have a game of cards.* ◇ *They often play cards in the evening.*

cardboard /'kɑːdbɔːd/ *noun* (no plural)
very thick paper that is used for making boxes, etc

cardigan /'kɑːdɪgən/ *noun*
a knitted woollen jacket

cardinal /'kɑːdɪnl/ *noun*
an important priest in the Roman Catholic church

care[1] /keə(r)/ *noun* (no plural)
thinking about what you are doing so that you do not make a mistake or break something: *Wash these glasses with care!*
care of somebody ☞ Look at **c/o**.
take care be careful: *Take care when you cross the road.*
take care of somebody or **something** look after somebody or something; do what is necessary: *Alison is taking care of her sister's baby today.* ◇ *I'll take care of the shopping if you do the cleaning.*

care[2] /keə(r)/ *verb* (**cares, caring, cared** /keəd/)
think that it is important: *The only thing he cares about is money.* ◇ *I don't care who wins – I'm not interested in football.*
⊙ You use expressions like **I don't care**, **who cares?** and **I couldn't care less** when you feel a little angry and want to be rude.
care for somebody or **something**
1 do the things for somebody that they need: *After the accident, her parents cared for her until she was better.* **2** like somebody or something: *Would you care for a cup of tea?*

career /kə'rɪə(r)/ *noun*
a job that you learn to do and then do for many years: *a career in teaching*

careful /'keəfl/ *adjective*
If you are careful, you think about what you are doing so that you do not make a mistake or have an accident: *Careful!*

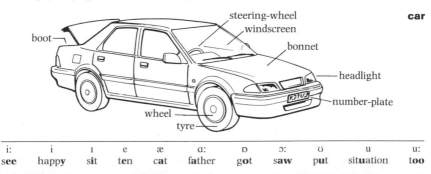

steering-wheel
windscreen
car
boot
bonnet
headlight
number-plate
wheel
tyre

i:	i	ɪ	e	æ	ɑ:	ɒ	ɔ:	ʊ	u	u:
see	happy	sit	ten	cat	father	got	saw	put	situation	too

The plate is very hot. ◇ *Be careful with those glasses.*
carefully /'keəfəli/ *adverb*
Please listen carefully.

careless /'keələs/ *adjective*
If you are careless, you do not think enough about what you are doing, so that you make mistakes: *Careless drivers can cause accidents.*
carelessly *adverb*
She carelessly threw her coat on the floor.
carelessness /'keələsnəs/ *noun* (no plural)
being careless

caretaker /'keəteɪkə(r)/ *noun*
a person whose job is to look after a large building like a school or a block of flats

cargo /'kɑ:gəʊ/ *noun* (*plural* **cargoes**)
the things that a ship or an aeroplane carries: *a cargo of wheat*

carnation /kɑ:'neɪʃn/ *noun*
a pink, white or red flower with a nice smell

carol /'kærəl/ *noun*
a religious song that people sing at Christmas

carpenter /'kɑ:pəntə(r)/ *noun*
a person who makes things from wood
carpentry /'kɑ:pəntri/ *noun* (no plural)
making things from wood

carpet /'kɑ:pɪt/ *noun*
a soft covering for a floor that is often made of wool and is usually the same size as the floor

carriage /'kærɪdʒ/ *noun*
1 one of the parts of a train where people sit: *The carriages at the back of the train were empty.*
2 a vehicle that is pulled by horses and is used at special times: *The Queen rode in a carriage through the streets of the city.*

carried *form of* **carry**

carrier bag /'kæriə bæg/, **carrier** *noun*
a large bag made from plastic or paper that you use for carrying shopping

carrot /'kærət/ *noun*
a long thin orange vegetable

carrot

carry /'kæri/ *verb* (**carries**, **carrying**, **carried** /'kærid/, **has carried**)
1 hold something and take it to another place or keep it with you: *He carried the suitcase to my room.* ◇ *I can't carry this box – it's too heavy.* ◇ *Do the police carry guns in your country?* ✪ Be careful! You use **wear**, not **carry**, to talk about having clothes on your body: *She is wearing a red dress and carrying a black bag.*
2 move people or things: *Special fast trains carry people to the city centre.*
carry on continue doing something: *Carry on with your work.* ◇ *If you carry on to the end of this road, you'll see the post office on the right.*
carry out do or finish what you have planned: *The swimming-pool was closed while they carried out the repairs.*

cart /kɑ:t/ *noun*
a wooden vehicle with two or four wheels that a horse usually pulls

carton /'kɑ:tn/ *noun*
a container made of cardboard or plastic: *a carton of milk* ☞ picture at **container**

cartoon /kɑ:'tu:n/ *noun*
1 a funny drawing, for example in a newspaper
2 a television or cinema film made with drawings, not pictures of real people and places: *a Mickey Mouse cartoon*

carve /kɑ:v/ *verb* (**carves**, **carving**, **carved** /kɑ:vd/)
1 cut wood or stone to make a picture or shape: *Her father carved a little horse for her out of wood.*
2 cut meat into thin pieces after you have cooked it

case /keɪs/ *noun*
1 a container like a box for keeping something in: *Put the camera back in its case.*
☞ Look also at **briefcase** and **suitcase**.
2 an example of something: *There were four cases of this disease in the school last month.*

3 something that happens or something that is true: *'There's no coffee.' 'Well, in that case we'll have tea.'*
4 a question that people in a court of law must decide about: *a divorce case*
5 a problem that the police must find an answer to: *a murder case*
in any case words that you use when you give a second reason for something: *I don't want to see the film, and in any case I'm too busy.*
in case because something might happen: *Take an umbrella in case it rains.*

cash¹ /kæʃ/ *noun* (no plural)
money in coins and notes: *How would you like to pay: cash or cheque?*
cash desk /'kæʃ desk/ *noun*
the place in a shop where you pay

cash² /kæʃ/ *verb* (**cashes**, **cashing**, **cashed** /kæʃt/)
give a cheque and get money for it: *I'd like to cash some traveller's cheques, please.*

cashier /kæ'ʃɪə(r)/ *noun*
the person who gives or takes money in a bank

cassette /kə'set/ *noun*
a plastic box with special tape inside for storing and playing sound, music or moving pictures: *a video cassette* ◇ *Put on (− play) your new cassette.*
cassette player /kə'set pleɪə(r)/, **cassette recorder** /kə'set rɪ,kɔːdə(r)/ *noun*
a machine that can put (**record**) sound or music on tape and play it again later

castle /'kɑːsl/ *noun*
a large old building that was built to keep people safe from their enemies: *Windsor Castle*

casual /'kæʒuəl/ *adjective*
1 showing that you are not worried about something; relaxed: *She gave us a casual wave as she passed.*
2 not for serious or important times: *I wear casual clothes like jeans and T-shirts when I'm not at work.*
casually /'kæʒuəli/ *adverb*
He was dressed too casually for the interview.

casualty /'kæʒuəlti/ *noun* (*plural* **casualties**)
a person who is hurt or killed in an accident or a war

casualty department /'kæʒuəlti dɪpɑːtmənt/, **casualty** *noun*
the place in a hospital where doctors help people who have been hurt in an accident

cat

cat — whiskers
kitten
tail
paw

cat /kæt/ *noun*
1 an animal that people keep as a pet and to catch mice ✪ A young cat is called a **kitten**.
2 the name of a group of large wild animals. Tigers and lions are cats.

catch /kætʃ/ *verb* (**catches**, **catching**, **caught** /kɔːt/, **has caught**)
1 take and hold something that is moving: *He threw the ball to me and I caught it.*
2 find and hold somebody or something: *They caught a fish in the river.* ◇ *The man ran so fast that the police couldn't catch him.*
3 see somebody when they are doing something wrong: *They caught the thief stealing the painting.*
4 be early enough for a bus, train, etc that is going to leave: *You should run if you want to catch the bus.* ✪ opposite: **miss**
5 get an illness: *She caught a cold.*
6 let something be held tightly: *I caught my fingers in the door.*
catch fire start to burn: *The house caught fire.*
catch up do something quickly so that you are not behind others: *If you miss a lesson, you can do some work at home to catch up.* ◇ *Quick! Run after the others and catch them up.*

caterpillar /'kætəpɪlə(r)/ *noun*
a thing like a long hairy worm that will become a butterfly or moth

cathedral /kə'θiːdrəl/ *noun*
a big important church

Catholic /'kæθəlɪk/ = Roman Catholic

cattle /'kætl/ *noun* (plural)
cows and bulls: *a herd of cattle*

p	b	t	d	k	g	tʃ	dʒ	f	v	θ	ð
pen	**bad**	**tea**	**did**	**cat**	**got**	**chain**	**jam**	**fall**	**van**	**thin**	**this**

caught *form of* **catch**

cauliflower
/'kɒliflaʊə(r)/ *noun*
a large vegetable
with green leaves
outside and a hard
white part in the
middle

cauliflower

cause¹ /kɔːz/ *noun*
1 the thing or person that makes something happen: *Bad driving is the cause of most road accidents.*
2 something that people care about and want to help: *They gave the money to a good cause – it was used to build a new hospital.*

cause² /kɔːz/ *verb* (**causes**, **causing**, **caused** /kɔːzd/)
be the reason why something happens: *Who caused the accident?* ◇ *The fire was caused by a cigarette.*

caution /'kɔːʃn/ *noun* (no plural)
great care: *Caution! Wet floor.*

cautious /'kɔːʃəs/ *adjective*
careful because there may be danger
cautiously *adverb*
Cautiously, he pushed open the door and looked into the room.

cave /keɪv/ *noun*
a large hole in the side of a mountain or under the ground: *Thousands of years ago, people lived in caves.*

CD /ˌsiː ˈdiː/ *short for* **compact disc**

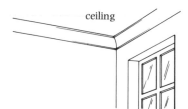

ceiling

ceiling /'siːlɪŋ/ *noun*
the part of a room over your head

celebrate /'seləbreɪt/ *verb* (**celebrates**, **celebrating**, **celebrated**)
enjoy yourself because you have a special reason to be happy: *If you pass your exams, we'll have a party to celebrate.*
celebration /ˌseləˈbreɪʃn/ *noun*
a time when you enjoy yourself because

you have a special reason to be happy: *birthday celebrations*

cell /sel/ *noun*
1 a small room where a prisoner lives
2 the smallest part of any living thing

cellar /'selə(r)/ *noun*
a room in the part of a building that is under the ground: *a wine cellar*

cello /'tʃeləʊ/ *noun* (*plural* **cellos**)
a musical instrument like a big violin. You sit and hold it between your knees when you are playing it.

Celsius /'selsiəs/ *noun* (no plural)
a way of measuring temperature. Water freezes at 0°Celsius and boils at 100°Celsius. ◌ The short way of writing 'Celsius' is **C**: *52° C*

cement /sɪ'ment/ *noun* (no plural)
grey powder that becomes hard like stone when you mix it with water and leave it to dry. Cement is used in building.

cemetery /'semətri/ *noun* (*plural* **cemeteries**)
an area of ground where dead people are put under the earth

cent /sent/ *noun*
a small coin that people use in the USA and some other countries. There are 100 cents in a **dollar**.

center *American English for* **centre**

centigrade /'sentɪgreɪd/ *another word for* **Celsius**

centiliter *American English for* **centilitre**

centilitre /'sentɪliːtə(r)/ *noun*
a measure of liquid. There are 100 centilitres in a **litre**. ◌ The short way of writing 'centilitre' is **cl**: *250 cl*

centimeter *American English for* **centimetre**

centimetre /'sentɪmiːtə(r)/ *noun*
a measure of length. There are 100 centimetres in a **metre**. ◌ The short way of writing 'centimetre' is **cm**: *98 cm*

central /'sentrəl/ *adjective*
in the middle part: *central London*
central heating /ˌsentrəl 'hiːtɪŋ/ *noun* (no plural)
a way of heating all the rooms in a house from one **boiler**

centre /'sentə(r)/ *noun*
1 the part in the middle: *the city centre* ◇ *The flower has a yellow centre with white petals.*
2 a place where people come to do something special: *a shopping centre* ◇ *Our town has a new sports centre.*

century /'sentʃəri/ *noun* (*plural* **centuries**)
1 100 years
2 a time of 100 years, that we use in dates: *We are living at the beginning of the twenty-first century.*

cereal /'sɪəriəl/ *noun*
1 (*plural* **cereals**) a plant that farmers grow so that we can eat the seed: *Wheat and oats are cereals.*
2 (no plural) special food made from rice, maize, wheat, etc that you can eat for breakfast: *a bowl of cereal with milk*

ceremony /'serəməni/ *noun* (*plural* **ceremonies**)
a time when you do something special and important: *the opening ceremony of the Olympic Games* ◇ *a wedding ceremony*

certain¹ /'sɜːtn/ *adjective*
without any doubt; sure: *I am certain that I have seen her before.* ◇ *It's not certain that they will come.*
for certain without any doubt: *I don't know for certain where she is.*
make certain check something so that you are sure about it: *Please make certain that the window is closed before you leave.*

certain² /'sɜːtn/ *adjective*
one or some that can be named: *It's cheaper to telephone at certain times of the day.* ◇ *Do you want the work to be finished by a certain date?*

certainly /'sɜːtnli/ *adverb*
1 without any doubt: *She is certainly the best swimmer in the team.*
2 yes: *'Will you open the door for me, please?' 'Certainly.'*
certainly not no: *'Can I borrow your bicycle?' 'Certainly not!'*

certificate /sə'tɪfɪkət/ *noun*
an important piece of paper that shows that something is true: *Your birth certificate shows when and where you were born.*

chain /tʃeɪn/ *noun*
metal rings that are joined together:

ILLUSTRATION 49

Round her neck she wore a gold chain. ◇ *My bicycle chain is broken.*
☞ picture at **bicycle**
chain *verb* (**chains**, **chaining**, **chained** /tʃeɪnd/)
attach somebody or something to a place with a chain: *The dog was chained to the fence.*

chair /tʃeə(r)/ *noun*
1 a piece of furniture with four legs, a seat and a back that one person can sit on: *a table and four chairs*
2 a person who controls a meeting
○ You can also say **chairman**/'tʃeəmən/, **chairwoman**/'tʃeəwʊmən/ or **chairperson**/'tʃeəpɜːsn/.

chalk /tʃɔːk/ *noun* (no plural)
1 soft white rock: *The cliffs are made of chalk.*
2 a piece of this rock that you use for writing on a **blackboard**

challenge /'tʃælɪndʒ/ *verb* (**challenges**, **challenging**, **challenged** /'tʃælɪndʒd/)
ask somebody to play a game with you or fight with you to see who wins: *The boxer challenged the world champion to a fight.*
challenge *noun*
a new or difficult thing that makes you try hard: *Climbing the mountain will be a real challenge.*

champagne /ʃæm'peɪn/ *noun* (no plural)
a French white wine with a lot of bubbles

champion /'tʃæmpiən/ *noun*
a person who is the best at a sport or game: *a chess champion* ◇ *the world champion*
championship /'tʃæmpiənʃɪp/ *noun*
a competition to find the champion: *Our team won the championship this year.*

chance /tʃɑːns/ *noun*
1 (*plural* **chances**) a time when you can do something: *It was their last chance to escape.* ◇ *I haven't had a chance to write to Jane today. I'll do it tomorrow.*
2 (*plural* **chances**) a possibility that something may happen: *He has a good chance*

of passing the exam because he has worked hard.

3 (no plural) something that happens that you cannot control; luck

by chance not because you have planned it: *We met by chance at the station.*

take a chance do something when it is possible that something bad may happen because of it

change¹ /tʃeɪndʒ/ *verb* (**changes, changing, changed** /tʃeɪndʒd/)

1 become different: *She has changed a lot since the last time I saw her – she looks much older.* ◇ *Water changes into ice when it gets very cold.*

2 make something different: *At this restaurant they change the menu every day.*

3 put or take something in place of another thing: *My new watch didn't work, so I took it back to the shop and changed it.* ◇ *I went to the bank to change my francs into dollars.* ◇ *Can you change a £5 note please? I need some pound coins.*

4 put on different clothes: *I must change before I go out.* ✪ You can also say **get changed**: *I must get changed before I go out.*

5 get off a train or bus and get on another one: *I have to change trains at Reading.*

change² /tʃeɪndʒ/ *noun*

1 (no plural) money that you get when you have paid too much: *I gave the shop assistant £1. The sweets cost 75 pence, so he gave me 25 pence change.*

2 (no plural) small pieces of money; coins: *I haven't got any change.*

3 (*plural* **changes**) a thing that is different now: *The new government has made a lot of changes.*

for a change because you want something different: *Today we had lunch in a restaurant for a change.*

channel /'tʃænl/ *noun*

1 a narrow place where water can go: *the English Channel* (= the sea between England and France)

2 one of the things you can choose on television: *Which channel are you watching?*

chapel /'tʃæpl/ *noun*

a room or a small church where Christians go to pray

chapter /'tʃæptə(r)/ *noun*

one of the parts of a book: *You start reading a book at the beginning of Chapter 1.*

character /'kærəktə(r)/ *noun*

1 (no plural) the way a person or thing is: *He has a strong character.* ◇ *The new factory will change the character of the village.*

2 (*plural* **characters**) a person in a play, book or film: *Tom and Jerry are famous cartoon characters.*

charge¹ /tʃɑ:dʒ/ *verb* (**charges, charging, charged** /tʃɑ:dʒd/)

1 ask somebody to pay a certain price for something: *The garage charged me £200 for the repairs.*

2 say that somebody has done something wrong: *The police have charged him with murder.*

3 move quickly and with a lot of force: *The bull charged.* ◇ *The children charged into the room.*

charge² /tʃɑ:dʒ/ *noun*

1 the money that you must pay for something: *There is a charge of £25 for the use of the hall.*

2 a statement that somebody has done something wrong: *a charge of murder*

be in charge of somebody or **something** look after or control somebody or something: *Tim is in charge of his baby brother while his mother is out.* ◇ *The headmaster is in charge of the school.*

charity /'tʃærəti/ *noun*

1 (*plural* **charities**) a group of people who collect money to help people who need it: *The Red Cross is a charity.*

2 (no plural) being kind and helping other people

charm /tʃɑ:m/ *noun*

1 (no plural) being able to make people like you: *Ann has a lot of charm.*

2 (*plural* **charms**) a small thing that you wear because you think it will bring good luck: *She wears a necklace with a lucky charm on it.*

charm *verb* (**charms, charming, charmed** /tʃɑ:md/)

make somebody like you: *The baby charmed everybody with her smile.*

charming /'tʃɑ:mɪŋ/ *adjective*

lovely; beautiful: *a charming little village*

ʌ	ɜː	ə	eɪ	əʊ	aɪ	aʊ	ɔɪ	ɪə	eə	ʊə
cup	bird	about	say	go	five	now	boy	near	hair	pure

chart /tʃɑːt/ *noun*
1 a drawing that gives information about something: *a temperature chart*
2 a map of the sea that sailors use

chase /tʃeɪs/ *verb* (**chases, chasing, chased** /tʃeɪst/)
run behind somebody or something and try to catch them: *The dog chased the cat around the garden.* ◊ *The police chased after the thief but he escaped.*
chase *noun*
In that film there is an exciting car chase.

chat /tʃæt/ *noun*
a friendly talk: *Let's have a chat about it later.*
chat *verb* (**chats, chatting, chatted**)
talk in a friendly way

chatter /'tʃætə(r)/ *verb* (**chatters, chattering, chattered** /'tʃætəd/)
talk quickly about things that are not very important: *Stop chattering and finish your work.*

cheap /tʃiːp/ *adjective* (**cheaper, cheapest**)
Something that is cheap does not cost a lot of money: *Tomatoes are cheaper in summer than in winter.* ◊ *That restaurant is very good and quite cheap.* ✿ opposite: **expensive** or **dear**

cheat /tʃiːt/ *verb* (**cheats, cheating, cheated**)
do something that is not honest or fair: *She cheated in the exam – she copied her friend's work.*
cheat *noun*
a person who cheats

check¹ /tʃek/ *verb* (**checks, checking, checked** /tʃekt/)
1 look at something to see that it is right, good, safe, etc: *Do the sums and then use a calculator to check your answers.* ◊ *At the garage the man checked the oil and water.* ◊ *Check that all the windows are closed before you leave.*
2 American English for **tick 2**
check in tell the person at the desk in a hotel or at an airport that you have arrived: *I have to check in an hour before my flight.*
check out pay your bill at a hotel, and leave

check² /tʃek/ *noun*
1 a look to see that everything is right,
good, safe, etc: *Have a quick check to see that you haven't forgotten anything.*
2 American English for **cheque**
3 American English for **bill 1**
4 American English for **tick 2**

check³ /tʃek/ *adjective*
a pattern of squares
checked /tʃekt/ *adjective*
with a pattern of squares: *a checked shirt*

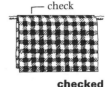
check

checked

checkers /'tʃekəz/ American English for **draughts**

checkout /'tʃekaʊt/ *noun*
one of the places in a supermarket where you pay for the things you are buying

check-up /'tʃek ʌp/ *noun*
an examination by a doctor to see if you are well

cheek /tʃiːk/ *noun*
1 (*plural* **cheeks**) one of the two round parts of your face under your eyes ☞ picture on page 126
2 (no plural) doing something without caring that it will make other people angry or unhappy: *What a cheek! Somebody has eaten my sandwiches.*

cheeky /'tʃiːki/ *adjective* (**cheekier, cheekiest**)
not polite: *Don't be so cheeky!* ◊ *She was punished for being cheeky to a teacher.*

cheer¹ /tʃɪə(r)/ *verb* (**cheers, cheering, cheered** /tʃɪəd/)
shout to show that you are pleased: *The crowd cheered loudly when the President arrived.*
cheer up make somebody happier; become happier: *We gave Julie some flowers to cheer her up.* ◊ *Cheer up! You will feel better soon.*

cheer² /tʃɪə(r)/ *noun*
a shout that shows that you are pleased: *The crowd gave a loud cheer as the singer came onto the stage.*
three cheers for ... Hip, hip, hurray! words that you shout when somebody has done something good: *Three cheers for the winner! Hip, hip, hurray!*

cheerful /'tʃɪəfl/ *adjective*
happy: *a cheerful smile* ◊ *You don't look very cheerful today. What's the matter?*

p	b	t	d	k	g	tʃ	dʒ	f	v	θ	ð
pen	**b**ad	**t**ea	**d**id	**c**at	**g**ot	**ch**ain	**j**am	**f**all	**v**an	**th**in	**th**is

cheers /tʃɪəz/
a word that you say to somebody when you have a drink together ✪ People sometimes say **cheers** instead of **thank you** or **goodbye**.

cheese /tʃi:z/ *noun*
yellow or white food made from milk: *bread and cheese*
cheeseburger /'tʃi:zbɜ:gə(r)/ *noun*
a hamburger with cheese in it

chef /ʃef/ *noun*
a person who cooks the food in a restaurant

chemical[1] /'kemɪkl/ *noun*
a solid or liquid substance that is used in chemistry or is made by chemistry

chemical[2] /'kemɪkl/ *adjective*
of chemistry or used in chemistry: *a chemical experiment*

chemist /'kemɪst/ *noun*
1 a person who makes and sells medicines ✪ The shop where a chemist works is called a **chemist's**. It sells things like soap and perfume as well as medicines.
2 a person who studies chemistry or who makes chemicals

chemistry /'kemɪstri/ *noun* (no plural)
the science that studies gases, liquids and solids to find out what they are and what they do

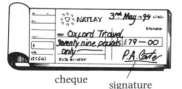

cheque   signature

cheque /tʃek/ *noun*
a piece of paper from a bank that you can write on and use to pay for things: *I gave him a cheque for £50.* ◇ *Can I pay by cheque?*
cheque-book /'tʃek bʊk/ *noun*
a book of cheques

cherry /'tʃeri/
noun (*plural* **cherries**)
a small round red or black fruit

cherry

chess /tʃes/ *noun* (no plural)
a game that two people play with pieces called **chessmen** on a board that has black and white squares on it (called a **chessboard**)

chest[1] /tʃest/ *noun*
the front part of your body below your shoulders and above your waist ☞ picture on page 126

chest[2] /tʃest/ *noun*
a large strong box with a lid
chest of drawers /ˌtʃest əv 'drɔ:z/ *noun* (*plural* **chests of drawers**)
a piece of furniture like a box with parts that you can pull out (**drawers**). It is usually used for keeping clothes in.

chew /tʃu:/ *verb* (**chews**, **chewing**, **chewed** /tʃu:d/)
use your teeth to make food soft

chewing-gum /'tʃu:ɪŋ gʌm/ *noun* (no plural)
sweet stuff that you can chew for a long time

chick /tʃɪk/ *noun*
a young bird, especially a young chicken: *a hen with her chicks*

chicken /'tʃɪkɪn/ *noun*
1 (*plural* **chickens**) a bird that people keep on farms for its eggs and meat

✪ A female chicken is called a **hen** and a male chicken is called a **cock**. A young chicken is a **chick**.

2 (no plural) meat from a chicken: *roast chicken*

chief[1] /tʃi:f/ *adjective*
most important: *Bad driving is one of the chief causes of road accidents.*
chiefly *adverb*
mostly; mainly: *They didn't enjoy their holiday, chiefly because the weather was so bad.*

chief[2] /tʃi:f/ *noun*
the leader or ruler of a group of people: *the chief of an African tribe*

child /tʃaɪld/ *noun* (*plural* **children** /'tʃɪldrən/)
1 a boy or girl: *There are 30 children in the class.*
2 a daughter or son. *One of her children got married last year.* ☞ picture on page 127

childhood /'tʃaɪldhʊd/ *noun* (no plural)
the time when you are a child: *She had a happy childhood.*

childish /'tʃaɪldɪʃ/ *adjective*
like a child, or for children: *childish games*

chilly /'tʃɪli/ *adjective* (**chillier, chilliest**)
cold: *a chilly morning*

chime /tʃaɪm/ *verb* (**chimes, chiming, chimed** /tʃaɪmd/)
make the sound that a bell makes: *The clock chimed midnight.*

chimney /'tʃɪmni/ *noun* (*plural* **chimneys**)
a large pipe over a fire that lets smoke go outside into the air ☞ picture at **house**

chimpanzee /ˌtʃɪmpæn'zi:/ *noun*
an African animal like a monkey with no tail

chin /tʃɪn/ *noun*
the part of your face below your mouth ☞ picture on page 126

china /'tʃaɪnə/ *noun* (no plural)
a hard white material made from earth, or things like plates and cups that are made from this: *a china cup*

chip¹ /tʃɪp/ *noun*
1 a small piece of wood, stone, china, etc that has broken off a larger piece
2 a piece of potato cooked in oil: *We had fish and chips for lunch.*
3 a microchip; a very small thing inside a computer, for example, that makes it work
4 *American English for* **crisp²**

chip² /tʃɪp/ *verb* (**chips, chipping, chipped** /tʃɪpt/)
break a small piece from something: *I chipped a cup.*

chirp /tʃɜːp/ *noun*
the short high sound that a small bird makes
chirp *verb* (**chirps, chirping, chirped** /tʃɜːpt/)
make this sound

chocolate /'tʃɒklət/ *noun*
1 (no plural) dark brown sweet food that is made from cocoa: *Do you like chocolate?* ◇ *a bar of chocolate* ◇ *a chocolate cake*
2 (*plural* **chocolates**) a sweet made of chocolate: *a box of chocolates*

choice /tʃɔɪs/ *noun*
1 deciding which one; choosing: *You made the right choice.* ◇ *We have no choice. We must go immediately.*
2 the number of things that you can choose: *There is a big choice of vegetables in the market.*

choir /'kwaɪə(r)/ *noun*
a big group of people who sing together: *a school choir* ◇ *the church choir*

choke /tʃəʊk/ *verb* (**chokes, choking, choked** /tʃəʊkt/)
not be able to breathe because something is in your throat

choose /tʃuːz/ *verb* (**chooses, choosing, chose** /tʃəʊz/, **has chosen** /'tʃəʊzn/)
take the thing or person that you like best: *Ann chose the biggest cake.*

chop¹ /tʃɒp/ *verb* (**chops, chopping, chopped** /tʃɒpt/)
cut something with a knife or an axe: *We chopped some wood for the fire.* ◇ *Chop the meat up into small pieces.*

chop² /tʃɒp/ *noun*
a thick slice of meat with a piece of bone in it: *a lamb chop*

chorus /'kɔːrəs/ *noun* (*plural* **choruses**)
a part of a song that you repeat

christen /'krɪsn/ *verb* (**christens, christening, christened** /'krɪsnd/)
give a first name to a baby and make him/her a member of the Christian church in a special ceremony
christening /'krɪsnɪŋ/ *noun*
the ceremony when a baby is christened

Christian /'krɪstʃən/ *noun*
a person who believes in Jesus Christ and what He taught
Christian *adjective*
the Christian church
Christian name /'krɪstʃən neɪm/ *noun*
a person's first name: *Her surname is Baker and her Christian name is Susan.* ☞ Note at **name**

Christianity /ˌkrɪsti'ænəti/ *noun* (no plural)
the religion that follows what Jesus Christ taught

Christmas /'krɪsməs/ *noun*
the special time when Christians remember the birth of Christ: *Merry Christmas!* ☞ Note on page 58

i:	i	ɪ	e	æ	ɑ:	ɒ	ɔ:	ʊ	u	u:
see	happy	sit	ten	cat	father	got	saw	put	situation	too

✪ Christmas is a very important festival in Britain and the USA. **Christmas Day** is on 25 December (the day before this is called **Christmas Eve** and the day after is called **Boxing Day**). Children believe that **Father Christmas** visits them at Christmas to bring **presents**, and we give presents and send **Christmas cards** to each other.
Many people go to church at Christmas and sing **carols**. We put special trees (**Christmas trees**) in our homes, and decorate them with coloured lights and other pretty things. On Christmas Day, a special **Christmas dinner** is eaten, usually with roast **turkey** and hot **Christmas pudding** (a kind of cake made with dried fruit).

church /tʃɜːtʃ/ *noun* (*plural* **churches**)
a building where Christians go to pray: *They go to church every Sunday.*
churchyard /'tʃɜːtʃjɑːd/ *noun*
a piece of land around a church

cigar /sɪ'gɑː(r)/ *noun*
a roll of tobacco leaves that you can smoke

cigarette /ˌsɪgə'ret/ *noun*
small pieces of tobacco in a tube of paper that you can smoke

cinema /'sɪnəmə/ *noun*
a place where you go to see a film: *Let's go to the cinema tonight.*

circle /'sɜːkl/ *noun*
a round shape: *There are 360 degrees in a circle.* ☞ picture on page 161

circular /'sɜːkjələ(r)/ *adjective*
with the shape of a circle; round: *A wheel is circular.*

circulate /'sɜːkjəleɪt/ *verb* (**circulates**, **circulating**, **circulated**)
move round: *Blood circulates in our bodies.*

circumference /sə'kʌmfərəns/ *noun*
the distance around a circle ☞ picture on page 161

circumstances /'sɜːkəmstənsɪz/ *noun* (plural)
the facts that are true when something happens
in or **under the circumstances** because things are as they are: *It was snowing, so under the circumstances we decided to stay at home.*
under no circumstances not at all; never: *Under no circumstances should you go out alone at night.*

circus /'sɜːkəs/ *noun* (*plural* **circuses**)
a show in a big tent, with clowns, acrobats and animals

citizen /'sɪtɪzn/ *noun*
a person who belongs to a country or a town: *She became a British citizen.*

city /'sɪti/ *noun* (*plural* **cities**)
1 a big and important town: *the city of Liverpool* ◇ *the city centre*
2 the City (no plural) the part of London with a lot of banks and offices

civil /'sɪvl/ *adjective*
of the people of a country: *civil rights*
the Civil Service /ˌsɪvl 'sɜːvɪs/ *noun* (no plural)
the people who work for the government
civil war /ˌsɪvl 'wɔː(r)/ *noun*
a war between groups of people in one country

civilian /sə'vɪliən/ *noun*
a person who is not a soldier

civilization /ˌsɪvəlaɪ'zeɪʃn/ *noun*
the way people live together in a certain place at a certain time: *ancient civilizations*

cl *short way of writing* **centilitre**

claim /kleɪm/ *verb* (**claims**, **claiming**, **claimed** /kleɪmd/)
1 ask for something because it is yours: *If nobody claims the camera you found, you can have it.*
2 say that something is true: *Manuel claims that he did the work without help.*
claim *noun*
The workers are making a claim for better pay.

clang /klæŋ/ *noun*
the loud sound that metal makes when you hit it with something: *The iron gates shut with a clang.*

clap /klæp/ *verb* (**claps**, **clapping**, **clapped** /klæpt/)
hit your hands together to make a noise, usually to show that you like something: *At the end of the concert the audience clapped loudly.*
clap *noun*
the sound that you make when you hit your hands together

ʌ	ɜː	ə	eɪ	əʊ	aɪ	aʊ	ɔɪ	ɪə	eə	ʊə
cup	**bird**	**about**	**say**	**go**	**five**	**now**	**boy**	**near**	**hair**	**pure**

clash /klæʃ/ verb (**clashes, clashing, clashed** /klæʃt/)
1 fight or argue: *Police clashed with football fans outside the stadium last Saturday.*
2 be at the same time: *The match clashed with my swimming lesson, so I couldn't watch it.*
3 If colours clash, they do not look nice together: *Your tie clashes with your shirt!*

class /klɑːs/ noun (*plural* **classes**)
1 a group of children or students who learn together: *The whole class passed the exam.* ◇ *There is a new girl in my class.*
2 the time when you learn something with a teacher: *Classes begin at nine o'clock.* ◇ *You mustn't eat in class.*
3 a group of people or things that are the same in some way: *There are many different classes of animals.*
4 how good, comfortable, etc something is: *It costs more to travel first class.*

classroom /'klɑːsruːm/ noun
a room where you have lessons in a school

classic /'klæsɪk/ noun
a book that is so good that people read it for many years after it was written: *'Alice in Wonderland' is a children's classic.*

classical /'klæsɪkl/ adjective
1 in a style that people have used for a long time because they think it is good: *classical music*
2 of ancient Greece or Rome: *classical Greek*

clatter /'klætə(r)/ noun (no plural)
a loud noise that hard things make when they hit each other: *the clatter of knives and forks*

clause /klɔːz/ noun
a part of a sentence that has a verb in it

claw /klɔː/ noun
one of the hard pointed parts on the feet of some animals and birds: *Cats have sharp claws.*

clay /kleɪ/ noun (no plural)
a kind of heavy earth that becomes hard when it is dry. Clay is used to make things like pots and tiles.

clean¹ /kliːn/ adjective (**cleaner, cleanest**)
not dirty: *clean clothes* ◇ *clean air*
☞ picture on page 263

clean² /kliːn/ verb (**cleans, cleaning, cleaned** /kliːnd/)
take away the dirt or marks from something; make something clean: *Sam helped his mother to clean the kitchen.* ◇ *Don't forget to clean your teeth before you go to bed.*
clean noun (no plural)
The car needs a clean.

clear¹ /klɪə(r)/ adjective (**clearer, clearest**)
1 easy to see, hear or understand: *She spoke in a loud clear voice.* ◇ *This photograph is very clear.* ◇ *It's clear that Jane is not happy.*
2 that you can see through: *clear glass*
3 with nothing in the way; empty: *The roads were very clear.*
4 bright; without clouds: *a clear day*

clear² /klɪə(r)/ verb (**clears, clearing, cleared** /klɪəd/)
1 take things away from a place because you do not need them there: *They cleared the snow from the path.* ◇ *When you have finished your meal, clear the table.*
2 become clear: *It rained in the morning, but in the afternoon the sky cleared.*
clear off go away: *He got cross and told them to clear off.*
clear out take everything out of a cupboard, room, etc so that you can clean it and make it tidy
clear up make a place clean and tidy: *She helped me to clear up after the party.*

clearly /'klɪəli/ adverb
1 in a way that is easy to see, hear or understand: *Please speak louder – I can't hear you very clearly.* ◇ *The notes explain very clearly what you have to do.*
2 without any doubt: *She is clearly very intelligent.*

clerk¹ /klɜːrk/ American English for **shop assistant**

clerk² /klɑːk/ noun
a person in an office or bank who does things like writing letters

clever /'klevə(r)/ adjective (**cleverer, cleverest**)
able to learn, understand or do something quickly and well: *a clever student*
cleverly adverb
The book is cleverly written.

p	b	t	d	k	g	tʃ	dʒ	f	v	θ	ð
pen	**b**ad	**t**ea	**d**id	**c**at	**g**ot	**ch**ain	**j**am	**f**all	**v**an	**th**in	**th**is

click /klɪk/ *noun*
a short sharp sound: *I heard a click as someone switched the light on.*
click *verb* (**clicks**, **clicking**, **clicked** /klɪkt/)
make this sound: *clicking cameras*

client /'klaɪənt/ *noun*
a person who pays another person, for example a lawyer or an accountant, for help or advice

cliff

cliff /klɪf/ *noun*
the high steep side of a hill by the sea

climate /'klaɪmət/ *noun*
the sort of weather that a place has: *Coffee will not grow in a cold climate.*

climb /klaɪm/ *verb* (**climbs**, **climbing**, **climbed** /klaɪmd/)
1 go up or down, walking or using your hands and feet: *The cat climbed to the top of the tree.* ◇ *They climbed the mountain.*
2 move to or from a place when it is not easy to do it: *The children climbed through a hole in the fence.*
3 move to a higher place: *The road climbs steeply.*
climb *noun* (no plural)
It was a long climb from the village to the top of the mountain.

climbing *noun* (no plural)
the sport of climbing mountains or rocks: *a pair of climbing boots* ○ We often say **go climbing**: *They usually go climbing in the Alps in the holidays.*

climber /'klaɪmə(r)/ *noun*
a person who goes up and down mountains or rocks as a sport

cling /klɪŋ/ *verb* (**clings**, **clinging**, **clung** /klʌŋ/, **has clung**)
hold or stick tightly to somebody or something: *The small child was crying and clinging to her mother.* ◇ *His wet clothes clung to his body.*

clinic /'klɪnɪk/ *noun*
a place where you can go to get special help from a doctor

clip /klɪp/ *noun*
a small piece of metal or plastic for holding things together: *a paper-clip*
clip *verb* (**clips**, **clipping**, **clipped** /klɪpt/)
join something to another thing with a clip: *I clipped the photo to the letter.*

cloak /kləʊk/ *noun*
a very loose coat that has no sleeves

cloakroom /'kləʊkruːm/ *noun*
1 a place in a building where you can leave your coat or bag
2 a toilet in a public building

clock /klɒk/ *noun*
a thing that shows you what time it is. It stands in a room or hangs on a wall: *an alarm clock* ○ A thing that shows the time and that you wear on your wrist is called a **watch**.

○ You say that a clock or watch is **fast** if it shows a time that is later than the real time. You say that it is **slow** if it shows a time that is earlier than the real time.

clockwise /'klɒkwaɪz/ *adjective, adverb*
in the direction that the hands of a clock move: *Turn the handle clockwise.* ○ opposite: **anticlockwise**

close¹ /kləʊs/ *adjective, adverb* (**closer**, **closest**)
1 near: *We live close to the station.* ◇ *You're too close to the fire.*
2 If people are close, they like or love each other very much: *I'm very close to my sister.* ◇ *John and I are close friends.*
3 with only a very small difference: *'Did David win the race?' 'No, but it was very close.'*
4 careful: *Keep a close watch on the children.*
close together with not much space between them: *The photographer asked us to stand closer together.*
closely *adverb*
in a close way: *We watched her closely.* ◇ *Paul entered, closely followed by Mike.*

close² /kləʊz/ *verb* (**closes**, **closing**, **closed** /kləʊzd/)
1 shut: *Please close the window.* ◇ *Close your eyes!* ◇ *The door closed quietly.*

s	z	ʃ	ʒ	h	m	n	ŋ	l	r	j	w
so	**zoo**	**shoe**	**vision**	**hat**	**man**	**no**	**sing**	**leg**	**red**	**yes**	**wet**

2 stop being open, so that people cannot go there: *The banks close at 4.30.*

❍ opposite: **open**
close down shut and stop working; make something shut and stop working: *The shop closed down when the owner died.*
closed *adjective*
not open; shut: *The shops are closed on Sundays.* ☞ picture on page 263

closet /'klɒzɪt/ *American English for* **cupboard**

cloth /klɒθ/ *noun*
1 (no plural) material that is made of wool, cotton, etc and that we use for making clothes and other things ❍ **Material** is the word that we usually use.
2 a piece of cloth that you use for a special job: *a tablecloth* (= for covering a table) ◇ *Wipe the floor with a cloth.*

clothes /kləʊðz/ *noun* (plural)
things like trousers, shirts and coats that you wear to cover your body: *She was wearing new clothes.* ◇ *Take off those wet clothes.*

clothing /'kləʊðɪŋ/ *noun* (no plural)
clothes: *skirts, trousers and other pieces of clothing*

cloud /klaʊd/ *noun*
1 a white or grey shape in the sky that is made of small drops of water: *Look at those dark clouds. It's going to rain.*
2 dust or smoke that looks like a cloud: *clouds of smoke*
cloudy *adjective* (**cloudier, cloudiest**)
with a lot of clouds: *a cloudy sky*

clown /klaʊn/ *noun*
a person in a circus who wears funny clothes and makes people laugh

club¹ /klʌb/ *noun*
a group of people who do something together, or the place where they meet: *I belong to the tennis club.* ☞ Look also at **nightclub**.
club *verb* (**clubs, clubbing, clubbed** /klʌbd/)
club together give money so that a group of people can buy something: *We all clubbed together to buy David and Lisa a wedding present.*

club² /klʌb/ *noun*
1 a heavy stick with a thick end

2 **clubs** (plural) the playing-cards that have the shape ♣ on them: *the three of clubs*

clue /kluː/ *noun*
something that helps to find the answer to a problem, or to know the truth: *The police have found a clue that may help them to catch the murderer.*
not have a clue not know something, or not know how to do something: *'What's his name?' 'I haven't a clue.'*

clumsy /'klʌmzi/ *adjective* (**clumsier, clumsiest**)
If you are clumsy, you often drop things or do things badly because you do not move in an easy or careful way: *I'm so clumsy! I've just broken a glass.*
clumsily /'klʌmzəli/ *adverb*
He clumsily knocked the cup off the table.

clung *form of* **cling**

clutch /klʌtʃ/ *verb* (**clutches, clutching, clutched** /klʌtʃt/)
hold something tightly: *The child clutched his mother's hand.*

cm *short way of writing* **centimetre**

Co /kəʊ/ *short for* **company 1**

c/o
You use **c/o** (short for **care of**) when you are writing to somebody who is staying at another person's house: *Mrs Jane Walker, c/o Miss P Smith*

coach¹ /kəʊtʃ/ *noun* (*plural* **coaches**)
1 a bus for taking people on long journeys
2 a vehicle with four wheels that is pulled by horses: *The Queen travelled to the wedding in the royal coach.*
3 one of the parts of a train where people sit

coach² /kəʊtʃ/ *noun* (*plural* **coaches**)
a person who teaches a sport: *a football coach*
coach *verb* (**coaches, coaching, coached** /kəʊtʃt/)
teach somebody: *She is coaching the British team for the Olympics.*

coal /kəʊl/ *noun* (no plural)
hard black stuff that comes from under the ground and gives heat when you burn it: *Put some more coal on the fire.*

i:	i	ɪ	e	æ	ɑ:	ɒ	ɔ:	ʊ	u	u:
see	happy	sit	ten	cat	father	got	saw	put	situation	too

coarse /kɔːs/ *adjective* (**coarser, coarsest**)
made of thick pieces so that it is not smooth: *coarse sand* ◊ *coarse material*

coast /kəʊst/ *noun*
the part of the land that is next to the sea: *Their house is near the coast.* ◊ *the west coast of France*

coastguard /'kəʊstgɑːd/ *noun*
a person whose job is to watch the sea and ships and help people who are in danger

coastline /'kəʊstlaɪn/ *noun*
the edge of the land next to the sea: *a rocky coastline*

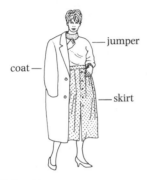
jumper
coat
skirt

coat /kəʊt/ *noun*
1 a piece of clothing that you wear over your other clothes when you go outside in cold weather or rain: *Put your coat on – it's cold today.* ◊ *a raincoat*
2 the hair or fur that covers an animal: *A tiger has a striped coat.*

coat *verb* (**coats, coating, coated**)
put a thin covering of something over another thing: *Their shoes were coated with mud.*

coat-hanger
/'kəʊt hæŋə(r)/ *noun*
a piece of wood, metal or plastic with a hook. You use it for hanging clothes on.

coat-hanger

cobweb
/'kɒbweb/ *noun*
a net that a spider makes to catch insects

Coca-Cola /ˌkəʊkə 'kəʊlə/ *noun*
1 (no plural) a sweet brown drink with bubbles in it

2 (*plural* **Coca-Colas**) a glass, bottle or can of Coca-Cola
✪ Coca-Cola is a trade mark.

cock /kɒk/ *noun*
1 a male bird
2 a male chicken

cockpit /'kɒkpɪt/ *noun*
the part of a plane where the pilot sits

cocktail /'kɒkteɪl/ *noun*
a drink made of alcohol, fruit juice, etc. mixed together

cocoa /'kəʊkəʊ/ *noun* (no plural)
1 a brown powder from the beans of a tree, that is used to make chocolate
2 a drink of hot milk mixed with this powder: *a cup of cocoa*

coconut /'kəʊkənʌt/ *noun*
a very large brown nut that grows on trees in hot countries. Coconuts are hard and hairy on the outside, and they have sweet white food and liquid inside.

cod /kɒd/ *noun* (*plural* **cod**)
a large fish that lives in the sea and that you can eat

code /kəʊd/ *noun*
1 a way of writing secret messages, using letters, numbers or special signs: *The list of names was written in code.*
2 a group of numbers or letters that helps you find something: *What's the code* (= the telephone number) *for Paris?*
3 a set of rules for a group of people: *the Highway Code* (= rules for people who are driving on the road)

coffee /'kɒfi/ *noun*
1 (no plural) brown powder made from the beans of a tree that grows in hot countries. You use it for making a drink.
2 (no plural) a drink of hot water mixed with this powder: *Would you like coffee or tea?* ◊ *a cup of coffee*
3 (*plural* **coffees**) a cup of this drink: *Two coffees, please.* **✪ White** coffee has milk in it and **black** coffee has no milk.

coffee-table /'kɒfi teɪbl/ *noun*
a small low table

coffin /'kɒfɪn/ *noun*
a box that you put a dead person's body in

coil /kɔɪl/ *noun*
a long piece of rope or wire that goes round in circles: *a coil of rope*

coil *verb* (**coils, coiling, coiled** /kɔɪld/)
make something into a lot of circles that
are joined together: *The snake coiled itself
round a branch.*

coin /kɔɪn/ *noun*
a round piece of money made of metal: *a
pound coin*

coincidence /kəʊ'ɪnsɪdəns/ *noun*
when things happen at the same time or in
the same place by chance: *What a coincidence! I was thinking about you when you
phoned!*

Coke /kəʊk/ *another word for* **Coca-Cola**
✪ **Coke** is a trade mark.

cola /'kəʊlə/ *noun*
1 (no plural) a sweet brown drink with
bubbles in it
2 (*plural* **colas**) a glass, bottle or can of
cola

cold¹ /kəʊld/ *adjective* (**colder, coldest**)
1 not hot or warm; with a low temperature. Ice and snow are cold: *Put your coat
on — it's cold outside.* ◇ *I'm cold. Will
you put the heater on?* ◇ *hot and cold water* ☞ picture on page 263
2 not friendly or kind: *a cold person*
coldly *adverb*
in an unfriendly way: *She looked at me
coldly.*

cold² /kəʊld/ *noun*
1 (no plural) cold weather: *Don't go out in
the cold.*
2 (*plural* **colds**) an illness that makes you
sneeze and cough: *I've got a cold.*
catch a cold become ill with a cold

collapse /kə'læps/ *verb* (**collapses, col-
lapsing, collapsed** /kə'læpst/)
fall down suddenly: *The building collapsed
in the earthquake.* ◇ *She collapsed in the
street and she was taken to hospital.*
collapse *noun*
the collapse of the bridge

collar /'kɒlə(r)/
noun
1 the part of your
clothes that goes
round your neck
2 a band that you
put round the neck
of a dog or cat

collar

colleague /'kɒliːg/ *noun*
a person who works with you

collect /kə'lekt/ *verb* (**collect, collecting, collected**)
1 take things from different people or
places and put them together: *The waiter
collected the dirty glasses.*
2 bring together things that are the same
in some way, to study or enjoy them: *My
son collects stamps.*
3 go and bring somebody or something
from a place: *She collects her children
from school at 3.30.*

collection /kə'lekʃn/ *noun*
1 a group of things that somebody has
brought together: *The Tate Gallery has a
large collection of modern paintings.* ◇ *a
record collection*
2 taking something from a place or from
people: *rubbish collection*

collector /kə'lektə(r)/ *noun*
a person who collects things as a hobby or
as a job: *a stamp collector* ◇ *a ticket collector at a railway station*

college /'kɒlɪdʒ/ *noun*
1 a place where people go to study more
difficult subjects after they have left school:
She's going to college next year. ◇ *My
brother is at college.*
2 a part of a university: *Kings College
London*

collide /kə'laɪd/ *verb* (**collides, collid-
ing, collided**)
move towards each other and hit each
other: *The two lorries collided.* ◇ *The
lorry collided with a bus.*

collision /kə'lɪʒn/ *noun*
when things or people collide: *The driver of
the car was killed in the collision.*

colon /'kəʊlən/ *noun*
a mark (:) that you use in writing, for example before a list

colonel /'kɜːnl/ *noun*
an officer in the army

colony /'kɒləni/ *noun* (*plural* **colonies**)
a country that is ruled by another country:
Kenya was once a British colony.

color *American English for* **colour**

colored *American English for* **coloured**

colorful *American English for* **colourful**

colour /'kʌlə(r)/ *noun*
Red, blue, yellow and green are all colours:
'What colour are your new shoes?'

'Black.' ◇ *The leaves change colour in autumn.*

❷ Some words that we use to talk about colours are **light**, **pale**, **dark**, **deep** and **bright**.

colour *verb* (**colours**, **colouring**, **coloured** /'kʌləd/)
put colours on something: *The children coloured their pictures with crayons.*

coloured /'kʌləd/ *adjective*
with a colour: *She was wearing a brightly coloured jumper.* ◇ *coloured paper*

colourful /'kʌləfl/ *adjective*
with a lot of bright colours: *The garden is very colourful in summer.*

column /'kɒləm/ *noun*
1 a tall piece of stone that is part of a building
2 a long thin piece of writing on one side or part of a page: *Each page of this dictionary has two columns.*

comb /kəʊm/ *noun*
a flat piece of metal or plastic with a line of thin parts like teeth. You use it to make your hair tidy.

comb

comb *verb* (**combs**, **combing**, **combed** /kəʊmd/)
make your hair tidy with a comb: *Have you combed your hair?*

combination /ˌkɒmbɪ'neɪʃn/ *noun*
two or more things mixed together: *The building is a combination of new and old styles.*

combine /kəm'baɪn/ *verb* (**combines**, **combining**, **combined** /kəm'baɪnd/)
join or mix together: *The two schools combined and moved to a larger building.*

come /kʌm/ *verb* (**comes**, **coming**, **came** /keɪm/, **has come**)
1 move towards the person who is speaking or the place that you are talking about: *Come here, please.* ◇ *The dog came when I called him.* ◇ *I'm sorry, but I can't come to your party.*
2 arrive: *If you go along that road, you will come to the river.* ◇ *A letter came for you this morning.*
3 be or happen: *June comes after May.*
4 go with the person who is speaking: *I'm going to a party. Do you want to come?*
come across something find some-

thing when you are not looking for it: *I came across these old photos yesterday.*
come apart break into pieces: *This old coat is coming apart.*
come back return: *I'm going to Italy tomorrow and I'm coming back in January.*
come from 1 be made from something: *Wool comes from sheep.* 2 The place that you come from is where you were born or where you live: *I come from Japan.* ◇ *Where do you come from?*
come on!, come along! words that you use for telling somebody to hurry or to try harder: *Come on! We'll be late!*
come out appear: *The rain stopped and the sun came out.* ◇ *This book came out in 1994.*
how come ...? why or how...?: *How come you're here so early?*
to come in the future: *I'll be very busy in the months to come.*

comedian /kə'miːdiən/ *noun*
a person whose job is to make people laugh

comedy /'kɒmədi/ *noun* (*plural* **comedies**)
a funny play or film

comfort /'kʌmfət/ *noun*
1 (no plural) having everything your body needs; being without pain or problems: *They have enough money to live in comfort.*
2 (*plural* **comforts**) a person or thing that helps you or makes life better: *Her children were a comfort to her when she was ill.*

comfort *verb* (**comforts**, **comforting**, **comforted**)
make somebody feel less unhappy or worried: *A mother was comforting her crying child.*

comfortable /'kʌmftəbl/ *adjective*
1 nice to sit in, to be in, or to wear: *This is a very comfortable bed.* ◇ *comfortable shoes*
2 with no pain or worry: *Sit down and make yourself comfortable.*
❷ opposite: **uncomfortable**
comfortably /'kʌmftəbli/ *adverb*
Are you sitting comfortably?

comic¹ /'kɒmɪk/, **comical** /'kɒmɪkl/ *adjective*
funny

comic² /'kɒmɪk/ *noun*
a magazine for children, with pictures that tell a story

s	z	ʃ	ʒ	h	m	n	ŋ	l	r	j	w
so	**zoo**	**shoe**	vision	**hat**	**man**	**no**	si**ng**	**leg**	**red**	**yes**	**wet**

comma /'kɒmə/ *noun* (*plural* **commas**)
a mark (,) that you use in writing to make
a short stop in a sentence

command /kə'mɑːnd/ *noun*
1 (*plural* **commands**) words that tell you
that you must do something: *The soldiers
must obey their general's commands.*
2 (no plural) the power to tell people what
to do: *Who is in command of this ship?*
command *verb* (**commands, commanding, commanded**)
tell somebody that they must do something: *He commanded us to leave immediately.* ✪ **Order** is the word that we
usually use.

comment /'kɒment/ *noun*
words that you say about something to
show what you think: *She made some interesting comments about the film.*
comment *verb* (**comments, commenting, commented**)
say what you think about something: *A lot
of people at school commented on my new
watch.*

commentary /'kɒməntri/ *noun* (*plural*
commentaries)
words that somebody says about something that is happening: *We listened to the
radio commentary on the football match.*
commentator /'kɒmənteɪtə(r)/ *noun*
a person who gives a commentary on radio
or television

commerce /'kɒmɜːs/ *noun* (no plural)
the work of buying and selling things

commercial /kə'mɜːʃl/ *adjective*
for or about buying and selling things: *a
commercial vehicle*
commercial *noun*
a short film on television or radio that
helps to sell something

commit /kə'mɪt/ *verb* (**commits, committing, committed**)
do something bad: *This man has committed a very serious crime.*

committee /kə'mɪti/ *noun*
a group of people that other people choose
to plan or organize something: *The members of the club choose a new committee
every year.*

common[1] /'kɒmən/ *adjective* (**commoner, commonest**)
1 that you often see or that often happens:
Smith is a common name in England.

2 that everybody in a group does or has:
The English and Australians have a common language.
have something in common be like
somebody in a certain way, or have the
same interests as somebody: *Paul and I are
good friends. We have a lot in common.*

common sense /ˌkɒmən 'sens/ *noun*
(no plural)
the ability to do the right thing and not
make stupid mistakes, because of what
you know about the world: *Jane's got no
common sense. She lay in the sun all day
and got sunburnt.*

common[2] /'kɒmən/ *noun*
a piece of land that everybody can use: *We
went for a walk on the common.*

communicate /kə'mjuːnɪkeɪt/ *verb*
(**communicates, communicating, communicated**)
talk or write to somebody: *The pilots communicate with the airport by radio.*
communication /kəˌmjuːnɪ'keɪʃn/
noun
1 (no plural) talking or writing to somebody: *Communication is difficult when
two people don't speak the same language.*
2 communications (plural) ways of
sending information or moving from one
place to another: *There are good communications with the islands.*

community /kə'mjuːnəti/ *noun* (*plural*
communities)
1 the people who live in a place: *Life in a
small fishing community is very different
from life in a big city.*
2 a group of people who join together, for
example because they have the same interests or religion: *the Asian community in
Britain*

commute /kə'mjuːt/ *verb* (**commutes,
commuting, commuted**)
travel a long way from home to work every
day: *She lives in the country and commutes to London.*
commuter *noun*
a person who commutes

compact disc /ˌkɒmpækt 'dɪsk/ *noun*
a small round piece of plastic, like a record.
You play it on a special machine called a
compact disc player. ✪ The short form is
CD. ☞ picture on next page

i:	i	ɪ	e	æ	ɑ:	ɒ	ɔ:	ʊ	u	u:
see	happy	sit	ten	cat	father	got	saw	put	situation	too

compact disc

companion /kəm'pæniən/ *noun*
a person who is with another person

company /'kʌmpəni/ *noun*
1 (*plural* **companies**) a group of people who work to make or sell things: *an advertising company*
2 (no plural) being with other people: *She lives alone so she likes company at weekends.*
keep somebody company be or go with somebody: *Please stay and keep me company for a while.*

comparative /kəm'pærətɪv/ *noun*
in the form of an adjective or adverb that shows more of something: *The comparative of 'bad' is 'worse'.*
comparative *adjective*
'Longer' is the comparative form of 'long'.

compare /kəm'peə(r)/ *verb* (**compares**, **comparing**, **compared** /kəm'peəd/)
think about or look at people or things together so that you can see how they are different: *I've compared the prices in the two shops and the prices here are cheaper.* ◇ *Compare your answers with those at the back of the book.*
compared *adjective*
if you compare somebody or something: *Stephen is quite small, compared with his friends.*

comparison /kəm'pærɪsn/ *noun*
seeing or understanding how things are different or the same: *We made a comparison of prices in three different shops.*
in or **by comparison with somebody or something** if you see or think about somebody or something together with another person or thing: *Britain is a small country in comparison with Australia.*

compartment /kəm'pɑːtmənt/ *noun*
1 a small room in a train: *The first-class compartments are at the front of the train.*
2 a separate part inside a box or bag: *The suitcase had a secret compartment at the back.*

compass /'kʌmpəs/ *noun* (*plural* **compasses**)
a thing with a needle that always shows where north is

compete /kəm'piːt/ *verb* (**competes**, **competing**, **competed**)
try to win a race or competition: *Teams from many countries compete in the World Cup.*

competition /ˌkɒmpə'tɪʃn/ *noun*
1 (*plural* **competitions**) a game or test that people try to win: *I entered the painting competition and won first prize.*
2 (no plural) trying to win or be best: *We were in competition with a team from another school.*

competitor /kəm'petɪtə(r)/ *noun*
a person who is trying to win a competition

complain /kəm'pleɪn/ *verb* (**complains**, **complaining**, **complained** /kəm'pleɪnd/)
say that you do not like something; say that you are unhappy or angry about something: *He complained to the waiter that his soup was cold.* ◇ *She was complaining about the weather.*

complaint /kəm'pleɪnt/ *noun*
saying that you do not like something: *We made a complaint to the hotel manager about the dirty rooms.*

complete¹ /kəm'pliːt/ *adjective*
1 with none of its parts missing: *I've got a complete set of Shakespeare's plays.*
✪ opposite: **incomplete**
2 finished: *The work is complete.*
3 in every way; total: *Their visit was a complete surprise.*

complete² /kəm'pliːt/ *verb* (**completes**, **completing**, **completed**)
finish doing or making something: *She was at university for two years but she did not complete her studies.* ◇ *When will the new building be completed?*

completely /kəm'pliːtli/ *adverb*
totally; in every way: *The money has completely disappeared.* ◇ *I completely forgot that it was your birthday!*

complex¹ /'kɒmpleks/ *adjective*
difficult to understand because it has a lot of different parts: *a complex problem*

complex² /'kɒmpleks/ *noun* (*plural* **complexes**)
a group of buildings: *a sports complex*

ʌ	ɜː	ə	eɪ	əʊ	aɪ	aʊ	ɔɪ	ɪə	eə	ʊə
cup	bird	about	say	go	five	now	boy	near	hair	pure

complicated /'kɒmplɪkeɪtɪd/ *adjective*
difficult to understand because it has a lot of different parts: *I can't explain how to play the game. It's too complicated.*

compliment /'kɒmplɪmənt/ *noun*
pay somebody a compliment say something nice about somebody: *Simon paid her a compliment on her speech.*
compliment *verb* (**compliments, complimenting, complimented**)
say something nice about somebody: *They complimented Frank on his cooking.*

compose /kəm'pəʊz/ *verb* (**composes, composing, composed** /kəm'pəʊzd/)
write something, especially music: *Verdi composed many operas.*
be composed of something be made of something; have something as parts: *Water is composed of oxygen and hydrogen.*

composer /kəm'pəʊzə(r)/ *noun*
a person who writes music: *My favourite composer is Mozart.*

composition /ˌkɒmpə'zɪʃn/ *noun*
a piece of writing or music

compound /'kɒmpaʊnd/ *noun*
1 something that is made of two or more parts: *Salt is a chemical compound.*
2 a word that is made from other words: *'Fingernail' and 'waiting-room' are compounds.*

comprehension /ˌkɒmprɪ'henʃn/ *noun* (no plural)
understanding something that you hear or read: *a test in listening comprehension*

comprehensive school
/ˌkɒmprɪ'hensɪv sku:l/, **comprehensive** *noun*
a school for pupils of all abilities between the ages of 11 and 18

compromise /'kɒmprəmaɪz/ *noun*
an agreement with another person or group, when you both do part of what the other person or group wants: *After long talks, the workers and management reached a compromise.*

compulsory /kəm'pʌlsəri/ *adjective*
If something is compulsory, you must do it: *School is compulsory for all children between the ages of five and sixteen.*

computer

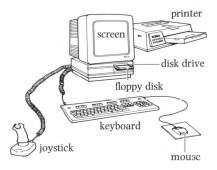

computer /kəm'pju:tə(r)/ *noun*
a machine that stores information and finds answers very quickly
computer program /kəm'pju:tə prəʊgræm/ *noun*
information that tells a computer what to do
computer programmer /kəm,pju:tə 'prəʊgræmə(r)/ *noun*
a person who writes computer programs
computing *noun* (no plural)
using computers to do work: *She is studying computing at college.*

conceal /kən'si:l/ *verb* (**conceals, concealing, concealed** /kən'si:ld/)
hide something: *They concealed the bomb in a suitcase.* ✪ **Hide** is the word that we usually use.

conceited /kən'si:tɪd/ *adjective*
too proud of yourself and what you can do

concentrate /'kɒnsntreɪt/ *verb* (**concentrates, concentrating, concentrated**)
think about what you are doing and not about anything else: *Stop looking out of the window and concentrate on your work!*
concentration /ˌkɒnsn'treɪʃn/ *noun* (no plural)
Concentration is very difficult when there's so much noise.

concern[1] /kən'sɜ:n/ *verb* (**concerns, concerning, concerned** /kən'sɜ:nd/)
1 be important or interesting to somebody: *This notice concerns all passengers travelling to Manchester.*
2 worry somebody: *It concerns me that she is always late.*
3 be about something: *The story concerns a young boy and his parents.*

p	b	t	d	k	g	tʃ	dʒ	f	v	θ	ð
pen	**b**ad	**t**ea	**d**id	**c**at	**g**ot	**ch**ain	**j**am	**f**all	**v**an	**th**in	**th**is

concerned *adjective*
worried: *They are very concerned about their son's illness.*

concern² /kən'sɜːn/ *noun*
1 (no plural) worry: *There is a lot of concern about this problem.*
2 (*plural* **concerns**) something that is important or interesting to somebody: *Her problems are not my concern.*

concerning /kən'sɜːnɪŋ/ *preposition*
about: *Thank you for your letter concerning the date of the next meeting . . .*

concert /'kɒnsət/ *noun*
music played for a lot of people: *a rock concert*

conclusion /kən'kluːʒn/ *noun*
what you believe or decide after thinking carefully: *We came to the conclusion* (= we decided) *that you were right.*

concrete /'kɒŋkriːt/ *noun* (no plural)
hard grey material used for building things: *a concrete path*

condemn /kən'dem/ *verb* (**condemns, condemning, condemned** /kən'demd/)
1 say that somebody must be punished in a certain way: *The murderer was condemned to death.*
2 say strongly that somebody or something is bad or wrong: *Many people condemned the government's decision.*

condition /kən'dɪʃn/ *noun*
1 (no plural) how a person, animal or thing is: *The car was cheap and in good condition, so I bought it.*
2 (*plural* **conditions**) something that must happen before another thing can happen: *One of the conditions of the job is that you agree to work on Saturdays.*
3 conditions (plural) how things are around you: *The prisoners lived in terrible conditions.*

on condition that only if: *You can go to the party on condition that you come home before midnight.*

conduct /kən'dʌkt/ *verb* (**conducts, conducting, conducted**)
1 stand in front of a group of musicians and control what they do: *The orchestra was conducted by Peter Jones.*
2 show somebody where to go: *She conducted us on a tour of the museum.*

conductor /kən'dʌktə(r)/ *noun*
1 a person who stands in front of a group of musicians and controls what they do
2 a person who sells tickets on a bus
3 *American English for* **guard²** 2

cone /kəʊn/ *noun*
1 a shape with one flat round end and one pointed end
☞ picture on page 161
2 the hard fruit of a **pine** or **fir** tree: *a pine cone*

cone 2

conference /'kɒnfərəns/ *noun*
a time when many people meet to talk about a special thing: *an international conference*

confess /kən'fes/ *verb* (**confesses, confessing, confessed** /kən'fest/)
say that you have done something wrong: *She confessed that she had stolen the money.* ◇ *He confessed to the crime.*

confession /kən'feʃn/ *noun*
something that you confess: *She made a confession to the police.*

confidence /'kɒnfɪdəns/ *noun* (no plural)
the feeling that you can do something well: *She answered the questions with confidence.*

have confidence in somebody feel sure that somebody will do something well: *I'm sure you'll pass the exam. I have great confidence in you.*

in confidence If somebody tells you something in confidence, it is a secret.

confident /'kɒnfɪdənt/ *adjective*
sure that you can do something well, or that something will happen: *I'm confident that our team will win.*

confirm /kən'fɜːm/ *verb* (**confirms, confirming, confirmed** /kən'fɜːmd/)
say that something is true or that something will happen: *Please write and confirm the date of your arrival.*

conflict /'kɒnflɪkt/ *noun*
a fight or an argument

confuse /kən'fjuːz/ *verb* (**confuses, confusing, confused** /kən'fjuːzd/)
1 mix somebody's ideas, so that they cannot think clearly or understand: *They confused me by asking so many questions.*
2 think that one thing or person is an-

other thing or person: *Don't confuse the word 'weather' with 'whether'*.

confused *adjective*
not able to think clearly: *The waiter got confused and brought everybody the wrong drink!*

confusing *adjective*
difficult to understand: *This map is very confusing.*

confusion /kən'fju:ʒn/ *noun* (no plural)
being confused: *He didn't speak any English and he looked at me in confusion when I asked him a question.*

congratulate /kən'grætʃuleɪt/ *verb* (**congratulates**, **congratulating**, **congratulated**)
tell somebody that you are pleased about something that they have done: *I congratulated Sue on passing her exam.*

congratulations /kən,grætʃu'leɪʃnz/ *noun* (plural)
a word that shows you are pleased about something that somebody has done: *Congratulations on your new job!*

congress /'kɒŋgres/ *noun*
1 (*plural* **congresses**) a meeting of many people to talk about important things
2 **Congress** (no plural) a group of people who make the laws in some countries, for example in the United States

conjunction /kən'dʒʌŋkʃn/ *noun*
a word that joins other words or parts of a sentence: *'And', 'or' and 'but' are conjunctions.*

conjuror /'kʌndʒərə(r)/ *noun*
a person who does clever tricks that seem to be magic: *The conjuror pulled a rabbit out of a hat.*

connect /kə'nekt/ *verb* (**connects**, **connecting**, **connected**)
join one thing to another thing: *This wire connects the video recorder to the television.* ◇ *The two cities are connected by a motorway.*

connection /kə'nekʃn/ *noun*
1 the way that one thing is joined to another: *We had a bad connection on the phone so I couldn't hear him very well.* ◇ *Is there a connection between violence on TV and crime?*
2 a train, plane or bus that leaves a place

soon after another arrives, so that people can change from one to the other: *The train was late, so I missed my connection.*
in connection with something about something: *The police want to talk to him in connection with the robbery.*

conscience /'kɒnʃəns/ *noun*
the feeling inside you about what is right and wrong
have a clear conscience feel that you have done nothing wrong
have a guilty conscience feel that you have done something wrong

conscious /'kɒnʃəs/ *adjective*
1 awake and able to think: *The patient was conscious during the operation.*
✪ opposite: **unconscious**
2 If you are conscious of something, you know about it: *I was conscious that somebody was watching me.*

consciousness /'kɒnʃəsnəs/ *noun* (no plural)
lose consciousness stop being conscious: *As she fell, she hit her head and lost consciousness.*

consent /kən'sent/ *noun* (no plural)
agreeing to let somebody do something: *Her parents gave their consent to the marriage.*

consequence /'kɒnsɪkwəns/ *noun*
what happens because of something: *I've just bought a car and, as a consequence, I've got no money.* ◇ *The mistake had terrible consequences.*

consequently /'kɒnsɪkwəntli/ *adverb*
because of that; therefore: *He didn't do any work, and consequently failed the exam.*

conservation /,kɒnsə'veɪʃn/ *noun* (no plural)
taking good care of the world and its forests, lakes, plants, and animals: *the conservation of the rain forests*

the Conservative Party
/ðə kən'sɜːvətɪv pɑːti/ *noun*
one of the important political parties in Britain ☞ Look at **the Labour Party** and **the Liberal Democrats**.

consider /kən'sɪdə(r)/ *verb* (**considers**, **considering**, **considered** /kən'sɪdəd/)
1 think carefully about something: *I'm*

considering going to Italy on holiday.
◇ *We must consider what to do next.*
2 think that something is true: *I consider her to be a good teacher.*
3 think about the feelings of other people when you do something: *I can't move to Australia next month! I have to consider my family.*

considerable /kən'sɪdərəbl/ *adjective*
great or large: *The car cost a considerable amount of money.*
considerably /kən'sɪdərəbli/ *adverb*
My flat is considerably smaller than yours.

considerate /kən'sɪdərət/ *adjective*
A person who is considerate is kind, and thinks and cares about other people: *Please be more considerate and don't play loud music late at night.* ○ opposite: **inconsiderate**

consideration /kən,sɪdə'reɪʃn/ *noun* (no plural)
1 thinking carefully about something: *After a lot of consideration, I decided not to accept the job.*
2 being kind, and caring about other people's feelings: *He shows no consideration for anybody else.*
take something into consideration think carefully about something when you are deciding: *We must take the cost into consideration when choosing where to go on holiday.*

consist /kən'sɪst/ *verb* (consists, consisting, consisted)
consist of something be made of something; have something as parts: *Jam consists of fruit and sugar.*

consistent /kən'sɪstənt/ *adjective*
always the same: *His work isn't very consistent – sometimes it's good and sometimes it's terrible!* ○ opposite: **inconsistent**

consonant /'kɒnsənənt/ *noun*
any letter of the alphabet that is not *a, e, i, o* or *u*, or the sound that you make when you say it ☞ Look at **vowel**.

constable /'kʌnstəbl/ *noun*
an ordinary police officer

constant /'kɒnstənt/ *adjective*
Something that is constant happens all the

time: *the constant noise of traffic*
constantly *adverb*
She talked constantly all evening.

constituency /kən'stɪtjuənsi/ *noun* (*plural* **constituencies**)
a town or an area that chooses one **Member of Parliament** (a person in the government)

constitution /,kɒnstɪ'tjuːʃn/ *noun*
the laws of a country: *the United States constitution*

construct /kən'strʌkt/ *verb* (**constructs, constructing, constructed**)
build something: *The bridge was constructed out of stone.* ○ **Build** is the word that we usually use.
construction /kən'strʌkʃn/ *noun*
1 (no plural) · building something: *the construction of a new motorway*
2 (*plural* **constructions**) something that people have built

consult /kən'sʌlt/ *verb* (**consults, consulting, consulted**)
ask somebody or look in a book when you want to know something: *If the pain doesn't go away, you should consult a doctor.*

consume /kən'sjuːm/ *verb* (**consumes, consuming, consumed** /kən'sjuːmd/)
eat, drink or use something: *This car consumes a lot of petrol.*
consumer *noun*
a person who buys or uses something: *There are laws to protect consumers.*
consumption /kən'sʌmpʃn/ *noun* (no plural)
eating, drinking or using something: *This car has a high petrol consumption* (= it uses a lot of petrol).

contact¹ /'kɒntækt/ *noun* (no plural)
meeting, talking to or writing to somebody: *Until Jane went to school, she didn't have much contact with other children.*
◇ *Are you still in contact with the people you met on holiday?* ◇ *Doctors come into contact with* (= meet) *a lot of people.*

contact² /'kɒntækt/ *verb* (**contacts, contacting, contacted**)
telephone or write to somebody, or go to see them: *If you see this man, please contact the police.*

Λ	ɜː	ə	eɪ	əʊ	aɪ	aʊ	ɔɪ	ɪə	eə	ʊə
cup	bird	about	say	go	five	now	boy	near	hair	pure

contact lens /'kɒntækt lenz/ *noun*
(*plural* **contact lenses**)
a small round piece of plastic or glass that you wear in your eye so that you can see better

contain /kən'teɪn/ *verb* (**contains, containing, contained** /kən'teɪnd/)
have something inside it: *This box contains pens and pencils.* ◇ *Chocolate contains a lot of sugar.*

container /kən'teɪnə(r)/ *noun*
a thing that you can put other things in. Boxes, bottles, bags and jars are all containers.

content /kən'tent/ *adjective*
happy with what you have. *She is not content with the money she has — she wants more.*
contented *adjective*
happy: *a contented smile* ◯ opposite: **discontented**

contents /'kɒntents/ *noun* (plural)
what is inside something: *I poured the contents of the bottle into a bowl.* ◇ *The contents page of a book tells you what is in it.*

contest /'kɒntest/ *noun*
a game or competition that people try to win: *a boxing contest*
contestant /kən'testənt/ *noun*
a person who tries to win a contest: *There are six contestants in the race.*

context /'kɒntekst/ *noun*
the words that come before and after another word or a sentence: *You can often understand the meaning of a word by looking at its context.*

continent /'kɒntɪnənt/ *noun*
one of the seven big pieces of land in the world, for example Africa, Asia or Europe ◯ In Britain, people sometimes say **the Continent** when they mean the main part of Europe.
continental /,kɒntɪ'nentl/ *adjective*
a continental climate

continual /kən'tɪnjuəl/ *adjective*
that happens often: *We have had continual problems with this machine.*
continually /kən'tɪnjuəli/ *adverb*
He is continually late for work.

continue /kən'tɪnju:/ *verb* (**continues, continuing, continued** /kən'tɪnju:d/)
1 not stop happening or doing something: *We continued working until five o'clock.* ◇ *The rain continued all afternoon.*
2 start again after stopping: *Let's have lunch now and continue the meeting this afternoon.*
3 go further: *We continued along the path until we came to the river.*

continuous /kən'tɪnjuəs/ *adjective*
Something that is continuous goes on and does not stop: *a continuous line* ◇ *a continuous noise*
continuously *adverb*
It rained continuously for five hours.

contract /'kɒntrækt/ *noun*
a piece of paper that says that somebody agrees to do something: *The company has signed a contract to build the new road.*

contradict /,kɒntrə'dɪkt/ *verb* (**contradicts, contradicting, contradicted**)
say that something is wrong or not true: *I*

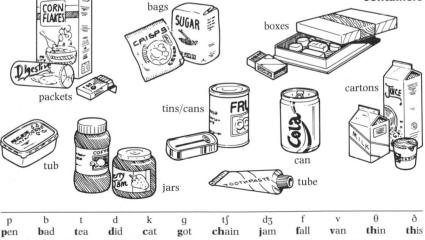

packets/
bags

CORN FLAKES

SUGAR

CRISPS

Digestive

packets

tins/cans

FR

containers

boxes

cartons   JUICE

COFF

Cola

can

tub

jars

TOOTHPASTE   tube

MILK

said we didn't have any coffee, but Jill contradicted me.

contrary¹ /'kɒntrəri/ noun (no plural)
on the contrary the opposite is true: 'You look ill, Ben.' 'On the contrary, I feel fine!'

contrary² /'kɒntrəri/ adjective
contrary to something very different from something; opposite to something: He didn't stay in bed, contrary to the doctor's orders.

contrast /kən'trɑːst/ verb (**contrasts, contrasting, contrasted**)
look at or think about two or more things together and see the differences between them: The book contrasts life today with life 100 years ago.
contrast /'kɒntrɑːst/ noun
a difference between things that you can see clearly: There is a big contrast between the weather in Spain and in Sweden.

contribute /kən'trɪbjuːt/ verb (**contributes, contributing, contributed**)
give something when other people are giving too: We contributed £10 each to pay for the party.
contribution /ˌkɒntrɪ'bjuːʃn/ noun
something that you give when other people are giving too: We are sending contributions of food and clothing to people in poor countries.

control¹ /kən'trəʊl/ noun
1 (no plural) the power to make people or things do what you want: Who has control of the government? ◇ A teacher must be in control of the class.
2 **controls** (plural) the parts of a machine that you press or move to make it work: the controls of an aeroplane
lose control not be able to make people or things do what you want: The driver lost control and the bus went into the river.
out of control If something is out of control, you cannot stop it or make it do what you want: The noise frightened the horse and it got out of control.
under control If something is under control, it is doing what you want it to do: The firemen have the fire under control.

control² /kən'trəʊl/ verb (**controls, controlling, controlled** /kən'trəʊld/)
make people or things do what you want:

He can't control his dog. ◇ This switch controls the heating.
controller noun
a person who controls something: an air traffic controller

convenience /kən'viːniəns/ noun (no plural)
being easy to use; making things easy: For convenience, I usually do all my shopping in the same place.

convenient /kən'viːniənt/ adjective
1 easy to use or go to: The house is very convenient for the station.
2 easy for somebody or something; suitable: Let's meet on Friday. What's the most convenient time for you?
◐ opposite: **inconvenient**
conveniently adverb
We live conveniently close to the shops.

convent /'kɒnvənt/ noun
a place where religious women, called **nuns**, live, work and pray

conversation /ˌkɒnvə'seɪʃn/ noun
a talk: She had a long conversation with her friend on the phone.

conversion /kən'vɜːʃn/ noun
changing something into another thing: the conversion of pounds into dollars

convert /kən'vɜːt/ verb (**converts, converting, converted**)
change into another thing: They converted the house into two flats.

convict /kən'vɪkt/ verb (**convicts, convicting, convicted**)
decide in a court of law that somebody has done something wrong: She was convicted of murder and sent to prison.

convince /kən'vɪns/ verb (**convinces, convincing, convinced** /kən'vɪnst/)
make somebody believe something: I couldn't convince him that I was right.
convinced adjective
certain: I'm convinced that I have seen her somewhere before.

cook¹ /kʊk/ verb (**cooks, cooking, cooked** /kʊkt/)
make food ready to eat by heating it: My father cooked the dinner. ◇ I am learning to cook.

◐ There are many words for ways of cooking food. Look at **bake, boil, fry, grill, roast, stew** and **toast**.

s	z	ʃ	ʒ	h	m	n	ŋ	l	r	j	w
so	**zoo**	**shoe**	vision	**hat**	**man**	**no**	sing	**leg**	**red**	**yes**	**wet**

cooking *noun* (no plural)
1 making food ready to eat: *Who does the cooking in your family?*
2 what you cook: *Italian cooking*

cook² /kʊk/ *noun*
a person who cooks: *She works as a cook in a big hotel.* ◊ *He is a good cook.*

cooker /ˈkʊkə(r)/ *noun*
a thing that you use in a kitchen for cooking food. It has an **oven** for cooking food inside it and places for heating pans on the top: *an electric cooker*

cookery /ˈkʊkəri/ *noun* (no plural)
making food ready to eat, often as a subject that you can study: *cookery lessons*

cookie /ˈkʊki/ *American English for* **biscuit**

cool¹ /kuːl/ *adjective* (**cooler, coolest**)
1 a little cold; not warm: *cool weather* ◊ *I'd like a cool drink.*
2 calm; not excited

cool² /kuːl/ *verb* (**cools, cooling, cooled** /kuːld/)
make something less hot; become less hot: *Take the cake out of the oven and leave it to cool.*
cool down 1 become less hot: *We swam in the river to cool down after our long walk.* **2** become less excited or angry

cooperate /kəʊˈɒpəreɪt/ *verb* (**cooperates, cooperating, cooperated**)
work together with someone else in a helpful way: *The two companies are cooperating with each other.*

cooperation /kəʊˌɒpəˈreɪʃn/ *noun* (no plural)
help: *Thank you for your cooperation.*

cooperative /kəʊˈɒpərətɪv/ *adjective*
happy to help: *The police asked her a lot of questions and she was very cooperative.*

cope /kəʊp/ *verb* (**copes, coping, coped** /kəʊpt/)
cope with somebody or **something**
do something well although it is difficult: *She has four young children. I don't know how she copes with them!*

copied *form of* **copy²**

copies
1 *plural of* **copy¹**
2 *form of* **copy²**

copper /ˈkɒpə(r)/ *noun* (no plural)
a metal with a colour between brown and red: *copper wire*

copy¹ /ˈkɒpi/ *noun* (*plural* **copies**)
1 a thing that is made to look exactly like another thing: *This isn't a real painting by Van Gogh. It's only a copy.* ◊ *The secretary made two copies of the letter.*
2 one example of a book or newspaper: *Two million copies of the newspaper are sold every day.*

copy² /ˈkɒpi/ *verb* (**copies, copying, copied** /ˈkɒpid/, **has copied**)
1 write or draw something so that it is exactly the same as another thing: *The teacher asked us to copy the list of words into our books.*
2 try to look or do the same as another person: *Tom always copies what his brother does.*

cord /kɔːd/ *noun*
strong thick string

core /kɔː(r)/ *noun*
the middle part of some kinds of fruit, where the seeds are: *an apple core*

core

cork /kɔːk/ *noun*
1 (no plural) light strong stuff that comes from the outside of a special tree
2 (*plural* **corks**) a piece of cork that you put in a bottle to close it

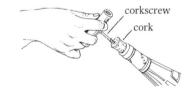
corkscrew
cork

corkscrew /ˈkɔːkskruː/ *noun*
a thing that you use for taking corks out of bottles

corn /kɔːn/ *noun* (no plural)
the seeds of plants like wheat or oats

corner /ˈkɔːnə(r)/ *noun*
a place where two lines, walls or roads meet ☞ picture on next page

cornflakes /ˈkɔːnfleɪks/ *noun* (plural)
food made from corn, that you eat with milk for breakfast. Cornflakes are a kind of **cereal**.

i:	i	ɪ	e	æ	ɑː	ɒ	ɔː	ʊ	u	u:
see	happy	sit	ten	cat	father	got	saw	put	situation	too

corner

The lamp is in the **corner**.

The bank is on the **corner**.

corporation /ˌkɔːpəˈreɪʃn/ *noun*
1 a big company: *the British Broadcasting Corporation*
2 a group of people that the people in a town choose, who meet to decide things

corpse /kɔːps/ *noun*
the body of a dead person

correct¹ /kəˈrekt/ *adjective*
right or true; with no mistakes: *All your answers were correct.* ◇ *What is the correct time, please?* ✪ opposite: **incorrect**
correctly *adverb*
Have I spelt your name correctly?

correct² /kəˈrekt/ *verb* (**corrects, correcting, corrected**)
show where the mistakes are in something and make it right: *The class did the exercises and the teacher corrected them.* ◇ *Please correct me if I make a mistake.*

correction /kəˈrekʃn/ *noun*
the right word or answer that is put in the place of what was wrong: *When the teacher gave my homework back to me it was full of corrections.*

correspond /ˌkɒrəˈspɒnd/ *verb* (**corresponds, corresponding, corresponded**)
be the same, or almost the same: *Does the name on the envelope correspond with the name inside the letter?*

correspondence /ˌkɒrəˈspɒndəns/ *noun* (no plural)
writing letters; the letters that somebody writes or receives: *Her secretary reads all her correspondence.*

corridor /ˈkɒrɪdɔː(r)/ *noun*
a long narrow part inside a building with rooms on each side of it

cosmetics /kɒzˈmetɪks/ *noun* (plural)
special powders or creams that you use on your face or hair to make yourself more beautiful

cost¹ /kɒst/ *noun*
1 the money that you must pay to have something: *The cost of the repairs was very high.*
2 what you lose or give to have another thing: *He saved the child at the cost of his own life.*
at all costs no matter what you must do to make it happen: *We must win at all costs.*

cost² /kɒst/ *verb* (**costs, costing, cost, has cost**)
1 have the price of: *This plant cost £5.* ◇ *How much did the book cost?*
2 make you lose something: *One mistake cost him his job.*

costly /ˈkɒstli/ *adjective* (**costlier, costliest**)
expensive: *The repairs were very costly.*

costume /ˈkɒstjuːm/ *noun*
the special clothes that people wear in a country or at a certain time: *The actors wore beautiful costumes.* ◇ *the national costume of Japan* ☞ Look also at **swimming-costume**.

cosy /ˈkəʊzi/ *adjective* (**cosier, cosiest**)
warm and comfortable: *a cosy room*

cot /kɒt/ *noun*
a baby's bed with high sides

cottage /ˈkɒtɪdʒ/ *noun*
a small house in the country

cotton /ˈkɒtn/ *noun* (no plural)
cloth or thread that is made from the soft white stuff on the seeds of a plant that grows in hot countries: *a cotton shirt* ◇ *a reel of cotton* ☞ picture at **sew**

cotton wool /ˌkɒtn ˈwʊl/ *noun* (no plural)
soft light stuff made from cotton: *The nurse cleaned the cut with cotton wool.*

couch /kaʊtʃ/ *noun* (plural **couches**)
a long seat that you can sit or lie on

ʌ	ɜː	ə	eɪ	əʊ	aɪ	aʊ	ɔɪ	ɪə	eə	ʊə
cup	bird	about	say	go	five	now	boy	near	hair	pure

cough /kɒf/ verb (**coughs, coughing, coughed** /kɒft/)
send air out of your throat with a sudden loud noise: *The smoke made me cough.*
cough noun
He gave a little cough before he started to speak. ◇ *I've got a bad cough.*

could /kʊd/ modal verb
1 the word for 'can' in the past: *He could run very fast when he was young.* ◇ *I could hear the birds singing.*
2 a word that shows what will perhaps happen or what is possible: *It could rain tomorrow.* ◇ *I don't know where Debbie is. She could be in the kitchen.*
3 a word that you use to ask something in a polite way: *Could you open the door?* ◇ *Could I have another drink, please?*

✪ The negative form of 'could' is **could not** or the short form **couldn't** /'kʊdnt/: *It was dark and I couldn't see anything.*
☞ Look at the Note on page 227 to find out more about **modal verbs**.

council /'kaʊnsl/ noun
a group of people who are chosen to work together and to make rules and decide things: *The city council is planning to build a new swimming-pool.*
councillor /'kaʊnsələ(r)/ noun
a member of a council
council-house /'kaʊnsl haʊs/ noun
a house that a town or city owns, that you can rent

count¹ /kaʊnt/ verb (**counts, counting, counted**)
1 say numbers one after the other in the right order: *The children are learning to count from one to ten.*
2 look at people or things to see how many there are: *I have counted the chairs – there are 32.*
3 include somebody or something: *There are five people in my family, counting me.*
4 be important: *He said that my ideas don't count because I'm only a child!*
count on somebody feel sure that somebody will do something for you: *Can I count on you to help me?*

count² /kaʊnt/ noun
a time when you count things: *After an election there is a count of all the votes.*
keep count of something know how

many there are of something: *Try to keep count of the number of tickets you sell.*
lose count of something not know how many there are of something

count³ /kaʊnt/ noun
a man in some countries who has a special title: *Count Dracula*

counter /'kaʊntə(r)/ noun
1 a long high table in a shop, bank or bar, that is between the people who work there and the people who want to buy things: *I put my money on the counter.*
2 a small round thing that you use when you play some games

countess /'kaʊntəs/ noun (plural **countesses**)
a woman who has a special title. She may be married to a **count** or an **earl**.

countless /'kaʊntləs/ adjective
very many: *I have tried to telephone him countless times.*

country /'kʌntri/ noun
1 (plural **countries**) an area of land with its own people and government: *France, Spain and Portugal are countries.*
2 **the country** (no plural) land that is not in a town: *Do you live in the town or the country?*

countryside /'kʌntrisaɪd/ noun (no plural)
land with fields, woods, farms, etc. that is away from towns: *The countryside near York is very beautiful.*

county /'kaʊnti/ noun (plural **counties**)
one of the parts of Britain or Ireland: *Kent and Oxfordshire are counties in England.*

couple /'kʌpl/ noun
two people who are married, living together, etc: *A young couple live next door.*
a couple of 1 two: *I invited a couple of friends to lunch.* **2** a few: *I'll be back in a couple of minutes.*

courage /'kʌrɪdʒ/ noun (no plural)
not being afraid, or not showing that you are afraid when you do something dangerous or difficult: *She showed great courage when she went into the burning building to save the child.*
courageous /kə'reɪdʒəs/ adjective
brave: *a courageous young man*

courgette /kɔː'ʒet/ noun
a long vegetable that is green on the outside and white on the inside

p	b	t	d	k	g	tʃ	dʒ	f	v	θ	ð
pen	**bad**	**tea**	**did**	**cat**	**got**	**chain**	**jam**	**fall**	**van**	**thin**	**this**

course /kɔːs/ *noun*
1 a set of lessons on a certain subject: *He's taking a course in computer programming.*
2 one part of a meal: *a three-course meal* ◇ *I had chicken for the main course.*
3 a piece of ground for some kinds of sport: *a golf-course* ◇ *a racecourse*
4 the direction that something moves in: *We followed the course of the river.*
5 the time when something is happening: *The telephone rang six times during the course of the evening.*
change course start to go in a different direction: *The plane had to change course because of the storm.*
of course certainly: *Of course I'll help you.* ◇ *'Can I use your telephone?' 'Of course you can.'* ◇ *'Are you angry with me?' 'Of course not!'*

court /kɔːt/ *noun*
1 (*also* **court of law**) a place where people (a **judge** or **jury**) decide if a person has done something wrong, and what the punishment will be: *The man will appear in court tomorrow.*
2 a piece of ground where you can play a certain sport: *a tennis-court*

courtyard /'kɔːtjɑːd/ *noun*
an open space without a roof, inside a building or between buildings

cousin /'kʌzn/ *noun*
the child of your aunt or uncle ☞ picture on page 127

cover¹ /'kʌvə(r)/ *verb* (**covers, covering, covered** /'kʌvəd/)
1 put one thing over another thing to hide it or to keep it safe or warm: *Cover the floor with a newspaper before you start painting.* ◇ *She covered her head with a scarf.*
2 be all over something: *Snow covered the ground.*
be covered with or **in something** have something all over yourself or itself: *The floor was covered in mud.*

cover² /'kʌvə(r)/ *noun*
1 a thing that you put over another thing, for example to keep it safe: *The computer has a plastic cover.*
2 the outside part of a book or magazine: *The book had a picture of a footballer on the cover.*

coveralls /'kʌvərɔːlz/ *American English for* **overalls**

covering /'kʌvərɪŋ/ *noun*
something that covers another thing: *There was a thick covering of snow on the ground.*

cow | bull | calf

cow /kaʊ/ *noun*
a big female farm animal that gives milk
❂ The male is called a **bull** and a young cow is called a **calf**. Meat from a cow is called **beef** and meat from a calf is called **veal**.

coward /'kaʊəd/ *noun*
a person who is afraid when there is danger or a problem

cowboy /'kaʊbɔɪ/ *noun*
a man who rides a horse and looks after cows on big farms in the USA

crab /kræb/ *noun*
an animal that lives in and near the sea. It has a hard shell and big claws.

crab

crack¹ /kræk/ *noun*
1 a thin line on something where it is nearly broken: *There's a crack in this glass.*
2 a sudden loud noise: *a crack of thunder*

crack² /kræk/ *verb* (**cracks, cracking, cracked** /krækt/)
break, but not into pieces: *The glass will crack if you pour boiling water into it.* ◇ *This cup is cracked.*

cracker /'krækə(r)/ *noun*
1 a thin dry biscuit that you can eat with cheese
2 a long round thing made of coloured paper with a small present inside. It makes a loud noise when two people pull the ends away from each other: *We often pull crackers at Christmas parties.*

crackle /'krækl/ *verb* (**crackles, crackling, crackled** /'krækld/)
make a lot of short sharp sounds: *Dry wood crackles when you burn it.*

cradle /'kreɪdl/ *noun*
a small bed for a baby

craft /krɑ:ft/ *noun*
a job in which you make things carefully and cleverly with your hands: *Pottery and weaving are crafts.*

cram /kræm/ *verb* (**crams, cramming, crammed** /kræmd/)
push too many people or things into something: *She crammed her clothes into a bag.*

crane

crane /kreɪn/ *noun*
a big machine with a long part for lifting heavy things

crash¹ /kræʃ/ *noun* (*plural* **crashes**)
1 an accident when something that is moving hits another thing: *He was killed in a car crash.* ◇ *a plane crash*
2 a loud noise when something falls or hits another thing: *I heard a crash as the tree fell.*

crash² /kræʃ/ *verb* (**crashes, crashing, crashed** /kræʃt/)
1 have an accident; hit something: *The bus crashed into a tree.*
2 make something hit another thing: *I crashed my father's car.*
3 fall or hit something with a loud noise: *A tree crashed through the window.*

crash-helmet /'kræʃ helmɪt/ *noun*
a hard hat that you wear to keep your head safe: *Motor cyclists must wear crash-helmets in Britain.*

crate /kreɪt/ *noun*
a big box for carrying bottles or other things

crawl

crawl /krɔ:l/ *verb* (**crawls, crawling, crawled** /krɔ:ld/)
1 move slowly on your hands and knees: *Babies crawl before they can walk.*
2 move slowly with the body close to the ground: *An insect crawled across the floor.*

crawl *noun* (no plural)
a way of swimming on your front

crayon /'kreɪən/ *noun*
a soft thick coloured pencil: *The children were drawing pictures with crayons.*

crazy /'kreɪzi/ *adjective* (**crazier, craziest**)
mad or very stupid: *You must be crazy to ride a bike at night with no lights.*
crazy about somebody or **something** If you are crazy about somebody or something, you like them very much: *She's crazy about football.* ◇ *He's crazy about her.*
go crazy become very angry or excited: *My mum will go crazy if I get home late.*

creak /kri:k/ *verb* (**creaks, creaking, creaked** /kri:kt/)
make a noise like a door that needs oil, or like an old wooden floor when you walk on it
creak *noun*
The door opened with a creak.

cream¹ /kri:m/ *noun*
1 (no plural) the thick liquid on the top of milk: *Do you want cream in your coffee?*
2 (*plural* **creams**) a thick liquid that you put on your skin

cream² /kri:m/ *adjective*
with a colour between white and yellow: *She was wearing a cream dress.*

creamy /'kri:mi/ *adjective*
1 with cream in it: *a creamy sauce*
2 like cream: *a creamy colour*

crease /kri:s/ *verb* (**creases, creasing, creased** /kri:st/)
1 make untidy lines in paper or cloth by not being careful with it: *Don't sit on my jacket – you'll crease it.*
2 become full of untidy lines: *This shirt creases easily.*
crease *noun*
a line in paper or cloth made by folding or pressing: *You need to iron this shirt – it's full of creases.*

create /kri'eɪt/ *verb* (**creates, creating, created**)
make something new: *Do you believe that God created the world?* ◇ *The company has created a new kind of engine.*

creation /kri'eɪʃn/ *noun*
1 (no plural) making something new: *the creation of the world*
2 (*plural* **creations**) a new thing that somebody has made: *Mickey Mouse was the creation of Walt Disney.*

creative /kri'eɪtɪv/ *adjective*
A person who is creative has a lot of new ideas or is good at making new things: *She's a very good painter – she's so creative.*

creator /kri'eɪtə(r)/ *noun*
a person who makes something new: *Walt Disney was the creator of Mickey Mouse.*

creature /'kri:tʃə(r)/ *noun*
any living thing that is not a plant: *birds, fish and other creatures* ◇ *This story is about creatures from another planet.*

credit[1] /'kredɪt/ *noun* (no plural)
buying something and paying for it later: *I bought the television on credit.*
credit card /'kredɪt kɑ:d/ *noun*
a plastic card from a bank that you can use to buy something and pay for it later: *Can I pay by credit card?*

credit[2] /'kredɪt/ *noun* (no plural)
saying that somebody or something is good: *I did all the work but John got all the credit for it!*

creep /kri:p/ *verb* (**creeps, creeping, crept** /krept/, **has crept**)
move quietly and carefully so that nobody hears or sees you; move along close to the ground: *The cat crept towards the bird.* ◇ *I crept into the room where the children were sleeping.*

crescent /'kreznt/ *noun*
1 the shape of the moon when it is less than half a circle ☞ picture on page 161
2 a street or line of houses with a curved shape: *I live at 34 Elgin Crescent.*

crew /kru:/ *noun*
all the people who work on a ship or an aeroplane

cricket[1] /'krɪkɪt/ *noun*
a small brown insect that makes a loud noise

cricket[2] /'krɪkɪt/ *noun* (no plural)
a game for two teams of eleven players who try to hit a small hard ball with a **bat** on a large field: *We watched a cricket match.*
cricketer *noun*
a person who plays cricket

cried *form of* **cry**[1]

cries
1 *form of* **cry**[1]
2 *plural of* **cry**[2]

crime /kraɪm/ *noun*
something that somebody does that is against the law: *Murder and robbery are serious crimes.*

criminal[1] /'krɪmɪnl/ *noun*
a person who does something that is against the law

criminal[2] /'krɪmɪnl/ *adjective*
1 against the law: *Stealing is a criminal act.*
2 of crime: *She is studying criminal law.*

crimson /'krɪmzn/ *adjective*
with a dark red colour, like blood

cripple /'krɪpl/ *verb* (**cripples, crippling, crippled** /'krɪpld/)
hurt your legs or back badly so that you cannot walk: *She was crippled in an accident.*

crisis /'kraɪsɪs/ *noun* (*plural* **crises** /'kraɪsi:z/)
a time when something very dangerous or serious happens: *a political crisis*

crisp[1] /krɪsp/ *adjective* (**crisper, crispest**)
1 hard and dry: *If you keep the biscuits in a tin, they will stay crisp.*
2 fresh and not soft: *crisp apples*

crisp[2] /krɪsp/ *noun*
a very thin piece of potato cooked in hot oil: *a packet of crisps*

crisps

critic /'krɪtɪk/ *noun*
1 a person who says that somebody or something is wrong or bad: *critics of the government*
2 a person who writes about a book, film or play and says if he/she likes it or not: *The critics liked his new film.*

critical /'krɪtɪkl/ *adjective*
1 If you are critical of somebody or something, you say that they are wrong or bad: *They were very critical of my work.*
2 very serious or dangerous: *a critical illness*
critically *adverb*
She's critically ill.

criticize /'krɪtɪsaɪz/ *verb* (**criticizes, criticizing, criticized** /'krɪtɪsaɪzd/)
say that somebody or something is wrong or bad: *He criticizes everything I do!*
criticism /'krɪtɪsɪzəm/ *noun*
what you think is bad about somebody or something: *I listened to all their criticisms of my plan.*

croak /krəʊk/ *noun*
the noise that a frog makes
croak *verb* (**croaks, croaking, croaked** /krəʊkt/)
make a noise like a frog makes

crockery /'krɒkəri/ *noun* (no plural)
plates, cups and dishes

crocodile /'krɒkədaɪl/ *noun*
a big long animal with sharp teeth. Crocodiles live in rivers in some hot countries: *A crocodile is a reptile.*

crooked /'krʊkɪd/ *adjective*
not straight: *She has crooked teeth.*

crop /krɒp/ *noun*
all the plants of one kind that a farmer grows at one time: *There was a good crop of potatoes last year.* ◇ *Rain is good for the crops.*

cross¹ /krɒs/ *noun* (*plural* **crosses**)
1 a mark like + or X: *The cross on the map shows where I live.*
2 something with the shape + or X: *She wears a cross around her neck.*

cross² /krɒs/ *verb* (**crosses, crossing, crossed** /krɒst/)
1 go from one side of something to the other: *Be careful when you cross the road.*
2 put one thing over another thing: *She sat down and crossed her legs.*
cross out draw a line through a word or words, for example because you have made a mistake: *I crossed the word out and wrote it again.*

cross³ /krɒs/ *adjective*
angry: *I was cross with her because she was late.*

crossing /'krɒsɪŋ/ *noun*
a place where cars must stop for people to cross the road

crossroads /'krɒsrəʊdz/ *noun* (*plural* **crossroads**)
a place where two roads cross each other

crosswalk /'krɒswɔːk/ *American English for* **pedestrian crossing**

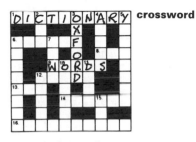

crossword

crossword puzzle /'krɒswɜːd pʌzl/, **crossword** *noun*
a game on paper where you write words in squares

crouch /kraʊtʃ/ *verb* (**crouches, crouching, crouched** /kraʊtʃt/)
bend your knees and back so that your body is close to the ground: *I crouched under the table to hide.*

crow¹ /krəʊ/ *noun*
a large black bird that makes a loud noise

crow² /krəʊ/ *verb* (**crows, crowing, crowed** /krəʊd/)
make a loud noise like a male chicken (a **cock**) makes early in the morning

crowd /kraʊd/ *noun*
a lot of people together: *There was a large crowd at the football match.* ☞ picture on page 261
crowd *verb* (**crowds, crowding, crowded**)
come together in a big group: *The journalists crowded round the Prime Minister.*
crowded *adjective*
full of people: *The streets were very crowded.* ◇ *a crowded bus*

crown /kraʊn/ *noun*
a special thing that a king or queen wears on his or her head at important times
crown *verb* (**crowns, crowning, crowned** /kraʊnd/)
put a crown on the head of a new king or queen: *Elizabeth II was crowned in 1952.*

p	b	t	d	k	g	tʃ	dʒ	f	v	θ	ð
pen	**bad**	**tea**	**did**	**cat**	**got**	**chain**	**jam**	**fall**	**van**	**thin**	**this**

crucial /ˈkruːʃl/ *adjective*
very important: *a crucial moment*

cruel /ˈkruːəl/ *adjective* (**crueller, cruellest**)
A person who is cruel is unkind and likes to hurt other people or animals: *I think it's cruel to keep animals in cages.*
cruelly /ˈkruːəli/ *adverb*
in a cruel way: *He was cruelly treated when he was a child.*
cruelty /ˈkruːəlti/ *noun* (no plural)
being cruel: *cruelty to animals*

cruise /kruːz/ *noun*
a holiday when you travel on a ship and visit a lot of different places: *They went on a world cruise.*
cruise *verb* (**cruises, cruising, cruised** /kruːzd/)
travel on a ship as a holiday: *They cruised around the Caribbean.*

crumb /krʌm/ *noun*
a very small piece of bread, cake or biscuit

crumble /ˈkrʌmbl/ *verb* (**crumbles, crumbling, crumbled** /ˈkrʌmbld/)
break into very small pieces: *The old castle walls are crumbling.*

crunch /krʌntʃ/ *verb* (**crunches, crunching, crunched** /krʌntʃt/)
1 make a loud noise when you eat something that is hard: *The dog was crunching a bone.*
2 make a noise like this when you press it hard: *The snow crunched under our feet as we walked.*

crush /krʌʃ/ *verb* (**crushes, crushing, crushed** /krʌʃt/)
press something very hard so that you break or damage it: *She sat on my hat and crushed it.*

crust /krʌst/ *noun*
the hard part on the outside of bread
crusty *adjective*
with a hard crust: *crusty bread*

crutch /krʌtʃ/ *noun* (plural **crutches**)
a long stick that you put under your arm to help you walk when you have hurt your leg: *He broke his leg and now he's on crutches* (= he walks using crutches).

cry[1] /kraɪ/ *verb* (**cries, crying, cried** /kraɪd/, **has cried**)
1 have drops of water falling from your eyes, usually because you are unhappy: *The baby cries a lot.*
2 shout or make a loud noise: *'Help!' he cried.* ◇ *She cried out in pain.*

cry[2] /kraɪ/ *noun* (plural **cries**)
a loud noise that you make to show pain, fear or excitement, for example: *We heard her cries and ran to help.* ◇ *the cry of a bird*

crystal /ˈkrɪstl/ *noun*
1 a kind of rock that looks like glass
2 a shape that some chemicals make when they are solid: *salt crystals*

cub /kʌb/ *noun*
a young lion, bear, wolf, fox or tiger

cube /kjuːb/ *noun*
a shape like a box with six square sides all the same size: *an ice-cube* ☞ picture on page 161
cubic /ˈkjuːbɪk/ *adjective*
a cubic metre (= a space like a cube that is one metre long on each side)

cuckoo /ˈkʊkuː/ *noun* (plural **cuckoos**)
a bird that makes a sound like its name

cucumber

cucumber /ˈkjuːkʌmbə(r)/ *noun*
a long vegetable with a green skin. You often eat it in salads.

cuddle /ˈkʌdl/ *verb* (**cuddles, cuddling, cuddled** /ˈkʌdld/)
hold somebody or something in your arms to show love: *He cuddled his baby.*
cuddle *noun*
give somebody a cuddle cuddle somebody: *I gave her a cuddle.*

cuff /kʌf/ *noun*
the end part of a sleeve, near your hand

cultivate /ˈkʌltɪveɪt/ *verb* (**cultivates, cultivating, cultivated**)
1 use land for growing plants: *Only a small area of the island was cultivated.*
2 keep and care for plants
cultivation /ˌkʌltɪˈveɪʃn/ *noun* (no plural)
cultivation of the land

cultural /'kʌltʃərəl/ adjective
1 about the art, ideas and way of life of a group of people: *There are many cultural differences between Britain and Japan.*
2 about things like art, music or theatre

culture /'kʌltʃə(r)/ noun
the art, ideas and way of life of a group of people: *She is studying the culture of the American Indians.*

cunning /'kʌnɪŋ/ adjective
clever; good at making people people believe something that is not true: *Their plan was quite cunning.*

cup /kʌp/ noun
1 a small round container with a handle, that you can drink from: *a cup and saucer*
◇ *a cup of coffee*

2 a large metal thing like a cup, that you get for winning in a sport

cupboard /'kʌbəd/ noun
a piece of furniture with shelves and doors, where you keep things like clothes or food

cure¹ /kjʊə(r)/ verb (**cures**, **curing**, **cured** /kjʊəd/)
1 make an ill person well again: *The doctors can't cure her.*
2 make an illness go away: *Can this disease be cured?*

cure² /kjʊə(r)/ noun
something that makes an illness go away: *a cure for cancer*

curiosity /ˌkjʊəri'ɒsəti/ noun (no plural)
wanting to know about things: *I was full of curiosity about the letter.*

curious /'kjʊəriəs/ adjective
1 If you are curious, you want to know about something: *I am curious to know where she found the money.*
2 strange or unusual: *a curious noise*
curiously adverb
'Where are you going?' she asked curiously.

curl¹ /kɜːl/ noun
a piece of hair in a round shape
curly adjective (**curlier**, **curliest**)
with a lot of curls: *He's got curly hair.*
☞ picture at **hair**

curl² /kɜːl/ verb (**curls**, **curling**, **curled** /kɜːld/)
bend into a round or curved shape: *The leaves were brown and curled.*
curl up put your arms, legs and head close to your body: *The cat curled up by the fire.*

currant /'kʌrənt/ noun
1 a small sweet dried fruit
2 a small soft fruit: *blackcurrants*

currency /'kʌrənsi/ noun (plural **currencies**)
the money that a country uses: *The currency of the USA is the dollar.*

current¹ /'kʌrənt/ adjective
Something that is current is happening or used now: *current fashions*
currently adverb
now: *We are currently living in London.*

current² /'kʌrənt/ noun
1 air or water that is moving: *It is dangerous to swim here because of the strong current.*
2 electricity that is going through a wire

curry /'kʌri/ noun (plural **curries**)
meat or vegetables cooked with spices. You often eat curry with rice: *We had a curry in an Indian restaurant.*

curse /kɜːs/ noun
words that wish for something bad to happen to somebody: *The witch put a curse on him and he became a frog.*

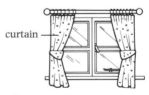

curtain

curtain /'kɜːtn/ noun
a piece of cloth that you move to cover a window

curve

curve /kɜːv/ noun
a line that is not straight; a bend

curve verb (**curves, curving, curved**
/kɜːvd/)
bend; make a round shape: The road
curves to the right.
curved adjective
a table with curved legs ◇ a curved line

cushion /'kʊʃn/ noun
a bag filled with something soft. You put it
on a chair and sit on it or rest your body
against it.

custard /'kʌstəd/ noun (no plural)
a sweet yellow sauce made with milk. You
eat it with fruit or puddings.

custom /'kʌstəm/ noun
something that a group of people usually
do: It is a custom to give presents at
Christmas.

customer /'kʌstəmə(r)/ noun
a person who buys things from a shop

customs /'kʌstəmz/ noun (plural)
the place at an airport or a port where you
must show what you have brought with
you from another country: a customs
officer

cut¹ /kʌt/ verb (**cuts, cutting, cut, has
cut**)
1 break or make a hole in something with
a knife or scissors, for example: I cut the
string and opened the parcel. ◇ I cut the
apple in half (= into two parts). ◇ She cut
her finger on some broken glass.
2 take one piece from something bigger:
Can you cut me a piece of cake, please?
3 make something shorter with a knife or
scissors, for example: Have you had your
hair cut?
be cut off be kept alone, away from

other people: Our house was cut off from
the village by the snow.
cut down **1** use, do or buy less of something: The doctor told me to cut down on
smoking. **2** cut something so that it falls
down: We cut down the old tree.
cut off stop something: The workmen cut
off the electricity.
cut out take something from the place
where it was by using scissors, etc: I cut
the picture out of the newspaper.
cut up break something into pieces with a
knife or scissors, for example

cut² /kʌt/ noun
a place where something has cut: I have a
cut on my leg.

cute /kjuːt/ adjective (**cuter, cutest**)
pretty: What a cute little puppy!

cutlery /'kʌtləri/ noun (no plural)
knives, forks and spoons

cycle /'saɪkl/ noun
a bicycle: a cycle shop
cycle verb (**cycles, cycling, cycled**
/'saɪkld/)
ride a bicycle: I cycle to school every day.
◒ When you talk about cycling as a sport
or for fun, you say **go cycling**: We went
cycling in Holland last year.
cyclist /'saɪklɪst/ noun
a person who rides a bicycle

cylinder /'sɪlɪndə(r)/ noun
a long round shape, like a tube or a tin of
food ☞ picture on page 161
cylindrical /sɪ'lɪndrɪkl/ adjective
with this shape

Dd

dab /dæb/ verb (**dabs, dabbing, dabbed**
/dæbd/)
touch something lightly and quickly: She
dabbed the cut with cotton wool.

dad /dæd/ noun
father: Hello, Dad. ◇ This is my dad.

daddy /'dædi/ noun (plural **daddies**)
a word for 'father' that children use

daffodil /'dæfədɪl/ noun
a yellow flower that grows in spring

daft /dɑːft/ adjective (**dafter, daftest**)
silly; stupid: I think you're daft to work for
nothing! ◇ Don't be daft!

dagger /'dægə(r)/ noun
a short pointed knife that people use as a
weapon

ʌ	ɜː	ə	eɪ	əʊ	aɪ	aʊ	ɔɪ	ɪə	eə	ʊə
cup	bird	about	say	go	five	now	boy	near	hair	pure

daily /'deɪli/ adjective, adverb
that happens or comes every day or once a day: There are daily flights between London and New York. ◇ a daily newspaper ◇ The museum is open daily from 9 a.m. to 5 p.m.

dainty /'deɪnti/ adjective (**daintier, daintiest**)
small and pretty: a dainty little girl

dairy /'deəri/ noun (plural **dairies**)
a place where milk is kept or where food like butter and cheese is made

daisy /'deɪzi/ noun (plural **daisies**)
a small flower with white petals and a yellow middle

dam /dæm/ noun
a wall that is built across a river to hold the water back

damage /'dæmɪdʒ/ verb (**damages, damaging, damaged** /'dæmɪdʒd/)
break or harm something: The house was badly damaged by fire.
damage noun (no plural)
He had an accident, but he didn't do any damage to his car.

damn /dæm/
a rude word that people sometimes use when they are angry: Damn! I've lost my key!

damp /dæmp/ adjective (**damper, dampest**)
a little wet: a cold damp house

dance[1] /dɑːns/ verb (**dances, dancing, danced** /dɑːnst/)
move your body to music: Ian dances well. ◇ I danced with her all night.
dancer noun
a person who dances: Nureyev was a famous ballet dancer. ◇ I'm not a very good dancer.
dancing noun (no plural)
moving to music: Will there be dancing at the party?

dance[2] /dɑːns/ noun
1 movements that you do to music
2 a party where people dance: My parents are going to a dance tonight.

danger /'deɪndʒə(r)/ noun
1 (no plural) the possibility that something bad may happen: You may be in danger if you travel alone late at night.
2 (plural **dangers**) a person or thing that

may bring harm or trouble: Smoking is a danger to health.

dangerous /'deɪndʒərəs/ adjective
A person or thing that is dangerous may hurt you: It's dangerous to drive a car at night without any lights. ◇ a dangerous illness
dangerously adverb
She drives dangerously.

dare /deə(r)/ verb (**dares, daring, dared** /deəd/)
1 be brave enough to do something: I daren't tell Debbie that I've lost her book. ◇ I didn't dare ask for more money.
2 ask somebody to do something dangerous or silly to see if they are brave enough: I dare you to jump off that wall!
don't you dare words that you use for telling somebody very strongly not to do something: Don't you dare read my letters!
how dare you words that show you are very angry about something that somebody has done: How dare you speak to me like that!

daring /'deərɪŋ/ adjective
not afraid to do dangerous things

dark[1] /dɑːk/ adjective (**darker, darkest**)
1 with no light, or not much light: It was so dark that I couldn't see anything. ◇ It gets dark very early in the winter. ✪ opposite: **light**
2 A dark colour is nearer to black than to white: a dark-green skirt ◇ He's got dark-brown eyes. ✪ opposite: **light** or **pale**
3 A person who is dark has brown or black hair or skin: a thin, dark woman ✪ opposite: **fair**

dark[2] /dɑːk/ noun (no plural)
where there is no light: Cats can see in the dark. ◇ Are you afraid of the dark?
after dark after the sun goes down: Don't go out alone after dark.
before dark before the sun goes down: Make sure you get home before dark.

darkness /'dɑːknəs/ noun (no plural)
where there is no light
in darkness with no light: The whole house was in darkness.

darling /'dɑːlɪŋ/ noun
a name that you call somebody that you love: Are you all right, darling?

dart[1] /dɑːt/ noun
a metal thing with a point at one end, that

p	b	t	d	k	g	tʃ	dʒ	f	v	θ	ð
pen	**bad**	**tea**	**did**	**cat**	**got**	**chain**	**jam**	**fall**	**van**	**thin**	**this**

you throw at a round board in a game called **darts**

dart² /dɑːt/ *verb* (**darts, darting, darted**) move quickly and suddenly: *He darted across the road.*

dash¹ /dæʃ/ *verb* (**dashes, dashing, dashed** /dæʃt/) run quickly: *I dashed into a shop when it started to rain.* ◇ *I must dash – I'm late for work.*

dash² /dæʃ/ *noun* (*plural* **dashes**)
1 a mark (–) that you use in writing to show a short stop or to separate two parts of a sentence
2 a sudden short run: *The robber made a dash for the door.*

data /'deɪtə/ *noun* (plural) facts or information: *We are studying the data that we have collected.*

date¹ /deɪt/ *noun* the number of the day, the month and sometimes the year: *'What's the date today?' 'The first of February.'* ◇ *Today's date is 11 September 1993.* ◇ *What is your date of birth?*
out of date 1 not modern: *The machinery they use is completely out of date.* 2 too old, so that you cannot use it: *This ticket is out of date.*
up to date 1 modern 2 with the newest information: *Is this list of names up to date?*

date² /deɪt/ *noun* a small sweet brown fruit

daughter /'dɔːtə(r)/ *noun* a girl or woman who is somebody's child: *They have two daughters and a son.* ◇ *My oldest daughter is a doctor.* ☞ picture on page 127

daughter-in-law /'dɔːtər ɪn lɔː/ *noun* (*plural* **daughters-in-law**) the wife of your son ☞ picture on page 127

dawn /dɔːn/ *noun* the time when the sun comes up

day /deɪ/ *noun* (*plural* **days**)
1 a time of 24 hours from midnight to the next midnight: *There are seven days in a week.* ◇ *I went to Italy for a few days.* ◇ *'What day is it today?' 'Tuesday.'*
2 the time when it is light outside: *Most*

people work during the day and sleep at night.
3 a time in the past: *In my grandparents' day, not many people had cars.*
one day 1 on a certain day in the past: *One day, a letter arrived.* ✪ We often use **one day** at the beginning of a story. 2 at some time in the future: *I hope to visit Canada one day.*
some day at some time in the future: *Some day I'll be rich and famous.*
the day after tomorrow not tomorrow, but the next day
the day before yesterday not yesterday, but the day before
the other day a few days ago: *I went to London the other day.*
these days now: *A lot of people work with computers these days.*

daylight /'deɪlaɪt/ *noun* (no plural) the light from the sun during the day: *These colours look different in daylight.*

day off /,deɪ 'ɒf/ *noun* (*plural* **days off**) a day when you do not go to work or school

daytime /'deɪtaɪm/ *noun* (no plural) the time when it is day and not night: *I prefer to study in the daytime and go out in the evening.*

dazzle /'dæzl/ *verb* (**dazzles, dazzling, dazzled** /'dæzld/) If a light dazzles you, it shines brightly in your eyes so that you cannot see for a short time: *I was dazzled by the car's lights.*

dead¹ /ded/ *adjective*
1 not living: *All my grandparents are dead.* ◇ *Throw away those dead flowers.*
2 very quiet: *This town is dead: everywhere is closed after ten o'clock at night.*
a dead end a street that is only open at one end
the dead *noun* (plural) dead people

dead² /ded/ *adverb* completely or very: *I'm dead tired.*

deadline /'dedlaɪn/ *noun* a day or time before which you must do something: *The deadline for finishing this essay is next Tuesday.*

s	z	ʃ	ʒ	h	m	n	ŋ	l	r	j	w
so	**zoo**	**shoe**	**vision**	**hat**	**man**	**no**	**sing**	**leg**	**red**	**yes**	**wet**

deadly /'dedli/ *adjective* (**deadlier, deadliest**)
Something that is deadly may kill people or other living things: *a deadly weapon*
deadly *adverb*
extremely: *I'm deadly serious.*

deaf /def/ *adjective*
not able to hear
the deaf *noun* (plural)
people who are deaf

deafen /'defn/ *verb* (**deafens, deafening, deafened** /'defnd/)
make a very loud noise so that somebody cannot hear well: *We were deafened by the sound of a plane flying over our heads.*

deafness /'defnəs/ *noun* (no plural)
being deaf

deal¹ /di:l/ *noun*
an agreement, usually about buying, selling or working: *Let's make a deal – I'll help you today if you help me tomorrow.*

deal² /di:l/ *noun*
a good deal or **a great deal** a lot; much: *I saw a good deal of France on my holiday.* ◇ *We ate a great deal.*

deal³ /di:l/ *verb* (**deals, dealing, dealt** /delt/, **has dealt**)
deal in something buy and sell something in business: *We deal in insurance.*
deal out give something to each person: *I dealt out the cards for the next game.*
deal with somebody or **something**
1 look after something and do what is necessary: *I am too busy to deal with this problem now.* **2** tell about something: *The first chapter of the book deals with letter-writing.*
dealer *noun*
a person who buys and sells things: *drug dealers*

dear /dɪə(r)/ *adjective* (**dearer, dearest**)
1 a word that you use before a person's name at the beginning of a letter: *Dear Mr Carter, ...* ◇ *Dear Sir or Madam, ...*
2 that you love very much: *She was a dear friend.*
3 that costs a lot of money; expensive: *Those strawberries are too dear.* ✪ opposite: **cheap**
dear *noun*
a word that you use when you are speaking to somebody that you know well or that you love: *Hello, dear.*

death /deθ/ *noun*
when a life finishes: *He became manager of the company after his father's death.* ◇ *There are thousands of deaths in car accidents every year.*
deathly (**deathlier, deathliest**) *adjective*
like death: *There was a deathly silence.*

debate /dɪ'beɪt/ *noun*
a public meeting where people talk about something important
debate *verb* (**debates, debating, debated**)
Parliament is debating the new law.

debt /det/ *noun*
money that you must pay back to somebody: *The company has borrowed a lot of money and it still has debts.*
in debt If you are in debt, you must pay money to somebody.

decay /dɪ'keɪ/ *verb* (**decays, decaying, decayed** /dɪ'keɪd/)
become bad or fall to pieces: *If you don't clean your teeth, they will decay.*
decay *noun* (no plural)
tooth decay

deceive /dɪ'si:v/ *verb* (**deceives, deceiving, deceived** /dɪ'si:vd/)
make somebody believe something that is not true: *Sophie's boyfriend deceived her – he didn't tell her he was already married.* ◇ *She deceived me into thinking she was a police officer.*

December /dɪ'sembə(r)/ *noun*
the twelfth month of the year

decent /'di:snt/ *adjective*
1 good enough; right: *You can't wear jeans for a job interview – you should buy some decent clothes.*
2 honest and good: *decent people*

decide /dɪ'saɪd/ *verb* (**decides, deciding, decided**)
choose something after thinking: *I can't decide what colour to paint my room.* ◇ *We've decided to go to France for our holidays.* ◇ *She decided that she didn't want to come.*

decimal /'desɪml/ *noun*
a part of a number, written after a dot (called a **decimal point**), for example 0.75 ✪ We say '0.75' as 'nought point seven five'.

i:	i	ɪ	e	æ	ɑ:	ɒ	ɔ:	ʊ	u	u:
see	happy	sit	ten	cat	father	got	saw	put	situation	too

decision /dɪ'sɪʒn/ *noun*
choosing something after thinking; deciding: *I must make a decision about what I'm going to do when I leave school.*

deck /dek/ *noun*
the floor of a ship or bus: *I always sit on the top deck when I travel by bus.*

deck-chair /'dek tʃeə(r)/ *noun*
a chair that you use outside, for example on the beach. You can fold it up and carry it.

declare /dɪ'kleə(r)/ *verb* (**declares, declaring, declared** /dɪ'kleəd/)
1 say very clearly what you think or what you will do, often to a lot of people: *He declared that he was not a thief.* ◇ *The country declared war on its enemy.*
2 In an airport or port you declare things that you have bought in another country so that you can pay tax on them: *Have you anything to declare?*
declaration /,deklə'reɪʃn/ *noun*
a declaration of independence

decorate /'dekəreɪt/ *verb* (**decorates, decorating, decorated**)
1 make something look nicer by adding beautiful things to it: *We decorated the room with flowers.*
2 put paint or paper on the walls of a room: *I am decorating the kitchen.*
decorations /,dekə'reɪʃnz/ *noun* (plural)
beautiful things that you add to something to make it look nicer: *Christmas decorations*

decrease /dɪ'kriːs/ *verb* (**decreases, decreasing, decreased** /dɪ'kriːst/)
become smaller or less; make something smaller or less: *The number of people in the village has decreased from 200 to 100.*
decrease /'diːkriːs/ *noun*
There was a decrease in the number of people living in the village.
◇ opposite: **increase**

deep /diːp/ *adjective* (**deeper, deepest**)
1 Something that is deep goes down a long way: *Be careful: the water is very deep.* ◇ *There were deep cuts in his face.* ◇ opposite: **shallow** ☞ picture on page 262
2 You use 'deep' to say or ask how far something is from the top to the bottom:

The hole was about six metres deep and three metres wide. ◇ The noun is **depth**.
3 A deep colour is strong and dark: *She has deep-blue eyes.* ◇ opposite: **pale** or **light**
4 A deep sound is low and strong: *He has a deep voice.*
5 Deep feelings are very strong: *deep sadness*
6 If you are in a deep sleep, it is difficult for somebody to wake you up: *She was in such a deep sleep that she didn't hear me calling her.*
deeply *adverb*
strongly or completely: *He is sleeping very deeply.*

deer

deer /dɪə(r)/ *noun* (*plural* **deer**)
a wild animal that eats grass and can run fast

defeat /dɪ'fiːt/ *verb* (**defeats, defeating, defeated**)
win a fight or game against a person or group of people: *Alexander the Great defeated the Persians in 334 BC.*
defeat *noun*
losing a game, fight or war

defence /dɪ'fens/ *noun*
fighting against people who attack, or keeping away dangerous people or things: *They fought the war in defence of their country.*

defend /dɪ'fend/ *verb* (**defends, defending, defended**)
1 fight to keep away people or things that attack: *They defended the city against the enemy.*
2 say that somebody has not done something wrong: *My sister defended me when my father said I was lazy.* ◇ *He had a lawyer to defend him in court.*
3 try to stop another person or team scoring goals or points in a game

defense *American English for* **defence**
defied, defies *forms of* **defy**

define /dɪ'faɪn/ verb (**defines, defining, defined** /dɪ'faɪnd/)
say what a word means: *How do you de-fine 'rich'?*

definite /'defɪnət/ adjective
sure; certain: *I want a definite answer, 'yes' or 'no'.* ◇ *I think it was Sally I saw but I'm not definite.*
definitely adverb
certainly: *I am definitely going to the theatre this evening – I have already bought my ticket.*

definition /ˌdefɪ'nɪʃn/ noun
a group of words that tell you what another word means

defy /dɪ'faɪ/ verb (**defies, defying, defied** /dɪ'faɪd/, **has defied**)
If you defy somebody or something, you do something that they say you should not do: *She defied her parents and stayed out all night.*

degree /dɪ'griː/ noun
1 a measurement of temperature: *Water boils at 100 degrees Celsius (100° C).*
2 a measurement of angles: *There are 90 degrees (90°) in a right angle.*
3 Universities and colleges give degrees to students who have completed special courses there: *She has a degree in Mathematics.*

delay¹ /dɪ'leɪ/ noun (plural **delays**)
a time when somebody or something is late: *There was a long delay at the airport.*
without delay immediately: *You must pay the money without delay.*

delay² /dɪ'leɪ/ verb (**delays, delaying, delayed** /dɪ'leɪd/)
1 make somebody or something late: *My train was delayed for two hours because of the bad weather.*
2 not do something until a later time: *I delayed my holiday because I was ill.*

deliberate /dɪ'lɪbərət/ adjective
that you want and plan to do, and do not do by mistake: *'Do you think it was an accident?' 'No, I'm sure it was deliberate.'*
deliberately adverb
The police think that somebody started the fire deliberately.

delicate /'delɪkət/ adjective
1 If something is delicate, you can break or damage it very easily: *I've got delicate skin, so I use special soap.*
2 pretty and fine; not strong: *delicate col-ours like pale pink and pale blue* ◇ *She had long, delicate fingers.*

delicious /dɪ'lɪʃəs/ adjective
very good to eat: *This soup is delicious.*

delight¹ /dɪ'laɪt/ verb (**delights, delighting, delighted**)
make somebody very pleased or happy
delighted adjective
very pleased or happy: *I'm delighted to meet you.*

delight² /dɪ'laɪt/ noun (no plural)
great happiness
delightful /dɪ'laɪtfl/ adjective
very nice; lovely: *We stayed in a delightful little hotel.*

deliver /dɪ'lɪvə(r)/ verb (**delivers, delivering, delivered** /dɪ'lɪvəd/)
take something to the place where it must go: *The postman delivered two letters this morning.*
delivery /dɪ'lɪvəri/ noun (plural **deliveries**)
We are waiting for a delivery of bread.

demand¹ /dɪ'mɑːnd/ verb (**demands, demanding, demanded**)
say strongly that you must have something: *The workers are demanding more money.* ◇ *She demanded to see the manager.*

demand² /dɪ'mɑːnd/ noun
saying strongly that you must have something
in demand wanted by a lot of people: *I'm in demand today – I've had eight telephone calls!*

democracy /dɪ'mɒkrəsi/ noun (plural **democracies**)
1 a system of government where the people choose their leader (by **voting**)
2 a country with a government that the people choose: *Great Britain is a democracy.*

democrat /'deməkræt/ noun
1 a person who wants democracy
2 **Democrat** a person in the Democratic Party in the USA ☞ Look at **Republican**.
democratic /ˌdemə'krætɪk/ adjective
If a country, etc is democratic, all the people in it can choose its leaders or decide about the way it is organized.

demolish /dɪ'mɒlɪʃ/ verb (**demolishes, demolishing, demolished** /dɪ'mɒlɪʃt/)
break a building so that it falls down: *They*

p	b	t	d	k	g	tʃ	dʒ	f	v	θ	ð
pen	**b**ad	**t**ea	**d**id	**c**at	**g**ot	**ch**ain	**j**am	**f**all	**v**an	**th**in	**th**is

demolished six houses and built a supermarket in their place.

demonstrate /'demənstreɪt/ verb
(**demonstrates, demonstrating, demonstrated**)
1 show something clearly: *He demonstrated how to operate the machine.*
2 walk or stand in public with a group of
people to show that you have strong feelings about something: *Thousands of
people demonstrated against the war.*

demonstration /,demən'streɪʃn/ noun
1 a group of people walking or standing
together in public to show that they have
strong feelings about something: *There
were demonstrations all over Eastern
Europe in 1989.*
2 showing how to do something, or how
something works: *He gave us a cookery
demonstration.*

den /den/ noun
the place where a wild animal lives

denied, denies forms of **deny**

denim /'denɪm/ noun (no plural)
strong cotton material that is used for
making jeans and other clothes. Denim is
often blue: *a denim jacket*

dense /dens/ adjective
1 with a lot of things or people close together: *dense forests*
2 thick and difficult to see through: *dense
fog*

dent /dent/ noun
a hollow place in something flat, that
comes when you hit it or press it hard:
There's a big dent in the side of my car.
dent verb (**dents, denting, dented**)
hit something and make a hollow place in
it: *I dropped the tin and dented it.*

dentist /'dentɪst/ noun
a person whose job is to look after your
teeth ✪ When we talk about visiting the
dentist, we say **go to the dentist's**: *I've got
toothache so I'm going to the dentist's.*
☞ Note at **tooth**

deny /dɪ'naɪ/ verb (**denies, denying,
denied** /dɪ'naɪd/, **has denied**)
say that something is not true: *He denied that he had stolen the car.* ◇ *They
denied breaking the window.* ✪ opposite:
admit

depart /dɪ'pɑːt/ verb (**departs, depart-
ing, departed**)
leave a place: *The next train to Birmingham departs from platform 3.* ✪ **Leave** is
the word that we usually use.

department /dɪ'pɑːtmənt/ noun
one of the parts of a university, school,
government, shop, big company, etc: *The
book department is on the second floor.*
◇ *Professor Jenkins is the head of the English department.*

department store /dɪ'pɑːtmənt stɔː(r)/
noun
a big shop that sells a lot of different things:
*Harrods is a famous department store in
London.*

departure /dɪ'pɑːtʃə(r)/ noun
leaving a place: *A board inside the airport
shows arrivals and departures.*

depend /dɪ'pend/ verb (**depends, de-
pending, depended**)
depend on somebody or **something 1** need somebody or something:
*She still depends on her parents for money
because she hasn't got a job.* **2** trust
somebody; feel sure that somebody or
something will do what you want: *I know I
can depend on my friends to help me.*
it depends, that depends words that
you use to show that something is not certain: *'Do you want to play tennis tomorrow?' 'It depends on the weather.'* ◇ *'Can
you lend me some money?' 'That depends.
How much do you want?'*

dependent /dɪ'pendənt/ adjective
If you are dependent on somebody or
something, you need them: *A baby is completely dependent on its parents.*

deposit /dɪ'pɒzɪt/ noun
1 money that you pay to show that you
want something and that you will pay the
rest later: *I paid a deposit on a holiday.*
2 money that you pay into a bank
3 extra money that you pay when you
rent something. You get it back if you do
not damage or lose what you have rented.
deposit verb (**deposits, depositing,
deposited**)
put something somewhere to keep it safe:
The money was deposited in the bank.

depress /dɪ'pres/ verb (**depresses, depressing, depressed** /dɪ'prest/)
make somebody feel unhappy: *This cold
winter weather really depresses me.*

s	z	ʃ	ʒ	h	m	n	ŋ	l	r	j	w
so	**zoo**	**shoe**	**vision**	**hat**	**man**	**no**	**sing**	**leg**	**red**	**yes**	**wet**

depressed *adjective*
If you are depressed, you are very unhappy: *He's been very depressed since he lost his job.*

depressing *adjective*
Something that is depressing makes you very unhappy: *That film about the war was very depressing.*

depression /dɪ'preʃn/ *noun* (no plural)
a feeling of unhappiness

depth /depθ/ *noun*
how deep something is; how far it is from the top of something to the bottom: *What is the depth of the swimming-pool?* ◇ *The hole was 2 m in depth.*

deputy /'depjəti/ *noun* (*plural* **deputies**)
the person in a company, school, etc, who does the work of the leader when he/she is not there: *a deputy headmaster*

derivative /dɪ'rɪvətɪv/ *noun*
a word that is made from another word: *'Sadness' is a derivative of 'sad'.*

descend /dɪ'send/ *verb* (**descends, descending, descended**)
go down: *The plane started to descend.*
✪ It is more usual to say **go down**.

descendant /dɪ'sendənt/ *noun*
Your descendants are your children, grandchildren and everybody in your family who lives after you: *Queen Elizabeth II is a descendant of Queen Victoria.*

descent /dɪ'sent/ *noun*
going down: *The plane began its descent to Munich airport.*

describe /dɪ'skraɪb/ *verb* (**describes, describing, described** /dɪ'skraɪbd/)
say what somebody or something is like or what happened: *Can you describe the man you saw?* ◇ *She described the accident to the police.*

description /dɪ'skrɪpʃn/ *noun*
words that tell what somebody or something is like or what happened: *I have given the police a description of the thief.*

desert¹ /'dezət/ *noun*
a large area of land that is usually covered with sand. Deserts are very dry and not many plants can grow there: *the Sahara Desert*
   desert island /ˌdezət 'aɪlənd/ *noun*
an island where nobody lives, in a hot part of the world

desert² /dɪ'zɜːt/ *verb* (**deserts, deserting, deserted**)
leave a person or place when it is wrong to go: *He deserted his wife and children.*

deserted /dɪ'zɜːtɪd/ *adjective*
empty, because all the people have left: *At night the streets are deserted.*

deserve /dɪ'zɜːv/ *verb* (**deserves, deserving, deserved** /dɪ'zɜːvd/)
be good or bad enough to have something: *You have worked very hard and you deserve a rest.* ◇ *They stole money from old people, so they deserve to go to prison.*

design¹ /dɪ'zaɪn/ *verb* (**designs, designing, designed** /dɪ'zaɪnd/)
draw a plan that shows how to make something: *The church was designed by a German architect.*

design² /dɪ'zaɪn/ *noun*
1 a drawing that shows how to make something: *Have you seen the designs for the new shopping centre?*
2 lines, shapes and colours on something: *The wallpaper has a design of blue and green squares on it.*

designer /dɪ'zaɪnə(r)/ *noun*
a person whose job is to make drawings that show how something will be made: *a fashion designer*

desire /dɪ'zaɪə(r)/ *noun*
a feeling of wanting something very much: *a desire for peace.*

desk

desk /desk/ *noun*
1 a table with drawers, where you sit to write or work
2 a table or place in a building where somebody gives information, etc: *Ask at the information desk.*

despair /dɪ'speə(r)/ *noun* (no plural)
a feeling of not having hope: *He was in despair because he had no money and nowhere to live.*

desperate /'despərət/ *adjective*
1 If you are desperate, you have no hope

and you are ready to do anything to get what you want: *She is so desperate for a job that she will work anywhere.*
2 very serious: *There is a desperate need for food in some parts of Africa.*
desperately *adverb*
He is desperately unhappy.

desperation /ˌdespə'reɪʃn/ *noun* (no plural)
the feeling of having no hope, that makes you do anything to get what you want: *In desperation, she sold her ring to get money for food.*

despise /dɪ'spaɪz/ *verb* (**despises, despising, despised** /dɪ'spaɪzd/)
hate somebody or something very much: *I despise people who tell lies.*

despite /dɪ'spaɪt/ *preposition*
although something is true; not noticing or not caring about something: *We decided to go out despite the bad weather.*

dessert /dɪ'zɜ:t/ *noun*
something sweet that you eat at the end of a meal: *We had ice-cream for dessert.*
dessertspoon /dɪ'zɜ:tspu:n/ *noun*
a spoon that you use for eating desserts

destination /destɪ'neɪʃn/ *noun*
the place where somebody or something is going: *They were very tired when they finally reached their destination.*

destroy /dɪ'strɔɪ/ *verb* (**destroys, destroying, destroyed** /dɪ'strɔɪd/)
break something completely so that you cannot use it again or so that it is gone: *The house was destroyed by fire.*

destruction /dɪ'strʌkʃn/ *noun* (no plural)
breaking something completely so that you cannot use it again or so that it is gone: *the destruction of the city by bombs*

detached /dɪ'tætʃt/ *adjective*
A detached house stands alone and is not joined to any other house.

detail /'di:teɪl/ *noun*
1 one of the very small parts that make the whole of something: *Tell me quickly what happened – I don't need to know all the details.*
2 details (plural) information about something: *For more details, please telephone this number.*

in detail with all the small parts: *Tell me about your plan in detail.*

detective /dɪ'tektɪv/ *noun*
a person whose job is to find out who did a crime. Detectives are usually police officers: *Sherlock Holmes is a famous detective in stories.*

detergent /dɪ'tɜ:dʒənt/ *noun*
a powder or liquid that you use for washing things

determination /dɪˌtɜ:mɪ'neɪʃn/ *noun* (no plural)
being certain that you want to do something: *She has shown great determination to succeed.*

determined /dɪ'tɜ:mɪnd/ *adjective*
very certain that you want do something: *She is determined to win the match.*

detest /dɪ'test/ *verb* (**detests, detesting, detested**)
hate somebody or something very much: *I detest spiders.*

detour /'di:tʊə(r)/ *noun*
a longer way to a place when you cannot go by the usual way: *The bridge was closed so we had to make a detour.*

develop /dɪ'veləp/ *verb* (**develops, developing, developed** /dɪ'veləpt/)
1 become bigger or more complete; make something bigger or more complete: *Children develop into adults.*
2 begin to have something: *She developed the disease at the age of 27.*
3 When a photograph is developed, special chemicals are used on the film so that you can see the picture.

development /dɪ'veləpmənt/ *noun*
1 (no plural) becoming bigger or more complete; growing: *We studied the development of babies in their first year of life.*
2 (*plural* **developments**) something new that happens: *There are new developments in science almost every day.*

device /dɪ'vaɪs/ *noun*
a tool or machine that you use for doing a special job: *a device for opening tins*

devil /'devl/ *noun*
1 the Devil (no plural) the most powerful evil spirit, in the Christian religion
2 an evil being or spirit

devote /dɪ'vəʊt/ *verb* (**devotes, devoting, devoted**)
give a lot of time or energy to something: *She devoted her life to helping the poor.*
devoted *adjective*
If you are devoted to somebody or something, you love them very much: *John is devoted to his wife and children.*

dew /dju:/ *noun* (no plural)
small drops of water that form on plants and grass in the night: *In the morning, the grass was wet with dew.*

diagonal /daɪ'æɡənl/ *adjective*
If you draw a diagonal line from one corner of a square to another, you make two triangles. ☞ picture on page 161

diagram /'daɪəɡræm/ *noun*
a picture that explains something: *This diagram shows all the parts of an engine.*

dial /'daɪəl/ *noun*
a circle with numbers or letters on it. Some telephones and clocks have dials.
dial *verb* (**dials, dialling, dialled** /'daɪəld/)
make a telephone call by moving a dial or pushing buttons: *You have dialled the wrong number.* ✪ In American English the spellings are **dialing** and **dialed**.

dialog *American English for* **dialogue**

dialogue /'daɪəlɒɡ/ *noun*
words that people say to each other in a book, play or film

diameter /daɪ'æmɪtə(r)/ *noun*
a straight line across a circle, through the centre ☞ picture on page 161

diamond /'daɪəmənd/ *noun*
1 a hard stone that looks like clear glass and is very expensive: *The ring has a large diamond in it.* ◇ *a diamond necklace*
2 the shape ♦
3 **diamonds** (plural) the playing-cards that have red shapes like diamonds on them: *the eight of diamonds*

diary /'daɪəri/ *noun* (*plural* **diaries**)
1 a book where you write what you are going to do: *I'll look in my diary to see if I'm free tomorrow.*
2 a book where you write what you have done each day
keep a diary write in a diary every day

dice /daɪs/ *noun*
(*plural* **dice**)
a small piece of wood or plastic with spots on the sides for playing games: *Throw the dice.*

dice

dictate /dɪk'teɪt/
verb (**dictates, dictating, dictated**)
1 say words so that another person can write them: *She dictated a letter to her secretary.*
2 tell somebody that they must do something: *You can't dictate to me where I should go.*

dictation /dɪk'teɪʃn/ *noun*
words that you say so that another person can write them: *We had a dictation in English today* (= a test when we wrote what the teacher said).

dictator /dɪk'teɪtə(r)/ *noun*
a person who has complete control of a country

dictionary /'dɪkʃənri/ *noun* (*plural* **dictionaries**)
a book that gives words from A to Z and explains what each word means

did *form of* **do**

didn't /'dɪdnt/ = **did not**

die /daɪ/ *verb* (**dies, dying, died** /daɪd/, **has died**)
stop living: *People, animals and plants die if they don't have water.*
die down slowly become less strong: *The storm died down.*
die of something stop living because of an illness: *She died of a heart attack.*

diesel /'di:zl/ *noun*
1 (*plural* **diesels**) (*also* **diesel engine**) an engine in buses, trains and some cars that uses oil, not petrol
2 (no plural) oil that is used in diesel engines

diet /'daɪət/ *noun*
1 the food that you usually eat: *It is important to have a healthy diet.*
2 special foods that you eat when you are ill or when you want to get thinner
be or **go on a diet** eat only special foods because you want to get thinner

difference /'dɪfrəns/ *noun*
the way that one thing is not the same as

p	b	t	d	k	ɡ	tʃ	dʒ	f	v	θ	ð
pen	**bad**	**tea**	**did**	**cat**	**got**	**chain**	**jam**	**fall**	**van**	**thin**	**this**

another thing: *There is a big difference between British and German schools.* ◇ *What's the difference in price between these two bikes?*

make a difference change something: *Your help has made a big difference – I understand the work much better now.*

make no difference not change anything; not be important: *It makes no difference which train you catch – the price of the ticket is the same.*

tell the difference see how one thing or person is different from another thing or person: *Sarah looks exactly like her sister – I can't tell the difference (between them).*

different /'dıfrǝnt/ *adjective*
1 not the same: *These two shoes are different sizes!* ◇ *Cricket is different from baseball.*
2 many and not the same: *They sell 30 different sorts of ice-cream.*

differently *adverb*
He's very quiet at home but he behaves differently at school.

difficult /'dıfıkǝlt/ *adjective*
1 not easy to do or understand: *a difficult problem* ◇ *The exam was very difficult.* ◇ *It's difficult to learn a new language.*
✪ opposite: **easy**
2 A person who is difficult is not easy to please or will not do what you want: *She's a very difficult child.*

difficulty /'dıfıkǝlti/ *noun* (*plural* **difficulties**)
a problem; something that is not easy to do or understand: *I have difficulty understanding German.*

with difficulty not easily: *My grandfather walks with difficulty now.*

dig /dıg/ *verb*
(**digs**, **digging**, **dug** /dʌg/, **has dug**)
move earth and make a hole in the ground: *You need to dig the garden before you plant the seeds.* ◇ *They dug a tunnel through the mountain for the new railway.*
dig up take

spade   **dig**

something from the ground by digging: *They dug up some Roman coins in their field.*

digest /daı'dʒest/ *verb* (**digests**, **digesting**, **digested**)
change food in your stomach so that your body can use it

digestion /daı'dʒestʃǝn/ *noun* (no plural)
changing food in your stomach so that your body can use it

dignified /'dıgnıfaıd/ *adjective*
calm, quiet and serious: *a dignified old lady*

dilute /daı'lju:t/ *verb* (**dilutes**, **diluting**, **diluted**)
add water to another liquid: *You need to dilute this paint before you use it.*

dim /dım/ *adjective* (**dimmer**, **dimmest**)
not bright or clear: *The light was so dim that we couldn't see anything.*

dimly *adverb*
The room was dimly lit.

din /dın/ *noun* (no plural)
a very loud unpleasant noise: *Stop making that terrible din!*

dinghy /'dıŋi/ *noun* (*plural* **dinghies**)
a small boat

dining-room /'daınıŋ ru:m/ *noun*
a room where people eat

dinner /'dınǝ(r)/ *noun*
the largest meal of the day. You have dinner in the evening, or sometimes in the middle of the day: *What time do you usually have dinner?* ◇ *What's for dinner?*

dinosaur
/'daınǝsɔ:(r)/ *noun*
a big wild animal that lived a very long time ago

dinosaur

dip /dıp/ *verb*
(**dips**, **dipping**, **dipped** /dıpt/)
put something into a liquid for a short time and then take it out again: *Dip your hand in the water to see how hot it is.*

diploma /dı'plǝʊmǝ/ *noun*
a piece of paper that shows you have passed an examination or finished special studies: *a teaching diploma*

s	z	ʃ	ʒ	h	m	n	ŋ	l	r	j	w
so	**zoo**	**shoe**	vision	**hat**	**man**	**no**	sing	**leg**	**red**	yes	**wet**

diplomat /'dɪpləmæt/ *noun*
a person whose job is to speak and do things for his/her country in another country
diplomatic /ˌdɪplə'mætɪk/ *adjective*
diplomatic talks

direct¹ /də'rekt/ *adjective, adverb*
1 as straight as possible, without turning or stopping: *Which is the most direct way to the town centre from here?* ◇ *We flew direct from Paris to New York.* ◇ *The 6.45 train goes direct to Oxford.*
2 from one person or thing to another person or thing with nobody or nothing between them: *You should keep this plant out of direct sunlight.*
☞ Look at **indirect**.

direct² /də'rekt/ *verb* (**directs, directing, directed**)
1 tell somebody how to get to a place: *Can you direct me to the station, please?*
2 tell or show somebody how to do something; control somebody or something: *He has directed many plays at the National Theatre.*

direction /də'rekʃn/ *noun*
where a person or thing is going or looking: *They got lost because they went in the wrong direction.*

directions /də'rekʃnz/ *noun* (plural)
words that tell you how to get to a place or how to do something: *I couldn't find the school so I asked a woman for directions.* ◇ *I didn't read the directions on the packet before I made the cake.*

directly /də'rektli/ *adverb*
1 exactly; in a direct way: *The teacher was looking directly at me.* ◇ *The post office is directly opposite the bank.*
2 very soon: *They left directly after breakfast.*

director /də'rektə(r)/ *noun*
1 a person who controls a business or a group of people
2 a person who controls a film or play, for example by telling the actors what to do

dirt /dɜːt/ *noun* (no plural)
stuff that is not clean, for example mud or dust: *The children came in from the garden covered in dirt.*

dirty /'dɜːti/ *adjective* (**dirtier, dirtiest**)
not clean: *Your hands are dirty – go and wash them!* ☞ picture on page 263

dis- *prefix*
You can add **dis-** to the beginning of some words to give them the opposite meaning, for example:
disagree = not agree
dishonest = not honest

disabled /dɪs'eɪbld/ *adjective*
not able to use a part of your body well: *Peter is disabled – he lost a leg in an accident.*
the disabled *noun* (plural)
people who are disabled

disadvantage /ˌdɪsəd'vɑːntɪdʒ/ *noun*
a problem that makes something difficult or less good: *One of the disadvantages of living in the countryside is that there is nowhere to go in the evenings.*

disagree /ˌdɪsə'griː/ *verb* (**disagrees, disagreeing, disagreed** /ˌdɪsə'griːd/)
say that another person's idea is wrong; not agree: *I said it was a good film, but Jason disagreed with me.* ◇ *My sister and I disagree about everything!*

disagreement /ˌdɪsə'griːmənt/ *noun*
a talk between people with different ideas; an argument: *My parents sometimes have disagreements about money.*

disappear /ˌdɪsə'pɪə(r)/ *verb* (**disappears, disappearing, disappeared** /ˌdɪsə'pɪəd/)
If a person or thing disappears, they go away so people cannot see them: *The sun disappeared behind the clouds.* ◇ *The police are looking for a woman who disappeared on Sunday.*
disappearance /ˌdɪsə'pɪərəns/ *noun*
Everybody was worried about the child's disappearance.

disappoint /ˌdɪsə'pɔɪnt/ *verb* (**disappoints, disappointing, disappointed**)
make you sad because what you wanted did not happen: *I'm sorry to disappoint you, but I can't come to your party.*
disappointed *adjective*
If you are disappointed, you feel sad because what you wanted did not happen: *Sue was disappointed when she didn't win the prize.*
disappointing *adjective*
If something is disappointing, it makes you feel sad because it is not as good as you hoped: *disappointing exam results*

disappointment /ˌdɪsə'pɔɪntmənt/ *noun*
1 (no plural) a feeling of sadness because what you wanted did not happen: *She couldn't hide her disappointment when she lost the match.*
2 (*plural* **disappointments**) something that makes you sad because it is not what you hoped: *Sarah's party was a disappointment – only four people came.*

disapprove /ˌdɪsə'pru:v/ *verb* (**disapproves**, **disapproving**, **disapproved** /ˌdɪsə'pru:vd/)
think that somebody or something is bad: *Joe's parents disapproved of his new girlfriend.*

disaster /dɪ'zɑ:stə(r)/ *noun*
1 something very bad that happens and that may hurt a lot of people: *Floods and earthquakes are disasters.*
2 something that is very bad: *Our holiday was a disaster! It rained all week!*

disastrous /dɪ'zɑ:strəs/ *adjective*
very bad; that causes great trouble: *The heavy rain brought disastrous floods.*

disc /dɪsk/ *noun*
1 a round flat thing
2 a round flat thing that makes music when you play it on a record-player
☞ Look also at **compact disc, floppy disk** and **hard disk.**

discipline /'dɪsəplɪn/ *noun* (no plural)
teaching you to control yourself and follow rules: *Children learn discipline at school.*
discipline *verb* (**disciplines**, **disciplining**, **disciplined** /'dɪsəplɪnd/)
You must discipline yourself to work harder.

disc jockey /'dɪsk dʒɒki/ *noun*
a person who plays records on the radio or at discos or nightclubs ✪ The short form is **DJ.**

disco /'dɪskəʊ/ *noun* (*plural* **discos**)
a place where people dance and listen to pop music

disconnect /ˌdɪskə'nekt/ *verb* (**disconnects**, **disconnecting**, **disconnected**)
stop electricity, gas, etc: *Your phone will be disconnected if you don't pay the bill.*

discount /'dɪskaʊnt/ *noun*
money that somebody takes away from the price of something to make it cheaper: *Students often get a discount on travel.*

discourage /dɪs'kʌrɪdʒ/ *verb* (**discourages**, **discouraging**, **discouraged** /dɪs'kʌrɪdʒd/)
make somebody not want to do something: *Jane's parents tried to discourage her from leaving school.* ✪ opposite: **encourage**

discover /dɪ'skʌvə(r)/ *verb* (**discovers**, **discovering**, **discovered** /dɪ'skʌvəd/)
find or learn something for the first time: *Who discovered Australia?* ◇ *I was in the shop when I discovered that I did not have any money.*
discovery /dɪ'skʌvəri/ *noun* (*plural* **discoveries**)
finding or learning something for the first time: *Scientists have made an important new discovery.*

discriminate /dɪ'skrɪmɪneɪt/ *verb* (**discriminates**, **discriminating**, **discriminated**)
treat one person or a group in a different way to others: *This company discriminates against women – it pays them less than men for doing the same work.*
discrimination /dɪˌskrɪmɪ'neɪʃn/ *noun* (no plural)
religious discrimination (= treating somebody in an unfair way because their religion is not the same as yours)

discuss /dɪ'skʌs/ *verb* (**discusses**, **discussing**, **discussed** /dɪ'skʌst/)
talk about something: *I discussed the problem with my parents.*
discussion /dɪ'skʌʃn/ *noun*
We had an interesting discussion about politics.

disease /dɪ'zi:z/ *noun*
an illness: *Cancer and measles are diseases.*

disgrace /dɪs'greɪs/ *noun* (no plural)
when other people stop thinking well of you, because you have done something bad: *He's in disgrace because he stole money from his brother.*

disgraceful /dɪs'greɪsfl/ *adjective*
Something that is disgraceful is very bad and makes you feel shame: *The way the football fans behaved was disgraceful.*

disguise /dɪs'gaɪz/ *verb* (**disguises**, **disguising**, **disguised** /dɪs'gaɪzd/)
make somebody or something different so that people will not know who or what

ʌ	ɜ:	ə	eɪ	əʊ	aɪ	aʊ	ɔɪ	ɪə	eə	ʊə
c**u**p	b**ir**d	**a**bout	s**ay**	g**o**	f**i**ve	n**ow**	b**oy**	n**ear**	h**air**	p**ure**

they are: *They disguised themselves as guards and escaped from the prison.*

disguise *noun*
things that you wear so that people do not know who you are: *We went to the party in disguise.*

disgust /dɪs'gʌst/ *noun* (no plural)
a strong feeling of not liking something: *They left the restaurant in disgust because the food was so bad.*

disgust *verb* (**disgusts, disgusting, disgusted**)
make somebody have a strong feeling of not liking something

disgusted *adjective*
If you are disgusted, you have a strong feeling of not liking something: *I was disgusted to find a fly in my soup.*

disgusting *adjective*
very bad: *What a disgusting smell!*

dish /dɪʃ/ *noun* (*plural* **dishes**)
1 a container for food. You can use a dish to cook food in an oven, or to put food on the table.
2 a part of a meal: *We had a fish dish and a vegetable dish.*
3 **the dishes** (plural) all the plates, bowls, cups, etc that you must wash after a meal: *I'll wash the dishes.*

dishonest /dɪs'ɒnɪst/ *adjective*
A person who is dishonest says things that are not true, or steals or cheats.

dishwasher /'dɪʃwɒʃə(r)/ *noun*
a machine that washes things like plates, glasses, knives and forks

disinfectant /ˌdɪsɪn'fektənt/ *noun*
a liquid that you use for cleaning something very well

disk /dɪsk/ *noun*
a flat thing that stores information for computers: *a floppy disk* ◇ *a hard disk*

disk drive /'dɪsk draɪv/ *noun*
the part of a computer where you can put floppy disks ☞ picture at **computer**

dislike /dɪs'laɪk/ *verb* (**dislikes, disliking, disliked** /dɪs'laɪkt/)
not like somebody or something: *I dislike getting up early.*

dislike *noun*
a feeling of not liking somebody or something: *I have a strong dislike of hospitals.*

dismal /'dɪzməl/ *adjective*
that makes you feel sad; not bright: *It was a wet, dismal day.*

dismay /dɪs'meɪ/ *noun* (no plural)
a strong feeling of surprise and worry: *John looked at me in dismay when I told him about the accident.*

dismayed /dɪs'meɪd/ *adjective*
I was dismayed to find that somebody had stolen my bike.

dismiss /dɪs'mɪs/ *verb* (**dismisses, dismissing, dismissed** /dɪs'mɪst/)
1 make somebody leave their job: *He was dismissed for stealing money from the company.* ◐ **Sack** and **fire** are the words that we usually use.
2 allow somebody to leave a place: *The lesson finished and the teacher dismissed the class.*

disobey /ˌdɪsə'beɪ/ *verb* (**disobeys, disobeying, disobeyed** /ˌdɪsə'beɪd/)
not do what somebody tells you to do; not obey: *She disobeyed her parents and went to the party.*

disobedient /ˌdɪsə'biːdiənt/ *adjective*
A person who is disobedient does not do what somebody tells him/her to do: *a disobedient child*

disobedience /ˌdɪsə'biːdiəns/ *noun* (no plural)
not doing what somebody tells you to do

display /dɪ'spleɪ/ *verb* (**displays, displaying, displayed** /dɪ'spleɪd/)
show something so that people can see it: *All kinds of toys were displayed in the shop window.*

display *noun* (*plural* **displays**)
something that people look at: *a firework display*
on display in a place where people can look at it: *The paintings are on display in the museum.*

dispose /dɪ'spəʊz/ *verb* (**disposes, disposing, disposed** /dɪ'spəʊzd/)
dispose of something throw something away or give something away because you do not want it: *Where can I dispose of this rubbish?*

disposal /dɪ'spəʊzl/ *noun* (no plural)
the disposal of nuclear waste

dispute /dɪ'spjuːt/ *noun*
an angry talk between people with different ideas: *There was a dispute about which driver caused the accident.*

dissatisfied /ˌdɪs'sætɪsfaɪd/ *adjective*
not pleased with something: *I am very dissatisfied with your work*

p	b	t	d	k	g	tʃ	dʒ	f	v	θ	ð
pen	**b**ad	**t**ea	**d**id	**c**at	**g**ot	**ch**ain	**j**am	**f**all	**v**an	**th**in	**th**is

distance /'dɪstəns/ *noun*
1 how far it is from one place to another place: *It's a short distance from my house to the station.* ◊ *We usually measure distance in miles or kilometres.*
2 a place that is far from somebody or something: *From a distance, he looks quite young.*
in the distance far away: *I could see a light in the distance.*

distant /'dɪstənt/ *adjective*
far away in space or time: *distant countries*

distinct /dɪ'stɪŋkt/ *adjective*
1 easy to hear, see or smell; clear: *There is a distinct smell of burning in this room.*
2 clearly different: *English and Welsh are two distinct languages.*
distinctly *adverb*
clearly: *I distinctly heard him say his name was Robert.*

distinguish /dɪ'stɪŋgwɪʃ/ *verb* (**distinguishes, distinguishing, distinguished** /dɪ'stɪŋgwɪʃt/)
see, hear, etc the difference between two things or people: *Some people can't distinguish between me and my twin sister.* ◊ *Can you distinguish butter from margarine?*

distinguished /dɪ'stɪŋgwɪʃt/ *adjective*
famous or important: *a distinguished actor*

distract /dɪ'strækt/ *verb* (**distracts, distracting, distracted**)
If a person or thing distracts you, he/she/it stops you thinking about what you are doing: *The noise distracted me from my homework.*

distress /dɪ'stres/ *noun* (no plural)
1 a strong feeling of pain or sadness
2 being in danger and needing help: *a ship in distress*

distribute /dɪ'strɪbjuːt/ (**distributes, distributing, distributed**)
give or send things to each person: *New books are distributed on the first day of school.*
distribution /ˌdɪstrɪ'bjuːʃn/ *noun* (no plural)
the distribution of newspapers

district /'dɪstrɪkt/ *noun*
a part of a country or town: *The Lake District is in the North-West of England.*

disturb /dɪ'stɜːb/ *verb* (**disturbs, disturbing, disturbed** /dɪ'stɜːbd/)
1 stop somebody doing something, for example thinking, working or sleeping: *My brother always disturbs me when I'm trying to do my homework.* ◊ *Do not disturb.* (a notice that you put on a door to tell people not to come in)
2 worry somebody: *We were disturbed by the news that John was ill.*

disturbance /dɪ'stɜːbəns/ *noun*
1 a thing that stops you doing something, for example thinking, working or sleeping
2 when a group of people fight or make a lot of noise and trouble: *The football fans were causing a disturbance outside the stadium.*

ditch /dɪtʃ/ *noun* (*plural* **ditches**)
a long narrow hole at the side of a road or field that carries away water

dive

dive /daɪv/ *verb* (**dives, diving, dived** /daɪvd/)
1 jump into water with your arms and head first: *Sam dived into the pool.*
2 go under water: *The birds were diving for fish.*
diver /'daɪvə(r)/ *noun*
a person who works under water: *Police divers found a body in the lake.*
diving (no plural)
the sport of jumping into water or swimming under water

diversion /daɪ'vɜːʃn/ *noun*
a way that you must go when the usual way is closed: *There was a diversion around Chester because of a road accident.*

divert /daɪ'vɜːt/ *verb* (**diverts, diverting, diverted**)
make something go a different way: *Our flight was diverted to another airport because of the bad weather.*

divide /dɪ'vaɪd/ verb (**divides, dividing, divided**)
1 share or cut something into smaller parts: *The teacher divided the class into groups of three.* ◇ *The book is divided into ten chapters.*
2 go into parts: *When the road divides, go left.*
3 find out how many times one number goes into a bigger number: *36 divided by 4 is 9 (36 ÷ 4 = 9).*

divine /dɪ'vaɪn/ adjective
of, like or from God or a god: *a divine message*

division /dɪ'vɪʒn/ noun
1 (no plural) finding out how many times one number goes into a bigger number
2 (no plural) sharing or cutting something into parts: *the division of Germany after the Second World War*
3 (plural **divisions**) one of the parts of a big company: *He works in the sales division.*

divorce /dɪ'vɔːs/ noun
the end of a marriage by law: *She is getting a divorce.*
divorce verb (**divorces, divorcing, divorced** /dɪ'vɔːst/)
He divorced his wife. ✪ We often say **get divorced**: *They got divorced last year.*
divorced adjective
I'm not married – I'm divorced.

DIY /ˌdiː aɪ 'waɪ/ noun (no plural)
making or repairing things in your house yourself. 'DIY' is short for **do-it-yourself**: *a DIY shop*

dizzy /'dɪzi/ adjective (**dizzier, dizziest**)
If you feel dizzy, you feel that everything is turning round and round and that you are going to fall: *The room was very hot and I started to feel dizzy.*

DJ /ˌdiː 'dʒeɪ/ short for **disc jockey**

do[1] /duː/, /də/ verb
1 a word that you use with another verb to make a question: *Do you want an apple?*
2 a word that you use with another verb when you are saying 'not': *I like football but I don't (= do not) like tennis.*
3 a word that you use in place of saying something again: *She doesn't speak English, but I do (= I speak English).*
4 a word that you use before another verb to make it stronger: *You do look nice!*

do[2] /duː/ verb (**does** /dʌz/, **doing, did** /dɪd/, **has done** /dʌn/)
1 carry out an action: *What are you doing?* ◇ *He did the cooking.* ◇ *What did you do with my key?* (= where did you put it?)
2 finish something; find the answer: *I have done my homework.* ◇ *I can't do this sum – it's too difficult.*
3 have a job or study something: *'Tell me what he does.' 'He's a doctor.'* ◇ *She's doing Economics at Hull University.*
4 be good enough; be enough: *Will this soup do for dinner?*
be or **have to do with somebody** or **something** be connected with somebody or something: *I'm not sure what his job is – I think it's something to do with computers.* ◇ *Don't read that letter. It has nothing to do with you!*
could do with something want or need something: *I could do with a drink.*
do up 1 fasten something: *Do up the buttons on your shirt.* ✪ opposite: **undo**
2 clean and repair something to make it look newer: *They bought an old house and now they are doing it up.*

dock /dɒk/ noun
a place by the sea or a river where ships go so that people can move things on and off them or repair them

doctor /'dɒktə(r)/ noun
1 a person whose job is to make sick

do[1]				
present tense		*negative short forms*		*past tense* **did** /dɪd/
I	**do**	I	**don't**	
you	**do**	you	**don't**	*present participle* **doing**
he/she/it	**does** /dʌz/	he/she/it	**doesn't**	*past participle* **done** /dʌn/
we	**do**	we	**don't**	
you	**do**	you	**don't**	
they	**do**	they	**don't**	

iː	i	ɪ	e	æ	ɑː	ɒ	ɔː	ʊ	u	uː
see	happy	sit	ten	cat	father	got	saw	put	situation	too

people well again: *Doctor Jones sees patients every morning.* ✪ When we talk about visiting the doctor, we say **go to the doctor's**: *If you're feeling ill you should go to the doctor's.*
2 a person who has the highest degree from a university
✪ When you write 'Doctor' as part of a person's name the short form is **Dr**.

document /'dɒkjumənt/ *noun*
a paper with important information on it: *a legal document*

documentary /ˌdɒkjuˈmentri/ *noun*
(*plural* **documentaries**)
a film about true things: *I watched an interesting documentary about Japan on TV last night.*

dodge /dɒdʒ/ *verb* (**dodges**, **dodging**, **dodged** /dɒdʒd/)
move quickly to avoid something or somebody: *He ran across the busy road, dodging the cars.*

does *form of* **do**

doesn't /'dʌznt/ = **does not**

dog /dɒg/ *noun*
an animal that many people keep as a pet or to do work ✪ A young dog is called a **puppy**.

doll /dɒl/ *noun*
a toy like a very small person

dollar /'dɒlə(r)/ *noun*
money that people use in the USA and some other countries. There are 100 **cents** in a dollar: *Those jeans cost 45 dollars.*
✪ We write **$**: *This shirt costs $30.*

dolphin

dolphin /'dɒlfɪn/ *noun*
an intelligent animal that lives in the sea

dome /dəʊm/ *noun*
the round roof of a building: *the dome of St Paul's Cathedral in London*

domestic /dəˈmestɪk/ *adjective*
1 of or about the home or family: *Cooking and cleaning are domestic jobs.* ◇ *Many*

cats and dogs are domestic animals (= animals that live in your home with you).
2 of or inside a country: *a domestic flight* (= to a place in the same country)

dominate /'dɒmɪneɪt/ *verb* (**dominates**, **dominating**, **dominated**)
control somebody or something because you are stronger or more important: *He dominates his younger brother.*

donate /dəʊ'neɪt/ *verb* (**donates**, **donating**, **donated**)
give something to people who need it: *They donated £1 000 to the hospital.*
donation /dəʊ'neɪʃn/ *noun*
something that you give to people who need it: *a donation of money*

done *form of* **do**

donkey /'dɒŋki/ *noun* (*plural* **donkeys**)
an animal like a small horse with long ears

don't /dəʊnt/ = **do not**

door /dɔ:(r)/ *noun*
the way into a building or room; a piece of wood, glass or metal that you use to open and close the way in to a building, room, cupboard, car, etc: *Can you close the door, please?* ◇ *Sophie knocked on the door.* 'Come in,' Peter said. ◇ *There is somebody at the door.* ☞ picture at **house**. A house often has a **front door** and a **back door**.
answer the door go to open the door when somebody knocks or rings the bell
next door in the next house, room or building: *Mary lives next door to us.*
out of doors outside; not in a building: *Farmers spend a lot of time out of doors.*

doorbell /'dɔ:bel/ *noun*
a bell outside a house that you ring to tell people inside that you want to go in

doorway /'dɔ:weɪ/ *noun*
an opening for going into a building or room: *Mike was waiting in the doorway when they arrived.*

dormitory /'dɔ:mətri/ *noun* (*plural* **dormitories**)
a big bedroom for a lot of people, usually in a school

dose /dəʊs/ *noun*
an amount of medicine that you take at one time: *Take a large dose of medicine before you go to bed.*

ʌ	ɜ:	ə	eɪ	əʊ	aɪ	aʊ	ɔɪ	ɪə	eə	ʊə
c**u**p	b**ir**d	**a**bout	s**ay**	g**o**	f**i**ve	n**ow**	b**oy**	n**ear**	h**air**	p**ure**

dot /dɒt/ *noun*
a small round mark: *The letter 'i' has a dot over it.*
on the dot at exactly the right time: *Please be here at nine o'clock on the dot.*

dotted line /ˌdɒtɪd 'laɪn/ *noun*
a line of dots that sometimes shows where you have to write something: *Please sign (= write your name) on the dotted line.*

double /'dʌbl/ *adjective*
1 two times as much or as many; twice as much or as many: *a double portion of chips*
2 with two parts that are the same: *double doors*
3 for two people: *a double bed* ◇ *a double room*
4 You use 'double' before a letter or a number to show that it comes two times: *'How do you spell your name, Mr Coombe?' 'C, double O, M, B, E.'* ◇ *My phone number is double four nine five one (44951).*
☞ Look at **single**.

double *verb* (**doubles, doubling, doubled** /'dʌbld/)
make something twice as much or as many; become twice as much or as many: *The price has doubled: last year it was £10 and this year it's £20.*

double-bass /ˌdʌbl 'beɪs/ *noun*
a musical instrument like a very big violin

double-decker /ˌdʌbl 'dekə(r)/ *noun*
a bus with places to sit upstairs and downstairs

doubt¹ /daʊt/ *noun*
a feeling that you are not sure about something: *She says the story is true but I have my doubts about it.*
in doubt not sure: *If you are in doubt, ask your teacher.*
no doubt I am sure: *Paul isn't here yet, but no doubt he will come later.*

doubt² /daʊt/ *verb* (**doubts, doubting, doubted**)
not feel sure about something; think that something is probably not true or probably will not happen: *I doubt if he will come.*

doubtful /'daʊtfl/ *adjective*
not certain or not likely: *It is doubtful whether he will walk again.*

doubtless /'daʊtləs/ *adverb*
almost certainly: *Doubtless she'll be late!*

dough /dəʊ/ *noun* (no plural)
flour, water and other things mixed together, for making bread

dove /dʌv/ *noun*
a bird that is often used as a sign of peace

down /daʊn/ *preposition, adverb*
1 in or to a lower place; not up: *The sun goes down in the evening.* ◇ *We ran down the hill.* ◇ *Put that box down on the floor.* ☞ picture on page 128
2 from standing to sitting or lying: *Sit down.* ◇ *Lie down on the bed.*
3 in a way that is smaller, less strong, etc: *Prices are going down.* ◇ *Turn that music down!* (= so that it is not so loud)
4 along: *'Can you tell me where the bank is, please?' 'Go down this road, then turn right at the end.'*
5 on paper: *Write these words down.*

downhill /ˌdaʊn'hɪl/ *adverb*
down, towards the bottom of a hill: *My bicycle can go fast downhill.*

downstairs /ˌdaʊn'steəz/ *adverb*
to or on a lower floor of a building: *I went downstairs to make breakfast.*
downstairs *adjective*
She lives in the downstairs flat.
✪ opposite: **upstairs**

downtown /ˌdaʊn'taʊn/ *American English for* **city centre**: *She works downtown.* ◇ *downtown Los Angeles*

downwards /'daʊnwədz/,
downward /'daʊnwəd/ *adverb*
down; towards a lower place or towards the ground: *She was lying face downward on the grass.* ✪ opposite: **upwards**

doze /dəʊz/ *verb* (**dozes, dozing, dozed** /dəʊzd/)
sleep lightly for a short time: *My grandfather was dozing in his armchair.*
doze off start dozing: *I dozed off in front of the television.*
doze *noun*
She had a doze after lunch.

dozen /'dʌzn/ *noun* (plural **dozen**)
twelve: *a dozen red roses* ◇ *two dozen boxes* ◇ *half a dozen eggs*
dozens of a lot of: *They've invited dozens of people to the party.*

Dr *short way of writing* **Doctor**

draft /drɑːft/, **drafty** /'drɑːfti/ *American English for* **draught, draughty**

p	b	t	d	k	g	tʃ	dʒ	f	v	θ	ð
pen	**bad**	**tea**	**did**	**cat**	**got**	**chain**	**jam**	**fall**	**van**	**thin**	**this**

drag /dræg/ *verb* (**drags, dragging, dragged** /drægd/)
1 pull something along the ground slowly, often because it is heavy: *He couldn't lift the sack, so he dragged it out of the shop.*
2 If something drags, it seems to go slowly because it is not interesting: *Time drags when you're waiting for a bus.*

dragon /'drægən/ *noun*
a big dangerous animal with fire in its mouth, that you find only in stories

drain¹ /dreɪn/ *noun*
a pipe that carries away dirty water from a building: *The drain is blocked.*

drain² /dreɪn/ *verb* (**drains, draining, drained** /dreɪnd/)
1 let liquid flow away from something, so that it becomes dry: *Wash the lettuce and then drain it.*
2 become dry because liquid is flowing away: *Let the dishes drain.*
3 flow away: *The water drained away slowly.*

drama /'drɑːmə/ *noun*
1 (*plural* **dramas**) a story that you watch in the theatre or on television, or listen to on the radio: *a TV drama*
2 (no plural) the study of plays and acting: *She went to drama school.*
3 (*plural* **dramas**) an exciting thing that happens: *There was a big drama at school when one of the teachers fell in the pond!*

dramatic /drə'mætɪk/ *adjective*
1 of plays or the theatre: *a dramatic society*
2 sudden, great or exciting: *The finish of the race was very dramatic.*
dramatically /drə'mætɪkli/ *adverb*
Prices went up dramatically.

dramatist /'dræmətɪst/ *noun*
a person who writes plays

drank *form of* **drink¹**

draught /drɑːft/ *noun*
cold air that comes into a room: *Can you shut the window? I can feel a draught.*
draughty /'drɑːfti/ *adjective* (**draughtier, draughtiest**)
a draughty house

draughts /drɑːfts/ *noun* (plural)
a game that two people play with round flat pieces on a board that has black and white squares on it: *Do you want a game of draughts?*

draw¹ /drɔː/ *verb* (**draws, drawing, drew** /druː/, **has drawn** /drɔːn/)
1 make a picture with a pencil, pen, chalk, etc: *She drew a picture of a horse.* ◇ *He has drawn a car.* ◇ *My sister draws well.*
2 pull or take something from a place: *He drew a knife from his pocket.*
3 move or come: *The train drew into the station.*
4 pull something to make it move: *The carriage was drawn by two horses.*
5 end a game with the same number of points for both players or teams: *Liverpool and Tottenham drew in last Saturday's match.*
6 open or close curtains: *I switched on the light and drew the curtains.*
draw out take money out of a bank: *I drew out £50 before I went shopping.*
draw up come to a place and stop: *A taxi drew up outside the house.*
draw something up write something: *They drew up a list of people that they wanted to invite to the wedding.*

draw² /drɔː/ *noun*
the result of a game when both players or teams have the same number of points: *The football match ended in a 1-1 draw.*

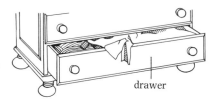
drawer

drawer /drɔː(r)/ *noun*
a thing like a box that you can pull out from a cupboard or desk, for example

drawing /'drɔːɪŋ/ *noun*
1 (*plural* **drawings**) a picture made with a pencil, pen, chalk, etc
2 (no plural) making pictures with a pencil, pen, chalk, etc: *Katherine is very good at drawing.*

drawing-pin /'drɔːɪŋ pɪn/ *noun*
a short pin with a flat round top, that you use for attaching paper to a wall or board: *I put the poster up with drawing-pins.*

drawn *form of* **draw¹**

---

dreadful /'dredfl/ *adjective*
very bad: *I had a dreadful journey – my train was two hours late!*

dreadfully /'dredfəli/ *adverb*
very: *I'm dreadfully sorry, but I must go now.*

dream /driːm/ *verb* (**dreams, dreaming, dreamt** /dremt/ or **dreamed** /driːmd/, **has dreamt** or **has dreamed**)
1 have a picture or idea in your mind when you are asleep: *I dreamt about you last night.* ◇ *I dreamt that I met the Queen.*
2 hope for something nice in the future: *She dreams of becoming a famous actress.*
dream *noun*
1 pictures or ideas in your mind when you are asleep: *I had a dream about school last night.* ✪ A bad or frightening dream is called a **nightmare**.
2 something nice that you hope for

dress¹ /dres/ *noun*
1 (*plural* **dresses**) a piece of clothing with a top part and a skirt, that a woman or girl wears
2 (no plural) clothes: *The group of dancers wore national dress.*

dress—
— tights

dress² /dres/ *verb*
(**dresses, dressing, dressed** /drest/)
1 put clothes on yourself or another person: *She dressed quickly and went out.* ◇ *He washed and dressed the baby.* ✪ opposite: **undress**
2 wear clothes: *She dresses like a film star.*
dressed in something wearing something: *He was dressed in black.*
dress up 1 put on your best clothes: *They dressed up to go to the theatre.*
2 put on special clothes for fun, so that you look like another person or a thing: *The children dressed up as ghosts.*
get dressed put on your clothes: *I got dressed and went downstairs for breakfast.* ✪ opposite: **get undressed**

dressing /'dresɪŋ/ *noun*
1 a thing for covering a part of your body that is hurt: *You should put a dressing on that cut.*
2 a mixture of oil, vinegar, etc that you put on a salad

dressing-gown /'dresɪŋ gaʊn/ *noun*
a piece of clothing like a coat that you wear over your pyjamas or nightdress

dressing-table /'dresɪŋ teɪbl/ *noun*
a piece of bedroom furniture like a table with drawers and a mirror

drew *form of* **draw**¹

dried *form of* **dry**²

drier¹ *form of* **dry**¹

drier² /'draɪə(r)/ *noun*
a machine for drying clothes: *Take the clothes out of the washing-machine and put them in the drier.* ☞ Look also at **hair-drier**.

dries *form of* **dry**²

driest *form of* **dry**¹

drift /drɪft/ *verb* (**drifts, drifting, drifted**)
move slowly in the air or on water: *The empty boat drifted along on the sea.* ◇ *The balloon drifted away.*

drill /drɪl/ *noun*
a tool that you use for making holes: *an electric drill* ◇ *a dentist's drill*
drill *verb* (**drills, drilling, drilled** /drɪld/)
make a hole using a drill

drink

drink¹ /drɪŋk/ *verb* (**drinks, drinking, drank** /dræŋk/, **has drunk** /drʌŋk/)
1 take in liquid, for example water, milk or coffee, through your mouth: *What do you want to drink?* ◇ *She was drinking a cup of tea.*
2 drink alcohol: *'Would you like some wine?' 'No, thank you. I don't drink.'*

drink² /drɪŋk/ *noun*
1 liquid, for example water, milk or coffee, that you take in through your mouth: *Would you like a drink?* ◇ *Can I have a drink of water?*
2 drink with alcohol in it, for example beer

iː	i	ɪ	e	æ	ɑː	ɒ	ɔː	ʊ	u	uː
see	happy	sit	ten	cat	father	got	saw	put	situation	too

or wine: *There was lots of food and drink at the party.*

drip /drɪp/ *verb* (**drips, dripping, dripped** /drɪpt/)
1 fall slowly in small drops: *Water was dripping through the roof.*
2 have liquid falling from it in small drops: *The tap is dripping.*

drive¹ /draɪv/ *verb* (**drives, driving, drove** /drəʊv/, **has driven** /'drɪvn/)
1 control a car, bus, etc and make it go where you want to go: *Can you drive?* ◇ *She usually drives to work.*
2 take somebody to a place in a car: *My parents drove me to the airport.*

drive² /draɪv/ *noun*
1 a journey in a car: *It's a long drive from Paris to Rome.* ◇ *We went for a drive in my sister's car.*
2 a road that goes from the street to one house: *You can park your car in the drive.*

driver /'draɪvə(r)/ *noun*
a person who controls a car, bus, train, etc: *John is a good driver.* ◇ *a taxi-driver*
driver's licence /'draɪvəz laɪsns/ *American English for* **driving-licence**

drive-in /'draɪv ɪn/ *noun*
a place where you can go to eat or to watch a film while you are sitting in your car

driving /'draɪvɪŋ/ *noun* (no plural)
controlling a car, bus, etc: *Driving in the fog can be dangerous.*
driving-licence /'draɪvɪŋ laɪsns/ *noun*
a piece of paper that shows that you are allowed to drive a car, etc
driving test /'draɪvɪŋ test/ *noun*
a test that you have to pass before you get your **driving-licence**

droop /druːp/ *verb* (**droops, drooping, drooped** /druːpt/)
bend or hang down: *Flowers droop if you don't put them in water.*

drop¹ /drɒp/ *verb* (**drops, dropping, dropped** /drɒpt/)
1 let something fall: *I dropped my watch and it broke.*
2 fall: *The glass dropped from her hands.*
3 become lower or less: *The temperature has dropped.*

drop

4 stop your car and let somebody get out: *Could you drop me at the station?*
5 stop doing something: *I'm going to drop geography at school next year.*
drop in visit somebody who does not know that you are coming: *Drop in to see me the next time you're in London.*
drop off fall asleep: *She dropped off in front of the TV.*
drop out stop doing something with a group of people: *I dropped out of the football team after I hurt my leg.*

drop² /drɒp/ *noun*
1 a very small amount of liquid: *a drop of blood* ☞ picture on page 261
2 a fall; going down: *a drop in temperature* ◇ *a drop in prices*

drought /draʊt/ *noun*
a long time when there is not enough rain: *Thousands of people died in the drought.*

drove *form of* **drive¹**

drown /draʊn/ *verb* (**drowns, drowning, drowned** /draʊnd/)
1 die under water because you cannot breathe: *The boy fell in the river and drowned.*
2 make a person or an animal die by putting them under water so that they cannot breathe: *They drowned the kittens.*

drug /drʌg/ *noun*
1 something that makes you better when you are ill
2 something that people eat, smoke or inject because it makes them feel happy or excited. In many countries it is against the law to use drugs: *She takes drugs.* ◇ *Heroin is a dangerous drug.*
drug addict /'drʌg ædɪkt/ *noun*
a person who cannot stop using drugs
drugstore /'drʌgstɔː(r)/ *noun*
a shop in the USA where you can buy medicines and a lot of other things

drum /drʌm/ *noun*
1 a musical instrument that you hit with sticks or with your hands: *He plays the drums in a band.*
2 a big round container for oil: *an oil drum*

drummer /'drʌmə(r)/ *noun*
a person who plays a drum

drunk¹ *form of* **drink¹**

ʌ	ɜː	ə	eɪ	əʊ	aɪ	aʊ	ɔɪ	ɪə	eə	ʊə
cup	bird	about	say	go	five	now	boy	near	hair	pure

drums

duck

drunk² /drʌŋk/ *adjective*
If a person is drunk, he/she has drunk too much alcohol.

dry¹ /draɪ/ *adjective* (**drier, driest**)
1 with no liquid in it or on it; not wet: *The washing isn't dry yet.* ☞ picture on page 263
2 with no rain: *dry weather*
3 not sweet: *dry white wine*

dry² /draɪ/ *verb* (**dries, drying, dried** /draɪd/, **has dried**)
1 become dry: *Our clothes were drying in the sun.*
2 make something dry: *Dry your hands on this towel.*
dry out become completely dry: *Leave your shoes by the fire to dry out.*
dry up 1 become completely dry: *There was no rain for several months and all the rivers dried up.* **2** dry things like plates, knives and forks with a towel after you have washed them: *If I wash the dishes, could you dry up?* ❸ You can also say **do the drying-up.**

dry-clean /ˌdraɪ ˈkliːn/ *verb* (**dry-cleans, dry-cleaning, dry-cleaned** /ˌdraɪ ˈkliːnd/)
make clothes clean by using chemicals, not water: *I had my suit dry-cleaned.*
dry-cleaner's *noun*
a shop where clothes and other things are dry-cleaned

dryer /ˈdraɪə(r)/ = **drier²**

dual carriageway /ˌdjuːəl ˈkærɪdʒweɪ/ *noun*
a wide road with grass or a fence between the two sides

duchess /ˈdʌtʃəs/ *noun* (*plural* **duchesses**)
1 a woman who has a special title
2 the wife of a **duke**

duck¹ /dʌk/ *noun*
a bird that lives on and near water. You of-

ten see ducks on farms or in parks. ❸ A young duck is called a **duckling.**

duck² /dʌk/ *verb* (**ducks, ducking, ducked** /dʌkt/)
move your head down quickly, so that something does not hit you or so that somebody does not see you: *He saw the ball coming towards him and ducked.*

duckling /ˈdʌklɪŋ/ *noun*
a young duck

due /djuː/ *adjective*
1 If something is due at a certain time, you expect it to happen or come then: *What time is the train due? ◇ The new motorway is due to open in April.*
2 If an amount of money is due, you must pay it: *My rent is due at the beginning of the month.*
due for something ready for something: *My car is due for a service.*
due to something because of something: *The accident was due to bad driving.*

duet /djuˈet/ *noun*
music for two people to sing or play on musical instruments: *James and Sarah sang a duet.*

dug *form of* **dig**

duke /djuːk/ *noun*
a man who has a special title ☞ Look at **duchess.**

dull /dʌl/ *adjective* (**duller, dullest**)
1 not bright: *It was a dull, cloudy day.*
2 not strong or loud: *a dull pain*
3 not interesting or exciting: *Life is never dull in a big city.*

dumb /dʌm/ *adjective*
1 not able to speak: *There are special schools for children who are deaf and dumb.*
2 not intelligent; stupid: *That was a dumb thing to do!*

dump /dʌmp/ *verb* (**dumps, dumping, dumped** /dʌmpt/)
1 take something to a place and leave it

p	b	t	d	k	g	tʃ	dʒ	f	v	θ	ð
pen	**bad**	**tea**	**did**	**cat**	**got**	**chain**	**jam**	**fall**	**van**	**thin**	**this**

there because you do not want it: *They dumped their rubbish by the side of the road.*
2 put something down without being careful: *Don't dump your clothes on the floor!*

dump *noun*
a place where you can take and leave things that you do not want

dune /dju:n/ *noun*
a small hill of sand near the sea or in a desert

dungarees /,dʌŋgə'ri:z/ *noun* (plural)
trousers with a part that covers the top of your body: *a new pair of dungarees*

dungeon /'dʌndʒən/ *noun*
a prison under the ground, for example in a castle

during /'djʊərɪŋ/ *preposition*
1 all the time that something is happening: *The sun gives us light during the day.*
2 at some time while something else is happening: *She died during the night.* ◇ *I fell asleep during the film.*

dusk /dʌsk/ *noun* (no plural)
the time in the evening when it is nearly dark

dust /dʌst/ *noun* (no plural)
dry dirt that is like powder: *The old table was covered in dust.*

dust *verb* (**dusts, dusting, dusted**)
take dust off something with a cloth: *I dusted the furniture.*

dustbin /'dʌstbɪn/ *noun*
a thing that you put rubbish in outside your house

duster /'dʌstə(r)/ *noun*
a cloth that you use for taking the dust off furniture

dustbin

dustman /'dʌstmən/ *noun* (plural **dustmen** /'dʌstmən/)
a person whose job is to take away rubbish from outside people's houses

dusty /'dʌsti/ *adjective* (**dustier, dustiest**)
covered with dust: *The furniture was very dusty.*

duty[1] /'dju:ti/ *noun* (plural **duties**)
something that you must do because it is part of your job or because you think it is right: *It's your duty to look after your parents when they get older.* ◇ *One of the duties of a secretary is to type letters.*

off duty not working: *The police officer was off duty.*

on duty working: *Some nurses at the hospital are on duty all night.*

duty[2] /'dju:ti/ *noun* (plural **duties**)
money (a **tax**) that you pay to the government when you bring things into a country from another country

duty-free /,dju:ti 'fri:/ *adjective, adverb*
that you can bring into a country without paying money to the government. You can buy duty-free goods on planes or ships and at airports.

duvet /'du:veɪ/ *noun*
a thick warm cover for a bed. Duvets are often filled with feathers.

dwarf /dwɔ:f/ *noun*
a person who is much smaller than the usual size

dye /daɪ/ *noun*
stuff that you use to change the colour of something, for example cloth or hair

dye *verb* (**dyes, dyeing, dyed** /daɪd/)
change the colour of something: *My parents were angry when I dyed my hair purple.*

dying *form of* **die**
be dying for something want to have something very much: *It's so hot! I'm dying for a drink.*

be dying to want to do something very much: *My brother is dying to meet you.*

Ee

each /iːtʃ/
adjective, pronoun
every person or
thing in a group:
*Each student buys a
book and a cassette.*
◇ *He gave a present
to each of the
children.*
each *adverb*
for one: *These
peaches cost 25p
each.*

They are looking
at **each other**.

each other words that show that some
body does the same thing as another person: *Gary and Susy looked at each other*
(= Gary looked at Susy and Susy looked at
Gary).

eager /ˈiːɡə(r)/ *adjective*
If you are eager to do something, you want
to do it very much: *She's eager to help
with the party.*
eagerly *adverb*
*The children were waiting eagerly for the
film to begin.*

eagle /ˈiːɡl/ *noun*
a large bird that catches and eats small
birds and animals

ear /ɪə(r)/ *noun*
one of the two parts of a person or an animal that are used for hearing: *Elephants
have big ears.* ☞ picture on page 126

earl /ɜːl/ *noun*
a British man who has a special title

early /ˈɜːli/ *adjective, adverb* (**earlier,
earliest**)
1 before the usual or right time: *The train
arrived ten minutes early.* ◇ *I was early
for the lesson.*
2 near the beginning of a time: *early afternoon* ◇ *She was in her early twenties*
(= between the ages of 20 and about 23 or
24). ◇ *I have to get up early tomorrow.*
○ opposite: **late**
an early night an evening when you go
to bed earlier than usual

earn /ɜːn/ *verb* (**earns, earning, earned**
/ɜːnd/)
1 get money by working: *How much do*

teachers earn in your country?* ◇ *She
earns about £900 a month.*
2 get something because you have
worked well or done something good:
You've earned a holiday!

earnings /ˈɜːnɪŋz/ *noun* (plural)
money that you get for working

earphones /ˈɪəfəʊnz/ *noun* (plural)
things that you put over your head and
ears for listening to a radio, cassette player,
etc

earring /ˈɪərɪŋ/
noun
a pretty thing that
you wear on your
ear

earth /ɜːθ/ *noun*
(no plural)
1 this world; the
planet that we live
on: *The moon
travels round the earth.*
2 what you grow plants in; soil: *Cover the
seeds with earth.*
on earth You use 'on earth' in questions
with words like 'how' and 'what' when
you are very surprised or do not know
what the answer will be: *Where on earth
is Paul? He's two hours late!* ◇ *What on
earth are you doing?*

earring

earthquake /ˈɜːθkweɪk/ *noun*
a sudden strong shaking of the ground

ease /iːz/ *noun* (no plural)
with ease with no difficulty: *She an
swered the questions with ease.*

easily /ˈiːzəli/ *adverb*
with no difficulty: *The cinema was almost
empty so we easily found a seat.*

east /iːst/ *noun* (no plural)
1 where the sun comes up in the morning:
Which way is east? ☞ picture at **north**
2 the East (no plural) the countries of
Asia, for example China and Japan
east *adjective, adverb*
They live on the east coast of Scotland.
◇ *an east wind* (= that comes from the

iː	i	ɪ	e	æ	ɑː	ɒ	ɔː	ʊ	u	uː
see	happy	sit	ten	cat	father	got	saw	put	situation	too

east) ◇ *We travelled east from San Francisco to New York.*

eastern /'i:stən/ *adjective*
in or of the east part of a place: *eastern Scotland*

Easter /'i:stə(r)/ *noun* (no plural)
a Sunday in March or April, and the days around it, when Christians think about Christ coming back to life: *I'm going on holiday at Easter.*

○ At Easter people often give eggs made of chocolate (**Easter eggs**) as presents.

easy /'i:zi/ *adjective* (**easier**, **easiest**)
1 If something is easy, you can do or understand it without any difficulty: *The homework was very easy.* ◇ *English isn't an easy language to learn.*
2 without problems or pain: *He has had an easy life.*
○ opposite: **difficult** or **hard**
take it easy, take things easy not worry or work too much: *After my exams I'm going to take it easy for a few days.*

eat /i:t/ *verb* (**eats**, **eating**, **ate** /et/, **has eaten** /'i:tn/)
take in food through your mouth: *Have you eaten all the chocolates?* ◇ *Do you want something to eat?*

echo /'ekəʊ/ *noun* (*plural* **echoes**)
a sound that a wall sends back so that you hear it again
echo *verb* (**echoes**, **echoing**, **echoed** /'ekəʊd/)
His footsteps echoed in the empty hall.

eclipse /i'klɪps/ *noun*
1 a time when the moon comes between the earth and the sun so that we cannot see the sun's light
2 a time when the earth comes between the sun and the moon so that we cannot see the moon's light

ecology /i'kɒlədʒi/ *noun* (no plural)
the study of the connection between living things and everything around them
ecological /ˌi:kə'lɒdʒɪkl/ *adjective*
The destruction of the rain forests is causing serious ecological problems.
ecologist /i'kɒlədʒɪst/ *noun*
a person who studies or knows a lot about ecology

economic /ˌi:kə'nɒmɪk/ *adjective*
about the way that a country spends its money and makes, buys and sells things:

The country is in serious economic difficulties.

economical /ˌi:kə'nɒmɪkl/ *adjective*
If something is economical, it does not cost a lot of money to use it: *This car is very economical to run* (= it does not use a lot of petrol).

economics /ˌi:kə'nɒmɪks/ *noun* (no plural)
the study of the way that countries spend money and make, buy and sell things

economist /i'kɒnəmɪst/ *noun*
a person who studies or knows a lot about economics

economy /i'kɒnəmi/ *noun* (*plural* **economies**)
1 the way that a country spends its money and makes, buys and sells things: *the economies of Japan and Germany*
2 using money or things well and carefully

edge /edʒ/ *noun*
the part along the end or side of something: *Don't sit on the edge of your chair – you might fall!*

edition /i'dɪʃn/ *noun*
one form of a book, magazine or newspaper: *The story was in the evening edition of the newspaper.*

editor /'edɪtə(r)/ *noun*
a person whose job is to prepare or control a magazine, newspaper, book or film

educate /'edʒukeɪt/ *verb* (**educates**, **educating**, **educated**)
teach somebody about things like reading, writing and mathematics at school or college: *Where was she educated?*
education /ˌedʒu'keɪʃn/ *noun* (no plural)
teaching somebody about things like reading, writing and mathematics at school or college: *He had a good education.* ◇ *The government spends a lot of money on education.*
educational /ˌedʒu'keɪʃənl/ *adjective*
an educational video

eel /i:l/ *noun*
a long fish that looks like a snake

effect /i'fekt/ *noun*
a change that happens because of something: *We are studying the effects of heat on different metals.*
have an effect on something make

something change: *His problems had a bad effect on his health.*

effective /ɪ'fektɪv/ *adjective*
Something that is effective works well: *Cycling is an effective way of keeping fit.*

efficient /ɪ'fɪʃnt/ *adjective*
A person or thing that is efficient works well and in the best way: *Our secretary is very efficient.* ○ opposite: **inefficient**
efficiency /ɪ'fɪʃnsi/ *noun* (no plural)
being efficient
efficiently *adverb*
You must use your time more efficiently.

effort /'efət/ *noun*
trying hard to do something; hard work: *Thank you for all your efforts.*
make an effort try hard to do something: *He made a big effort to arrive on time.*

eg /ˌiː 'dʒiː/ *short for* **for example**: *She travels to a lot of European countries, eg Spain, Greece and Italy.*

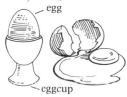

egg

eggcup

egg /eg/ *noun*
1 a round or oval thing that has a baby bird, fish, insect or snake inside it: *The hen has laid an egg.*
2 an egg from a hen that we eat: *Do you want eggs and bacon for breakfast?*
eggcup /'egkʌp/ *noun*
a small cup that holds a boiled egg while you are eating it

eight /eɪt/ *number* 8
eighth /eɪtθ/ *adjective, adverb, noun*
1 8th
2 one of eight equal parts of something; 1/8

eighteen /ˌeɪ'tiːn/ *number*
18
eighteenth /ˌeɪ'tiːnθ/ *adjective, adverb, noun*
18th

eighty /'eɪti/ *number*
1 80
2 **the eighties** (plural) the numbers, years or temperature between 80 and 89

in your eighties between the ages of 80 and 89
eightieth /'eɪtiəθ/ *adjective, adverb, noun*
80th

either¹ /'aɪðə(r)/, /'iːðə(r)/ *adjective, pronoun*
1 one of two things or people: *There is cake and ice-cream. You can have either.*
◇ *Either of us will help you.*
2 each: *There are trees along either side of the street.*

either² /'aɪðə(r)/, /'iːðə(r)/
(used in sentences with 'not') also: *Lydia can't swim and I can't (swim) either.*
either ... or words that show two different things or people that you can choose: *You can have either tea or coffee.* ◇ *I will either write or telephone.*

elaborate /ɪ'læbərət/ *adjective*
not simple; with a lot of different parts: *The carpet has a very elaborate pattern on it.*

elastic /ɪ'læstɪk/ *noun* (no plural)
material that becomes longer when you pull it and then goes back to its usual size: *His trousers have elastic in the top to stop them falling down.*
elastic *adjective*
elastic material
elastic band /ɪˌlæstɪk 'bænd/ *noun*
a thin circle of rubber that you use for holding things together

elbow /'elbəʊ/ *noun*
the part in the middle of your arm where it bends ☞ picture on page 126

elder /'eldə(r)/ *adjective*
older of two people: *My elder brother lives in France and the younger one lives in London.*

elderly /'eldəli/ *adjective*
quite old: *She is elderly and can't hear very well.*

eldest /'eldɪst/ *adjective*
oldest of three or more people: *Their eldest son is at university but the other two are at school.*

elect /ɪ'lekt/ *verb* (**elects, electing, elected**)
choose somebody to be a leader (by **voting**): *The new president was elected in 1990.*

p	b	t	d	k	g	tʃ	dʒ	f	v	θ	ð
pen	bad	tea	did	cat	got	chain	jam	fall	van	thin	this

election /ɪ'lekʃn/ *noun*
a time when people choose somebody to be a leader by voting: *The election will be held on Wednesday.*

electric /ɪ'lektrɪk/ *adjective*
using electricity to make it work: *an electric cooker* ◇ *an electric guitar*

electrical /ɪ'lektrɪkl/ *adjective*
of or using electricity: *an electrical engineer*

electrician /ɪ,lek'trɪʃn/ *noun*
a person whose job is to work with electricity: *This light isn't working – we need an electrician to mend it.*

electricity /ɪ,lek'trɪsəti/ *noun* (no plural)
power that comes through wires. Electricity can make heat and light and makes things work.

electronic /ɪ,lek'trɒnɪk/ *adjective*
Things like computers, calculators and radios are electronic. They use **microchips** or **transistors** to make them work: *an electronic typewriter*

electronics /ɪ,lek'trɒnɪks/ *noun* (no plural)
using **microchips** or **transistors** to make things like computers, calculators and radios: *the electronics industry*

elegant /'elɪgənt/ *adjective*
with a beautiful style or shape: *She looked very elegant in her black dress and diamond earrings.* ◇ *an elegant chair with long thin legs*

element /'elɪmənt/ *noun*
a simple chemical, for example oxygen or gold: *Water is made of the elements hydrogen and oxygen.*

elementary /,elɪ'mentri/ *adjective*
for beginners; not difficult to do or understand: *an elementary dictionary*

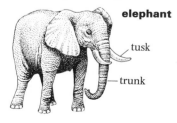
elephant
tusk
trunk

elephant /'elɪfənt/ *noun*
a very big wild animal from Africa or Asia, with a long nose (called a **trunk**) that hangs down

elevator /'eləveɪtə(r)/ *American English* for **lift** ² **1**

eleven /ɪ'levn/ *number*
11
eleventh /ɪ'levnθ/ *adjective, adverb, noun*
11th

else /els/ *adverb*
1 more; extra: *What else would you like?* ◇ *Is anyone else coming to the party?*
2 different; other: *The Grand Hotel was full, so we stayed somewhere else.* ◇ *It's not mine – it must be somebody else's.* ◇ *There was nothing else to eat so we had pizza again.*
○ You use **else** after words like **anybody**, **nothing** and **somewhere**, and after question words like **where** and **who**.
or else if not, then: *Go now, or else you'll be late.*

elsewhere /els'weə(r)/ *adverb*
in or to another place: *He can't find a job in Liverpool so he's looking elsewhere for work.*

embarrass /ɪm'bærəs/ *verb* (**embarrasses**, **embarrassing**, **embarrassed** /ɪm'bærəst/)
make somebody feel shy or worried about what other people think of them: *Mark embarrassed his friends by singing very loudly on the bus.*
embarrassed *adjective*
If you are embarrassed, you feel shy or worried about what other people think of you: *Everyone laughed when I fell off my chair – I was really embarrassed!*
embarrassing *adjective*
Something that is embarrassing makes you feel embarrassed: *I couldn't remember her name – it was so embarrassing!*
embarrassment *noun*
the feeling that you have when you are embarrassed; a person or thing that embarrasses you: *His face was red with embarrassment.*

embassy /'embəsi/ *noun* (*plural* **embassies**)
a place where people work whose job is to speak and act for their government in an-

other country: *To get a visa to travel in America, you should apply to the American embassy.*

embroider /ɪmˈbrɔɪdə(r)/ *verb* (**embroiders, embroidering, embroidered** /ɪmˈbrɔɪdəd/)
make pictures with thread on cloth
embroidered *adjective*
an embroidered blouse
embroidery /ɪmˈbrɔɪdəri/ *noun* (no plural)
something that has been embroidered

emerald /ˈemərəld/ *noun*
a green jewel: *an emerald ring*
emerald, emerald green *adjective*
bright green in colour

emerge /ɪˈmɜːdʒ/ *verb* (**emerges, emerging, emerged** /ɪˈmɜːdʒd/)
come out from a place: *The moon emerged from behind the clouds.*

emergency /ɪˈmɜːdʒənsi/ *noun* (*plural* **emergencies**)
a sudden dangerous situation, when people must help quickly: *Come quickly, doctor! It's an emergency!* ◇ *I can lend you some money in an emergency.*

emigrate /ˈemɪɡreɪt/ *verb* (**emigrates, emigrating, emigrated**)
leave your country to live in another country: *They emigrated to Australia in the 1960s to find work.*
emigration /ˌemɪˈɡreɪʃn/ *noun* (no plural)
the emigration of Soviet Jews to Israel

emotion /ɪˈməʊʃn/ *noun*
a strong feeling, for example love or anger
emotional /ɪˈməʊʃənl/ *adjective*
1 about feelings: *She's got emotional problems – her boyfriend has left her.*
2 If you are emotional, you have strong feelings and you show them: *He got very emotional when we said goodbye.*

emperor /ˈempərə(r)/ *noun*
a man who rules a group of countries (called an **empire**): *the Emperor Napoleon* ☞ Look at **empress**.

emphasize /ˈemfəsaɪz/ *verb* (**emphasizes, emphasizing, emphasized** /ˈemfəsaɪzd/)
say something strongly to show that it is important: *She emphasized the importance of hard work.*

empire /ˈempaɪə(r)/ *noun*
a group of countries that is controlled by one country: *the Roman Empire*

employ /ɪmˈplɔɪ/ *verb* (**employs, employing, employed** /ɪmˈplɔɪd/)
pay somebody to do work for you: *The factory employs 800 workers.* ☞ Look at **unemployed**.

employee /ɪmˈplɔɪiː/ *noun*
a person who is paid to work: *This company treats its employees very well.*

employer /ɪmˈplɔɪə(r)/ *noun*
a person or company that pays other people to do work

employment /ɪmˈplɔɪmənt/ *noun* (no plural)
having a job that you are paid to do: *She went to London and found employment as a taxi-driver.* ☞ Look at **unemployment**.

empress /ˈemprəs/ *noun* (plural **empresses**)
a woman who rules a group of countries (called an **empire**), or the wife of an emperor

empty¹ /ˈempti/ *adjective* (**emptier, emptiest**)
with nothing or nobody inside or on it: *My glass is empty.* ◇ *The cinema was almost empty.* ☞ picture at **full**

empty² /ˈempti/ *verb* (**empties, emptying, emptied** /ˈemptid/, **has emptied**)
1 take everything out of something: *The waiter emptied the ashtrays.* ◇ *We emptied our bags out onto the floor.*
2 become empty. *The film finished and the cinema started to empty.*

enable /ɪˈneɪbl/ *verb* (**enables, enabling, enabled** /ɪˈneɪbld/)
make it possible for somebody to do something: *Your help enabled me to finish the job.*

enclose /ɪnˈkləʊz/ *verb* (**encloses, enclosing, enclosed** /ɪnˈkləʊzd/)
1 put something inside a letter or parcel: *I enclose a cheque for £10.*
2 put something, for example a wall or fence, around a place on all sides: *The prison is enclosed by a high wall.*

encourage /ɪnˈkʌrɪdʒ/ *verb* (**encourages, encouraging, encouraged** /ɪnˈkʌrɪdʒd/)
give somebody hope or help so that they do

iː	i	ɪ	e	æ	ɑː	ɒ	ɔː	ʊ	u	uː
see	happy	sit	ten	cat	father	got	saw	put	situation	too

something or continue doing something: *We encouraged him to write a book about his adventures.*

encouragement /ɪnˈkʌrɪdʒmənt/ *noun* (no plural)
giving somebody hope or help so that they do something or continue doing something: *Kim's parents gave her a lot of encouragement when she was taking her exams.*

encouraging *adjective*
Something that is encouraging gives encouragement: *Ann's school report is very encouraging.*

encyclopedia /ɪn,saɪkləˈpiːdiə/ *noun* (*plural* **encyclopedias**)
a book or set of books that gives information about a lot of different things from A to Z: *an encyclopedia of world history*

end¹ /end/ *noun*
the furthest or last part of something: *Turn right at the end of the street.* ◊ *They were sitting at the other end of the room.* ◊ *I'm going on holiday at the end of June.*

come to an end stop: *The holiday was coming to an end and we started to think about going back to work.*

end to end in a line with the ends touching: *They put the tables end to end.*

for ... on end for a very long time: *He watches TV for hours on end.*

in the end finally; at last: *I looked for the keys for hours and in the end I found them in the car.*

make ends meet have enough money for your needs: *After her husband died it was difficult to make ends meet.*

put an end to something stop something happening: *We must put an end to this terrible war.*

end² /end/ *verb* (**ends, ending, ended**)
1 stop: *What time does the film end?* ◊ *The road ends here.* ◊ *Most adverbs in English end in '-ly'.*
2 finish something: *We ended our holiday in France with a trip to Paris.*

end up finally be in a place or doing something when you did not plan it: *If she continues to steal, she'll end up in prison.* ◊ *He ended up as a teacher.*

ending /ˈendɪŋ/ *noun*
the last part of something, for example a word, story or film: *All these words have the same ending: criticize, organize and realize.* ◊ *The film has a happy ending.*

endless /ˈendləs/ *adjective*
never stopping or finishing; very long: *The journey seemed endless.*

endlessly *adverb*
He talks endlessly about nothing.

enemy /ˈenəmi/ *noun* (*plural* **enemies**)
1 a person who hates you: *The President has many enemies.*
2 the enemy (no plural) the army or country that your country is fighting against in a war: *The enemy is attacking from the north.*

make enemies do things that make people hate you: *In business, you often make enemies.*

energetic /,enəˈdʒetɪk/ *adjective*
full of energy so that you can do a lot of things

energy /ˈenədʒi/ *noun* (no plural)
1 the power that your body has to do things: *You need a lot of energy to work with young children.*
2 the power from electricity, gas, coal, etc that is used to make machines work and to make heat and light: *It is important to try to save energy.* ◊ *atomic energy*

engaged /ɪnˈgeɪdʒd/ *adjective*
1 If two people are engaged, they have agreed to get married: *Louise is engaged to Michael.* ◊ *They got engaged last year.*
2 (used about a telephone) being used: *I tried to phone him but his number was engaged.*

engagement /ɪnˈgeɪdʒmənt/ *noun*
an agreement to marry somebody

engine /ˈendʒɪn/ *noun*
1 a machine that makes things move: *a car engine*
2 the front part of a train which pulls the rest.

engineer /,endʒɪˈnɪə(r)/ *noun*
a person whose job is to plan, make or repair things like machines, roads or bridges: *My brother is an electrical engineer.*

engineering /,endʒɪˈnɪərɪŋ/ *noun* (no plural)
planning and making things like machines, roads or bridges: *She's studying engineering at college.* ◊ *He works in chemical engineering.*

ʌ	ɜː	ə	eɪ	əʊ	aɪ	aʊ	ɔɪ	ɪə	eə	ʊə
cup	**bird**	**about**	**say**	**go**	**five**	**now**	**boy**	**near**	**hair**	**pure**

enjoy /ɪn'dʒɔɪ/ *verb* (**enjoys, enjoying, enjoyed** /ɪn'dʒɔɪd/)
like something very much: *I enjoy playing football.* ◇ *Did you enjoy your dinner?*
enjoy yourself have a happy time; have fun: *I really enjoyed myself at the party last night. Did you?*

enjoyable /ɪn'dʒɔɪəbl/ *adjective*
Something that is enjoyable makes you happy: *Thank you for a very enjoyable evening.*

enjoyment /ɪn'dʒɔɪmənt/ *noun* (no plural)
a feeling of enjoying something; pleasure: *I get a lot of enjoyment from travelling.*

enlarge /ɪn'lɑːdʒ/ *verb* (**enlarges, enlarging, enlarged** /ɪn'lɑːdʒd/)
make something bigger: *Can you enlarge this photograph for me?*
enlargement /ɪn'lɑːdʒmənt/ *noun*
a photograph that somebody has made bigger.

enormous /ɪ'nɔːməs/ *adjective*
very big: *an enormous dog*

enormously /ɪ'nɔːməsli/ *adverb*
very or very much: *London has changed enormously since my grandmother was a child.*

enough /ɪ'nʌf/ *adjective, adverb, pronoun*
as much or as many as you need: *There isn't enough food for ten people.* ◇ *You're too thin – you don't eat enough.* ◇ *Is she old enough to drive?*

enquire /ɪn'kwaɪə(r)/, **enquiry** /ɪn'kwaɪəri/ = **inquire, inquiry**

enrol /ɪn'rəʊl/ *verb* (**enrols, enrolling, enrolled** /ɪn'rəʊld/)
join a group, for example a school, college, course or club. You usually pay money (a **fee**) when you enrol: *I've enrolled for English classes at the college.*

ensure /ɪn'ʃʊə(r)/ *verb* (**ensures, ensuring, ensured** /ɪn'ʃʊəd/)
make certain: *Please ensure that all the lights are switched off before you leave.*

enter /'entə(r)/ *verb* (**enters, entering, entered** /'entəd/)
1 come or go into a place: *They stopped talking when she entered the room.* ◇ *Do not enter without knocking.* ✪ In this

sense, it is more usual to say **go in(to)** or **come in(to)**.
2 write a name or other information: *Please enter your name, address and date of birth at the bottom of the form.*
3 give your name to somebody because you want to do something like take an examination or run in a race: *I entered a competition last month and won £50.*

enterprise /'entəpraɪz/ *noun*
a plan to do something new and difficult, often to get money: *a business enterprise*

entertain /,entə'teɪn/ *verb* (**entertains, entertaining, entertained** /,entə'teɪnd/)
1 make somebody have a good time: *She entertained us all with her funny stories.*
2 give food and drink to visitors in your house: *We're entertaining friends this evening.*

entertaining /,entə'teɪnɪŋ/ *adjective*
funny or interesting: *The play was really entertaining.*

entertainment /,entə'teɪnmənt/ *noun*
anything that entertains people, for example films, plays or concerts: *There isn't much entertainment for young people in this town.*

enthusiasm /ɪn'θjuːziæzəm/ *noun* (no plural)
a strong feeling of wanting to do something or liking something: *They didn't show much enthusiasm when I asked them to help me with the shopping.*
enthusiastic /ɪn,θjuːzi'æstɪk/ *adjective*
full of enthusiasm: *She's starting a new job next week and she's very enthusiastic about it.*

entire /ɪn'taɪə(r)/ *adjective*
whole or complete; with no parts missing: *We spent the entire day on the beach.*

entirely /ɪn'taɪəli/ *adverb*
completely: *She looks entirely different from her sister.* ◇ *I entirely agree with you.*

entrance /'entrəns/ *noun*
1 (*plural* **entrances**) where you go into a place: *I'll meet you at the entrance to the museum.*
2 (*plural* **entrances**) coming or going into a place: *He made his entrance onto the stage.*
3 (no plural) the right to go into a place:

p	b	t	d	k	g	tʃ	dʒ	f	v	θ	ð
pen	**b**ad	**t**ea	**d**id	**c**at	**g**ot	**ch**ain	**j**am	**f**all	**v**an	**th**in	**th**is

They were refused entrance to the club because they were wearing jeans.

entry /'entri/ *noun* (*plural* **entries**)
1 (no plural) the right to go into a place: *You can't go into that room – there's a sign on the door that says 'No Entry'.*
2 (*plural* **entries**) where you go into a place

envelope /'envələʊp/ *noun*
a paper cover for a letter: *Have you written his address on the envelope?* ☞ picture on page 299

envied, envies *forms of* **envy**

envious /'enviəs/ *adjective*
wanting what somebody else has: *She's envious of her sister's success.*

environment /ɪn'vaɪərənmənt/ *noun*
1 everything around you: *The children need a happy home environment.*
2 the environment (no plural) the air, water, land, animals and plants around us: *We must do more to protect the environment.*
environmental /ɪn,vaɪərən'mentl/ *adjective*
We talked about pollution and other environmental problems.

envy /'envi/ *noun* (no plural)
a sad or angry feeling of wanting what another person has: *I was filled with envy when I saw her new bike.*
envy *verb* (**envies, envying, envied** /'envid/, **has envied**)
I envy you! You always seem so happy!

epidemic /,epɪ'demɪk/ *noun*
a disease that many people in a place have at the same time: *a flu epidemic*

episode /'epɪsəʊd/ *noun*
a programme on radio or television that is part of a longer story: *You can see the final episode of the series on Monday.*

equal¹ /'i:kwəl/ *adjective*
the same; as big, as much or as good as another: *Women want equal pay for equal work.* ◇ *I gave the two children equal numbers of sweets.*

equal² /'i:kwəl/ *verb* (**equals, equalling, equalled** /'i:kwəld/)
1 be exactly the same amount as something: *Two plus two equals four* (2 + 2 = 4).
2 be as good as somebody or something:

He ran the race in 21.2 seconds, equalling the world record.
✪ In American English the spellings are **equaling** and **equaled**.

equality /ɪ'kwɒləti/ *noun* (no plural)
being the same or having the same rights: *In some countries black people are still fighting for equality.*

equally /'i:kwəli/ *adverb*
1 in equal parts: *Don't eat all the chocolates yourself – share them out equally!*
2 in the same way: *You can wear the jacket with jeans but it looks equally good with a skirt.*

equator /ɪ'kweɪtə(r)/ *noun* (no plural)
the line on maps around the middle of the world. Countries near the equator are very hot.

equip /ɪ'kwɪp/ *verb* (**equips, equipping, equipped** /ɪ'kwɪpt/)
give somebody, or put in a place, all the things that are needed for doing something: *Before you go climbing, you must equip yourselves with things like boots and ropes.* ◇ *The kitchen is well equipped.*

equipment /ɪ'kwɪpmənt/ *noun* (no plural)
special things that you need for doing something: *sports equipment*

eraser /ɪ'reɪzə(r)/ *American English for* **rubber 2**

error /'erə(r)/ *noun*
a thing that is done wrongly; a mistake: *The letter was sent to the wrong address because of a computer error.*

erupt /ɪ'rʌpt/ *verb* (**erupts, erupting, erupted**)
When a **volcano** erupts, very hot liquid rock (called **lava**) suddenly comes out: *When Mount Vesuvius erupted, it buried Pompeii.*
eruption /ɪ'rʌpʃn/ *noun*
a volcanic eruption

escalator /'eskəleɪtə(r)/ *noun*
stairs that move and carry people up and down

escape /ɪ'skeɪp/ *verb* (**escapes, escaping, escaped** /ɪ'skeɪpt/)
1 get free from somebody or something:

The bird escaped from the cage. ◇ The prisoner escaped, but he was caught.
2 If a liquid or gas escapes, it comes out of a place.

escape noun
make your escape get free; get away from a place: They jumped out of a window and made their escape.

escort /ɪ'skɔːt/ verb (**escorts, escorting, escorted**)
go with somebody, for example to make sure that they arrive somewhere: The police escorted him out of the building.

especially /ɪ'speʃəli/ adverb
1 very; more than usual or more than others: I hate getting up early, especially in winter. ◇ The food in that restaurant is not especially good.
2 for a particular person or thing: I bought these flowers especially for you.

essay /'eseɪ/ noun
a short piece of writing about a subject: Our teacher asked us to write an essay on our favourite author.

essential /ɪ'senʃl/ adjective
If something is essential, you must have or do it: It is essential that you work hard for this exam.

establish /ɪ'stæblɪʃ/ verb (**establishes, establishing, established** /ɪ'stæblɪʃt/)
start something new: This company was established in 1852.

estate /ɪ'steɪt/ noun
1 land with a lot of houses or factories on it: We live on a housing estate. ◇ an industrial estate
2 a large piece of land in the country that one person or family owns

estate agent /ɪ'steɪt eɪdʒənt/ noun
a person whose job is to sell buildings and land for other people

estate car /ɪ'steɪt kɑː(r)/ noun
a long car with a door at the back and space behind the back seat for carrying things

estimate /'estɪmeɪt/ verb (**estimates, estimating, estimated**)
say how much you think something will cost, how big something is, how long it will take to do something, etc: The builders estimated that it would take a week to repair the roof.

estimate /'estɪmət/ noun
The estimate for repairing the roof was £2 000.

estuary /'estʃuəri/ noun (plural **estuaries**)
the wide part of a river where it goes into the sea: the Thames Estuary

etc /et'setərə/
You use 'etc' at the end of a list to show that there are other things but you are not going to name them all: We bought coffee, milk, bread, etc at the shop.

ethnic /'eθnɪk/ adjective
of or from another country or race: There are a lot of different ethnic groups living in London.

evacuate /ɪ'vækjueɪt/ verb (**evacuates, evacuating, evacuated**)
take people away from a dangerous place to a safer place: The area near the factory was evacuated after the explosion.
evacuation /ɪ,vækju'eɪʃn/ noun
the evacuation of cities during the war

evaporate /ɪ'væpəreɪt/ verb (**evaporates, evaporating, evaporated**)
If a liquid evaporates, it changes into a gas: Water evaporates if you heat it.

eve /iːv/ noun
the day before a special day: 24 December is Christmas Eve. ◇ I went to a party on New Year's Eve (= 31 December).

even¹ /'iːvn/ adjective
1 flat and smooth: I fell over because the floor wasn't even. ✪ opposite: **uneven**
2 the same; equal: Sara won the first game and I won the second, so we're even.
3 Even numbers can be divided exactly by two: 4, 6 and 8 are even numbers. ✪ opposite: **odd**
get even with somebody hurt somebody who has hurt you

even² /'iːvn/ adverb
1 a word that you use to say that something is surprising: The game is so easy that even a child can play it. ◇ He didn't laugh – he didn't even smile.
2 a word that you use to make another word stronger: That car is big, but this one is even bigger.
even if it does not change anything if: Even if you run, you won't catch the bus.
even so although that is true: I didn't

have any lunch today, but even so I'm not
hungry.
even though although: I went to the
party, even though I was tired.

evening /'i:vnɪŋ/ noun
the part of the day between the afternoon
and when you go to bed: What are you
doing this evening? ◇ We went for a long
walk and in the evening we saw a film.
◇ John came on Monday evening.

event /ɪ'vent/ noun
1 something important that happens: My
sister's wedding was a big event for our
family.
2 a race or competition: The next event
will be the high-jump.

eventually /ɪ'ventʃʊəli/ adverb
after a long time: I waited for him for three
hours, and eventually he came.

ever /'evə(r)/ adverb
at any time: 'Have you ever been to
Africa?' 'No, I haven't.' ◇ Do you ever
see Peter?
ever since in all the time since: I have
known Lucy ever since we were children.
ever so, ever such a very: I'm ever so
hot. ◇ It's ever such a good film.
for ever for all time; always: I will love
you for ever.

evergreen /'evəgri:n/ noun
a tree that has green leaves all the year

every /'evri/ adjective
1 all of the people or things in a group: She
knows every student in the school.
2 once in each: He phones every evening.
**every now and then, every now
and again, every so often** sometimes,
but not often: I see Robert every now and
then.
every other: She comes every other day
(= for example on Monday, Wednesday
and Friday but not on Tuesday or
Thursday).

everybody /'evribɒdi/, **everyone**
/'evriwʌn/ pronoun
each person; all people: Everybody at
school likes my coat. ◇ If everybody is
here then we can start.

everyday /'evrideɪ/ adjective
normal; not special: Computers are now
part of everyday life.

everything /'evriθɪŋ/ pronoun
each thing; all things: Everything in that
shop is very expensive.

everywhere /'evriweə(r)/ adverb
in all places or to all places: I've looked
everywhere for my pen, but I can't find it.

evidence /'evɪdəns/ noun (no plural)
a thing that makes you believe that something has happened or that helps you
know who did something: The police
searched the room, looking for evidence.
◇ a piece of evidence
give evidence tell what you know
about somebody or something in a court of
law: The man who saw the accident will
give evidence in court.

evident /'evɪdənt/ adjective
easy to see or understand: It was evident
that he was lying, because he didn't look
at me when he was speaking.
evidently adverb
clearly

evil /'i:vl/ adjective
very bad: an evil person

exact /ɪg'zækt/ adjective
completely correct; without any mistakes:
Have you got the exact time?

exactly /ɪg'zæktli/ adverb
1 You use 'exactly' when you are asking
for or giving information that is completely
correct: Can you tell me exactly what happened? ◇ It cost £10 exactly.
2 just: This shirt is exactly what I
wanted.
3 You use 'exactly' to agree with somebody: 'So you've never met this man before?' 'Exactly.'

exaggerate /ɪg'zædʒəreɪt/ verb (exag-
gerates, exaggerating, exaggerated)
say that something is bigger, better, worse,
etc than it really is: Don't exaggerate! I
was only two minutes late, not twenty.
exaggeration /ɪg,zædʒə'reɪʃn/ noun
It's an exaggeration to say you don't
know any English!

examination /ɪg,zæmɪ'neɪʃn/ noun
1 (also **exam**) a test of what you know or
can do: We've got an exam in English
next week.

❂ You **sit** or **take** an examination. If you
do well, you **pass** and if you do badly, you
fail: I took an examination at the end of
the year. ◇ Did she pass all her exams?

2 looking carefully at somebody or something: She went into hospital for an
examination.

ʌ	ɜː	ə	eɪ	əʊ	aɪ	aʊ	ɔɪ	ɪə	eə	ʊə
cup	bird	about	say	go	five	now	boy	near	hair	pure

examine /ɪg'zæmɪn/ verb (**examines, examining, examined** /ɪg'zæmɪnd/)
1 ask questions to find out what somebody knows or what they can do: *You will be examined on everything you have learnt this year.*
2 look carefully at something or somebody: *I had my chest examined by the doctor.* ◇ *I examined the car before I bought it.*

example /ɪg'zɑːmpl/ noun
something that shows what other things of the same kind are like: *This dictionary gives many examples of how words are used in sentences.*
for example let me give you an example: *Do you speak any other languages, for example French or German?*

exceed /ɪk'siːd/ verb (**exceeds, exceeding, exceeded**)
do or be more than something: *The price will not exceed £50.*

excellent /'eksələnt/ adjective
very good: *She speaks excellent Japanese.*

except /ɪk'sept/ preposition
but not: *The restaurant is open every day except Sunday.* ◇ *Everyone went to the party except for me.*
except that only that: *I don't know what he looks like, except that he's very tall.*

exception /ɪk'sepʃn/ noun
a person or thing that is not the same as the others: *Most of his films are good but this one is an exception.*
with the exception of somebody or **something** if you do not count somebody or something: *I like all vegetables with the exception of cabbage.*

exceptional /ɪk'sepʃənl/ adjective
1 not usual: *It's exceptional to have such hot weather at this time of year.*
2 very good: *She is an exceptional pianist.*
exceptionally /ɪk'sepʃənəli/ adverb
He was an exceptionally good student.

exchange /ɪks'tʃeɪndʒ/ verb (**exchanges, exchanging, exchanged** /ɪks'tʃeɪndʒd/)
give one thing and get another thing for it: *My new radio didn't work so I exchanged it for another one.* ◇ *We exchanged telephone numbers at the end of the holiday.*
exchange noun
in exchange for something If you get one thing in exchange for another thing, you give one thing and get another thing for it: *I gave her English lessons in exchange for a room in her house.*

exchange rate /ɪks'tʃeɪndʒ reɪt/ noun
how much money from one country you can buy with money from another country: *The exchange rate is one pound to eight francs.*

excite /ɪk'saɪt/ verb (**excites, exciting, excited**)
make somebody have strong feelings of happiness or interest so that they are not calm: *Please don't excite the children too much or they won't sleep tonight.*
excited adjective
not calm, for example because you are happy about something that is going to happen: *He's getting very excited about his holiday.*
excitement /ɪk'saɪtmənt/ noun (no plural)
a feeling of being excited: *There was great excitement in the stadium before the match began.*
exciting adjective
Something that is exciting makes you have strong feelings of happiness or interest: *an exciting film* ◇ *She's got a very exciting job – she travels all over the world and meets lots of famous people.*

exclaim /ɪk'skleɪm/ verb (**exclaims, exclaiming, exclaimed** /ɪk'skleɪmd/)
say something suddenly and loudly because you are surprised, angry, etc: *'I don't believe it!' she exclaimed.*
exclamation /ˌekskləˈmeɪʃn/ noun
exclamation mark /ekskləˈmeɪʃn mɑːk/ noun
a mark (!) that you use in writing to show loud or strong words or surprise

exclude /ɪk'skluːd/ verb (**excludes, excluding, excluded**)
shut or keep a person or thing out: *We cannot exclude the students from the meeting. Their ideas are important.* ☞ Look at **include.**
excluding preposition
without; if you do not count: *The meal cost £35, excluding drinks.*

excursion /ɪk'skɜːʃn/ noun
a short journey to see something interesting or to enjoy yourself: *We're going on an excursion to the seaside on Sunday.*

p	b	t	d	k	g	tʃ	dʒ	f	v	θ	ð
pen	**b**ad	**t**ea	**d**id	**c**at	**g**ot	**ch**ain	**j**am	**f**all	**v**an	**th**in	**th**is

excuse¹ /ɪk'skjuːs/ *noun*
words you say or write to explain why you have done something wrong: *You're late! What's your excuse this time?*

excuse² /ɪk'skjuːz/ *verb* (**excuses, excusing, excused** /ɪk'skjuːzd/)
say that it is not important that a person has done something wrong: *Please excuse us for being late.*
excuse me You use 'excuse me' when you want to stop somebody who is speaking, or when you want to speak to somebody you don't know. You can also use 'excuse me' to say that you are sorry: *Excuse me, could you tell me the time, please?* ◇ *Did I stand on your foot? Excuse me.*

execute /'eksɪkjuːt/ *verb* (**executes, executing, executed**)
kill somebody to punish them
execution /,eksɪ'kjuːʃn/ *noun*
the execution of prisoners

executive /ɪg'zekjʊtɪv/ *noun*
an important businessman or businesswoman

exercise¹ /'eksəsaɪz/ *noun*
1 (*plural* **exercises**) a piece of work that you do to learn something: *The teacher asked us to do exercises 1 and 2 for homework.*
2 (no plural) moving your body to keep it strong and well: *Swimming is very good exercise.*
3 (*plural* **exercises**) a special movement that you do to keep your body strong and well: *Touch your toes and stand up 20 times. This exercise is good for your legs, stomach and back.*
exercise book /'eksəsaɪz bʊk/ *noun*
a book with clean pages that you use at school for writing in

exercise² /'eksəsaɪz/ *verb* (**exercises, exercising, exercised** /'eksəsaɪzd/)
move your body to keep it strong and well: *They exercise in the park every morning.*

exhaust¹ /ɪg'zɔːst/ *verb* (**exhausts, exhausting, exhausted**)
make somebody very tired: *The long journey exhausted us.*
exhausted *adjective*
very tired: *I'm exhausted – I think I'll go to bed.*

exhaust² /ɪg'zɔːst/ *noun*
a pipe that takes gas out from an engine, for example on a car

exhibition /,eksɪ'bɪʃn/ *noun*
a group of things in a place so that people can look at them: *an exhibition of paintings by Monet*

exile /'eksaɪl/ *noun*
1 (no plural) having to live away from your own country, for example as a punishment: *Napoleon spent the last years of his life in exile.*
2 (*plural* **exiles**) a person who must live away from his/her own country

exist /ɪg'zɪst/ *verb* (**exists, existing, existed**)
be real; live: *Does life exist on other planets?* ◇ *That word does not exist.*
existence /ɪg'zɪstəns/ *noun* (no plural)
being real; existing: *Do you believe in the existence of God?*

exit /'eksɪt/ *noun*
a way out of a building: *Where is the exit?*
make an exit go out of a place: *He made a quick exit.*

exotic /ɪg'zɒtɪk/ *adjective*
strange or interesting because it comes from another country: *exotic fruits*

expand /ɪk'spænd/ *verb* (**expands, expanding, expanded**)
become bigger or make something bigger: *Metals expand when they are heated.*
expansion /ɪk'spænʃn/ *noun* (no plural)
getting bigger: *The company needs bigger offices because of the expansion.*

expect /ɪk'spekt/ *verb* (**expects, expecting, expected**)
1 think that somebody or something will come or that something will happen: *I expect she'll be late. She usually is.* ◇ *We expected it to be hot in San Francisco, but it was quite cold.* ◇ *She's expecting (= she is going to have) a baby in June.*
2 think that something is probably true: *They haven't had lunch yet, so I expect they're hungry.*
3 If you are expected to do something, you must do it: *I am expected to work every Saturday.*
I expect so You say 'I expect so' when you think that something will happen or that something is true: *'Is Ian coming?' 'Oh yes, I expect so.'*

s	z	ʃ	ʒ	h	m	n	ŋ	l	r	j	w
so	**zoo**	**shoe**	vision	**hat**	**man**	**no**	sing	**leg**	**red**	yes	**wet**

expedition /ˌekspə'dɪʃn/ *noun*
a journey to find or do something special: *Scott's expedition to the South Pole*

expel /ɪk'spel/ *verb* (**expels, expelling, expelled** /ɪk'speld/)
send somebody away from a school or club: *The boys were expelled from school for smoking.*

expense /ɪk'spens/ *noun*
1 the cost of something: *Having a car is a big expense.*
2 expenses (plural) money that you spend on a certain thing: *The company pays our travelling expenses.*
at somebody's expense If you do something at somebody's expense, they pay for it: *We had dinner at the company's expense.*

expensive /ɪk'spensɪv/ *adjective*
Something that is expensive costs a lot of money: *expensive clothes* ✪ opposite: **cheap** or **inexpensive**

experience /ɪk'spɪəriəns/ *noun*
1 (no plural) knowing about something because you have seen it or done it: *She has four years' teaching experience.* ◇ *Do you have much experience of working with children?*
2 (*plural* **experiences**) something that has happened to you: *He wrote a book about his experiences in Africa.* ◇ *What's the most frightening experience you have ever had?*

experienced /ɪk'spɪəriənst/ *adjective*
If you are experienced, you know about something because you have done it many times before: *She's an experienced driver.*
✪ opposite: **inexperienced**

experiment /ɪk'sperɪmənt/ *noun*
You do an experiment to find out what will happen or to see if something is true: *They are doing experiments to find out if the drug is safe for humans.*
experiment *verb* (**experiments, experimenting, experimented**)
I don't think it's right to experiment on animals.

expert /'ekspɜːt/ *noun*
a person who knows a lot about something: *He's an expert on Shakespeare.* ◇ *a computer expert*

explain /ɪk'spleɪn/ *verb* (**explains, explaining, explained** /ɪk'spleɪnd/)
1 tell somebody about something so that

they understand it: *The teacher usually explains the new words to us.* ◇ *He explained how to use the machine.*
2 give a reason for something: *I explained why we needed the money.*

explanation /ˌeksplə'neɪʃn/ *noun*
telling somebody about something so that they understand it, or giving a reason for something: *What explanation did they give for being late?*

explode /ɪk'spləʊd/ *verb* (**explodes, exploding, exploded**)
burst suddenly with a very loud noise: *A bomb exploded in the city centre, killing two people.* ✪ The noun is **explosion**.

exploit /ɪk'splɔɪt/ *verb* (**exploits, exploiting, exploited**)
treat somebody badly to get what you want: *People who work at home are often exploited – they work long hours for very little money.*

explore /ɪk'splɔː(r)/ *verb* (**explores, exploring, explored** /ɪk'splɔːd/)
travel around a new place to learn about it: *Indiana Jones explored the jungles of South America.*
exploration /ˌeksplə'reɪʃn/ *noun*
the exploration of space
explorer *noun*
a person who travels around a new place to learn about it: *The first European explorers arrived in America in the 15th century.*

explosion /ɪk'spləʊʒn/ *noun*
bursting suddenly with a very loud noise: *There was an explosion and pieces of glass flew everywhere.* ✪ The verb is **explode**.

explosive /ɪk'spləʊsɪv/ *adjective*
Something that is explosive can cause an explosion: *an explosive gas*
explosive *noun*
a substance that can make things explode: *Dynamite is an explosive.*

export /ɪk'spɔːt/ *verb* (**exports, exporting, exported**)
sell things to another country: *Japan exports cars to Britain.*
export /'ekspɔːt/ *noun*
1 (no plural) selling things to another country: *These cars are made for export.*
2 (*plural* **exports**) something that you sell to another country: *The country's biggest exports are tea and cotton.*
✪ opposite: **import**

i:	i	ɪ	e	æ	ɑ:	ɒ	ɔ:	ʊ	u	u:
see	happy	sit	ten	cat	father	got	saw	put	situation	too

expose /ɪk'spəʊz/ *verb* (**exposes, exposing, exposed** /ɪk'spəʊzd/)
show something that is usually covered or hidden: *A baby's skin should not be exposed to the sun for too long.* ◇ *The newspaper exposed his terrible secret.*

express[1] /ɪk'spres/ *verb* (**expresses, expressing, expressed** /ɪk'sprest/)
say or show how you think or feel: *She expressed her ideas well.*

express[2] /ɪk'spres/ *adjective*
that goes or is sent very quickly: *an express letter*
express *adverb*
I sent the parcel express.

express[3] (*plural* **expresses**), **express train** *noun*
a fast train that does not stop at all stations

expression /ɪk'spreʃn/ *noun*
1 a word or group of words; a way of saying something: *The expression 'to drop off' means 'to fall asleep'.*
2 the look on your face that shows how you feel: *an expression of surprise*

expressway /ɪk'spresweɪ/ *American English for* **motorway**

extend /ɪk'stend/ *verb* (**extends, extending, extended**)
1 make something longer or bigger: *I'm extending my holiday for another week.*
2 continue or stretch: *The park extends as far as the river.*

extension /ɪk'stenʃn/ *noun*
1 a part that you add to something to make it bigger: *They've built an extension on the back of the house.*
2 one of the telephones in a building that is connected to the main telephone: *Can I have extension 4110, please?*

extent /ɪk'stent/ *noun* (no plural)
how big something is: *I didn't know the full extent of the problem* (= how big it was) *until he explained it to me.* ◇ You use expressions like **to a certain extent** and **to some extent** to show that you do not think something is completely true: *I agree with you to a certain extent.*

exterior /ɪk'stɪəriə(r)/ *noun*
the outside part: *We painted the exterior of the house white.*
exterior *adjective*
an exterior door
◇ opposite: **interior**

external /ɪk'stɜːnl/ *adjective*
on, of or from the outside: *external walls*
◇ opposite: **internal**

extinct /ɪk'stɪŋkt/ *adjective*
If a type of animal or plant is extinct, it does not exist now: *Dinosaurs became extinct millions of years ago.*

extra /'ekstrə/ *adjective, adverb*
more than what is usual: *I have put an extra blanket on your bed because it's cold tonight.* ◇ *The room costs £20 and you have to pay extra for breakfast.*

extraordinary /ɪk'strɔːdnri/ *adjective*
very unusual or strange: *I had an extraordinary dream last night – I dreamt that I could fly.* ◇ *Have you seen that extraordinary building with the pink roof?*
extraordinarily /ɪk'strɔːdnrəli/ *adverb*
extremely: *She's extraordinarily clever.*

extravagant /ɪk'strævəgənt/ *adjective*
1 If you are extravagant, you spend too much money.
2 Something that is extravagant costs too much money: *He buys her a lot of extravagant presents.*

extreme /ɪk'striːm/ *adjective*
1 very great or strong: *the extreme cold of the Arctic*
2 as far away as possible: *They came from the extreme north of Scotland.*
3 If you say that a person is extreme, you mean that his/her ideas are too strong.
extremely *adverb*
very: *He's extremely good-looking.*

eye /aɪ/ *noun*
one of the two parts in your head that you see with: *She's got blue eyes.* ◇ *Open your eyes!* ☞ picture on page 126
catch somebody's eye 1 If you catch somebody's eye, you make them look at you: *Try to catch the waiter's eye the next time he comes this way.* **2** If something catches your eye, you see it suddenly: *Her bright-yellow hat caught my eye.*
in somebody's eyes as somebody thinks: *Richard is 42, but in his mother's eyes, he's still a little boy!*
keep an eye on somebody or **something** look after or watch somebody or something: *Will you keep an eye on my bag while I go to the toilet?*
see eye to eye with somebody agree with somebody: *Mr Harper doesn't always see eye to eye with his neighbours.*

ʌ	ɜː	ə	eɪ	əʊ	aɪ	aʊ	ɔɪ	ɪə	eə	ʊə
cup	bird	about	say	go	five	now	boy	near	hair	pure

eyebrow /ˈaɪbraʊ/ *noun*
one of the two lines of hair above your eyes ☞ picture on page 126

eyelash /ˈaɪlæʃ/ *noun* (*plural* **eyelashes**)
one of the hairs that grow in a line on your eyelid: *She's got beautiful long eyelashes.* ☞ picture on page 126

eyelid /ˈaɪlɪd/ *noun*
the piece of skin that can move to close your eye

eyesight /ˈaɪsaɪt/ *noun* (no plural)
the power to see: *Your eyesight is very good.*

Ff

F *short way of writing* **Fahrenheit**

fable /ˈfeɪbl/ *noun*
a short story, usually about animals, that teaches people something

fabulous /ˈfæbjʊləs/ *adjective*
very good; wonderful: *The food smells fabulous!*

face¹ /feɪs/ *noun*
1 the front part of your head: *Have you washed your face?* ◇ *She had a smile on her face.*
2 the front or one side of something: *a clock face* ◇ *He put the cards face down on the table.*
face to face If two people are face to face, they are looking straight at each other: *They stood face to face.*
keep a straight face not smile or laugh when something is funny: *I couldn't keep a straight face when he dropped his watch in the soup!*
make or **pull a face** move your mouth and eyes to show that you do not like something: *She made a face when she saw what I had made for dinner.*
let's face it we must agree that it is true: *Let's face it – you're not very good at maths.*

face² /feɪs/ *verb* (**faces, facing, faced** /feɪst/)
1 have the face or the front towards something: *Can you all face the front of the class, please?* ◇ *My bedroom faces the garden.*
2 be brave enough to meet somebody unfriendly or something difficult: *I can't face going to work today – I feel too ill.*

facilities /fəˈsɪlətiz/ *noun* (plural)
things in a place for you to use: *Our school has very good sports facilities.*

fact /fækt/ *noun*
something that you know has happened or is true: *It's a fact that the earth travels around the sun.*
in fact, in actual fact words that you use to show that something is true; really: *I thought she was Swedish, but in actual fact she's from Norway.* ◇ *I think I saw him – I'm certain, in fact.*

factory /ˈfæktəri/ *noun* (*plural* **factories**)
a place where people make things, usually with machines: *He works at the car factory.*

fade /feɪd/ *verb* (**fades, fading, faded**)
become less bright and colourful: *Will this shirt fade when I wash it?* ◇ *faded jeans*

Fahrenheit /ˈfærənhaɪt/ *noun* (no plural)
a way of measuring temperature. Water freezes at 32° Fahrenheit and boils at 212° Fahrenheit. ✪ The short way of writing 'Fahrenheit' is **F**: *110° F*

fail /feɪl/ *verb* (**fails, failing, failed** /feɪld/)
1 not pass an exam or test: *She failed her driving test again.* ◇ *How many students failed last term?*
2 try to do something but not be able to do it: *He played quite well but failed to win the match.*
3 not do something that you should do: *The driver failed to stop at a red light.*

p	b	t	d	k	g	tʃ	dʒ	f	v	θ	ð
pen	**b**ad	**t**ea	**d**id	**c**at	**g**ot	**ch**ain	**j**am	**f**all	**v**an	**th**in	**th**is

fail *noun*
without fail certainly: *Be there at twelve o'clock without fail!*

failure /'feɪljə(r)/ *noun*
1 (no plural) not being successful: *The search for the missing children ended in failure.*
2 (*plural* **failures**) a person or thing that does not do well: *I felt that I was a failure because I didn't have a job.*

faint¹ /feɪnt/ *adjective* (**fainter, faintest**)
1 not clear or strong: *We could hear the faint sound of music in the distance.*
2 If you feel faint, you feel that you are going to fall, for example because you are ill or tired.

faint² /feɪnt/ *verb* (**faints, fainting, fainted**)
fall down suddenly, for example because you are weak, ill or shocked: *She almost fainted when she saw the blood on her leg.*

fair¹ /feə(r)/ *adjective* (**fairer, fairest**)
1 Somebody or something that is fair treats people equally or in the right way: *a fair judge* ◇ *It's not fair! I have to go to bed but you can stay up and watch TV!* ☺ opposite: **unfair**
2 with a light colour: *He's got fair hair.* ◇ *He is fair-haired.* ☺ opposite: **dark**
3 quite good or quite large: *They've invited a fair number of people to their party.*
4 good, without rain: *fair weather*

fair² /feə(r)/ *noun*
a place outside where you can ride on big machines and play games to win prizes. Fairs usually travel from town to town.

fairly /'feəli/ *adverb*
1 in a way that is right and honest: *This company treats its workers fairly.* ☺ opposite: **unfairly**
2 quite; not very: *She speaks French fairly well.* ◇ *I'm fairly certain it was him.*

fairy /'feəri/ *noun* (*plural* **fairies**)
a very small person in stories. Fairies have wings and can do magic.

fairy tale /'feəri teɪl/, **fairy story** /'feəri stɔːri/ (*plural* **fairy stories**) *noun*
a story for children that is about magic

faith /feɪθ/ *noun*
1 (no plural) feeling sure that somebody or something is good, right, honest, etc: *I've got great faith in your ability to do the job* (= I'm sure that you can do it).
2 (*plural* **faiths**) a religion: *the Muslim faith*

faithful /'feɪθfl/ *adjective*
always ready to help your friends and to do what you have promised to do: *a faithful friend*

faithfully /'feɪθfəli/ *adverb*
Yours faithfully words that you write at the end of a letter, before your name

fake /feɪk/ *noun*
a copy of something, made to trick people: *This painting is not really by Van Gogh – it's a fake.*

fake *adjective*
a fake ten-pound note

fall¹ /fɔːl/ *verb* (**falls, falling, fell** /fel/, **has fallen** /'fɔːlən/)
1 go down quickly; drop: *The book fell off the table.* ◇ *She fell down the stairs and broke her arm.*
2 (*also* **fall over**) suddenly stop standing: *He slipped on the ice and fell.* ◇ *I fell over and hurt my leg.*
3 become lower or less: *In the desert the temperature falls at night.* ◇ *Prices have fallen again.* ☺ opposite: **rise**
4 come or happen: *Darkness was falling.*
fall apart break into pieces: *The chair fell apart when I sat on it.*
fall asleep start sleeping: *She was so tired that she fell asleep in the armchair.*
fall behind become slower than others, or not do something when you should do it: *She's falling behind with her school work because she goes out every evening.*
fall for somebody start to love somebody: *He has fallen for someone he met on holiday.*
fall out with somebody argue with somebody so that you stop being friends: *John has fallen out with his girlfriend.*
fall through If a plan falls through, it does not happen.

fall² /fɔːl/ *noun*
1 a sudden drop from a higher place to a lower place: *He had a fall from his horse.*
2 becoming lower or less: *a fall in the price of oil*
3 **falls** (plural) a place where water falls

s	z	ʃ	ʒ	h	m	n	ŋ	l	r	j	w
so	**zoo**	**shoe**	**vision**	**hat**	**man**	**no**	**sing**	**leg**	**red**	**yes**	**wet**

from a high place to a low place: *the Victoria Falls*
4 *American English for* **autumn**

false /fɔːls/ *adjective*
1 not true; wrong: *A spider has eight legs – true or false?* ◇ *She gave a false name to the police.*
2 not real or not natural: *People who have lost their own teeth wear false teeth* (= teeth that are made of plastic).
false alarm /ˌfɔːls əˈlɑːm/ *noun*
a warning about something bad that does not happen: *Everyone thought there was a fire, but it was a false alarm.*

fame /feɪm/ *noun* (no plural)
being known by many people ✪ The adjective is **famous**

familiar /fəˈmɪliə(r)/ *adjective*
that you know well: *I heard a familiar voice in the next room.*
be familiar with something know something well: *I'm not familiar with this computer.*
✪ opposite: **unfamiliar**

family /ˈfæməli/ *noun* (*plural* **families**)
1 parents and children: *How many people are there in your family?* ◇ *My family have all got red hair.* ◇ *His family lives on a farm.* ✪ Sometimes 'family' means not just parents and children but other people too, for example grandparents, aunts, uncles and cousins.
2 a group of plants or animals: *Lions belong to the cat family.*
family tree /ˌfæməli ˈtriː/ *noun*
a plan that shows all the people in a family ☞ picture on page 127

famine /ˈfæmɪn/ *noun*
A famine happens when there is not enough food in a country: *There is a famine in many parts of Africa.*

famous /ˈfeɪməs/ *adjective*
known by many people: *Oxford is famous for its university.* ◇ *Marilyn Monroe was a famous actress.* ✪ The noun is **fame**.

fan¹ /fæn/ *noun*
a thing that moves the air to make you cooler: *an electric fan on the ceiling*
fan *verb* (**fans, fanning, fanned** /fænd/)
make somebody or something cooler by moving the air: *I fanned my face with the newspaper.*

fans

fan² /fæn/ *noun*
a person who likes somebody or something, for example a singer or a sport, very much: *She was a fan of the Beatles.* ◇ *football fans*

fancy¹ /ˈfænsi/ *verb* (**fancies, fancying, fancied** /ˈfænsid/, **has fancied**)
1 feel that you would like something: *Do you fancy a drink?*
2 a word that shows you are surprised: *Fancy seeing you here!*

fancy² /ˈfænsi/ *adjective* (**fancier, fanciest**)
not simple or ordinary: *She wore a very fancy hat to the wedding.*
fancy dress /ˌfænsi ˈdres/ *noun* (no plural)
special clothes that you wear at a party so that you look like a different person or a thing: *It was a fancy dress party so I went as Charlie Chaplin.*

fantastic /fænˈtæstɪk/ *adjective*
1 very good; wonderful: *We had a fantastic holiday.*
2 strange or difficult to believe: *He told us fantastic stories about his adventures.*

fantasy /ˈfæntəsi/ *noun* (*plural* **fantasies**)
something nice that you think about and that you hope will happen

far¹ /fɑː(r)/ *adjective* (**farther** /ˈfɑːðə(r)/ or **further** /ˈfɜːðə(r)/, **farthest** /ˈfɑːðɪst/ or **furthest** /ˈfɜːðɪst/)
1 a long way away: *Let's walk – it's not far.*
2 other: *They live on the far side of town.*

far² /fɑː(r)/ *adverb* (**farther** /ˈfɑːðə(r)/ or **further** /ˈfɜːðə(r)/, **farthest** /ˈfɑːðɪst/ or **furthest** /ˈfɜːðɪst/)
1 a long way: *My house isn't far from the station.* ◇ *It's too far to drive in one day.* ◇ *I walked much farther than you.*
2 You use 'far' to ask about the distance

from one place to another place: *How far is it to Liverpool from here?* ✪ We usually use 'far' only in questions and negative sentences, and after 'too' and 'so'. In other sentences we use **a long way**: *It's a long way to walk – let's take the bus.*
3 very much: *He's far taller than his brother.* ◇ *That's far too expensive.*
as far as to a place: *We walked as far as the village and then came back.*
as far as I know words that you use when you think something is true but you are not certain: *As far as I know, she's well, but I haven't seen her for a long time.*
by far You use 'by far' to show that a person or thing is much better, bigger, etc than anybody or anything else: *She's by far the best player in the team.*
far apart If two things or people are far apart, they are a long way from each other: *I don't see him very often because we live too far apart.*
far from not at all: *I'm far from certain.*
so far until now: *So far the work has been easy.*

fare /feə(r)/ *noun*
the money that you pay to travel by bus, train, plane, etc: *How much is the train fare to Manchester?*

farewell /ˌfeə'wel/ *noun*
saying goodbye: *We are having a farewell party for Mike because he is going to live in Australia.*

farm /fɑːm/ *noun*
land and buildings where people keep animals and grow crops: *They work on a farm.* ◇ *farm animals*
farm *verb* (**farms**, **farming**, **farmed** /fɑːmd/)
He's farming in Scotland.
farmer *noun*
a person who owns or looks after a farm
farmhouse /'fɑːmhaʊs/ *noun*
the house on a farm where the farmer lives
farmyard /'fɑːmjɑːd/ *noun*
the outside space near a farmhouse. A farmyard has buildings or walls around it.

farther, farthest *forms of* **far**

fascinating /'fæsɪneɪtɪŋ/ *adjective*
very interesting: *She told us fascinating stories about her journey through Africa.*

fashion /'fæʃn/ *noun*
1 a way of dressing or doing something

that people like and try to copy for a short time: *In the 1960s it was the fashion for women to wear very short skirts.*
2 the way you do something: *He spoke in a very strange fashion.*
in fashion If something is in fashion, people like it at the moment: *Long hair is coming into fashion again.*
out of fashion If something is out of fashion, people do not like it at the moment: *Bright colours have gone out of fashion.*
fashionable /'fæʃnəbl/ *adjective*
in the newest fashion: *She was wearing a fashionable black hat.* ✪ opposite: **unfashionable** or **old-fashioned**
fashionably /'fæʃnəbli/ *adverb*
He was fashionably dressed.

fashion designer /'fæʃn dɪzaɪnə(r)/ *noun*
a person whose job is to design clothes

fast¹ /fɑːst/ *adjective* (**faster**, **fastest**)
1 A person or thing that is fast can move quickly: *a fast car*
2 If a clock or watch is fast, it shows a time that is later than the real time: *My watch is five minutes fast.*
✪ opposite: **slow**
fast food /ˌfɑːst 'fuːd/ *noun* (no plural)
food like hamburgers and chips that can be cooked and eaten quickly

fast² /fɑːst/ *adverb* (**faster**, **fastest**)
quickly: *Don't talk so fast – I can't understand what you're saying.* ✪ opposite: **slowly**
fast asleep sleeping very well: *The baby was fast asleep.*

fast³ /fɑːst/ *verb* (**fasts**, **fasting**, **fasted**)
not eat food for a certain time: *Muslims fast during Ramadan.*

fasten /'fɑːsn/ *verb* (**fastens**, **fastening**, **fastened** /'fɑːsnd/)
1 close something so that it will not come open: *Please fasten your seat-belts.* ◇ *Can you fasten this suitcase for me?*
2 join one thing to another thing: *Fasten this badge to your jacket.*

fat¹ /fæt/ *adjective* (**fatter**, **fattest**)
with a large round body: *You'll get fat if you eat too much chocolate.* ✪ opposite: **thin** ☞ picture on page 262

fat² /fæt/ *noun*
1 (no plural) the oily substance under the

skins of animals and people: *Cut the fat off the meat.*
2 (*plural* **fats**) oil that you use for cooking: *Heat some fat in a frying-pan.*

fatal /ˈfeɪtl/ *adjective*
1 Something that is fatal causes death: *a fatal car accident*
2 Something that is fatal has very bad results: *I made the fatal mistake of signing a paper I had not read properly.*
fatally /ˈfeɪtəli/ *adverb*
She was fatally injured in the crash.

fate /feɪt/ *noun*
1 (no plural) the power that some people believe controls everything that happens
2 (*plural* **fates**) what will happen to somebody or something: *What will be the fate of the prisoners?*

father /ˈfɑːðə(r)/ *noun*
a man who has a child: *Where do your mother and father live?* ☞ picture on page 127 ☞ Look at **dad** and **daddy**.
Father Christmas /ˌfɑːðə ˈkrɪsməs/ *noun*
an old man with a red coat and a long white beard. Children believe that he brings presents at Christmas.

father-in-law /ˈfɑːðər ɪn lɔː/ *noun*
(*plural* **fathers-in-law**)
the father of your husband or wife ☞ picture on page 127

faucet /ˈfɔːsɪt/ *American English for* **tap¹**

fault /fɔːlt/ *noun*
1 (no plural) If something bad is your fault, you made it happen: *It's Sophie's fault that we are late.*
2 (*plural* **faults**) something that is wrong or bad in a person or thing: *There is a serious fault in the machine.*
faulty *adjective*
not working well: *This light doesn't work – the switch is faulty.*

favor *American English for* **favour**

favorite *American English for* **favourite**

favour /ˈfeɪvə(r)/ *noun*
something that you do to help somebody: *Would you do me a favour and open the door?* ◇ *Could I ask you a favour – will you take me to the station this evening?*
be in favour of something like or agree with something: *Are you in favour of higher taxes on cigarettes?*

favourite /ˈfeɪvərɪt/ *adjective*
Your favourite person or thing is the one that you like more than any other: *What's your favourite food?*
favourite *noun*
a person or thing that you like more than any other: *I like all chocolates but these are my favourites.*

fax /fæks/ *verb* (**faxes, faxing, faxed** /fækst/)
send a copy of something like a letter or picture using telephone lines and a machine called a **fax machine**: *The drawings were faxed from New York.*
fax *noun* (*plural* **faxes**)
a copy of something that is sent by a fax machine

fear /fɪə(r)/ *noun*
the feeling that you have when you think that something bad might happen: *I have a terrible fear of dogs.*
fear *verb* (**fears, fearing, feared** /fɪəd/)
1 be afraid of somebody or something: *We all fear illness and death.*
2 feel that something bad might happen: *I fear we will be late.*
● It is more usual to say **be afraid (of)** or **be frightened (of)**.

feast /fiːst/ *noun*
a large special meal for a lot of people: *a wedding feast*

feat /fiːt/ *noun*
something you do that is clever, difficult or dangerous: *Climbing Mount Everest was an amazing feat.*

feather /ˈfeðə(r)/ *noun*
Birds have feathers on their bodies to keep them warm and to help them fly.

feather

feature /ˈfiːtʃə(r)/ *noun*
1 an important part of something: *Pictures are a feature of this dictionary.*
2 features (plural) the parts of the face, for example the eyes, nose or mouth
3 an important piece of writing in a magazine or newspaper, or a programme on TV: *The magazine has a special feature on Paris on the centre pages.*

February /ˈfebruəri/ *noun*
the second month of the year

fed *form of* **feed**

fed up /ˌfed ˈʌp/ *adjective*
unhappy or bored because you have had or done too much of something: *I'm fed up with watching TV – let's go out.*

federal /ˈfedərəl/ *adjective*
A federal country has several smaller countries or states that are joined together: *the Federal Government of the United States*

federation /ˌfedəˈreɪʃn/ *noun*
a group of states or companies that work together

fee /fiː/ *noun*
1 money that you pay to somebody for special work: *The lawyer's fee was £200.*
2 money that you pay to do something, for example to join a club: *How much is the entrance fee?*
3 fees (plural) the money that you pay for lessons at school, college or university: *Who pays your college fees?*

feeble /ˈfiːbl/ *adjective* (**feebler, feeblest**)
not strong; weak: *a feeble old man*

feed /fiːd/ *verb* (**feeds, feeding, fed** /fed/, **has fed**)
give food to a person or an animal: *The baby's crying – I'll go and feed her.*

feel /fiːl/ *verb* (**feels, feeling, felt** /felt/, **has felt**)
1 know something because your body tells you: *How do you feel? ◇ I don't feel well. ◇ I'm feeling tired. ◇ He felt somebody touch his arm.*
2 be rough, smooth, wet, dry, etc when you touch it: *The water felt cold. ◇ This towel feels wet – can I have a dry one?*
3 think; believe: *I feel that we should talk about this.*
4 touch something to learn about it: *Feel this wool – it's really soft.*

feel for something If you feel for something, you try to get something you cannot see with your hands: *She felt in her pocket for some matches.*

feel like want something: *Do you feel like a cup of tea? ◇ I don't feel like going out tonight.*

feeling /ˈfiːlɪŋ/ *noun*
1 (plural **feelings**) something that you feel inside yourself, like happiness or anger: *a feeling of sadness*
2 (no plural) the ability to feel in your body: *I was so cold that I had no feeling in my feet.*
3 (plural **feelings**) an idea that you are not certain about: *I have a feeling that she isn't telling the truth.*

hurt somebody's feelings do or say something that makes somebody sad: *Don't tell him you don't like his shirt – you'll hurt his feelings.*

feet *plural of* **foot**

fell *form of* **fall**¹

fellow¹ /ˈfeləʊ/ *noun*
a man: *What is that fellow doing?*

fellow² /ˈfeləʊ/ *adjective*
a word that you use to talk about people who are the same as you: *She doesn't know many of her fellow students.*

felt *form of* **feel**

felt-pen /ˌfelt ˈpen/, **felt-tip pen** /ˌfelt tɪp ˈpen/ *noun*
a pen with a soft point

female /ˈfiːmeɪl/ *adjective*
A female animal or person belongs to the sex that can have babies.
female *noun*
My cat is a female.
☞ Look at **male**.

feminine /ˈfemənɪn/ *adjective*
of or like a woman; right for a woman: *feminine clothes* ☞ Look at **masculine**.

fence

fence /fens/ *noun*
a thing like a wall that is made of pieces of wood or metal. Fences are put round gardens and fields.

ferocious /fəˈrəʊʃəs/ *adjective*
very fierce and wild: *A rhinoceros is a ferocious animal.*

ferry /ˈferi/ *noun* (plural **ferries**)
a boat that takes people or things on short journeys across a river or sea: *We travelled to France by ferry.*

fertile /ˈfɜːtaɪl/ *adjective*
where plants grow well: *fertile soil* ✪ opposite: **infertile**

Prepositions 1

Prepositions of place

The lamp is **above** the table.

The meat is **on** the table.

The cat is **under** the table.

The bird is **in/inside** the cage.

The temperature is **below** zero.

The lorry is **in front of** the car.

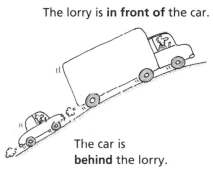

The car is **behind** the lorry.

Sam is **between** Tom and Kim.

Kim is **next to/beside** Sam.

The girl is leaning **against** the wall.

Kim is **opposite** Tom.

The house is **among** the trees.

The Human Body

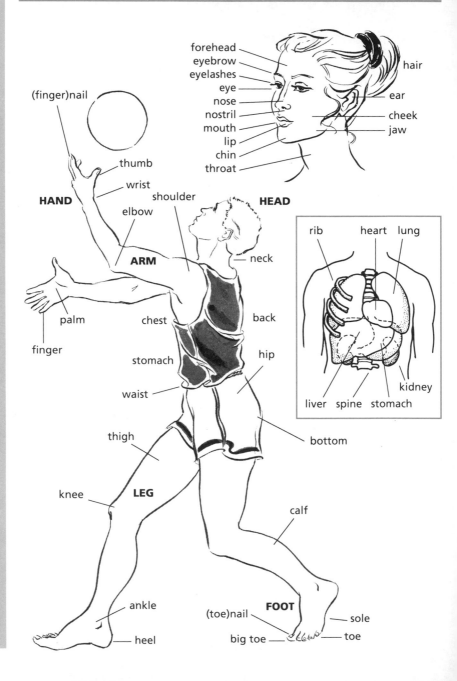

forehead
eyebrow
eyelashes
eye
nose
nostril
mouth
lip
chin
throat

hair
ear
cheek
jaw

(finger)nail

thumb
wrist

HAND

shoulder
elbow

HEAD

neck

ARM

palm
finger

chest

back

stomach

hip

waist

rib   heart   lung

liver   spine   stomach

kidney

thigh

bottom

knee

LEG

calf

ankle

heel

FOOT

(toe)nail

big toe

sole
toe

The Family

GRANDPARENTS

grandmother grandfather

This is Sarah's family. The people in the pictures are Sarah's **relations**.

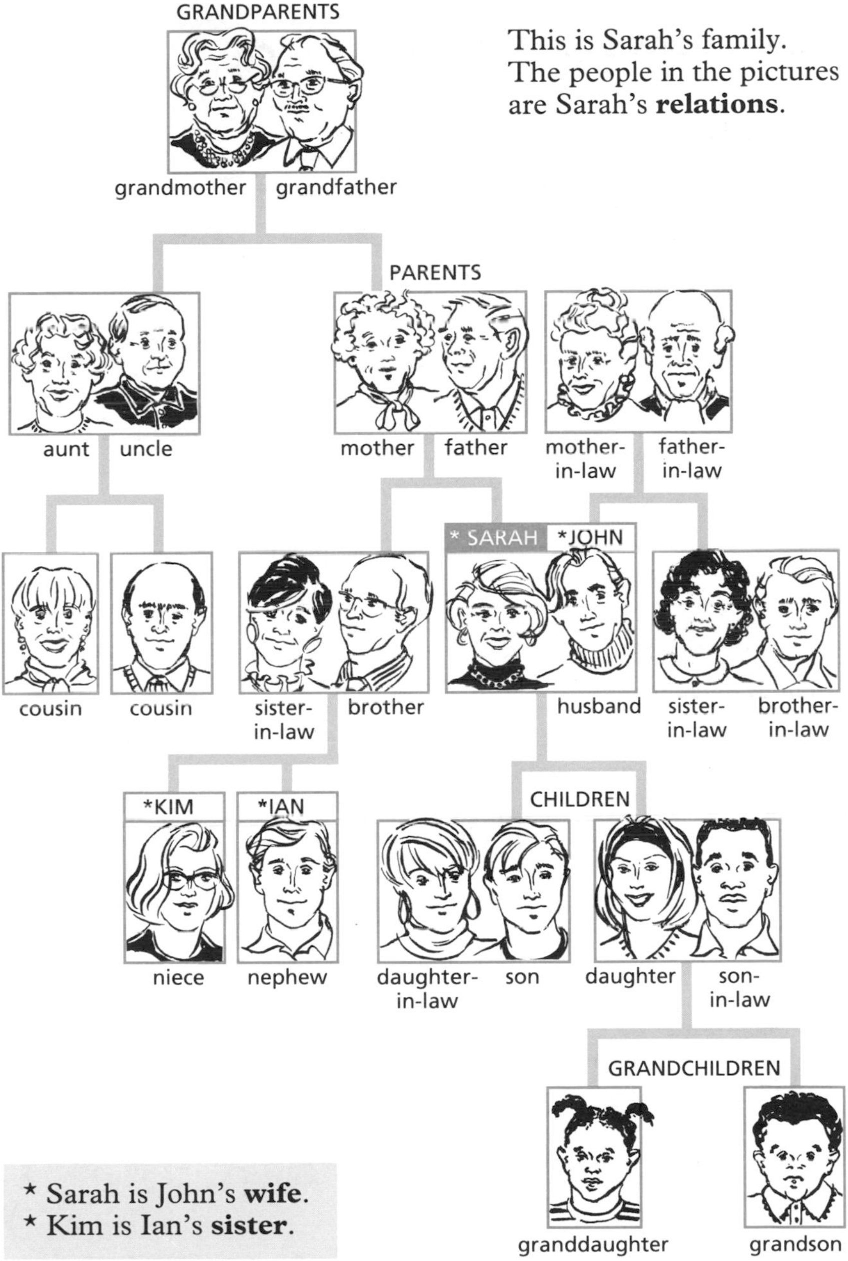

PARENTS

aunt uncle

mother father

mother-in-law father-in-law

* SARAH *JOHN

cousin cousin

sister-in-law brother

husband

sister-in-law brother-in-law

*KIM *IAN

niece nephew

CHILDREN

daughter-in-law son

daughter son-in-law

GRANDCHILDREN

granddaughter grandson

★ Sarah is John's **wife**.
★ Kim is Ian's **sister**.

Prepositions 2

Prepositions of movement

up the ladder

along the pole

down the slide

into the pool

across the pool

out of the pool

FINISH

towards the finish

through the tunnel

over the wall

round the track

fertilizer /'fɜːtəlaɪzə(r)/ *noun*
food for plants

festival /'festɪvl/ *noun*
1 a time when people do special things because they are happy about something: *Christmas is an important Christian festival.*
2 a time when there are a lot of plays, concerts, etc in one place: *the Cannes Film Festival*

fetch /fetʃ/ *verb* (**fetches, fetching, fetched** /fetʃt/)
1 go and bring back somebody or something: *Can you fetch me the books from the cupboard?* ◇ *I went to fetch Andy from the station.* ☞ picture at **bring**
2 If something fetches a certain price, somebody pays this price for it: *The house fetched £50 000.*

fête /feɪt/ *noun*
a party outside where you can buy things and play games to win prizes. Schools and churches often have fêtes to get money: *the summer fête*

fever /'fiːvə(r)/ *noun*
If you have a fever, your body is too hot because you are ill.
feverish /'fiːvərɪʃ/ *adjective*
If you are feverish, your body is too hot because you are ill.

few /fjuː/ *adjective, pronoun* (**fewer, fewest**)
not many: *Few people live to the age of 100.* ◇ *There are fewer buses in the evenings.*
a few some but not many: *Only a few people came to the meeting.* ◇ *She has written a lot of books, but I have only read a few of them.*

fiancé /fi'ɒnseɪ/ *noun*
A woman's fiancé is the man she is going to marry: *Can I introduce my fiancé, David? We've just got engaged.*
fiancée /fi'ɒnseɪ/ *noun*
A man's fiancée is the woman he is going to marry.

fib /fɪb/ *noun*
something you say that you know is not true; a small lie: *Don't tell fibs!*
fib *verb* (**fibs, fibbing, fibbed** /fɪbd/)
I was fibbing when I said I liked her hat.
fibber *noun*
a person who tells fibs

fiction /'fɪkʃn/ *noun* (no plural)
stories that somebody writes and that are not true: *I enjoy reading fiction.*

fiddle /'fɪdl/ *verb* (**fiddles, fiddling, fiddled** /'fɪdld/)
touch something a lot with your fingers: *Stop fiddling with your pen and do some work!*

field /fiːld/ *noun*
1 a piece of land that has a fence or hedge around it. Fields are used for growing crops or keeping animals in.
2 one thing that you study: *Dr Smith is one of the most famous scientists in his field.*
3 a piece of land used for something special: *a sports field* ◇ *an airfield* (= a place where aeroplanes land and take off)
4 a place where people find oil, coal, gold, etc: *the oilfields of Texas* ◇ *a coalfield*

fierce /fɪəs/ *adjective* (**fiercer, fiercest**)
1 angry and wild: *a fierce dog*
2 very strong: *the fierce heat of the sun*

fifteen /ˌfɪf'tiːn/ *number*
15
fifteenth /ˌfɪf'tiːnθ/ *adjective, adverb, noun*
15th

fifth /fɪfθ/ *adjective, adverb, noun*
1 5th
2 one of five equal parts of something; ⅕

fifty /'fɪfti/ *number*
1 50
2 the fifties (plural) the numbers, years or temperature between 50 and 59: *He was born in the fifties* (= in the 1950s).
in your fifties between the ages of 50 and 59
fiftieth /'fɪftiəθ/ *adjective, adverb, noun*
50th

fig /fɪg/ *noun*
a soft sweet fruit that is full of small seeds

fight¹ /faɪt/ *verb* (**fights, fighting, fought** /fɔːt/, **has fought**)
1 When people fight, they try to hurt or kill each other using their hands, knives or guns: *What are the children fighting about?*
2 try very hard to stop something: *He fought against the illness for two years.*
3 talk in an angry way; argue
fight for something try very hard to

do or get something: *The workers are fighting for better pay.*

fighter *noun*
1 a person who fights as a sport
2 a small aeroplane that shoots other aeroplanes

fight² /faɪt/ *noun*
an act of fighting: *There was a fight outside the restaurant last night.*

figure /'fɪgə(r)/ *noun*
1 one of the symbols (0-9) that we use to show numbers: *Shall I write the numbers in words or figures?*
2 an amount or price: *What are our sales figures for Spain this year?*
3 the shape of a person's body: *She's got a good figure.*
4 a shape of a person that you cannot see clearly: *I saw a tall figure outside the window.*
5 figures (plural) working with numbers to find an answer; arithmetic: *I'm not very good at figures.*

figure of speech words that you use in an unusual way to make your meaning stronger: *I didn't really mean that she was mad – it was just a figure of speech.*

file

file¹ /faɪl/ *noun*
1 a box or cover for keeping papers in
2 a collection of information on a computer

file *verb* (**files, filing, filed** /faɪld/)
put papers into a file: *Can you file these letters, please?*

file² /faɪl/ *noun*
a tool with rough sides that you use for making things smooth: *a nail-file*

file *verb* (**files, filing, filed** /faɪld/)
make something smooth with a file: *She filed her nails.*

file³ /faɪl/ *verb* (**files, filing, filed** /faɪld/)
walk in a line, one behind the other: *The students filed into the classroom.*

in single file in a line with each person following the one in front: *The children walked into the hall in single file.*

fill /fɪl/ *verb* (**fills, filling, filled** /fɪld/)
1 make something full: *Can you fill this glass with water, please?*
2 become full: *His eyes filled with tears.*

fill in write facts or answers in the spaces that have been left for them: *She gave me a form and told me to fill it in.*

fill up become or make something completely full: *He filled up the tank with petrol.*

filling /'fɪlɪŋ/ *noun*
something that you put into a space or hole: *I've got three fillings in my teeth.*
◇ *What filling do you want in your sandwiches: cheese or ham?*

film¹ /fɪlm/ *noun*
1 moving pictures that you see at a cinema or on television: *There's a good film on at the cinema this week.*
2 the special thin plastic that you use in a camera for taking photographs: *I bought a roll of black and white film.*

film² /fɪlm/ *verb* (**films, filming, filmed** /fɪlmd/)
use a camera to make moving pictures of a story, news, etc: *A TV company are filming outside my house.*

filter /'fɪltə(r)/ *noun*
a thing used for holding back the solid parts in a liquid or gas: *a coffee filter*
filter *verb* (**filters, filtering, filtered** /'fɪltəd/)
You should filter the water before you drink it.

filthy /'fɪlθi/ *adjective* (**filthier, filthiest**)
very dirty: *Go and wash your hands. They're filthy!*

fin /fɪn/ *noun*
one of the thin flat parts on a fish that help it to swim ☞ *picture at* **fish**

final¹ /'faɪnl/ *adjective*
last; at the end: *The final word in this dictionary is 'zoom'.*

final² /'faɪnl/ *noun*
1 the last game in a competition to decide who wins
2 finals (plural) the last examinations that you take at university

finally /'faɪnəli/ adverb
1 after a long time; in the end: *After a long wait the bus finally arrived.*
2 You use 'finally' before saying the last thing in a list: *And finally, I would like to thank my parents for all their help.*

finance /'faɪnæns/ noun
1 (no plural) money; planning how to get, save and use money for a business, country, etc: *the French Minister of Finance*
2 **finances** (plural) the money you have that you can spend: *My finances aren't very good* (= I haven't got much money).
finance verb (**finances, financing, financed** /'faɪnænst/)
give money to pay for something: *The building was financed by the government.*

financial /faɪ'nænʃl/ adjective
of or about money: *financial problems*

find /faɪnd/ verb (**finds, finding, found** /faʊnd/, **has found**)
1 see or get something after looking or trying: *I can't find my glasses.* ◇ *She hasn't found a job yet.* ◇ *Has anybody found the answer to this question?*
2 see or get something that you did not expect: *I found some money in the street.* ◇ *I woke up and found myself in hospital.*
3 think or have an idea about something because you have felt, tried, seen it, etc: *I didn't find that book very interesting.* ◇ *He finds it difficult to sleep at night.*
find out discover something, for example by asking or studying: *Can you find out what time the train leaves?* ◇ *Has she found out that you broke the window?*

fine¹ /faɪn/ adjective (**finer, finest**)
1 well or happy: *'How are you?' 'Fine thanks. And you?'*
2 good enough; okay: *'Let's meet on Monday.' 'Fine.'* ◇ *'Do you want some more milk in your coffee?' 'No, that's fine.'*
3 beautiful or of good quality: *There's a fine view from the cathedral.* ◇ *This is one of Monet's finest paintings.*
4 (used about the weather) sunny; not raining: *I hope it stays fine for our picnic.*
5 in very thin pieces: *I've got very fine hair.* ○ opposite: **thick**
6 in very small pieces: *Salt is finer than sugar.* ○ opposite: **coarse**

fine² /faɪn/ noun
money that you must pay because you have done something wrong: *You'll get a fine if you park your car there.*
fine verb (**fines, fining, fined** /faɪnd/)
make somebody pay a fine: *I was fined £100 for speeding* (= driving too fast).

finger /'fɪŋgə(r)/ noun
one of the five parts at the end of each hand: *She wears a ring on her little* (= smallest) *finger.* ☞ picture on page 126
keep your fingers crossed hope that somebody or something will be successful: *I'll keep my fingers crossed for you in your exams.*

fingernail /'fɪŋgəneɪl/ noun
the hard part at the end of your finger ☞ picture on page 126

fingerprint /'fɪŋgəprɪnt/ noun
the mark that a finger makes when it touches something: *The police found his fingerprints on the gun.*

finish¹ /'fɪnɪʃ/ verb (**finishes, finishing, finished** /'fɪnɪʃt/)
1 stop happening: *School finishes at four o'clock.*
2 stop doing something; come to the end of something: *I finish work at half past five.* ◇ *Hurry up and finish your dinner!* ◇ *Have you finished cleaning your room?*
finish off do or eat the last part of something: *He finished off all the milk.*
finish with somebody or **something** not want or need somebody or something any more: *Can I read this book when you've finished with it?*

finish² /'fɪnɪʃ/ noun (plural **finishes**)
the last part of something; the end: *the finish of a race* ○ opposite: **start**

fir /fɜː(r)/, **fir-tree** /'fɜː triː/ noun
a tall tree with thin sharp leaves (called **needles**) that do not fall off in winter

fire¹ /'faɪə(r)/ noun
1 the heat and bright light that comes from burning things: *Many animals are afraid of fire.* ◇ *There was a big fire at the factory last night.*
2 burning wood or coal that you use for keeping a place warm or for cooking: *They lit a fire to keep warm.*
3 a thing that uses electricity or gas to keep a room warm: *Switch on the fire.*

p	b	t	d	k	g	tʃ	dʒ	f	v	θ	ð
pen	**b**ad	**t**ea	**d**id	**c**at	**g**ot	**ch**ain	**j**am	**f**all	**v**an	**th**in	**th**is

catch fire start to burn: *She dropped her cigarette and the chair caught fire.*
on fire burning: *My house is on fire!*
put out a fire stop something from burning: *We put out the fire with buckets of water.*
set fire to something, set something on fire make something start to burn: *Somebody set the house on fire.*

fire² /ˈfaɪə(r)/ *verb* (**fires, firing, fired** /ˈfaɪəd/)
1 shoot with a gun: *The soldiers fired at the enemy.*
2 tell somebody to leave their job: *He was fired because he was always late for work.*

fire-alarm /ˈfaɪər əlɑːm/ *noun*
a bell that rings to tell people that there is a fire

fire brigade /ˈfaɪə brɪˌɡeɪd/ *noun*
a group of people whose job is to stop fires: *Call the fire brigade!*

fire-engine /ˈfaɪər endʒɪn/ *noun*
a vehicle that takes people and equipment to stop fires

fire-escape /ˈfaɪər ɪskeɪp/ *noun*
stairs on the outside of a building where people can leave quickly when there is a fire inside

fire extinguisher /ˈfaɪər ɪkˌstɪŋɡwɪʃə(r)/ *noun*
a metal container full of chemicals for stopping a fire

fireman /ˈfaɪəmən/ (*plural* **firemen** /ˈfaɪəmən/), **fire-fighter** /ˈfaɪə faɪtə(r)/ *noun*
a person whose job is to stop fires

fireplace /ˈfaɪəpleɪs/ *noun*
the place in a room where you can have a fire to make the room warm

fire station /ˈfaɪə steɪʃn/ *noun*
a building where fire-engines are kept

firework /ˈfaɪəwɜːk/ *noun*
a container with special powder in it that sends out coloured lights and smoke or makes a loud noise when you burn it: *We watched a firework display in the park.*

firm¹ /fɜːm/ *adjective* (**firmer, firmest**)
1 Something that is firm is quite hard or does not move easily: *Wait until the glue is firm.* ◇ *The shelf isn't very firm, so don't put too many books on it.*
2 showing that you will not change your ideas: *She's very firm with her children (=*

she makes them do what she wants). ◇ *a firm promise*
firmly *adverb*
Nail the pieces of wood together firmly.

firm² /fɜːm/ *noun*
a group of people working together in a business; a company: *My father works for a building firm.*

first¹ /fɜːst/ *adjective*
before all the others: *January is the first month of the year.*
firstly *adverb*
a word that you use when you are giving the first thing in a list: *We were angry firstly because he didn't come, and secondly because he didn't telephone.*

first² /fɜːst/ *adverb*
1 before all the others: *I arrived at the house first.*
2 for the first time: *I first met Paul in 1986.*
3 before doing anything else: *First fry the onions, then add the potatoes.*
at first at the beginning: *At first she was afraid of the water, but she soon learned to swim.*
first of all before anything else: *I'm going to cook dinner, but first of all I need to buy some food.*

first³ /fɜːst/ *noun* (no plural)
a person or thing that comes earliest or before all others: *I was the first to arrive at the party.* ◇ *Today is the first of May (May 1st).*

first aid /ˌfɜːst ˈeɪd/ *noun* (no plural)
quick simple help that you give to a person who is hurt, before a doctor comes

first class /ˌfɜːst ˈklɑːs/ *noun* (no plural)
1 the part of a train, plane, etc that it is more expensive to travel in: *I got a seat in first class.*
2 the fastest, most expensive way of sending letters
first-class /ˌfɜːst ˈklɑːs/ *adjective, adverb*
a first-class stamp ◇ *It costs more to travel first-class.*
☞ Look at **second class** and at the Note at **stamp**.

first name /ˈfɜːst neɪm/ *noun*
the name that your parents choose for you

s	z	ʃ	ʒ	h	m	n	ŋ	l	r	j	w
so	**zoo**	**shoe**	vision	**hat**	**man**	**no**	sing	**leg**	**red**	**yes**	**wet**

when you are born: *'What is Mr Carter's first name?' 'Paul.'* ☞ Note at **name**

fin — fish

tail

fish¹ /fɪʃ/ *noun* (*plural* **fish** or **fishes**)
an animal that lives and breathes in water and uses its fins and tail for swimming: *I caught a big fish.* ◇ *We had fish and chips for dinner.*

fish² /fɪʃ/ *verb* (**fishes, fishing, fished** /fɪʃt/)
try to catch fish ✪ When you talk about spending time fishing as a sport, you often say **go fishing**: *I go fishing at weekends.*
fishing *noun* (no plural)
catching fish

fisherman /'fɪʃəmən/ *noun* (*plural* **fishermen** /'fɪʃəmən/)
a person who catches fish as a job or sport

fist /fɪst/ *noun*
a hand with the fingers closed tightly: *She banged on the door with her fist.*

fit¹ /fɪt/ *adjective* (**fitter, fittest**)
1 healthy and strong: *I keep fit by going swimming every morning.*
2 good enough; right: *This food isn't fit to eat* ◇ *Do you think she's fit for the job?*
✪ opposite: **unfit**
fitness /'fɪtnəs/ *noun* (no plural)
being healthy and strong

fit² /fɪt/ *verb* (**fits, fitting, fitted**)
1 be the right size and shape for somebody or something: *These jeans don't fit me – they're too tight.* ◇ *This key doesn't fit the lock.*
2 put something in the right place: *Can you fit these pieces of the puzzle together?*
fit in 1 have space for somebody or something: *I can only fit five people in the car.*
2 have time to do something or see somebody: *The doctor can fit you in at 10.30.*

fit³ /fɪt/ *noun*
1 a sudden illness
2 doing something suddenly that you cannot stop: *He was so funny – we were in fits of laughter.* ◇ *I had a coughing fit.*

five /faɪv/ *number*
5

fix /fɪks/ *verb* (**fixes, fixing, fixed** /fɪkst/)
1 put something in a place so that it will not move: *We fixed the shelf to the wall.*
2 repair something: *The light isn't working – can you fix it?*
3 decide something; make a plan for something: *They've fixed a date for the wedding.* ◇ *Have you fixed up your holiday yet?*
fixed *adjective*
Something that is fixed does not change or move: *a fixed price*

fizz /fɪz/ *verb* (**fizzes, fizzing, fizzed** /fɪzd/)
If a drink fizzes, it makes a lot of small bubbles.
fizzy *adjective* (**fizzier, fizziest**)
Do you like fizzy drinks?

flag /flæg/ *noun*
a piece of cloth with a special pattern on it joined to a stick (called a **flagpole**). Every country has its own flag.

flag

flake /fleɪk/ *noun*
a small thin piece of something: *snowflakes* ◇ *Flakes of paint were coming off the wall.*
flake *verb* (**flakes, flaking, flaked** /fleɪkt/)
Paint was flaking off the wall.

flame /fleɪm/ *noun*
a hot bright pointed piece of fire ☞ picture at **candle**
in flames burning: *The house was in flames.*

flap¹ /flæp/ *noun*
a flat piece of something that hangs down, for example to cover an opening. A flap is joined to something by one side: *the flap of an envelope*

flap² /flæp/ *verb* (**flaps, flapping, flapped** /flæpt/)
move quickly up and down or from side to side: *Birds flap their wings when they fly.* ◇ *The sails of the boat flapped in the wind.*

flare /fleə(r)/ *verb* (**flares, flaring, flared** /fleəd/)
flare up If a fire flares up, it suddenly burns more brightly or strongly.

flash¹ /flæʃ/ *verb* (**flashes, flashing, flashed** /flæʃt/)
1 send out a bright light that comes and

goes quickly: *The disco lights flashed on and off.*
2 make something send out a sudden bright light: *She flashed a torch into the dark room.*
3 come and go very quickly: *I saw something flash past the window.*

flash² /flæʃ/ *noun* (*plural* **flashes**)
1 a bright light that comes and goes quickly: *a flash of lightning*
2 a bright light that you use with a camera for taking photographs
in a flash very quickly: *Wait for me – I'll be back in a flash.*

flashlight /'flæʃlaɪt/ *American English for* **torch**

flat¹ /flæt/ *noun*
a group of rooms for living in. A flat is usually on one floor of a house or big building.
❍ A tall building with a lot of flats in it is called a **block of flats**.

flat² /flæt/ *adjective* (**flatter**, **flattest**)
1 smooth, with no parts that are higher or lower than the rest: *The countryside in Holland is very flat.* ◇ *A table has a flat top.*
2 A tyre that is flat does not have enough air inside it.
flat *adverb*
with no parts that are higher or lower than the rest: *He lay flat on his back on the floor.*

flatten /'flætn/ *verb* (**flattens**, **flattening**, **flattened** /'flætnd/)
make something flat: *I sat on the box and flattened it.*

flatter /'flætə(r)/ *verb* (**flatters**, **flattering**, **flattered** /'flætəd/)
1 try to please somebody by saying too many nice things about them that are not completely true
2 If you are flattered by something, you like it because it makes you feel important: *I felt flattered when she asked for my advice.*
flattery /'flætəri/ *noun* (no plural)
saying too many nice things about somebody to please them

flavor *American English for* **flavour**

flavour /'fleɪvə(r)/ *noun*
the taste of food: *They sell 20 different flavours of ice-cream.*

flavour *verb* (**flavours**, **flavouring**, **flavoured** /'fleɪvəd/)
chocolate-flavoured milk

flea /fliː/ *noun*
a very small insect without wings that can jump and that lives on and bites animals and people: *Our cat has got fleas.*

flee /fliː/ *verb* (**flees**, **fleeing**, **fled** /fled/, **has fled**)
run away from something bad or dangerous: *During the war, thousands of people fled the country.*

fleet /fliːt/ *noun*
a big group of ships

flesh /fleʃ/ *noun* (no plural)
the soft part of your body under your skin
❍ The flesh of an animal that we eat is called **meat**.

flew *form of* **fly²**

flex /fleks/ *noun* (*plural* **flexes**)
a long piece of wire covered with plastic that brings electricity to things like lamps, irons, etc

flexible /'fleksəbl/ *adjective*
1 that can bend easily without breaking
2 that can change easily: *It's not important to me when we go – my plans are quite flexible.*

flies
1 *plural of* **fly¹**
2 *form of* **fly²**

flight /flaɪt/ *noun*
1 (*plural* **flights**) a journey in an aeroplane: *Our flight from New York leaves at 10 a.m.* ◇ *a direct flight from London to San Francisco*
2 (no plural) flying: *Have you ever seen an eagle in flight?*
flight of stairs /ˌflaɪt əv 'steəz/ *noun*
a group of steps

fling /flɪŋ/ *verb* (**flings**, **flinging**, **flung** /flʌŋ/, **has flung**)
throw something strongly or without care: *She flung a book and it hit me.*

flirt /flɜːt/ *verb* (**flirts**, **flirting**, **flirted**)
show somebody that you like them in a sexual way: *Who was that boy she was flirting with at the party?*
flirt *noun*
a person who flirts a lot

float /fləʊt/ *verb* (**floats, floating, floated**)
1 stay on top of a liquid: *Wood floats on water.* ☞ Look at **sink**.
2 move slowly in the air: *Clouds were floating across the sky.*

flock /flɒk/ *noun*
a group of birds, sheep or goats: *a flock of seagulls*

flood /flʌd/ *noun*
1 When there is a flood, a lot of water covers the land: *Many homes were destroyed in the flood.*
2 a lot of something: *My dad had a flood of cards when he was in hospital.*
flood *verb* (**floods, flooding, flooded**)
A pipe burst and flooded the kitchen.

floor /flɔː(r)/ *noun*
1 the part of a room that you walk on: *There weren't any chairs so we sat on the floor.*
2 all the rooms at the same height in a building: *I live on the top floor.* ◇ *Our hotel room was on the sixth floor.* ☞ picture at **house**
○ The part of a building that is on the same level as the street is called the **ground floor** in British English and the **first floor** in American English.

floppy disk /ˌflɒpi 'dɪsk/ *noun*
a small flat piece of plastic that stores information for a computer ☞ picture at **computer**

florist /'flɒrɪst/ *noun*
a person who sells flowers ○ A shop that sells flowers is called a **florist's**.

flour /'flaʊə(r)/ *noun* (no plural)
soft white or brown powder that we use to make bread, cakes, etc

flourish /'flʌrɪʃ/ *verb* (**flourishes, flourishing, flourished** /'flʌrɪʃt/)
1 grow well: *The garden flourished after all the rain.*
2 become strong or successful: *Their business is flourishing.*

flow /fləʊ/ *verb* (**flows, flowing, flowed** /fləʊd/)
move along like a river: *This river flows into the North Sea.*
flow *noun* (no plural)
I used a handkerchief to stop the flow of blood.

flower /'flaʊə(r)/ *noun*
the brightly coloured part of a plant that comes before the seeds or fruit: *She gave me a bunch of flowers.* ☞ picture at **plant**
flowery /'flaʊəri/, **flowered** /'flaʊəd/ *adjective*
with a pattern of flowers on it: *a flowery dress*

flown *form of* **fly²**

flu /fluː/ *noun* (no plural)
an illness like a bad cold that makes you ache and feel very hot: *I think I've got flu.*

fluent /'fluːənt/ *adjective*
1 able to speak easily and correctly: *Ramon is fluent in English and French.*
2 spoken easily and correctly: *fluent German*
fluently *adverb*
She speaks five languages fluently.

fluff /flʌf/ *noun* (no plural)
soft light stuff that comes off wool, animals, etc

fluid /'fluːɪd/ *noun*
anything that can flow; a liquid: *Water is a fluid.*

flung *form of* **fling**

flush /flʌʃ/ *verb* (**flushes, flushing, flushed** /flʌʃt/)
1 clean something by sending water through it: *Please flush the toilet.*
2 If you flush, your face becomes red: *He flushed with anger.*

flute

flute /fluːt/ *noun*
a musical instrument with holes, that you blow

fly¹ /flaɪ/ *noun*
(*plural* **flies**)
a small insect with two wings

fly² /flaɪ/ *verb*
(**flies, flying, flew** /fluː/, **has flown** /fləʊn/)

fly

1 move through the air: *In autumn some birds fly to warmer countries.*
2 make an aircraft move through the air: *A pilot is a person who flies an aircraft.*
3 travel in an aeroplane: *I'm flying to Brussels tomorrow.*
4 move quickly: *The door suddenly flew open and John came in.* ◇ *A stone came flying through the window.*

flying /ˈflaɪɪŋ/ *adjective*
able to fly: *flying insects*

flying saucer /ˌflaɪɪŋ ˈsɔːsə(r)/ *noun*
a flying object that some people think they have seen, and that may come from another planet

flyover /ˈflaɪəʊvə(r)/ *noun*
a bridge that carries a road over other roads

foal /fəʊl/ *noun*
a young horse

foam /fəʊm/ *noun* (no plural)
a lot of very small white bubbles that you see when you move liquid quickly

focus /ˈfəʊkəs/ *verb* (**focuses, focusing, focused** /ˈfəʊkəst/)
move parts of a camera, microscope, etc so that you can see things through it clearly
focus *noun* (no plural)
in focus If a photograph is in focus, it is clear.
out of focus If a photograph is out of focus, it is not clear: *Your face is out of focus in this photo.*

fog /fɒg/ *noun* (no plural)
thick cloudy air near the ground, that is difficult to see through: *The fog will clear by late morning.*
foggy *adjective* (**foggier, foggiest**)
a foggy day ◇ *It was very foggy this morning.*

foil /fɔɪl/ *noun* (no plural)
metal that is very thin like paper. Foil is used for covering food: *I wrapped the meat in foil and put it in the oven.*

fold¹ /fəʊld/ *verb* (**folds, folding, folded**)
1 (*also* **fold up**) bend something so that one part is on top of another part: *I folded the letter and put it in the envelope.* ◇ *Fold up your clothes.* ✪ opposite: **unfold**
2 If you fold your arms, you cross them in front of your chest.
folding *adjective*
that can be made flat: *a folding bed*

fold

fold² /fəʊld/ *noun*
a line that is made when you bend cloth or paper

folder /ˈfəʊldə(r)/ *noun*
a cover made of cardboard or plastic for keeping papers in

folk /fəʊk/ *noun* (plural)
people: *There are a lot of old folk living in this village.*

folk-dance /ˈfəʊk dɑːns/ *noun*
an old dance of the people of a particular place: *the folk-dances of Turkey*

folk-song /ˈfəʊk sɒŋ/ *noun*
an old song of the people of a particular place

follow /ˈfɒləʊ/ *verb* (**follows, following, followed** /ˈfɒləʊd/)
1 come or go after somebody or something: *Follow me and I'll show you the way.* ◇ *I think that car is following us!*
2 go along a road, path, etc: *Follow this road for about a mile and then turn right.*
3 do what somebody says you should do: *Did you follow my advice?*
4 understand something: *Has everyone followed the lesson so far?*
as follows as you will now hear or read: *The dates of the meetings will be as follows: 21 March, 3 April, 19 April.*

following /ˈfɒləʊɪŋ/ *adjective*
next: *I came back from holiday on Sunday and went to work on the following day.*

fond /fɒnd/ *adjective* (**fonder, fondest**)
be fond of somebody or **something**
like somebody or something a lot: *They are very fond of their uncle.*

food /fuːd/ *noun* (no plural)
People and animals eat food so that they can live and grow: *Let's go and get some*

food — I'm hungry. ◇ *They gave the horses food and water.*

fool[1] /fuːl/ *noun*
a person who is silly or who does something silly: *You fool! You forgot to lock the door!*
make a fool of somebody do something that makes somebody look silly: *He always makes a fool of himself at parties.*

fool[2] /fuːl/ *verb* (**fools, fooling, fooled** /fuːld/)
make somebody think something that is not true; trick somebody: *You can't fool me! I know you're lying!*
fool about, fool around do silly things: *Stop fooling about with that knife*

foolish /ˈfuːlɪʃ/ *adjective*
stupid; silly: *a foolish mistake*
foolishly *adverb*
I foolishly forgot to bring a coat.

foot /fʊt/ *noun*
1 (*plural* **feet** /fiːt/) the part of your leg that you stand on: *I've been walking all day and my feet hurt.* ☞ picture on page 126
2 (*plural* **foot** or **feet**) a measure of length (= 30.48 centimetres). There are twelve **inches** in a foot, and three feet in a **yard**: *'How tall are you?' 'Five foot six (= five feet and six inches).'* ◑ The short way of writing 'foot' is **ft**.
◑ In the past, people in Britain used **inches, feet, yards** and **miles** to measure distances, not **centimetres, metres** and **kilometres**. Now many people use and understand both ways.
3 the lowest part; the bottom: *She was standing at the foot of the stairs.*
on foot walking: *Shall we go by car or on foot?*
put your feet up rest: *If you're tired, put your feet up and listen to the radio.*
put your foot down say strongly that something must or must not happen: *My mum put her foot down when I asked if I could stay out all night.*

football /ˈfʊtbɔːl/ *noun*
1 (no plural) a game for two teams of eleven players who try to kick a ball into a **goal** on a field called a **pitch**: *He plays football for England.* ◇ *I'm going to a football match on Saturday.*

2 (*plural* **footballs**) a ball for playing this game
footballer *noun*
a person who plays football

footpath /ˈfʊtpɑːθ/ *noun*
a path in the country for people to walk on

footprint /ˈfʊtprɪnt/ *noun*
a mark that your foot or shoe makes on the ground

footstep /ˈfʊtstep/ *noun*
the sound of a person walking: *I heard footsteps, and then a knock on the door.*

for[1] /fə(r)/, /fɔː(r)/ *preposition*
1 a word that shows who will get or have something: *These flowers are for you.*
2 a word that shows how something is used or why something is done: *We had fish and chips for dinner.* ◇ *Take this medicine for your cold.* ◇ *He was sent to prison for murder.*
3 a word that shows how long: *She has lived here for 20 years.* ☞ Note at **since**
4 a word that shows how far: *We walked for miles.*
5 a word that shows where a person or thing is going: *Is this the train for Glasgow?*
6 a word that shows the person or thing you are talking about: *It's time for us to go.*
7 a word that shows how much something is: *I bought this book for £2.*
8 a word that shows that you like an idea: *Some people were for the strike and others were against it.*
9 on the side of somebody or something: *He plays football for Italy.*
10 with the meaning of: *What is the word for 'table' in German?*

for[2] /fə(r)/ *conjunction*
because: *She was crying, for she knew they could never meet again.* ◑ **Because** and **as** are the words that we usually use.

forbid /fəˈbɪd/ *verb* (**forbids, forbidding, forbade** /fəˈbæd/, **has forbidden** /fəˈbɪdn/)
say that somebody must not do something: *My parents have forbidden me to see him again.* ◇ *Smoking is forbidden (= not allowed) inside the building.*

force[1] /fɔːs/ *noun*
1 (no plural) power or strength: *He was killed by the force of the explosion.*
2 (*plural* **forces**) a group of people, for example police or soldiers, who do a special job: *the police force*
by force using a lot of strength, for example by pushing, pulling or hitting: *I lost the key so I had to open the door by force.*

force[2] /fɔːs/ *verb* (**forces**, **forcing**, **forced** /fɔːst/)
1 make somebody do something that they do not want to do: *They forced him to give them the money.*
2 do something by using a lot of strength: *The thief forced the window open.*

forecast /'fɔːkɑːst/ *noun*
what somebody thinks will happen: *The weather forecast said that it would snow today.*

foreground /'fɔːɡraʊnd/ *noun*
the part of a picture that seems nearest to you: *The man in the foreground is my father.* ✪ opposite: **background**

forehead /'fɔːhed/ *noun*
the part of your face above your eyes ☞ picture on page 126

foreign /'fɒrən/ *adjective*
of or from another country: *We've got some foreign students staying at our house.* ◇ *a foreign language*
foreigner *noun*
a person from another country ☞ Note at **stranger**

forest /'fɒrɪst/ *noun*
a big piece of land with a lot of trees: *We went for a walk in the forest.*

✪ A forest is larger than a **wood**. A **jungle** is a forest in a very hot country.

forever /fər'evə(r)/ *adverb*
1 for all time; always: *I will love you forever.*
2 very often: *I can't read because he is forever asking me questions!*

forgave *form of* **forgive**

forge /fɔːdʒ/ *verb* (**forges**, **forging**, **forged** /fɔːdʒd/)
make a copy of something because you want to trick people and make them think it is real: *He was put in prison for forging money.*

forgery /'fɔːdʒəri/ *noun*
1 (no plural) making a copy of something to trick people: *Forgery is a crime.*
2 (*plural* **forgeries**) a copy of something made to trick people: *This painting is not really by Picasso – it's a forgery.*

forget /fə'ɡet/ *verb* (**forgets**, **forgetting**, **forgot** /fə'ɡɒt/, **has forgotten** /fə'ɡɒtn/)
1 not remember something; not have something in your mind any more: *I've forgotten her name.* ◇ *Don't forget to feed the cat.*
2 not bring something with you: *I couldn't see the film very well because I had forgotten my glasses.*
3 stop thinking about something: *Forget about your exams and enjoy yourself!*

forgive /fə'ɡɪv/ *verb* (**forgives**, **forgiving**, **forgave** /fə'ɡeɪv/, **has forgiven** /fə'ɡɪvn/)
stop being angry with somebody for a bad thing that they did: *He never forgave me for forgetting his birthday.*

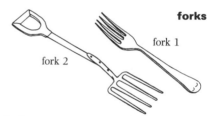

forks

fork 1

fork 2

fork /fɔːk/ *noun*
1 a thing with long points at one end, that you use for putting food in your mouth
2 a large tool with points at one end, that you use for digging the ground
3 a place where a road or river divides into two parts: *When you get to the fork in the road, go left.*

form[1] /fɔːm/ *noun*
1 a type of something: *Cars, trains and buses are all forms of transport.*
2 a piece of paper with spaces for you to answer questions: *You need to fill in this form to get a new passport.*
3 the shape of a person or thing: *For her birthday I made her a cake in the form of a cat.*
4 one of the ways you write or say a word: *'Forgot' is a form of 'forget'.*

5 a class in a school: *Which form are you in?*

form² /fɔːm/ *verb* (**forms, forming, formed** /fɔːmd/)
1 make something or give a shape to something: *We formed a line outside the cinema.* ◇ *In English we usually form the past tense by adding 'ed'.*
2 grow; take shape: *Ice forms when water freezes.*
3 start a group, etc: *They formed a club for French people living in London.*

formal /'fɔːml/ *adjective*
You use formal language or behave in a formal way at important or serious times and with people you do not know very well: *'Yours faithfully' is a formal way of ending a letter.* ◇ *I wore a suit and tie because it was a formal dinner.* ✪ opposite: **informal**
formally /'fɔːməli/ *adverb*
They were dressed too formally for a disco.

former /'fɔːmə(r)/ *adjective*
of a time before now: *the former Prime Minister, Mrs Thatcher*
former *noun* (no plural)
the first of two things or people: *I have visited both Budapest and Vienna, and I prefer the former.* ☞ Look at **latter**.

formerly /'fɔːməli/ *adverb*
before this time: *Sri Lanka was formerly called Ceylon.*

formula /'fɔːmjulə/ *noun* (*plural* **formulae** /'fɔːmjuliː/ or **formulas**)
1 a group of letters, numbers or symbols that show a rule in mathematics or science: *The formula for finding the area of a circle is πr^2.*
2 a list of the substances that you need to make something: *a formula for a new drug*

fort /fɔːt/ *noun*
a strong building that was made to protect a place against its enemies

fortieth /'fɔːtiəθ/ *adjective, adverb, noun*
40th

fortnight /'fɔːtnaɪt/ *noun*
two weeks: *I'm going on holiday for a fortnight.*
fortnightly *adjective, adverb*
We have fortnightly meetings.

fortress /'fɔːtrəs/ *noun* (*plural* **fortresses**)
a large strong building that was made to protect a place against its enemies

fortunate /'fɔːtʃənət/ *adjective*
lucky: *I was very fortunate to get the job.*
✪ opposite: **unfortunate**
fortunately *adverb*
There was an accident but fortunately nobody was hurt.

fortune /'fɔːtʃuːn/ *noun*
1 (no plural) things that happen that you cannot control; luck: *I had the good fortune to get the job.*
2 (*plural* **fortunes**) a lot of money: *He made a fortune selling old cars.*
tell somebody's fortune say what will happen to somebody in the future: *The old lady said she could tell my fortune by looking at my hand.*

forty /'fɔːti/ *number*
1 40
2 the forties (plural) the numbers, years or temperature between 40 and 49
in your forties between the ages of 40 and 49

forward¹ /'fɔːwəd/, **forwards** /'fɔːwədz/ *adverb*
1 in the direction that is in front of you: *Move forwards to the front of the train.*
✪ opposite: **backwards**
2 to a later time: *When you travel from London to Paris, you need to put your watch forward.*
look forward to something wait for something with pleasure: *We're looking forward to seeing you again.*

forward² /'fɔːwəd/ *verb* (**forwards, forwarding, forwarded**)
send a letter to somebody at their new address: *Could you forward all my post to me while I'm in Liverpool?*

✪ If you are writing to somebody who has moved to a new house but you do not know their address, you can write the old address and **please forward** on the envelope.

fossil /'fɒsl/ *noun*
a part of a dead plant or an animal that has been in the ground for a very long time and has become hard

fought *form of* **fight**

p	b	t	d	k	g	tʃ	dʒ	f	v	θ	ð
pen	**bad**	**tea**	**did**	**cat**	**got**	**chain**	**jam**	**fall**	**van**	**thin**	**this**

foul[1] /faʊl/ *adjective*
1 dirty, or with a bad smell or taste: *What a foul smell!*
2 very bad: *We had foul weather all week.*

foul[2] /faʊl/ *noun*
something you do that is against the rules of a game, for example football: *He was sent off the field for a foul on the goalkeeper.*
foul *verb* (**fouls, fouling, fouled** /faʊld/)
Johnson was fouled twice.

found[1] *form of* **find**

found[2] /faʊnd/ *verb* (**founds, founding, founded**)
start something, for example a school or business: *This school was founded in 1865.*
founder *noun*
a person who founds something

foundation /faʊn'deɪʃn/ *noun*
1 (no plural) starting a group, building, etc: *the foundation of a new school*
2 **foundations** (plural) the strong parts of a building which you build first under the ground

fountain
/'faʊntən/ *noun*
water that shoots up into the air and then falls down again. You often see fountains in gardens and parks.

fountain

fountain-pen
/'faʊntən pen/ *noun*
a pen that you fill with ink

four /fɔː(r)/ *number*
4
on all fours with your hands and knees on the ground: *We went through the tunnel on all fours.*
four-legged /,fɔː 'legɪd/ *adjective*
with four legs. A horse is a four-legged animal.

fourth /fɔːθ/ *adjective, adverb, noun*
4th

fourteen /,fɔː'tiːn/ *number*
14
fourteenth /,fɔː'tiːnθ/ *adjective, adverb, noun*
14th

fox /fɒks/ *noun* (*plural* **foxes**)
a wild animal that looks like a dog and has a long thick tail and red fur

fraction /'frækʃn/ *noun*
1 an exact part of a number: $1/4$ (= a quarter) *and* $1/3$ (= a third) *are fractions.*
2 a very small part of something: *For a fraction of a second I thought you were my sister.*

fracture /'fræktʃə(r)/ *verb* (**fractures, fracturing, fractured** /'fræktʃəd/)
break a bone in your body: *She fell and fractured her leg.*
fracture *noun*
a fracture of the arm

fragile /'frædʒaɪl/ *adjective*
A thing that is fragile breaks easily: *Be careful with those glasses. They're very fragile.*

fragment /'frægmənt/ *noun*
a very small piece that has broken off something: *The window broke and fragments of glass went everywhere.*

frail /freɪl/ *adjective* (**frailer, frailest**)
not strong or healthy: *a frail old woman*

frame[1] /freɪm/ *noun*
1 a thin piece of wood or metal round the edge of a picture, window, mirror, etc
2 strong pieces of wood or metal that give something its shape: *The frame of this bicycle was made in Britain and the wheels were made in Japan.*
frame of mind /,freɪm əv 'maɪnd/ *noun*
how you feel: *I'm not in the right frame of mind for a party.*

frame[2] /freɪm/ *verb* (**frames, framing, framed** /freɪmd/)
put a picture in a frame: *She had her daughter's photograph framed.*

framework /'freɪmwɜːk/ *noun*
the strong part of something that gives it shape: *The bridge has a steel framework.*

frank /fræŋk/ *adjective* (**franker, frankest**)
If you are frank, you say exactly what you think: *To be frank, I don't really like that shirt you're wearing.*
frankly *adverb*
Tell me frankly what you think of my work.

fraud /frɔːd/ *noun*
1 (no plural) doing things that are not

honest to get money: *Two of the company directors were sent to prison for fraud.*
2 (*plural* **frauds**) a person or thing that is not what he/she/it seems to be: *He said he was a police officer but I knew he was a fraud.*

freckles /'freklz/ *noun* (plural)
small light brown spots on a person's skin: *A lot of people with red hair have freckles.*

free¹ /fri:/ *adjective, adverb* (**freer, freest**)
1 If you are free, you can go where you want and do what you want: *After five years in prison she was finally free.*
2 If something is free, you do not have to pay for it: *We've got some free tickets for the concert.* ◇ *Children under five travel free on trains.*
3 not busy: *Are you free this afternoon?* ◇ *I don't have much free time.*
4 not being used: *Excuse me, is this seat free?*
5 not fixed: *Take the free end of the rope in your left hand.*
free from something, free of something without something bad: *It's nice to be on holiday, free from all your worries.*
set free let a person or animal go out of a prison or cage: *We set the bird free and it flew away.*

free² /fri:/ *verb* (**frees, freeing, freed** /fri:d/)
make somebody or something free: *He was freed after ten years in prison.*

freedom /'fri:dəm/ *noun* (no plural)
being free: *They gave their children too much freedom.*

freeway /'fri:weɪ/ *American English for* **motorway**

freeze /fri:z/ *verb* (**freezes, freezing, froze** /frəʊz/, **has frozen** /'frəʊzn/)
1 become hard because it is so cold. When water freezes, it becomes ice.
2 make food very cold so that it stays fresh for a long time: *frozen food*
3 stop suddenly and stay very still: *The cat froze when it saw the bird.*
freeze to death be so cold that you die

freezer /'fri:zə(r)/ *noun*
a big metal box for making food very cold, like ice, so that you can keep it for a long time

freezing /'fri:zɪŋ/ *adjective*
very cold: *Can you close the window? I'm freezing!*

freight /freɪt/ *noun* (no plural)
things that lorries, ships, trains and aeroplanes carry from one place to another: *a freight train*

French fries /ˌfrentʃ 'fraɪz/ *American English for* **chips**¹ **2**

frequent /'fri:kwənt/ *adjective*
Something that is frequent happens often: *How frequent are the buses to the airport?*
frequently *adverb*
often: *Simon is frequently late for school.*

fresh /freʃ/ *adjective* (**fresher, freshest**)
1 made or picked not long ago; not old: *I love the smell of fresh bread.* ◇ *These flowers are fresh – I picked them this morning.*
2 new or different: *fresh ideas*
3 not frozen or from a tin: *fresh fruit*
4 clean and cool: *Open the window and let some fresh air in.*
fresh water /ˌfreʃ 'wɔːtə/ *noun*
not sea water
freshly *adverb*
freshly baked bread

Friday /'fraɪdeɪ/ *noun*
the sixth day of the week, next after Thursday

fridge /frɪdʒ/ *noun*
a big metal box for keeping food and drink cold and fresh: *Is there any milk in the fridge?*

fried *form of* **fry**

friend /frend/ *noun*
a person that you like and know very well: *David is my best friend.* ◇ *We are very good friends.*
make friends with somebody become a friend of somebody: *Have you made friends with any of the students in your class?*

friendly /'frendli/ *adjective* (**friendlier, friendliest**)
A person who is friendly is kind and helpful: *My neighbours are very friendly.* � *opposite:* **unfriendly**
be friendly with somebody If you are friendly with somebody, he/she is your friend: *Jane is friendly with a girl who lives in the same street.*

i:	i	ɪ	e	æ	ɑ:	ɒ	ɔ:	ʊ	u	u:
see	happy	sit	ten	cat	father	got	saw	put	situation	too

friendship /'frendʃɪp/ *noun*
being friends with somebody

fries *form of* **fry**

fright /fraɪt/ *noun*
a sudden feeling of fear: *Why didn't you knock on the door before you came in? You gave me a fright!*

frighten /'fraɪtn/ *verb* (**frightens**, **frightening**, **frightened** /'fraɪtnd/)
make somebody feel afraid: *Sorry, did I frighten you?*
frightened *adjective*
If you are frightened, you are afraid of something: *He's frightened of spiders.*
frightening /'fraɪtnɪŋ/ *adjective*
Something that is frightening makes you feel afraid: *That was the most frightening film I have ever seen.*

fringe /frɪndʒ/ *noun*
1 the short hair that hangs down above your eyes ☞ picture at **hair**
2 threads that hang from the edge of a piece of material
3 the edge of a place: *We live on the fringes of town.*

fro /frəʊ/ *adverb*
to and fro first one way and then the other way, many times: *She travels to and fro between Oxford and London.*

frog /frɒg/ *noun*
a small animal that lives in and near water. Frogs have long back legs and they can jump.

frog

from /frəm/, /frɒm/ *preposition*
1 a word that shows where something starts: *We travelled from New York to Boston.*
2 a word that shows where somebody lives or was born: *I come from Spain.*
3 a word that shows when somebody or something starts: *The shop is open from 9.30 until 5.30.*
4 a word that shows who gave or sent something: *I had a letter from Lyn.* ◇ *I borrowed a dress from my sister.*
5 a word that shows the place where you find something: *He took the money from my bag.*
6 a word that shows how far away something is: *The house is two miles from the village.*
7 a word that shows how something

changes: *The sky changed from blue to grey.*
8 a word that shows the lowest number or price: *The tickets cost from £5 to £15.*
9 a word that shows what is used to make something: *Paper is made from wood.*
10 a word that shows difference: *My book is different from yours.*
11 a word that shows why: *Children are dying from this disease.*

front /frʌnt/ *noun*
the side or part of something that faces forwards and that you usually see first: *The book has a picture of a lion on the front.*
◇ *John and I sat in the front of the car and the children sat in the back.* ☞ picture at **back**
in front of somebody or **something**
1 further forward than another person or thing: *Alice was sitting in front of the television.* ☞ picture on page 125 **2** when other people are there: *Please don't talk about it in front of my parents.*
front *adjective*
the front door ◇ *the front seat of a car*

frontier /'frʌntɪə(r)/ *noun*
the line where one country joins another country

frost /frɒst/ *noun*
ice like white powder that covers the ground when the weather is very cold: *There was a frost last night.*
frosty *adjective* (**frostier**, **frostiest**)
a frosty morning

frown /fraʊn/ *verb* (**frowns**, **frowning**, **frowned** /fraʊnd/)
move your eyebrows together to make lines on your forehead. You frown when you are worried, angry or thinking hard: *John frowned at me when I came in. 'You're late,' he said.*
frown *noun*
She looked at me with a frown.

froze, frozen *forms of* **freeze**
frozen food /ˌfrəʊzn 'fuːd/ *noun* (no plural)
food that is very cold, like ice, when you buy it. You keep frozen food in a **freezer**.

fruit /fruːt/ *noun*
the part of a plant or tree that holds the seeds and that you can eat. Bananas, or-

ʌ	ɜː	ə	eɪ	əʊ	aɪ	aʊ	ɔɪ	ɪə	eə	ʊə
cup	**bird**	**about**	**say**	**go**	**five**	**now**	**boy**	**near**	**hair**	**pure**

anges and apples are kinds of fruit. ☼ Be careful! We do not usually say 'a fruit'. We say 'a piece of fruit' or 'some fruit ': *Would you like a piece of fruit?* ◇ *'Would you like some fruit?' 'Yes please − I'll have a pear.'*

frustrating /frʌ'streɪtɪŋ/ *adjective*
If something is frustrating, it makes you angry because you cannot do what you want to do: *It's very frustrating when you can't say what you mean in a foreign language.*

fry /fraɪ/ *verb* (**fries, frying, fried** /fraɪd/, **has fried**)
cook something or be cooked in hot oil: *Fry the onions in butter.* ◇ *fried eggs*
fry-pan /'fraɪ pæn/ *American English for* **frying-pan**
frying-pan
/'fraɪɪŋ pæn/ *noun*
a flat metal container with a long handle that you use for frying food

frying-pan

ft *short way of writing* **foot 2**

fuel /'fjuːəl/ *noun* (no plural)
anything that you burn to make heat or power. Wood, coal and oil are kinds of fuel.

fulfil /fʊl'fɪl/ *verb* (**fulfils, fulfilling, fulfilled** /fʊl'fɪld/)
do what you have planned or promised to do: *Jane fulfilled her dream of travelling around the world.*

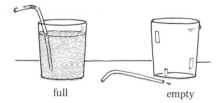

full   empty

full /fʊl/ *adjective* (**fuller, fullest**)
1 with a lot of people or things in it, so that there is no more space: *My glass is full.* ◇ *The bus was full so we waited for the next one.* ◇ *These socks are full of holes.*
2 complete; with nothing missing: *Please tell me the full story.*
3 as much, big, etc as possible: *The train was travelling at full speed.*
full up with no space for anything or any-

body else: *'Would you like anything else to eat?' 'No thank you, I'm full up.'*
in full completely; with nothing missing: *Please write your name in full.*

full stop /ˌfʊl 'stɒp/ *noun*
a mark (.) that you use in writing to show the end of a sentence, or after the short form of a word

full-time /ˌfʊl 'taɪm/ *adjective, adverb*
for all the normal working hours of the day or week: *My mother has a full-time job.* ◇ *Do you work full-time?* ☞ Look at **part-time.**

fully /'fʊli/ *adverb*
completely; totally: *'Do you have a room for tonight, please?' 'No, I'm sorry, we're fully booked.'*

fun /fʌn/ *noun* (no plural)
something that you enjoy; pleasure: *Skiing is fun if you like the snow.* ◇ *We had great fun at the Christmas party.* ◇ *Have fun!* (= enjoy yourself!)
for fun to enjoy yourself: *I don't need English for my work − I'm learning it just for fun.*
make fun of somebody laugh about somebody in an unkind way: *The other children make fun of him because he wears glasses.*

function /'fʌŋkʃn/
the special work that a person or thing does: *The function of the heart is to send blood round the body.*
function *verb* (**functions, functioning, functioned** /'fʌŋkʃnd/)
work. *The engine will not function without oil.*

fund /fʌnd/ *noun*
money that will be used for something special: *The money from the concert will go into a fund to help homeless people.*

fundamental /ˌfʌndə'mentl/ *adjective*
most important; basic: *You are making a fundamental mistake.*

funeral /'fjuːnərəl/ *noun*
the time when a dead person is buried or burned

funnel /'fʌnl/ *noun*
1 a tube that is wide at the top to help you pour things into bottles
2 a large pipe on a ship or railway engine that smoke comes out of

p	b	t	d	k	g	tʃ	dʒ	f	v	θ	ð
pen	**b**ad	**t**ea	**d**id	**c**at	**g**ot	**ch**ain	**j**am	**f**all	**v**an	**th**in	**th**is

funny /'fʌni/ *adjective* (**funnier, funniest**)
1 A person or thing that is funny makes you laugh or smile: *a funny story*
2 strange or surprising: *There's a funny smell in this room.*

fur /fɜː(r)/ *noun*
the soft thick hair on animals. Cats and rabbits have fur.
furry /'fɜːri/ *adjective* (**furrier, furriest**)
a furry animal

furious /'fjʊəriəs/ *adjective*
very angry: *My parents were furious with me when I came home late again.*

furnace /'fɜːnɪs/ *noun*
a very hot fire in a closed place, used for heating metals, making glass, etc

furnished /'fɜːnɪʃt/ *adjective*
with furniture already in it: *I live in a furnished flat.* ✪ opposite: **unfurnished**

furniture /'fɜːnɪtʃə(r)/ *noun* (no plural)
tables, chairs, beds, etc: *They've bought some furniture for their new house.* ◇ *All the furniture is very old.* ◇ *The only piece of furniture in the room was a large bed.*

further /'fɜːðə(r)/ *adjective, adverb*
1 more far: *Which is further – London or Birmingham?* ◇ *We couldn't go any further because the road was closed.*
2 more; extra: *Do you have any further questions?*
further education /ˌfɜːðər edʒuˈkeɪʃn/ *noun*
studying that you do after you leave school at the age of 16

furthest *form of* **far**

fuse /fjuːz/ *noun*
a small piece of wire that stops too much electricity going through something. Plugs usually have fuses in them.

fuss¹ /fʌs/ *noun* (no plural)
a lot of excitement or worry about small things that are not important: *He makes a fuss when I'm five minutes late.*
make a fuss of somebody be kind to somebody; do a lot of small things for somebody: *I like visiting my grandfather because he always makes a fuss of me.*
fussy *adjective* (**fussier, fussiest**)
A fussy person cares a lot about small things that are not important, and is difficult to please: *Rod is fussy about his food – he won't eat anything with onions in it.*

fuss² /fʌs/ *verb* (**fusses, fussing, fussed** /fʌst/)
worry and get excited about a lot of small things that are not important: *Stop fussing!*

future¹ /'fjuːtʃə(r)/ *noun*
1 the time that will come: *Nobody knows what will happen in the future.* ◇ *The company's future is uncertain.*
2 **the future** (no plural) the form of a verb that shows what will happen after now
in future after now: *You must work harder in future.*
☞ Look at **past** and **present**.

future² /'fjuːtʃə(r)/ *adjective*
of the time that will come: *Have you met John's future wife?*

Gg

g *short way of writing* **gram**

gadget /'gædʒɪt/ *noun*
a small machine or tool: *Their kitchen is full of electrical gadgets.*

gain /geɪn/ *verb* (**gains, gaining, gained** /geɪnd/)
1 get more of something: *She gained useful experience from her holiday job.* ◇ *I have gained a lot of weight.*
2 get what you want or need: *The police*

are trying to gain more information about the robbery.

galaxy /'gæləksi/ *noun* (*plural* **galaxies**)
a very large group of stars and planets

gale /geɪl/ *noun*
a very strong wind: *The trees were blown down in the gale.*

gallery /'gæləri/ *noun* (*plural* **galleries**)
a building or room where people can go to

s	z	ʃ	ʒ	h	m	n	ŋ	l	r	j	w
so	**zoo**	**shoe**	vision	**hat**	**man**	**no**	sing	**leg**	**red**	**yes**	**wet**

look at paintings: *We visited the art galleries in Florence.*

gallon /'gælən/ *noun*
a measure of liquid (= 4.5 litres). There are eight **pints** in a gallon: *a gallon of petrol* ☞ Note at **pint**

gallop /'gæləp/ *verb* (**gallops, galloping, galloped** /'gæləpt/)
When a horse gallops, it runs very fast with all its feet off the ground at the same time: *The horses galloped round the field.*
gallop *noun*
I took the horse for a gallop.

gamble /'gæmbl/ *verb* (**gambles, gambling, gambled** /'gæmbld/)
1 try to win money by playing games that need luck: *He gambled a lot of money on the last race.*
2 do something, although there is a chance that you might lose: *We bought the food for the picnic the day before, and gambled on the weather staying fine.*
gamble *noun*
something that you do without knowing if you will win or lose
gambler /'gæmblə(r)/ *noun*
a person who tries to win money by playing games that need luck
gambling /'gæmblɪŋ/ *noun* (no plural)
playing games that need luck, to try to win money

game /geɪm/ *noun*
1 (*plural* **games**) something you play that has rules: *Shall we have a game of football?* ◇ *We played a game of cards, and I won.*
2 (no plural) wild animals or birds that people shoot and sometimes eat
3 **games** (plural) sports that you play at school or in a competition: *the Olympic Games*

gang /gæŋ/ *noun*
1 a group of people who do bad things together: *a street gang*
2 a group of friends who often meet: *The whole gang is coming to the party tonight.*
3 a group of workers: *a gang of road menders*
gang *verb* (**gangs, ganging, ganged** /gæŋd/)
gang up on or **against somebody**
join together against another person: *The other boys ganged up on Tim because he was much smaller than them.*

gangster /'gæŋstə(r)/ *noun*
one of a group of dangerous criminals: *Al Capone was a famous Chicago gangster.*

gangway /'gæŋweɪ/ *noun*
1 a bridge from the side of a ship to the land so that people can go on and off
2 the long space between two rows of seats in a cinema, theatre, etc

gaol /dʒeɪl/ = **jail**

gap /gæp/ *noun*
a space in something or between two things; a space where something should be: *The sheep got out through a gap in the fence.* ◇ *Write the correct word in the gap.*

gape /geɪp/ *verb* (**gapes, gaping, gaped** /geɪpt/)
look at somebody or something with your mouth open because you are surprised: *She gaped at me when I said I was getting married.*
gaping *adjective*
wide open: *There was a gaping hole in the ground.*

garage /'gærɑːʒ/ *noun*
1 a building where you keep your car
2 a place where cars are repaired
3 a place where you can buy petrol

garbage /'gɑːbɪdʒ/ *American English for* **rubbish**

garbage can /'gɑːbɪdʒ kæn/ *American English for* **dustbin**

garden /'gɑːdn/ *noun*
1 a piece of land by your house where you can grow flowers, fruit and vegetables: *Let's have lunch in the garden.*
2 **gardens** (plural) a public park: *Kensington Gardens*
garden *verb* (**gardens, gardening, gardened** /'gɑːdnd/)
work in a garden: *My mother was gardening all weekend.*
gardener /'gɑːdnə(r)/ *noun*
a person who works in a garden
gardening /'gɑːdnɪŋ/ *noun* (no plural)
My father does the gardening on Sundays.

garlic /'gɑːlɪk/ *noun* (no plural)
a plant like a small onion with a strong taste and smell, that you use in cooking

gas /gæs/ *noun*
1 (*plural* **gases**) anything that is like air: *Hydrogen and oxygen are gases.*
2 (no plural) a gas with a strong smell,

i:	i	ɪ	e	æ	ɑː	ɒ	ɔː	ʊ	u	u:
see	happy	sit	ten	cat	father	got	saw	put	situation	too

that you burn to make heat: *Do you use electricity or gas for cooking?* ◇ *a gas fire*

3 *American English for* **petrol**

gas station /'gæs steɪʃn/ *American English for* **petrol station, service station, garage 3**

gasoline /'gæsəli:n/ *American English for* **petrol**

gasp /gɑ:sp/ *verb* (**gasps, gasping, gasped** /gɑ:spt/)
breathe in quickly and noisily through your mouth: *She gasped in surprise when she heard the news.* ◇ *He was gasping for air when they pulled him out of the water.*

gasp *noun*
a gasp of surprise

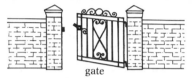
gate

gate /geɪt/ *noun*
1 a kind of door in a fence or wall outside: *We closed the gate to stop the cows getting out of the field.*
2 a door in an airport that you go through to reach the aeroplane: *Please go to gate 15.*

gateway /'geɪtweɪ/ *noun*
a way in or out of a place that has a gate to close it

gather /'gæðə(r)/ *verb* (**gathers, gathering, gathered** /'gæðəd/)
1 come together in a group; meet: *A crowd gathered to watch the fight.*
2 take things that are in different places and bring them together: *I gathered up all the books and papers and put them in my bag.*
3 understand something: *I gather that you know my sister.*

gathering /'gæðərɪŋ/ *noun*
a time when people come together: *There was a large gathering outside the palace.*

gauge /geɪdʒ/ *noun*
an instrument that measures how much of something there is: *Where is the petrol gauge in this car?*

gauge *verb* (**gauges, gauging, gauged** /geɪdʒd/)
measure something

gave *form of* **give**

gay /geɪ/ *adjective*
1 attracted to people of the same sex; homosexual
2 happy and full of fun ✪ We do not often use 'gay' with this meaning now.

gaze /geɪz/ *verb* (**gazes, gazing, gazed** /geɪzd/)
look at somebody or something for a long time: *She sat and gazed out of the window.* ◇ *He was gazing at her.*

GCSE /,dʒi: si: es 'i:/ *noun*
an examination in one subject that children at schools in England, Wales and Northern Ireland take when they are 16 ✪ 'GCSE' is short for **General Certificate of Secondary Education**.

gear /gɪə(r)/ *noun*
1 (*plural* **gears**) a set of wheels that work together in a machine to pass power from one part to another. The gears of a car or bicycle help to control it when it goes up and down hills and help it to go faster or slower: *You need to change gear to go round the corner.*
2 (no plural) special clothes or things that you need for a job or sport: *camping gear*

geese *plural of* **goose**

gem /dʒem/ *noun*
a beautiful stone that is very valuable; a jewel

general¹ /'dʒenrəl/ *adjective*
1 of, by or for most people or things: *Is this car park for general use?*
2 not in detail: *The back cover gives you a general idea of what the book is about.*
in general usually: *I don't eat much meat in general.*

general election /,dʒenrəl ɪ'lekʃn/ *noun*
a time when people choose a new government: *Did you vote in the last general election?*

general knowledge /,dʒenrəl 'nɒlɪdʒ/ *noun* (no plural)
what you know about a lot of different things

general² /'dʒenrəl/ *noun*
a very important officer in the army

generally /'dʒenrəli/ *adverb*
usually; mostly: *I generally get up at about eight o'clock.*

generate /ˈdʒenəreɪt/ *verb* (**generates, generating, generated**)
make heat, electricity, etc: *Power stations generate electricity.*

generation /ˌdʒenəˈreɪʃn/ *noun*
1 the children, or the parents, or the grandparents, in a family: *This photo shows three generations of my family.*
2 all the people who were born at about the same time: *The older and the younger generations listen to different music.*

generosity /ˌdʒenəˈrɒsəti/ *noun* (no plural)
liking to give things to other people

generous /ˈdʒenərəs/ *adjective*
1 always ready to give things or to spend money: *She is very generous – she often buys me presents.*
2 large: *generous amounts of food*
generously *adverb*
Please give generously.

genius /ˈdʒiːniəs/ *noun* (*plural* **geniuses**)
a very clever person: *Einstein was a genius.*

gentle /ˈdʒentl/ *adjective* (**gentler, gentlest**)
quiet and kind; not rough: *Be gentle with the baby.* ◇ *a gentle voice* ◇ *It was a hot day, but there was a gentle breeze* (= a soft wind).
gently /ˈdʒentli/ *adverb*
Close the door gently or you'll wake the children up.

gentleman /ˈdʒentlmən/ *noun* (*plural* **gentlemen** /ˈdʒentlmən/)
1 a polite way of saying 'man': *There is a gentleman here to see you.*
2 a man who is polite and kind to other people
☞ Look at **lady.**

Gents /dʒents/ *noun* (no plural)
a public toilet for men: *Do you know where the Gents is, please?*

genuine /ˈdʒenjuɪn/ *adjective*
real and true: *Those aren't genuine diamonds – they're pieces of glass!*
genuinely *adverb*
really: *Do you think he's genuinely sorry?*

geography /dʒiˈɒgrəfi/ *noun* (no plural)
the study of the earth and its countries, mountains, rivers, weather, etc

geographical /ˌdʒiːəˈgræfɪkl/ *adjective*
geographical names (=names of countries, seas, cities, etc)

geology /dʒiˈɒlədʒi/ *noun* (no plural)
the study of rocks and soil and how they were made
geologist /dʒiˈɒlədʒɪst/ *noun*
a person who studies or knows a lot about geology

geometry /dʒiˈɒmətri/ *noun* (no plural)
the study of things like lines, angles and shapes

geranium /dʒəˈreɪniəm/ *noun*
a plant with red, white or pink flowers

germ /dʒɜːm/ *noun*
a very small living thing that can make you ill: *flu germs*

gesture /ˈdʒestʃə(r)/ *noun*
a movement of your head or hand to show how you feel or what you want

get /get/ *verb* (**gets, getting, got** /gɒt/, **has got**)
1 buy or take something: *Will you get some bread when you go shopping?*
2 receive something: *I got a lot of presents for my birthday.*
3 become: *He is getting fat.* ◇ *Mum got angry.* ◇ *It's getting cold.*
4 go and bring back somebody or something: *Jenny will get the children from school.*
5 arrive somewhere: *We got to London at ten o'clock.*
6 start to have an illness: *I think I'm getting a cold.*
7 understand or hear something: *I don't get the joke.*
8 a word that you use with part of another verb to show that something happens to somebody or something: *She got caught by the police.*
9 travel on a train, bus, etc: *I didn't walk – I got the train.*
10 make somebody do something: *I got Peter to help me.*
get away with something do something bad and not be punished for it: *He lied but he got away with it.*
get back return: *When did you get back from your holiday?*
get in come to a place: *My train got in at 7.15.*
get in, get into something climb into a car: *Tom got into the car.*

get off leave a train, bus, bicycle, etc: *Where did you get off the bus?*

get on **1** words that you use to say or ask how well somebody does something: *Patrick is getting on well at school.* ◇ *How did you get on in the exam?* **2** become late: *I must go home – the time is getting on.* **3** become old: *My grand-father is getting on – he's nearly 80.*

get on, get onto something climb onto a bus, train or bicycle: *I got on the train.*

get on with somebody live or work in a friendly way with somebody: *We get on well with our neighbours.*

get out leave a car, etc: *I opened the door and got out.*

get out of something not do something that you do not like: *I'll come swimming with you if I can get out of cleaning my room.*

get something out take something from the place where it was: *She opened her bag and got out a pen.*

get over something become well or happy again after you have been ill or sad: *He still hasn't got over his wife's death.*

get through be able to speak to somebody on the telephone; be connected: *I tried to ring Kate but I couldn't get through.*

get through something **1** use or finish a certain amount of something: *I got through a lot of work today.* **2** pass an examination, etc

get together meet; come together in a group: *The whole family got together for Christmas.*

get up stand up; get out of bed: *What time do you usually get up?*

get up to something **1** do something, usually something bad: *I must go and see what the children are getting up to.* **2** come as far as a place in a book, etc: *I've got up to page 180.*

have got have something: *She has got brown eyes.* ◇ *Have you got any money?*

have got to If you have got to do something, you must do it: *I have got to leave soon.*

ghost /gəʊst/ *noun*
the form of a dead person that a living person thinks he/she sees: *Do you believe in ghosts?*

ghostly *adjective*
of or like a ghost: *ghostly noises*

giant /'dʒaɪənt/ *noun*
a very big tall person in stories: *Goliath was a giant.*
giant *adjective*
very big: *a giant insect*

gift /gɪft/ *noun*
1 something that you give to or get from somebody; a present: *wedding gifts*
2 something that you can do well or learn easily: *She has a gift for languages.*

gigantic /dʒaɪ'gæntɪk/ *adjective*
very big

giggle /'gɪgl/ *verb* (**giggles, giggling, giggled** /'gɪgld/)
laugh in a silly way: *The children couldn't stop giggling.*
giggle *noun*
There was a giggle from the back of the class.

gill /gɪl/ *noun*
the part on each side of a fish that it breathes through ☞ picture at **fish**

ginger¹ /'dʒɪndʒə(r)/ *noun* (no plural)
a plant with a very hot strong taste, that is used in cooking: *a ginger biscuit*
gingerbread /'dʒɪndʒəbred/ *noun* (no plural)
a dark brown cake with ginger in it

ginger² /'dʒɪndʒə(r)/ *adjective*
with a colour between brown and orange: *My brother has got ginger hair.* ◇ *a ginger cat*

gipsy /'dʒɪpsi/ = **gypsy**

giraffe /dʒə'rɑːf/ *noun*
a big animal from Africa with a very long neck and long legs

girl /gɜːl/ *noun*
a female child; a young woman

girlfriend /'gɜːlfrend/ *noun*
a girl or woman who is somebody's special friend: *Have you got a girlfriend?*

Girl Guide /ˌgɜːl 'gaɪd/ *noun*
a member of a special club for girls

give /gɪv/ *verb* (**gives, giving, gave** /geɪv/, **has given** /'gɪvn/)
1 let somebody have something: *She gave*

s	z	ʃ	ʒ	h	m	n	ŋ	l	r	j	w
so	**zoo**	**shoe**	vision	**hat**	**man**	**no**	sing	leg	**red**	yes	**wet**

me a watch for my birthday. ◇ *I gave my ticket to the man at the door.* ◇ *I gave John £60 for his bike.*
2 make somebody have or feel something: *That noise is giving me a headache.*
3 make a sound, movement, etc: *Jo gave me an angry look.* ◇ *He gave a shout.* ◇ *She gave him a kiss.*

give away give something to somebody without getting money for it: *I've given all my old clothes away.*

give somebody back something, give something back to somebody return something to somebody: *Can you give me back the cassette I lent you last week?*

give in say that you will do something that you do not want to do, or agree that you will not win: *My parents finally gave in and said I could go to the party.*

give something in give work, etc to somebody: *The teacher asked us to give in our essays today.*

give out give something to many people: *Could you give out these books to the class, please?*

give up stop trying to do something, because you know that you cannot do it: *I give up – what's the answer?*

give something up stop doing or having something: *I'm trying to give up smoking.*

glacier /'glæsɪə(r)/ *noun*
a large river of ice that moves slowly down a mountain

glad /glæd/ *adjective*
happy; pleased: *He was glad to see us.*
gladly *adverb*
If you do something gladly, you are happy to do it: *I'll gladly help you.*

glance /glɑːns/ *verb* (**glances, glancing, glanced** /glɑːnst/)
look quickly at somebody or something: *Sue glanced at her watch.*
glance *noun*
a glance at the newspaper
at a glance with one look: *I could see at a glance that he was ill.*

glare /gleə(r)/ *verb* (**glares, glaring, glared** /gleəd/)
1 look angrily at somebody: *He glared at the children.*

2 shine with a strong light that hurts your eyes: *The sun glared down.*
glare *noun*
1 (no plural) strong light that hurts your eyes: *the glare of the car's headlights*
2 (*plural* **glares**) a long angry look: *I tried to say something, but he gave me a glare.*

glass /glɑːs/ *noun*
1 (no plural) hard stuff that you can see through. Bottles and windows are made of glass: *I cut myself on some broken glass.* ◇ *a glass jar*

glass

2 (*plural* **glasses**) a thing made of glass that you drink from: *Could I have a glass of milk, please?* ◇ *a wineglass*

glasses /'glɑːsɪz/ *noun* (plural)
two pieces of special glass (called **lenses**) in a frame that people wear over their eyes to help them see better: *Does she wear glasses?* ☞ Look also at **sunglasses**.

glasses

○ Be careful! You cannot say 'a glasses'. You can say **a pair of glasses**: *I need a new pair of glasses.* (or: *I need (some) new glasses.*)

gleam /gliːm/ *verb* (**gleams, gleaming, gleamed** /gliːmd/)
shine with a soft light: *The lake gleamed in the moonlight.*
gleam *noun*
I could see a gleam of light through the trees.

glide /glaɪd/ *verb* (**glides, gliding, glided**)
move smoothly and silently: *The bird glided through the air.*

glider /'glaɪdə(r)/ *noun*
an aeroplane without an engine
gliding *noun* (no plural)
flying in a glider as a sport

glimmer /'glɪmə(r)/ *verb* (**glimmers, glimmering, glimmered** /'glɪməd/)
shine with a small, weak light

glimmer *noun*
the glimmer of a candle

glimpse /glɪmps/ *verb* (**glimpses,
glimpsing, glimpsed** /glɪmpst/)
see somebody or something quickly, but
not clearly: *I just glimpsed a plane between the clouds.*
glimpse *noun*
catch a glimpse of somebody or
something see somebody or something
quickly, but not clearly: *I caught a glimpse
of myself in the mirror as I walked past.*

glisten /'glɪsn/ *verb* (**glistens, glisten-
ing, glistened** /'glɪsnd/)
shine because it is wet or smooth: *His eyes
glistened with tears.*

glitter /'glɪtə(r)/ *verb* (**glitters, glittering, glittered** /'glɪtəd/)
shine brightly with a lot of small flashes of
light: *The broken glass glittered in the
sun.* ◇ *glittering diamonds*
glitter *noun* (no plural)
the glitter of jewels

global /'gləʊbl/ *adjective*
of or about the whole world: *Pollution is a
global problem.*

globe /gləʊb/ *noun*
1 a ball with a map of the world on it
2 **the globe** (no plural) the earth: *He's
travelled all over the globe.*

gloomy /'gluːmi/ *adjective* (**gloomier,
gloomiest**)
1 dark and sad: *What a gloomy day!*
2 sad and without hope: *He's feeling very
gloomy because he can't get a job.*
gloomily /'gluːmɪli/ *adverb*
*She looked gloomily out of the window at
the rain.*

glorious /'glɔːriəs/ *adjective*
1 wonderful or beautiful: *The weather
was glorious.*
2 famous and full of glory: *a glorious
history*

glory /'glɔːri/ *noun* (no plural)
1 fame and respect that you get when you
do great things: *the glory of winning at the
Olympics*
2 great beauty: *Autumn is the best time
to see the forest in all its glory.*

glossy /'glɒsi/ *adjective* (**glossier,
glossiest**)
smooth and shiny: *glossy hair*

glove /glʌv/ *noun*
a thing that you
wear to keep your
hand warm or safe:
*I need a new pair of
gloves.* ◇ *rubber
gloves*

gloves

glow /gləʊ/ *verb* (**glows, glowing,
glowed** /gləʊd/)
send out soft light or heat without flames
or smoke: *His cigarette glowed in the dark.*
glow *noun*
the glow of the sky at sunset

glue /gluː/ *noun* (no plural)
a thick liquid that you use for sticking
things together
glue *verb* (**glues, gluing, glued** /gluːd/)
stick one thing to another thing with glue:
Glue the two pieces of wood together.

gnaw /nɔː/ *verb* (**gnaws, gnawing,
gnawed** /nɔːd/)
bite something for a long time: *The dog
was gnawing a bone.*

go[1] /gəʊ/ *verb* (**goes, going, went**
/went/, **has gone** /gɒn/)
1 move from one place to another: *I went
to London by train.* ◇ *Her new car goes
very fast.*
2 travel to a place to do something: *Paul
has gone shopping.* ◇ *Are you going to
Dave's party?* ◇ *I'll go and make some
coffee.*
3 leave a place: *What time does the train
go?* ◇ *I must go now – it's four o'clock.*
4 become: *Her hair has gone grey.*
5 have as its place: *'Where do these plates
go?' 'In that cupboard.'*
6 lead to a place: *Does this road go to the
station?*
7 work: *Jane dropped the clock and now it
doesn't go.*
8 happen in a certain way: *How is your
new job going?* ◇ *The week went very
quickly.*
9 disappear: *My headache has gone.*
10 be or look good with something else:
Does this jumper go with my skirt?
11 make a certain sound: *Cows go 'moo'.*
go ahead begin or continue to do something: *'Can I borrow your pen?' 'Yes, go
ahead.'*
go away leave: *Go away! I'm doing my
homework.* ◇ *They have gone away for
the weekend.*

go back go again to a place where you were before; return: *We're going back to school tomorrow.*

go by pass: *The holidays went by very quickly.*

go down well be something that people like: *The film went down very well in America.*

go off 1 explode: *A bomb went off in the station today.* **2** When food or drink goes off, it becomes too old to eat or drink: *This milk has gone off – it smells horrible.*

go off somebody or **something** stop liking somebody or something

go on 1 happen: *What's going on?* **2** continue; not stop: *I went on working.* **3** words that you use when you want somebody to do something: *Oh, go on! Come to the party with me!*

go out 1 leave the place where you live or work: *I went out for a walk.* ◇ *We're going out tonight.* **2** stop shining or burning: *The fire has gone out.*

go out with somebody have somebody as a boyfriend or girlfriend: *She's going out with a boy at school.*

go over something look at or explain something carefully from the beginning to the end: *Go over your work before you give it to the teacher.*

go round 1 be enough for everybody: *Is there enough wine to go round?* **2** go to somebody's home: *We're going round to Jo's this evening.*

go through something 1 look at or explain something carefully from the beginning to the end: *The teacher went through our homework.* **2** suffer something: *She went through a difficult time when her husband was ill.*

go up become higher or more: *The price of petrol has gone up again.*

go² /gəʊ/ *noun* (*plural* **goes**)
the time when you can or should do something: *Get off the bike – it's my go!*

have a go try to do something: *I'll have a go at mending your bike.*

in one go with one try: *There are too many books here to carry in one go.*

goal

goalkeeper

goal /gəʊl/ *noun*
1 the place where the ball must go to win a point in a game like football: *He kicked the ball into the goal.*
2 a point that a team wins in a game like football when the ball goes into the goal: *Liverpool won by three goals to two.* ◇ *Jones has scored another goal.*

goalkeeper /ˈgəʊlkiːpə(r)/ *noun*
a player in a game like football who must stop the ball from going into the goal

goat
horn
kid   goat

goat /gəʊt/ *noun*
an animal with horns. People keep goats for their milk. ❸ A young goat is called a **kid**.

god /gɒd/ *noun*
1 (*plural* **gods**) a being that people believe controls them and nature: *Mars was the Roman god of war.*
2 **God** (no plural) the one great being that Christians, Jews and Muslims believe made the world and controls everything

goddess /ˈgɒdes/ *noun* (*plural* **goddesses**)
a female god: *Venus was the Roman goddess of love.*

p	b	t	d	k	g	tʃ	dʒ	f	v	θ	ð
pen	**b**ad	**t**ea	**d**id	**c**at	**g**ot	**ch**ain	**j**am	**f**all	**v**an	**th**in	**th**is

goes *form of* **go¹**

goggles /'gɒglz/ *noun* (plural)
big glasses that you wear so that water, dust, wind, etc cannot get in your eyes. Swimmers, skiers and motor cyclists often wear goggles: *a pair of goggles*

going *form of* **go¹**
be going to 1 words that show what you plan to do in the future: *Joe's going to cook the dinner tonight.* **2** words that you use when you are sure that something will happen: *It's going to rain.*

gold /gəʊld/ *noun* (no plural)
a yellow metal that is very valuable: *Is your ring made of gold?* ◇ *a gold watch*
gold *adjective*
with the colour of gold: *gold paint*

golden /'gəʊldən/ *adjective*
1 made of gold: *a golden crown*
2 with the colour of gold: *golden hair*

goldfish /'gəʊldfɪʃ/ *noun* (plural **goldfish**)
a small orange fish that people keep as a pet

golf /gɒlf/ *noun* (no plural)
a game that you play by hitting a small ball into holes with a long stick (called a **golf club**): *My mother plays golf on Sundays.*
golf-course /'gɒlf kɔ:s/ *noun*
a large piece of land, covered in grass, where people play golf

gone *form of* **go¹**

good¹ /gʊd/ *adjective* (**better, best**)
1 that does what you want; done or made very well: *It's a good knife – it cuts very well.* ◇ *The film was really good.*
2 that you enjoy; nice: *Have a good evening!* ◇ *The weather was very good.*
3 able to do something well: *She's a good driver.*
4 kind, or doing the right thing: *It's good of you to help.* ◇ *The children were very good while you were out.*
5 right or suitable: *This is a good place for a picnic.*
6 big, long, complete, etc: *Take a good look at this photo.*
7 a word that you use when you are pleased: *Is everyone here? Good. Now let's begin.*
○ The adverb is **well**.
good at something able to do something well: *James is very good at tennis.*
good for you If something is good for you, it makes you well, happy, etc: *Fresh fruit and vegetables are good for you.*

good² /gʊd/ *noun* (no plural)
something that is right or helpful
be no good, not be any good not be useful: *This jumper isn't any good. It's too small.* ◇ *It's no good asking mum for money – she hasn't got any.*
do somebody good make somebody well or happy: *It will do you good to go to bed early tonight.*
for good for all time; for ever: *She has gone to Australia for good.*

good afternoon /,gʊd ɑ:ftə'nu:n/
words that you say when you see or speak to somebody in the afternoon ○ Often we just say **Afternoon**: *'Good afternoon, Laura.' 'Afternoon, Mike.'*

goodbye /,gʊd'baɪ/
a word that you say when somebody goes away, or when you go away: *Goodbye! See you tomorrow.*

good evening /,gʊd 'i:vnɪŋ/
words that you say when you see or speak to somebody in the evening ○ Often we just say **Evening**: *'Good evening, Mr James.' 'Evening, Miss Evans.'*

Good Friday /,gʊd 'fraɪdeɪ/ *noun*
the Friday before Easter when Christians remember the death of Christ

good-looking /,gʊd 'lʊkɪŋ/ *adjective*
nice to look at; handsome: *He's a good-looking boy.* ☞ Note at **beautiful**

good morning /,gʊd 'mɔ:nɪŋ/
words that you say when you see or speak to somebody in the morning ○ Often we just say **Morning**: *'Good morning, Jack.' 'Morning.'*

good-natured /,gʊd 'neɪtʃəd/ *adjective*
friendly and kind

goodness /'gʊdnəs/ *noun* (no plural)
1 something in food that is good for your health: *Fresh vegetables have a lot of goodness in them.*
2 being good or kind
for goodness' sake words that show anger: *For goodness' sake, hurry up!*
goodness, goodness me words that show surprise: *Goodness! What a big cake!*
thank goodness words that show you are happy because a problem or danger

s	z	ʃ	ʒ	h	m	n	ŋ	l	r	j	w
so	**zoo**	**sh**oe	vi**si**on	**h**at	**m**an	**no**	si**ng**	**l**eg	**r**ed	**y**es	**w**et

has gone away: *Thank goodness it's stopped raining.*

good night /ˌgʊd 'naɪt/
words that you say when you leave somebody in the evening

goods /gʊdz/ *noun* (plural)
1 things that you buy or sell: *That shop sells electrical goods.*
2 things that a train or lorry carries: *a goods train*

good-tempered /ˌgʊd 'tempəd/ *adjective*
not often angry: My dad is very good-tempered.

goose /guːs/ *noun* (plural **geese** /giːs/)
a big bird with a long neck. People keep geese on farms for their eggs and meat.

gooseberry /'gʊzbəri/ *noun* (plural **gooseberries**)
a small green fruit with hairs

gorgeous /'gɔːdʒəs/ *adjective*
very good; wonderful: *The weather was gorgeous!* ◇ *What a gorgeous dress!*

gorilla /gə'rɪlə/ *noun*
an African animal like a very big black monkey

gosh /gɒʃ/
a word that shows surprise: *Gosh! What a big house!*

gossip /'gɒsɪp/ *noun* (no plural)
talk about other people that is often unkind: *Don't believe all the gossip you hear.*
gossip *verb* (**gossips, gossiping, gossiped** /'gɒsɪpt/)
They were gossiping about Jane's new boyfriend.

got *form of* **get**

govern /'gʌvn/ *verb* (**governs, governing, governed** /'gʌvnd/)
control a country or part of a country: *Britain is governed by Parliament.* .

government /'gʌvənmənt/ *noun*
a group of people who control a country: *The leaders of all the European governments will meet today in Brussels.* ◇ *The Government have discussed the plan.*

governor /'gʌvənə(r)/ *noun*
1 a person who controls part of a country: *the Governor of California*
2 a person who controls a place like a prison or hospital

gown /gaʊn/ *noun*
1 a long dress that a woman wears at a special time
2 a long loose piece of clothing that people wear to do a special job. Judges and university teachers sometimes wear gowns.

grab /græb/ *verb* (**grabs, grabbing, grabbed** /græbd/)
take something quickly and roughly: *The thief grabbed her bag and ran away.*

grace /greɪs/ *noun* (no plural)
1 a beautiful way of moving: *She dances with grace.*
2 thanks to God that people say before or after they eat

graceful /'greɪsfl/ *adjective*
A person or thing that is graceful moves in a beautiful way: *a graceful dancer*
gracefully /'greɪsfəli/ *adverb*
He moves very gracefully.

grade¹ /greɪd/ *noun*
1 how good something is; the level or quality of something: *Which grade of petrol does your car use?*
2 a number or letter that a teacher gives for your work to show how good it is: *She got very good grades in all her exams.*
3 a class in a school in the USA where all the children are the same age: *My sister is in the fifth grade.*

grade² /greɪd/ *verb* (**grades, grading, graded**)
sort things or people into sizes, kinds, etc: *The eggs are graded by size.*

grade crossing /'greɪd krɒsɪŋ/ *American English for* **level crossing**

gradual /'grædʒuəl/ *adjective*
Something that is gradual happens slowly: *I am making gradual progress with my work.*
gradually /'grædʒuəli/ *adverb*
We all become gradually older.

graduate¹ /'grædʒuət/ *noun*
a person who has finished studying at a university or college and who has passed his/her last exams: *an Oxford graduate*

graduate² /'grædʒueɪt/ *verb* (**graduates, graduating, graduated**)
finish your studies at a university or college and pass your last exams: *I graduated from Exeter University in 1994.*

graffiti /grə'fiːti/ *noun* (plural)
funny, rude or angry words or pictures

iː	i	ɪ	e	æ	ɑː	ɒ	ɔː	ʊ	u	uː
see	happy	sit	ten	cat	father	got	saw	put	situation	too

that people write or draw on walls: *The walls of the old building were covered with graffiti.*

grain /greɪn/ *noun*
1 (no plural) the seeds of a plant like wheat or rice that we eat
2 (*plural* **grains**) a seed or a small hard piece of something: *grains of rice* ◇ *a grain of sand*

gram, **gramme** /græm/ *noun*
a measure of weight. There are 1 000 grams in a **kilogram**. ✪ The short way of writing 'gram' is **g**: *30 g of butter*

grammar /'græmə(r)/ *noun* (no plural)
the rules that tell you how to put words together when you speak or write

grammar school /'græmə skuːl/ *noun*
a school for children between the ages of 11 and 18 who are good at studying

grammatical /grə'mætɪkl/ *adjective*
1 of or about grammar: *What is the grammatical rule for making plurals in English?*
2 correct because it follows the rules of grammar: *The sentence 'They is happy' is not grammatical.* ✪ opposite: **ungrammatical**
grammatically /grə'mætɪkli/ *adverb*
The sentence is not grammatically correct.

gran /græn/ *noun*
grandmother

grand /grænd/ *adjective* (**grander**, **grandest**)
very big, important, rich, etc: *They live in a grand house in the centre of London.*

grandad /'grændæd/ *noun*
grandfather

grandchild /'græntʃaɪld/ *noun* (*plural* **grandchildren** /'græntʃɪldrən/)
the child of your child ☞ picture on page 127

granddaughter /'grændɔːtə(r)/ *noun*
the daughter of your child ☞ picture on page 127

grandfather /'grænfɑːðə(r)/ *noun*
the father of your mother or father ☞ picture on page 127

grandma /'grænmɑː/ *noun*
grandmother

grandmother /'grænmʌðə(r)/ *noun*
the mother of your mother or father ☞ picture on page 127

grandpa /'grænpɑː/ *noun*
grandfather

grandparents /'grænpeərənts/ *noun* (plural)
the mother and father of your mother or father ☞ picture on page 127

grandson /'grænsʌn/ *noun*
the son of your child ☞ picture on page 127

grandstand /'grændstænd/ *noun*
lines of seats, with a roof over them, where you sit to watch a sport

granny, grannie /'græni/ *noun* (*plural* **grannies**)
grandmother

grant¹ /grɑːnt/ *noun*
money that you give for a special reason: *The government gives grants to some young people so they can study at university.*

grant² /grɑːnt/ *verb* (**grants**, **granting**, **granted**)
give somebody what they have asked for: *They granted him a visa to leave the country.*

a bunch of grapes

grape /greɪp/ *noun*
a small green or purple fruit that we eat or make into wine: *a bunch of grapes*

grapefruit /'greɪpfruːt/ *noun* (*plural* **grapefruit** or **grapefruits**)
a fruit that looks like a big orange, but is yellow

grapevine /'greɪpvaɪn/ *noun*
the grapevine the way that news is passed from one person to another: *I heard it on the grapevine that you are getting married.*

ʌ	ɜː	ə	eɪ	əʊ	aɪ	aʊ	ɔɪ	ɪə	eə	ʊə
cup	bird	about	say	go	five	now	boy	near	hair	pure

graph /grɑ:f/ *noun*
a picture that shows how numbers, amounts, etc are different from each other

graph

grasp /grɑ:sp/ *verb* (**grasps**, **grasping**, **grasped** /grɑ:spt/)
1 hold something tightly: *Claire grasped my arm to stop herself from falling.*
2 understand something: *He could not grasp what I was saying.*
grasp *noun* (no plural)
The ball fell from my grasp.

grass /grɑ:s/ *noun* (no plural)
a plant with thin green leaves that covers fields and gardens. Cows and sheep eat grass: *Don't walk on the grass.*
grassy *adjective*
covered with grass

grate /greɪt/ *verb* (**grates**, **grating**, **grated**)
If you grate food you rub it over a metal tool (called a **grater**) so that it is in very small pieces: *Can you grate some cheese?*
◇ *grated carrot*

grateful /'greɪtfl/ *adjective*
If you are grateful, you feel or show thanks to somebody: *We are grateful to you for the help you have given us.* ✪ opposite: **ungrateful**

gratitude /'grætɪtjuːd/ *noun* (no plural)
the feeling of being grateful: *We gave David a present to show our gratitude for all his help.*

grave¹ /greɪv/ *adjective* (**graver**, **gravest**)
very bad or serious ✪ **Serious** is the word that we usually use.

grave² /greɪv/ *noun*
a hole in the ground where a dead person's body is put: *We put flowers on the grave.*
gravestone /'greɪvstəʊn/ *noun*
a piece of stone on a grave that shows the name of the dead person
graveyard /'greɪvjɑːd/ *noun*
a piece of land near a church where dead people are put in the ground

gravel /'grævl/ *noun* (no plural)
very small stones that are used for making roads

gravity /'grævəti/ *noun* (no plural)
the force that pulls everything towards the earth

gravy /'greɪvi/ *noun* (no plural)
a hot brown liquid that you eat with meat and vegetables

gray *American English for* **grey**

graze¹ /greɪz/ *verb* (**grazes**, **grazing**, **grazed** /greɪzd/)
hurt your skin by rubbing it against something rough: *He fell and grazed his arm.*
graze *noun*
Her legs were covered with grazes.

graze² /greɪz/ *verb* (**grazes**, **grazing**, **grazed** /greɪzd/)
eat grass: *The sheep were grazing in the fields.*

grease /griːs/ *noun* (no plural)
fat from animals, or any thick stuff that is like oil: *You will need very hot water to get the grease off these plates.*

greasy /'griːsi/ *adjective* (**greasier**, **greasiest**)
with a lot of grease on or in it: *Greasy food is not good for you.* ◇ *greasy hair*

great¹ /greɪt/ *adjective* (**greater**, **greatest**)
1 very large or very much: *It's a great pleasure to meet you.*
2 important or special: *Einstein was a great scientist.*
3 very; very good: *They are great friends.* ◇ *There's a great big dog in the garden!*
4 very good; wonderful: *I had a great weekend.* ◇ *It's great to see you!*
a great many very many: *He knows a great many people.*

great-² /greɪt/ *prefix*
a word that you put before other words to show some parts of a family. For example, your **great-grandmother** is the mother of your grandmother or grandfather, and your **great-grandson** is the son of your grandson or granddaughter.

greatly /'greɪtli/ *adverb*
very much: *I wasn't greatly surprised to see her.*

p	b	t	d	k	g	tʃ	dʒ	f	v	θ	ð
pen	**b**ad	**t**ea	**d**id	**c**at	**g**ot	**ch**ain	**j**am	**f**all	**v**an	**th**in	**th**is

greed /gri:d/ *noun* (no plural)
the feeling that you want more of something than you need
greedy *adjective* (**greedier, greediest**)
A person who is greedy wants or takes more of something than he/she needs: *She's so greedy – she's eaten all the chocolates!*

green /gri:n/ *adjective* (**greener, greenest**)
with the colour of leaves and grass: *My brother has green eyes.* ◇ *dark green*
green *noun*
1 the colour of leaves and grass: *She was dressed in green.*
2 a place in the centre of a village that is covered with grass

greengrocer /'gri:ngrəʊsə(r)/ *noun*
a person who sells fruit and vegetables in a small shop (called a **greengrocer's**)

greenhouse /'gri:nhaʊs/ *noun* (*plural* **greenhouses** /'gri:nhaʊzɪz/)
a building made of glass, where plants grow

greet /gri:t/ *verb* (**greets, greeting, greeted**)
say or do something when you meet somebody: *He greeted me with a smile.*

greeting /'gri:tɪŋ/ *noun*
1 words that you say when you meet somebody: *'Hello' and 'Good morning' are greetings.*
2 **greetings** (plural) words that you write to somebody at a special time: *a greetings card* (= a card that you send at Christmas or on a birthday, for example)

grew *form of* **grow**

grey /greɪ/ *adjective* (**greyer, greyest**)
with a colour like black and white mixed together: *My grandmother has grey hair.* ◇ *a grey-haired old man* ◇ *The sky was grey.*
grey *noun*
He was dressed in grey.

grid /grɪd/ *noun*
lines that cross each other to make squares, for example on a map

grief /gri:f/ *noun* (no plural)
great sadness

grieve /gri:v/ *verb* (**grieves, grieving, grieved** /gri:vd/)
feel great sadness: *She is grieving for her dead son.*

grill /grɪl/ *verb* (**grills, grilling, grilled** /grɪld/)
cook meat, fish, etc on metal bars under or over heat: *grilled steak*
grill *noun*
the part of a cooker, or a special metal thing, where you grill food

grin /grɪn/ *verb* (**grins, grinning, grinned** /grɪnd/)
have a big smile on your face: *She grinned at me.*
grin *noun*
He had a big grin on his face.

grind /graɪnd/ *verb* (**grinds, grinding, ground** /graʊnd/, **has ground**)
make something into very small pieces or powder by crushing it: *They ground the wheat into flour.* ◇ *ground coffee*

grip /grɪp/ *verb* (**grips, gripping, gripped** /grɪpt/)
hold something tightly: *Marie gripped my hand as we crossed the road.*
grip *noun* (no plural)
He kept a tight grip on the rope.

grit /grɪt/ *noun* (no plural)
very small pieces of stone

groan /grəʊn/ *verb* (**groans, groaning, groaned** /grəʊnd/)
make a deep sad sound, for example because you are unhappy or in pain: *'I've got a headache,' he groaned.*
groan *noun*
'I've got to do my homework,' she said with a groan.

groceries /'grəʊsəriz/ *noun* (plural)
food that you buy in packets, tins, jars, etc

groom /gru:m/ *noun*
1 a person whose job is to look after horses
2 a man on the day of his wedding; a bridegroom

groove /gru:v/ *noun*
a long thin cut: *The needle moves along a groove in the record.*

grope /grəʊp/ *verb* (**gropes, groping, groped** /grəʊpt/)
try to find something by using your hands, when you cannot see: *I groped in the dark for the door.*

ground[1] *form of* **grind**

ground[2] /graʊnd/ *noun*
1 (no plural) the top part of the earth: *We sat on the ground to eat our picnic.*
2 (*plural* **grounds**) a piece of land that is

used for something special: *a sports ground* ◇ *a playground* (= a place where children play)
3 grounds (plural) the land around a large building: *the grounds of the hospital*
ground floor /ˌgraʊnd ˈflɔː(r)/ *noun*
the part of a building that is at the same height as the street: *My office is on the ground floor.* ☞ picture at **house**

group /gruːp/ *noun*
1 a number of people or things together: *A group of people were standing outside the shop.*
2 people who play pop music together

grow /grəʊ/ *verb* (**grows, growing, grew** /gruː/, **has grown** /grəʊn/)
1 become bigger: *Children grow very quickly.*
2 When a plant grows somewhere, it lives there: *Oranges grow in warm countries.*
3 plant something in the ground and look after it: *We grow potatoes and carrots in our garden.*
4 let something grow: *Mark has grown a beard.*
5 become: *It was growing dark.* ✪ In this sense, it is more usual to say **get** or **become**.
grow into something get bigger and become something: *Kittens grow into cats.*
grow out of something become too big to do or wear something: *She's grown out of her shoes.*
grow up become an adult; change from a child to a man or woman: *I want to be a doctor when I grow up.*

growl /graʊl/ *verb* (**growls, growling, growled** /graʊld/)
If an animal growls, it makes a low angry sound: *The dog growled at the stranger.*
growl *noun*
The dog gave a fierce growl.

grown-up /ˈgrəʊn ʌp/ *noun*
a man or woman, not a child; an adult: *Ask a grown-up to help you.*
grown-up /ˌgrəʊn ˈʌp/ *adjective*
She has a grown-up son.

growth /grəʊθ/ *noun* (no plural)
getting bigger; growing: *the growth of a baby*

grubby /ˈgrʌbi/ *adjective* (**grubbier, grubbiest**)
dirty: *grubby hands*

grumble /ˈgrʌmbl/ *verb* (**grumbles, grumbling, grumbled** /ˈgrʌmbld/)
say many times that you do not like something: *The children often grumble about the food at school.*

grumpy /ˈgrʌmpi/ *adjective* (**grumpier, grumpiest**)
a little angry; bad-tempered: *She gets grumpy when she's tired.*

grunt /grʌnt/ *verb* (**grunts, grunting, grunted**)
make a short rough sound, like a pig makes
grunt *noun*
She didn't say anything – she just gave a grunt.

guarantee /ˌgærənˈtiː/ *noun*
1 a special promise on paper that a company will repair a thing you have bought, or give you a new one, if it goes wrong: *This watch has a two-year guarantee.*
2 a promise that something will happen: *I want a guarantee that you will do the work today.*
guarantee *verb* (**guarantees, guaranteeing, guaranteed** /ˌgærənˈtiːd/)
1 say that you will repair a thing that somebody buys, or give them a new one, if it goes wrong: *The television is guaranteed for three years.*
2 promise something: *I can't guarantee that I will be able to help you, but I'll try.*

guard¹ /gɑːd/ *verb* (**guards, guarding, guarded**)
keep somebody or something safe from other people, or stop somebody from escaping: *The house was guarded by two large dogs.*

guard² /gɑːd/ *noun*
1 a person who keeps somebody or something safe from other people, or who stops somebody from escaping: *There are guards outside the palace.*
2 a person whose job is to look after people and things on a train
on guard guarding: *The soldiers were on guard outside the airport.*

guardian /ˈgɑːdiən/ *noun*
a person who looks after a child with no parents

guerrilla /gəˈrɪlə/ *noun*
a person who is not in an army but who fights secretly against the government or an army

iː	i	ɪ	e	æ	ɑː	ɒ	ɔː	ʊ	u	uː
see	happy	sit	ten	cat	father	got	saw	put	situation	too

guess /ges/ *verb* (**guesses, guessing, guessed** /gest/)
give an answer when you do not know if it is right: *Can you guess how old he is?*
guess *noun* (*plural* **guesses**)
If you don't know the answer, have a guess!

guest /gest/ *noun*
1 a person that you invite to your home, to a party, etc: *There were 200 guests at the wedding.*
2 a person who is staying in a hotel
guest-house /'gest haʊs/ *noun* (*plural* **guest-houses** /'gest haʊzɪz/)
a small hotel

guidance /'gaɪdns/ *noun* (no plural)
help and advice: *I want some guidance on how to find a job.*

guide[1] /gaɪd/ *noun*
1 a person who shows other people where to go and tells them about a place: *The guide took us round the castle.*
2 (*also* **guidebook**) a book that tells you about a town, country, etc
3 a book that tells you about something, or how to do something: *a guide to skiing*
4 Guide = Girl Guide

guide[2] /gaɪd/ *verb* (**guides, guiding, guided**)
show somebody where to go or what to do: *He guided us through the busy streets to our hotel.*

guilt /gɪlt/ *noun* (no plural)
1 having done something wrong: *The police could not prove his guilt.* ✪ opposite: **innocence**
2 the feeling that you have when you know that you have done something wrong: *She felt terrible guilt after stealing the money.*

guilty /'gɪlti/ *adjective* (**guiltier, guiltiest**)
1 If you are guilty, you have done something wrong: *He is guilty of murder.* ✪ opposite: **innocent**
2 If you feel guilty, you feel that you have done something wrong: *I feel guilty about lying to her.*

guinea-pig /'gɪni pɪg/ *noun*
1 a small animal that people keep as a pet
2 a person who is used in an experiment

guitar

guitar /gɪ'tɑ:(r)/ *noun*
a musical instrument with strings: *I play the guitar in a band.*
guitarist /gɪ'tɑ:rɪst/ *noun*
a person who plays the guitar

gulf /gʌlf/ *noun*
a large part of the sea that has land almost all the way around it: *the Gulf of Mexico*

gull /gʌl/ *noun*
a large grey or white bird that lives by the sea; a seagull

gulp /gʌlp/ *verb* (**gulps, gulping, gulped** /gʌlpt/)
eat or drink something quickly: *He gulped down a cup of tea and left.*
gulp *noun*
She took a gulp of coffee.

gum /gʌm/ *noun*
1 (*plural* **gums**) Your gums are the hard pink parts of your mouth that hold the teeth.
2 (no plural) thick liquid that you use for sticking pieces of paper together
☞ Look also at **chewing-gum**.

gun /gʌn/ *noun*
a thing that shoots out pieces of metal (called **bullets**) to kill or hurt people or animals: *He pointed the gun at the bird and fired.*

gun

gunman /'gʌnmən/ *noun* (*plural* **gunmen** /'gʌnmən/)
a man who shoots another person with a gun

gunpowder /'gʌnpaʊdə(r)/ *noun* (no plural)
powder that explodes. It is used in guns and fireworks.

gush /gʌʃ/ *verb* (**gushes, gushing, gushed** /gʌʃt/)
flow out suddenly and strongly: *Blood was gushing from the cut in her leg.*

gust /gʌst/ *noun*
a sudden strong wind: *A gust of wind blew his hat off.*

gutter /ˈgʌtə(r)/ *noun*
1 a pipe under the edge of a roof to carry away rainwater
2 the part at the edge of a road where water is carried away

guy /gaɪ/ *noun*
1 a man: *He's a nice guy!*
2 a big doll that children make and burn on **Guy Fawkes Night**

> ○ In Britain, **Guy Fawkes Night** or **Bonfire Night** is the evening of 5 November, when people have a party outside with a **bonfire** and **fireworks**. Guy Fawkes was a man who tried to destroy the **Houses of Parliament** in 1605.

gymnasium /dʒɪmˈneɪziəm/ *noun*
a room where you do exercises for your body ○ The short form is **gym**.

gymnastics /dʒɪmˈnæstɪks/ *noun* (plural)
exercises for your body ○ The short form is **gym**.

gypsy /ˈdʒɪpsi/ *noun* (*plural* **gypsies**)
Gypsies are people who live in **caravans** and travel around from one place to another.

Hh

habit /ˈhæbɪt/ *noun*
something that you do very often: *Smoking is a bad habit.* ◇ *She's got a habit of phoning me when I'm in bed.*

habitat /ˈhæbɪtæt/ *noun*
the natural place where a plant or animal lives

had *form of* **have**

hadn't /ˈhædnt/ = **had not**

ha! ha! /ˌhɑ: ˈhɑ:/
words that you write to show that somebody is laughing

hail /heɪl/ *noun* (no plural)
frozen rain that falls in small hard balls (called **hailstones**)
hail *verb* (**hails**, **hailing**, **hailed** /heɪld/)
It's hailing.

hair /heə(r)/ *noun*
1 (*plural* **hairs**) one of the long thin things that grow on the skin of people and animals: *There's a hair in my soup.*
2 (no plural) all the hairs on a person's head: *She's got long black hair.* ☞ picture on page 126

> ○ You wash your hair with **shampoo** and make it tidy with a **hairbrush** or a **comb**. Some words that you can use to talk about the colour of a person's hair are **black**, **dark**, **brown**, **ginger**, **red**, **fair**, **blond** and **grey**.

hairbrush /ˈheəbrʌʃ/ *noun* (*plural* **hairbrushes**)
a brush that you use to make your hair tidy

haircut /ˈheəkʌt/ *noun*
1 when somebody cuts your hair: *I need a haircut.*
2 the way that your hair is cut: *I like your new haircut.*

hair

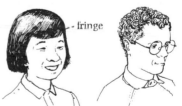

She's got straight hair. He's got curly hair.

She's got wavy hair. He's bald.

p	b	t	d	k	g	tʃ	dʒ	f	v	θ	ð
pen	**bad**	**tea**	**did**	**cat**	**got**	**chain**	**jam**	**fall**	**van**	**thin**	**this**

hairdresser /'heədresə(r)/ *noun*
a person whose job is to wash, cut and arrange hair ✪ The place where a hairdresser works is called a **hairdresser's**: *I'm going to the hairdressers to get my hair cut.*

hair-drier, hair-dryer /'heə draɪə(r)/ *noun*
a machine that dries hair by blowing hot air on it

hairstyle /'heəstaɪl/ *noun*
the way that your hair is cut and arranged

hairy /'heəri/ *adjective* (**hairier, hairiest**)
covered with hair: *He has got hairy legs.*

half /hɑːf/ *noun* (*plural* **halves** /hɑːvz/), *adjective, pronoun*
one of two equal parts of something; ½: *Half of six is three.* ◇ *I lived in Rome for two and a half years.* ◇ *The journey takes an hour and a half.* ◇ *She gave me half of her apple.*
in half so that there are two equal parts: *Cut the cake in half.*
half *adverb*
50%; partly: *The bottle is half empty.*
half past 30 minutes after an hour on the clock: *It's half past nine.* ☞ Look at page 164.

half-price /,hɑːf 'praɪs/ *adjective, adverb*
for half the usual price: *Children travel half-price on most trains and buses.*

half-term /,hɑːf 'tɜːm/ *noun*
a short school holiday in the middle of a term

half-time /,hɑːf 'taɪm/ *noun* (no plural)
a short time in the middle of a game like football, when you are not playing

halfway /,hɑːf'weɪ/ *adverb*
in the middle: *They live halfway between London and Oxford.* ◇ *She went out halfway through the lesson.*

hall /hɔːl/ *noun*
1 a big room or building where a lot of people meet: *a concert hall* ◇ *We did our exams in the school hall.*
2 the room in a house that is near the front door and has doors to other rooms: *You can leave your coat in the hall.*

hallo = hello

Hallowe'en /,hæləʊ'iːn/ *noun* (no plural)
31 October. Some people believe that at Hallowe'en, witches and ghosts appear.

halt /hɔːlt/ *noun* (no plural)
come to a halt stop: *The car came to a halt.*

halve /hɑːv/ *verb* (**halves, halving, halved** /hɑːvd/)
divide something into two parts that are the same: *There were two of us, so I halved the orange.*

halves *plural of* **half**

ham /hæm/ *noun* (no plural)
meat from a pig's leg that you can keep for a long time because salt or smoke was used to prepare it ☞ Note at **pig**

hamburger /'hæmbɜːgə(r)/ *noun*
meat cut into very small pieces and made into a flat round shape, that you eat between two pieces of bread: *A hamburger and chips, please.*

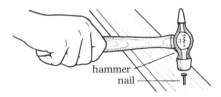
hammer
nail

hammer /'hæmə(r)/ *noun*
a tool with a handle and a heavy metal part, that you use for hitting **nails** into things
hammer *verb* (**hammers, hammering, hammered** /'hæməd/)
1 hit something with a hammer: *I hammered the nail into the wood.*
2 hit something hard: *He hammered on the door until somebody opened it.*

hammock /'hæmək/ *noun*
a bed made of cloth or rope that you hang up at the two ends

hamster /'hæmstə(r)/ *noun*
a small animal that people keep as a pet. Hamsters can keep food in the sides of their mouths.

hand¹ /hænd/ *noun*
1 the part at the end of your arm: *She held the letter in her hand.* ☞ picture on page 126
2 one of the parts of a clock or watch that move to show the time
a hand some help: *Could you give me a hand with my homework?*

Shapes and sizes

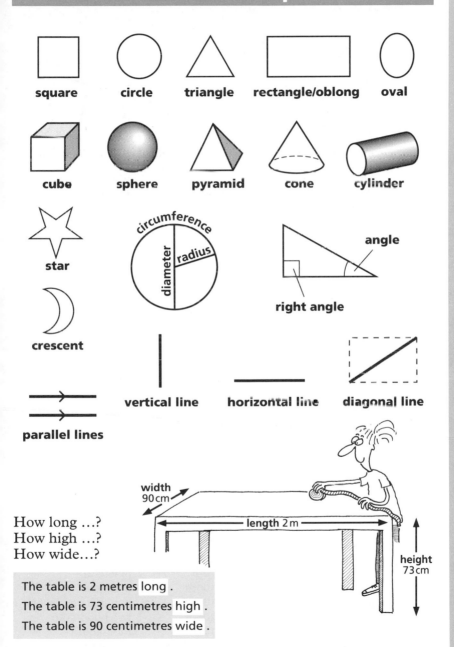

square **circle** **triangle** **rectangle/oblong** **oval**

cube **sphere** **pyramid** **cone** **cylinder**

star

circumference

diameter radius

angle

right angle

crescent

vertical line **horizontal line** **diagonal line**

parallel lines

width
90 cm

length 2 m

How long ...?
How high ...?
How wide...?

height
73 cm

The table is 2 metres long .

The table is 73 centimetres high .

The table is 90 centimetres wide .

Numbers

*He has got **three** children.*

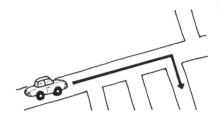

*Take the **third** road on the right.*

1	one	1st	first
2	two	2nd	second
3	three	3rd	third
4	four	4th	fourth
5	five	5th	fifth
6	six	6th	sixth
7	seven	7th	seventh
8	eight	8th	eighth
9	nine	9th	ninth
10	ten	10th	tenth
11	eleven	11th	eleventh
12	twelve	12th	twelfth
13	thirteen	13th	thirteenth
14	fourteen	14th	fourteenth
15	fifteen	15th	fifteenth
16	sixteen	16th	sixteenth
17	seventeen	17th	seventeenth
18	eighteen	18th	eighteenth
19	nineteen	19th	nineteenth
20	twenty	20th	twentieth
21	twenty-one	21st	twenty-first
30	thirty	30th	thirtieth
40	forty	40th	fortieth
50	fifty	50th	fiftieth
60	sixty	60th	sixtieth
70	seventy	70th	seventieth
80	eighty	80th	eightieth
90	ninety	90th	ninetieth
100	a/one hundred	100th	hundredth
101	a/one hundred and one	101st	hundred and first
200	two hundred	200th	two hundredth
1 000	a/one thousand	1 000th	thousandth
1 000 000	a/one million	1 000 000th	millionth

Saying numbers

267

4 302

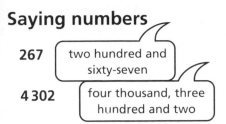

267 two hundred and sixty-seven

4 302 four thousand, three hundred and two

Writing numbers

We put a small space or a comma (,) between *thousands* and *hundreds* in numbers, for example:

15 000 or 15,000

Saying '0'

We usually say **nought** or **zero**:

nought point five (0.5)

In telephone numbers, we usually say **o** (you say it like **oh**):

My telephone number is 29035 (two nine **o** three five).

When we talk about temperature, we use **zero**:

It was very cold ~ the temperature was below **zero**.

In scores of games like football, we say **nil**:

The score was two-**nil**.

Fractions

	$1/2$	a half
	$1/3$	a/one third
	$1/4$	a/one quarter
	$1/8$	an/one eighth
	$1/16$	a/one sixteenth
	$3/4$	three quarters
	$1 2/5$	one and two fifths

☞ To find out more about how to say **telephone numbers**, look at page 300.

☞ To find out more about how to say and write **numbers in dates**, look at page 297.

We use . (NOT ,) in **decimals**.

Symbols		We write:	We say:
.	point	3.2	three point two
+	plus	5 + 6	five plus six
-	minus	10 - 4	ten minus four
x	multiplied by/	4 x 6	four multiplied by six
	times		four times six
÷	divided by	4 ÷ 2	four divided by two
%	per cent	78%	seventy-eight per cent
=	equals	1 + 3 = 4	one plus three equals four

Time

ten o'clock

(a) quarter past five
five fifteen

half past six
six thirty

(a) quarter to four
three forty-five

ten past eleven
eleven ten

twenty to twelve
eleven forty

seven minutes past two
two o seven *

What time is it?

What's the time?

It's ten o'clock.

To show what part of the day we mean, we can use:

a.m. *or* **in the morning**

The meeting is at 10 a.m.
The telephone rang at four o'clock in the morning.

p.m. *or* **in the afternoon**
       in the evening
       at night

The shop closes at 6 p.m.
She came home at eight o'clock in the evening.

* We do not often use the 'twenty-four
hour clock' when we say times (so we do
not say 'fourteen o seven'). We occasionally use it when we are reading a time from
a bus or train timetable.

60 seconds	= 1 minute
60 minutes	= 1 hour
24 hours	= 1 day

by hand without using a machine: *The curtains were made by hand.*

get out of hand become difficult to control: *The party got out of hand.*

hand in hand with your hand in another person's hand

hands up 1 put one hand in the air if you can answer the question 2 put your hands in the air because somebody has a gun

hold hands have another person's hand in your hand

in good hands well looked after: *Don't worry – your son is in good hands.*

on hand near and ready to help: *There is a doctor on hand 24 hours a day.*

hold hands

on the one hand ... on the other hand words that show the good and bad things about an idea: *On the one hand the hotel has a lovely view, but on the other hand it doesn't have a restaurant.*

hand² /hænd/ *verb* (**hands, handing, handed**)
put something into somebody's hand: *Can you hand me the scissors, please?* ◇ *I handed the money to the shop assistant.*

hand down pass a thing, story, etc from an older person to a younger one: *He never had new clothes – they were handed down from his older brothers.*

hand in give something to somebody: *The teacher asked us to hand in our homework.*

hand out give something to many people: *Please hand out these books.*

hand over give something to somebody: *'Hand over that knife!' said the police officer.*

handbag /'hændbæg/ *noun*
a small bag for carrying things like money and keys

handcuffs /'hændkʌfs/ *noun* (plural)
two metal rings with a chain that are put on a prisoner's arms so that he/she cannot use his/her hands

handful /'hændfʊl/ *noun*
1 as much as you can hold in one hand: *a handful of stones*
2 a small number: *Only a handful of people came to the meeting.*

handicap /'hændikæp/ *noun*
something that stops you doing well: *a school for children with physical handicaps*

handicapped /'hændikæpt/ *adjective*
not able to use a part of your body well: *They have a handicapped son.*

handkerchief /'hæŋkətʃɪf/ *noun*
a square piece of cloth or paper that you use for cleaning your nose

handles

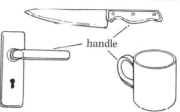

handle

handle¹ /'hændl/ *noun*
the part of a thing that you hold in your hand: *I turned the handle and opened the door.* ◇ *Hold that knife by the handle.*

handle² /'hændl/ *verb* (**handles, handling, handled** /'hændld/)
1 touch something with your hands: *Please wash your hands before you handle the food.*
2 control somebody or something: *That dog is too big for a small child to handle*
3 look after something and do what is necessary: *My secretary handles all letters.*

handlebars /'hændlbɑːz/ *noun* (plural)
the part at the front of a bicycle or motorcycle that you hold when you are riding it ☞ picture at **bicycle**

hand-luggage /'hænd lʌgɪdʒ/ *noun* (no plural)
a small bag or anything that you carry with you on an aeroplane

handmade /ˌhænd'meɪd/ *adjective*
made by a person, not by a machine: *handmade chocolates*

handsome /'hænsəm/ *adjective*
good-looking: *a handsome man* ☞ Note at **beautiful**

handwriting /'hændraɪtɪŋ/ *noun* (no plural)

the way you write: *Her handwriting is difficult to read.*

handy /'hændi/ *adjective* (**handier, handiest**)
1 useful: *This bag will be handy for carrying my books.*
2 near and easy to find or reach: *Have you got a pen handy?*
come in handy be useful: *Don't throw that box away – it might come in handy for something.*

hang /hæŋ/ *verb*
1 (**hangs, hanging, hung** /hʌŋ/, **has hung**) fix something, or be fixed at the top so that the lower part is free: *Hang your coat (up) on the hook.* ◇ *I hung the washing on the line to dry.*
2 (**hangs, hanging, hanged** /hæŋd/, **has hanged**) kill somebody by holding them above the ground by a rope around the neck: *She was hanged for murder.*
hang about, hang around stay somewhere with nothing special to do: *My plane was late so I had to hang about in the airport all morning.*
hang on wait: *Hang on – I'm not ready.*
hang on to somebody or **something** hold something firmly: *Hang on to your purse.*
hang up end a telephone call by putting the telephone down

hanger /'hæŋə(r)/ *noun*
a coat-hanger; a piece of metal, wood or plastic with a hook. You use it for hanging clothes on. ☞ picture at **coat-hanger**

hang-glider /'hæŋ glaɪdə(r)/ *noun*
a thing made of a very large piece of material on a frame, which you hang from and fly through the air
hang-gliding *noun* (no plural)
the sport of flying in a hang-glider

hanky, hankie /'hæŋki/ *noun* (*plural* **hankies**)
a handkerchief

happen /'hæpən/ *verb* (**happens, happening, happened** /'hæpənd/)
take place: *How did the accident happen?* ◇ *Did you hear what happened to me yesterday?*
happen to do something by chance: *I happened to meet Tim yesterday.*

happy /'hæpi/ *adjective* (**happier, happiest**)

1 If you are happy, you feel very pleased. People often laugh or smile when they are happy: *She looks very happy.* ◇ *That was one of the happiest days of my life.* ✪ opposite: **unhappy** or **sad** ☞ picture on page 262
2 a word that you use to say that you hope somebody will enjoy a special time: *Happy New Year!* ◇ *Happy Christmas!* ◇ *Happy Birthday!* ✪ **Many happy returns (of the day)** means the same as **Happy Birthday**.

happily /'hæpɪli/ *adverb*
1 in a happy way
2 it is lucky that: *Happily, the accident was not serious.*

happiness /'hæpɪnəs/ *noun* (no plural)
being happy

harbor *American English for* **harbour**

harbour /'hɑːbə(r)/ *noun*
a place where ships can stay safely in the water

hard¹ /hɑːd/ *adjective* (**harder, hardest**)
1 not soft; firm: *These apples are very hard.* ◇ *I couldn't sleep because the bed was too hard.* ✪ opposite: **soft** ☞ picture on page 263
2 difficult to do or understand: *The exam was very hard.* ◇ *hard work* ☞ Look at **easy**.
3 full of problems: *He's had a hard life.*
4 not kind or gentle: *She is very hard on her children.*

hard² /hɑːd/ *adverb*
1 a lot: *She works very hard.* ◇ *You must try harder!*
2 strongly: *It's raining hard.* ◇ *She hit him hard.*

hardback /'hɑːdbæk/ *noun*
a book with a hard cover ☞ Look at **paperback**.

hard disk /ˌhɑːd 'dɪsk/ *noun*
a plastic part inside a computer that stores information

harden /'hɑːdn/ *verb* (**hardens, hardening, hardened** /'hɑːdnd/)
become hard: *Wait for the cement to harden.*

hardly /'hɑːdli/ *adverb*
almost not; only just: *She spoke so quietly that I could hardly hear her.* ◇ *There's hardly any* (= almost no) *coffee left.*

hare /heə(r)/ *noun*
an animal like a big rabbit. Hares have long ears and can run very fast.

harm[1] /hɑːm/ *noun* (no plural)
hurt or damage
come to harm be hurt or damaged: *Make sure the children don't come to any harm.*
there is no harm in nothing bad will happen if you do something: *I don't know if she'll help you, but there's no harm in asking.*

harm[2] /hɑːm/ *verb* (**harms, harming, harmed** /hɑːmd/)
hurt or damage somebody or something: *The dog won't harm you.*

harmful /ˈhɑːmfl/ *adjective*
Something that is harmful can hurt or damage people or things: *Strong sunlight can be harmful to young babies.*

harmless /ˈhɑːmləs/ *adjective*
not dangerous: *Don't be frightened – these insects are harmless.*

harmony /ˈhɑːməni/ *noun*
1 (no plural) having the same ideas, etc, with no arguments: *The different races live together in harmony.*
2 (*plural* **harmonies**) musical notes that sound nice together: *They sang in harmony.*

harsh /hɑːʃ/ *adjective* (**harsher, harshest**)
1 rough and unpleasant to see or hear: *a harsh voice*
2 not kind; cruel: *a harsh punishment*

harvest /ˈhɑːvɪst/ *noun*
1 the time when fruit, corn or vegetables are ready to cut or pick: *The apple harvest is in September.*
2 all the fruit, corn or vegetables that are cut or picked: *We had a good harvest this year.*
harvest *verb* (**harvests, harvesting, harvested**)
When does the farmer harvest his wheat?

has *form of* **have**

hasn't /ˈhæznt/ = **has not**

haste /heɪst/ *noun* (no plural)
doing things too quickly: *In his haste to get up, he knocked over the chair.*
in haste quickly; in a hurry: *The letter was written in haste.*

hasty /ˈheɪsti/ *adjective* (**hastier, hastiest**)
1 If you are hasty, you do something too quickly: *Don't be too hasty. This is a very important decision.*
2 said or done quickly: *We ate a hasty lunch, then left.*
hastily /ˈheɪstɪli/ *adverb*
He put the money hastily into his pocket.

hats

hat /hæt/ *noun*
a thing that you wear on your head: *She's wearing a hat.*

hatch /hætʃ/ *verb* (**hatches, hatching, hatched** /hætʃt/)
When baby birds, insects, fish, etc hatch, they come out of an egg.

hate /heɪt/ *verb* (**hates, hating, hated**)
have a very strong feeling of not liking somebody or something: *Most cats hate water.* ◇ *I hate waiting for buses.*
hate, hatred /ˈheɪtrɪd/ *noun* (no plural)
a very strong feeling of not liking somebody or something

haul /hɔːl/ *verb* (**hauls, hauling, hauled** /hɔːld/)
pull something heavy: *They hauled the boat out of the river.*

haunt /hɔːnt/ *verb* (**haunts, haunting, haunted**)
1 If a ghost haunts a place, it visits it often: *A ghost haunts the castle.*
2 If something sad or unpleasant haunts you, you often think of it: *Her unhappy face still haunts me.*
haunted *adjective*
often visited by ghosts: *a haunted house*

have[1] /həv/, /hæv/ *verb*
a word that you use with parts of other verbs to show that something happened or started in the past: *I have seen that film.* ◇ *We have been in England for six months.* ◇ *When we arrived, Paul had already left.* ☞ verb table on next page

have[2] /hæv/ *verb* (**has** /hæz/, **having, had** /hæd/, **has had**)
1 (*also* **have got**) own or keep some

have¹

present tense		short forms	negative short forms	
I	**have**	I**'ve**	I	**haven't**
you	**have**	you**'ve**	you	**haven't**
he/she/it	**has** /hæz/	he**'s**/she**'s**/it**'s**	he/she/it	**hasn't**
we	**have**	we**'ve**	we	**haven't**
you	**have**	you**'ve**	you	**haven't**
they	**have**	they**'ve**	they	**haven't**

past tense **had** /hæd/

present participle **having**

past participle **had**

past tense short forms
I**'d**
you**'d**
he**'d**/she**'d**/it**'d**
we**'d**
you**'d**
they**'d**

thing: *She has blue eyes.* ◇ *They have got a big car.* ◇ *Do you have any brothers and sisters?*
2 be ill with something; feel something: *She has got a headache.*
3 eat or drink something: *What time do you have breakfast?*
4 a word that shows that something happens to somebody or something: *I had a shower.* ◇ *He has had an accident.* ◇ *Did you have a good holiday?*
5 (*also* **have got**) a word that you use with some nouns: *I have an idea.* ◇ *Have you got time to help me?*
have to, have got to must: *I have to/ have got to go to school tomorrow.* ◇ *We don't have to/ haven't got to get up early tomorrow.* ◇ *Do we have to/ have we got to pay for this now?*
have something done let somebody do something for you: *I had my hair cut yesterday.* ◇ *Have you had your car mended?*

haven't /'hævnt/ = **have not**

hawk /hɔːk/ *noun*
a big bird that catches and eats other birds and small animals

hay /heɪ/ *noun* (no plural)
dry grass that is used as food for farm animals
hay fever /'heɪ fiːvə(r)/ *noun* (no plural)
an illness like a cold. Grass and other plants can cause hay fever.

hazard /'hæzəd/ *noun*
a danger: *Ice is a hazard for drivers.*
hazardous /'hæzədəs/ *adjective*
dangerous: *Motor racing is a hazardous sport.*

hazelnut /'heɪzlnʌt/ *noun*
a small nut that you can eat

he /hiː/ *pronoun* (*plural* **they**)
the man or boy that the sentence is about: *I saw Mike when he arrived.* ◇ *'Where is John?' 'He's* (= he is) *at home.'*

head¹ /hed/ *noun*
1 the part of your body above your neck, that has your eyes, ears, nose and mouth in it: *She turned her head to look at me.* ☞ picture on page 126
2 what you use for thinking: *A strange thought came into his head.*
3 the top, front or most important part: *She sat at the head of the table.*
4 the most important person: *The Pope is the head of the Roman Catholic church.*
5 **heads** (plural) the side of a coin that has the head of a person on it ✪ You say **heads or tails** when you are throwing a coin in the air to decide something, for example who will start a game.
a head, per head for one person: *The meal cost £12 a head.*
go to your head make you too pleased with yourself: *Winning a prize for his*

painting went to his head, and he began to think he was a great artist.

head first with your head before the rest of your body

> ❍ In Britain, you **nod** your head (move it up and down) to say 'yes' or to show that you agree, and you **shake** your head (move it from side to side) to say 'no' or to show that you disagree.

head² /hed/ *verb* (**heads, heading, headed**)
1 be at the front or top of a group: *Michael's name heads the list.*
2 hit a ball with your head
head for go towards a place: *Let's head for home.*

headache /'hedeɪk/ *noun*
a pain in your head: *I've got a headache.*

heading /'hedɪŋ/ *noun*
the words at the top of a piece of writing to show what it is about; a title

headlight /'hedlaɪt/, **headlamp** /'hedlæmp/ *noun*
one of the two big strong lights on the front of a car ☞ **picture at car**

headline /'hedlaɪn/ *noun*
1 words in big letters at the top of a newspaper story
2 **the headlines** (plural) the most important news on radio or television: *Here are the news headlines.*

headmaster /,hed'mɑːstə(r)/ *noun*
a man who is in charge of a school

headmistress /,hed'mɪstrəs/ *noun* (*plural* **headmistresses**)
a woman who is in charge of a school

headphones

headphones /'hedfəʊnz/ *noun* (plural)
things that you put over your head and ears for listening to a radio, cassette player, etc

headquarters /,hed'kwɔːtəz/ *noun* (plural)
the main offices where the leaders work:

The company's headquarters are in London. ❍ The short form is **HQ.**

headway /'hedweɪ/ *noun* (no plural)
make headway go forward: *We haven't made much headway in our discussions.*

heal /hiːl/ *verb* (**heals, healing, healed** /hiːld/)
become well again; make something well again: *The cut on his leg healed slowly.*

health /helθ/ *noun* (no plural)
how well your body is; how you are: *Smoking is bad for your health.*

healthy /'helθi/ *adjective* (**healthier, healthiest**)
1 well; not ill: *healthy children*
2 that helps to make or keep you well: *healthy food*
❍ opposite: **unhealthy**

heap /hiːp/ *noun*
1 a lot of things on top of one another in an untidy way; a large amount of something: *She left her clothes in a heap on the floor.*
2 **heaps** (plural) a lot: *heaps of time*
heap *verb* (**heaps, heaping, heaped** /hiːpt/)
put a lot of things on top of one another: *She heaped food onto my plate.*

hear /hɪə(r)/ *verb* (**hears, hearing, heard** /hɜːd/, **has heard**)
1 get sounds with your ears: *Can you hear that noise?* ◇ *I heard somebody laughing in the next room.*

> **hear** or **listen**?
>
> **Hear** and **listen** are used in different ways. When you **hear** something, sounds come to your ears:
>
> *I **heard** the door close.*
>
> When you **listen to** something, you are trying to hear it:
>
> *I **listen to** the radio every morning.*

2 learn about something with your ears: *Have you heard the news?*
hear from somebody get a letter or a phone call from somebody: *Have you heard from your sister?*
hear of somebody or **something**

iː	i	ɪ	e	æ	ɑː	ɒ	ɔː	ʊ	u	uː
see	happy	sit	ten	cat	father	got	saw	put	situation	too

know about somebody or something: *Who is he? I've never heard of him.*

will not hear of something will not agree to something: *My father wouldn't hear of me paying for the meal.*

hearing /'hɪərɪŋ/ *noun* (no plural)
the power to hear: *Speak louder – her hearing isn't very good.*

heart /hɑːt/ *noun*
1 the part of a person's or animal's body that makes the blood go round inside: *Your heart beats faster when you run.* ☞ picture on page 126
2 your feelings: *She has a kind heart.*
3 the centre; the middle part: *They live in the heart of the countryside.*
4 the shape ♥
5 **hearts** (plural) the playing-cards that have red shapes like hearts on them: *the six of hearts*

break somebody's heart make somebody very sad: *It broke his heart when his wife died.*

by heart so that you know every word: *I have learned the poem by heart.*

lose heart stop hoping: *Don't lose heart – you can still win if you try.*

your heart sinks you suddenly feel unhappy: *My heart sank when I saw the first question on the exam paper.*

heart attack /'hɑːt ətæk/ *noun*
a sudden dangerous illness, when your heart stops working properly: *She had a heart attack and died.*

heartbeat /'hɑːtbiːt/ *noun*
the movement or sound of your heart as it pushes blood around your body: *The doctor listened to my heartbeat.*

heartless /'hɑːtləs/ *adjective*
not kind; cruel

heat /hiːt/ *noun*
1 (no plural) the feeling of something hot: *the heat of the sun*
2 (plural **heats**) one of the first parts of a race or competition: *The winner of this heat will swim in the semifinal.*

heat, **heat up** *verb* (**heats**, **heating**, **heated**)
make something hot; become hot: *I heated some milk in a saucepan.* ◇ *Wait for the oven to heat up before you put the food in.*

heater *noun*
a thing that makes a place warm or heats

water: *Switch on the heater if you feel cold.* ◇ *a water-heater*

heath /hiːθ/ *noun*
a big piece of wild land where there are no farms

heating /'hiːtɪŋ/ *noun* (no plural)
the way you make a building warm: *What kind of heating do you have?*

heave /hiːv/ *verb* (**heaves**, **heaving**, **heaved** /hiːvd/)
lift or pull something heavy: *We heaved the suitcase up the stairs.*

heaven /'hevn/ *noun* (no plural)
Many people believe that God lives in heaven and that good people go to heaven when they die. ☞ Look at **hell**.

Good Heavens! words that you use to show surprise: *Good Heavens! I've won £100!*

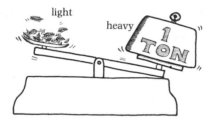

light   heavy

heavy /'hevi/ *adjective* (**heavier**, **heaviest**)
1 with a lot of weight, so it is difficult to lift or move: *I can't carry this bag – it's too heavy.*
2 larger, stronger or more than usual: *heavy rain* ◇ *The traffic was very heavy this morning.*
✪ opposite: **light**

heavy metal /,hevi 'metl/ *noun* (no plural)
a kind of very loud rock music

heavily /'hevəli/ *adverb*
It was raining heavily.

hectare /'hekteə(r)/ *noun*
a measure of land. There are 10 000 **square metres** in a hectare.

hectic /'hektɪk/ *adjective*
very busy: *I had a hectic day at work.*

he'd /hiːd/
1 = he had
2 = he would

hedge /hedʒ/ *noun*
a line of small trees that makes a kind of wall around a garden or field

hedgehog /'hedʒhɒg/ *noun*
a small animal covered with hairs that are like sharp needles

heel /hi:l/ *noun*
1 the back part of your foot ☞ picture on page 126
2 the back part of a shoe under the heel of your foot
3 the part of a sock that covers the heel of your foot

height /haɪt/ *noun*
1 (*plural* **heights**) how far it is from the bottom to the top of somebody or something: *What is the height of this mountain?* ◇ *The wall is two metres in height.* ◇ *She asked me my height, weight and age.* ☞ picture on page 161
2 (*plural* **heights**) a high place: *I'm afraid of heights.*
3 (no plural) the strongest or most important part of something: *the height of summer*

heir /eə(r)/ *noun*
a person who receives money, goods, etc when another person dies: *Prince Charles is Queen Elizabeth's heir.*
heiress /'eəres/ *noun* (*plural* **heiresses**)
an heir who is a woman

held *form of* **hold¹**

helicopter

helicopter /'helɪkɒptə(r)/ *noun*
a kind of small aircraft that can go straight up in the air. It has long metal parts on top that turn to help it fly.

hell /hel/ *noun* (no plural)
Some people believe that bad people go to hell when they die. ☞ Look at **heaven**.

he'll /hi:l/ = he will

hello /hə'ləʊ/
a word that you say when you meet somebody or when you answer the telephone

helmet /'helmɪt/ *noun*
a hard hat that keeps your head safe: *Motor cyclists in Britain must wear helmets.*

help /help/ *verb* (**helps**, **helping**, **helped** /helpt/)
1 do something useful for somebody; make somebody's work easier: *Will you help me with the washing-up?* ◇ *She helped me to carry the box.*
2 a word that you shout when you are in danger: *Help! I can't swim!*
can't help If you can't help doing something, you can't stop yourself doing it: *It was so funny that I couldn't help laughing.*
help yourself take what you want: *Help yourself to a drink.* ◇ *'Can I have a sandwich?' 'Of course. Help yourself!'*
help *noun* (no plural)
1 helping somebody: *Thank you for all your help.* ◇ *Do you need any help?*
2 a person or thing that helps: *He was a great help to me when I was ill.*

helpful /'helpfl/ *adjective*
A person or thing that is helpful gives help: *The woman in the shop was very helpful.* ◇ *helpful advice* ✪ opposite: **unhelpful**

helping /'helpɪŋ/ *noun*
the amount of food on your plate: *I had a big helping of pie.*

helpless /'helpləs/ *adjective*
not able to do things without help: *Babies are totally helpless.*

hem /hem/ *noun*
the bottom edge of something like a shirt or trousers, that is folded and sewn

hemisphere /'hemɪsfɪə(r)/ *noun*
one half of the earth: *the northern/southern hemisphere*

hen /hen/ *noun*
1 a female bird that people keep on farms for its eggs ☞ Note at **chicken**
2 any female bird
✪ A male bird is a **cock**.

her¹ /hɜ:(r)/ *pronoun* (*plural* **them**)
a word that shows a woman or girl: *Tell Jane that I'll see her tonight.* ◇ *I wrote to her yesterday.*

her² /hɜ:(r)/ *adjective*
of the woman or girl that you have just talked about: *That's her book.* ◇ *Jill has hurt her leg.*

p	b	t	d	k	g	tʃ	dʒ	f	v	θ	ð
pen	**b**ad	**t**ea	**d**id	**c**at	**g**ot	**ch**ain	**j**am	**f**all	**v**an	**th**in	**th**is

herb /hɜːb/ *noun*
a plant that people use to make food taste good, or in medicine

herd /hɜːd/ *noun*
a big group of animals of the same kind: *a herd of cows* ◇ *a herd of elephants*

here /hɪə(r)/ *adverb*
in, at or to this place: *Your glasses are here.* ◇ *Come here, please.* ◇ *Here's my car.* ◇ *Where's Bill? Oh, here he is.*

here and there in different places: *There were groups of people here and there along the beach.*

here goes words that you say before you do something exciting or dangerous: *'Here goes,' said Sue, and jumped into the river.*

here you are words that you say when you give something to somebody: *'Can I borrow a pen, please?' 'Yes, here you are.'*

here's /hɪəz/ = **here is**

hero /'hɪərəʊ/ *noun* (*plural* **heroes**)
1 a person who has done something brave or good: *Everybody said that Mark was a hero after he rescued his sister from the fire.*
2 the most important man or boy in a book, play or film

heroic /hə'rəʊɪk/ *adjective*
very brave

heroin /'herəʊɪn/ *noun* (no plural)
a very strong drug that can be dangerous

heroine /'herəʊɪn/ *noun*
1 a woman who has done something brave or good
2 the most important woman or girl in a book, play or film

hers /hɜːz/ *pronoun*
something that belongs to her: *Gina says this book is hers.* ◇ *Are these keys hers?*

herself /hɜː'self/ *pronoun* (*plural* **themselves** /ðəm'selvz/)
1 a word that shows the same woman or girl that you have just talked about: *She fell and hurt herself.*
2 a word that makes 'she' stronger: *'Who told you that Jane was married?' 'She told me herself.'*
by herself 1 alone; without other people: *She lives by herself.* **2** without help: *She can carry the box by herself.*

he's /hiːz/
1 = **he is**
2 = **he has**

hesitate /'hezɪteɪt/ *verb* (**hesitates**, **hesitating**, **hesitated**)
stop for a moment before you do or say something because you are not sure about it: *He hesitated before answering the question.*
hesitation /,hezɪ'teɪʃn/ *noun* (no plural)
They agreed without hesitation.

hexagon /'heksəgən/ *noun*
a shape with six sides
hexagonal /hek'sægənl/ *adjective*
with six sides: *a hexagonal box*

hey /heɪ/
a word that you shout to make somebody listen to you, or when you are surprised: *Hey! Where are you going?*

hi /haɪ/
a word that you say when you meet somebody; hello: *Hi Tony! How are you?*

hiccup, hiccough /'hɪkʌp/ *noun*
a sudden noise that you make in your throat. You sometimes get hiccups when you have eaten or drunk too quickly.

hide /haɪd/ *verb* (**hides**, **hiding**, **hid** /hɪd/, **has hidden** /'hɪdn/)
1 put something where people cannot find it: *I hid the money under the bed.*
2 be or get in a place where people cannot see or find you: *Somebody was hiding behind the door.*
3 not tell or show something to somebody: *She tried to hide her feelings.*
hide-and-seek /,haɪd n 'siːk/ *noun* (no plural)
a game that children play. Some children hide and one child tries to find them.

hideous /'hɪdiəs/ *adjective*
very ugly: *That shirt is hideous!*

hiding /'haɪdɪŋ/ *noun* (no plural)
be in hiding, go into hiding be in, or go into a place where people will not find you: *The prisoners escaped and went into hiding.*

hi-fi /'haɪ faɪ/ *noun*
a machine for playing records, cassettes and compact discs

high /haɪ/ *adjective* (**higher**, **highest**)
1 Something that is high goes up a long way: *a high wall* ◇ *Mount Everest is the highest mountain in the world.* ☞ opposite: **low** ☞ picture on page 262
2 You use 'high' to say or ask how far

s	z	ʃ	ʒ	h	m	n	ŋ	l	r	j	w
so	**zoo**	**shoe**	vision	**hat**	**man**	**no**	sing	**leg**	**red**	**yes**	**wet**

something is from the bottom to the top: *The table is 80 cm high.* ☞ picture on page 161
❂ We use **tall**, not **high**, to talk about people: *How tall are you?* ◊ *He's 1.72 metres tall.*
3 far from the ground: *a high shelf*
4 great: *The car was travelling at high speed.* ◊ *high temperatures*
5 at the top of sound; not deep: *I heard the high voice of a child.*
☞ Look at **low**.
high *adverb*
a long way above the ground: *The plane flew high above the clouds.*
high and low everywhere: *I've looked high and low for my keys, but I can't find them anywhere.*

high-jump /'haɪ dʒʌmp/ *noun* (no plural)
a sport where people jump over a high bar

highlands /'haɪləndz/ *noun* (plural)
the part of a country with hills and mountains: *the Scottish Highlands*

highlight /'haɪlaɪt/ *noun*
the best or most exciting part of something: *The highlight of our holiday was a visit to the palace.*

highly /'haɪli/ *adverb*
1 very or very much: *Their children are highly intelligent.* ◊ *She has a highly paid job.*
2 very well: *I think very highly of your work* (= I think it is very good).

Highness /'haɪnəs/ *noun* (plural **Highnesses**)
a word that you use when speaking to or about a royal person: *His Highness the Prince of Wales*

high school /'haɪ skuːl/ *noun*
1 a school in Britain for children between the ages of 11 and 18
2 a school in the USA for children between the ages of 15 and 18

high street /'haɪ striːt/ *noun*
the biggest or most important street in a town: *There is a bookshop on the High Street.*

highway /'haɪweɪ/ *noun*
a big road between towns ❂ **Highway** is used mostly in American English.

hijack /'haɪdʒæk/ *verb* (**hijacks**, **hijacking**, **hijacked** /'haɪdʒækt/)
take control of an aeroplane or a car and make the pilot or driver take you somewhere
hijacker *noun*
a person who hijacks a plane or car

hill /hɪl/ *noun*
a high piece of land that is not as high as a mountain: *I pushed my bike up the hill.* ◊ *Their house is at the top of the hill.*
☞ Look also at **uphill** and **downhill**.
hilly *adjective* (**hillier**, **hilliest**)
with a lot of hills: *The countryside is very hilly where I live.*

him /hɪm/ *pronoun* (plural **them**)
a word that shows a man or boy: *Where's Andy? I can't see him.* ◊ *I spoke to him yesterday.*

himself /hɪm'self/ *pronoun* (plural **themselves** /ðəm'selvz/)
1 a word that shows the same man or boy that you have just talked about: *Paul looked at himself in the mirror.*
2 a word that makes 'he' stronger: *Did he make this cake himself?*
by himself 1 alone; without other people: *Dad went shopping by himself.*
2 without help: *He did it by himself.*

Hindu /'hɪnduː/ *noun*
a person who follows one of the religions of India, called **Hinduism**

hinge /hɪndʒ/ *noun*
a piece of metal that joins two sides of a box, door, etc together so that it can open and close

hint /hɪnt/ *verb* (**hints**, **hinting**, **hinted**)
say something, but not in a direct way: *Sarah looked at her watch, hinting that she wanted to go home.*
hint *noun*
1 something that you say, but not in a direct way: *When he said he had no money, it was a hint that he wanted you to pay for his dinner.*
2 a small amount of something: *There's a hint of garlic in this soup.*

hip /hɪp/ *noun*
the place where your leg joins the side of your body ☞ picture on page 126

hippopotamus /ˌhɪpə'pɒtəməs/ *noun* (plural **hippopotamuses** or **hippopotami** /ˌhɪpə'pɒtəmaɪ/)
a large African animal with thick skin that

| iː | i | ɪ | e | æ | ɑː | ɒ | ɔː | ʊ | u | uː |
| see | happy | sit | ten | cat | father | got | saw | put | situation | too |

lives near water ✪ The short form is
hippo.

hire /ˈhaɪə(r)/ *verb* (**hires**, **hiring**, **hired**
/ˈhaɪəd/)
1 pay to use something for a short time:
We hired a car when we were on holiday.
2 pay somebody to do a job for you: *We
hired somebody to mend the roof.*
hire out let somebody hire something
from you: *They hire out bicycles.*
hire *noun* (no plural)
Have you got any boats for hire?

his /hɪz/ *adjective*
of him: *John came with his sister.* ◇ *He
has hurt his arm.*
his *pronoun*
something that belongs to him: *Are these
books yours or his?*

hiss /hɪs/ *verb* (**hisses**, **hissing**, **hissed**
/hɪst/)
make a noise like a very long **S**: *The cat
hissed at me.*
hiss *noun* (*plural* **hisses**)
the hiss of steam

historic /hɪˈstɒrɪk/ *adjective*
important in history: *It was a historic
moment when man first walked on the
moon.*

historical /hɪˈstɒrɪkl/ *adjective*
of or about past times: *She writes historical novels.*

history /ˈhɪstri/ *noun* (no plural)
1 the study of things that happened in the
past: *History is my favourite subject at
school.*
2 all the things that happened in the past:
It was an important moment in history.

hit¹ /hɪt/ *verb* (**hits**, **hitting**, **hit**, **has hit**)
touch somebody or something hard: *He
hit me on the head with a book.* ◇ *The car
hit a wall.*

hit² /hɪt/ *noun*
1 touching somebody or something hard:
That was a good hit! (in a game of cricket
or baseball, for example)
2 a person or a thing that a lot of people
like: *This song was a hit in America.*

hitchhike /ˈhɪtʃhaɪk/, **hitch** *verb*
(**hitchhikes**, **hitchhiking**, **hitchhiked**

/ˈhɪtʃhaɪkt/, **hitches**, **hitching**, **hitched**
/hɪtʃt/)
travel by asking for free rides in cars and
lorries: *We hitchhiked across Europe.*
hitchhiker *noun*
a person who hitchhikes

hive /haɪv/ *noun*
a box where bees live

hoard /hɔːd/ *noun*
a secret store of something, for example
food or money
hoard *verb* (**hoards**, **hoarding**,
hoarded)
save and keep things secretly: *The old man
hoarded the money in a box under his bed.*

hoarse /hɔːs/ *adjective*
If your voice is hoarse, it is rough and
quiet, for example because you have a
cold.

hoax /həʊks/ *noun* (*plural* **hoaxes**)
a trick that makes somebody believe something that is not true: *There wasn't really
a bomb in the station – it was a hoax.*

hobby /ˈhɒbi/ *noun* (*plural* **hobbies**)
something that you like doing when you
are not working: *My hobbies are reading
and swimming.*

hockey /ˈhɒki/ *noun* (no plural)
a game for two teams of eleven players
who hit a small ball with long curved
sticks on a field (called a **pitch**)

hold¹ /həʊld/ *verb* (**holds**, **holding**, **held**
/held/, **has held**)
1 have something in your hand or arms:
She was holding a gun. ◇ *He held the
baby in his arms.*
2 keep something in a certain way: *Hold
your hand up.*
3 have space for a certain number or
amount: *The car holds five people.*
4 make something happen: *The meeting
was held in the town hall.*
5 have something: *He holds a Swiss
passport.*
hold somebody or **something back**
stop somebody or something from moving
forwards: *The police held back the crowd.*
Hold it! Wait! Don't move!
hold on 1 wait: *Hold on, I'm coming.*
2 not stop holding something tightly: *The
child held on to her mother's hand.*
hold up 1 make somebody or something late: *The plane was held up for 40*

minutes. **2** try to steal from a place, using a gun: *Two men held up a bank in Bristol today.*

hold² /həʊld/ *noun* (no plural)
having something in your hand: *Can you get hold of* (= take and hold) *the other end of the table and help me move it?*
get hold of somebody find somebody so that you can speak to them: *I'm trying to get hold of Peter but he's not at home.*
get hold of something find something: *I can't get hold of the book I need.*

hold³ /həʊld/ *noun*
the part of a ship or an aeroplane where you keep the goods

hole /həʊl/ *noun*
an empty space or opening in something: *I'm going to dig a hole in the garden.* ◇ *The dentist filled the hole in my tooth.* ◇ *My socks are full of holes.*

holiday /'hɒlədeɪ/ *noun*
a day or days when you do not go to work or school, and when you may go and stay away from home: *The school holidays start next week.* ◇ *We're going to France for our summer holidays.* ❂ A day when everybody in a country has a holiday is called a **bank holiday** or a **public holiday** in Britain.
on holiday not at work or school: *Mrs Smith isn't here this week. She's on holiday.*

hollow /'hɒləʊ/ *adjective*
with an empty space inside: *A drum is hollow.*

holly /'hɒli/ *noun*
a tree that has leaves with a lot of sharp points, and red berries ❂ People often put holly in their houses at Christmas.

holy /'həʊli/ *adjective* (**holier**, **holiest**)
1 very special because it is about God or a god: *The Bible is the holy book of Christians.*
2 A holy person lives a good and religious life.

home¹ /həʊm/ *noun*
1 the place where you live: *Simon left home at the age of 18.*
2 a place where they look after people, for example children who have no parents, or old people: *My grandmother lives in a home.*
at home in your house or flat: *I stayed at home yesterday.* ◇ *Is Sara at home?*

home² /həʊm/ *adverb*
to the place where you live ❂ Be careful! We do not use **to** before **home**: *Let's go home.* ◇ *What time did you arrive home last night?*

home³ /həʊm/ *adjective*
of your home or your country: *What is your home address?*

homeless /'həʊmləs/ *adjective*
If you are homeless, you have nowhere to live: *The floods made many people homeless.*

home-made /ˌhəʊm 'meɪd/ *adjective*
made in your house, not bought in a shop: *home-made bread*

homesick /'həʊmsɪk/ *adjective*
sad because you are away from home

homework /'həʊmwɜːk/ *noun* (no plural)
work that a teacher gives to you to do at home: *Have you done your French homework?* ☞ Note at **housework**

homosexual /ˌhəʊɒmə'sekʃʊəl/ *adjective*
attracted to people of the same sex

honest /'ɒnɪst/ *adjective*
A person who is honest says what is true and does not steal or cheat: *She's a very honest person.* ◇ *Be honest – do you really like this dress?* ❂ opposite: **dishonest**

honestly *adverb*
Try to answer the questions honestly. ◇ *Honestly, I don't know where your money is.*

honesty /'ɒnəsti/ *noun* (no plural)
being honest

honey /'hʌni/ *noun* (no plural)
the sweet food that bees make

honeymoon /'hʌnimuːn/ *noun*
a holiday that a man and woman have just after they get married

honor *American English for* **honour**

honour /'ɒnə(r)/ *noun* (no plural)
1 something that makes you proud and pleased: *It was a great honour to be invited to Buckingham Palace.*
2 the respect from other people that a person or country gets because of something very good that they have done: *They are fighting for the honour of their country.*
in honour of somebody to show that

p	b	t	d	k	g	tʃ	dʒ	f	v	θ	ð
pen	**b**ad	**t**ea	**d**id	**c**at	**g**ot	**ch**ain	**j**am	**f**all	**v**an	**th**in	**th**is

you respect somebody: *There is a party to-night in honour of our visitors.*

hood /hʊd/ *noun*
1 the part of a coat or jacket that covers your head and neck
2 *American English for* **bonnet 1**

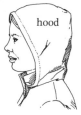
hood

hoof /hu:f/ *noun*
(*plural* **hoofs** or **hooves** /hu:vz/)
the hard part of the foot of horses and some other animals ☞ picture at **horse**

hook /hʊk/ *noun*
a curved piece of metal or plastic for hanging things on, or for catching something: *Hang your coat on that hook.* ◇ *a fish-hook*
off the hook If a telephone is off the hook, the part that you speak into (the **receiver**) is not in place so that the telephone will not ring.

hooks

hooligan /'hu:lɪɡən/ *noun*
a young person who behaves in a noisy way and fights other people: *football hooligans*

hoot /hu:t/ *noun*
the sound that an owl or a car's horn makes
hoot *verb* (**hoots, hooting, hooted**)
make this sound: *The driver hooted at the dog.*

Hoover /'hu:və(r)/ *noun*
a machine that cleans carpets by sucking up dirt ✪ **Hoover** is a trade mark.

hooves *plural of* **hoof**

hop /hɒp/ *verb*
(**hops, hopping, hopped** /hɒpt/)
1 jump on one foot
2 jump with two or all feet together: *The frog hopped onto the stone.*

hop

hope¹ /həʊp/ *noun*
1 a feeling of wanting something to happen and thinking that it will: *He hasn't*

worked very hard so there is not much hope that he will pass the exam.
2 a person or thing that gives you hope: *Can you help me? You're my only hope.*
give up hope stop thinking that what you want will happen: *Don't give up hope. The letter may come tomorrow.*

hope² /həʊp/ *verb* (**hopes, hoping, hoped** /həʊpt/)
want something that may happen: *I hope you have a nice holiday.* ◇ *I hope to see you tomorrow.* ◇ *We're hoping that Dave will come to the party.* ◇ *She's hoping for a bike for her birthday.*
I hope not I do not want that to happen: *'Do you think it will rain?' 'I hope not.'*
I hope so I want that to happen: *'Will you be at the party?' 'I'm not sure – I hope so.'*

hopeful /'həʊpfl/ *adjective*
If you are hopeful, you think that something that you want will happen: *I'm hopeful about getting a job.*
hopefully /'həʊpfəli/ *adverb*
1 in a hopeful way: *The cat looked hopefully at our plates.*
2 I hope: *Hopefully he won't be late.*

hopeless /'həʊpləs/ *adjective*
1 very bad: *I'm hopeless at tennis.*
2 useless: *It's hopeless trying to work when my brother is here – he's so noisy!*
hopelessly *adverb*
We got hopelessly lost in the forest.

horizon /hə'raɪzn/ *noun*
the line between the earth or sea and the sky: *We could see a ship on the horizon.*

horizontal /ˌhɒrɪ'zɒntl/ *adjective*
Something that is horizontal goes from side to side, not up and down: *a horizontal line* ☞ picture on page 161

horn /hɔ:n/ *noun*
1 one of the hard pointed things that some animals have on their heads ☞ picture at **goat**
2 a thing in a car, ship, etc that makes a loud sound to warn people: *Don't sound your horn late at night.*
3 a musical instrument that you blow

horoscope /'hɒrəskəʊp/ *noun*
something that tells you what will happen, using the planets and your date of birth: *Have you read your horoscope today?* (in a newspaper, for example)

s	z	ʃ	ʒ	h	m	n	ŋ	l	r	j	w
so	**zoo**	**shoe**	vision	**hat**	**man**	**no**	sing	**leg**	**red**	**yes**	**wet**

horrible /'hɒrəbl/ *adjective*
1 Something that is horrible makes you feel afraid or shocked: *There was a horrible murder here last week.*
2 very bad: *What horrible weather!*

horrid /'hɒrɪd/ *adjective*
very bad or unkind: *Don't be so horrid!*

horrify /'hɒrɪfaɪ/ *verb* (**horrifies, horrifying, horrified** /'hɒrɪfaɪd/, **has horrified**)
shock and frighten somebody: *We were horrified by the photos of the car crash.*

horror /'hɒrə(r)/ *noun* (no plural)
a feeling of fear or shock: *They watched in horror as the child ran in front of the bus.*
horror film /'hɒrə fɪlm/ *noun*
a film that shows frightening things

horse

horse /hɔːs/ *noun*
a big animal that can carry people and pull heavy things: *Can you ride a horse?* ✪ A young horse is called a **foal**.
on horseback sitting on a horse: *We saw a lot of policemen on horseback.*

horseshoe /'hɔːs ʃuː/ *noun*
a piece of metal like a U that a horse wears on its foot

hose /həʊz/, **hose-pipe** /'həʊz paɪp/ *noun*
a long soft tube that you use to bring water, for example in the garden or when there is a fire

hospital /'hɒspɪtl/ *noun*
a place where doctors and nurses look after people who are ill or hurt: *My brother is in hospital – he's broken his leg.* ◇ *The ambulance took her to hospital.*

✪ A room in a hospital where people sleep is called a **ward**. A person who is staying in hospital is called a **patient**.

hospitality /ˌhɒspɪ'tæləti/ *noun* (no plural)
being friendly to people who are visiting you, and looking after them well: *We thanked them for their hospitality.*

host /həʊst/ *noun*
a person who invites guests, for example to a party: *The host offered me a drink.*

hostage /'hɒstɪdʒ/ *noun*
a prisoner that you keep until people give you what you want: *The hijackers have freed all the hostages.*
hold somebody hostage keep somebody as a hostage: *They held his daughter hostage until he paid them the money.*
take somebody hostage catch somebody and keep them as a hostage

hostel /'hɒstl/ *noun*
a place like a cheap hotel where people can stay. *a youth hostel*

hostess /'həʊstəs/ *noun* (*plural* **hostesses**)
a woman who invites guests, for example to a party ☞ Look also at **air-hostess**.

hostile /'hɒstaɪl/ *adjective*
very unfriendly: *a hostile army*

hot /hɒt/ *adjective* (**hotter, hottest**)
1 not cold. A fire is hot: *I'm hot. Can you open the window?* ◇ *It's hot today, isn't it?* ◇ *hot water* ☞ picture on page 263
2 Food that is hot has a strong, burning taste: *a hot curry*

hotel /həʊ'tel/ *noun*
a place where you pay to sleep and eat: *I stayed at a hotel near the airport.*

hour /'aʊə(r)/ *noun*
1 a measure of time. There are 60 **minutes** in an hour: *The journey took two hours.* ◇ *I've been waiting for an hour.* ◇ *half an hour*
2 **hours** (plural) the time when somebody is working, or when a shop or office is open: *Our office hours are 9 a.m. to 5 p.m.*

house

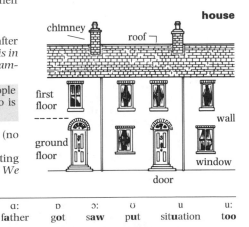

hourly /'aʊəli/ *adjective, adverb*
that happens or comes once an hour:
There is an hourly bus to Oxford.

house /haʊs/ *noun* (*plural* **houses**
/'haʊzɪz/)
1 a building where a person or a family
lives. A house has more than one floor:
*How many rooms are there in your
house?* ◇ *We're having dinner at Jane's
house tonight.* ☞ Look at **bungalow**,
cottage and **flat**. ☞ picture on page 177
2 a building for a special use: *a warehouse*

housewife /'haʊswaɪf/ *noun* (*plural*
housewives /'haʊswaɪvz/)
a woman who works for her family in the
house

housework /'haʊswɜːk/ *noun* (no
plural)
work that you do in your house, for example cleaning and washing ✪ Be careful! Work that a teacher gives you to do at
home is called **homework**.

housing /'haʊzɪŋ/ *noun* (no plural)
flats and houses for people to live in: *We
need more housing for young people.*
housing estate /'haʊzɪŋ ɪsteɪt/ *noun*
a big group of houses that were built at the
same time: *We live on a housing estate.*

hover /'hɒvə(r)/ *verb* (**hovers**, **hovering**,
hovered /'hɒvəd/)
stay in the air in one place: *A helicopter
hovered above the building.*

hovercraft /'hɒvəkrɑːft/ *noun* (*plural*
hovercraft)
a kind of boat that moves over the top of
water on air that it pushes out

how /haʊ/ *adverb*
1 in what way: *How does this machine
work?* ◇ *She told me how to get to the
station.* ◇ *Do you know how to spell
'elementary'?*
2 a word that you use to ask if somebody is
well: *'How is your sister?' 'She's very
well, thank you.'* ✪ You use 'how' only
when you are asking about somebody's
health. When you are asking somebody to
describe another person or a thing you use
what ... like?: *'What is your sister like?'
'She's tall with brown hair.'*
3 a word that you use to ask if something
is good: *How was the film?*
4 a word that you use to ask questions
about amount, etc: *How old are you?*

◇ *How many brothers and sisters have
you got?* ◇ *How much does this cost?*
◇ *How long have you lived here?*
5 a word that shows surprise or strong
feeling: *How kind of you to help!*
how about ...? words that you use
when you suggest something: *How about
a drink?* ◇ *How about going for a walk?*
how are you? do you feel well?: *'How
are you?' 'Fine, thanks.'*
how do you do? polite words that you
say when you meet somebody for the first
time ✪ When somebody says 'How do
you do?', you also answer 'How do you
do?'

however¹ /haʊ'evə(r)/ *adverb*
1 it does not matter how: *I never win,
however hard I try.*
2 a way of saying 'how' more strongly:
However did you find me?

however² /haʊ'evə(r)/ *conjunction*
but: *She's very intelligent. However, she's
quite lazy.*

howl /haʊl/ *noun*
a long loud sound, like a dog makes
howl *verb* (**howls**, **howling**, **howled**
/haʊld/)
make this sound: *The dogs howled all
night.* ◇ *The wind howled around the
house.*

HQ /ˌeɪtʃ 'kjuː/ *short for* **headquarters**

hug /hʌɡ/ *verb* (**hugs**, **hugging**, **hugged**
/hʌɡd/)
put your arms around somebody to show
that you love them: *She hugged her parents and said goodbye.*
hug *noun*
He gave his brother a hug.

huge /hjuːdʒ/ *adjective*
very big: *They live in a huge house.*

hullo = **hello**

hum /hʌm/ *verb* (**hums**, **humming**,
hummed /hʌmd/)
1 make a sound like bees
2 sing with your lips closed: *If you don't
know the words of the song, hum it.*

human /'hjuːmən/ *adjective*
of or like people, not animals or machines:
the human body
human, human being *noun*
a person: *Human beings have lived on
earth for thousands of years.*

the human race /ðə ˌhjuːmən ˈreɪs/ noun (no plural)
all the people in the world

humble /ˈhʌmbl/ adjective
1 A humble person does not think he/she is better or more important than other people: *Becoming rich and famous has not changed her – she is still very humble.*
2 simple or poor: *a humble cottage*

humor American English for **humour**

humorous /ˈhjuːmərəs/ adjective
A person or thing that is humorous makes you smile or laugh: *a humorous story*

humour /ˈhjuːmə(r)/ noun (no plural)
being funny: *a story full of humour*
have a sense of humour be able to laugh and make other people laugh at funny things: *Dave has a good sense of humour.*

hump /hʌmp/ noun
a round lump: *A camel has a hump on its back.*

hundred /ˈhʌndrəd/ number
100: *We invited a hundred people to the party.* ◇ *two hundred pounds* ◇ *four hundred and twenty* ◇ *hundreds of people*
hundredth /ˈhʌndrədθ/ adjective, adverb, noun
100th

hung form of **hang** 1

hunger /ˈhʌŋgə(r)/ noun (no plural)
the feeling that you want or need to eat
✪ Be careful! You cannot say 'I have hunger' in English. You must say 'I am hungry'.

hungry /ˈhʌŋgri/ adjective (**hungrier**, **hungriest**)
If you are hungry, you want to eat: *Let's eat soon – I'm hungry!*

hunt /hʌnt/ verb (**hunts**, **hunting**, **hunted**)
chase animals to kill them as a sport or for food: *Young lions have to learn to hunt.*
✪ When you talk about spending time hunting, you say **go hunting**: *They went hunting in the forest.*
hunt for something try to find something: *I've hunted everywhere for my watch but I can't find it.*

hunt noun
a fox-hunt ◇ *a hunt for my keys*
hunter noun
a person who chases and kills animals
hunting noun (no plural)
chasing and killing animals

hurl /hɜːl/ verb (**hurls**, **hurling**, **hurled** /hɜːld/)
throw something strongly: *She hurled the book across the room.*

hurray, hooray /həˈreɪ/, **hurrah** /həˈrɑː/
a word that you shout when you are very pleased about something: *Hurray! She's won!*

hurricane /ˈhʌrɪkən/ noun
a storm with very strong winds

hurry¹ /ˈhʌri/ noun
in a hurry If you are in a hurry, you need to do something quickly: *I can't talk to you now – I'm in a hurry.*

hurry² /ˈhʌri/ verb (**hurries**, **hurrying**, **hurried** /ˈhʌrid/)
move or do something quickly: *We hurried home after school.*
hurry up move or do something more quickly: *Hurry up or we'll be late!*

hurt /hɜːt/ verb (**hurts**, **hurting**, **hurt**, has **hurt**)
1 make somebody or something feel pain: *I fell and hurt my leg.* ◇ *Did you hurt yourself?* ◇ *You hurt her feelings* (= made her unhappy) *when you said she was fat.* ◇ *These shoes hurt – they are too small.*
2 feel pain: *My leg hurts.*

husband /ˈhʌzbənd/ noun
the man that a woman is married to
☞ picture on page 127

hut /hʌt/ noun
a small building with one room. Huts are usually made of wood or metal.

hydrogen /ˈhaɪdrədʒən/ noun (no plural)
a light gas that you cannot see or smell: *Water is made of hydrogen and oxygen.*

hygiene /ˈhaɪdʒiːn/ noun (no plural)
keeping yourself and things around you clean: *Good hygiene is very important when you are preparing food.*

p	b	t	d	k	g	tʃ	dʒ	f	v	θ	ð
pen	**b**ad	**t**ea	**d**id	**c**at	**g**ot	**ch**ain	**j**am	**f**all	**v**an	**th**in	**th**is

hygienic /haɪˈdʒiːnɪk/ *adjective*
clean ✪ opposite: **unhygienic**

hymn /hɪm/ *noun*
a song that Christians sing in church

hyphen /ˈhaɪfn/ *noun*
a mark (-) that you use in writing. It joins words together (for example *ice-cream*) or shows that a word continues on the next line.

Ii

I /aɪ/ *pronoun (plural* **we**)
the person who is speaking: *I am German.* ◇ *I'll* (= I will) *see you tomorrow.* ◇ *I'm early, aren't I?*

ice /aɪs/ *noun* (no plural)
water that has become hard because it is very cold: *Do you want ice in your drink?*

iceberg /ˈaɪsbɜːg/ *noun*
a very big piece of ice in the sea

ice-cream /ˌaɪs ˈkriːm/ *noun*
very cold sweet food made from milk: *Do you like ice-cream?* ◇ *Two chocolate ice-creams, please.*

ice-cube /ˈaɪs kjuːb/ *noun*
a small piece of ice that you put in a drink to make it cold

iced /aɪst/ *adjective*
1 very cold: *iced water*
2 covered with **icing**: *iced cakes*

ice hockey /ˈaɪs hɒki/ *noun* (no plural)
a game that two teams play on ice

ice lolly /ˌaɪs ˈlɒli/ *noun* (*plural* **ice lollies**)
a piece of sweet ice on a stick

ice-rink /ˈaɪs rɪŋk/ *noun*
a special place where you can skate

ice-skating /ˈaɪs skeɪtɪŋ/ *noun* (no plural)
moving on ice in special boots (called **ice-skates**) that have long sharp pieces of metal on the bottom

icicle /ˈaɪsɪkl/ *noun*
a long piece of ice that hangs down from something

icing /ˈaɪsɪŋ/ *noun* (no plural)
sweet stuff that you use for covering cakes: *a cake with pink icing*

icy /ˈaɪsi/ *adjective* (**icier**, **iciest**)
1 covered with ice: *icy roads*
2 very cold: *an icy wind*

ID /ˌaɪ ˈdiː/ *short for* **identification 2**

I'd /aɪd/
1 = **I had**
2 = **I would**

idea /aɪˈdɪə/ *noun*
1 a plan or new thought: *It was a good idea to give Martin a pen for his birthday.* ◇ *I've got an idea. Let's have a party!*
2 a picture in your mind: *The film gives you a good idea of what Iceland is like.* ◇ *I've got no idea* (= I do not know) *where she is.*
3 what you believe: *My parents have very strict ideas about who I go out with.*

ideal /aɪˈdiːəl/ *adjective*
the best or exactly right: *This is an ideal place for a picnic.*

identical /aɪˈdentɪkl/ *adjective*
exactly the same: *These two cameras are identical.* ◇ *identical twins*

identify /aɪˈdentɪfaɪ/ *verb* (**identifies**, **identifying**, **identified** /aɪˈdentɪfaɪd/ **has identified**)
say or know who somebody is or what something is: *The police have not identified the dead man yet.*

identification /aɪˌdentɪfɪˈkeɪʃn/ *noun* (no plural)
1 identifying somebody or something: *The identification of bodies after the accident was difficult.*
2 something that shows who you are, for example a passport: *Do you have any identification?* ✪ The short form is **ID**.

identity /aɪˈdentəti/ *noun* (*plural* **identities**)
who or what a person or thing is: *The identity of the killer is not known.*

identity card /aɪˈdentəti kɑːd/ *noun*
a card that shows who you are

s	z	ʃ	ʒ	h	m	n	ŋ	l	r	j	w
so	**zoo**	**shoe**	vision	**hat**	**man**	**no**	sing	**leg**	**red**	**yes**	**wet**

idiom /'ɪdɪəm/ *noun*
a group of words with a special meaning:
*The idiom 'break somebody's heart'
means 'make somebody very unhappy'.*
idiomatic /ˌɪdɪə'mætɪk/ *adjective*
using idioms: *idiomatic English*

idiot /'ɪdɪət/ *noun*
a person who is stupid or does something
silly: *I was an idiot to forget my key.*

idol /'aɪdl/ *noun*
1 something that people worship as a god
2 a famous person that people love: *Madonna is the idol of millions of teenagers.*

ie /ˌaɪ 'i:/
this is what I mean: *You can buy hot
drinks, ie tea and coffee, on the train.* ○ **ie**
is usually used in writing.

if /ɪf/ *conjunction*
1 a word that you use to say what is possible or true when another thing happens
or is true: *If you press this button, the machine starts.* ◇ *If you see him, give him
this letter.* ◇ *If your feet were smaller,
you could wear my shoes.* ◇ *If I had a
million pounds, I would buy a big house.*
◇ *I may see you tomorrow. If not, I'll see
you next week.*
2 a word that shows a question; whether:
Do you know if Paul is at home? ◇ *She
asked me if I wanted to go to a party.*
as if in a way that makes you think something: *She looks as if she has been on
holiday.*
if only words that show that you want
something very much: *If only I could
drive!*

ignorance /'ɪɡnərəns/ *noun* (no plural)
not knowing about something: *Her ignorance surprised me.*

ignorant /'ɪɡnərənt/ *adjective*
If you are ignorant, you do not know about
something: *I'm very ignorant about
computers.*

ignore /ɪɡ'nɔː(r)/ *verb* (**ignores**, **ignor-
ing**, **ignored** /ɪɡ'nɔːd/)
know about somebody or something, but
do not do anything about it: *He ignored
the warning and put his head in the lion's
cage.* ◇ *I said hello to her, but she ignored
me!*

il- *prefix*
You can add **il**- to the beginning of some

words to give them the opposite meaning, for example:
illegal = not legal

ill /ɪl/ *adjective*
1 not well; not in good health: *Mark is in
bed because he is ill.* ◇ *I feel too ill to go to
work.* ○ The noun is **illness**.
2 bad: *ill health*
be taken ill become ill: *Josie was taken
ill on holiday.*

I'll /aɪl/ = **I shall, I will**

illegal /ɪ'liːɡl/ *adjective*
not allowed by the law; not legal: *It is illegal to drive a car in Britain if you are under the age of 17.*
illegally /ɪ'liːɡəli/ *adverb*
She came into the country illegally.

illness /'ɪlnəs/ *noun* (*plural* **illnesses**)
being ill: *Cancer is a serious illness.* ◇ *He
could not come to the meeting because of
illness.*

ill-treat /ˌɪl'triːt/ *verb* (**ill-treats, ill-
treating, ill-treated**)
do unkind things to a person or an animal:
This dog has been ill-treated.

illustrate /'ɪləstreɪt/ *verb* (**illustrates,
illustrating, illustrated**)
add pictures to show something more
clearly: *The book is illustrated with colour
photographs.*

illustration /ˌɪlə'streɪʃn/ *noun*
a picture: *This dictionary has a lot of
illustrations.*

im- *prefix*
You can add **im**- to the beginning of
some words to give them the opposite
meaning, for example:
impatient = not patient

I'm /aɪm/ = **I am**

image /'ɪmɪdʒ/ *noun*
1 a picture in people's minds of somebody
or something: *A lot of people have an image of London as cold and rainy.*
2 a picture on paper or in a mirror: *images
of war*

imaginary /ɪ'mædʒɪnəri/ *adjective*
not real; only in your mind: *The film is
about an imaginary country.*

i:	i	ɪ	e	æ	ɑ:	ɒ	ɔ:	ʊ	u	u:
see	happy	sit	ten	cat	father	got	saw	put	situation	too

imagination /ɪˌmædʒɪˈneɪʃn/ *noun*
being able to think of new ideas or make pictures in your mind: *You need a lot of imagination to write stories for children.* ◇ *You didn't really see a ghost – it was just your imagination.*

imagine /ɪˈmædʒɪn/ *verb* (**imagines, imagining, imagined** /ɪˈmædʒɪnd/)
1 make a picture of something in your mind: *Can you imagine life without electricity?* ◇ *I closed my eyes and imagined I was lying on a beach.*
2 think that something will happen or that something is true: *I imagine Mehmet will come by car.*

imitate /ˈɪmɪteɪt/ *verb* (**imitates, imitating, imitated**)
try to do the same as somebody or something; copy somebody or something: *He imitated his teacher's voice.*

imitation /ˌɪmɪˈteɪʃn/ *noun*
something that you make to look like another thing; a copy: *It's not a diamond, it's only a glass imitation.* ◇ *imitation leather*

immediate /ɪˈmiːdiət/ *adjective*
happening at once: *I can't wait – I need an immediate answer.*
immediately /ɪˈmiːdiətli/ *adverb*
now; at once: *Come to my office immediately!*

immense /ɪˈmens/ *adjective*
very big: *immense problems*
immensely /ɪˈmensli/ *adverb*
very or very much: *We enjoyed the party immensely.*

immigrant /ˈɪmɪɡrənt/ *noun*
a person who comes to another country to live there: *Many immigrants to Britain have come from Asia.*

immigration /ˌɪmɪˈɡreɪʃn/ *noun* (no plural)
coming to another country to live there

immune /ɪˈmjuːn/ *adjective*
safe, so that you cannot get a disease: *You're immune to measles if you've had it before.*

impatience /ɪmˈpeɪʃns/ *noun* (no plural)
not being calm when you are waiting: *He showed his impatience by looking at his watch five or six times.*

impatient /ɪmˈpeɪʃnt/ *adjective*
If you are impatient, you do not want to wait for something: *Don't be so impatient! The bus will be here soon.*
impatiently *adverb*
'Hurry up!' she said impatiently.

imperative /ɪmˈperətɪv/ *noun*
the form of a verb that you use for telling somebody to do something: *'Listen!' and 'Go away!' are in the imperative.*

imply /ɪmˈplaɪ/ *verb* (**implies, implying, implied** /ɪmˈplaɪd/, **has implied**)
mean something without saying it: *He asked if I had any work to do. He was implying that I was lazy.*

import /ɪmˈpɔːt/ *verb* (**imports, importing, imported**)
buy things from another country and bring them into your country: *Britain imports oranges from Spain.* ◯ opposite: **export**
import /ˈɪmpɔːt/ *noun*
a thing that is imported ◯ opposite: **export**
importer /ɪmˈpɔːtə(r)/ *noun*
a person, company or country that imports things

important /ɪmˈpɔːtnt/ *adjective*
1 If something is important, you must do, have or think about it: *It is important to sleep well the night before an exam.* ◇ *I think that happiness is more important than money.*
2 powerful or special: *The prime minister is a very important person.*
◯ opposite: **unimportant**
importance /ɪmˈpɔːtns/ *noun* (no plural)
being important; value: *Oil is of great importance to industry.*

impossible /ɪmˈpɒsəbl/ *adjective*
If something is impossible, you cannot do it, or it cannot happen: *It is impossible to finish this work by five o'clock.* ◇ *The house was impossible to find.*
impossibility /ɪmˌpɒsəˈbɪləti/ *noun* (*plural* **impossibilities**)
I can't lend you £1000. It's an impossibility!

impress /ɪmˈpres/ *verb* (**impresses, impressing, impressed** /ɪmˈprest/)
make somebody have good feelings or thoughts about you or about something

that is yours: *He was so impressed by Cindy's singing that he asked her to sing on the radio.*

impressive /ɪmˈpresɪv/ *adjective*
If something is impressive, it impresses people, for example because it is very good or very big: *an impressive building* ◇ *Your work is very impressive.*

impression /ɪmˈpreʃn/ *noun*
feelings or thoughts you have about somebody or something: *My first impressions of London were not very good.* ◇ *What's your impression of the new teacher?*
make an impression give somebody a certain idea of yourself: *He made a good impression on his first day at work.*

imprison /ɪmˈprɪzn/ *verb* (**imprisons, imprisoning, imprisoned** /ɪmˈprɪznd/)
put somebody in prison: *He was imprisoned for killing his wife.*
imprisonment /ɪmˈprɪznmənt/ *noun* (no plural)
being in prison: *two years' imprisonment*

improve /ɪmˈpruːv/ *verb* (**improves, improving, improved** /ɪmˈpruːvd/)
become better or make something better: *Your English has improved a lot this year.* ◇ *You must improve your spelling.*
improvement /ɪmˈpruːvmənt/ *noun*
a change that makes something better than it was before: *There has been a big improvement in Sam's work.*

impulse /ˈɪmpʌls/ *noun*
a sudden strong wish to so something: *She felt an impulse to run away.*

in¹ /ɪn/ *adverb*
1 to a place, from outside: *I opened the door and went in.*
2 at home or at work: *'Can I speak to Helen, please?' 'I'm sorry – she's not in.'*

in² /ɪn/ *preposition*
1 a word that shows where: *Glasgow is in Scotland.* ◇ *He put his hand in the water* ◇ *Julie is in bed.* ☞ picture on page 125
2 a word that shows when: *My birthday is in May.* ◇ *He started school in 1987.* ☞ Look at page 297.
3 a word that shows how long; after: *I'll be ready in ten minutes.*
4 a word that shows how somebody or something is: *This room is in a mess.* ◇ *Jenny was in tears* (= she was crying).

5 a word that shows what clothes somebody is wearing: *He was dressed in a suit.*
6 a word that shows what way, what language, etc: *Write your name in capital letters.* ◇ *They were speaking in French.*
7 a word that shows somebody's job: *He's in the army.*
8 making something: *There are 100 centimetres in a metre.* ◇ *Sit in a circle.*

in-³ *prefix*
You can add **in-** to the beginning of some words to give them the opposite meaning, for example:
incomplete = not complete

inability /ˌɪnəˈbɪləti/ *noun* (no plural)
not being able to do something: *He has an inability to talk about his problems.*

inaccurate /ɪnˈækjərət/ *adjective*
not correct; with mistakes in it: *The report in the newspaper was inaccurate.*

inadequate /ɪnˈædɪkwət/ *adjective*
not as much as you need, or not good enough: *These shoes are inadequate for cold weather.* ◇ *inadequate food*

inch /ɪntʃ/ *noun* (*plural* **inches**)
a measure of length (= 2.54 centimetres). There are twelve inches in a **foot**: *I am five foot six inches tall.* ◇ *a twelve-inch ruler*
☞ Note at **foot**

incident /ˈɪnsɪdənt/ *noun*
something that happens: *Josie told us about a funny incident at school, when her teacher fell in the pond!*

incidentally /ˌɪnsɪˈdentəli/ *adverb*
a word that you say when you are going to talk about something different: *Charles helped us to move the table. Incidentally, he has a new car.*

inclined /ɪnˈklaɪnd/ *adjective*
be inclined to 1 be likely to do something: *I don't want to tell Susy about this – she's inclined to get angry.* **2** want to do something: *I'm inclined to agree with you.*

include /ɪnˈkluːd/ *verb* (**includes, including, included**)
1 have somebody or something as one part of the whole: *The price of the room includes breakfast.*
2 make somebody or something part of a

p	b	t	d	k	g	tʃ	dʒ	f	v	θ	ð
pen	**b**ad	**t**ea	**d**id	**c**at	**g**ot	**ch**ain	**j**am	**f**all	**v**an	**th**in	**th**is

group: *Have you included tea on the list of things to buy?*
☞ Look at **exclude**.

including *preposition*
with; if you count: *There were five people in the car, including the driver.*

income /'ɪnkʌm/ *noun*
all the money that you receive for your work, for example: *What was your income last year?*

income tax /'ɪnkʌm tæks/ *noun* (no plural)
the money that you pay to the government from the money that you earn

incomplete /ˌɪnkəm'pliːt/ *adjective*
not finished; with parts missing: *This list is incomplete.*

inconsiderate /ˌɪnkən'sɪdərət/ *adjective*
A person who is inconsiderate does not think or care about other people and their feelings: *It's inconsiderate of you to make so much noise when people are asleep.*

inconsistent /ˌɪnkən'sɪstənt/ *adjective*
not always the same: *She's very inconsistent – sometimes her work is good and sometimes it's bad.*

inconvenience /ˌɪnkən'viːniəns/ *noun* (no plural)
problems or difficulty: *The snow caused a lot of inconvenience to drivers.*

inconvenient /ˌɪnkən'viːniənt/ *adjective*
If something is inconvenient, it gives you problems or difficulty: *She came at an inconvenient time – I was on the telephone.*

incorrect /ˌɪnkə'rekt/ *adjective*
not correct; not right or true: *It is incorrect to say that two plus two equals five.*
incorrectly *adverb*
The name was incorrectly spelt.

increase /ɪn'kriːs/ *verb* (**increases**, **increasing**, **increased** /ɪn'kriːst/)
become bigger or more; make something bigger or more: *The number of women who go to work has increased.*
increase /'ɪnkriːs/ *noun*
There has been an increase in road accidents. ◇ *a price increase*
○ opposite: **decrease**

incredible /ɪn'kredəbl/ *adjective*
1 surprising and very difficult to believe:

Mike told us an incredible story about his grandmother catching a thief.
2 very great: *She earns an incredible amount of money.*

incredibly /ɪn'kredəbli/ *adverb*
extremely: *He's incredibly clever.*

indeed /ɪn'diːd/ *adverb*
1 a word that makes 'very' stronger: *Thank you very much indeed.* ◇ *She's very happy indeed.*
2 really; certainly: *'Did you have a good holiday?' 'I did indeed.'*

indefinite /ɪn'defɪnət/ *adjective*
not definite; not clear or certain: *They are staying for an indefinite length of time.*
indefinitely /ɪn'defɪnətli/ *adverb*
for a long time, perhaps for ever: *I can't wait indefinitely.*

independence /ˌɪndɪ'pendəns/ *noun* (no plural)
being free from another person, thing or country: *America declared its independence from Britain in 1776.*

independent /ˌɪndɪ'pendənt/ *adjective*
1 not controlled by another person, thing or country: *Zimbabwe has been independent since 1980.*
2 A person who is independent does not need help: *She lives alone now and she is very independent.*

index /'ɪndeks/ *noun* (plural **indexes**)
a list of words from A to Z at the end of a book. It tells you what things are in the book and where you can find them.

indicate /'ɪndɪkeɪt/ *verb* (**indicates**, **indicating**, **indicated**)
1 show something, usually by pointing with your finger: *Can you indicate your school on this map?*
2 give a sign about something: *Black clouds indicate that it's going to rain.*
3 show that your car is going to turn by using a light: *You should indicate left now.*
indication /ˌɪndɪ'keɪʃn/ *noun*
something that shows something: *He gave no indication that he was angry.*

indicator /'ɪndɪkeɪtə(r)/ *noun*
a light on a car that shows that it is going to turn left or right

indignant /ɪn'dɪgnənt/ *adjective*
angry because somebody has done or said something that you do not like or agree

s	z	ʃ	ʒ	h	m	n	ŋ	l	r	j	w
so	**zoo**	**shoe**	vi**s**ion	**hat**	**man**	**no**	si**ng**	**leg**	**red**	**yes**	**wet**

with: *She was indignant when I said she was lazy.*
indignantly *adverb*
'I'm not late,' he said indignantly.
indignation /ˌɪndɪg'neɪʃn/ *noun* (no plural)
a feeling of anger and surprise
indirect /ˌɪndə'rekt/ *adjective*
not straight or direct: *We came an indirect way to avoid the city centre.*
indirectly *adverb*
in an indirect way
individual¹ /ˌɪndɪ'vɪdʒuəl/ *adjective*
1 for only one person or thing: *He had individual lessons to help him learn to read.*
2 single and different: *Each individual country has its own flag.*
individually /ˌɪndɪ'vɪdʒuəli/ *adverb*
separately; alone; not together: *The teacher spoke to each student individually.*
individual² /ˌɪndɪ'vɪdʒuəl/ *noun*
one person: *Teachers must treat each child as an individual.*
indoor /'ɪndɔː(r)/ *adjective*
done or used inside a building: *an indoor swimming-pool* ◇ *indoor games* ✿ opposite: **outdoor**
indoors /ˌɪn'dɔːz/ *adverb*
in or into a building: *Let's go indoors. I'm cold.* ✿ opposite: **outdoors**
industrial /ɪn'dʌstriəl/ *adjective*
1 of or about making things in factories: *industrial machines*
2 with a lot of factories: *Leeds is an industrial city.*
industry /'ɪndəstri/ *noun*
1 (no plural) the work of making things in factories: *Is there much industry in your country?*
2 (plural **industries**) all the companies that make the same thing: *Japan has a big car industry.*
inefficient /ˌɪnɪ'fɪʃnt/ *adjective*
A person or thing that is inefficient does not work well or in the best way: *This machine is very old and inefficient.*
inevitable /ɪn'evɪtəbl/ *adjective*
If something is inevitable, it will certainly happen: *The accident was inevitable – he was driving too fast.*
inevitably /ɪn'evɪtəbli/ *adverb*
Building the new hospital inevitably cost a lot of money.

inexperienced /ˌɪnɪk'spɪəriənst/ *adjective*
If you are inexperienced, you do not know about something because you have not done it many times before: *a young inexperienced driver*
infant school /'ɪnfənt skuːl/ *noun*
a school for children between the ages of five and seven
infect /ɪn'fekt/ *verb* (**infects, infecting, infected**)
give a disease to somebody: *He infected the other children in the class with his cold.*
infected *adjective*
full of small living things (called **germs**) that can make you ill: *Clean that cut or it could become infected.*
infection /ɪn'fekʃn/ *noun*
a disease: *Mike has an ear infection.*
infectious /ɪn'fekʃəs/ *adjective*
that goes easily from one person to another: *This disease is infectious.*
inferior /ɪn'fɪəriə(r)/ *adjective*
not as good or important as another person or thing: *Lisa's work is so good that she makes the other students feel inferior.*
✿ opposite: **superior**
infinite /'ɪnfɪnət/ *adjective*
with no end; too much or too many to count or measure: *There is an infinite number of stars in the sky.*
infinitive /ɪn'fɪnətɪv/ *noun*
the simple form of a verb: *'Eat', 'go' and 'play' are all infinitives.*
inflate /ɪn'fleɪt/ *verb* (**inflates, inflating, inflated**)
fill something with air or gas to make it bigger: *He inflated the tyre.* ✿ It is more usual to say **blow up** or **pump up.**
inflation /ɪn'fleɪʃn/ *noun* (no plural)
a general rise in prices in a country: *The government is trying to control inflation.*
influence /'ɪnfluəns/ *noun*
1 (no plural) the power to change what somebody believes or does: *Television has a strong influence on people.*
2 (plural **influences**) a person or thing that can change somebody or something: *Paul's new girlfriend is a good influence on him.*
influence *verb* (**influences, influencing, influenced** /'ɪnfluənst/)
change somebody or something; make

somebody do what you want: *She is easily influenced by her friends.*

inform /ɪnˈfɔːm/ *verb* (**informs, informing, informed** /ɪnˈfɔːmd/)
tell something to somebody: *You should inform the police of the accident.*

informal /ɪnˈfɔːml/ *adjective*
You use informal language or behave in an informal way in situations that are friendly and easy, not serious or important, and with people that you know well. You do not usually use informal words when you write (except in letters to people that you know well): *I wear a suit when I'm at work, but more informal clothes, like jeans and T-shirts, at weekends.* ◊ *an informal letter*

informally /ɪnˈfɔːməli/ *adverb*
The students talked informally to each other.

information /ˌɪnfəˈmeɪʃn/ *noun* (no plural)
what you tell somebody; facts: *Can you give me some information about trains to London?* ✪ Be careful! You cannot say 'an information'. You can say 'some information' or 'a piece of information': *She gave me an interesting piece of information.*

ingredient /ɪnˈɡriːdiənt/ *noun*
one of the things that you put in when you make something to eat: *The ingredients for this cake are flour, butter, sugar and eggs.*

inhabitant /ɪnˈhæbɪtənt/ *noun*
a person or an animal that lives in a place: *The town has 30 000 inhabitants.*

inhabited /ɪnˈhæbɪtɪd/ *adjective*
be inhabited have people or animals living there: *The South Pole is inhabited by penguins.*

inherit /ɪnˈherɪt/ *verb* (**inherits, inheriting, inherited**)
receive something from somebody who has died: *Sabine inherited some money from her grandmother.*

inheritance /ɪnˈherɪtəns/ *noun*
something that you inherit

initial /ɪˈnɪʃl/ *adjective*
first: *Our initial idea was to go to Greece, but then we decided to go to Spain.*

initially /ɪˈnɪʃəli/ *adverb*
in the beginning; at first: *Initially I hated England, but now I love it!*

initials /ɪˈnɪʃlz/ *noun* (plural)
the first letters of your names: *Julie Ann Smith's initials are J. A. S.*

inject /ɪnˈdʒekt/ *verb* (**injects, injecting, injected**)
use a special needle to put a drug into a person's body
injection /ɪnˈdʒekʃn/ *noun*
The doctor gave the baby an injection.

injure /ˈɪndʒə(r)/ *verb* (**injures, injuring, injured** /ˈɪndʒəd/)
hurt somebody or something: *She injured her arm when she was playing tennis.* ◊ *Joe was injured in a car accident.*
injured *adjective*
The injured woman was taken to hospital.

injury /ˈɪndʒəri/ *noun* (plural **injuries**)
damage to the body of a person or an animal: *He had serious head injuries.*

injustice /ɪnˈdʒʌstɪs/ *noun* (no plural)
not being fair or right: *People are angry about the injustice of the new tax.*

ink /ɪŋk/ *noun*
a coloured liquid for writing and printing: *The words on this page are printed in black ink.*

inland /ˈɪnlənd/ *adjective*
in the middle of a country, not near the sea: *an inland lake*
inland /ˌɪnˈlænd/ *adverb*
in or towards the middle of a country

inn /ɪn/ *noun*
a house or small hotel where you can buy drinks and food: *We went to the 'Bear Inn' for lunch.* ✪ **Inn** is an old word that we do not use much now, except in names. The usual words are **pub** or **hotel**.

inner /ˈɪnə(r)/ *adjective*
of the inside; in the centre: *the inner city* ✪ opposite: **outer**

innocent /ˈɪnəsnt/ *adjective*
If you are innocent, you have not done wrong: *The police say John stole the money, but I think he's innocent.* ✪ opposite: **guilty**
innocence /ˈɪnəsns/ *noun* (no plural)
The prisoner's family are sure of her innocence. ✪ opposite: **guilt**

inquire /ɪnˈkwaɪə(r)/ *verb* (**inquires, inquiring, inquired** /ɪnˈkwaɪəd/)
ask: *I inquired about trains to Leeds.*

◇ *'Are you hungry?' he inquired.* ✪ **Ask** is the word that we usually use.

inquire into something try to find out more about something that happened: *The police are inquiring into the murder.*

inquiry /ɪn'kwaɪəri/ *noun* (*plural* **inquiries**)
a question that you ask about something: *The police are making inquiries about the robbery.*

insane /ɪn'seɪn/ *adjective*
mad

insect /'ɪnsekt/ *noun*
a very small animal that has six legs: *Ants, flies, butterflies and beetles are all insects.*

insecure /ˌɪnsɪ'kjʊə(r)/ *adjective*
1 not safe or firm: *An actor's job is very insecure.*
2 worried and not sure about yourself: *Since their father left, the children have felt very insecure.*

insecurity /ˌɪnsɪ'kjʊərəti/ *noun* (no plural)
She had feelings of insecurity.

insert /ɪn'sɜːt/ *verb* (**inserts, inserting, inserted**)
put something into something or between two things: *Insert the key in the lock.*

inside¹ /ɪn'saɪd/ *noun*
the part near the middle of something: *The inside of a pear is white and the outside is green or yellow.* ◇ *He did not see the inside of the house before he bought it.*
inside out with
the wrong side on
the outside: *You've
got your jumper on
inside out.*   ILLUS 130

inside² /'ɪnsaɪd/
adjective
in or near the
middle: *the inside
pages of a newspaper*

inside³ /ɪn'saɪd/ *preposition, adverb*
in or to the inside of something: *What's inside the box?* ◇ *It's raining – let's go inside* (= into the building). ☞ picture on page 125

insist /ɪn'sɪst/ *verb* (**insists, insisting, insisted**)
1 say very strongly that you must do or have something or that something must

happen: *I said I would walk to the station, but Paul insisted on driving me there.*
2 say very strongly that something is true, when somebody does not believe you: *Mum insists that she saw a ghost.*

inspect /ɪn'spekt/ *verb* (**inspects, inspecting, inspected**)
1 look at something carefully: *I inspected the car before I bought it.*
2 visit a place or a group of people to see that work is done well: *The kitchens are inspected every week.*

inspection /ɪn'spekʃn/ *noun*
The police made an inspection of the house.

inspector /ɪn'spektə(r)/ *noun*
1 a person whose job is to see that things are done correctly: *On the train, the inspector asked to see my ticket.* ◇ *a factory inspector*
2 a police officer

inspiration /ˌɪnspə'reɪʃn/ *noun*
a person or thing that gives you ideas which help you do something good, for example write or paint: *The beauty of the mountains is a great inspiration to many artists.*

inspire /ɪn'spaɪə(r)/ *verb* (**inspires, inspiring, inspired** /ɪn'spaɪəd/)
1 give somebody ideas that help them do something good, for example write or paint: *His wife inspired him to write this poem.*
2 make somebody feel or think something: *Her words inspired us all with hope.*

install /ɪn'stɔːl/ *verb* (**installs, installing, installed** /ɪn'stɔːld/)
put a new thing in its place so it is ready to use: *She installed a new washing-machine.*

installment *American English for* **instalment**

instalment /ɪn'stɔːlmənt/ *noun*
1 one part of a long story on radio or television, or in a magazine: *Did you read the last instalment?*
2 a part of the cost of something that you pay each week or month, for example: *She's paying for her new car in twelve monthly instalments.*

instance /'ɪnstəns/ *noun*
an example: *There have been many instances of forest fires this year.*
for instance as an example: *There are*

p	b	t	d	k	g	tʃ	dʒ	f	v	θ	ð
pen	**b**ad	**t**ea	**d**id	**c**at	**g**ot	**ch**ain	**j**am	**f**all	**v**an	**th**in	**th**is

many things to see in London — for instance Big Ben and Buckingham Palace.

instant¹ /'ɪnstənt/ adjective
1 that happens very quickly; immediate: *The film was an instant success.*
2 quick and easy to prepare: *an instant meal*

instant coffee /ˌɪnstənt 'kɒfi/ noun (no plural)
coffee that you make quickly with coffee powder and hot water

instantly adverb
immediately; at once: *I asked him a question and he replied instantly.*

instant² /'ɪnstənt/ noun
a very short time; a moment: *She thought for an instant before she answered.*

instead /ɪn'sted/ adverb
in the place of somebody or something: *We haven't got any coffee. Would you like tea instead?* ◇ *Stuart can't go to the meeting so I will go instead.*

instead of preposition
in the place of: *He's been playing football all afternoon instead of studying.* ◇ *Can you come at 7.30 instead of 8.00?*

instinct /'ɪnstɪŋkt/ noun
something that makes people and animals do certain things without thinking or learning about them: *Birds build their nests by instinct.*

instinctive /ɪn'stɪŋktɪv/ adjective
Animals have an instinctive fear of fire.

institute /'ɪnstɪtjuːt/ noun
a group of people who meet to study or talk about a special thing; the building where they meet: *the Institute of Science*

institution /ˌɪnstɪ'tjuːʃn/ noun
a big building like a bank, hospital, prison or school, and all the people in it: *Most of the hospitals and schools in Britain are government institutions* (= the government controls them).

instruct /ɪn'strʌkt/ verb (instructs, instructing, instructed)
1 tell somebody what they must do: *He instructed the driver to take him to the palace.*
2 teach somebody: *She instructed me in how to use the computer.*

instruction /ɪn'strʌkʃn/ noun
1 (plural **instructions**) words that tell you what you must do or how to do something: *Read the instructions on the box before you make the cake.*
2 (no plural) teaching or being taught something: *driving instruction*

instructor /ɪn'strʌktə(r)/ noun
a person who teaches you how to do something: *a driving instructor*

instrument /'ɪnstrəmənt/ noun
1 a thing that you use for doing a special job: *A telescope is an instrument used for looking at things that are a long way away.* ◇ *medical instruments* (= used by doctors)
2 a thing that you use for playing music: *Violins and trumpets are musical instruments.* ◇ *What instrument do you play?*

insult /ɪn'sʌlt/ verb (insults, insulting, insulted)
be rude to somebody: *She insulted my brother by saying he was fat.*

insult /'ɪnsʌlt/ noun
something rude that you say or do to somebody: *The boys shouted insults at each other.*

insurance /ɪn'ʃʊərəns/ noun (no plural)
an agreement where you pay money to a company so that it will give you a lot of money if something bad happens: *When I crashed my car, the insurance paid for the repairs.*

insure /ɪn'ʃʊə(r)/ verb (insures, insuring, insured /ɪn'ʃʊəd/)
1 pay money to a company, so that it will give you money if something bad happens: *Have you insured your house against fire?* ◇ *My car isn't insured.*
2 American English for **ensure**

intelligence /ɪn'telɪdʒəns/ noun (no plural)
being able to think, learn and understand quickly and well: *He is a man of great intelligence.* ◇ *an intelligence test*

intelligent /ɪn'telɪdʒənt/ adjective
able to think, learn and understand quickly and well: *Their daughter is very intelligent.*

intend /ɪn'tend/ verb (intends, intending, intended)
plan to do something: *When do you intend to go to London?*

be intended for somebody or

something be for somebody or something: *This dictionary is intended for elementary learners of English.*

intense /ɪn'tens/ *adjective*
very great or strong: *intense pain* ◇ *The heat from the fire was intense.*

intention /ɪn'tenʃn/ *noun*
what you plan to do: *They have no intention of getting married.*

intentional /ɪn'tenʃənl/ *adjective*
that you want and plan to do, and do not do by mistake: *I'm sorry I upset you – it wasn't intentional!* ❂ opposite: **unintentional**

intentionally /ɪn'tenʃənəli/ *adverb*
They broke the window intentionally – it wasn't an accident.

interest[1] /'ɪntrəst/ *noun*
1 (no plural) wanting to know or learn about somebody or something: *He read the story with interest.*
2 (*plural* **interests**) something that you like doing or learning about: *His interests are computers and rock music.*
3 (no plural) the extra money that you pay back if you borrow money or that you receive if you put money in a bank
take an interest in somebody or **something** want to know about somebody or something: *He takes no interest in politics.*

interest[2] /'ɪntrəst/ *verb* (**interests, interesting, interested**)
make somebody want to know more: *Religion doesn't interest her.*

interested *adjective*
If you are interested in somebody or something, you want to know more about them: *Are you interested in cars?* ❂ opposite: **uninterested**

interesting *adjective*
A person or thing that is interesting makes you want to know more about him/her/it: *This book is very interesting.* ◇ *That's an interesting idea!* ❂ opposite: **uninteresting** or **boring**

interfere /ˌɪntə'fɪə(r)/ *verb* (**interferes, interfering, interfered** /ˌɪntə'fɪəd/)
1 try to do something with or for somebody, when they do not want your help: *Don't interfere! Let John decide what he wants to do.*
2 stop something from being done well:

His interest in football often interferes with his studies.
3 change or touch something without asking if you can: *Who's been interfering with the clock? It's stopped.*

interference /ˌɪntə'fɪərəns/ *noun*
Go away! I don't want any interference when I'm working!

interior /ɪn'tɪəriə(r)/ *noun*
the inside part: *We painted the interior of the house white.*

interior *adjective*
interior walls
❂ opposite: **exterior**

intermediate /ˌɪntə'miːdiət/ *adjective*
that comes between two people or things; in the middle: *She's in an intermediate class.*

internal /ɪn'tɜːnl/ *adjective*
of or on the inside: *He has internal injuries* (= inside his body). ❂ opposite: **external**

internally /ɪn'tɜːnəli/ *adverb*
on the inside

international /ˌɪntə'næʃnəl/ *adjective*
between different countries: *an international football match* ◇ *an international flight*

interpret /ɪn'tɜːprɪt/ *verb* (**interprets, interpreting, interpreted**)
say in one language what somebody has said in another language: *I can't speak Italian – can you interpret for me?*

interpreter *noun*
a person who interprets: *The President had an interpreter when he went to China.*

interrupt /ˌɪntə'rʌpt/ *verb* (**interrupts, interrupting, interrupted**)
1 stop somebody speaking or doing something by saying or doing something yourself: *Please don't interrupt me when I'm speaking.*
2 stop something for a time: *The war interrupted travel between the two countries.*

interruption /ˌɪntə'rʌpʃn/ *noun*
I can't do my homework here. There are too many interruptions.

interval /'ɪntəvl/ *noun*
a short time between two parts of a play or concert: *We bought drinks in the interval.*

interview /'ɪntəvjuː/ *noun*
1 a meeting when somebody asks you

iː	i	ɪ	e	æ	ɑː	ɒ	ɔː	ʊ	u	uː
see	happy	sit	ten	cat	father	got	saw	put	situation	too

questions to decide if you will have a job: *I've got an interview for a new job tomorrow.*
2 a meeting when somebody answers questions for a newspaper or for a television or radio programme: *There was an interview with the Prime Minister on TV last night.*

interview verb (**interviews, interviewing, interviewed** /'ɪntəvjuːd/)
ask somebody questions in an interview: *They interviewed six people for the job.*

interviewer noun
a person who asks questions in an interview: *The interviewer asked me why I wanted the job.*

into /'ɪntə/, /'ɪntu/, /'ɪntuː/ preposition
1 to the middle or the inside of something: *Come into the house.* ◇ *I went into town.* ◇ *He fell into the river.* ☞ picture on page 128
2 a word that shows how somebody or something changes: *When it is very cold, water changes into ice.* ◇ *They made the room into a bedroom.*
3 against something: *The car crashed into a tree.*
4 a word that you use when you divide a number: *4 into 12 is 3.*

be into something like something; be interested in something: *What sort of music are you into?*

introduce /ˌɪntrə'djuːs/ verb (**introduces, introducing, introduced** /ˌɪntrə'djuːst/)
1 bring people together for the first time and tell each of them the name of the other: *She introduced me to her brother.*
2 bring in something new: *This law was introduced in 1990.*

introduce yourself tell somebody your name: *He introduced himself to me.*

introduction /ˌɪntrə'dʌkʃn/ noun
1 (plural **introductions**) bringing people together to meet each other
2 (plural **introductions**) a piece of writing at the beginning of a book that tells you about the book
3 (no plural) bringing in something new: *the introduction of computers into schools*

invade /ɪn'veɪd/ verb (**invades, invading, invaded**)
go into another country to attack it: *They invaded the country with tanks and guns.*

invader noun
a person who invades

invalid /'ɪnvəlɪd/ noun
a person who is very ill and needs another person to look after him/her: *She has been an invalid since the accident.*

invaluable /ɪn'væljuəbl/ adjective
very useful: *Your help was invaluable.*

invariably /ɪn'veəriəbli/ adverb
almost always: *He invariably arrives late.*

invasion /ɪn'veɪʒn/ noun
a time when an army from one country goes into another country to attack it: *Germany's invasion of Poland in 1939*

invent /ɪn'vent/ verb (**invents, inventing, invented**)
1 make or think of something for the first time: *Who invented the bicycle?*
2 tell something that is not true: *She invented a story about where she was last night.*

inventor /ɪn'ventə(r)/ noun
a person who makes or thinks of something new

invention /ɪn'venʃn/ noun
1 (plural **inventions**) a thing that somebody has made for the first time
2 (no plural) inventing something: *The invention of the telephone changed the world.*

inverted commas /ɪn,vɜːtɪd 'kɒməz/ noun (plural)
the signs " " or ' ' that you use in writing before and after words that somebody said

invest /ɪn'vest/ verb (**invests, investing, invested**)
give money to a business or bank so that you will get more money back: *He invested all his money in the company.*

investment /ɪn'vestmənt/ noun
investing money; money that you invest: *an investment of £10 000*

investigate /ɪn'vestɪgeɪt/ verb (**investigates, investigating, investigated**)
try to find out about something: *The police are investigating the murder.*

investigation /ɪn,vestɪ'geɪʃn/ noun
The police are holding an investigation into the fire.

invisible /ɪnˈvɪzəbl/ *adjective*
If something is invisible, you cannot see it:
Wind is invisible.

invitation /ˌɪnvɪˈteɪʃn/ *noun*
If you have an invitation to go somewhere,
somebody has spoken or written to you
and asked you to go: *Joe sent me an invitation to his party.*

invite /ɪnˈvaɪt/ *verb* (**invites, inviting,
invited**)
ask somebody to come to a party or a meeting, for example: *Anna invited me to her
party.* ◇ *Let's invite them for dinner.*

invoice /ˈɪnvɔɪs/ *noun*
a list that shows how much you must pay
for things that somebody has sold you, or
for work that somebody has done for you

involve /ɪnˈvɒlv/ *verb* (**involves, invol-
ving, involved** /ɪnˈvɒlvd/)
1 have something as a part: *The job involves using a computer.*
2 make somebody take part in something:
*A lot of people were involved in planning
the wedding.*

inward /ˈɪnwəd/, **inwards** /ˈɪnwədz/
adverb
towards the inside or centre: *The doors
open inwards.* ○ opposite: **outward** or
outwards

> **ir-** *prefix*
> You can add **ir-** to the beginning of some
> words to give them the opposite mean-
> ing, for example:
> **irregular** = not regular

iron /ˈaɪən/ *noun*
1 (no plural) a strong hard metal: *The
gates are made of iron.* ◇ *an iron bar*
2 (*plural* **irons**) an electrical thing that
gets hot and that you use for making
clothes smooth
iron *verb* (**irons, ironing, ironed**
/ˈaɪənd/)
make clothes smooth with an iron: *Can
you iron this shirt for me?* ○ When we
talk about ironing a lot of clothes, we often
say **do the ironing**: *I've done the ironing.*

ironing *noun* (no plural)
clothes that you must iron: *There's a pile
of ironing on the chair.*

ironing-board /ˈaɪənɪŋ bɔːd/ *noun*
a special long table where you iron
clothes

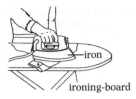

iron

ironing-board

irregular /ɪˈregjələ(r)/ *adjective*
1 that happens again and again, but with
different amounts of time in between:
Their visits were irregular.
2 A word that is irregular does not have
the usual verb forms or plural: *'Catch' is
an irregular verb.*

irrelevant /ɪˈreləvənt/ *adjective*
not connected with something and not important: *We are good friends. She is older
than me, but that is irrelevant.*

irritate /ˈɪrɪteɪt/ *verb* (**irritates, irritat-
ing, irritated**)
1 make somebody quite angry: *He irritates me when he asks so many questions.*
2 make a part of your body hurt a little: *Cigarette smoke irritates my eyes.*
irritation /ˌɪrɪˈteɪʃn/ *noun*
This plant causes irritation to your skin.

is *form of* **be**

Islam /ˈɪzlɑːm/ *noun* (no plural)
the religion of Muslim people. Islam
teaches that there is only one God and that
Muhammad is his messenger.
Islamic /ɪzˈlæmɪk/ *adjective*
Islamic law

island /ˈaɪlənd/ *noun*
a piece of land with water all around it:
Malta is an island.

Isle /aɪl/ *noun*
an island: *the British Isles* ○ **Isle** is usually used in names of islands.

isn't /ˈɪznt/ = **is not**

isolated /ˈaɪsəleɪtɪd/ *adjective*
far from other people or things: *an isolated
house in the mountains*

isolation /ˌaɪsəˈleɪʃn/ *noun* (no plural)
being away from other people or things: *A
lot of old people live in isolation.*

issue¹ /ˈɪʃuː/ *noun*
1 an important problem that people talk
about: *Pollution is a serious issue.*

p	b	t	d	k	g	tʃ	dʒ	f	v	θ	ð
pen	**b**ad	**t**ea	**d**id	**c**at	**g**ot	**ch**ain	**j**am	**f**all	**v**an	**th**in	**th**is

2 a magazine or newspaper of a particular day, week or month: *Have you read this week's issue of the magazine?*

issue² /'ɪʃu:/ *verb* (**issues, issuing, issued** /'ɪʃu:d/)
give something to people: *The soldiers were issued with uniforms.*

it /ɪt/ *pronoun* (*plural* **they, them**)
1 a word that shows a thing or an animal: *I've got a new shirt. It's* (= it is) *blue.* ◇ *Where is the coffee? I can't find it.*
2 a word that points to an idea that follows: *It is difficult to learn Japanese.*
3 a word that shows who somebody is: *'Who's on the telephone?' 'It's Jo.'*
4 a word at the beginning of a sentence about time, the weather, distance, etc: *It's six o'clock.* ◇ *It's hot today.* ◇ *It's 100 kilometres to London.*

italics /ɪ'tælɪks/ *noun* (plural)
letters that lean to the side: *This sentence is in italics.*

itch /ɪtʃ/ *verb* (**itches, itching, itched** /ɪtʃt/)
have a feeling on your skin that makes you want to rub or scratch it: *My nose itches.* ◇ *This jumper makes me itch.*
itch *noun* (*plural* **itches**)
I've got an itch.
itchy *adjective*
If something is itchy, it itches or it makes you itch: *itchy skin*

it'd /'ɪtəd/
1 = **it had**
2 = **it would**

item /'aɪtəm/ *noun*
1 one thing in a list or group of things: *She had the most expensive item on the menu.* ◇ *an item of clothing*
2 a piece of news: *There was an interesting item on TV about South Africa.*

it'll /'ɪtl/ = **it will**

its /ɪts/ *adjective*
of the thing or animal that you have just talked about: *The dog has hurt its leg.* ◇ *The company has its factory in Hull.*

it's /ɪts/
1 = **it is**
2 = **it has**

itself /ɪt'self/ *pronoun* (*plural* **themselves** /ðəm'selvz/)
1 a word that shows the same thing or animal that you have just talked about: *The cat was washing itself.*
2 a word that makes 'it' stronger: *The hotel itself was nice but I didn't like the town.*
by itself **1** alone: *The house stands by itself in the forest.* **2** without being controlled by a person: *The machine will start by itself.*

I've /aɪv/ = **I have**

ivory /'aɪvəri/ *noun* (no plural)
the hard white stuff that an elephant's **tusks** are made of

ivy /'aɪvi/ *noun* (no plural)
a plant with dark green leaves, that climbs up walls or trees

Jj

jack /dʒæk/ *noun*
the playing-card that has a picture of a young man on it: *the jack of hearts*

jacket /'dʒækɪt/ *noun*
a short coat with sleeves ☞ picture at **suit**

jacket potato /ˌdʒækɪt pə'teɪtəʊ/ *noun* (*plural* **jacket potatoes**)
a potato that you cook in the oven without taking the skin off

jagged /'dʒæɡɪd/ *adjective*
rough, with a lot of sharp points: *jagged rocks*

jaguar /'dʒæɡjuə(r)/ *noun*
a wild animal like a big cat. It has yellow fur with black spots.

jail /dʒeɪl/ *noun*
a prison: *He was sent to jail for two years.*
jail *verb* (**jails, jailing, jailed** /dʒeɪld/)

s	z	ʃ	ʒ	h	m	n	ŋ	l	r	j	w
so	**zoo**	**shoe**	**vision**	**hat**	**man**	**no**	**sing**	**leg**	**red**	**yes**	**wet**

put somebody in prison: *She was jailed for killing her husband.*

jam¹ /dʒæm/ *noun* (no plural)
food made from fruit and sugar. You eat jam on bread: *a jar of strawberry jam*

jam² /dʒæm/ *verb* (**jams, jamming, jammed** /dʒæmd/)
1 push something into a place where there is not much space: *She jammed all her clothes into a suitcase.*
2 fix something or become fixed so that you cannot move it: *I can't open the window. It's jammed.*

jam³ /dʒæm/ *noun*
a lot of people or things in a place, so that it is difficult to move: *a traffic jam*

January /'dʒænjuəri/ *noun*
the first month of the year

jar /dʒɑ:(r)/ *noun*
a glass container for food: *a jar of coffee* ◇ *a jamjar* ☞ picture at **container**

javelin /'dʒævəlɪn/ *noun*
a long pointed stick that people throw as a sport

jaw /dʒɔ:/ *noun*
one of the two bones in the head of a person or an animal that hold the teeth ☞ picture on page 126

jazz /dʒæz/ *noun* (no plural)
a kind of music with a strong beat

jealous /'dʒeləs/ *adjective*
1 angry or sad because you want what another person has: *Ben was jealous of his brother's new car.*
2 angry or sad because you are afraid of losing somebody's love: *Sarah's boyfriend gets jealous if she speaks to other boys.*
jealousy /'dʒeləsi/ *noun* (no plural)
being jealous

jeans /dʒi:nz/ *noun* (plural)
trousers made of strong cotton material, called **denim**. Jeans are usually blue: *a pair of jeans* ◇ *She wore jeans and a T-shirt.*

Jeep /dʒi:p/ *noun*
a strong car that can go well over rough land ◆ **Jeep** is a trade mark.

jelly /'dʒeli/ *noun* (plural **jellies**)
a soft food made from fruit juice and sugar, that shakes when you move it

jellyfish /'dʒelifɪʃ/ *noun* (plural **jellyfish** or **jellyfishes**)
a sea animal like jelly, that you can see through: *I saw a jellyfish on the beach.*

jerk /dʒɜ:k/ *noun*
a sudden pull or other movement: *The bus started with a jerk.*
jerk *verb* (**jerks, jerking, jerked** /dʒɜ:kt/)
The car jerked forward. ◇ *She jerked the door open.*

jet /dʒet/ *noun*
1 an aeroplane that flies when its engines push out hot gas
2 liquid or gas that is coming very fast out of a small hole: *a jet of gas* ◇ *Jets of water*
jet lag /'dʒet læg/ *noun* (no plural)
a very tired feeling that you may have after a long journey by aeroplane

Jew /dʒu:/ *noun*
a person who follows the old religion of Israel, called **Judaism**
Jewish /'dʒu:ɪʃ/ *adjective*
She is Jewish.

jewel /'dʒu:əl/ *noun*
a beautiful stone, for example a diamond, that is very valuable
jeweller *noun*
a person who sells, makes or repairs jewellery and watches ◆ A shop that sells jewellery and watches is called a **jeweller's**.
jewellery /'dʒu:əlri/ *noun* (no plural)
things like rings, bracelets and necklaces: *She wears a lot of jewellery.*

jeweler, jewelry *American English for* **jeweller, jewellery**

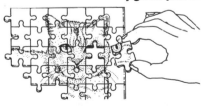

jigsaw puzzle

jigsaw, jigsaw puzzle /'dʒɪgsɔ: pʌzl/ *noun*
a picture in many pieces that you must put together

job /dʒɒb/ *noun*
1 the work that you do for money: *He has*

left school but he hasn't got a job. ◇ *She's looking for a new job.*
2 a piece of work that you must do: *I have a lot of jobs to do in the house.*
a good job a good or lucky thing: *It's a good job that I was at home when you phoned.*
make a good job of something do something well: *You made a good job of the painting.*
out of a job If you are out of a job, you do not have work that you are paid to do.

jockey /'dʒɒki/ *noun* (*plural* **jockeys**)
a person who rides horses in races

jog /dʒɒg/ *verb* (**jogs, jogging, jogged** /dʒɒgd/)
1 run slowly for exercise: *I jogged round the park.* ♦ We often say **go jogging**: *I go jogging every morning.*
2 push or touch something a little, so that it moves: *She jogged my arm and I spilled my drink.*
jog *noun* (no plural)
a slow run for exercise: *I went for a jog.*
jogger *noun*
a person who jogs
jogging *noun* (no plural)
running slowly for exercise

join /dʒɔɪn/ *verb* (**joins, joining, joined** /dʒɔɪnd/)
1 bring or fix one thing to another thing: *The tunnel joins Britain to France.* ◇ *Join the two pieces of wood together.*
2 come together with somebody or something: *This road joins the motorway soon.* ◇ *Will you join us for dinner?*
3 become a member of a group: *He joined the army.*
join in do something with other people: *We're playing football. Do you want to join in?*

joint¹ /dʒɔɪnt/ *noun*
1 a part of the body where two bones come together. Elbows and knees are joints.
2 a place where two parts of something join together: *the joints of a pipe*
3 a big piece of meat that you cook: *a joint of beef*

joint² /dʒɔɪnt/ *adjective*
that people do or have together: *Paul and Ian gave a joint party.*

joke¹ /dʒəʊk/ *noun*
something that you say or do to make people laugh: *She told us a joke.*
play a joke on somebody do something to somebody to make other people laugh; trick somebody: *They played a joke on their teacher – they hid his books.*

joke² /dʒəʊk/ *verb* (**jokes, joking, joked** /dʒəʊkt/)
say things that are not serious; say funny things: *I didn't really mean what I said – I was only joking.*

jolly /'dʒɒli/ *adjective* (**jollier, jolliest**)
happy and full of fun
jolly *adverb*
very: *It was a jolly good meal.*

jolt /dʒəʊlt/ *noun*
a sudden movement: *The train stopped with a jolt.*
jolt *verb* (**jolts, jolting, jolted**)
move or move something suddenly and quickly: *The van jolted along the rough road.*

jot /dʒɒt/ *verb* (**jots, jotting, jotted**)
jot down write something quickly: *I jotted down his phone number.*

journal /'dʒɜːnl/ *noun*
a magazine about one special thing: *a medical journal*

journalism /'dʒɜːnəlɪzəm/ *noun* (no plural)
the work of writing about the news for newspapers, magazines, television or radio

journalist /'dʒɜːnəlɪst/ *noun*
a person whose job is to write about the news for newspapers, magazines, television or radio

journey /'dʒɜːni/ *noun* (*plural* **journeys**)
going from one place to another: *Did you have a good journey?* ◇ *The plane journey from London to Paris takes an hour.*

joy /dʒɔɪ/ *noun* (no plural)
a very happy feeling: *Their children give them so much joy.*

joystick /'dʒɔɪstɪk/
a handle that you move to control something, for example a computer or an aeroplane ☞ picture at **computer**

Judaism /'dʒuːdeɪɪzəm/ *noun* (no plural)
the religion of the Jewish people

ʌ	ɜː	ə	eɪ	əʊ	aɪ	aʊ	ɔɪ	ɪə	eə	ʊə
cup	bird	about	say	go	five	now	boy	near	hair	pure

judge¹ /dʒʌdʒ/ *noun*
1 the person in a court of law who decides how to punish somebody: *The judge sent the man to prison for 20 years for killing his wife.*
2 a person who chooses the winner of a competition

judge² /dʒʌdʒ/ *verb* (**judges, judging, judged** /dʒʌdʒd/)
1 decide if something is good or bad, right or wrong, for example
2 decide who or what wins a competition: *The headmaster judged the painting competition.*

judgement /'dʒʌdʒmənt/ *noun*
1 what a judge in a court of law decides
2 what you think about somebody or something: *In my judgement, she will do the job very well.*

judo /'dʒuːdəʊ/ *noun* (no plural)
a sport where two people fight and try to throw each other onto the floor

jug

jug /dʒʌg/ *noun*
a container with a handle that you use for holding or pouring water or milk, for example

juggle

juggle /'dʒʌgl/ *verb* (**juggles, juggling, juggled** /'dʒʌgld/)
keep two or more things in the air by throwing and catching them quickly: *The clown juggled three oranges.*
juggler /'dʒʌglə(r)/ *noun*
a person who juggles

juice /dʒuːs/ *noun* (no plural)
the liquid from fruit and vegetables: *a glass of orange juice* ◇ *lemon juice*

juicy /'dʒuːsi/ *adjective* (**juicier, juiciest**)
with a lot of juice: *big juicy tomatoes*

jukebox /'dʒuːkbɒks/ *noun* (*plural* **jukeboxes**)
a machine in a café or bar that plays music when you put money in it

July /dʒu'laɪ/ *noun*
the seventh month of the year

jumble /'dʒʌmbl/ *verb* (**jumbles, jumbling, jumbled** /'dʒʌmbld/)
jumble up mix things so that they are untidy or in the wrong place: *I can't find the photo I was looking for – they are all jumbled up in this box.*
jumble *noun* (no plural)
a lot of things that are mixed together in an untidy way: *a jumble of old clothes and books*

jumble sale /'dʒʌmbl seɪl/ *noun*
a sale of things that people do not want any more. Clubs, churches and schools often have jumble sales to get money.

jump /dʒʌmp/ *verb* (**jumps, jumping, jumped** /dʒʌmpt/)
1 move quickly off the ground, using your legs to push you up: *The cat jumped onto the table.* ◇ *The horse jumped over the wall.*

jump

2 move quickly: *He jumped into the car and drove away.*
3 move suddenly because you are surprised or frightened: *A loud noise made me jump.*
jump *noun*
With one jump, the horse was over the fence.

jumper /'dʒʌmpə(r)/ *noun*
a warm piece of clothing with sleeves, that you wear on the top part of your body. Jumpers are often made of wool. ☞ picture at **coat**

jump-rope /'dʒʌmp rəʊp/ *American English for* **skipping-rope**

junction /'dʒʌŋkʃn/ *noun*
a place where roads or railway lines meet: *Turn right at the next junction.*

p	b	t	d	k	g	tʃ	dʒ	f	v	θ	ð
pen	**b**ad	**t**ea	**d**id	**c**at	**g**ot	**ch**ain	**j**am	**f**all	**v**an	**th**in	**th**is

June /dʒuːn/ *noun*
the sixth month of the year

jungle /'dʒʌŋgl/ *noun*
a thick forest in a hot part of the world:
There are jungles in South America.

junior /'dʒuːniə(r)/ *adjective*
1 less important: *He's a junior officer in the army.*
2 younger: *a junior pupil*
○ opposite: **senior**

junior school /'dʒuːniə skuːl/ *noun*
a school for children between the ages of seven and eleven

junk /dʒʌŋk/ *noun* (no plural)
things that are old or useless: *The cupboard is full of junk.*

junk food /'dʒʌŋk fuːd/ *noun*
food that is not very good for you, but that is easy to prepare or ready to eat

jury /'dʒʊəri/ *noun* (*plural* **juries**)
a group of people in a court of law who decide if somebody has done something wrong or not: *The jury decided that the woman was guilty of killing her husband.*

just¹ /dʒʌst/ *adverb*
1 a very short time before: *Jim isn't here – he's just gone out.*

2 at this or that moment; now or very soon: *I'm just going to make some coffee.*
◊ *She phoned just as I was going to bed.*
3 only: *It's just a small present.*
4 almost not: *I ran to the station and I just caught the train.*
5 a word that makes what you say stronger: *Just look at that funny little dog!*
just a minute, just a moment wait for a short time: *Just a minute – there's someone at the door.*
just now 1 at this time; now: *I can't talk to you just now. I'm busy.* **2** a short time before: *Where's Liz? She was here just now.*

just² /dʒʌst/ *adjective*
fair and right: *a just punishment* **○** opposite: **unjust**

justice /'dʒʌstɪs/ *noun* (no plural)
1 being fair and right: *Justice for all!*
○ opposite: **injustice**
2 the law: *British justice*

justify /'dʒʌstɪfaɪ/ *verb* (**justifies, justifying, justified** /'dʒʌstɪfaɪd/, **has justified**)
be or give a good reason for something:
Can you justify what you did?

Kk

kangaroo

kangaroo /ˌkæŋgə'ruː/ *noun* (*plural* **kangaroos**)
an animal in Australia that jumps on its strong back legs

karate /kə'rɑːti/ *noun* (no plural)
a Japanese sport where people fight with their hands and feet

keen /kiːn/ *adjective* (**keener, keenest**)
1 If you are keen, you want to do something and are interested in it: *Ian was keen to go out but I wanted to stay at home.*
◊ *Louise is a keen swimmer.*
2 very good or strong: *keen eyesight*
be keen on somebody or **something** like somebody or something very much: *Katie is keen on football.*

keep /kiːp/ *verb* (**keeps, keeping, kept** /kept/, **has kept**)
1 have something and not give it to another person: *You can keep that book – I don't need it.*
2 continue in the same way and not change: *Keep still – I want to take your photograph.*
3 make somebody or something stay the

same and not change: *Keep this door closed.* ◇ *You must keep the baby warm.*
4 have something in a special place: *Where do you keep the coffee?*
5 not stop doing something; do something many times: *Keep driving until you see the cinema, then turn left.* ◇ *She keeps forgetting my name.*
6 look after and buy food and other things for a person or an animal: *It costs a lot to keep a family of four.* ◇ *They keep sheep and pigs on their farm.*
7 stay fresh: *Will this fish keep until tomorrow?*
keep away from somebody or **something** not go near somebody or something: *Keep away from the river please, children.*
keep somebody from stop somebody from doing something: *You can't keep me from going out!*
keep going continue; not stop: *I was very tired but I kept going to the end of the race.*
keep off something not go on something: *Keep off the grass!*
keep on not stop doing something; do something many times: *We kept on driving all night!* ◇ *That man keeps on looking at me.*
keep out stay outside: *The sign on the door said 'Danger. Keep out!'*
keep somebody or **something out** stop somebody or something from going in: *We put a fence round the garden to keep the sheep out.*
keep up with somebody or **something** go as fast as another person or thing so that you are together: *Don't walk so quickly – I can't keep up with you.*

keeper /'kiːpə(r)/ *noun*
a person who looks after something: *He's a keeper at the zoo – he looks after the lions.*
☞ Look also at **goalkeeper**.

kennel /'kenl/ *noun*
a small house where a dog sleeps

kept *form of* **keep**

kerb /kɜːb/ *noun*
the edge of a path next to a road: *They stood on the kerb waiting to cross the road.*

ketchup /'ketʃəp/ *noun* (no plural)
a cold sauce made from tomatoes: *Do you want ketchup on your chips?*

kettle

kettle /'ketl/ *noun*
a metal or plastic pot that you use for making water hot: *Put the kettle on* (= fill it with water and make it start to get hot).

key

key¹ /kiː/ *noun*
1 a piece of metal that opens or closes a lock: *He turned the key and opened the door.*
2 one of the parts of a typewriter, computer, piano, etc that you press with your fingers: *Pianos have black and white keys.*
3 answers to questions: *Check your answers with the key at the back of the book.*

key² /kiː/ *verb* (**keys, keying, keyed** /kiːd/)
key in put words or numbers into a computer by pressing the keys: *Key in your name.*

keyboard /'kiːbɔːd/ *noun*
1 all the keys on a piano, computer or typewriter, for example ☞ picture at **computer**
2 a musical instrument like a small electrical piano: *a keyboard player*

keyhole /'kiːhəʊl/ *noun*
a hole in a lock where you put a key

kg short way of writing **kilogram**

kick¹ /kɪk/ *verb* (**kicks, kicking, kicked** /kɪkt/)
1 hit somebody or something with your foot: *I kicked the ball to Chris.*
2 move your foot or feet up quickly: *The child was kicking and screaming.*
kick off start a game of football
kick somebody out make somebody leave a place: *The boys were kicked out of the cinema because they were noisy.*

kick² /kɪk/ *noun*
1 hitting something or somebody with

your foot, or moving your foot or feet up quickly: *Jan gave the ball a kick.*
2 a feeling of excitement
kick-off /'kɪk ɒf/ *noun*
the start of a game of football: *The kick-off is at 2.30.*

kid /kɪd/ *noun*
1 a child: *How old are your kids?* ❍ This is an informal word.
2 a young goat ☞ picture at **goat**

kidnap /'kɪdnæp/ *verb* (**kidnaps**, **kidnapping**, **kidnapped** /'kɪdnæpt/)
take somebody away and hide them, so that their family or friends will pay you money to free them: *The son of a rich businessman was kidnapped today.*
kidnapper *noun*
a person who kidnaps somebody

kidney /'kɪdni/ *noun* (*plural* **kidneys**)
one of two parts inside your body ☞ picture on page 126

kill /kɪl/ *verb* (**kills**, **killing**, **killed** /kɪld/)
make somebody or something die: *The police do not know who killed the old man.* ◇ *Three people were killed in the accident.*
killer *noun*
a person, animal or thing that kills

kilogram, kilogramme
/'kɪləgræm/, **kilo** /'kiːləʊ/ (*plural* **kilos**) *noun*
a measure of weight. There are 1 000 **grams** in a kilogram: *I bought two kilos of potatoes.* ❍ The short way of writing 'kilogram' is **kg**: *1 kg of bananas*

kilometer *American English for* **kilometre**

kilometre /'kɪləmiːtə(r)/, /kɪ'lɒmɪtə(r)/ *noun*
a measure of length. There are 1 000 **metres** in a kilometre. ❍ The short way of writing 'kilometre' is **km**: *They live 100 km from Paris.*

kilt /kɪlt/ *noun*
a skirt that men in Scotland sometimes wear

kind¹ /kaɪnd/ *adjective* (**kinder**, **kindest**)
friendly and good to other people: *'Can I carry your bag?' 'Thanks. That's very kind of you.'* ◇ *Be kind to animals.*
❍ opposite: **unkind**

kind-hearted /ˌkaɪnd 'hɑːtɪd/ *adjective*
A person who is kind-hearted is kind and gentle to other people.

kindness /'kaɪndnəs/ *noun* (no plural)
being kind: *Thank you for your kindness.*

kind² /kaɪnd/ *noun*
a group of things or people that are the same in some way; a sort or type: *What kind of car do you have?* ◇ *The shop sells ten different kinds of bread.*
kind of words that you use when you are not sure about something: *He looks kind of tired.*

kindly¹ /'kaɪndli/ *adverb*
in a kind way: *She kindly drove me to the station.*

kindly² /'kaɪndli/ *adjective* (**kindlier**, **kindliest**)
kind and friendly: *a kindly old man*

king /kɪŋ/ *noun*
a man who rules a country and who is from a royal family: *King Juan Carlos of Spain* ☞ Look at **queen**.

kingdom /'kɪŋdəm/ *noun*
a country where a king or queen rules: *the United Kingdom*

kiosk /'kiːɒsk/ *noun*
a small shop in a street where you can buy things like sweets and newspapers through an open window ☞ Look also at **telephone kiosk**.

kiss /kɪs/ *verb* (**kisses**, **kissing**, **kissed** /kɪst/)
touch somebody with your lips to show love or to say hello or goodbye: *She kissed me on the cheek.* ◇ *Mark and Lucy were kissing in the park.*
kiss (*plural* **kisses**) *noun*
Give me a kiss!

kit /kɪt/ *noun*
1 all the clothes or other things that you need to do something or to play a sport: *Where is my football kit?* ◇ *a tool kit*
2 a set of small pieces that you put together to make something: *a kit for making a model aeroplane*

kitchen /'kɪtʃɪn/ *noun*
a room where you cook food

kite /kaɪt/ *noun*
a light toy made of paper or cloth on a long

ʌ	ɜː	ə	eɪ	əʊ	aɪ	aʊ	ɔɪ	ɪə	eə	ʊə
cup	bird	about	say	go	five	now	boy	near	hair	pure

string. You can make a kite fly in the wind: *The children were flying kites on the hill.*

kitten /'kɪtn/ *noun*
a young cat ☞ picture at **cat**

km *short way of writing* **kilometre**

knee /ni:/ *noun*
the part in the middle of your leg where it bends: *I fell and cut my knee.* ☞ picture on page 126

kneel /ni:l/ *verb*
(**kneels, kneeling, knelt** /nelt/ or **kneeled** /ni:ld/, **has knelt** or **has kneeled**)
go down or stay with your knees on the ground: *He knelt down to pray.* ◇ *Jane was kneeling on the floor.*

kneel

knew *form of* **know**

knickers /'nɪkəz/ *noun* (plural)
a small piece of clothing that a woman or girl wears under her other clothes, between the middle of her body and the top of her legs: *a pair of knickers*

knife

knife /naɪf/ *noun* (*plural* **knives** /naɪvz/)
a sharp metal thing with a handle, that you use to cut things or to fight

knight /naɪt/ *noun*
1 a man who has a special title and who can use 'Sir' in front of his name
2 a soldier who rode a horse and fought a long time ago

knit /nɪt/ *verb*
(**knits, knitting, knitted**)
use long sticks (called **knitting-needles**) to make clothes from wool: *My grandmother knitted this hat for me.*

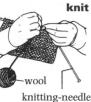
knit
wool
knitting-needle

knitting *noun* (no plural)
1 making clothes from wool: *Her hobbies are knitting and football.*
2 something that you are knitting

knitting-needle /'nɪtɪŋ ni:dl/ *noun*
a long metal or plastic stick that you use for knitting

knives *plural of* **knife**

knob /nɒb/ *noun*
1 a round handle on a door or drawer: *a wooden doorknob*
2 a round thing that you turn to control part of a machine

knock¹ /nɒk/ *verb* (**knocks, knocking, knocked** /nɒkt/)
1 hit something to make a noise: *I knocked on the door, but nobody answered.*
2 hit something hard: *I knocked my head on the car door.* ◇ *She knocked a glass off the table.*
knock somebody down, knock somebody over hit somebody so that they fall onto the ground: *The little boy was knocked down by a car.*
knock something down break a building so that it falls down: *They knocked down the old houses and built a supermarket in their place.*
knock somebody out hit somebody hard so that they cannot get up again for a while
knock something over hit something so that it falls: *I knocked over a vase of flowers.*

knock² /nɒk/ *noun*
hitting something hard or the sound that this makes: *I heard a knock at the door.*

knot /nɒt/ *noun*
a place where you have tied two ends of rope, string, etc tightly together: *I tied a knot in the rope.* ◇ *Can you undo this knot (= make it loose)?*

knot

knot *verb* (**knots, knotting, knotted**)
tie a knot in something: *He knotted the ends of the rope together.*

know /nəʊ/ *verb* (**knows, knowing, knew** /nju:/, **has known** /nəʊn/)
1 have something in your head, because you have learned it: *I don't know her name.* ◇ *He knows a lot about cars.* ◇ *Do you know how to use this machine?* ◇ *'You're late!' 'Yes, I know.'*
2 have met or seen somebody or something before, perhaps many times: *I have*

known Mario for six years. ◇ I know Paris quite well.

get to know somebody start to know somebody well: *I liked him when I got to know him.*

let somebody know tell somebody: *Let me know if you need any help.*

you know words that you use when you are thinking about what to say next

✪ You use expressions like **God knows** and **Heaven knows** to show very strongly that you do not know something: *'Where is Lisa?' 'God knows!'*

knowledge /'nɒlɪdʒ/ *noun* (no plural) what you know and understand about

something: *He has a good knowledge of European history.*

knuckle /'nʌkl/ *noun* the bones where your fingers join your hand and where your hands bend

koala /kəʊ'ɑːlə/ *noun* a wild animal, like a small bear, that lives in Australia

kph a way of measuring how fast something is moving. 'Kph' is short for **kilometres per hour**.

Ll

l *short way of writing* **litre**

lab /læb/ *short for* **laboratory**

label   **labels**

label /'leɪbl/ *noun* a piece of paper or plastic on something that tells you about it: *The label on the bottle says 'Made in Mexico'.*
label *verb* (**labels, labelling, labelled** /'leɪbld/) put a label on something: *I labelled all the boxes with my name and address.* ✪ In American English the spellings are **labeling** and **labeled**.

labor *American English for* **labour**

laboratory /lə'bɒrətri/ *noun* (*plural* **laboratories**) a special room where scientists work ✪ The short form of 'laboratory' is **lab**.

laborer *American English for* **labourer**

labour /'leɪbə(r)/ *noun* (no plural) hard work that you do with your hands and body
the Labour Party /ðə 'leɪbə pɑːti/ *noun* one of the important political parties in

Britain ☞ Look at **the Conservative Party** and **the Liberal Democrats**.

labourer /'leɪbərə(r)/ *noun* a person who does hard work with his/her hands and body: *a farm labourer*

lace

lace /leɪs/ *noun*
1 (no plural) thin pretty material with a pattern of very small holes in it: *lace curtains* ◇ *a handkerchief with lace round the edge*
2 (*plural* **laces**) a string that you tie to close a shoe

lack /læk/ *verb* (**lacks, lacking, lacked** /lækt/) not have something, or not have enough of something: *The children lacked the food they needed.*
be lacking be needed: *Money is lacking for a new school.*
lack *noun* (no plural) *There is a lack of good teachers.*

lad /læd/ *noun* a boy or young man

ladder /ˈlædə(r)/
noun
two tall pieces of
metal or wood with
shorter pieces
(called **rungs**)
between them. You
use a ladder for
climbing up
something.

— rung

ladder

Ladies /ˈleɪdiz/
noun (no plural)
a public toilet for women: *Where is the Ladies, please?*

lady /ˈleɪdi/ *noun* (*plural* **ladies**)
1 a polite way of saying 'woman': *an old lady* ☞ Look at **gentleman**.
2 **Lady** a woman with a special title: *Before she married Charles, her name was Lady Diana Spencer.* ☞ Look at **Lord**.

lager /ˈlɑːgə(r)/ *noun*
1 (no plural) a light beer: *I'll have a pint of lager, please.*
2 (*plural* **lagers**) a glass, bottle or can of lager

laid *form of* **lay²**

lain *form of* **lie²**

lake /leɪk/ *noun*
a big area of water with land all around it: *Lake Victoria* ◇ *We went swimming in the lake.*

lamb /læm/ *noun*
1 (*plural* **lambs**) a young sheep ☞ picture at **sheep**
2 (no plural) meat from a lamb: *We had roast lamb for lunch.*

lame /leɪm/ *adjective*
If an animal is lame, it cannot walk well because it has hurt its leg or foot: *My horse is lame, so I can't ride her.*

lamp

— lampshade

lamp /læmp/ *noun*
a thing that gives light: *It was dark, so I switched on the lamp.*

lamppost /ˈlæmp pəʊst/ *noun*
a tall thing in the street with a light on the top

lampshade /ˈlæmpʃeɪd/ *noun*
a cover for a lamp

land¹ /lænd/ *noun*
1 (no plural) the part of the earth that is not the sea: *After two weeks in a boat, we were happy to see land.*
2 (no plural) a piece of ground: *They have bought some land and they are going to build a house on it.* ◇ *farming land*
3 (*plural* **lands**) a country: *She returned to the land where she was born.* ✿ In this sense, **country** is the word that we usually use.

land² /lænd/ *verb* (**lands**, **landing**, **landed**)
1 come onto the ground from the air or from the sea: *The plane landed at Heathrow airport.* ◇ *The boat has landed.*
2 bring an aircraft down onto the ground: *The pilot landed the plane safely.*

landing /ˈlændɪŋ/ *noun*
1 coming down onto the ground: *The plane made a safe landing in a field.*
2 a flat place at the top of stairs in a building: *There's a telephone on the landing.*

landlady /ˈlændleɪdi/ *noun* (*plural* **landladies**)
1 a woman who has a house and lets you live there if you pay her money
2 a woman who has a pub or a small hotel

landlord /ˈlændlɔːd/ *noun*
1 a man who has a house and lets you live there if you pay him money
2 a man who has a pub or a small hotel

landmark /ˈlændmɑːk/ *noun*
a big building or another thing that you can see easily from far away: *Big Ben is one of London's most famous landmarks.*

landscape /ˈlændskeɪp/ *noun*
everything you can see in an area of land: *The Scottish landscape is very beautiful.*

lane /leɪn/ *noun*
1 a narrow road in the country
2 one part of a wide road: *We were driving in the middle lane of the motorway.*

i:	i	ɪ	e	æ	ɑː	ɒ	ɔː	ʊ	u	u:
see	happy	sit	ten	cat	father	got	saw	put	situation	too

language /'læŋgwɪdʒ/ *noun*
1 (no plural) words that people say or write
2 (*plural* **languages**) words that a certain group of people say and write: *'Do you speak any foreign languages?' 'Yes, I speak French and Italian.'*

lap¹ /læp/ *noun*
the flat part at the top of your legs when you are sitting: *The child sat on his mother's lap.*

lap² /læp/ *noun*
going once round the track in a race: *The runner fell on the last lap.*

large /lɑːdʒ/ *adjective* (**larger**, **largest**)
big: *They live in a large house.* ◇ *She has a large family.* ◇ *Have you got this shirt in a large size?* ✪ opposite: **small** ☞ picture on page 262

largely /'lɑːdʒli/ *adverb*
mostly; mainly: *The room is largely used for meetings.*

laser /'leɪzə(r)/ *noun*
an instrument that makes a very strong line of light (called a **laser beam**). Some lasers are used to cut metal and others are used by doctors in operations.

last¹ /lɑːst/ *adjective*
1 after all the others: *December is the last month of the year.*
2 just before now: *It's June now, so last month was May.* ◇ *I was at school last week, but this week I'm on holiday.*
3 only one left: *Who wants the last cake?*
last night yesterday in the evening or in the night: *Did you go out last night?*
lastly *adverb*
finally, as the last thing: *Lastly, I want to thank my parents for all their help.*

last² /lɑːst/ *adverb*
1 after all the others: *He finished last in the race.*
2 at a time that is nearest to now: *I last saw Penny in 1993.*

last³ /lɑːst/ *noun* (no plural)
a person or thing that comes after all the others; what comes at the end: *I was the last to arrive at the party.*
at last in the end; after some time: *She waited all week, and at last the letter arrived.*

last⁴ /lɑːst/ *verb* (**lasts**, **lasting**, **lasted**)
1 continue for a time: *The film lasted for*

three hours. ◇ *I hope the good weather will last until the weekend.*
2 be enough for a certain time: *We have enough food to last us till next week.*

late /leɪt/ *adjective, adverb* (**later**, **latest**)
1 after the usual or right time: *I went to bed late last night.* ◇ *I was late for school today* (= I arrived late). ◇ *My train was late.* ✪ opposite: **early**
2 near the end of a time: *They arrived in the late afternoon.* ◇ *She's in her late twenties* (= between the ages of about 25 and 29). ✪ opposite: **early**
3 no longer alive; dead: *Her late husband was a doctor.*
a late night an evening when you go to bed later than usual
at the latest not later than: *Please be here by twelve o'clock at the latest.*
later on at a later time: *Bye – I'll see you later on.*

lately /'leɪtli/ *adverb*
not long ago; recently: *Have you seen Mark lately?* ◇ *The weather has been very bad lately.*

latest /'leɪtɪst/ *adjective*
newest: *the latest fashions*

latter /'lætə(r)/ *adjective*
last: *She lived in Liverpool in the latter part of her life.*
latter *noun* (no plural)
the second of two things or people: *I study both French and German, but I prefer the latter.* ☞ Look at **former**.

laugh /lɑːf/ *verb* (**laughs**, **laughing**, **laughed** /lɑːft/)
make sounds that show you are happy or that you think something is funny: *His jokes always make me laugh.*
laugh at somebody or **something** laugh to show that you think somebody or something is funny or silly: *The children laughed at the clown.* ◇ *They all laughed at me when I said I was frightened of dogs.*
laugh *noun*
My brother has a loud laugh. ◇ *She told us a joke and we all had a good laugh.*
for a laugh as a joke; for fun: *The boys put a spider in her bed for a laugh.*

laughter /'lɑːftə(r)/ *noun* (no plural)
the sound of laughing: *I could hear laughter in the next room.*

ʌ	ɜː	ə	eɪ	əʊ	aɪ	aʊ	ɔɪ	ɪə	eə	ʊə
cup	bird	about	say	go	five	now	boy	near	hair	pure

launch /lɔːntʃ/ *verb* (**launches, launching, launched** /lɔːntʃt/)
1 put a ship into the water or a spacecraft into the sky: *This ship was launched in 1967.*
2 start something new: *The magazine was launched last year.*

launderette /ˌlɔːndəˈret/ *noun*
a shop where you pay to wash and dry your clothes in machines

laundromat /ˈlɔːndrəmæt/ *American English for* **launderette**

laundry /ˈlɔːndri/ *noun*
1 (no plural) clothes that you must wash or that you have washed: *a laundry basket*
2 (*plural* **laundries**) a place where you send things like sheets and clothes so that somebody can wash them for you

lava /ˈlɑːvə/ *noun* (no plural)
hot liquid rock that comes out of a **volcano**

lavatory /ˈlævətri/ *noun* (*plural* **lavatories**)
a large bowl with a seat that you use when you need to empty waste from your body. The room that it is in is also called a **lavatory**: *Where's your lavatory, please?*
○ **Toilet** is the word that we usually use.

law /lɔː/ *noun*
1 a rule of a country that says what people may and may not do: *There is a law against stealing.* ☞ Look at **legal**.
2 **the law** (no plural) all the laws of a country
against the law not allowed by the rules of a country: *Murder is against the law.*
break the law do something that the laws of a country say you must not do: *I have never broken the law.*

lawcourt /ˈlɔːkɔːt/ *noun*
a place where people (a **judge** or **jury**) decide if somebody has done something wrong, and what the punishment will be

lawn /lɔːn/ *noun*
a piece of short grass in a garden or park: *They were sitting on the lawn.*

lawnmower /ˈlɔːnməʊə(r)/ *noun*
a machine that cuts grass

lawyer /ˈlɔːjə(r)/ *noun*
a person who has studied the law and who helps people or talks for them in a court of law

lay¹ *form of* **lie**²

lay² /leɪ/ *verb* (**lays, laying, laid** /leɪd/, **has laid**)
1 put something carefully on another thing: *I laid the papers on the desk.*
2 make an egg: *Birds and insects lay eggs.*

layer /ˈleɪə(r)/ *noun*
something flat that lies on another thing or that is between other things: *The table was covered with a thin layer of dust.* ◇ *The cake has a layer of jam in the middle.*

lazy /ˈleɪzi/ *adjective* (**lazier, laziest**)
A person who is lazy does not want to work: *Don't be so lazy – come and help me!* ◇ *My teacher said I was lazy.*
lazily /ˈleɪzɪli/ *adverb*
in a slow, lazy way: *She walked lazily across the room.*
laziness /ˈleɪzinəs/ *noun* (no plural)
being lazy

lb *short way of writing* **pound 2**

lead¹ /led/ *noun*
1 (no plural) a soft grey metal that is very heavy. Lead is used to make things like water-pipes and roofs.
2 (*plural* **leads**) the grey part inside a pencil

lead² /liːd/ *verb* (**leads, leading, led** /led/, **has led**)
1 take a person or an animal somewhere by going in front: *He led me to my room.*
2 be the first or the best, for example in a race or game: *Who's leading in the race?*
3 go to a place: *This path leads to the river.*
4 control a group of people: *The team was led by Gary Hollis.*
lead to something make something happen: *Smoking can lead to heart disease.*

lead³ /liːd/ *noun* (no plural)
going in front or doing something first
be in the lead be in front: *At the start of the race her horse was in the lead.*

lead⁴ /liːd/ *noun*
1 a long piece of leather or a chain that you tie to a dog's neck so that it walks with you
2 a long piece of wire that brings electricity to things like lamps and machines

p	b	t	d	k	g	tʃ	dʒ	f	v	θ	ð
pen	**bad**	**tea**	**did**	**cat**	**got**	**chain**	**jam**	**fall**	**van**	**thin**	**this**

leader /'liːdə(r)/ *noun*
1 a person who controls a group of people: *They chose a new leader.*
2 a person or group that is the first or the best: *The leader is ten metres in front of the other runners.*

leadership /'liːdəʃɪp/ *noun* (no plural)
controlling a group of people: *The country is under new leadership* (= has new leaders).

leading /'liːdɪŋ/ *adjective*
best or very important: *a leading writer*

leaf /liːf/ *noun* (*plural* **leaves** /liːvz/)
one of the flat green parts that grow on a plant or tree: *Leaves fall from the trees in autumn.* ☞ pictures at **plant** and **tree**

leaflet /'liːflət/ *noun*
a piece of paper with writing on it that tells you about something: *The man at the tourist information office gave me a leaflet about buses to the airport.*

league /liːg/ *noun*
1 a group of teams that play against each other in a sport: *the football league*
2 a group of people or countries that work together to do something: *the League of Nations*

leak /liːk/ *verb* (**leaks, leaking, leaked** /liːkt/)
1 have a hole that liquid or gas can go through: *The roof of our house leaks when it rains.* ◇ *The boat is leaking.*
2 go out through a hole: *Water is leaking from the pipe.*
leak *noun*
There's a leak in the roof.

lean¹ /liːn/ *adjective* (**leaner, leanest**)
1 thin but strong: *He is tall and lean.*
2 Lean meat does not have very much fat.

lean

She is **leaning** against a tree. ▨ He is **leaning** out of a window.

lean² /liːn/ *verb* (**leans, leaning, leant** /lent/ or **leaned** /liːnd/, **has leant** or **has leaned**)
1 not be straight; bend forwards, backwards or to the side
2 put your body or a thing against another thing: *Lean your bike against the wall.*

leap /liːp/ *verb* (**leaps, leaping, leapt** /lept/ or **leaped** /liːpt/, **has leapt** or **has leaped**)
make a big jump: *The cat leapt onto the table.*
leap *noun*
a big jump: *With one leap, he was over the wall.*

leap year /'liːp jɪə(r)/ *noun*
a year when February has 29 days. Leap years happen every four years.

learn /lɜːn/ *verb* (**learns, learning, learnt** /lɜːnt/ or **learned** /lɜːnd/, **has learnt** or **has learned**)
1 find out something, or how to do something, by studying or by doing it often: *Jodie is learning to swim.* ◇ *I learnt English at school.* ◇ *Learn this list of words for homework* (= so you can remember them). ☞ Look at **teach**.
2 hear about something: *I was sorry to learn of your father's death.*

learner /'lɜːnə(r)/ *noun*
a person who is learning: *This dictionary is for learners of English.*

leash /liːʃ/ *American English for* **lead⁴ 1**

least¹ /liːst/ *adjective, pronoun*
the smallest amount of something: *Sue has a lot of money, Jane has less, and Kate has the least.* ☞ Look at **less**.

least² /liːst/ *adverb*
less than all others: *This is the least expensive camera in the shop.*
at least 1 not less than: *It will cost at least £150.* **2** although other things are bad: *We're not rich, but at least we're happy.*
not in the least not at all: *'Are you angry?' 'Not in the least!'*

leather /'leðə(r)/ *noun* (no plural)
the skin of an animal that is used to make things like shoes, jackets or bags: *a leather jacket*

leave[1] /li:v/ *verb* (**leaves, leaving, left** /left/, **has left**)
1 go away from somebody or something: *The train leaves at 8.40.* ◇ *She left home when she was 18.* ◇ *I left my job in May.*
2 let somebody or something stay in the same place or in the same way: *John left the door open.*
3 not bring something with you: *I left my books at home.*
4 make something stay; not use something: *Leave some cake for me!*
leave somebody alone not speak to or touch somebody: *Leave me alone – I'm busy!*
leave something alone not touch or take something: *Leave that bag alone – it's mine!*
leave somebody or something behind not take somebody or something with you: *She went shopping and left the children behind.*
leave for start a journey to a place: *Jane is leaving for France tomorrow.*
leave out not put in or do something; not include somebody or something: *The other children left him out of the game.* ◇ *I left out question 3 in the exam because it was too difficult.*
leave something to somebody
1 let somebody do a job for you: *I left the cooking to John.* **2** give something to somebody when you die: *She left all her money to her sons.*

leave[2] /li:v/ *noun* (no plural)
a time when you do not go to work: *I have 25 days' leave each year.*
on leave having a holiday from your job: *He's on leave from the army.*

leaves *plural of* **leaf**

lecture /'lektʃə(r)/ *noun*
a talk to a group of people to teach them about something: *She gave an interesting lecture on Spanish history.*
lecture *verb* (**lectures, lecturing, lectured** /'lektʃəd/)
Professor Sims lectures on Modern Art.
lecturer *noun*
a person whose job is to lecture: *He is a university lecturer.*

led *form of* **lead**[2]

ledge /ledʒ/ *noun*
a long narrow flat place, for example under

a window or on the side of a mountain: *a window-ledge*

leek /li:k/ *noun*
a vegetable like a long white onion with green leaves: *leek and potato soup*

left[1] *form of* **leave**[1]
be left be there after the rest has gone: *There is only a small piece of cake left.*

left[2] /left/ *adjective, adverb*
opposite of right: *Turn left at the church.* ◇ *My left leg hurts.*
left *noun* (no plural)
The house is on your left. ◇ *In Britain we drive on the left.*

left-hand /'left hænd/ *adjective*
of or on the left: *Your heart is on the left-hand side of your body.*
left-handed /,left 'hændɪd/ *adjective*
If you are left-handed, you use your left hand more easily than your right-hand, for example when you write.

leg /leg/ *noun*
1 one of the long parts of a the body of a person or an animal that is used for walking and standing: *A dog has four legs.*
☞ picture on page 126
2 one of the parts of a pair of trousers that covers your leg
3 one of the long parts that a table or chair stands on
pull somebody's leg try to make somebody believe something that is not true, for fun: *I didn't really see an elephant – I was only pulling your leg!*

legal /'li:gl/ *adjective*
1 allowed by the law: *In many parts of America, it is legal to carry a gun.* ✪ opposite: **illegal** or **against the law**
2 of or about the law: *legal advice*
legally /'li:gəli/ *adverb*
They are not legally married.

legend /'ledʒənd/ *noun*
an old story that is perhaps not true: *the legend of Robin Hood*

leisure /'leʒə(r)/ *noun* (no plural)
the time when you are not working and can do what you want
leisure centre /'leʒə sentə(r)/ *noun*
a place where you can play sports and do other things in your free time

i:	i	ɪ	e	æ	ɑ:	ɒ	ɔ:	ʊ	u	u:
see	happy	sit	ten	cat	father	got	saw	put	situation	too

lemon /'lemən/ *noun*
a yellow fruit with a
sour taste

lemonade
/ˌleməˈneɪd/ *noun*
1 (no plural) a

lemon
sweet clear drink with bubbles in it
2 (*plural* **lemonades**) a glass of this drink

lend /lend/ *verb* (**lends**, **lending**, **lent**
/lent/, **has lent**)
give something to somebody for a short
time: *Rick lent me his car for an hour.*
☞ picture at **borrow**

length /leŋθ/ *noun* (no plural)
how long something is: *The table is two
metres in length.* ◊ *We measured the
length of the garden.* ☞ picture on page
161

lengthen /'leŋθn/ *verb* (**lengthens**,
lengthening, **lengthened** /'leŋθnd/)
become longer or make something longer

lengthy /'leŋθi/ *adjective* (**lengthier**,
lengthiest)
long: *a lengthy meeting*

lens /lenz/ *noun* (*plural* **lenses**)
a special piece of glass in things like cameras, microscopes or glasses ☞ Look also
at **contact lens**.

lent *form of* **lend**

lentil /'lentl/ *noun*
a small round dried seed. You cook lentils
in water before you eat them: *lentil soup*

leopard /'lepəd/ *noun*
a wild animal like a big cat with yellow fur
and dark spots

less[1] /les/ *adjective, pronoun*
a smaller amount of something; not so
much: *A poor person has less money than
a rich person.* ◊ *I'm too fat – I should eat
less.* ☞ Look at **least**.

less[2] /les/ *adverb*
not so much: *It rains less in summer.*
◊ *He's less intelligent than his sister.*
☞ Look at **least**.

lesson /'lesn/ *noun*
a time when you learn something with a
teacher: *We have a French lesson after
lunch.*

let[1] /let/ *verb* (**lets**, **letting**, **let**, **has let**)
allow somebody or something to do some-
thing: *Her parents won't let her go out
with her boyfriend.* ◊ *Let me carry your*
bag. ◊ *Don't let the fire go out.* ◊ *Let the
dog in* (= let it come in).

let somebody down not do something
that you promised to do for somebody:
*Claire has let me down. We agreed to meet
at eight o'clock but she didn't come.*

let go of somebody or **something,**
let somebody or **something go** stop
holding somebody or something: *Let go of
my hand!* ◊ *Hold the rope and don't let
go.*

let somebody off not punish somebody: *He wasn't sent to prison – the judge
let him off.*

let's You use 'let's' to ask somebody to do
something with you: *Let's go to the
theatre this evening.*

let[2] /let/ *verb* (**lets**, **letting**, **let**, **has let**)
allow somebody to use your house or land
if they pay you: *Have you got any rooms
to let?*

letter /'letə(r)/ *noun*
1 a sign in writing: *Z is the last letter in
the English alphabet.*

> **❂** A, B and C are **capital** letters, and a, b,
> and c are **small** letters.

2 a piece of writing that one person sends
to another person: *Did you post my letter?* ◊ *She wrote a letter to her mother.*

letter-box /'letə bɒks/ *noun* (*plural*
letter-boxes)
1 a hole for letters in the door of a house
2 a box for letters outside a house
3 a box in the street where you put letters
that you want to send

lettuce /'letɪs/ *noun*
a plant with big leaves that you eat without cooking, in salads

level[1] /'levl/ *adjective*
1 with no part higher than another part;
flat: *We need level ground to play football
on.* ◊ *This shelf isn't level.*
2 with the same heights, points or posi-
tions, for example: *The two teams are level
with 40 points each.* ◊ *His head is level
with his mother's shoulder.*

level[2] /'levl/ *noun*
how high something is: *The town is 500
metres above sea level.* ◊ *an elementary-
level English class*

level crossing /ˌlevl ˈkrɒsɪŋ/ *noun*
a place where a railway line goes over a
road

lever /'li:və(r)/ *noun*
1 a bar for lifting something heavy or opening something. You put one end under the thing you want to lift or open, and push the other end.
2 a thing that you pull or push to make a machine work: *Pull this lever.*

liable /'laɪəbl/ *adjective*
If you are liable to do something, you usually do it or you will probably do it: *He's liable to get angry if you don't do what he says.*

liar /'laɪə(r)/ *noun*
a person who says or writes things that are not true: *I don't believe her – she's a liar.*

liberal /'lɪbərəl/ *adjective*
A person who is liberal lets other people do and think what they want: *Kim's parents are very liberal, but mine are quite strict.*
the Liberal Democrats /ðə ˌlɪbərəl 'deməkræts/ *noun* (plural)
one of the important political parties in Britain ☞ Look at **the Conservative Party** and **the Labour Party**.

liberate /'lɪbəreɪt/ *verb* (**liberates, liberating, liberated**)
make somebody or something free: *France was liberated in 1945.*

liberty /'lɪbəti/ *noun* (no plural)
being free to go where you want and do what you want

library /'laɪbrəri/ *noun* (*plural* **libraries**)
a room or building where you go to borrow or read books ✪ Be careful! You cannot buy books from a **library**. The place where you buy books is called a **bookshop**.
librarian /laɪ'breəriən/ *noun*
a person who works in a library

licence /'laɪsns/ *noun*
1 a piece of paper that shows you are allowed to do or have something: *Do you have a driving-licence?*
2 *American English for* **license**

license /'laɪsns/ *verb* (**licenses, licensing, licensed** /'laɪsnst/)
1 give somebody a licence: *This shop is licensed to sell guns.*
2 *American English for* **licence**

license plate /'laɪsns pleɪt/ *American English for* **number-plate**

lick /lɪk/ *verb* (**licks, licking, licked** /lɪkt/)
move your tongue over something: *The cat was licking its paws.*
lick *noun*
Can I have a lick of your ice-cream?

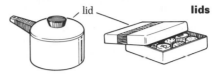

lid /lɪd/ *noun*
the top part of a box, pot or other container that covers it and that you can take off
☞ Look also at **eyelid**.

lie¹ /laɪ/ *verb* (**lies, lying, lied** /laɪd/, **has lied**)
say something that you know is not true: *He lied about his age. He said he was 16 but really he's 14.*
lie *noun*
something you say that you know is not true: *She told me a lie.*
☞ A person who lies is a **liar**.

lie² /laɪ/ *verb* (**lies, lying, lay** /leɪ/, **has lain** /leɪn/)
1 put your body flat on something so that you are not sitting or standing: *He lay on the bed and went to sleep.*
2 have your body flat on something: *The baby was lying on its back.*
3 be or stay on something: *Snow lay on the ground.*
lie down put or have your body flat on something: *She lay down on the bed.*

lieutenant /lef'tenənt/ *noun*
an officer in the army or navy

life /laɪf/ *noun*
1 (no plural) People, animals and plants have life, but things like stone, metal and water do not: *Do you believe there is life after death?* ◇ *Is there life on the moon?*
2 (*plural* **lives** /laɪvz/) being alive: *Many people lost their lives (= died) in the fire.* ◇ *The doctor saved her life (= stopped her dying).*
3 (*plural* **lives**) the time that you have been alive: *He has lived here all his life.*
4 (no plural) the way that you live: *an unhappy life.*
5 (no plural) energy; being busy and interested: *Young children are full of life.*
lead a life live in a certain way: *She leads a busy life.*

p	b	t	d	k	g	tʃ	dʒ	f	v	θ	ð
pen	**b**ad	**t**ea	**d**id	**c**at	**g**ot	**ch**ain	**j**am	**f**all	**v**an	**th**in	**th**is

lifebelt /ˈlaɪfbelt/ *noun*
a big ring that you hold or wear if you fall into water to stop you from drowning

lifeboat /ˈlaɪfbəʊt/ *noun*
a boat that goes to help people who are in danger at sea

life-jacket /ˈlaɪf dʒækɪt/ *noun*
a special jacket that you wear in a boat to stop you from drowning if you fall in the water

lifestyle /ˈlaɪfstaɪl/ *noun*
the way that you live: *They have a healthy lifestyle.*

lifetime /ˈlaɪftaɪm/ *noun*
all the time that you are alive: *There have been a lot of changes in my grandmother's lifetime.*

lift¹ /lɪft/ *verb* (**lifts**, **lifting**, **lifted**)
move somebody or something up: *I can't lift this box. It's too heavy.* ◇ *Lift your arm.*

lift² /lɪft/ *noun*
1 a machine that takes people and things up and down in a high building: *Shall we use the stairs or take the lift?*
2 a free journey in another person's car: *Can you give me a lift to the station?*

light¹ /laɪt/ *noun*
1 (no plural) Light comes from the sun, fire and lamps. It makes us able to see things: *sunlight* ◇ *The light was not very good so it was difficult to read.*
2 (*plural* **lights**) a thing that gives light, for example an electric lamp ☞ Look also at **traffic-lights**.

○ A light can be **on** or **off**. You can **put**, **turn** or **switch** a light **on**, **off** or **out**: *Turn the lights off before you go to bed.* ◇ *It's getting dark. Shall I switch the light on?*

3 (no plural) something, for example a match, that you use to start a cigarette burning: *Have you got a light?*
set light to something make something start to burn

light² /laɪt/ *adjective* (**lighter**, **lightest**)
1 with a lot of light; not dark: *In summer it's light until about ten o'clock.* ◇ *The room has a lot of windows so it's very light.*
2 with a pale colour; not dark: *a light-blue shirt*

3 easy to lift or move; not heavy: *Will you carry this bag for me? It's very light.*
☞ picture at **heavy**
4 not very much or not very strong: *light rain* ◇ *I had a light breakfast.*
lightly *adverb*
She touched me lightly on the arm.

light³ /laɪt/ *verb* (**lights**, **lighting**, **lit** /lɪt/ or **lighted**, **has lit** or **has lighted**)
1 make something start to burn: *Will you light the fire?*
2 give light to something: *The room is lit by two big lamps.*

light-bulb /ˈlaɪt bʌlb/ *noun*
the glass part of an electric lamp that gives light

lighter /ˈlaɪtə(r)/ *noun*
a thing for lighting cigarettes

lighthouse /ˈlaɪthaʊs/ *noun* (*plural* **lighthouses** /ˈlaɪthaʊzɪz/)
a tall building by or in the sea, with a strong light to show ships that there are rocks

lighting /ˈlaɪtɪŋ/ *noun* (no plural)
the kind of lights that a place has: *street lighting*

lightning /ˈlaɪtnɪŋ/ *noun* (no plural)
a sudden bright light in the sky when there is a storm: *He was struck* (= hit) *by lightning.* ☞ Look at **thunder**.

like¹ /laɪk/ *verb* (**likes**, **liking**, **liked** /laɪkt/)
feel that somebody or something is good or nice; enjoy something: *Do you like Jane's new boyfriend?* ◇ *I don't like carrots.* ◇ *I like playing tennis.* ○ opposite: **dislike**
if you like if you want: *'Shall we go out?' 'Yes, if you like.'*
○ **Would like** is a more polite way of saying **want**: *Would you like some coffee?* ◇ *I'd like to speak to the manager.*

like² /laɪk/ *preposition, conjunction*
1 the same as somebody or something: *She is wearing a dress like mine.* ◇ *John looks like his father.* ☞ Look at **unlike**
2 in the same way as somebody or something: *She acted like a child.*
3 for example: *I bought a lot of things, like books and clothes.*
what is ... like? words that you say

when you want to know more about somebody or something: *'What's that book like?' 'It's very interesting.'*

likely /ˈlaɪkli/ *adjective* (**likelier, likeliest**)
If something is likely, it will probably happen: *It's likely that she will agree.* ◇ *They are likely to be late.* ✪ opposite: **unlikely**

likeness /ˈlaɪknəs/ *noun* (no plural)
being or looking the same: *There's a strong likeness between John and his brother.*

likewise /ˈlaɪkwaɪz/ *adverb*
the same: *I sat down and John did likewise.*

lily /ˈlɪli/ *noun* (*plural* **lilies**)
a plant with big flowers

limb /lɪm/ *noun*
an arm or a leg

lime /laɪm/ *noun*
a small green fruit like a lemon

limit /ˈlɪmɪt/ *noun*
the most that is possible or allowed: *What is the speed limit?* (= how fast are you allowed to go?)
limit *verb* (**limits, limiting, limited**)
do or have no more than a certain amount or number: *The theatre only has 100 seats, so we must limit the number of tickets we sell.*

limp /lɪmp/ *verb* (**limps, limping, limped** /lɪmpt/)
walk with difficulty because you have hurt your foot or leg
limp *noun* (no plural)
She walks with a limp.

line¹ /laɪn/ *noun*
1 a long thin mark like this _____:
Draw a straight line. ◇ *Two yellow lines at the side of the road mean that you can't park there.*
2 people or things beside each other or one after the other: *Stand in a line.*
3 all the words that are beside each other on a page: *How many lines are there on this page?* ◇ *I don't know the next line of the poem.*
4 a long piece of string or rope: *Hang the washing on the line to dry.*
5 what a train moves along
6 a very long wire for telephones or electricity: *I tried to phone him but the line was busy.*

line² /laɪn/ *verb* (**lines, lining, lined** /laɪnd/)
1 stand or be in lines along something: *People lined the street to watch the race.*
2 cover the inside of something with a different material: *The boots are lined with fur.*
line up stand in a line or make a line: *We lined up to buy tickets.*

linen /ˈlɪnɪn/ *noun* (no plural)
1 a kind of strong cloth: *a linen jacket*
2 things like tablecloths and sheets that are made of cotton or linen

liner /ˈlaɪnə(r)/ *noun*
1 a big ship that carries people a long way
2 a bag that you put inside something to keep it clean: *a dustbin liner*

linger /ˈlɪŋgə(r)/ *verb* (**lingers, lingering, lingered** /ˈlɪŋgəd/)
stay somewhere for a long time: *They lingered in the park after the end of the concert.*

lining /ˈlaɪnɪŋ/ *noun*
material that covers the inside of something: *My coat has a thick lining so it's very warm.*

link /lɪŋk/ *noun*
1 something that joins things or people together: *There's a link between smoking and heart disease.*
2 one of the round parts in a chain
link *verb* (**links, linking, linked** /lɪŋkt/)
join two people or things: *The new tunnel links Britain to France.*

lioness
lion

lion /ˈlaɪən/ *noun*
a wild animal like a big cat with yellow fur. Lions live in Africa and parts of Asia.
✪ A female lion is called a **lioness** and a young lion is called a **cub**.

lip /lɪp/ *noun*
one of the two soft red parts above and below your mouth ☞ picture on page 126

lipstick /'lɪpstɪk/ *noun*
colour that you put on your lips: *I put on some lipstick.*

liquid /'lɪkwɪd/ *noun*
anything that is not a solid or a gas. Water, oil and milk are liquids.
liquid *adjective*
liquid gold

list /lɪst/ *noun*
a lot of names or other things that you write, one after another: *a shopping list* (= of things that you must buy)
list *verb* (**lists**, **listing**, **listed**)
write or say a list: *The teacher listed all our names.*

listen /'lɪsn/ *verb* (**listens**, **listening**, **listened** /'lɪsnd/)
hear something when you are trying to hear it: *I was listening to the radio.* ◇ *Listen! I want to tell you something.* ☞ Note at **hear**

lit *form of* **light³**

liter *American English for* **litre**

literature /'lɪtrətʃə(r)/ *noun* (no plural)
books, plays and poetry: *He is studying English literature.*

litre /'li:tə(r)/ *noun*
a measure of liquid. There are 100 **centilitres** in a litre: *ten litres of petrol* ✪ The short way of writing 'litre' is **l**: *20 l*

litter¹ /'lɪtə(r)/ *noun*
1 (no plural) pieces of paper and other things that people leave on the ground: *The park was full of litter after the concert.*
2 (*plural* **litters**) all the baby animals that are born to the same mother at the same time: *Our dog had a litter of six puppies.*

litter² /'lɪtə(r)/ *verb* (**litters**, **littering**, **littered** /'lɪtəd/)
be or make something untidy with litter: *My desk was littered with papers.*

little¹ /'lɪtl/ *adjective*
1 not big; small: *a little village* ☞ picture on page 262
2 young: *a little girl*
3 not much: *We have very little money.*
a little some but not much: *I speak a little French.*

little² /'lɪtl/ *adverb*
not much: *I'm tired – I slept very little last night.*
a little quite; rather: *This skirt is a little

too short for me.*
little by little slowly: *Little by little she started to feel better.*

little³ /'lɪtl/ *pronoun*
a small amount; not much: *I've got some ice-cream. Would you like a little?* ◇ *I did very little today.*

live¹ /lɪv/ *verb* (**lives**, **living**, **lived** /lɪvd/)
1 be or stay alive: *You can't live without water.* ◇ *He lived to the age of 93.*
2 have your home somewhere: *Where do you live?*
3 spend your life in a certain way: *They live a quiet life in the country.*
live on something 1 eat or drink only one thing: *Cows live on grass.* **2** have a certain amount of money: *They live on £70 a week.*

live² /laɪv/ *adjective*
1 not dead: *The snake ate a live mouse.*
2 If a radio or television programme is live, you see or hear it at the same time as it happens: *a live football match*
3 with electricity passing through it: *Don't touch that wire – it's live!*

lively /'laɪvli/ *adjective* (**livelier**, **liveliest**)
full of life; always moving or doing things: *The children are very lively.*

liver /'lɪvə(r)/ *noun*
the part inside the body of a person or an animal that cleans the blood ☞ picture on page 126

lives *plural of* **life**

living¹ /'lɪvɪŋ/ *adjective*
alive; not dead: *Some people say he is the greatest living writer.*

living² /'lɪvɪŋ/ *noun*
1 the way that you get money: *What do you do for a living?*
2 the way that you live

living-room /'lɪvɪŋ ru:m/ *noun*
a room in a house where people sit and watch television or talk, for example

lizard /'lɪzəd/ *noun*
a small animal that has four legs, a long tail and rough skin

lizard

load¹ /ləʊd/ *noun*
1 something that is carried: *The lorry brought another load of wood.*
2 loads (plural) a lot: *We've got loads of time.*

load² /ləʊd/ *verb* (**loads, loading, loaded**)
1 put things in or on something, for example a car or ship, that will carry them: *Two men loaded the furniture into the van.* ◇ *They're loading the plane now.*
○ opposite: **unload**
2 put bullets in a gun or film in a camera

loaf /ləʊf/ *noun* (*plural* **loaves** /ləʊvz/)
a big piece of bread: *a loaf of bread* ☞ picture at **bread**

loan /ləʊn/ *noun*
money that somebody lends you: *The bank gave me a loan of £1 000 to buy a new car.*
loan *verb* (**loans, loaning, loaned** /ləʊnd/)
lend something: *This book is loaned from the library.*

lobster /'lɒbstə(r)/ *noun*
a sea animal with a hard shell, two big claws, eight legs and a long tail

local /'ləʊkl/ *adjective*
of a place near you: *Her children go to the local school.* ◇ *a local newspaper* ◇ *local government*
locally /'ləʊkəli/ *adverb*
Do you work locally?

located /ləʊ'keɪtɪd/ *adjective*
in a place: *The factory is located near Glasgow.*

location /ləʊ'keɪʃn/ *noun*
a place: *The house is in a quiet location on top of a hill.*

lock¹ /lɒk/ *noun*
a metal thing that keeps a door, gate, box, etc closed so that you cannot open it without a key

lock

lock² /lɒk/ *verb*
(**locks, locking, locked** /lɒkt/)
close with a key: *Don't forget to lock the door when you leave.* **○** opposite: **unlock**
lock away put something in a place that you close with a key: *The paintings are locked away at night.*

lock in lock a door so that somebody cannot go out: *The prisoners are locked in.*
lock out lock a door so that somebody cannot go in
lock up lock all the doors and windows of a building

locker /'lɒkə(r)/ *noun*
a small cupboard, with a lock, for keeping things in, for example in a school or at a station

lodge /lɒdʒ/ *verb* (**lodges, lodging, lodged** /lɒdʒd/)
pay to live in another person's house: *I lodged with a family when I was studying in Oxford.*
lodger *noun*
a person who pays to live in another person's house

loft /lɒft/ *noun*
the room or space under the roof of a house: *My old books are in a box in the loft.*

log /lɒg/ *noun*
a thick round piece of wood from a tree: *Put another log on the fire.*

log

lollipop /'lɒlipɒp/,
lolly /'lɒli/ (*plural* **lollies**) *noun*
a big sweet on a stick ☞ Look also at **ice lolly**.

lonely /'ləʊnli/ *adjective* (**lonelier, loneliest**)
1 unhappy because you are not with other people: *I was very lonely when I first came to London.*
2 far from other places: *a lonely house in the hills*
loneliness /'ləʊnlinəs/ *noun* (no plural)
being lonely

long¹ /lɒŋ/ *adjective* (**longer** /'lɒŋgə(r)/, **longest** /'lɒŋgɪst/)
1 far from one end to the other: *This is the longest road in Britain.* ◇ *She has long black hair.* **○** opposite: **short** ☞ picture on page 262
2 You use 'long' to say or ask how far something is from one end to the other: *How long is the table?* ◇ *The wall is 5 m long.* ☞ picture on page 161

p	b	t	d	k	g	tʃ	dʒ	f	v	θ	ð
pen	**b**ad	**t**ea	**d**id	**c**at	**g**ot	**ch**ain	**j**am	**f**all	**v**an	**th**in	**th**is

3 that continues for a lot of time: *a long film* ✪ opposite: **short**
4 You use 'long' to say or ask about the time from the beginning to the end of something: *How long is the lesson?*

long² /lɒŋ/ *adverb*
for a lot of time: *I can't stay long.*
as long as, so long as if: *You can borrow the book as long as you promise not to lose it.*
long after at a time much after
long ago many years in the past: *Long ago there were no cars.*
long before at a time much before: *My grandfather died long before I was born.*
no longer, not any longer not now; not as before: *She doesn't live here any longer.*

long³ /lɒŋ/ *noun* (no plural)
a lot of time: *She went shopping but she was not out for long.*

long⁴ /lɒŋ/ *verb* (**longs, longing, longed** /lɒŋd/)
want something very much: *I long to see my family again.* ◇ *She's longing for a letter from her boyfriend.*
longing *noun*
a strong feeling of wanting something

long-jump /ˈlɒŋ dʒʌmp/ *noun* (no plural)
a sport where you try to jump as far as you can

loo /luː/ *noun* (*plural* **loos**)
toilet: *I need to go to the loo.* ✪ This is an informal word.

look¹ /lʊk/ *verb* (**looks, looking, looked** /lʊkt/)
1 turn your eyes towards somebody or something and try to see them: *Look at this picture.* ◇ *You should look both ways before you cross the road.* ☞ Note at **see**
2 seem to be; appear: *You look tired!*
3 You say 'look' to make somebody listen to you: *Look, I need some money.*
look after somebody or **something** take care of somebody or something: *Can you look after my cat when I'm on holiday?*
look as if, look as though seem or appear: *It looks as if it's going to rain.*
look for somebody or **something** try to find somebody or something: *I'm looking for my keys.*

look forward to something wait for something with pleasure: *I'm looking forward to seeing you again.*
look into something study something carefully: *We will look into the problem.*
look like somebody or **something**
1 seem to be something: *That looks like a good film.* **2** words that you use to ask about somebody's appearance: 'What does he look like?' 'He's tall with dark hair.' **3** have the same appearance as somebody or something: *She looks like her mother.*
look out! be careful!: *Look out! There's a car coming!*
look out for somebody or **something** pay attention and try to see somebody or something: *Look out for thieves!*
look round visit a place: *We looked round the cathedral.*

look² /lʊk/ *noun*
1 turning your eyes towards somebody or something; looking: *Paula gave me an angry look!*
2 the way something seems: *I don't like the look of this weather. I think it's going to rain.*
3 looks (plural) how a person's face and body is: *good looks*
have a look **1** see something: *Can I have a look at your photos?* **2** try to find something: *I've had a look for your pen, but I can't find it.*
have a look round see many parts of a place: *We had a look round the museum.*

loop /luːp/ *noun*
a round shape made by something like string or rope

loop

loose /luːs/
adjective (**looser, loosest**)
1 not tied or fixed: *The dog broke its chain and got loose.* ◇ *One of his teeth is loose.*
2 not tight: *a loose white dress* ☞ picture on page 263
loosely *adverb*
not tightly or firmly: *The rope was tied loosely round a tree.*

loosen /ˈluːsn/ *verb* (**loosens, loosening, loosened** /ˈluːsnd/)
become looser or make something looser: *Can you loosen this knot? It's too tight.* ✪ opposite: **tighten**

s	z	ʃ	ʒ	h	m	n	ŋ	l	r	j	w
so	**zoo**	**shoe**	vision	**hat**	**man**	**no**	sing	**leg**	**red**	**yes**	**wet**

Lord /lɔːd/ *noun*
1 Lord a man who has a special title:
Lord Fraser ☞ Look at **Lady**.
2 the Lord (no plural) God or Jesus
Christ

lorry

lorry /ˈlɒri/ *noun* (*plural* **lorries**)
a big vehicle for carrying heavy things

lose /luːz/ *verb* (**loses, losing, lost** /lɒst/,
has lost)
1 not be able to find something: *I can't
open the door because I've lost my key.*
2 not have somebody or something that
you had before: *I lost my job when the
factory closed.*
3 not win: *Our team lost the match.*

loser /ˈluːzə(r)/ *noun*
a person who does not win a game, race or
competition ☺ opposite: **winner**

loss /lɒs/ *noun* (*plural* **losses**)
1 losing something: *Has she told the police about the loss of her car?* ◇ *job losses*
2 how much money a business loses: *The
company made a loss of £5 million.*
at a loss If you are at a loss, you do not
know what to do or say.

lost[1] *form of* **lose**

lost[2] /lɒst/ *adjective*
1 If you are lost, you do not know where
you are: *I took the wrong road and now
I'm lost.* ◇ *Take this map so that you
don't get lost!*
2 If something is lost, you cannot find it.
lost property /ˌlɒst ˈprɒpəti/ *noun* (no
plural)
things that people have lost: *I left my bag
on the train, so I went to the lost property
office at the station.*

lot[1] /lɒt/ *noun*
a lot very much; a big amount or number:
We ate a lot.
a lot of, lots of a big number or amount
of something: *She's got a lot of friends.*
◇ *Lots of love from Jane* (= words at the
end of a letter).

lot[2] /lɒt/ *adverb*
a lot very much or often: *Your flat is a lot*

bigger than mine. ◇ *I go to the cinema a
lot.*

lotion /ˈləʊʃn/ *noun*
liquid that you put on your skin: *suntan
lotion*

loud /laʊd/ *adjective, adverb* (**louder,
loudest**)
that makes a lot of noise; not quiet: *I
couldn't hear what he said because the
music was too loud.* ◇ *loud voices*
◇ *Please speak a bit louder – I can't hear
you.* ☞ picture on page 263
out loud so that other people can hear it:
I read the story out loud.
loudly *adverb*
She laughed loudly.

loudspeaker /ˌlaʊdˈspiːkə(r)/ *noun*
an instrument for making sounds louder:
Music was coming from the loudspeakers.

lounge /laʊndʒ/ *noun*
a room in a house or hotel where you can
sit in comfortable chairs

love[1] /lʌv/ *verb* (**loves, loving, loved**
/lʌvd/)
1 have a strong warm feeling for somebody: *I love him very much.* ◇ *She loves
her parents.*
2 like something very much: *I love skiing.* ◇ *I would love to go to America.*

love[2] /lʌv/ *noun*
1 (no plural) a strong warm feeling of liking somebody or something: *Their love for
each other was very strong.* ◇ *a love of
football*
2 (*plural* **loves**) a person that you love:
Yes, my love.
3 (no plural) (*also* **love from**) a way of
ending a letter to somebody that you know
well: *Lots of love from Peter.*
4 (no plural) a word in tennis that means
zero: *The score is 15-love.*
be in love with somebody love somebody: *He says he is in love with her and
they are going to get married.*
fall in love with somebody begin to
love somebody: *He fell in love with Anna
the first time they met.*

lovely /ˈlʌvli/ *adjective* (**lovelier, loveli-
est**)
beautiful or very nice: *That's a lovely
dress.* ◇ *We had a lovely holiday.* ◇ *It's
lovely to see you again.*

iː	i	ɪ	e	æ	ɑː	ɒ	ɔː	ʊ	u	uː
see	happy	sit	ten	cat	father	got	saw	put	situation	too

lover /'lʌvə(r)/ *noun*
a person who you have sex with, but who is not your husband or wife

loving /'lʌvɪŋ/ *adjective*
feeling or showing love: *loving parents*

low /ləʊ/ *adjective* (**lower**, **lowest**)
1 near the ground; not high: *There was a low wall round the garden.* ◇ *a low bridge* ☞ picture on page 262
2 less than usual: *low temperatures* ◇ *low pay*
3 soft and quiet: *I heard low voices in the next room.*
4 deep; not high: *a low sound*
low *adverb*
near the ground: *The plane flew low over the fields.*

lower¹ /'ləʊə(r)/ *verb* (**lowers**, **lowering**, **lowered** /'ləʊəd/)
1 move somebody or something down: *They lowered the flag.*
2 make something less: *Please lower your voice* (= speak more quietly).
◯ opposite: **raise**

lower² /'ləʊə(r)/ *adjective*
that is under another; bottom: *the lower lip* ◯ opposite: **upper**

loyal /'lɔɪəl/ *adjective*
A person who is loyal does not change his/her friends or beliefs: *a loyal friend* ◇ *He is loyal to the company he works for.*
loyalty /'lɔɪəlti/ *noun* (no plural)
being loyal: *Loyalty to your friends is very important.*

LP /ˌel 'piː/ *noun*
a record with about 25 minutes of music on each side ☞ Look at **single**.

L-plate /'el pleɪt/ *noun*
a sign with a big red letter L on it, that you put on your car when you are learning to drive

luck /lʌk/ *noun* (no plural)
1 things that happen to you that you cannot control; chance
2 good things that happen to you that you cannot control: *Wish me luck for my exams!*
bad luck, **hard luck** words that you say to somebody when you are sorry that they did not have good luck
be in luck have good things happen to you: *I was in luck – the shop had the book I wanted.*

good luck words that you say to somebody when you hope that they will do well: *Good luck! I'm sure you'll get the job.*

lucky /'lʌki/ *adjective* (**luckier**, **luckiest**)
1 If you are lucky, you have good luck: *She had a bad accident and she is lucky to be alive.*
2 Something that is lucky brings good luck: *My lucky number is 3.*
◯ opposite: **unlucky**
luckily /'lʌkɪli/ *adverb*
it is lucky that: *I was late, but luckily they waited for me.*

luggage /'lʌgɪdʒ/ *noun* (no plural)
bags and suitcases that you take with you when you travel: *'How much luggage have you got?' 'Only one suitcase.'*

lump /lʌmp/ *noun*
1 a hard piece of something: *two lumps of sugar* ◇ *a lump of coal* ☞ picture on page 261
2 a part in or on your body which has become hard and bigger: *I've got a lump on my head where I hit it.*

lunch /lʌntʃ/ *noun* (*plural* **lunches**)
a meal that you eat in the middle of the day: *What would you like for lunch?* ◇ *What time do you usually have lunch?*
lunch-time /'lʌntʃ taɪm/ *noun*
the time when you eat lunch: *I'll meet you at lunch-time.*

lung /lʌŋ/ *noun*
one of the two parts inside your body that you use for breathing ☞ picture on page 126

luxurious /lʌg'ʒʊəriəs/ *adjective*
very comfortable and expensive: *a luxurious hotel*

luxury /'lʌkʃəri/ *noun*
1 (no plural) a way of living when you have all the expensive and beautiful things that you want: *They live in luxury in a beautiful house in the West Indies.* ◇ *a luxury hotel*
2 (*plural* **luxuries**) something that is very nice and expensive that you do not really need: *Eating in a restaurant is a luxury for most people.*

lying *form of* **lie**

ʌ	ɜː	ə	eɪ	əʊ	aɪ	aʊ	ɔɪ	ɪə	eə	ʊə
cup	bird	about	say	go	five	now	boy	near	hair	pure

Mm

m *short way of writing* **metre**

mac /mæk/ *noun*
a light coat that you wear when it rains

machine /məˈʃiːn/ *noun*
a thing with parts that move to do work or to make something. Machines often use electricity: *a washing-machine* ◇ *This machine does not work.*

machine-gun /məˈʃiːn gʌn/ *noun*
a gun that can send out a lot of bullets very quickly

machinery /məˈʃiːnəri/ *noun* (no plural)
1 the parts of a machine: *the machinery inside a clock*
2 a group of machines: *The factory has bought some new machinery.*

mad /mæd/ *adjective* (**madder, maddest**)
1 ill in your mind
2 very stupid; crazy: *I think you're mad to go out in this snow!*
3 very angry: *He was mad at me for losing his watch.*
be mad about somebody or **something** like somebody or something very much: *Mina is mad about computer games.* ◇ *He's mad about her.*
drive somebody mad make somebody very angry: *This noise is driving me mad!*
go mad 1 become ill in your mind: *He went mad and killed himself.* **2** become very angry: *Mum will go mad when she finds out what you did at school.*

madam /ˈmædəm/ *noun* (no plural)
1 a polite way of speaking to a woman, instead of using her name: *'Can I help you, madam?' asked the shop assistant.*
2 Madam a word that you use at the beginning of a business letter to a woman: *Dear Madam . . .*
☞ Look at **sir**.

made *form of* **make¹**
made of something from this material: *This shirt is made of cotton.*

madness /ˈmædnəs/ *noun* (no plural)
being ill in your mind

magazine /ˌmægəˈziːn/ *noun*
a kind of thin book with a paper cover that

you can buy every week or every month. It has a lot of different stories and pictures inside.

magic /ˈmædʒɪk/ *noun* (no plural)
1 a special power that can make strange or impossible things happen: *The witch changed the prince into a frog by magic.*
2 clever tricks that somebody can do to surprise people

magic, magical /ˈmædʒɪkl/ *adjective*
magic tricks ◇ *The witch had magical powers.*

magician /məˈdʒɪʃn/ *noun*
1 a man in stories who has strange, unusual powers: *The magician turned the boy into a dog.*
2 a person who does clever tricks to surprise people

magistrate /ˈmædʒɪstreɪt/ *noun*
a judge in a court of law who decides how to punish people for small crimes

magnet /ˈmægnət/ *noun*
a piece of metal that can make other metal things move towards it
magnetic /mægˈnetɪk/ *adjective*
with the power of a magnet: *Is this metal magnetic?*

magnificent /mægˈnɪfɪsnt/ *adjective*
very good or beautiful: *What a magnificent cathedral!*

magnify /ˈmægnɪfaɪ/ *verb* (**magnifies, magnifying, magnified** /ˈmægnɪfaɪd/, **has magnified**)
make something look bigger than it really is: *We magnified the insect under a microscope.*
magnifying glass /ˈmægnɪfaɪɪŋ glɑːs/ *noun* (*plural* **magnifying glasses**)
a special piece of glass that you hold in your hand. It makes things look bigger than they really are.

maid /meɪd/ *noun*
a woman who does work like cleaning in a hotel or large house

mail /meɪl/ *noun* (no plural)
1 the way of sending and receiving letters, parcels, etc; post: *airmail*

2 letters and parcels that you send or receive; post: *Is there any mail for me?*

mail *verb* (**mails, mailing, mailed** /meɪld/)
send something in the mail: *I'll mail the money to you.*

○ Mail is more usual in American English. In British English you usually say **post**.

mailbox /ˈmeɪlbɒks/ *American English for* **letter-box, pillar-box, postbox**

mailman /ˈmeɪlmæn/ *American English for* **postman**

main /meɪn/ *adjective*
most important: *My main reason for learning English is to get a better job.*

main course /ˌmeɪn ˈkɔːs/ *noun*
the most important part of a meal: *I had fish for the main course.*

main road /ˌmeɪn ˈrəʊd/ *noun*
a big important road between towns

mainly *adverb*
mostly: *The students here are mainly from Japan.* ◇ *She eats mainly vegetables.*

maintain /meɪnˈteɪn/ *verb* (**maintains, maintaining, maintained** /meɪnˈteɪnd/)
1 continue with something: *If he can maintain this speed, he'll win the race.*
2 keep something working well: *The roads are well maintained.*

maintenance /ˈmeɪntənəns/ *noun* (no plural)
things that you do to keep something working well: *maintenance of a machine*

maize /meɪz/ *noun* (no plural)
a tall plant with big yellow seeds that you can eat

Majesty /ˈmædʒəsti/ *noun* (*plural* **Majesties**)
a word that you use to talk to or about a king or queen: *Her Majesty Queen Elizabeth II*

major¹ /ˈmeɪdʒə(r)/ *adjective*
very large, important or serious: *There are airports in all the major cities.* ◇ *major problems* **○** opposite: **minor**

major² /ˈmeɪdʒə(r)/ *noun*
an officer in the army

majority /məˈdʒɒrəti/ *noun* (no plural)
most things or people in a group: *The majority of families in Japan have a colour television.* ☞ Look at **minority**.

make¹ /meɪk/ *verb* (**makes, making, made** /meɪd/, **has made**)
1 put things together so that you have a new thing: *They make cars in that factory.* ◇ *He made a box out of some pieces of wood.*
2 cause something to be or to happen; produce something: *The plane made a loud noise when it landed.* ◇ *Chocolates make you fat.* ◇ *That film made me cry.* ◇ *I made a mistake.*
3 force somebody to do something: *My father made me stay at home.*
4 a word that you use with money, numbers and time: *She makes* (= earns) *a lot of money.* ◇ *Five and seven make twelve.* ◇ *'What's the time?' 'I make it six o'clock.'*
5 give somebody a job: *They made him President.*
6 be able to go somewhere: *I'm sorry, but I can't make the meeting on Friday.*

make do with something use something that is not very good, because there is nothing better: *We didn't have a table, but we made do with some boxes.*

make something into something change something so that it becomes a different thing: *They made the bedroom into an office.*

make out be able to see or understand something that is not clear: *It was dark and I couldn't make out the words on the sign.*

make up **1** tell something that is not true: *Nobody believes that story – he made it up!* **2** end a quarrel with somebody: *Jane and Tom had an argument last week, but they've made up now.*

make² /meɪk/ *noun*
the name of the company that made something: *'What make is your car?' 'It's a Ford.'*

maker /ˈmeɪkə(r)/ *noun*
a person or company that makes something: *a film maker*

make-up /ˈmeɪk ʌp/ *noun* (no plural)
special powders and creams that you put on your face to make yourself more beautiful. Actors also wear make-up to make themselves look different: *She put on her make-up.*

s	z	ʃ	ʒ	h	m	n	ŋ	l	r	j	w
so	**zoo**	**shoe**	vision	**hat**	**man**	**no**	sing	**leg**	**red**	**yes**	**wet**

male /meɪl/ *adjective*
A male animal or person belongs to the sex that cannot have babies: *A cock is a male chicken.*
male *noun*
If you look at these fish you can see that the males are bigger than the females.
☞ Look at **female**.

mammal /'mæml/ *noun*
any animal that drinks milk from its mother's body when it is young: *Dogs, horses, whales and people are all mammals.*

man /mæn/ *noun*
1 (*plural* **men** /men/) a grown-up male person: *I saw a tall man with dark hair.*
2 (*plural* **men**) any person: *All men must have water to live.*
3 (no plural) all human beings; people: *How long has man lived on the earth?*

manage /'mænɪdʒ/ *verb* (**manages, managing, managed** /'mænɪdʒd/)
1 be able to do something that is difficult: *The box was heavy but she managed to carry it to the car.*
2 control somebody or something: *She manages a department of 30 people.*

management /'mænɪdʒmənt/ *noun*
1 (no plural) control of something, for example a business, and the people who work in it: *good management*
2 (*plural* **management**) all the people who control a business: *The management have decided to close the factory.*

manager /'mænɪdʒə(r)/ *noun*
a person who controls a business, bank or hotel, for example: *Clive is the manager of a shoe shop.* ◇ *a bank manager*

manageress /ˌmænɪdʒə'res/ *noun*
a woman who controls a shop or restaurant

managing director /ˌmænɪdʒɪŋ də'rektə(r)/ *noun*
the person who controls a big business

mane /meɪn/ *noun*
the long hair on the neck of a horse or lion

mango /'mæŋgəʊ/ *noun* (*plural* **mangoes** or **mangos**)
a fruit that is yellow or red on the outside and yellow on the inside. Mangoes grow in hot countries.

mankind /mæn'kaɪnd/ *noun* (no plural)
all the people in the world

man-made /ˌmæn 'meɪd/ *adjective*
made by people; not natural: *man-made materials*

manner /'mænə(r)/ *noun*
1 the way that you do something or the way that something happens: *Don't get angry. Let's try to talk about this in a calm manner.*
2 **manners** (plural) the way you behave when you are with other people: *It's bad manners to talk with your mouth full.*

mansion /'mænʃn/ *noun*
a very big house

mantelpiece /'mæntlpiːs/ *noun*
a long flat piece of wood, etc above a fireplace: *She has photographs of her children on the mantelpiece.*

manual¹ /'mænjuəl/ *adjective*
that you do with your hands: *Do you prefer manual work or office work?*
manually /'mænjuəli/ *adverb*
using your hands: *This machine is operated manually.*

manual² /'mænjuəl/ *noun*
a book that tells you how to do something: *Do you have a manual for this video recorder?*

manufacture /ˌmænju'fæktʃə(r)/ *verb* (**manufactures, manufacturing, manufactured** /ˌmænju'fæktʃəd/)
make things in a factory using machines: *The company manufactures radios.*
manufacture *noun* (no plural)
the manufacture of plastic from oil
manufacturer *noun*
If it doesn't work, send it back to the manufacturers.

many /'meni/ *adjective* (**many, more, most**), *pronoun*
a large number of people or things: *Many people in this country are very poor.* ◇ *There aren't many students in my class.* ◇ *Many of these books are very old.* ◇ *There are too many mistakes in your homework.*
as many as the same number that: *Take as many cakes as you want.*
how many ...? words that you use to ask about the number of people or things: *How many brothers and sisters have you got?*
☞ Look at **much**.

map /mæp/ *noun*
a drawing of a town, a country or the

iː	i	ɪ	e	æ	ɑː	ɒ	ɔː	ʊ	u	uː
see	happy	sit	ten	cat	father	got	saw	put	situation	too

world. It shows things like mountains, rivers and roads: *Can you find Glasgow on the map?* ◊ *a street map of Exeter* ✪ A book of maps is called an **atlas**.

marathon /'mærəθən/ *noun*
a very long race when people run about 42 kilometres

marble /'mɑ:bl/ *noun*
1 (no plural) very hard stone that is used to make buildings and statues: *Marble is always cold when you touch it.*
2 (*plural* **marbles**) a small glass ball that you use in a children's game: *They are playing marbles.*

March /mɑ:tʃ/ *noun*
the third month of the year

march /mɑ:tʃ/ *verb* (**marches, marching, marched** /mɑ:tʃt/)
1 walk like a soldier: *The soldiers marched along the road.*
2 walk with a large group of people to show that you have strong feelings about something: *They marched through the town shouting 'Stop the war!'*
march *noun* (*plural* **marches**)
1 marching: *The soldiers were tired after the long march.*
2 a long walk by a large group of people to show that they have strong feelings about something: *a peace march*

margarine /,mɑ:dʒə'ri:n/ *noun* (no plural)
soft yellow food that looks like butter, but is not made of milk. You put it on bread or use it in cooking.

margin /'mɑ:dʒɪn/ *noun*
the space at the side of a page that has no writing or pictures in it

mark¹ /mɑ:k/ *noun*
1 a spot or line that makes something less good than it was before: *There's a dirty mark on the front of your shirt.*
2 a shape or special sign on something: *This mark shows that the ring is made of silver.*
3 a number or letter that a teacher gives for your work to show how good it is: *She got very good marks in the exam.*

mark² /mɑ:k/ *verb* (**marks, marking, marked** /mɑ:kt/)
1 put a sign on something by writing or drawing on it: *The price is marked on the bottom of the box.*
2 put a tick (✓) or cross (✗) on school work to show if it is right or wrong, or write a number or letter to show how good it is: *The teacher marked all my answers wrong.*
3 show where something is: *This cross marks the place where he died.*

market /'mɑ:kɪt/ *noun*
1 a place where people go to buy and sell things, usually outside: *There is a fruit and vegetable market in the town square.*
2 the people who want to buy something: *There is a big market for personal computers in the USA.*

marmalade /'mɑ:məleɪd/ *noun* (no plural)
soft sweet food made from oranges or lemons: *We had toast and marmalade for breakfast.*

marriage /'mærɪdʒ/ *noun*
1 the time when two people are together as husband and wife: *They had a long and happy marriage.*
2 the time when a man and woman become husband and wife; a wedding: *The marriage will take place in church.*

marry /'mæri/ *verb* (**marries, marrying, married** /'mærid/, **has married**)
take somebody as your husband or wife: *Will you marry me?* ◊ *They married when they were very young.* ✪ It is more usual to say **get married**.
married *adjective*
How long have you been married? ◊ *Ian is married to Helen.* ✪ opposite: **single** or **unmarried**
get married take somebody as your husband or wife: *Sue and Mike got married last year.*

marsh /mɑ:ʃ/ *noun* (*plural* **marshes**)
soft wet ground

marvelous American English for **marvellous**

marvellous /'mɑ:vələs/ *adjective*
very good; wonderful: *I had a marvellous holiday.*

masculine /'mæskjʊlɪn/ *adjective*
of or like a man; right for a man: *a masculine voice* ☞ Look at **feminine**.

ʌ	ɜ:	ə	eɪ	əʊ	aɪ	aʊ	ɔɪ	ɪə	eə	ʊə
cup	bird	about	say	go	five	now	boy	near	hair	pure

mash /mæʃ/ verb (**mashes**, **mashing**, **mashed** /mæʃt/)
press and mix food to make it soft: *mashed potatoes*

masks

mask /mɑːsk/ noun
a thing that you wear over your face to hide or protect it: *The thieves were wearing masks.* ◇ *The doctor wore a mask.*

Mass /mæs/ noun (plural **Masses**)
a service in the Roman Catholic church

mass /mæs/ noun (plural **masses**)
a large amount or number of something: *a mass of rock* ◇ *masses of people*

massacre /'mæsəkə(r)/ noun
the cruel killing of a lot of people
massacre verb (**massacres**, **massacring**, **massacred** /'mæsəkəd/)
The army massacred hundreds of women and children.

massive /'mæsɪv/ adjective
very big: *The house is massive – it has 16 bedrooms!*

mast /mɑːst/ noun
1 a tall piece of wood or metal that holds the sails on a boat
2 a very tall metal thing that sends out sounds or pictures for radio or television

master¹ /'mɑːstə(r)/ noun
a man who has people or animals in his control: *The dog ran to its master.*

master² /'mɑːstə(r)/ verb (**masters**, **mastering**, **mastered** /'mɑːstəd/)
learn how to do something well: *It takes a long time to master a foreign language.*

masterpiece /'mɑːstəpiːs/ noun
a very good painting, book, film, etc: *'War and Peace' was Tolstoy's masterpiece.*

mat /mæt/ noun
1 a small thing that covers a part of the floor: *Wipe your feet on the doormat before you go in.*
2 a small thing that you put on a table under a hot dish or cup or a glass: *a table-mat*

match¹ /mætʃ/
noun (plural **matches**)
a special short thin piece of wood that makes fire when you rub it on something rough: *He struck a match and lit his cigarette.* ◇ *a box of matches*

matches

matchbox /'mætʃbɒks/ noun
a small box for matches

match² /mætʃ/ noun (plural **matches**)
a game between two people or teams: *a football match* ◇ *a boxing match*

match³ /mætʃ/ verb (**matches**, **matching**, **matched** /mætʃt/)
1 have the same colour, shape or pattern as something else, or look good with something else: *That scarf doesn't match your blouse.*
2 find something that is like another thing or that you can put with it: *Match the word with the right picture.*
match noun (no plural)
something that looks good with something else, for example because it has the same colour, shape or pattern: *Your shoes and dress are a good match.*
matching adjective
She was wearing a blue skirt and matching jacket.

mate /meɪt/ noun
1 a friend: *He went out with his mates last night.* ❸ This is an informal word.
2 a person who lives, works or studies with you: *André is one of my classmates.* ◇ *a flatmate*
3 one of two animals that come together to make young animals: *The bird is looking for a mate.*
mate verb (**mates**, **mating**, **mated**)
When animals mate, they come together to make young animals.

material /mə'tɪəriəl/ noun
1 what you use for making or doing something: *Wood and stone are building materials.* ◇ *writing materials* (= pens, pencils and paper, for example)
2 stuff that is made of wool, cotton, etc

p	b	t	d	k	g	tʃ	dʒ	f	v	θ	ð
pen	**b**ad	**t**ea	**d**id	**c**at	**g**ot	**ch**ain	**j**am	**f**all	**v**an	**th**in	**th**is

and that you use for making clothes and other things; cloth: *I don't have enough material to make a dress.*

math /mæθ/ *American English for* **maths**

mathematics /ˌmæθəˈmætɪks/, **maths** /mæθs/ *noun* (no plural)
the study of numbers, measurements and shapes: *Maths is my favourite subject.*
mathematical /ˌmæθəˈmætɪkl/ *adjective*
a mathematical problem

matter¹ /ˈmætə(r)/ *noun*
something that you must talk about or do: *There is a matter I would like to discuss with you.*
as a matter of fact words that you use when you say something true, important or interesting: *I'm going home early today. As a matter of fact, it's my birthday.*
be the matter with somebody or **something** be the reason for problems or unhappiness, for example: *Julie is crying. What's the matter with her?* ◇ *There is something the matter with my eye.*
no matter how, what, when, who, etc however, whatever, whenever, whoever, etc: *No matter how hard I try, I can't open the door.*

matter² /ˈmætə(r)/ *verb* (**matters, mattering, mattered** /ˈmætəd/)
be important: *It doesn't matter if you're late – we'll wait for you.*

mattress

mattress /ˈmætrəs/ *noun* (plural **mattresses**)
the thick soft part of a bed

mature /məˈtjʊə(r)/ *adjective*
like an adult; fully grown

mauve /məʊv/ *adjective*
purple

maximum /ˈmæksɪməm/ *noun* (no plural)
the most; the biggest possible size, amount

or number: *This plane can carry a maximum of 150 people.*
maximum *adjective*
We drove at a maximum speed of 110 kilometres per hour.
❍ opposite: **minimum**

May /meɪ/ *noun*
the fifth month of the year

may /meɪ/ *modal verb*
1 a word that shows what will perhaps happen or what is possible: *I may go to Spain next year.* ◇ *He may not be here.*
2 be allowed to do something: *May I open the window?* ◇ *You may stay here tonight.*
3 I hope that this will happen: *May God be with you.* ☞ Look at the Note on page 227 to find out more about **modal verbs**.

maybe /ˈmeɪbi/ *adverb*
perhaps; possibly: *'Are you going out tonight?' 'Maybe.'* ◇ *Maybe you should phone him.*

mayor /meə(r)/ *noun*
the leader of a **council** (a group of people who control a town or city)
mayoress /meəˈres/ *noun* (plural **mayoresses**)
a mayor who is a woman, or the wife of a mayor

me /mi:/ *pronoun* (plural **us**)
the person who is speaking: *When he saw me he told me about the accident.* ◇ *'Who broke the window?' 'It was me.'*

meadow /ˈmedəʊ/ *noun*
a field of grass

meal /mi:l/ *noun*
food that you eat at a certain time of the day: *Breakfast is the first meal of the day.*
❍ **Breakfast, lunch** and **dinner** (and sometimes **tea** and **supper**) are the usual meals of the day.

mean¹ /mi:n/ *verb* (**means, meaning, meant** /ment/, **has meant**)
1 say or show something in a different way; have as a meaning: *What does 'medicine' mean?* ◇ *The red light means that you have to stop here.*
2 plan or want to say something: *She said 'yes' but she really meant 'no'.* ◇ *I don't understand what you mean.*
3 plan or want to do something: *I didn't*

mean to hurt you. ◇ *I meant to phone you, but I forgot.*
4 make something happen: *This snow means there will be no sport today.*
be meant to 1 If you are meant to do something, you should do it: *You're not meant to smoke on the train.* **2** If something is meant to be true, people say it is true: *This is meant to be a good film.*
mean something to somebody be important to somebody: *My family means a lot to me.*

mean² /miːn/ *adjective* (**meaner, meanest**)
1 A person who is mean does not like to give things or to spend money: *Jim is very mean – he never buys anybody a drink.*
○ opposite: **generous**
2 unkind: *It was mean of you to say that Peter was fat.*

meaning /'miːnɪŋ/ *noun*
what something means or shows: *This word has two different meanings.*

means /miːnz/ *noun* (*plural* **means**)
a way of doing something; a way of going somewhere: *I don't have a car and there are no trains, so I haven't got any means of getting to London.*
by means of something by using something: *We crossed the river by means of a small bridge.*
by no means not at all: *I am by no means certain that I can come.*

meant *form of* **mean**¹

meantime /'miːntaɪm/ *noun* (no plural)
in the meantime in the time between two things happening: *The police will be here soon – in the meantime you should stay calm.*

meanwhile /'miːnwaɪl/ *adverb*
1 at the same time as another thing is happening: *Neil cooked the dinner and meanwhile Anna cleaned the house.*
2 in the time between two things happening: *I'm going to buy a bed next week, but meanwhile I'm sleeping on the floor.*

measles /'miːzlz/ *noun* (no plural)
an illness that makes small red spots come on your skin: *My little brother has got measles.*

measure¹ /'meʒə(r)/ *verb* (**measures, measuring, measured** /'meʒəd/)
1 find the size, weight or amount of some-

body or something: *I measured the box with a ruler.*
2 be a certain size or amount: *This room measures six metres across.*

measure² /'meʒə(r)/ *noun*
a way of showing the size or amount of something: *A metre is a measure of length.*

measurement /'meʒəmənt/ *noun*
how long, wide, high, etc something is: *What are the measurements of the kitchen?*

meat /miːt/ *noun* (no plural)
the parts of an animal's body that you can eat: *You can buy meat at a butcher's.*

mechanic /mə'kænɪk/ *noun*
a person whose job is to repair or work with machines: *a car mechanic*

mechanical /mə'kænɪkl/ *adjective*
moved, done or made by a machine: *a mechanical toy*

mechanics /mə'kænɪks/ *noun* (no plural)
the study of how machines work

medal /'medl/ *noun*
a piece of metal with words and pictures on it that is given to somebody who has done something very good: *She won a gold medal in the Olympic Games.*

media /'miːdiə/ *noun* (plural)
the media
television, radio and newspapers: *The media are always interested in the lives of film stars.*

medical /'medɪkl/ *adjective*
of or about medicine, hospitals or doctors: *a medical student* ◇ *medical treatment*

medicine /'medsn/ *noun*
1 (no plural) the science of understanding illnesses and making sick people well again: *He studied medicine for five years before becoming a doctor.*
2 (*plural* **medicines**) pills or special drinks that help you to get better when you are ill: *Take this medicine every morning.*

medieval /,medi'iːvl/ *adjective*
of the years between about 1100 and 1500 in Europe: *a medieval castle*
☞ Look at **the Middle Ages**.

medium /'miːdiəm/ *adjective*
not big and not small; middle: *Would you*

like a small, medium or large coke? ◇ *He is of medium height.*

meet /miːt/ *verb* (**meets, meeting, met** /met/, **has met**)
1 come together at a certain time and place when you have planned it: *Let's meet outside the cinema at eight o'clock.*
2 see and say hello to somebody: *I met Kate in the library today.*
3 see and speak to somebody for the first time: *Have you met Anne?*
4 go to a place and wait for somebody to arrive: *Can you meet me at the airport?*
5 join together with something: *The two rivers meet in Oxford.*

meeting /'miːtɪŋ/ *noun*
1 a time when a group of people come together for a special reason: *We had a meeting to talk about the plans for the new swimming-pool.*
2 two or more people coming together: *Do you remember your first meeting with your husband?*

melody /'melədi/ *noun* (*plural* **melodies**)
a group of musical notes that make a nice sound when you play or sing them together; a tune: *This song has a lovely melody.*

melon /'melən/ *noun*
a big round yellow or green fruit with a lot of seeds inside

melt /melt/ *verb* (**melts, melting, melted**)
warm something so that it becomes liquid; get warmer so that it becomes liquid: *Melt the butter in a saucepan.* ◇ *The snow melted in the sunshine.*

member /'membə(r)/ *noun*
a person who is in a group: *I'm a member of the school football team.*
Member of Parliament /,membər əv 'pɑːləmənt/ *noun*
a person that the people of a town or city choose to speak for them in politics ◐ The short form is **MP**.
membership /'membəʃɪp/ *noun* (no plural)
being in a group: *Membership of the club costs £20 a year.*

memo /'meməʊ/ (*plural* **memos**), **memorandum** /,memə'rændəm/ (*plural* **memoranda**) *noun*
a note that you write to a person who

works with you: *I sent you a memo about the meeting on Friday.*

memorable /'memərəbl/ *adjective*
easy to remember because it is special in some way: *Their wedding was a very memorable day.*

memorial /mə'mɔːriəl/ *noun*
something that people build or do to help us remember somebody, or something that happened: *The statue is a memorial to all the soldiers who died in the war.*

memorize /'meməraɪz/ *verb* (**memorizes, memorizing, memorized** /'meməraɪzd/)
learn something so that you can remember it exactly: *We have to memorize a poem for homework.*

memory /'meməri/ *noun* (*plural* **memories**)
1 the power to remember things: *She's got a very good memory – she never forgets people's names.*
2 something that you remember: *I have very happy memories of that holiday.*
3 the part of a computer that holds information

men *plural of* **man**

mend /mend/ *verb* (**mends, mending, mended**)
make something good again when it was broken; repair something: *Can you mend this chair?*

mental /'mentl/ *adjective*
of or in your mind: *mental illness*
mentally /'mentəli/ *adverb*
He is mentally ill.

mention /'menʃn/ *verb* (**mentions, mentioning, mentioned** /'menʃnd/)
speak or write a little about something: *When Liz telephoned, she mentioned that she was going to buy a new car.* ◇ *He didn't mention Anna in his letter.*
don't mention it polite words that you say when somebody says 'thank you': *'Thanks very much.' 'Don't mention it.'*
mention *noun*
There was no mention of the accident in the newspaper.

menu /'menjuː/ *noun* (*plural* **menus**)
1 a list of the food that you can choose in a

restaurant: *What's on the menu tonight?*
◇ *Can I have the menu, please?*
2 a list on the screen of a computer that shows what you can do

merchant /'mɜːtʃənt/ *noun*
a person who buys and sells things, especially from and to other countries: *She's a wine merchant.*

mercy /'mɜːsi/ *noun* (no plural)
being kind and not hurting somebody who has done wrong: *The prisoners asked the king for mercy.*
be at the mercy of somebody or **something** have no power against somebody or something: *Farmers are at the mercy of the weather.*

mere /mɪə(r)/ *adjective*
only; not more than: *She was a mere child when her parents died.*
merely *adverb*
only: *I don't want to buy the book – I am merely asking how much it costs.*

merge /mɜːdʒ/ *verb* (**merges, merging, merged** /mɜːdʒd/)
join together with something else: *The two small companies merged into one large one.*

merit /'merɪt/ *noun*
what is good about somebody or something: *What are the merits of this plan?*

mermaid /'mɜːmeɪd/ *noun*
a woman in stories who has a fish's tail and lives in the sea

merry /'meri/ *adjective* (**merrier, merriest**)
happy and full of fun: *Merry Christmas!*

merry-go-round /'meri gəʊ raʊnd/ *noun*
a big round machine at a fair. It has model animals or cars on it that children can ride on as it turns.

mess¹ /mes/ *noun* (no plural)
1 a lot of untidy or dirty things all in the wrong place: *There was a terrible mess after the party.*
2 a person or thing that is untidy or dirty: *My hair is a mess!*
be in a mess **1** be untidy: *My bedroom is in a mess.* **2** have problems: *She's in a mess – she's got no money and nowhere to live.*

mess² /mes/ *verb* (**messes, messing, messed** /mest/)
mess about, mess around do something in a silly way; play when you should be working: *Stop messing around and finish your work!*
mess up **1** do something badly or make something go wrong: *The bad weather messed up our plans for the weekend.*
2 make something untidy or dirty

message /'mesɪdʒ/ *noun*
words that one person sends to another: *Could you give a message to Jane, please? Please tell her I will be late.* ◇ *Mr Willis is not here at the moment. Can I take a message?*
messenger /'mesɪndʒə(r)/ *noun*
a person who brings a message

messy /'mesi/ *adjective* (**messier, messiest**)
1 untidy or dirty: *a messy kitchen*
2 that makes you untidy or dirty: *Painting is a messy job.*

met *form of* **meet**

metal /'metl/ *noun*
Iron, lead, tin and gold are all metals: *This chair is made of metal.* ◇ *a metal box*

meter /'miːtə(r)/ *noun*
1 a machine that measures or counts something: *An electricity meter shows how much electricity you have used.*
2 *American English for* **metre**

method /'meθəd/ *noun*
a way of doing something: *What is the best method of cooking beef?*

metre /'miːtə(r)/ *noun*
a measure of length. There are 100 **centimetres** in a metre: *The wall is eight metres long.* ◑ The short way of writing 'metre' is **m**: *2 m*

metric /'metrɪk/ *adjective*
using metres, grams, litres, etc to measure things

miaow /mi'aʊ/ *noun*
a sound that a cat makes
miaow *verb* (**miaows, miaowing, miaowed** /mi'aʊd/)
make this sound

mice *plural of* **mouse**

microchip /'maɪkrəʊtʃɪp/ *noun*
a very small thing inside a computer, for example, that makes it work

p	b	t	d	k	g	tʃ	dʒ	f	v	θ	ð
pen	**bad**	**tea**	**did**	**cat**	**got**	**chain**	**jam**	**fall**	**van**	**thin**	**this**

microcomputer

/'maɪkrəʊkəmpju:tə(r)/ *noun*
a small computer

microphone

microphone /'maɪkrəfəʊn/ *noun*

an electrical thing that makes sounds louder or records them so you can listen to them later

microscope /'maɪkrəskəʊp/ *noun*

an instrument with special glass in it, that makes very small things look much bigger: *The scientist looked at the hair under the microscope.*

microwave /'maɪkrəweɪv/, **microwave oven** /ˌmaɪkrəweɪv 'ʌvn/ *noun*

a special oven that cooks food very quickly

mid, mid- /mɪd/ *adjective*

(in) the middle of: *I'm going on holiday in mid July.* ◇ *mid-morning coffee*

midday /ˌmɪd'deɪ/ *noun* (no plural)

twelve o'clock in the day: *We met at midday.*

middle /'mɪdl/ *noun*

1 the part that is the same distance from the sides, edges or ends of something: *A peach has a stone in the middle.*
2 the time after the beginning and before the end: *The phone rang in the middle of the night.*
be in the middle of be busy doing something: *I can't speak to you now – I'm in the middle of cooking dinner.*
middle *adjective*
There are three houses and ours is the middle one.

middle-aged /ˌmɪdl 'eɪdʒd/ *adjective*

not old and not young; between the ages of about 40 and 60: *a middle-aged man*

the Middle Ages /ðə ˌmɪdl 'eɪdʒɪz/ *noun* (plural)

the years between about 1100 and 1500 in Europe ☞ Look at **medieval**.

middle school /'mɪdl sku:l/ *noun*

a school for children between the ages of 9 and 13

midnight /'mɪdnaɪt/ *noun* (no plural)

twelve o'clock at night: *We left the party at midnight.*

midway /ˌmɪd'weɪ/ *adverb*

in the middle: *The village is midway between London and Birmingham.*

might /maɪt/ *modal verb*

1 a word for 'may' in the past: *He said he might be late, but he was early.*
2 a word that shows what will perhaps happen or what is possible: *Don't run because you might fall.* ◇ *'Where's Anne?' 'I don't know – she might be in the kitchen.'*
3 a word that you use to ask something in a very polite way: *Might I say something?* ☞ Look at the Note on page 227 to find out more about **modal verbs**.

mighty /'maɪti/ *adjective* (**mightier**, **mightiest**)

very great, strong or powerful: *a mighty ocean*

mild /maɪld/ *adjective* (**milder**, **mildest**)

1 gentle; not strong or rough: *This cheese has a mild taste.*
2 not too hot and not too cold: *a mild winter*

mile /maɪl/ *noun*

a measure of length that is used in Britain and the USA (= 1.6 kilometres): *We live three miles from the sea.* ☞ Note at **foot**

military /'mɪlətri/ *adjective*

of or for soldiers or the army: *a military camp* ◇ *military action*

milk /mɪlk/ *noun* (no plural)

the white liquid that a mother makes in her body to give to her baby. People drink the milk that cows and some other animals make: *Do you want milk in your coffee?*
milk *verb* (**milks**, **milking**, **milked** /mɪlkt/)
take milk from a cow or another animal

milkman /'mɪlkmən/ *noun* (plural **milkmen** /'mɪlkmən/)

a person who brings milk to your house

milky /'mɪlki/ *adjective*

with a lot of milk in it: *milky coffee*

mill /mɪl/ *noun*
1 a building where a machine makes corn into flour ☞ Look also at **windmill**.
2 a factory for making things like steel or paper: *a paper-mill*

millimeter *American English for* **millimetre**

millimetre /ˈmɪlɪmiːtə(r)/ *noun*
a measure of length. There are ten millimetres in a **centimetre**. ✪ The short way of writing 'millimetre' is **mm**: *60 mm*

million /ˈmɪljən/ *number*
1 000 000; one thousand thousand: *About 56 million people live in this country.* ◊ *millions of dollars* ◊ *six million pounds*
millionth /ˈmɪljənθ/ *adjective, adverb, noun*
1 000 000th

millionaire /ˌmɪljəˈneə(r)/ *noun*
a very rich person who has more than a million pounds, dollars, etc

mime /maɪm/ *verb* (**mimes, miming, mimed** /maɪmd/)
tell something by your actions, not by speaking

mince /mɪns/ *verb* (**minces, mincing, minced** /mɪnst/)
cut meat into very small pieces, using a special machine: *minced beef*
mince *noun* (no plural)
meat in very small pieces

mind¹ /maɪnd/ *noun*
the part of you that thinks and remembers: *He has a very quick mind.*
change your mind have an idea, then decide to do something different: *I planned a holiday in France and then changed my mind and went to Italy.*
have something on your mind be worried about something: *I've got a lot on my mind at the moment.*
make up your mind decide something: *Shall I buy the blue shirt or the red one? I can't make up my mind.*

mind² /maɪnd/ *verb* (**minds, minding, minded**)
1 feel unhappy or angry about something: *'Do you mind if I smoke?' 'No, I don't mind.'* (= you may smoke)
2 be careful of somebody or something: *Mind the step!* ◊ *Mind! There's a dog in the road.*

do you mind ...?, would you mind ...? please could you. . .?: *It's cold — would you mind closing the window?*
I don't mind it is not important to me which thing: *'Do you want tea or coffee?' 'I don't mind.'*
never mind don't worry; there is no problem; it doesn't matter: *'I forgot your book.' 'Never mind, I don't need it today.'*

mine¹ /maɪn/ *noun*
a very big hole in the ground where people work to get things like coal, gold or diamonds: *a coalmine*
mine *verb* (**mines, mining, mined** /maɪnd/)
dig in the ground for things like coal or gold
miner *noun*
a person who works in a mine: *His father was a miner.*

mine² /maɪn/ *pronoun*
something that belongs to me: *That bike is mine.* ◊ *Are those books mine or yours?*

mineral /ˈmɪnərəl/ *noun*
Minerals are things like coal, gold, salt or oil that come from the ground and that people use.
mineral water /ˈmɪnərəl ˈwɔːtə(r)/ *noun*
water with minerals in it, that comes from the ground: *a bottle of mineral water*

mini- /ˈmɪni/ *prefix*
very small: *The school has a minibus that can carry twelve people.*

miniature /ˈmɪnətʃə(r)/ *noun*
a very small copy of something larger: *a miniature railway*

minimum /ˈmɪnɪməm/ *noun* (no plural)
the smallest size, amount or number that is possible: *We need a minimum of six people to play this game.*
minimum *adjective*
What is the minimum age for leaving school in your country?
✪ opposite: **maximum**

minister /ˈmɪnɪstə(r)/ *noun*
1 one of the most important people in a government: *the Minister of Education*
2 a priest in some Christian churches

ministry /ˈmɪnɪstri/ *noun* (*plural* **ministries**)
a part of the government that controls one special thing: *the Ministry of Defence*

minor

minor /'maɪnə(r)/ *adjective*
not very big or important: *Don't worry –
it's only a minor problem.* ◇ *a minor
road* ✪ opposite: **major**

minority /maɪ'nɒrəti/ *noun* (no plural)
the smaller part of a group: *Only a minority of the students speak English.* ☞ Look
at **majority**.

mint /mɪnt/ *noun*
1 (no plural) a small plant with a strong
fresh taste and smell, that you put in food
and drinks: *mint chewing-gum*
2 (*plural* **mints**) a sweet made from this

minus /'maɪnəs/ *preposition*
1 less; when you take away: *Six minus
two is four* (6 – 2 = 4). ☞ Look at **plus**.
2 below zero: *The temperature will fall to
minus ten degrees.*

minute¹ /'mɪnɪt/ *noun*
a measure of time. There are 60 **seconds**
in a minute and 60 minutes in an **hour**:
It's nine minutes past six. ◇ *The train
leaves in ten minutes.*
in a minute very soon: *I'll be ready in a
minute.*
the minute as soon as: *Phone me the
minute you arrive.*

minute² /maɪ'njuːt/ *adjective*
very small: *I can't read his writing – it's
minute.*

miracle /'mɪrəkl/ *noun*
a wonderful and surprising thing that happens and that you cannot explain: *It's a
miracle that he wasn't killed when he fell
from the window.*
miraculous /mɪ'rækjʊləs/ *adjective*
wonderful and surprising: *a miraculous
escape*

mirror /'mɪrə(r)/ *noun*
a piece of special glass where you can see
yourself: *Look in the mirror.*

mis- *prefix*
You can add **mis-** to the beginning of
some words to show that something is
done wrong or badly, for example:
misbehave = behave badly
misunderstand = not understand
correctly

miserable /'mɪzrəbl/ *adjective*
1 If you are miserable, you are very sad: *I

waited in the rain for an hour, feeling cold,
wet and miserable.*
2 If something is miserable, it makes you
very sad: *miserable weather*

mirror

misery /'mɪzəri/ *noun* (no plural)
great unhappiness

misfortune /ˌmɪs'fɔːtʃuːn/ *noun*
something bad that happens; bad luck: *She
had the misfortune to crash her car and
lose her job on the same day.*

mislead /ˌmɪs'liːd/ *verb* (**misleads,
misleading, misled** /ˌmɪs'led/, **has
misled**)
make somebody believe something that is
not true: *You misled me when you said
you could give me a job.*

Miss /mɪs/
a word that you use before the name of
a girl or woman who is not married:
Dear Miss Smith, ... ☞ Look at **Mrs** and
Ms.

miss /mɪs/ *verb* (**misses, missing, missed** /mɪst/)
1 not hit or catch something: *I tried to hit
the ball but I missed.*
2 feel sad about somebody or something
that has gone: *I'll miss you when you go
to Canada.*
3 be too late for a train, bus, plane or boat:
I just missed my bus.
4 not see, hear, etc something: *You missed a good programme on TV last night.*
miss out not put in or do something; not
include something: *I didn't finish the
exam – I missed out two questions.*

missile /'mɪsaɪl/ *noun*
a thing that you throw or send through
the air to hurt somebody: *The boys were
throwing stones, bottles and other missiles.* ◇ *nuclear missiles*

missing /'mɪsɪŋ/ *adjective*
lost, or not in the usual place: *The police
are looking for the missing child.* ◇ *My
purse is missing. Have you seen it?*

ʌ	ɜː	ə	eɪ	əʊ	aɪ	aʊ	ɔɪ	ɪə	eə	ʊə
cup	bird	about	say	go	five	now	boy	near	hair	pure

mission /'mɪʃn/ *noun*
a journey to do a special job: *They were sent on a mission to the moon.*

missionary /'mɪʃənri/ *noun* (*plural* **missionaries**)
a person who goes to another country to teach people about a religion

mist /mɪst/ *noun*
thin cloud near the ground, that is difficult to see through: *Early in the morning, the fields were covered in mist.*
misty *adjective* (**mistier, mistiest**)
a misty morning

mistake¹ /mɪ'steɪk/ *noun*
something that you think or do that is wrong: *You have made a lot of spelling mistakes in this letter.* ◊ *It was a mistake to go by bus – the journey took two hours!*
by mistake when you did not plan to do it: *I took your book by mistake – I thought it was mine.*

mistake² /mɪ'steɪk/ *verb* (**mistakes, mistaking, mistook** /mɪ'stʊk/, **has mistaken** /mɪ'steɪkən/)
think that somebody or something is a different person or thing: *I'm sorry – I mistook you for my cousin.*
mistaken *adjective*
wrong: *I said she was Spanish but I was mistaken – she's Portuguese.*

misunderstand /ˌmɪsˌʌndə'stænd/ *verb* (**misunderstands, misunderstanding, misunderstood** /ˌmɪsˌʌndə'stʊd/, **has misunderstood**)
not understand something correctly: *I'm sorry, I misunderstood what you said.*
misunderstanding *noun*
not understanding something correctly: *I think there's been a misunderstanding. I ordered two tickets, not four.*

mitten /'mɪtn/ *noun*
a thing that you wear to keep your hand warm. It has one part for your thumb and another part for your other fingers.

mix /mɪks/ *verb* (**mixes, mixing, mixed** /mɪkst/)
1 put different things together to make something new: *Mix yellow and blue paint together to make green.*
2 join together to make something new: *Oil and water don't mix.*
3 be with and talk to other people: *In my job, I mix with a lot of different people.*
mix up 1 think that one person or thing

is a different person or thing: *People often mix Mark up with his brother.* **2** make things untidy: *Don't mix up my papers!*

mixed /mɪkst/ *adjective*
of different kinds: *a mixed salad* ◊ *a mixed class* (of boys and girls together)

mixer /'mɪksə(r)/ *noun*
a machine that mixes things: *a food-mixer*

mixture /'mɪkstʃə(r)/ *noun*
something that you make by mixing different things together: *Air is a mixture of gases.* ◊ *a cake mixture*

mm *short way of writing* **millimetre**

moan /məʊn/ *verb* (**moans, moaning, moaned** /məʊnd/)
1 make a long sad sound when you are hurt or very unhappy: *He was moaning with pain.*
2 talk a lot about something that you do not like: *He's always moaning about the weather.*
moan *noun*
I heard a loud moan.

mob /mɒb/ *noun*
a big noisy group of people who are shouting or fighting

mobile /'məʊbaɪl/ *adjective*
able to move easily from place to place: *A mobile library visits the village every week.*

modal verb /ˌməʊdl 'vɜːb/ *noun*
a verb, for example 'might', 'can' or 'must', that you use with another verb

---

Modal verbs

Can, could, may, might, should, must, will, shall, would and **ought to** are modal verbs.

Modal verbs do not have an 's' in the 'he/she' form:

She can drive. (NOT: *She cans drive.*)

After modal verbs (except **ought to**), you use the infinitive without 'to':

I must go now. (NOT: *I must to go.*)

You make questions and negative sentences without 'do' or 'did':

Will you come with me? (NOT: *Do you will come?*)

They might not know. (NOT: *They don't might know.*)

---

model¹ /ˈmɒdl/ *noun*
1 a small copy of something: *a model of the Taj Mahal* ◇ *a model aeroplane*
2 a person who wears clothes at a special show or for photographs, so that people will see them and buy them
3 one of the cars, machines, etc that a certain company makes: *Have you seen the latest model of the Ford Sierra?*
4 a person who sits or stands so that an artist can draw, paint or photograph him/her

model² /ˈmɒdl/ *verb* (**models, modelling, modelled** /ˈmɒdld/)
wear and show clothes as a model: *Kate modelled swimsuits at the fashion show.*

moderate /ˈmɒdərət/ *adjective*
in the middle; not too much and not too little; not too big and not too small: *Cook the vegetables over a moderate heat.*

modern /ˈmɒdn/ *adjective*
of the present time; of the kind that is usual now: *modern art* ◇ *The airport is very modern.*

modest /ˈmɒdɪst/ *adjective*
A person who is modest does not talk much about good things that he/she has done or about things that he/she can do well: *You didn't tell me you could sing so well – you're very modest!*
modestly *adverb*
He spoke quietly and modestly about his success.
modesty /ˈmɒdəsti/ *noun* (no plural)
being modest

moist /mɔɪst/ *adjective*
a little wet: *Keep the earth moist or the plant will die.*

moisture /ˈmɔɪstʃə(r)/ *noun* (no plural)
small drops of water on something or in the air

mold, moldy American English for **mould, mouldy**

mole¹ /məʊl/ *noun*
a small grey or brown animal that lives under the ground and makes tunnels

mole² /məʊl/ *noun*
a small dark spot on a person's skin

mom /mɒm/ *American English for* **mum**

moment /ˈməʊmənt/ *noun*
a very short time: *He thought for a mo-*
ment before he answered. ◇ *Can you wait a moment?*
at the moment now: *She's on holiday at the moment, but she'll be back next week.*
in a moment very soon: *He'll be here in a moment.*
the moment as soon as: *Tell Jim to phone me the moment he arrives.*

momma /ˈmɒmə/, **mommy** /ˈmɒmi/ *American English for* **mummy**

monarch /ˈmɒnək/ *noun*
a king or queen
monarchy /ˈmɒnəki/ *noun* (*plural* **monarchies**)
a country that has a king or queen

monastery /ˈmɒnəstri/ *noun* (*plural* **monasteries**)
a place where religious men, called **monks**, live, work and pray

Monday /ˈmʌndeɪ/ *noun*
the second day of the week, next after Sunday

money /ˈmʌni/ *noun* (no plural)
small round metal things (called **coins**) and pieces of paper (called **notes**) that you use when you buy or sell something: *How much money did you spend?* ◇ *This jacket cost a lot of money.*
make money get or earn money

monk /mʌŋk/ *noun*
a religious man who lives with other religious men in a **monastery**

monkey

monkey /ˈmʌŋki/ *noun* (*plural* **monkeys**)
an animal with a long tail, that can climb trees

monster /ˈmɒnstə(r)/ *noun*
an animal in stories that is big, ugly and frightening: *A dragon is a kind of monster.*

month /mʌnθ/ *noun*
1 one of the twelve parts of a year: *December is the last month of the year.* ◇ *We*

s	z	ʃ	ʒ	h	m		n	ŋ	l	r	j	w
so	**zoo**	**shoe**	**vision**	**hat**	**man**		**no**	**sing**	**leg**	**red**	**yes**	**wet**

went on holiday last month. ◇ *My exams start at the end of the month.* **2** about four weeks: *She was in hospital for a month.*

monthly /'mʌnθli/ *adjective, adverb*
that happens or comes every month or once a month: *a monthly magazine* ◇ *I am paid monthly.*

monument /'mɒnjumənt/ *noun*
a thing that is built to help people remember a person or something that happened: *This is a monument to Queen Victoria.*

moo /muː/ *noun*
the sound that a cow makes
moo *verb* (**moos, mooing, mooed** /muːd/)
make this sound

mood /muːd/ *noun*
how you feel: *Dad is in a bad mood because he's lost his glasses.* ◇ *Our teacher was in a very good mood today.*
be in the mood for something feel that you want something: *I'm not in the mood for a party.*

moon /muːn/ *noun*
the moon (no plural)
the big thing that shines in the sky at night
full moon /ˌfʊl 'muːn/ *noun*
the time when you can see all of the moon
new moon /ˌnjuː 'muːn/ *noun*
the time when you can see only the first thin part of the moon

moonlight /'muːnlaɪt/ *noun* (no plural)
the light from the moon

moor¹ /mʊə(r)/ *noun*
wild land on hills that has grass and low plants, but not many trees: *the Yorkshire moors* ◇ *We went walking on the moor.*

moor² /mʊə(r)/ *verb* (**moors, mooring, moored** /mʊəd/)
tie a boat or ship to something so that it will stay in one place

mop /mɒp/ *noun*
a thing with a long handle that you use for washing floors
mop *verb* (**mops, mopping, mopped** /mɒpt/)
clean something with a cloth or mop: *I mopped the floor.*

moped /'məʊped/ *noun*
a thing like a bicycle with a small engine

moral¹ /'mɒrəl/ *adjective*
about what you think is right or wrong: *Some people do not eat meat for moral reasons.* ◇ *a moral problem*
morally /'mɒrəli/ *adverb*
It's morally wrong to tell lies.

moral² /'mɒrəl/ *noun*
a lesson about what is right and wrong, that you can learn from a story or from something that happens: *The moral of the story is that we should be kind to animals.*

more¹ /mɔː(r)/ *adjective, pronoun*
a bigger amount or number of something: *You've got more money than I have.* ◇ *Can I have some more sugar in my tea?* ◇ *We need two more chairs.* ◇ *There aren't any more chocolates.* ☞ Look at **most**.

more² /mɔː(r)/ *adverb*
1 a word that makes an adjective or adverb stronger: *Your book was more expensive than mine.* ◇ *Please speak more slowly.*
2 a bigger amount or number: *I like Anna more than her brother.*
☞ Look at **most**.
more or less almost, but not exactly: *We are more or less the same age.*
not any more not as before; not any longer: *They don't live here any more.*
once more again: *Spring will soon be here once more.*

morning /'mɔːnɪŋ/ *noun*
the first part of the day, between the time when the sun comes up and midday: *I went swimming this morning.* ◇ *I'm going to London tomorrow morning.* ◇ *The letter arrived on Tuesday morning.* ◇ *I felt ill all morning.*
in the morning 1 not in the afternoon or evening: *I start work at nine o'clock in the morning.* **2** tomorrow during the morning: *I'll see you in the morning.*

mortgage /'mɔːɡɪdʒ/ *noun*
money that you borrow to buy a house

Moslem /'mɒzləm/ = Muslim

mosque /mɒsk/ *noun*
a building where Muslims go to pray

mosquito /mə'skiːtəʊ/ *noun* (plural **mosquitoes**)
a small flying insect that bites people and animals and drinks their blood

iː	i	ɪ	e	æ	ɑː	ɒ	ɔː	ʊ	u	uː
see	happy	sit	ten	cat	father	got	saw	put	situation	too

moss /mɒs/ *noun* (no plural)
a soft green plant that grows like a carpet on things like trees and stones

most[1] /məʊst/ *adjective, pronoun*
the biggest amount or number of something: *Jo did a lot of work, but I did the most.* ◇ *He was ill for most of last week.*
☞ Look at **more**.
at most, at the most not more than; but not more: *We can stay two days at the most.*
make the most of something use something in the best way: *We only have one free day, so let's make the most of it.*

most[2] /məʊst/ *adverb*
more than all others: *It's the most beautiful garden I have ever seen.* ◇ *Which part of your holiday did you most enjoy?*

mostly /ˈməʊstli/ *adverb*
almost all: *The students in my class are mostly Japanese.*

motel /məʊ'tel/ *noun*
a hotel for people who are travelling by car

moth /mɒθ/ *noun*
an insect with big wings that flies at night

mother /ˈmʌðə(r)/ *noun*
a woman who has a child: *My mother is a doctor.* ☞ picture on page 127. Look at **mum** and **mummy**.

mother-in-law /ˈmʌðər ɪn lɔː/ *noun*
(*plural* **mothers-in-law**)
the mother of your husband or wife
☞ picture on page 127

motion /ˈməʊʃn/ *noun* (no plural)
in motion moving: *Don't put your head out of the window while the train is in motion.*

motive /ˈməʊtɪv/ *noun*
a reason for doing something: *Was there a motive for the murder?*

motor /ˈməʊtə(r)/ *noun*
the part inside a machine that makes it move or work: *an electric motor*

motor bike

motor bike /ˈməʊtə baɪk/, **motor cycle** /ˈməʊtə saɪkl/ *noun*
a large bicycle with an engine
motor cyclist /ˈməʊtə saɪklɪst/ *noun*
a person who rides a motor cycle

motor boat /ˈməʊtə bəʊt/ *noun*
a small fast boat that has an engine

motorist /ˈməʊtərɪst/ *noun*
a person who drives a car

motor racing /ˈməʊtə reɪsɪŋ/ *noun* (no plural)
a sport where people drive cars very fast on a special road (called a **track**) to try to win races: *He watched the motor racing on TV.*

motorway /ˈməʊtəweɪ/ *noun*
a wide road where cars, lorries and coaches can travel a long way fast: *The motorway around London is called the M25.*

mould[1] /məʊld/ *noun* (no plural)
soft green, grey or blue stuff that grows on food that is too old
mouldy *adjective*
covered with mould: *mouldy cheese*

mould[2] /məʊld/ *verb* (**moulds, moulding, moulded**)
make something soft into a certain shape: *The children moulded animals out of clay.*
mould *noun*
an empty container for making things into a certain shape: *They poured the hot metal into the mould.*

mound /maʊnd/ *noun*
1 a small hill
2 a pile of things: *a mound of newspapers*

Mount /maʊnt/ *noun*
You use 'Mount' before the name of a mountain: *Mount Everest* ✪ The short way of writing 'Mount' is **Mt**: *Mt Etna*

mountain /ˈmaʊntən/ *noun*
a very high hill: *Everest is the highest mountain in the world.* ◇ *We climbed the mountain.*

mountaineer /ˌmaʊntə'nɪə(r)/ *noun*
a person who climbs mountains
mountaineering /ˌmaʊntə'nɪərɪŋ/ *noun* (no plural)
the sport of climbing mountains

mourn /mɔːn/ *verb* (**mourns, mourning, mourned** /mɔːnd/)
feel very sad, usually because somebody

has died: *She is still mourning for her husband.*

mourning /'mɔːnɪŋ/ *noun* (no plural)
a time when people are very sad because somebody has died: *They are in mourning for their son.*

mouse /maʊs/
noun (*plural* **mice** /maɪs/)
1 a small animal with a long tail: *Our cat caught a mouse.*

mouse

2 a thing that you move with your hand to tell a computer what to do ☞ picture at **computer**

moustache /mə'stɑːʃ/ *noun*
the hair above a man's mouth, below his nose: *He has got a moustache.*

mouth /maʊθ/
noun (*plural* **mouths** /maʊðz/)
1 the part of your face below your nose that you use for eating and speaking: *Open your mouth, please!* ☞ picture on page 126

moustache

2 the place where a river goes into the sea

mouthful /'maʊθfʊl/ *noun*
the amount of food or drink that you can put in your mouth at one time: *a mouthful of food*

move¹ /muːv/ *verb* (**moves, moving, moved** /muːvd/)
1 go from one place to another; change the way you are standing or sitting: *Don't get off the bus while it's moving.* ◇ *We moved to the front of the cinema.*
2 put something in another place or another way: *Can you move your car, please?*
3 go to live in another place: *They sold their house in London and moved to Liverpool.* ◇ *We are moving house soon.*
move in go to live in a house or flat: *I've got a new flat – I'm moving in next week.*
move out leave a house or flat where you were living

move² /muːv/ *noun*
1 going from one place to another; chan-

ging the way you are standing or sitting: *The police are watching every move she makes.*
2 going to live in a new place: *We need a big van for the move.*
get a move on hurry: *Get a move on or you'll be late for work!*

movement /'muːvmənt/ *noun*
1 moving or being moved: *The old man's movements were slow and painful.*
2 a group of people who have the same ideas or beliefs: *a political movement*

movie /'muːvi/ *noun*
1 a film that you see at the cinema: *Would you like to see a movie?*
2 **the movies** (plural) the cinema: *We went to the movies last night.*
♦ **Movie** is the American English word. In British English we usually use **film** and **cinema**.

mow /məʊ/ *verb* (**mows, mowing, mowed** /məʊd/, *has* **mown** /məʊn/)
cut grass: *Sally is mowing the grass.*
mower *noun*
a machine that cuts grass; a lawnmower

MP /ˌem 'piː/ *short for* **Member of Parliament**

mph
a way of measuring how fast something is moving. 'Mph' is short for **miles per hour**: *The train was travelling at 125 mph.*

Mr /'mɪstə(r)/
a word that you use before the name of a man: *Mr John Smith* ◇ *Mr Major*

Mrs /'mɪsɪz/
a word that you use before the name of a woman who is married: *Mrs Sandra Williams* ◇ *Mrs Mills* ☞ Look at **Miss** and **Ms**.

Ms /məz/, /mɪz/
a word that you use before the name of any woman, instead of **Mrs** or **Miss**: *Ms Fiona Green*

Mt *short way of writing* **Mount**

much¹ /mʌtʃ/ *adjective* (**much, more, most**), *pronoun*
a big amount of something; a lot of something: *I haven't got much money.* ◇ *There was so much food that we couldn't eat it all.* ◇ *'Do you like it?' 'No,*

not much.' ✪ We usually use 'much' only in negative sentences, in questions, and after 'too', 'so', 'as' and 'how'. In other sentences we use **a lot (of)**: *She's got a lot of money.* ☞ Look at **many**.
as much as the same amount that: *Eat as much as you can.*
how much ...? 1 what amount?: *How much paper do you want?* 2 what price?: *How much is this shirt?*

much² /mʌtʃ/ *adverb*
a lot: *I don't like him very much.* ◇ *Your flat is much bigger than mine.*

mud /mʌd/ *noun* (no plural)
soft wet earth: *Phil came home from the football match covered in mud.*

muddle /'mʌdl/ *verb* (**muddles, muddling, muddled** /'mʌdld/)
muddle somebody up mix somebody's ideas so that they cannot understand or think clearly: *Don't ask so many questions – you're muddling me up.*
muddle somebody or **something up** think that one person or thing is a different person or thing: *I always muddle Jane up with her sister.*
muddle something up make something untidy: *You've muddled all my papers up!*
muddle *noun*
in a muddle untidy or not thinking clearly: *Your room is in a terrible muddle.* ◇ *I was in such a muddle that I couldn't find anything.*

muddy /'mʌdi/ *adjective* (**muddier, muddiest**)
covered with mud: *When it rains, the roads get very muddy.*

mug¹ /mʌg/ *noun*
a big cup with straight sides: *a mug of tea*

mug

mug² /mʌg/ *verb*
(**mugs, mugging, mugged** /mʌgd/)
attack somebody in the street and take their money
mugger *noun*
a person who mugs somebody

mule /mju:l/ *noun*
an animal whose parents were a horse and a donkey

multicoloured /ˌmʌlti'kʌləd/ *adjective*
with many colours: *multicoloured birds*

multiply /'mʌltɪplaɪ/ *verb* (**multiplies, multiplying, multiplied** /'mʌltɪplaɪd/, **has multiplied**)
make a number bigger by a certain number of times: *Two multiplied by three is six* (2 x 3 = 6). ◇ *Multiply 3 and 7 together.*
multiplication /ˌmʌltɪplɪ'keɪʃn/ *noun* (no plural)
multiplying a number

multi-storey /ˌmʌlti 'stɔːri/ *adjective*
with many floors: *a multi-storey car park*

mum /mʌm/ *noun*
mother: *This is my mum.* ◇ *Can I have an apple, Mum?*

mumble /'mʌmbl/ *verb* (**mumbles, mumbling, mumbled** /'mʌmbld/)
speak quietly in a way that is not clear, so that people cannot hear you well: *She mumbled something about a party, but I didn't hear what she said.*

mummy /'mʌmi/ *noun* (plural **mummies**)
a word for 'mother' that children use

murder /'mɜːdə(r)/ *verb* (**murders, murdering, murdered** /'mɜːdəd/)
kill somebody when you have decided to do it: *She was murdered with a knife.*
murder *noun*
murdering somebody: *He was sent to prison for the murder of a police officer.*
murderer *noun*
a person who has murdered somebody: *The police have caught the murderer.*

murmur /'mɜːmə(r)/ *verb* (**murmurs, murmuring, murmured** /'mɜːməd/)
speak in a low quiet voice or make a low sound that is not very clear: *'I love you,' she murmured in his ear.*
murmur *noun*
I heard the murmur of voices from the next room. ◇ *the murmur of the wind in the trees*

muscle /'mʌsl/ *noun*
one of the parts inside your body that become tight or loose to help you move

museum /mju'ziːəm/ *noun*
a building where people can look at old or interesting things: *Have you ever been to the British Museum?*

mushroom

/'mʌʃrum/ *noun*
a plant that you can
eat, with a flat top
and no leaves

music /'mju:zɪk/
noun (no plural)

mushroom

1 the sounds that
you make by singing, or by playing instruments: *What sort of music do you like?*
2 signs on paper to show people what to sing or play: *Can you read music?*

○ Some types of music are **pop, rock, jazz, soul, reggae, rap** and **classical**.

musical /'mju:zɪkl/ *adjective*
1 of music: *musical instruments* (= the piano, the guitar or the trumpet, for example)
2 good at making music: *She's a very musical child – she plays the piano and the violin.*
musical *noun*
a play or film that has singing and dancing in it

musician /mju'zɪʃn/ *noun*
a person who writes music or plays a musical instrument

Muslim /'mʊzlɪm/ *noun*
a person who follows the religion of **Islam**
Muslim *adjective*
the Muslim way of life

must /məst/, /mʌst/ *modal verb*
1 a word that you use to tell somebody what to do or what is necessary: *You must look before you cross the road.*

○ You use **must not** or the short form **mustn't** to tell people **not** to do something:

*You **mustn't** be late.*

When you want to say that somebody can do something if they want, but that it is not necessary, you use **don't have to**:

*You **don't have to** do your homework today* (= you can do it if you want, but it is not necessary).

2 a word that shows that you are sure something is true: *You must be tired after your long journey.* ◇ *I can't find my keys. I must have left them at home.*

☞ Look at the Note on page 227 to find out more about **modal verbs.**

mustache *American English for* **moustache**

mustard /'mʌstəd/ *noun* (no plural)
a thick yellow sauce with a very strong taste, that you eat with meat

mustn't /'mʌsnt/ = **must not**

mutter /'mʌtə(r)/ *verb* (**mutters, muttering, muttered** /'mʌtəd/)
speak in a low quiet voice that is difficult to hear: *He muttered something about going home, and left the room.*

my /maɪ/ *adjective*
of me: *Where is my watch?* ◇ *These are my books, not yours.* ◇ *I've hurt my arm.*

myself /maɪ'self/ *pronoun* (*plural* **ourselves**)
1 a word that shows the same person as the one who is speaking: *I hurt myself.* ◇ *I bought myself a new shirt.*
2 a word that makes 'I' stronger: *'Did you buy this cake?' 'No, I made it myself.'*
by myself 1 alone; without other people: *I live by myself.* **2** without help: *I made dinner by myself.*

mysterious /mɪ'stɪəriəs/ *adjective*
Something that is mysterious is strange and you do not know about it or understand it: *The house is empty but some people say they have seen mysterious lights there in the night.*
mysteriously *adverb*
The plane disappeared mysteriously.

mystery /'mɪstri/ *noun* (*plural* **mysteries**)
something strange that you cannot understand or explain: *The police say that the man's death is still a mystery.*

myth /mɪθ/ *noun*
1 a very old story
2 a story or belief that is not true

i:	i	ɪ	e	æ	ɑ:	ɒ	ɔ:	ʊ	u	u:
see	**happy**	**sit**	**ten**	**cat**	**father**	**got**	**saw**	**put**	**situation**	**too**

Nn

nail /neɪl/ *noun*
1 the hard part at the end of a finger or toe: *toenails* ◇ *fingernails* ☞ picture on page 126
2 a small thin piece of metal with one sharp end which you hit into wood (with a **hammer**) to fix things together ☞ picture at **hammer**
nail *verb* (**nails, nailing, nailed** /neɪld/)
fix something to another thing with a nail: *I nailed the pieces of wood together.*

naked /ˈneɪkɪd/ *adjective*
If you are naked, you are not wearing any clothes.

name¹ /neɪm/ *noun*
a word or words that you use to call or talk about a person or thing: *My name is Chris Eaves.* ◇ *What's your name?* ◇ *Do you know the name of this flower?*

○ Your **first name** is the name that your parents give you when you are born. In Christian countries this is also called your **Christian name**. Your **surname** is the name that everybody in your family has. A **nickname** is a name that your friends or family sometimes call you instead of your real name.

call somebody names say bad, unkind words about somebody: *Joe cried because the other children were calling him names.*

name² /neɪm/ *verb* (**names, naming, named** /neɪmd/)
1 give a name to somebody or something: *They named their baby Sophie.*
2 know and say the name of somebody or something: *The headmaster could name every one of his 600 pupils.*

namely /ˈneɪmli/ *adverb*
You use 'namely' when you are going to name a person or thing that you have just said something about: *Only two students were late, namely Sergio and Antonio.*

nanny /ˈnæni/ *noun* (*plural* **nannies**)
a woman whose job is to look after the children of a family

nap /næp/ *noun*
a short sleep that you have during the day: *I had a nap after lunch.*

napkin /ˈnæpkɪn/ *noun*
a piece of cloth or paper that you use when you are eating to clean your mouth and hands and to keep your clothes clean

nappy /ˈnæpi/ *noun* (*plural* **nappies**)
a piece of cloth or strong paper that a baby wears around its bottom and between its legs

narrow /ˈnærəʊ/ *adjective* (**narrower, narrowest**)
not far from one side to the other: *The road was too narrow for two cars to pass.*
○ opposite: **wide** or **broad** ☞ picture on page 262
have a narrow escape If you have a narrow escape, something bad almost happens to you: *You had a very narrow escape – your car nearly hit a tree.*
narrowly *adverb*
only just: *The car narrowly missed hitting me.*

nasty /ˈnɑːsti/ *adjective* (**nastier, nastiest**)
bad; not nice: *There's a nasty smell in this room.* ◇ *Don't be so nasty!*

nation /ˈneɪʃn/ *noun*
a country and all the people who live in it

national /ˈnæʃnəl/ *adjective*
of or for all of a country: *She wore the national costume of Greece.* ◇ *national newspapers*
national anthem /ˌnæʃnəl ˈænθəm/ *noun*
the song of a country
national park /ˌnæʃnəl ˈpɑːk/ *noun*
a large area of beautiful land that the government looks after

nationality /ˌnæʃəˈnæləti/ *noun* (*plural* **nationalities**)
belonging to a certain country: *'What nationality are you?' 'I'm French.'*

native /ˈneɪtɪv/ *adjective*
(of) the place where you were born: *I returned to my native country.*
native *noun*
a person who was born in a place: *He lives in London but he's a native of Liverpool.*

natural /ˈnætʃrəl/ *adjective*
1 made by nature, not by people: *This part*

of Scotland is an area of great natural beauty. ◇ Earthquakes and floods are natural disasters.
2 normal or usual: It's natural for parents to feel sad when their children leave home. ✪ opposite: **unnatural**

naturally /'nætʃrəli/ adverb
1 in a way that is not made or caused by people: Is your hair naturally curly?
2 of course: You didn't answer the telephone, so I naturally thought you were out.
3 in a normal way: Try to stand naturally while I take a photo.

nature /'neɪtʃə(r)/ noun
1 (no plural) everything in the world that was not made by people: the beauty of nature
2 (plural **natures**) the way a person or thing is: Our cat has a very friendly nature.

naughty /'nɔːti/ adjective (**naughtier, naughtiest**)
You say that a child is naughty when he/she does bad things or does not do what you ask him/her to do: She's the naughtiest child in the class.

naval /'neɪvl/ adjective
of a navy: a naval officer

navigate /'nævɪgeɪt/ verb (**navigates, navigating, navigated**)
use a map, etc to find which way a ship, an aeroplane or a car should go: Long ago, explorers used the stars to navigate.
navigator /'nævɪgeɪtə(r)/ noun
a person who navigates

navy /'neɪvi/ noun (plural **navies**)
the ships that a country uses when there is a war, and the people who work on them: Mark is in the navy.

navy blue /,neɪvi 'bluː/ adjective
dark blue

near /nɪə(r)/ adjective, adverb (**nearer, nearest**)
not far; close: Let's walk to my house. It's quite near. ◇ Where's the nearest hospital? ◇ My parents live quite near.
near preposition
close to somebody or something: I don't need a car because I live near the city centre.

nearby /'nɪəbaɪ/ adjective
not far away; close: We took her to a nearby hospital.
nearby /nɪə'baɪ/ adverb
Let's go and see Tim – he lives nearby.

nearly /'nɪəli/ adverb
almost; not quite: I'm nearly 16 – it's my birthday next week. ◇ She was so ill that she nearly died.
not nearly not at all: The book wasn't nearly as good as the film.

neat /niːt/ adjective (**neater, neatest**)
with everything in the right place; tidy: Keep your room neat and tidy.
neatly adverb
Write your name neatly.

necessarily /,nesə'serəli/ adverb
not necessarily not always: Big men aren't necessarily strong.

necessary /'nesəsəri/ adjective
If something is necessary, you must have or do it: Warm clothes are necessary in winter.

necessity /nə'sesəti/ noun (plural **necessities**)
something that you must have: Food and clothes are necessities of life.

neck /nek/ noun
1 the part of your body between your shoulders and your head: Helen wore a thick scarf round her neck. ☞ picture on page 126
2 the part of a jumper, T-shirt, etc that goes round your neck
3 the thin part at the top of a bottle

necklace /'nekləs/ noun
a pretty thing that you wear round your neck: a diamond necklace

necklace

need¹ /niːd/ verb (**needs, needing, needed**)
1 must have something; want something important and necessary that is not there: All plants and animals need water. ◇ You don't need your coat – it's not cold.
2 If you need to do something, you must do it, or it is very important to do it: James is very ill. He needs to go to hospital.

p	b	t	d	k	g	tʃ	dʒ	f	v	θ	ð
pen	**b**ad	**t**ea	**d**id	**c**at	**g**ot	**ch**ain	**j**am	**f**all	**v**an	**th**in	**th**is

◇ *'Do we need to pay now, or can we pay next week?' 'You needn't pay now.'/'You don't need to pay now.'*

need² /niːd/ *noun*
be in need of something want something important and necessary that is not there: *She's in need of a rest.*

needle /'niːdl/ *noun*
1 a small thin piece of metal with a hole at one end and a sharp point at the other. You use a needle for sewing: *If you give me a needle and cotton, I'll sew the button on your shirt.* ☞ picture at **sew**
2 something that is like a needle: *the needle of a compass*
3 a very thin pointed leaf. **Pine trees** and **fir-trees** have needles.
☞ Look also at **knitting-needle**.

needn't /'niːdnt/ = need not

negative /'negətɪv/ *adjective*
using words like 'no', 'not' and 'never': *'I don't like British food' is a negative sentence.*
negative *noun*
a piece of film that you use to make a photograph. On a negative, dark things are light and light things are dark.

neglect /nɪ'glekt/ *verb* (**neglects, neglecting, neglected**)
not take care of somebody or something: *The dog was dirty and thin because its owner had neglected it.*
neglect *noun* (no plural)
The house was in a state of neglect.

neigh /neɪ/ *noun*
the sound that a horse makes
neigh *verb* (**neighs, neighing, neighed** /neɪd/)
make this sound

neighbor, neighboring American English for **neighbour, neighbouring**

neighborhood American English for **neighbourhood**

neighbour /'neɪbə(r)/ *noun*
a person who lives near you: *Don't make so much noise or you'll wake the neighbours.* ✪ Your **next-door neighbour** is the person who lives in the house next to your house.
neighbouring *adjective*
that is near: *We played football against a team from the neighbouring village.*

neighbourhood /'neɪbəhʊd/ *noun*
a part of a town: *They live in a friendly neighbourhood.*

neither¹ /'naɪðə(r)/, /'niːðə(r)/ *adjective, pronoun*
not one and not the other of two things or people: *Neither book was very interesting.* ◇ *Neither of the children liked the film.*

neither² /'naɪðə(r)/, /'niːðə(r)/ *adverb*
(used in sentences with 'not') also not: *Lydia can't swim and neither can I.* ◇ *'I don't like rice.' 'Neither do I.'*
neither ... nor not ... and not: *Neither Paul nor I went to the party.*

nephew /'nefjuː/ *noun*
the son of your brother or sister ☞ picture on page 127

nerve /nɜːv/ *noun*
1 (*plural* **nerves**) one of the long thin things inside your body that carry feelings and messages to and from your brain
2 **nerves** (plural) being worried or afraid: *John breathed deeply to calm his nerves.*
3 (no plural) being brave or calm when there is danger: *You need a lot of nerve to be a racing driver.*
get on somebody's nerves annoy somebody: *Stop making that noise – you're getting on my nerves!*

nervous /'nɜːvəs/ *adjective*
1 worried or afraid: *I'm quite nervous about starting my new job.*
2 of the nerves in your body: *the nervous system*
nervously *adverb*
He laughed nervously because he didn't know what to say.
nervousness /'nɜːvəsnəs/ *noun* (no plural)
being nervous

nest /nest/ *noun*
a place where a bird, a snake, an insect, etc lives and lays its eggs or keeps its babies: *a bird's nest*
nest *verb* (**nests, nesting, nested**)
make and live in a nest: *The ducks are nesting by the river.*

net /net/ *noun*
material that is made of long pieces of string, etc with holes between them: *a fishing net* ◇ *a tennis net*

s	z	ʃ	ʒ	h	m	n	ŋ	l	r	j	w
so	**zoo**	**shoe**	**vision**	**hat**	**man**	**no**	**sing**	**leg**	**red**	**yes**	**wet**

nets

netball /'netbɔːl/ noun (no plural)
a game where two teams of seven players try to throw a ball through a high round net

nettle /'netl/ noun
a wild plant covered with hairs that can hurt you if you touch them

network /'netwɜːk/ noun
a large group of things that are connected to one another across a country, etc: the railway network

never /'nevə(r)/ adverb
not at any time; not ever: She never works on Saturdays. ◇ I've never been to America. ◇ I will never forget you.

nevertheless /ˌnevəðə'les/ conjunction, adverb
but; however; although that is true: They played very well. Nevertheless, they didn't win.

new /njuː/ adjective (newer, newest)
1 Something that is new has just been made or bought: I bought a new pair of shoes yesterday. ◇ Have you seen Spike Lee's new film? ☞ picture on page 263
2 that you have not seen, had, learnt, etc before: Our new flat is much bigger than our old one. ◇ The teacher usually explains the new words to us.
new to something If you are new to something, you are at a place or doing something for the first time: They are new to the town and they don't have any friends there.
new year the beginning of the year; the time around 1 January: Happy New Year! ○ 1 January is called **New Year's Day** and 31 December is called **New Year's Eve**.

newcomer /'njuːkʌmə(r)/ noun
a person who has just come to a place

newly /'njuːli/ adverb
not long ago; recently: Our school is newly built.

news /njuːz/ noun (no plural)
1 words that tell people about things that have just happened: Have you heard the news? Stuart is getting married. ◇ I've got some good news for you. ○ Be careful! You cannot say 'a news'. You can say 'some news' or 'a piece of news': Julie told us an interesting piece of news.
2 **the news** (no plural) a programme on television or radio that tells people about important things that have just happened: We heard about the plane crash on the news.
break the news tell somebody about something important that has happened: Have you broken the news to your wife?

newsagent /'njuːzeɪdʒənt/ noun
a person who has a shop that sells things like newspapers, magazines, sweets and cigarettes ○ The shop where a newsagent works is called a **newsagent's**.

newspaper /'njuːzpeɪpə(r)/ noun
large pieces of paper with news, advertisements and other things printed on them, that you can buy every day or every week

next¹ /nekst/ adjective
1 that comes after this one: I'm going on holiday next week. ◇ Go straight on, then take the next road on the right.
2 nearest to this one: I live in the next village.
next to at the side of somebody or something; beside: The bank is next to the post office. ☞ picture on page 125

next² /nekst/ adverb
after this; then: I've finished this work. What shall I do next?

next³ /nekst/ noun (no plural)
the person or thing that comes after this one: Susy came first and Paul was the next to arrive.

next door /ˌnekst 'dɔː(r)/ adjective, adverb
in or to the nearest house: Who lives next door? ◇ next-door neighbours

nibble /'nɪbl/ verb (nibbles, nibbling, nibbled /'nɪbld/)
eat something in very small bites: The mouse nibbled the cheese.

nice /naɪs/ adjective (nicer, nicest)
pleasant, good or kind: Did you have a nice holiday? ◇ I met a nice boy at the party. ◇ It's nice to see you.
nice and ... words that show that you

iː	i	ɪ	e	æ	ɑː	ɒ	ɔː	ʊ	u	uː
see	happy	sit	ten	cat	father	got	saw	put	situation	too

like something: *It's nice and warm by the fire.*

nicely *adverb*
You can have a cake if you ask nicely.

nickname /'nɪkneɪm/ *noun*
a name that your friends or family sometimes call you instead of your real name

niece /niːs/ *noun*
the daughter of your brother or sister
☞ picture on page 127

night /naɪt/ *noun*
1 the time when it is dark because there is no light from the sun: *Most people sleep at night.* ◇ *She stayed at my house last night.* ◇ *The baby cried all night.*
2 the part of the day between the afternoon and when you go to bed: *We went to a party on Saturday night.*
○ **Tonight** means the night or evening of today.

nightclub /'naɪtklʌb/ *noun*
a place where you can go late in the evening to drink and dance, for example

nightdress /'naɪtdres/ (*plural* **nightdresses**), **nightie** /'naɪti/ *noun*
a loose dress that a woman or girl wears in bed

nightly /'naɪtli/ *adjective, adverb*
that happens or comes every night: *a nightly TV show*

nightmare /'naɪtmeə(r)/ *noun*
1 a dream that frightens you: *I had a nightmare last night.*
2 something that is very bad or frightening: *Travelling through the snow was a nightmare.*

night-time /'naɪt taɪm/ *noun* (no plural)
the time when it is dark: *She is afraid to go out at night-time.*

nil /nɪl/ *noun* (no plural)
nothing: *Our team won the match by two goals to nil.*

nine /naɪn/ *number*
9
ninth /naɪnθ/ *adjective, adverb, noun*
1 9th
2 one of nine equal parts of something; ⅑

nineteen /ˌnaɪn'tiːn/ *number*
19
nineteenth /ˌnaɪn'tiːnθ/ *adjective, adverb, noun*
19th

ninety /'naɪnti/ *number*
1 90
2 **the nineties** (plural) the numbers, years or temperatures between 90 and 99
in your nineties between the ages of 90 and 99: *My grandmother is in her nineties.*
ninetieth /'naɪntiəθ/ *adjective, adverb, noun*
90th

nitrogen /'naɪtrədʒən/ *noun* (no plural)
a gas in the air

no¹, No *short way of writing* **number 1**

no² /nəʊ/ *adjective*
1 not one; not any: *I have no money – my purse is empty.*
2 a word that shows you are not allowed to do something: *The sign said 'No Smoking'.*
no *adverb*
not any: *My flat is no bigger than yours.*

no³ /nəʊ/
a word that you use to show that something is not right or true, or that you do not want something; not yes: *'Do you want a drink?' 'No, thank you.'* ◇ *'He's Italian.' 'No he isn't. He's French.'*
oh no! words that you say when something bad happens: *Oh no! I've broken my watch!*

noble /'nəʊbl/ *adjective* (**nobler, noblest**)
1 of a rich important family: *a noble prince*
2 good, honest and not selfish: *noble thoughts*

nobody /'nəʊbədi/ *pronoun*
no person; not anybody: *Nobody in our class speaks Greek.* ◇ *There was nobody at home.*

nod /nɒd/ *verb* (**nods, nodding, nodded**)
move your head down and up again quickly as a way of saying 'yes' or 'hello' to somebody: *'Do you understand?' asked the teacher, and everybody nodded.*
nod *noun*
Jim gave me a nod when I arrived.

noise /nɔɪz/ *noun*
1 something that you hear; a sound: *I heard a noise upstairs.*
2 a loud sound that you do not like: *Don't make so much noise!* ◇ *What a terrible noise!*

ʌ	ɜː	ə	eɪ	əʊ	aɪ	aʊ	ɔɪ	ɪə	eə	ʊə
cup	bird	about	say	go	five	now	boy	near	hair	pure

noisy /ˈnɔɪzi/ *adjective* (**noisier, noisiest**)
1 full of loud noise: *The restaurant was too noisy.*
2 If a person or thing is noisy, he/she/it makes a lot of noise: *The children are very noisy.*
✪ opposite: **quiet**
noisily /ˈnɔɪzɪli/ *adverb*
He ate his dinner noisily.

> **non-** /nɒn/ *prefix*
> You can add **non-** to the beginning of some words to give them the opposite meaning, for example:
> a **non-smoker** = a person who does not smoke
> a **non-stop** train = a train that goes from one place to another without stopping at the other stations between

none /nʌn/ *pronoun*
not any; not one: *She has eaten all the chocolates − there are none in the box.* ◇ *I went to every bookshop, but none of them had the book I wanted.*

nonsense /ˈnɒnsns/ *noun* (no plural)
words or ideas that have no meaning or that are not true: *It's nonsense to say that Jackie is lazy.*

noodles /ˈnuːdlz/ *noun* (plural)
long thin pieces of food made from flour, eggs and water

noon /nuːn/ *noun* (no plural)
twelve o'clock in the middle of the day: *I met Sally at noon.*

no one /ˈnəʊ wʌn/ *pronoun*
no person; not anybody: *There was no one in the classroom.* ◇ *No one saw me go into the house.*

nor /nɔː(r)/ *conjunction*
(used after 'neither' and 'not') also not: *If Alan doesn't go, nor will Lucy.* ◇ *'I don't like eggs.' 'Nor do I.'* ◇ *Neither Tom nor I eat meat.*

normal /ˈnɔːml/ *adjective*
usual and ordinary; not different or special: *I will be home at the normal time.*
normally /ˈnɔːməli/ *adverb*
1 usually: *I normally go to bed at about eleven o'clock.*
2 in a normal way: *He isn't behaving normally.*

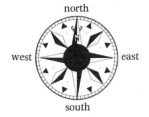

north /nɔːθ/ *noun* (no plural)
the direction that is on your left when you watch the sun come up in the morning: *the north of England*
north *adjective, adverb*
They live in North London. ◇ *a north wind* (= that comes from the north) ◇ *We travelled north from London to Scotland.*
northern /ˈnɔːðən/ *adjective*
in or of the north part of a place: *Newcastle is in northern England.*

nose /nəʊz/ *noun*
1 the part of your face, above your mouth, that you use for breathing and smelling ☞ picture on page 126
2 the front part of a plane
blow your nose blow air through your nose to empty it, into a piece of cloth or paper (a **handkerchief** or a **tissue**)

nostril /ˈnɒstrəl/ *noun*
one of the two holes in your nose ☞ picture on page 126

nosy /ˈnəʊzi/ *adjective* (**nosier, nosiest**)
too interested in other people's lives and in things that you should not be interested in: *'Where are you going?' 'Don't be so nosy!'*

not /nɒt/ *adverb*
a word that gives the opposite meaning to another word or a sentence: *I'm not hungry.* ◇ *They did not arrive.* ◇ *I can come tomorrow, but not on Tuesday.* ◇ *'Are you angry with me?' 'No, I'm not.'* ✪ We often say and write **n't**: *John isn't* (= is not) *here.* ◇ *I haven't* (= have not) *got any sisters.*
not at all **1** no; not a little bit: *'Are you tired?' 'Not at all.'* **2** polite words that you say when somebody has said 'thank you': *'Thanks for your help.' 'Oh, not at all.'*

note¹ /nəʊt/ *noun*
1 some words that you write quickly to help you remember something: *I made a note of her address.*

2 a short letter: *Dave sent me a note to thank me for the present.*
3 a piece of paper money: *He gave me a £10 note.*
4 a short piece of extra information about something in a book: *Look at the note on page 39.*
5 one sound in music, or a mark on paper that shows a sound in music: *I can play a few notes of this song.*
take notes write when somebody is speaking so that you can remember their words later: *The teacher asked us to take notes in the lesson.*

note² /nəʊt/ *verb* (**notes, noting, noted**)
notice and remember something: *Please note that all the shops are closed on Mondays.*
note down write something so that you can remember it: *The police officer noted down my name and address.*

notebook /'nəʊtbʊk/ *noun*
a small book where you write things that you want to remember

notepad /'nəʊtpæd/ *noun*
some pieces of paper that are joined together at one edge, where you write things that you want to remember

notepaper /'nəʊtpeɪpə(r)/ *noun* (no plural)
paper that you write letters on

nothing /'nʌθɪŋ/ *pronoun*
not anything; no thing: *There's nothing in this bottle – it's empty.* ◇ *I've finished all my work and I've got nothing to do.*
for nothing 1 for no money; free: *You can have these books for nothing. I don't want them.* **2** without a good result: *I went to the station for nothing – she wasn't on the train.*
have nothing on If you have nothing on, you are not wearing any clothes.
nothing but only: *He eats nothing but salad.*
nothing like not the same as somebody or something in any way: *He's nothing like his brother.*

notice¹ /'nəʊtɪs/ *noun*
1 (*plural* **notices**) a piece of writing that tells people something: *The notice on the wall says 'NO SMOKING'.*
2 (no plural) a warning that something is

going to happen: *Our teacher gave us two weeks' notice of the history exam.*
at short notice with not much time to get ready: *We left for Scotland at very short notice and I forgot to take my coat.*
give in or **hand in your notice** tell the person you work for that you are going to leave your job
take no notice of somebody or **something** not listen to or look at somebody or something; not pay attention to somebody or something: *Take no notice of what she said – she's not feeling well today.*

notice² /'nəʊtɪs/ *verb* (**notices, noticing, noticed** /'nəʊtɪst/)
see somebody or something: *Did you notice what she was wearing?* ◇ *I noticed that he was driving a new car.*

noticeable /'nəʊtɪsəbl/ *adjective*
easy to see: *I've got a mark on my shirt. Is it noticeable?*

notice-board /'nəʊtɪs bɔːd/ *noun*
a flat piece of wood on a wall. You put papers on a notice-board so everybody can read them: *The teacher put the exam results on the notice-board.*

nought /nɔːt/ *noun*
the number 0: *We say 0.5 as 'nought point five'.*

noun /naʊn/ *noun*
a word that is the name of a person, place, thing or idea: *'Anne', 'London', 'cat' and 'happiness' are all nouns.*

novel /'nɒvl/ *noun*
a book that tells a story about people and things that are not real: *'David Copperfield' is a novel by Charles Dickens.*
novelist /'nɒvəlɪst/ *noun*
a person who writes novels

November /nəʊ'vembə(r)/ *noun*
the eleventh month of the year

now¹ /naʊ/ *adverb*
1 at this time: *I can't see you now – can you come back later?* ◇ *She was in Paris but she's living in Rome now.* ◇ *Don't wait – do it now!*
2 a word that you use when you start to talk about something new, or to make people listen to you: *I've finished writing this letter. Now, what shall we have for dinner?* ◇ *Be quiet, now!*

s	z	ʃ	ʒ	h	m	n	ŋ	l	r	j	w
so	**zoo**	**shoe**	**vision**	**hat**	**man**	**no**	**sing**	**leg**	**red**	**yes**	**wet**

from now on after this time; in the future: *From now on your teacher will be Mr Hancock.*
now and again, now and then sometimes, but not often: *We go to the cinema now and again.*

now[2] /naʊ/ *conjunction*
because something has happened: *Now that Mark has arrived we can start dinner.*

nowadays /'naʊədeɪz/ *adverb*
at this time: *A lot of people work with computers nowadays.*

nowhere /'naʊweə(r)/ *adverb*
not anywhere; at, in or to no place: *There's nowhere to stay in this village.*
nowhere near not at all: *Ruichi's English is nowhere near as good as yours.*

nuclear /'njuːkliə(r)/ *adjective*
1 of or about the inside part of **atoms**: *nuclear physics*
2 using the great power that is made by breaking or joining parts of atoms: *nuclear energy* ◇ *nuclear weapons*

nudge /nʌdʒ/ *verb* (**nudges, nudging, nudged** /nʌdʒd/)
touch or push somebody or something with your elbow: *Nudge me if I fall asleep.*
nudge *noun*
Liz gave me a nudge.

nuisance /'njuːsns/ *noun*
a person or thing that causes you trouble: *I've lost my keys. What a nuisance!*

numb /nʌm/ *adjective*
not able to feel anything: *My fingers were numb with cold.*

number /'nʌmbə(r)/ *noun*
1 a word like 'two' or 'fifteen', or a symbol or group of symbols like 7 or 130: *Choose a number between ten and one hundred.* ◇ *My phone number is Oxford 56767.*
◐ We sometimes write **No** or **no**: *I live at no 47.*
2 a group of more than one person or thing: *A large number of our students come from Japan.* ◇ *There are a number of ways you can cook an egg.*
number *verb* (**numbers, numbering, numbered** /'nʌmbəd/)
give a number to something: *Number the pages from one to ten.*

number-plate /'nʌmbə pleɪt/ *noun*
the flat piece of metal on the front and back of a car that has numbers and letters on it (its **registration number**) ☞ picture at **car**

numerous /'njuːmərəs/ *adjective*
very many: *He writes a lot of letters because he has numerous friends.*

nun /nʌn/ *noun*
a religious woman who lives with other religious women in a **convent**

nurse[1] /nɜːs/ *noun*
a person whose job is to look after people who are sick or hurt: *My sister works as a nurse in a hospital.*

nurse[2] /nɜːs/ *verb* (**nurses, nursing, nursed** /nɜːst/)
look after somebody who is sick or hurt: *I nursed my father when he was ill.*

nursery /'nɜːsəri/ *noun* (*plural* **nurseries**)
1 a place where young children can stay when their parents are at work
2 a place where people grow and sell plants
nursery rhyme /'nɜːsəri raɪm/ *noun*
a song or poem for young children
nursery school /'nɜːsəri skuːl/ *noun*
a school for children between the ages of three and five

nursing /'nɜːsɪŋ/ *noun* (no plural)
the job of being a nurse: *He has decided to go into nursing when he leaves school.*

nut /nʌt/ *noun*
1 the hard fruit of a tree or bush: *walnuts, hazelnuts and peanuts*
2 a small piece of metal with a hole in the middle that you put on the end of a long piece of metal (called a **bolt**). You use nuts and bolts for fixing things together.

nuts

nylon /'naɪlɒn/ *noun* (no plural)
very strong material made by machines. Nylon is used for making clothes and other things: *a nylon brush*

Oo

O /əʊ/
1 = **Oh**
2 a way of saying the number '0'

oak /əʊk/ *noun*
1 (*plural* **oaks**) a kind of large tree
2 (no plural) the wood of an oak tree: *an oak table*

OAP /,əʊ eɪ 'piː/ *short for* **old-age pensioner**

oar /ɔː(r)/ *noun*
a long piece of wood with one flat end. You use oars to move a small boat through water (to **row**). ☞ picture at **row**

oasis /əʊ'eɪsɪs/ *noun* (*plural* **oases** /əʊ'eɪsiːz/)
a place in a desert that has trees and water

oath /əʊθ/ *noun*
a serious promise: *I took an oath in front of a lawyer.*

oats /əʊts/ *noun* (plural)
a plant with seeds that we use as food for people and animals: *We make porridge from oats.*

obedient /ə'biːdiənt/ *adjective*
An obedient person does what somebody tells him/her to do: *He was an obedient child.* ✪ opposite: **disobedient**
obedience /ə'biːdiəns/ *noun* (no plural)
being obedient
obediently *adverb*
I called the dog and it followed me obediently.

obey /ə'beɪ/ *verb* (**obeys**, **obeying**, **obeyed** /ə'beɪd/)
do what somebody or something tells you to do: *You must obey the law.*

object¹ /'ɒbdʒɪkt/ *noun*
1 a thing that you can see and touch: *There was a small round object on the table.*
2 what you plan to do: *His object in life is to become as rich as possible.*
3 In the sentence 'Jane painted the door', the object of the sentence is 'the door'.

object² /əb'dʒekt/ *verb* (**objects**, **objecting**, **objected**)
not like something or not agree with something: *I object to the plan.*
objection /əb'dʒekʃn/ *noun*
saying or feeling that you do not like something or that you do not agree with something: *I have no objections to the plan.*

obligation /,ɒblɪ'geɪʃn/ *noun*
something that you must do: *We have an obligation to help.*

oblige /ə'blaɪdʒ/ *noun* (**obliges**, **obliging**, **obliged** /ə'blaɪdʒd/)
be obliged to If you are obliged to do something, you must do it: *You are not obliged to come if you do not want to.*

oblong /'ɒblɒŋ/ *noun*
a shape with two long sides, two short sides and four angles of 90 degrees ☞ picture on page 161
oblong *adjective*
This page is oblong.

observation /,ɒbzə'veɪʃn/ *noun* (no plural)
watching or being watched carefully
be under observation be watched carefully: *The police kept the house under observation.*

observe /ə'bzɜːv/ *verb* (**observes**, **observing**, **observed** /ə'bzɜːvd/)
watch somebody or something carefully; see somebody or something: *The police observed a man leaving the house.*

obsess /əb'ses/ *verb* (**obsesses**, **obsessing**, **obsessed** /əb'sest/)
be obsessed with somebody or **something** think about somebody or something all the time: *Debbie is obsessed with football.*
obsession /əb'seʃn/ *noun*
a person or thing that you think about all the time: *Cars are his obsession.*

obstacle /'ɒbstəkl/ *noun*
1 something that is in front of you, that you must go over or round before you can go on: *The horse jumped over the obstacle.*
2 a problem that stops you doing something

obstinate /'ɒbstɪnət/ *adjective*
An obstinate person does not change his/her ideas or do what other people want him/her to do: *He's too obstinate to say he's sorry.*

ʌ	ɜː	ə	eɪ	əʊ	aɪ	aʊ	ɔɪ	ɪə	eə	ʊə
cup	bird	about	say	go	five	now	boy	near	hair	pure

obstruct /əb'strʌkt/ verb (**obstructs, obstructing, obstructed**)
be in the way so that somebody or something cannot go past: *Please move your car – you're obstructing the traffic.*
obstruction /əb'strʌkʃn/ noun
a thing that stops somebody or something from going past: *The train had to stop because there was an obstruction on the line.*

obtain /əb'teɪn/ verb (**obtains, obtaining, obtained** /əb'teɪnd/)
get something: *Where can I obtain tickets for the play?* ○ **Get** is the word that we usually use.

obvious /'ɒbviəs/ adjective
very clear and easy to see or understand: *It's obvious that she's not happy.*
obviously adverb
it is easy to see or understand that; clearly: *He obviously learned English at school – he speaks it very well.*

occasion /ə'keɪʒn/ noun
1 a time when something happens: *I've been to Paris on three or four occasions.*
2 a special time: *A wedding is a big family occasion.*

occasional /ə'keɪʒənl/ adjective
that happens sometimes, but not very often: *We get the occasional visitor.*
occasionally /ə'keɪʒənəli/ adverb
sometimes, but not often: *I go to London occasionally.*

occupation /ˌɒkju'peɪʃn/ noun
1 (plural **occupations**) a job: *What is your mother's occupation?* ○ **Job** is the word that we usually use.
2 (plural **occupations**) something that you do in your free time: *Fishing is his favourite occupation.*
3 (no plural) living in a house, room, etc: *The new house is now ready for occupation.*
4 (no plural) taking and keeping a town or country in war

occupy /'ɒkjupaɪ/ verb (**occupies, occupying, occupied** /'ɒkjupaɪd/, **has occupied**)
1 live or be in a place: *Who occupies the house next door?*
2 make somebody busy; take somebody's time: *The children occupy most of her free time.*
3 take and keep control of a country,

town, etc in a war: *The Normans occupied England from 1066.*
occupied adjective
1 busy: *This work will keep me occupied all week.*
2 being used: *Excuse me – is this seat occupied?*

occur /ə'kɜ:(r)/ verb (**occurs, occurring, occurred** /ə'kɜ:d/)
happen: *The accident occurred this morning.*
occur to somebody come into somebody's mind: *It occurred to me that she didn't know our new address.*

ocean /'əʊʃn/ noun
a very big sea: *the Atlantic Ocean*

o'clock /ə'klɒk/ adverb
a word that you use after the numbers one to twelve for saying what time it is ○ Be careful! 'O'clock' is only used with full hours: *I left home at four o'clock and arrived in London at half past five (NOT at half past five o'clock).* ☞ Look at page 164.

October /ɒk'təʊbə(r)/ noun
the tenth month of the year

octopus /'ɒktəpəs/ noun (plural **octopuses**)
a sea animal with eight arms

odd /ɒd/ adjective (**odder, oddest**)
1 strange or unusual: *It's odd that he left without telling anybody.*
2 Odd numbers cannot be divided exactly by two: *1, 3, 5 and 7 are all odd numbers.* ○ opposite: **even**
3 part of a pair when the other one is not there: *You're wearing odd socks! One is black and the other is green!*
the odd one out one that is different from all the others: *'Apple', 'orange', 'cabbage' – which is the odd one out?*
oddly adverb
strangely: *She behaved very oddly.*

odds and ends /ˌɒdz ənd 'endz/ noun (plural)
different small things that are not important: *Sarah went out to buy a few odds and ends for the party.*

of /əv/, /ɒv/ preposition
1 a word that shows who or what has or owns something: *the back of the chair*

p	b	t	d	k	g	tʃ	dʒ	f	v	θ	ð
pen	**b**ad	**t**ea	**d**id	**c**at	**g**ot	**ch**ain	**j**am	**f**all	**v**an	**th**in	**th**is

◇ *What's the name of this mountain?*
◇ *the plays of Shakespeare*
2 a word that you use after an amount, etc: *a litre of water* ◇ *the fourth of July*
3 a word that shows what something is or what is in something: *a piece of wood* ◇ *a cup of tea* ◇ *Is this shirt made of cotton?*
4 a word that shows who: *That's very kind of you.*
5 a word that shows that somebody or something is part of a group: *One of her friends is a doctor.*
6 a word that you use with some adjectives and verbs: *I'm proud of you.* ◇ *This perfume smells of roses.*

off /ɒf/ *preposition, adverb*
1 down or away from something: *He fell off the roof.* ◇ *We got off the bus.* ◇ *The thief ran off.*
2 away from the place where it was: *If you're hot, take your coat off.* ◇ *Can you clean that paint off the carpet?*
3 not working; not being used: *All the lights are off.*
4 away: *My birthday is not far off.*
5 not at work or school: *I had the day off yesterday.*
6 joined to something: *The bathroom is off the bedroom.*
7 not fresh: *This milk is off.*

offence /ə'fens/ *noun*
something you do that is against the law: *It is an offence to drive at night without lights.*
take offence become angry or unhappy: *He took offence because I said his spelling was bad.*

offend /ə'fend/ *verb* (**offends, offending, offended**)
make somebody feel angry or unhappy; hurt somebody's feelings: *She was offended when you said she was fat.*

offense *American English for* **offence**

offer /'ɒfə(r)/ *verb* (**offers, offering, offered** /'ɒfəd/)
say or show that you will do or give something if another person wants it: *She offered me a cake.* ◇ *I offered to help her.*
offer *noun*
Thanks for the offer, but I don't need any help.

office /'ɒfɪs/ *noun*
1 a room or building with desks and tele-

phones, where people work: *I work in an office.*
2 a room or building where you can buy something or get information: *The ticket office is at the front of the station.* ◇ *the post office*
3 one part of the government: *the Foreign Office*

officer /'ɒfɪsə(r)/ *noun*
1 a person in the army, navy or air force who gives orders to other people: *a naval officer*
2 a person who does important work, especially for the government: *a prison officer* ◇ *police officers*

official¹ /ə'fɪʃl/ *adjective*
of or from the government or somebody who is important: *an official report* ◇ *The news is now official – they are getting married!* ◯ opposite: **unofficial**
officially *adverb*
I think I've got the job, but they will tell me officially on Friday.

official² /ə'fɪʃl/ *noun*
a person who does important work, especially for the government: *government officials*

off-licence /'ɒf laɪsns/ *noun*
a shop where you can buy drinks like beer and wine

often /'ɒfn/ *adverb*
many times: *We often play football on Sundays.* ◇ *I've often seen her on the train.* ◇ *I don't write to him very often.* ◇ *How often do you visit her?*
every so often sometimes, but not often: *Every so often she phones me.*

oh /əʊ/
1 a word that shows a strong feeling, like surprise or fear: *Oh no! I've lost my keys!*
2 a word that you say before other words: *'What time is it?' 'Oh, about two o'clock.'*
Oh dear words that show you are surprised or unhappy: *Oh dear – have you hurt yourself?*
Oh well words that you use when you are not happy about something, but you cannot change it: *'I'm too busy to go out tonight.' 'Oh well, I'll see you tomorrow then.'*

oil /ɔɪl/ *noun* (no plural)
1 a thick liquid that comes from plants or

s	z	ʃ	ʒ	h	m	n	ŋ	l	r	j	w
so	**zoo**	**shoe**	vision	**hat**	**man**	**no**	sing	leg	red	yes	**wet**

animals and that you use in cooking: *Fry the onions in oil.*
2 a thick liquid that comes from under the ground or the sea. We burn oil or use it in machines.

oil-painting /'ɔɪl peɪntɪŋ/ *noun*
a picture that has been done with paint made from oil

oil rig /'ɔɪl rɪg/ *noun*
a special building with machines that dig for oil under the sea or on land

oily /'ɔɪli/ *adjective* (**oilier, oiliest**)
like oil or covered with oil: *I don't like oily food.* ◇ *an oily liquid*

OK, okay /ˌəʊ 'keɪ/
yes; all right: *'Do you want to go to a party?' 'OK.'*
OK, okay *adjective, adverb*
all right; good or well enough: *Is it okay to sit here?*

old /əʊld/ *adjective* (**older, oldest**)
1 If you are old, you have lived for a long time: *My grandfather is very old.* ◇ *My sister is older than me.* ❂ opposite: **young** ☞ picture on page 262
2 made or bought a long time ago: *an old house* ❂ opposite: **new** ☞ picture on page 263
3 You use 'old' to show the age of somebody or something: *He's nine years old.* ◇ *How old are you?* ◇ *a six-year-old boy*
4 that you did or had before now: *My old job was more interesting than this one.* ❂ opposite: **new**
5 that you have known for a long time: *Jane is an old friend – we were at school together.*
the old *noun* (plural)
old people
old age /ˌəʊld 'eɪdʒ/ *noun* (no plural)
the part of your life when you are old
old-age pension /ˌəʊld eɪdʒ 'penʃn/ *noun* (no plural)
money that you get from a government or a company when you are old and do not work any more (when you are **retired**)
old-age pensioner /ˌəʊld eɪdʒ 'penʃənə(r)/ *noun*
a person who has an old-age pension ❂ The short form is **OAP**.

old-fashioned /ˌəʊld 'fæʃnd/ *adjective*
not modern; that people do not often use or wear now: *Clothes from the 1970s look*

old-fashioned now.

olive /'ɒlɪv/ *noun*
a small green or black fruit, that people eat or make into oil

omelette /'ɒmlət/ *noun*
eggs that you mix together and cook in oil: *a cheese omelette*

omit /ə'mɪt/ *verb* (**omits, omitting, omitted**)
not include something; leave something out: *Omit question 2 and do question 3.*
❂ It is more usual to say **leave out**.

on /ɒn/ *preposition, adverb*
1 a word that shows where: *Your book is on the table.* ◇ *The number is on the door.* ◇ *There is a good film on TV tonight.* ◇ *I've got a cut on my hand.*
☞ picture on page 125
2 a word that shows when: *My birthday is on 6 May.* ◇ *I'll see you on Monday.*
☞ Look at page 297.
3 a word that shows that somebody or something continues: *You can't stop here – drive on.*
4 about: *a book on cars*
5 working; being used: *Is the light on or off?*
6 using something: *I spoke to Jane on the telephone.* ◇ *I came here on foot* (= walking).
7 covering your body: *Put your coat on.*
8 happening: *What's on at the cinema?*
9 when something happens: *She telephoned me on her return from New York.*
on and on without stopping: *He went* (= talked) *on and on about his girlfriend.*

once /wʌns/ *adverb*
1 one time: *I've only been to Spain once.* ◇ *He phones us once a week* (= once every week).
2 at some time in the past: *This house was once a school.*
at once **1** immediately; now: *Come here at once!* **2** at the same time: *I can't do two things at once!*
for once this time only: *For once I agree with you.*
once again, once more again, as before: *Can you explain it to me once more?*
once or twice a few times; not often: *I've only met them once or twice.*
once *conjunction*
as soon as: *Once you've finished your homework you can go out.*

one[1] /wʌn/ *noun, adjective*
1 the number 1: *One and one make two* (1 + 1 = 2). ◇ *Only one person spoke.* ◇ *One of my friends is an actress.*
2 a: *I saw her one day last week.*
3 only: *You are the one person I can trust.*
4 the same: *All the birds flew in one direction.*
one by one first one, then the next, etc; one at a time: *Please come in one by one.*

one[2] /wʌn/ *pronoun*
a word that you say instead of the name of a person or thing: *I've got some bananas. Do you want one?* ◇ *'Which shirt do you prefer?' 'This one.'* ◇ *Here are some books – take the ones you want.*
one another words that show that somebody does the same thing as another person: *John and Mark looked at one another* (= John looked at Mark and Mark looked at John).

one[3] /wʌn/ *pronoun*
any person; a person: *One can fly to New York in three hours.* ✪ It is formal to use 'one' in this way. We often use **you**.

oneself /wʌn'self/ *pronoun*
1 a word that shows the same person as 'one' in a sentence: *to hurt oneself*
2 a word that makes 'one' stronger: *One can do it oneself.*
by oneself 1 alone; without other people **2** without help

one-way /ˌwʌn 'weɪ/ *adjective*
1 A one-way street is a street where you can drive in one direction only.
2 A one-way ticket is a ticket to travel to a place, but not back again. ✪ opposite: **return**

onion /'ʌniən/ *noun*
a round vegetable with a strong taste and smell: *onion soup* ◇ *Cutting onions can make you cry.*

onion

only[1] /'əʊnli/ *adjective*
with no others: *She's the only girl in her class – all the other students are boys.*
an only child a child who has no brothers or sisters

only[2] /'əʊnli/ *adverb*
and nobody or nothing else; no more than: *I invited twenty people to the party, but*
only five came. ◇ *We can't have dinner now. It's only four o'clock!* ◇ *We only waited five minutes.*
only just 1 a short time before: *We've only just arrived.* **2** almost not: *We only just had enough money to pay for the meal.*

only[3] /'əʊnli/ *conjunction*
but: *I like this bag, only it's too expensive.*

onto, on to /'ɒntə/, /'ɒntu/, /'ɒntuː/ *preposition*
to a place on somebody or something: *The cat jumped on to the table.* ◇ *The bottle fell onto the floor.*

onwards /'ɒnwədz/, **onward** /'ɒnwəd/ *adverb*
1 and after: *I shall be at home from eight o'clock onwards.*
2 forward; further: *The soldiers marched onwards until they came to a bridge.*

open[1] /'əʊpən/ *adjective*
1 not closed, so that people or things can go in or out: *Leave the windows open.* ☞ picture on page 263
2 not closed or covered, so that you can see inside: *The book lay open on the table.* ◇ *an open box*
3 ready for people to go in: *The bank is open from 9 a.m. to 4 p.m.*
4 that anybody can do or visit, for example: *The competition is open to all children under the age of 14.*
5 with not many buildings, trees, etc: *open fields*
in the open air outside: *We had our lunch in the open air.*

open[2] /'əʊpən/ *verb* (**opens**, **opening**, **opened** /'əʊpənd/)
1 move so that people or things can go in, out or through: *It was hot, so I opened a window.* ◇ *The door opened and a man came in.*
2 move so that something is not closed or covered: *Open your eyes!*
3 fold something out or back, to show what is inside: *Open your books.*
4 be ready for people to use; start: *Banks don't open on Sundays.*
5 say that something can start or is ready: *The President opened the new hospital.*
✪ opposite: **close** or **shut**

open[3] /'əʊpən/ *noun* (no plural)
in the open outside: *I like to be out in the open at weekends.*

open-air /ˌəʊpən 'eə(r)/ *adjective*
outside: *an open-air concert*

opener /'əʊpnə(r)/ *noun*
a thing that you use for opening tins or bottles: *a tin-opener*

opening /'əʊpnɪŋ/ *noun*
1 a hole or space in something where people or things can go in and out; a hole: *The sheep got out of the field through an opening in the fence.*
2 when something is opened: *the opening of the new theatre*

openly /'əʊpənli/ *adverb*
not secretly; without trying to hide anything: *She told me openly that she didn't agree.*

opera /'ɒprə/ *noun*
a play where the actors sing most of the words: *Do you like opera?* ◇ *We went to see an opera by Verdi..*

opera-house /'ɒprə haʊs/ *noun*
a building where you can see operas

operate /'ɒpəreɪt/ *verb* (**operates, operating, operated**)
1 work or make something work: *How do you operate this machine?* ◇ *I don't know how this computer operates.*
2 cut a person's body to take out or mend a part inside: *The doctor will operate on her leg tomorrow.*
○ A doctor who operates is called a **surgeon**. A surgeon's work is called **surgery**.

operation /ˌɒpə'reɪʃn/ *noun*
1 cutting a person's body to take out or mend a part inside: *He had an operation on his eye.*
2 something that happens, that needs a lot of people or careful planning: *a military operation*

operator /'ɒpəreɪtə(r)/ *noun*
1 a person who makes a machine work: *She's a computer operator.*
2 a person who works for a telephone company and helps people to make calls: *In Britain, you dial 100 for the operator.*

opinion /ə'pɪnɪən/ *noun*
what you think about something: *What's your opinion of his work?* ◇ *In my opinion, (= I think that) she's wrong.*

opponent /ə'pəʊnənt/ *noun*
a person that you fight or argue with, or

play a game against: *The team beat their opponents easily.*

opportunity /ˌɒpə'tju:nəti/ *noun* (*plural* **opportunities**)
a time when you can do something that you want to do; a chance: *I was only in Paris for two days and I didn't get the opportunity to visit the Louvre.*

oppose /ə'pəʊz/ *verb* (**opposes, opposing, opposed** /ə'pəʊzd/)
try to stop or change something because you do not like it: *A lot of people opposed the new law.*
as opposed to something words that you use to show that you are talking about one thing, not something different: *She teaches at the college, as opposed to the university.*
be opposed to something disagree strongly with something: *I am opposed to the plan.*

opposite¹ /'ɒpəzɪt/ *adjective, adverb, preposition*
1 across from where somebody or something is; on the other side: *The church is on the opposite side of the road from my flat.* ◇ *You sit here, and I'll sit opposite.* ◇ *The bank is opposite the supermarket.*
☞ picture on page 125
2 as different as possible: *North is the opposite direction to south.*

opposite² /'ɒpəzɪt/ *noun*
a word or thing that is as different as possible from another word or thing: *'Hot' is the opposite of 'cold'.*

opposition /ˌɒpə'zɪʃn/ *noun* (no plural)
disagreeing with something and trying to stop it: *There was a lot of opposition to the plan.*

optician /ɒp'tɪʃn/ *noun*
a person who finds out how well you can see and sells you glasses ○ The place where an optician works is called an **optician's**.

optimism /'ɒptɪmɪzəm/ *noun* (no plural)
thinking that good things will happen
○ opposite: **pessimism**

optimist /'ɒptɪmɪst/ *noun*
a person who always thinks that good things will happen

optimistic /ˌɒptɪ'mɪstɪk/ *adjective*
If you are optimistic, you think that good

p	b	t	d	k	g	tʃ	dʒ	f	v	θ	ð
pen	**b**ad	**t**ea	**d**id	**c**at	**g**ot	**ch**ain	**j**am	**f**all	**v**an	**th**in	**th**is

things will happen: *I'm optimistic about winning.*

option /ˈɒpʃn/ *noun*
a thing that you can choose: *If you're going to France, there are two options – you can go by plane or by boat.*

optional /ˈɒpʃənl/ *adjective*
that you can choose or not choose: *All students must learn English, but German is optional.* ○ opposite: **compulsory**

or /ɔː(r)/ *conjunction*
1 a word that joins the words for different things that you can choose: *Is it blue or green?* ◇ *Are you coming or not?* ◇ *You can have soup, salad or sandwiches.*
2 if not, then: *Go now, or you'll be late.*

oral /ˈɔːrəl/ *adjective*
spoken, not written: *an oral test in English*

orange[1] /ˈɒrɪndʒ/
noun
a round fruit with a colour between red and yellow, and a thick skin: *orange juice*

orange

orange[2] /ˈɒrɪndʒ/ *adjective*
with a colour that is between red and yellow: *orange paint*
orange *noun*
Orange is my favourite colour.

orbit /ˈɔːbɪt/ *noun*
the path of one thing that is moving round another thing in space
orbit *verb* (**orbits, orbiting, orbited**)
move round something in space: *The spacecraft is orbiting the moon.*

orchard /ˈɔːtʃəd/ *noun*
a place where a lot of fruit trees grow

orchestra /ˈɔːkɪstrə/ *noun*
a big group of people who play different musical instruments together

ordeal /ɔːˈdiːl/ *noun*
a very bad or painful thing that happens to somebody: *He was lost in the mountains for a week without food or water – it was a terrible ordeal.*

order[1] /ˈɔːdə(r)/ *noun*
1 (no plural) the way that you place people or things together: *The names are in alphabetical order* (= with the names that begin with A first, then B, then C, etc).
2 (no plural) when everything is in the

right place or everybody is doing the right thing: *Our teacher likes order in the classroom.*
3 (*plural* **orders**) words that tell somebody to do something: *Soldiers must always obey orders.*
4 (*plural* **orders**) asking somebody to make, send or bring you something: *The waiter came and took our order* (= we told him what we wanted to eat).
in order with everything in the right place: *Are these papers in order?*
in order to so that you can do something: *We arrived early in order to buy our tickets.*
out of order not working: *I couldn't ring you – the phone was out of order.*

order[2] /ˈɔːdə(r)/ *verb* (**orders, ordering, ordered** /ˈɔːdəd/)
1 tell somebody that they must do something: *The doctor ordered me to stay in bed.*
2 say that you want something to be made, sent, brought, etc: *The shop didn't have the book I wanted, so I ordered it.* ◇ *When the waiter came I ordered an omelette.*

ordinary /ˈɔːdnri/ *adjective*
normal; not special or unusual: *Simon was wearing a suit, but I was in my ordinary clothes.*
out of the ordinary unusual; strange: *Did you see anything out of the ordinary?*

ore /ɔː(r)/ *noun*
rock or earth from which you get metal: *iron ore*

organ /ˈɔːgən/ *noun*
1 a part of the body that has a special purpose, for example the heart or the liver
2 a big musical instrument like a piano, with pipes that air goes through to make sounds: *She plays the organ in church.*

organic /ɔːˈgænɪk/ *adjective*
1 of living things: *organic chemistry*
2 grown in a natural way, without using chemicals: *organic vegetables*

organization /ˌɔːgənaɪˈzeɪʃn/ *noun*
1 (*plural* **organizations**) a group of people who work together for a special purpose: *He works for an organization that helps old people.*
2 (no plural) planning or arranging something: *She's busy with the organization of her daughter's wedding.*

s	z	ʃ	ʒ	h	m	n	ŋ	l	r	j	w
so	**zoo**	**shoe**	vision	**hat**	**man**	**no**	sing	**leg**	**red**	**yes**	**wet**

organize /'ɔ:gənaɪz/ *verb* (**organizes, organizing, organized** /'ɔ:gənaɪzd/)
plan or arrange something: *Our teacher has organized a visit to the museum.*

oriental /ˌɔ:ri'entl/ *adjective*
of or from eastern countries, for example China or Japan: *oriental art*

origin /'ɒrɪdʒɪn/ *noun*
the beginning; the start of something: *Many English words have Latin origins.*

original /ə'rɪdʒənl/ *adjective*
1 first; earliest: *I have the car now, but my sister was the original owner.*
2 new and different: *His poems are very original.*
3 real, not copied: *original paintings*
original *noun*
This is a copy of the painting – the original is in the National Gallery.

originally /ə'rɪdʒənəli/ *adverb*
in the beginning; at first: *This building was originally the home of a rich family, but now it's a hotel.*

ornament /'ɔ:nəmənt/ *noun*
a thing that we have because it is beautiful, not because it is useful: *Their house is full of china ornaments.*

ornamental /ˌɔ:nə'mentl/ *adjective*
There is an ornamental pond in the garden.

orphan /'ɔ:fn/ *noun*
a child whose mother and father are dead

ostrich /'ɒstrɪtʃ/ *noun* (*plural* **ostriches**)
a very big bird from Africa. Ostriches have very long legs and can run fast, but they cannot fly.

other /'ʌðə(r)/ *adjective, pronoun*
as well as or different from the one or ones I have said: *Carmen and Maria are Spanish, but the other students in my class are Japanese.* ◊ *I can only find one other.* ◊ *Have you seen the other one?* ◊ *I saw her on the other side of the road.* ◊ *John and Claire arrived at nine o'clock, but the others* (= the other people) *were late.*
other than except; apart from: *I haven't told anybody other than you.*
some . . . or other words that show you are not sure: *I can't find my glasses. I know I put them somewhere or other.*
the other day not many days ago: *I saw your brother the other day.*

otherwise /'ʌðəwaɪz/ *adverb*
1 in all other ways: *The house is a bit small, but otherwise it's very nice.*
2 in a different way: *Most people agreed, but Rachel thought otherwise.*
otherwise *conjunction*
if not: *Hurry up, otherwise you'll be late.*

ouch /aʊtʃ/
You say 'ouch' when you suddenly feel pain: *Ouch! That hurts!*

ought to /'ɔ:t tə/, /'ɔ:t tu/, /'ɔ:t tu:/ *modal verb*
1 words that you use to tell or ask somebody what is the right thing to do: *It's late – you ought to go home.* ◊ *Ought I to ring her?*
2 words that you use to say what you think will happen or what you think is true: *Tim has worked very hard, so he ought to pass the exam.* ◊ *That film ought to be good.*
☞ Look at the Note on page 227 to find out more about **modal verbs**.

ounce /aʊns/ *noun*
a measure of weight (= 28.35 grams). There are 16 ounces in a **pound**: *four ounces of flour* ✪ The short way of writing 'ounce' is **oz**: *6 oz butter*
☞ Note at **pound**

our /ɑ:(r)/, /'aʊə(r)/ *adjective*
of us: *This is our house.*

ours /ɑ:z/, /'aʊəz/ *pronoun*
something that belongs to us: *Your car is the same as ours.*

ourselves /ɑ:'selvz/, /aʊə'selvz/ *pronoun* (plural)
1 a word that shows the same people that you have just talked about: *We made ourselves some coffee.*
2 a word that makes 'we' stronger: *We built the house ourselves.*
by ourselves **1** alone; without other people: *We went on holiday by ourselves.*
2 without help

out /aʊt/ *adjective, adverb*
1 away from a place; from inside: *When you go out, please close the door.* ◊ *She opened the box and took out a gun.*
2 not at home or not in the place where you work: *I phoned Steve but he was out.* ◊ *I went out to the cinema last night.*
3 not burning or shining: *The fire went out.*
4 not hidden; that you can see: *Look! The*

sun is out! ◇ *All the flowers are out* (= open).
5 in a loud voice: *She cried out in pain.*

outbreak /'aʊtbreɪk/ *noun*
the sudden start of something: *There have been outbreaks of fighting in the city.*

outdoor /'aʊtdɔ:(r)/ *adjective*
done or used outside a building: *Football and cricket are outdoor games.* ○ opposite: **indoor**

outdoors /ˌaʊt'dɔ:z/ *adverb*
outside a building: *In summer we sometimes eat outdoors.* ○ opposite: **indoors**

outer /'aʊtə(r)/ *adjective*
on the outside; far from the centre: *I live in outer London.* ○ opposite: **inner**

outfit /'aʊtfɪt/ *noun*
a set of clothes that you wear together: *I've bought a new outfit for the party.*

outing /'aʊtɪŋ/ *noun*
a short journey to enjoy yourself: *We went on an outing to the zoo last Saturday.*

outline /'aʊtlaɪn/ *noun*
a line that shows the shape or edge of something: *It was dark, but we could see the outline of the castle on the hill.*

outlook /'aʊtlʊk/ *noun*
what will probably happen: *The outlook for the weekend: dry and sunny weather in all parts of Britain.*

out of /'aʊt əv/ *preposition*
1 words that show where from: *She took a cake out of the box.* ◇ *She got out of bed.* ☞ picture on page 128
2 not in: *Fish can't live out of water.*
3 by using something; from: *He made a table out of some old pieces of wood.*
4 from that number: *Nine out of ten people think that the government is right.*
5 because of: *Ann helped us out of kindness.*
6 without: *She's been out of work for six months.*

output /'aʊtpʊt/ *noun* (no plural)
the amount of things that somebody or something has made or done: *What was the factory's output last year?*

outside¹ /ˌaʊt'saɪd/ *noun*
the part of something that is away from the middle: *The outside of a pear is green or yellow and the inside is white.*

outside² /ˌaʊt'saɪd/ *adjective*
away from the middle of something: *the outside walls of a house*

outside³ /ˌaʊt'saɪd/ *preposition, adverb*
not in; in or to a place that is not inside a building: *I left my bicycle outside the shop.* ◇ *Come outside and see the garden!*

outskirts /'aʊtskɜ:ts/ *noun* (plural)
the parts of a town or city that are far from the centre: *The airport is on the outskirts of the city.*

outstanding /ˌaʊt'stændɪŋ/ *adjective*
very good; much better than others: *Her work is outstanding.*

outward /'aʊtwəd/, **outwards** /'aʊtwədz/ *adverb*
towards the outside: *The windows open outwards.* ○ opposite: **inward** or **inwards**

oval /'əʊvl/ *noun*
a shape like an egg ☞ picture on page 161
oval *adjective*
with a shape like an egg: *an oval mirror*

oven /'ʌvn/ *noun*
the part of a cooker that has a door. You put food inside an oven to cook it.

over¹ /'əʊvə(r)/ *adverb, preposition*
1 above something; higher than something: *A plane flew over our heads.* ◇ *There is a picture over the fireplace.*
2 on somebody or something so that it covers them: *She put a blanket over the sleeping child.*
3 down: *I fell over in the street.*
4 across; to the other side of something: *The dog jumped over the wall.* ◇ *a bridge over a river* ☞ picture on page 128
5 so that the other side is on top: *Turn the cassette over.*
6 more than a number, price, etc: *She lived in Spain for over 20 years.* ◇ *This game is for children of ten and over.*
7 not used: *There are a lot of cakes left over from the party.*
8 from one place to another: *Come over and see us on Saturday.*
9 a word that shows that you repeat something: *He said the same thing over and over again* (= many times). ◇ *The audience liked the song so much that she*

ʌ	ɜ:	ə	eɪ	əʊ	aɪ	aʊ	ɔɪ	ɪə	eə	ʊə
cup	**bird**	**about**	**say**	**go**	**five**	**now**	**boy**	**near**	**hair**	**pure**

sang it all over again (= again, from the beginning).
10 finished: *My exams are over.*
all over in every part: *She travels all over the world.*
over here here: *Come over here!*
over there there: *Go over there and see if you can help.*

over-² /'əʊvə(r)/ *prefix*
You can add **over-** to the beginning of a lot of words to give them the meaning 'too much', for example:
overeat = eat too much
oversleep = sleep too long

overall¹ /ˌəʊvər'ɔːl/ *adjective*
of everything; total: *The overall cost of the repairs will be about £350.*
overall *adverb*
How much will it cost overall?

overall² /'əʊvərɔːl/ *noun*
a kind of coat that you wear over your clothes to keep them clean when you are working
overalls /'əʊvərɔːlz/ *noun* (plural)
a piece of clothing that covers your legs, body and arms. You wear it over your other clothes to keep them clean when you are working.

overboard /'əʊvəbɔːd/ *adverb*
over the side of a boat and into the water: *She fell overboard.*

overcoat /'əʊvəkəʊt/ *noun*
a long thick coat that you wear in cold weather

overcome /ˌəʊvə'kʌm/ *verb* (**overcomes**, **overcoming**, **overcame** /ˌəʊvə'keɪm/, **has overcome**)
find an answer to a difficult thing in your life; control something: *He overcame his fear of flying.*

overcrowded /ˌəʊvə'kraʊdɪd/ *adjective*
too full of people: *The trains are overcrowded on Friday evenings.*

overdue /ˌəʊvə'djuː/ *adjective*
late: *Our landlady is angry because the rent is overdue.*

overflow /ˌəʊvə'fləʊ/ *verb* (**overflows**, **overflowing**, **overflowed** /ˌəʊvə'fləʊd/)
come over the edge of something because

there is too much in it: *After the rain, the river overflowed its banks.*

overgrown /ˌəʊvə'grəʊn/ *adjective*
covered with plants that have grown too big: *The house was empty and the garden was overgrown.*

overhead /'əʊvəhed/ *adjective*
above your head: *an overhead light*
overhead /ˌəʊvə'hed/ *adverb*
A plane flew overhead.

overhear /ˌəʊvə'hɪə(r)/ *verb* (**overhears**, **overhearing**, **overheard** /ˌəʊvə'hɜːd/, **has overheard**)
hear what somebody is saying when they are speaking to another person, not to you: *I overheard Louise saying that she was unhappy.*

overlap /ˌəʊvə'læp/ *verb* (**overlaps**, **overlapping**, **overlapped** /ˌəʊvə'læpt/)
When two things overlap, part of one thing covers part of the other thing: *The tiles on the roof overlap.*

overlook /ˌəʊvə'lʊk/ *verb* (**overlooks**, **overlooking**, **overlooked** /ˌəʊvə'lʊkt/)
1 look down on something from above: *My room overlooks the garden.*
2 not see or notice something: *He overlooked a spelling mistake.*

overnight /ˌəʊvə'naɪt/ *adjective, adverb*
for or during the night: *They stayed at our house overnight.* ◇ *an overnight journey*

overpass /'əʊvəpɑːs/ *American English for* **flyover**

overseas /ˌəʊvə'siːz/ *adjective, adverb*
in, to or from another country across the sea: *There are many overseas students in Britain.* ◇ *She travels overseas a lot.*

oversleep /ˌəʊvə'sliːp/ *verb* (**oversleeps**, **oversleeping**, **overslept** /ˌəʊvə'slept/, **has overslept**)
sleep too long and not wake up at the right time: *I overslept and was late for work.*

overtake /ˌəʊvə'teɪk/ *verb* (**overtakes**, **overtaking**, **overtook** /ˌəʊvə'tʊk/, **has overtaken** /ˌəʊvə'teɪkən/)
go past somebody or something that is going more slowly: *The car overtook a bus.*

overtime /'əʊvətaɪm/ *noun* (no plural)
extra time that you spend at work: *I have done a lot of overtime this week.*

p	b	t	d	k	g	tʃ	dʒ	f	v	θ	ð
pen	**bad**	**tea**	**did**	**cat**	**got**	**chain**	**jam**	**fall**	**van**	**thin**	**this**

overweight /ˌəʊvə'weɪt/ *adjective*
too heavy or fat: *The doctor said I was overweight and that I should eat less.*

overwhelming /ˌəʊvə'welmɪŋ/ *adjective*
very great or strong: *an overwhelming feeling of loneliness*

ow /aʊ/
You say 'ow' when you suddenly feel pain: *Ow! You're standing on my foot.*

owe /əʊ/ *verb* (**owes, owing, owed** /əʊd/)
1 have to pay money to somebody because they have given you something: *I lent you £5 last week and £5 the week before, so you owe me £10.*
2 feel that you have something because of what another person has done: *She owes her life to the man who pulled her out of the river.*

owing to /'əʊɪŋ tu/ *preposition*
because of: *The train was late owing to the bad weather.*

owl /aʊl/ *noun*
a bird that flies at night and eats small animals

owl

own¹ /əʊn/
adjective, pronoun
You use 'own' to say that something belongs to a person or thing: *Is that your own camera or did you borrow it?* ◇ *I have my own room* (= for me and nobody else). ✪ Be careful! You cannot use 'own' after 'a' or 'the'. You cannot say: *I would like an own room.* You say: *I would like my own room.* (or: *I would like a room of my own.*)

get your own back on somebody do something bad to somebody who has done something bad to you: *He said he would get his own back on me for breaking his watch.*

of your own that belongs to you and not to anybody else: *I want a home of my own.*

on your own 1 alone: *She lives on her own.* **2** without help: *I can't move this box on my own – can you help me?*

own² /əʊn/ *verb* (**owns, owning, owned** /əʊnd/)
have something that is yours: *We don't own our flat – we rent it.*

own up say that you have done something wrong: *Nobody owned up to breaking the window.*

owner /'əʊnə(r)/ *noun*
a person who has something: *Who is the owner of that red car?*

ox /ɒks/ *noun* (*plural* **oxen** /'ɒksn/)
a male cow. Oxen are sometimes used to pull or carry heavy things on farms.

oxygen /'ɒksɪdʒən/ *noun* (no plural)
a gas in the air. Plants and animals need oxygen to live.

oz *short way of writing* **ounce**

ozone /'əʊzəʊn/ *noun* (no plural)
a gas in the air

Pp

p
1 /piː/ *short for* **pence**
2 *short way of writing* **page 1**

pace /peɪs/ *noun*
1 a step: *Take two paces forward!*
2 how fast you do something or how fast something happens: *The race began at a fast pace.*
keep pace with somebody or **something** go as fast as somebody or something: *She couldn't keep pace with the other runners.*

pack¹ /pæk/ *noun*
1 a group of things that you buy together: *I bought a pack of five exercise books.*
2 a group of animals that hunt together: *a pack of wolves*
3 *American English for* **packet**
pack of cards /ˌpæk əv 'kɑːdz/ *noun*
a set of 52 playing-cards ☞ Look at **card.**

s	z	ʃ	ʒ	h	m	n	ŋ	l	r	j	w
so	**zoo**	**shoe**	vision	**hat**	**man**	**no**	sing	**leg**	**red**	**yes**	**wet**

pack² /pæk/ *verb* (**packs, packing, packed** /pækt/)
1 put things into a bag or suitcase before you go somewhere: *Have you packed your suitcase?* ◇ *Don't forget to pack your toothbrush.*
2 put things into a box, bag, etc: *Pack all these books into boxes.*
⊙ opposite: **unpack**
pack up 1 stop doing something: *At two o'clock we packed up and went home.* **2** If a machine packs up, it stops working.

packed lunch /ˌpækt ˈlʌntʃ/ *noun*
sandwiches and other things that you take with you to eat at school or work

package /ˈpækɪdʒ/ *noun*
something that is wrapped in paper

package holiday /ˌpækɪdʒ ˈhɒlədeɪ/, **package tour** /ˈpækɪdʒ tʊə(r)/ *noun*
a complete holiday where a travel company sells you your hotel, flight, etc together

packaging /ˈpækɪdʒɪŋ/ *noun* (no plural)
material like paper, cardboard or plastic that is used to wrap things that you buy or that you send

packed /pækt/ *adjective*
full: *The train was packed.*

packet /ˈpækɪt/ *noun*
a small box or bag that you buy things in: *a packet of cigarettes* ◇ *an empty cigarette packet* ◇ *a packet of biscuits* ☞ picture at **container**

pact /pækt/ *noun*
an important agreement to do something: *The two countries signed a peace pact.*

pad /pæd/ *noun*
1 some pieces of paper that are joined together at one end: *a writing pad*
2 a thick flat piece of soft material: *Footballers wear pads on their legs to protect them.* ◇ *I used a pad of cotton wool to clean the cut.*

paddle¹ /ˈpædl/ *noun*
a piece of wood with a flat end, that you use for moving a small boat through water
paddle *verb* (**paddles, paddling, paddled** /ˈpædld/)
move a small boat through water with a paddle: *We paddled up the river.*

paddle² /ˈpædl/ *verb* (**paddles, paddling, paddled** /ˈpædld/)
walk in water that is not deep, with no shoes on your feet: *The children were paddling in the sea.*

padlock /ˈpædlɒk/ *noun*
a lock that you use on things like gates and bicycles

page /peɪdʒ/ *noun*
1 one side of a piece of paper in a book, magazine or newspaper: *Please turn to page 120.* ◇ *What page is the story on?*
⊙ The short way of writing 'page' is **p.**
2 one piece of paper in a book, magazine or newspaper

paid *form of* **pay¹**

pain /peɪn/ *noun*
1 (*plural* **pains**) the feeling that you have in your body when you are hurt or ill: *I've got a pain in my leg.* ◇ *He's in pain.*
2 (no plural) unhappiness

painful /ˈpeɪnfl/ *adjective*
Something that is painful gives pain: *I've cut my leg – it's very painful.*

paint

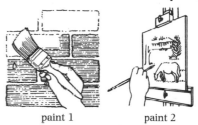

paint 1   paint 2

paint /peɪnt/ *noun*
a coloured liquid that you put on things with a brush, to change the colour or to make a picture: *red paint* ◇ *Is the paint dry yet?*
paint *verb* (**paints, painting, painted**)
1 put paint on something to change the colour: *We painted the walls grey.*
2 make a picture of somebody or something with paints: *I'm painting some flowers.* ◇ *My sister paints very well.*

paintbrush /ˈpeɪntbrʌʃ/ *noun* (*plural* **paintbrushes**)
a brush that you use for painting

painter /ˈpeɪntə(r)/ *noun*
1 a person whose job is to paint things like walls or houses

2 a person who paints pictures: *Picasso was a famous painter.*

painting /'peɪntɪŋ/ *noun*
a picture that somebody makes with paint: *a painting by Rembrandt*

pair /peə(r)/ *noun*
1 two things of the same kind that you use together: *a pair of shoes* ◇ *a pair of earrings* ☞ picture on page 261
2 a thing with two parts that are joined together: *a pair of glasses* ◇ *a pair of scissors* ◇ *I bought two pairs of trousers.*
3 two people or animals together: *a pair of ducks*
in pairs with two things or people together: *Shoes are only sold in pairs.*

pajamas *American English for* **pyjamas**

palace /'pæləs/ *noun*
a very large house where a king, queen or another important person lives: *The Queen lives at Buckingham Palace.*

pale /peɪl/ *adjective* (**paler, palest**)
1 with not much colour in your face; white: *Are you ill? You look pale.*
2 with a light colour; not strong or dark: *a pale-blue dress* ○ opposite: **dark** or **deep**

palm /pɑːm/ *noun*
1 the flat part of the front of your hand ☞ picture on page 126
2 (*also* **palm-tree**) a tree that grows in hot countries, with no branches and a lot of big leaves at the top: *a coconut palm*

pan /pæn/ *noun*
a metal pot that you use for cooking: *a frying-pan* ◇ *a saucepan*

pancake /'pænkeɪk/ *noun*
a very thin round thing that you eat. You make pancakes with flour, eggs and milk and cook them in a frying-pan.

panda /'pændə/ *noun*
a large black and white animal like a bear, that lives in China

pane /peɪn/ *noun*
a piece of glass in a window

panel /'pænl/ *noun*
1 a flat piece of wood, metal or glass that is part of a door, wall or ceiling
2 a flat part on a machine, where there are

things to help you control it: *the control panel of a TV*

panic /'pænɪk/ *noun*
a sudden feeling of fear that you cannot control and that makes you do things without thinking carefully: *There was panic in the shop when the fire started.*
panic *verb* (**panics, panicking, panicked** /'pænɪkt/)
Don't panic!

pant /pænt/ *verb* (**pants, panting, panted**)
take in and let out air quickly through your mouth, for example after running or because you are very hot: *The dog was panting.*

panther /'pænθə(r)/ *noun*
a wild animal like a big cat. Panthers are usually black.

pantomime /'pæntəmaɪm/ *noun*
a funny play for children, with singing and dancing. You can usually see pantomimes at Christmas.

pants /pænts/ *noun* (plural)
1 a small piece of clothing that you wear under your other clothes, between the middle of your body and the top of your legs: *a pair of pants*
2 *American English for* **trousers**

paper /'peɪpə(r)/ *noun*
1 (no plural) thin material for writing or drawing on or for wrapping things in: *The pages of this book are made of paper.* ◇ *a sheet of paper* ◇ *a paper bag*
2 (*plural* **papers**) a newspaper: *Have you seen today's paper?*
3 **papers** (plural) important pieces of paper with writing on them: *The police officer asked to see my papers* (= for example, a passport or an identity card).
4 (*plural* **papers**) a group of questions in an examination: *The English paper was easy.*

paperback /'peɪpəbæk/ *noun*
a book with a paper cover ☞ Look at **hardback**.

paper-clip /'peɪpə klɪp/
a small metal thing that you use for holding pieces of paper together

paper-clip

parachute
/'pærəʃuːt/ *noun*
a thing like a big
umbrella that you
have on your back
when you jump out
of an aeroplane and
that opens so that
you will fall to the
ground slowly

parade /pə'reɪd/
noun   **parachute**
a line of people who
are walking together for a special reason,
while other people watch them: *a military
parade*

paradise /'pærədaɪs/ *noun* (no plural)
the place where some people think good
people go after they die; heaven

paragraph /'pærəgrɑːf/ *noun*
a group of lines of writing. A paragraph always begins on a new line.

parallel /'pærəlel/ *adjective*
Parallel lines are straight lines that are always the same distance from each other.
☞ picture on page 161

paralysed /'pærəlaɪzd/ *adjective*
If you are paralysed, you cannot move
your body or a part of it: *After the accident
she was paralysed in both legs.*

paralyzed *American English for* **paralysed**

parcel /'pɑːsl/
noun
something with
paper around it, that
you send or carry:
*She sent a parcel of
books to her aunt.*

                                              parcel

pardon /'pɑːdn/
verb (**pardons, pardoning, pardoned**
/'pɑːdnd/)
forgive somebody for something bad that
they have done ✪ **Forgive** is the word
that we usually use.
pardon? What did you say?
pardon me 1 What did you say? **2** I am
sorry.

parent /'peərənt/ *noun*
a mother or father: *Her parents live in
Italy.* ☞ picture on page 127

parish /'pærɪʃ/ *noun* (*plural* **parishes**)
an area that has its own church and priest

park¹ /pɑːk/ *noun*
a large place with grass and trees, where
anybody can go to walk, play games, etc:
We had a picnic in the park. ◊ *Hyde Park*

park² /pɑːk/ *verb* (**parks, parking,
parked** /pɑːkt/)
stop and leave a car, lorry, etc somewhere
for a time: *You can't park in this street.*
◊ *My car is parked opposite the bank.*
parking *noun* (no plural)
The sign says 'No Parking'. ◊ *I can't find
a parking space.*
parking-lot /'pɑːkɪŋ lɒt/ *American
English for* **car park**
parking-meter /'pɑːkɪŋ miːtə(r)/ *noun*
a machine that you put money into to pay
for parking a car next to it

parliament /'pɑːləmənt/ *noun*
the people who make the laws in a country: *the French parliament*

✪ In the United Kingdom, the group of
people who make the laws meet in the
Houses of Parliament in London. The
two parts of the Houses of Parliament are
called the **House of Commons** (where
the **Members of Parliament** meet) and
the **House of Lords.**

parrot /'pærət/ *noun*
a bird with very bright feathers that can
copy what people say

parsley /'pɑːsli/ *noun* (no plural)
a small plant that you use in cooking

part¹ /pɑːt/ *noun*
1 some, but not all of something; one of
the pieces of something: *We spent part of
the day on the beach.* ◊ *Which part of
Spain do you come from?*
2 a piece of a machine: *Is there a shop
near here that sells bicycle parts?*
3 the person you are in a play or film: *She
played the part of Ophelia.*
take part in something do something
together with other people: *All the students took part in the concert.*

part² /pɑːt/ *verb* (**parts, parting, parted**)
go away from each other: *We parted at the
station. John got on the train and I went
home.*

participate /pɑː'tɪsɪpeɪt/ *verb* (**particip-
ates, participating, participated**)
do something together with other people:

p	b	t	d	k	g	tʃ	dʒ	f	v	θ	ð
pen	**bad**	**tea**	**did**	**cat**	**got**	**chain**	**jam**	**fall**	**van**	**thin**	**this**

Ten countries participated in the discussions.

participant /pɑːˈtɪsɪpənt/ *noun*
a person who does something together with other people

participation /pɑːˌtɪsɪˈpeɪʃn/ *noun* (no plural)
doing something together with other people

participle /ˈpɑːtɪsɪpl/ *noun*
a form of a verb: *The present participle of 'eat' is 'eating' and the past participle is 'eaten'.*

particular /pəˈtɪkjələ(r)/ *adjective*
1 one only, and not any other: *You need a particular kind of flour to make bread.*
2 special or more than usual: *The road is very icy, so take particular care when you are driving.*
3 If you are particular, you want something to be exactly right: *He's very particular about the food he eats.*
in particular more than others: *Is there anything in particular you want to do this weekend?*

particularly /pəˈtɪkjələli/ *adverb*
more than others; especially: *I'm particularly tired today.* ◇ *I don't particularly like fish.*

parties *plural of* **party**

parting /ˈpɑːtɪŋ/ *noun*
1 a line that you make on your head by combing your hair in different directions
2 when people leave each other: *It was a sad parting for Sarah and Tom.*

partly /ˈpɑːtli/ *adverb*
not completely but in some way: *The window was partly open.* ◇ *The accident was partly my fault and partly the other driver's.*

partner /ˈpɑːtnə(r)/ *noun*
1 your husband, wife, boyfriend or girlfriend
2 a person you are dancing with, or playing a game with
3 one of the people who owns a business

partnership /ˈpɑːtnəʃɪp/ *noun*
being partners: *The two sisters went into partnership and opened a shop.*

part of speech /ˌpɑːt əv ˈspiːtʃ/ *noun*
'Noun', 'verb', 'adjective' and 'adverb' are parts of speech.

part-time /ˌpɑːt ˈtaɪm/ *adjective, adverb*
for only a part of the day or week: *I've got a part-time job as a secretary.* ◇ *Jane works part-time.* ☞ Look at **full-time**.

party /ˈpɑːti/ *noun* (*plural* **parties**)
1 a meeting of friends, often in somebody's house, to eat, drink and perhaps dance: *We're having a party this Saturday. Can you come?* ◇ *a birthday party*
2 a group of people who have the same ideas about politics: *the Labour Party*
3 a group of people who are travelling or working together: *a party of tourists*

pass¹ /pɑːs/ *noun* (*plural* **passes**)
1 a special piece of paper or card that says you can go somewhere or do something: *You need a pass to get into the factory.*
2 kicking, throwing or hitting a ball to somebody in a game
3 doing well enough in an examination: *How many passes did you get in your exams?*
4 a road or way through mountains: *the Brenner Pass*

pass² /pɑːs/ *verb* (**passes**, **passing**, **passed** /pɑːst/)
1 go by somebody or something: *She passed me in the street.* ◇ *Do you pass any shops on your way to the station?*
2 give something to somebody: *Could you pass me the salt, please?*
3 go by: *A week passed before his letter arrived.*
4 do well enough in an examination or test: *Did you pass your driving test?* ✪ opposite: **fail**
5 spend time: *How did you pass the time in hospital?*

pass on give or tell something to another person: *Will you pass on a message to Mike for me?*

pass through go through a place: *The train passes through Oxford on its way to London.*

passage /ˈpæsɪdʒ/ *noun*
1 a short part of a book or speech: *We studied a passage from the story for homework.*
2 a narrow way, for example between two buildings

passenger /ˈpæsɪndʒə(r)/ *noun*
a person who is travelling in a car, bus,

s	z	ʃ	ʒ	h	m	n	ŋ	l	r	j	w
so	**zoo**	**shoe**	vision	**hat**	**man**	**no**	sing	**leg**	**red**	**yes**	**wet**

train, plane, etc, but not the person who is driving it: *The plane was carrying 200 passengers.*

passer-by /ˈpɑːsə baɪ/ *noun* (*plural* **passers-by**)
a person who is walking past you in the street: *I asked a passer-by where the museum was.*

passion /ˈpæʃn/ *noun*
a very strong feeling, usually of love, but sometimes of anger or hate
passionate /ˈpæʃənət/ *adjective*
with very strong feelings: *a passionate kiss*

passive /ˈpæsɪv/ *noun* (no plural)
the form of a verb that shows that the action is done by a person or thing to another person or thing: *In the sentence 'The car was stolen by thieves', the verb is in the passive.* ✪ opposite: **active**

passport /ˈpɑːspɔːt/ *noun*
a small book with your name and photograph in it. You must take it with you when you travel to other countries.

password /ˈpɑːswɜːd/ *noun*
a secret word that you must say to enter a place

past¹ /pɑːst/ *noun* (no plural)
1 the time before now, and the things that happened then: *We learn about the past in history lessons.* ◇ *In the past, many people had large families.*
2 (*also* **past tense**) the form of a verb that you use to talk about the time before now: *The past tense of the verb 'go' is 'went'.*
☞ Look at **present** and **future**.
past *adjective*
1 of the time that has gone: *We will forget your past mistakes.*
2 last; just before now: *He has been ill for the past week.*

past² /pɑːst/ *preposition, adverb*
1 a word that shows how many minutes after the hour: *It's two minutes past four.* ◇ *It's half past seven.* ☞ Look at page 164.
2 from one side of somebody or something to the other; by; on the other side of somebody or something: *Go past the cinema, then turn left.* ◇ *The bus went past without stopping.*

paste /peɪst/ *noun*
soft wet stuff, sometimes used for sticking paper to things: *Mix the powder with wa-*

ter to make a paste.

pastime /ˈpɑːstaɪm/ *noun*
something that you like doing when you are not working: *Painting is her favourite pastime.*

pastry /ˈpeɪstri/ *noun*
1 (no plural) a mixture of flour, fat and water that is used for making pies
2 (*plural* **pastries**) a small cake made with pastry

pat /pæt/ *verb* (**pats**, **patting**, **patted**)
touch somebody or something lightly with your hand flat: *She patted the dog on the head.*
pat *noun*
He gave me a pat on the shoulder.

patch /pætʃ/ *noun* (*plural* **patches**)
1 a piece of cloth that you use to cover a hole in things like clothes: *I sewed a patch on my jeans.*
2 a small piece of something that is not the same as the other parts: *a black cat with a white patch on its back*

pâté /ˈpæteɪ/ *noun* (no plural)
thick food made from meat, fish or vegetables, that you eat on bread

path /pɑːθ/ *noun* (*plural* **paths** /pɑːðz/)
a way across a piece of land, where people can walk: *a path through the woods*

patience /ˈpeɪʃns/ *noun* (no plural)
staying calm and not getting angry when you are waiting for something, or when you have problems: *Learning to play the piano takes hard work and patience.*
✪ opposite: **impatience**
lose patience with somebody become angry with somebody: *She was walking so slowly that her sister finally lost patience with her.*

patient¹ /ˈpeɪʃnt/ *adjective*
able to stay calm and not get angry when you are waiting for something or when you have problems: *Just sit there and be patient. Your mum will be here soon.*
✪ opposite: **impatient**
patiently *adverb*
She waited patiently for the bus.

patient² /ˈpeɪʃnt/ *noun*
a sick person that a doctor is looking after

patrol /pəˈtrəʊl/ *noun*
a group of people, ships, aircraft, etc that

i:	i	ɪ	e	æ	ɑː	ɒ	ɔ:	ʊ	u	u:
see	happy	sit	ten	cat	father	got	saw	put	situation	too

go round a place to see that everything is all right: *an army patrol*
on patrol going round a place to see that everything is all right: *During the carnival there will be 30 police cars on patrol.*
patrol *verb* (**patrols**, **patrolling**, **patrolled** /pə'trəʊld/)
A guard patrols the gate at night.

patter /'pætə(r)/ (**patters**, **pattering**, **pattered** /'pætəd/)
make quick light sounds: *Rain pattered against the window.*
patter *noun*
the patter of children's feet on the stairs

pattern /'pætn/ *noun*
1 shapes and colours on something: *The curtains had a pattern of flowers and leaves.*
2 a thing that you copy when you make something: *I bought some material and a pattern to make a new skirt.*
patterned /'pætnd/ *adjective*
with shapes and colours on it: *a patterned shirt*

pause /pɔːz/ *noun*
a short stop: *She played for 30 minutes without a pause.*
pause *verb* (**pauses**, **pausing**, **paused** /pɔːzd/)
stop for a short time: *He paused before answering my question.*

pavement /'peɪvmənt/ *noun*
the part at the side of a road where people can walk

paw /pɔː/ *noun*
the foot of an animal, for example a dog, cat or bear ☞ picture at **cat**

pay¹ /peɪ/ *verb* (**pays**, **paying**, **paid** /peɪd/, **has paid**)
1 give money to get something: *She paid £4 000 for her car.* ◇ *Are you paying in cash or by cheque?*
2 give money for work that somebody does: *I paid the builder for mending the roof.*
pay back give back the money that somebody has lent to you: *Can you lend me £5? I'll pay you back* (= pay it back to you) *next week.*
pay for something give money for what you buy: *Have you paid for your hotel room yet?*

pay² /peɪ/ *noun* (no plural)
the money that you get for work

payment /'peɪmənt/ *noun*
1 (no plural) paying or being paid: *This cheque is in payment for the work you have done.*
2 (*plural* **payments**) an amount of money that you pay: *I make monthly payments of £50.*

pay phone /'peɪ fəʊn/ *noun*
a telephone that you put money in to make a call

PC /ˌpiː 'siː/ *noun*
1 a small computer. 'PC' is short for **personal computer**.
2 a policeman. 'PC' is short for **police constable**: *PC Smith*

PE /ˌpiː 'iː/ *short for* **physical education**

pea /piː/ *noun*
a very small round green vegetable. Peas grow in **pods**.

peace /piːs/ *noun* (no plural)
1 a time when there is no war, fighting or trouble between people or countries
2 being quiet and calm: *the peace of the countryside at night* ◇ *Go away and leave me in peace!*
make peace agree to end a war or fight: *The two countries made peace.*

peaceful /'piːsfl/ *adjective*
1 with no fighting: *a peaceful demonstration*
2 quiet and calm: *a peaceful evening*
peacefully /'piːsfəli/ *adverb*
She's sleeping peacefully.

peach /piːtʃ/ *noun*
(*plural* **peaches**)
a soft round fruit
with a yellow and
red skin and a large
stone in the centre

peach

peacock /'piːkɒk/ *noun*
a large bird with beautiful long blue and green feathers in its tail

peak /piːk/ *noun*
1 the pointed top of a mountain
2 the time when something is highest, biggest, etc: *The traffic is at its peak between five and six in the evening.*
3 the pointed front part of a hat that is above your eyes

peanut /'piːnʌt/ *noun*
a nut that you can eat

ʌ	ɜː	ə	eɪ	əʊ	aɪ	aʊ	ɔɪ	ɪə	eə	ʊə
cup	bird	about	say	go	five	now	boy	near	hair	pure

pear /peə(r)/ *noun*
a fruit that is green or yellow on the outside and white on the inside

pear

pearl /pɜːl/ *noun*
a small round white thing that comes from an **oyster** (a kind of shellfish). Pearls are used to make things like necklaces and earrings: *a pearl necklace*

peasant /'peznt/ *noun*
a poor person who lives in the country and works on a small piece of land

pebble /'pebl/ *noun*
a small round stone

peck /pek/ *verb* (**pecks, pecking, pecked** /pekt/)
When a bird pecks something, it cuts or bites it with its beak: *The hens were pecking at the corn.*

peculiar /pɪ'kjuːliə(r)/ *adjective*
strange; not usual: *What's that peculiar smell?*

pedal /'pedl/ *noun*
a part of a bicycle or other machine that you move with your feet ☞ picture at **bicycle**

pedestrian /pə'destriən/ *noun*
a person who is walking in the street
pedestrian crossing /pə,destriən 'krɒsɪŋ/ *noun*
a place where cars must stop so that people can cross the road
pedestrian precinct /pə,destriən 'priːsɪŋkt/ *noun*
a part of a town where there are a lot of shops and where cars cannot go

peel /piːl/ *noun* (no plural)
the outside part of some fruit and vegetables: *orange peel*
peel *verb* (**peels, peeling, peeled** /piːld/)
1 take the outside part off a fruit or vegetable: *Can you peel the potatoes?*
2 come off in thin pieces: *The paint is peeling off the walls.*

peep /piːp/ *verb* (**peeps, peeping, peeped** /piːpt/)
1 look at something quickly or secretly: *I peeped through the window and saw her.*
2 come out for a short time: *The moon peeped out from behind the clouds.*

peer /pɪə(r)/ *verb* (**peers, peering, peered** /pɪəd/)
look closely at something because you cannot see well: *I peered outside but I couldn't see anything because it was dark.*

peg /peg/ *noun*
1 a small thing on a wall or door where you can hang clothes: *Your coat is on the peg.*
2 a small wooden or plastic thing that holds wet clothes on a line when they are drying: *a clothes-peg*

pen¹ /pen/ *noun*
a thing that you use for writing with a coloured liquid (called **ink**)

pen² /pen/ *noun*
a small place with a fence around it for keeping animals in

penalty /'penlti/ *noun* (*plural* **penalties**)
a punishment: *The penalty for travelling without a ticket is £300* (= you must pay £300).

pence *plural of* **penny**

pencil /'pensl/ *noun*
a thin piece of wood with grey or coloured stuff inside it. Pencils are used for writing or drawing.

pen-friend /'pen frend/, **pen-pal** /'pen pæl/ *noun*
a person that you write to but have probably never met

penguin

penguin /'peŋgwɪn/ *noun*
a black and white bird that lives in very cold places. Penguins can swim but they cannot fly.

penknife /'pen naɪf/ *noun* (*plural* **penknives** /'pen naɪvz/)
a small knife that you can carry in your pocket ☞ picture on next page

p	b	t	d	k	g	tʃ	dʒ	f	v	θ	ð
pen	**b**ad	**t**ea	**d**id	**c**at	**g**ot	**ch**ain	**j**am	**f**all	**v**an	**th**in	**th**is

penknife

penny /'peni/ noun (plural **pence** /pens/ or **pennies**)
a small coin that people use in Britain. There are 100 pence in a **pound**: *These pencils cost 40 pence each.* ✪ The short form of 'pence' is **p**: *Can you lend me 50p?*

pension /'penʃn/ noun
money that you get from a government or a company when you are old and do not work any more (when you are **retired**)
pensioner /'penʃənə(r)/ noun
a person who has a pension

people /'piːpl/ noun (plural)
more than one person: *How many people came to the meeting?* ◇ *People often arrive late at parties.*

pepper /'pepə(r)/ noun
1 (no plural) powder with a hot taste that you put on food: *salt and pepper*
2 (plural **peppers**) a red, green or yellow vegetable with a lot of white seeds inside

peppermint /'pepəmɪnt/ noun
1 (no plural) a plant with a strong fresh taste and smell. It is used to make things like sweets and medicines.
2 (plural **peppermints**) a sweet made from this

per /pə(r)/ preposition
for each; in each: *These apples cost 40p per pound.* ◇ *I was driving at 60 miles per hour.*

per cent /pə 'sent/ noun (no plural)
%; in each hundred: *90 per cent of the people who work here are men* (= in 100 people there are 90 men).
percentage /pə'sentɪdʒ/ noun
'What percentage of students passed the exam?' 'Oh, about eighty per cent.'

perch /pɜːtʃ/ noun (plural **perches**)
a place where a bird sits
perch verb (**perches, perching, perched** /pɜːtʃt/)
sit on something narrow: *The bird perched on a branch.*

perfect /'pɜːfɪkt/ adjective
1 so good that it cannot be better; with

nothing wrong: *Her English is perfect.*
◇ *The weather is perfect for a picnic.*
2 made from 'has', 'have' or 'had' and the **past participle** of a verb: *perfect tenses*

perfectly /'pɜːfɪktli/ adverb
1 completely; very: *I'm perfectly all right.*
2 in a perfect way: *She played the piece of music perfectly.*

perform /pə'fɔːm/ verb (**performs, performing, performed** /pə'fɔːmd/)
1 do a piece of work: *The doctor performed an operation to save her life.*
2 be in a play, concert, etc: *The band is performing at the Odeon tonight.*
performer noun
a person who is in a play, concert, etc

performance /pə'fɔːməns/ noun
1 (plural **performances**) a time when a play, etc is shown or music is played in front of a lot of people: *We went to the evening performance of the play.*
2 (no plural) how well you do something: *My parents were pleased with my performance in the exam.*

perfume /'pɜːfjuːm/ noun
1 a nice smell
2 a liquid with a nice smell that you put on your body: *a bottle of perfume*

perhaps /pə'hæps/ adverb
a word that you use when you are not sure about something: *I don't know where she is – perhaps she's still at work.* ◇ *There were three men, or perhaps four.*

period /'pɪəriəd/ noun
1 an amount of time: *He was ill four times in a period of six months.*
2 a certain time in the life of a person or the history of a country: *What period of history are you studying?*
3 a lesson: *We have five periods of German a week.*
4 the time when a woman loses blood from her body each month
5 *American English for* **full stop**

permanent /'pɜːmənənt/ adjective
Something that is permanent continues for ever or for a very long time and does not change: *I'm looking for a permanent job.*
☞ Look at **temporary**.
permanently adverb
Has he left permanently or is he coming back?

Words that go together 1

a **pair** of shoes

a **string** of beads

a **bar** of chocolate

a **row** of houses

a **bundle** of newspapers

a **drop** of water

a **bunch** of flowers

a **crowd** of people

a **ball** of string

a **slice/piece** of pizza

a **pile** of books

a **queue** (of people)

a **lump** of coal

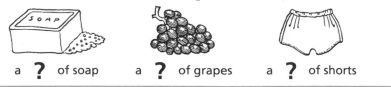

This dictionary tells you about words that often go together.
Do you know what word is missing in each of these
expressions? You can use the dictionary (look up **soap**, **grape**
and **shorts** and read the example sentences) to find out.

a **?** of soap   a **?** of grapes   a **?** of shorts

Opposites

big/large

little/small

thick

thin

tall

short

wide/broad

narrow

high

low

shallow

deep

long

short

happy

sad

fat

thin

old

young

Opposites

old · new

clean · dirty

weak · strong

cheap · expensive

hot · cold

open · closed/shut

soft · hard

loud · quiet

wet · dry

loose · tight

We give opposites for many of the words in this dictionary.
If you want to know the opposite of **tidy**, for example, look up
this word and you will find ✺ opposite: **untidy** after it.

Words that go together 2

She has _____ a lot of mistakes.

When you learn a new word it is important to remember what other words you often see with it. This dictionary can help you to decide what word goes with another word. For example, if you look up **mistake** in the dictionary, you will see:

> **mistake**¹ /mɪˈsteɪk/ *noun*
> something that you think or do that is wrong: *You have made a lot of spelling mistakes in this letter.* ◇ *It was a mistake to go by bus – the journey took two hours!*
> **by mistake** when you did not plan to do it: *I took your book by mistake – I thought*

The example sentence shows you that you use **make** with **mistake**.

You can use your dictionary to check which words below go together. Find the words in **B** and use the example sentences.

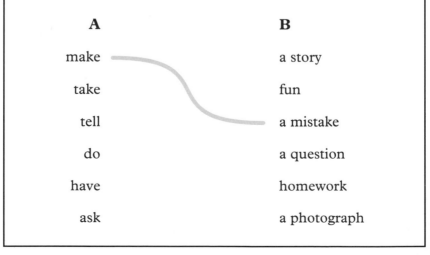

A	B
make	a story
take	fun
tell	a mistake
do	a question
have	homework
ask	a photograph

permission /pə'mɪʃn/ noun (no plural)
allowing somebody to do something: *She
gave me permission to leave early.*

permit¹ /pə'mɪt/ verb (**permits, per-
mitting, permitted**)
allow somebody to do something: *You are
not permitted to smoke in the hospital.*
✪ **Allow** is the word that we usually use.

permit² /'pɜːmɪt/ noun
a piece of paper that says you can do something or go somewhere: *Have you got a
work permit?*

person /'pɜːsn/ noun (plural **people**
/'piːpl/)
a man or woman: *I think she's the best
person for the job.*
in person seeing somebody, not just
speaking on the telephone or writing a letter: *I want to speak to her in person.*

personal /'pɜːsənl/ adjective
of or for one person; private: *This letter is
personal, so I don't want anyone else to
read it.*
personal stereo /ˌpɜːsənl 'steriəʊ/
noun (plural **personal stereos**)
a small cassette player or radio with **headphones,** that is easy to carry

personality /ˌpɜːsə'næləti/ noun (plural **personalities**)
1 what sort of person you are; your character: *Mark has a great personality.*
2 a famous person: *a television personality*

personally /'pɜːsənəli/ adverb
You say 'personally' when you are saying
what you think about something: *Personally, I like her, but a lot of people don't.*

persuade /pə'sweɪd/ verb (**persuades,
persuading, persuaded**)
make somebody think or do something by
talking to them: *The man in the shop persuaded me to buy the most expensive pen.*
persuasion /pə'sweɪʒn/ noun (no
plural)
persuading somebody or being persuaded:
*After a lot of persuasion she agreed to
come.*

pessimism /'pesɪmɪzəm/ noun (no
plural)
thinking that bad things will happen
✪ opposite: **optimism**

pessimist /'pesɪmɪst/ noun
a person who always thinks that bad
things will happen
pessimistic /ˌpesɪ'mɪstɪk/ adjective
If you are pessimistic, you think that bad
things will happen: *Don't be so
pessimistic!*

pest /pest/ noun
1 an insect or animal that damages plants
or food
2 a person or thing that makes you a little
angry: *My sister won't leave me alone
when I'm working – she's a real pest!*

pet /pet/ noun
1 an animal that you keep in your home:
I've got two pets – a cat and a goldfish.
2 a child that a teacher or a parent likes
best: *She's the teacher's pet.*

petal /'petl/ noun
one of the coloured parts of a flower

petition /pə'tɪʃn/ noun
a special letter, from a group of people, that
asks for something: *Hundreds of people
signed the petition for a new pedestrian
crossing.*

petrol /'petrəl/ noun (no plural)
a liquid that you put in a car to make the
engine work
petrol station /'petrəl steɪʃn/ noun
a place where you can buy petrol

phantom /'fæntəm/ noun
a ghost

pharmacist /'fɑːməsɪst/ another word
for **chemist 1**

phase /feɪz/ noun
a time when something is changing or
growing: *My first year at university was
a very exciting phase of my life.*

philosophy /fə'lɒsəfi/ noun
1 (no plural) the study of ideas about the
meaning of life
2 (plural **philosophies**) what one person
thinks about life: *Enjoy yourself today and
don't worry about tomorrow – that's my
philosophy!*
philosopher /fə'lɒsəfə(r)/ noun
a person who studies philosophy

phone /fəʊn/ noun
a telephone; an instrument that you use
for talking to somebody who is in another
place: *The phone's ringing – can you answer it?* ◇ *What's your phone number?*
◇ *I need to make a phone call.*

on the phone using a telephone to speak to somebody: *Anna was on the phone for an hour.*

phone *verb* (**phones, phoning, phoned** /fəʊnd/)
use a telephone: *I phoned Di last night.*

phone book /'fəʊn bʊk/ *noun*
a book of people's names, addresses and telephone numbers

phone box /'fəʊn bɒks/ (*plural* **phone boxes**), **phone booth** /'fəʊn buːð/ *noun*
a public telephone in the street

phonecard /'fəʊnkɑːd/ *noun*
a small plastic card that you can use to pay for a call to somebody from a **phone box**

phonetics /fə'netɪks/ *noun* (no plural)
the study of the sounds that people make when they speak

phonetic *adjective*
using special signs to show how to say words: *The phonetic alphabet is printed at the bottom of this page.*

photocopy /'fəʊtəʊkɒpi/ *noun* (*plural* **photocopies**)
a copy of something on paper that you make with a special machine (called a **photocopier**)

photocopy *verb* (**photocopies, photocopying, photocopied** /'fəʊtəʊkɒpid/, **has photocopied**)
Can you photocopy this letter for me?

photograph /'fəʊtəgrɑːf/, **photo** /'fəʊtəʊ/ (*plural* **photos**) *noun*
a picture that you take with a camera: *I took a photo of the Eiffel Tower.*

photograph *verb* (**photographs, photographing, photographed** /'fəʊtəgrɑːft/)
take a photograph of somebody or something: *The winner was photographed holding his prize.*

photographer /fə'tɒɡrəfə(r)/ *noun*
a person who takes photographs

photographic /ˌfəʊtə'ɡræfɪk/ *adjective*
about photographs or photography: *photographic equipment*

photography /fə'tɒɡrəfi/ *noun* (no plural)
taking photographs

phrase /freɪz/ *noun*
a group of words that you use together as part of a sentence: *'First of all' and 'a bar of chocolate' are phrases.*

physical /'fɪzɪkl/ *adjective*
You use 'physical' about things that you feel or do with your body: *physical exercise*

physically /'fɪzɪkli/ *adverb*
I'm not physically fit.

physical education /ˌfɪzɪkl edʒu'keɪʃn/ *noun* (no plural)
sports that you do at school ✪ The short form is **PE**.

physics /'fɪzɪks/ *noun* (no plural)
the study of things like heat, light and sound

physicist /'fɪzɪsɪst/ *noun*
a person who studies or knows a lot about physics

piano /pi'ænəʊ/ *noun* (*plural* **pianos**)
a big musical instrument that you play by pressing black and white bars (called **keys**): *Can you play the piano?*

pianist /'piːənɪst/ *noun*
a person who plays the piano

pick¹ /pɪk/ *verb* (**picks, picking, picked** /pɪkt/)
1 take the person or thing you like best; choose: *They picked Simon as their captain.*
2 take a flower, fruit or vegetable from the place where it grows: *I've picked some flowers for you.*

pick out be able to see somebody or something in a lot of others: *Can you pick out my father in this photo?*

pick up **1** take and lift somebody or something: *She picked up the bags and put them on the table.* ◇ *The phone stopped ringing just as I picked it up.* **2** come to take somebody or something away: *My father picks me up from school.* **3** learn something without really studying it: *Did you pick up any Japanese while you were in Tokyo?*

pick² /pɪk/ *noun* (no plural)
what you choose; your choice

take your pick choose what you like: *We've got orange juice, lemonade or milk. Take your pick.*

picket /'pɪkɪt/ *verb* (**pickets, picketing, picketed**)
stand outside the place where you work

ʌ	ɜː	ə	eɪ	əʊ	aɪ	aʊ	ɔɪ	ɪə	eə	ʊə
cup	bird	about	say	go	five	now	boy	near	hair	pure

when there is a **strike**, and try to stop other people going to work
picket *noun*
a person or group of people who picket: *There was a picket outside the hospital.*

pickpocket /'pɪkpɒkɪt/ *noun*
a person who steals things from people's pockets

picnic /'pɪknɪk/ *noun*
a meal that you eat outside, away from home: *We had a picnic by the river.*
picnic *verb* (**picnics, picnicking, picnicked** /'pɪknɪkt/)
have a picnic: *We picnicked on the beach yesterday.*

picture /'pɪktʃə(r)/ *noun*
1 a drawing, painting or photograph: *Julie drew a picture of her dog.* ◇ *They showed us some pictures of their wedding.*
2 the pictures (plural) the cinema: *We're going to the pictures this evening.*
take a picture photograph something: *I took a picture of the house.*

pie /paɪ/ *noun*
meat, fruit, vegetables, etc with pastry: *an apple pie*

piece /piːs/ *noun*   **pie**
1 a part of something: *Would you like another piece of cake?* ◇ *a piece of broken glass* ☞ picture on page 261
2 one single thing: *Have you got a piece of paper?* ◇ *That's an interesting piece of news.*
3 a coin: *a 50p piece*
fall to pieces break into pieces: *The chair fell to pieces when I sat on it.*
in pieces broken: *The teapot lay in pieces on the floor.*
take something to pieces divide something into its parts: *I took the bed to pieces because it was too big to go through the door.*

pier /pɪə(r)/ *noun*
a long thing that is built from the land into the sea, where people can walk or get on and off boats

pierce /pɪəs/ *verb* (**pierces, piercing, pierced** /pɪəst/)
make a hole in something with a sharp point: *The nail pierced her skin.*

piercing /'pɪəsɪŋ/ *adjective*
A piercing sound is very loud and sharp: *a piercing cry*

pig /pɪg/ *noun*
1 a fat animal that people keep on farms for its meat

❍ A young pig is called a **piglet**. Meat from a pig is called **pork**, **bacon** or **ham**.

2 an unkind person or a person who eats too much: *You've eaten all the biscuits, you pig!*

pigeon /'pɪdʒɪn/ *noun*
a grey bird that you often see in towns

piglet /'pɪglət/ *noun*
a young pig

pigsty /'pɪgstaɪ/ *noun* (*plural* **pigsties**)
a small building where pigs live

pile /paɪl/ *noun*
a lot of things on top of one another; a large amount of something: *There's a pile of clothes on the floor.* ◇ *a pile of earth* ☞ picture on page 261
pile *verb* (**piles, piling, piled** /paɪld/)
put a lot of things on top of one another: *She piled the boxes on the table.*

pilgrim /'pɪlgrɪm/ *noun*
a person who travels a long way to a place because it has a special religious meaning
pilgrimage /'pɪlgrɪmɪdʒ/ *noun*
a journey that a pilgrim makes

pill /pɪl/ *noun*
a small round hard piece of medicine that you swallow: *Take one of these pills.*

pillar /'pɪlə(r)/ *noun*
a tall strong piece of stone, wood or metal that holds up a building

pillar-box /'pɪlə bɒks/ *noun* (*plural* **pillar-boxes**)
a tall red box in the street for sending letters

pillow /'pɪləʊ/ *noun*
a soft thing that you put your head on when you are in bed ☞ picture on next page
pillowcase /'pɪləʊkeɪs/ *noun*
a cover for a pillow

pilot /'paɪlət/ *noun*
1 a person who flies an aircraft
2 a person who guides a ship along a river, into a harbour, etc

p	b	t	d	k	g	tʃ	dʒ	f	v	θ	ð
pen	**b**ad	**t**ea	**d**id	**c**at	**g**ot	**ch**ain	**j**am	**f**all	**v**an	**th**in	**th**is

pillow

pin¹ /pɪn/ *noun*
a small thin piece of metal with a flat part at one end and a sharp point at the other. You use a pin for holding pieces of cloth or paper together. ☞ Look also at **drawing-pin** and **safety pin**.
pins and needles /ˌpɪnz ən 'niːdlz/ *noun* (plural)
the feeling that you sometimes get in a part of your body when you have not moved it for a long time

pin² /pɪn/ *verb* (**pins, pinning, pinned** /pɪnd/)
1 fix things together with a pin or pins: *Pin the pieces of material together before you sew them.* ◇ *Could you pin this notice to the board?*
2 hold somebody or something so that they cannot move: *He tried to get away, but they pinned him against the wall.*

pinch /pɪntʃ/ *verb* (**pinches, pinching, pinched** /pɪntʃt/)
1 press somebody's skin tightly between your thumb and finger: *Don't pinch me – it hurts!*
2 steal something: *Who's pinched my pen?* ✪ This is an informal use.
pinch *noun* (*plural* **pinches**)
1 pinching something: *He gave my leg a pinch.*
2 how much of something you can hold between your thumb and finger: *Add a pinch of salt to the soup.*

pine /paɪn/, **pine tree** /'paɪn triː/ *noun*
a tall tree with thin sharp leaves (called **needles**) that do not fall off in winter

pineapple /'paɪnæpl/ *noun*
a big fruit that has a rough brown skin and a yellow inside part

ping-pong /'pɪŋ pɒŋ/ *noun* (no plural)
a game where players use a round **bat** to hit a small light ball over a net on a big table; table tennis

pink /pɪŋk/ *adjective*
with a light red colour: *a pink jumper*
pink *noun*
She was dressed in pink.

pint /paɪnt/ *noun*
a measure of liquid (= 0.57 litres). There are eight pints in a **gallon**: *a pint of beer* ◇ *two pints of milk* ✪ The short way of writing 'pint' is **pt**.

✪ In the past, people in Britain used **pints** and **gallons** to measure liquids, not **litres**. Now, many people use and understand both ways.

pioneer /ˌpaɪə'nɪə(r)/ *noun*
a person who goes somewhere or does something before other people: *the pioneers of the American West*

pip /pɪp/ *noun*
the seed of some fruits. Lemons, oranges and apples have pips.

pipe /paɪp/ *noun*
1 a long tube that takes water, oil, gas, etc from one place to another
2 a thing that you put tobacco in to smoke it
3 a musical instrument that you blow

pipeline /'paɪplaɪn/ *noun*
a big pipe that carries oil or gas a long way

pirate /'paɪrət/ *noun*
a person on a ship who robs other ships

pistol /'pɪstl/ *noun*
a small gun

pit /pɪt/ *noun*
1 a deep hole in the ground
2 a deep hole that people make in the ground to take out coal

pitch¹ /pɪtʃ/ *noun* (*plural* **pitches**)
1 a piece of ground where you play games like football or cricket
2 how high or low a sound is

pitch² /pɪtʃ/ *verb* (**pitches, pitching, pitched** /pɪtʃt/)
put up a tent: *We pitched our tent under a big tree.*

pineapple

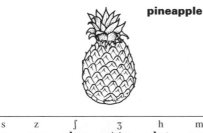

s	z	ʃ	ʒ	h	m	n	ŋ	l	r	j	w
so	**zoo**	**shoe**	**vision**	**hat**	**man**	**no**	**sing**	**leg**	**red**	**yes**	**wet**

pitcher /'pɪtʃə(r)/ *American English for* jug

pity[1] /'pɪti/ *noun* (no plural)
sadness for a person or an animal who is in pain or who has problems: *I felt pity for the old dog so I gave him some food.*
it's a pity, what a pity it is sad: *It's a pity you can't come to the party.*
take pity on somebody help somebody because you feel sad for them: *I took pity on her and gave her some money.*

pity[2] /'pɪti/ *verb* (**pities, pitying, pitied** /'pɪtid/, **has pitied**)
feel sad for somebody who is in pain or who has problems: *I really pity people who haven't got anywhere to live.*

pizza /'piːtsə/ *noun* (*plural* **pizzas**)
a flat round piece of bread with tomatoes, cheese and other things on top, that is cooked in an oven

place[1] /pleɪs/ *noun*
1 where somebody or something is: *Put the book back in the right place.*
2 a building, town, country, etc: *Budapest is a very interesting place.* ◇ *Do you know a good place to have lunch?*
3 a seat or space for one person: *An old man was sitting in my place.*
4 where you are in a race, test, etc: *Alice finished in second place.*
in place where it should be; in the right place: *She tied her hair with a ribbon to keep it in place.*
in place of somebody or **something** instead of somebody or something: *Joe became goalkeeper in place of Martin, who had broken his leg.*
take place happen: *The wedding of John and Sara will take place on 22 May.*

place[2] /pleɪs/ *verb* (**places, placing, placed** /pleɪst/)
put something somewhere: *The waiter placed the meal in front of me.*

plain[1] /pleɪn/ *adjective* (**plainer, plainest**)
1 with no pattern; all one colour: *She wore a plain blue dress.*
2 simple and ordinary: *plain food*
3 easy to see, hear or understand; clear: *It's plain that he's unhappy.*
4 not pretty: *She was a plain child.*
plainly *adverb*
clearly: *They were plainly very angry.*

plain[2] /pleɪn/ *noun*
a large piece of flat land

plait /plæt/ *verb* (**plaits, plaiting, plaited**)
put long pieces of hair, rope, etc over and under each other to make one thick piece: *Her hair is plaited.*
plait *noun*
a long piece of hair that somebody has plaited: *She wears her hair in plaits.*

plan[1] /plæn/ *noun*
1 something that you have decided to do, and how to do it: *What are your holiday plans?* ◇ *They have plans to build a new school.*
2 a map: *a street plan of London*
3 a drawing for a new building, machine, etc: *Have you seen the plans for the new shopping centre?*

plan[2] /plæn/ *verb* (**plans, planning, planned** /plænd/)
decide what you are going to do and how you are going to do it: *They're planning a holiday in Australia next summer.* ◇ *I'm planning to go to university.*

plane /pleɪn/ *noun*
an aeroplane: *I like travelling by plane.* ◇ *What time does your plane land?*
☞ picture at **aeroplane**

planet /'plænɪt/ *noun*
a large round thing in space that moves around the sun: *Earth, Mars and Venus are planets.*

plank /plæŋk/ *noun*
a long flat piece of wood

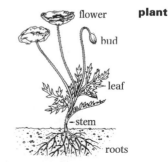
flower **plant**
bud
leaf
stem
roots

plant[1] /plɑːnt/ *noun*
anything that grows from the ground: *Don't forget to water the plants.*

plant² /plɑ:nt/ *verb* (**plants**, **planting**, **planted**)
put plants or seeds in the ground to grow: *We planted some roses in the garden.*

plantation /plɑ:n'teɪʃn/ *noun*
a piece of land where things like tea, cotton or tobacco grow: *a sugar plantation*

plaster /'plɑ:stə(r)/ *noun*
1 (no plural) soft stuff that becomes hard and smooth when it is dry. Plaster is used for covering walls.
2 (*plural* **plasters**) a small piece of sticky material that you put over a cut on your body to keep it clean
3 (no plural) white stuff that you put round a broken arm or leg. It becomes hard and keeps the arm or leg safe until it is better: *When I broke my leg it was in plaster for two months.*

plastic /'plæstɪk/ *noun* (no plural)
a strong light material that is made in factories. Plastic is used for making a lot of different things: *These chairs are made of plastic.* ◇ *plastic cups*

plate /pleɪt/ *noun*
a round flat thing that you put food on ☞ Look also at **number-plate**.

plate

platform /'plætfɔ:m/ *noun*
1 the part of a railway station where you stand to wait for a train: *The train to London leaves from platform 5.*
2 a place that is higher than the floor, where people stand so that other people can see and hear them: *The headmaster went up to the platform to make his speech.*

play¹ /pleɪ/ *verb* (**plays**, **playing**, **played** /pleɪd/)
1 have fun; do something to enjoy yourself: *The children were playing with their toys.*
2 take part in a game: *I like playing tennis.* ◇ *Do you know how to play chess?*
3 make music with a musical instrument: *My sister plays the piano very well.*
✪ We always use **the** before the names of musical instruments: *I'm learning to play the violin.*
4 put a record, tape or compact disc in a machine and listen to it: *Shall I play the tape again?*
5 be somebody in a play in the theatre or on television or radio: *Hamlet was played by Michael Kent.*

play² /pleɪ/ *noun*
1 (*plural* **plays**) a story that you watch in the theatre or on television, or listen to on the radio: *We went to see a play at the National Theatre.*
2 (no plural) games; what children do for fun: *work and play* ✪ Be careful! We **play** football, cards, etc or we **have a game of** football, cards, etc (NOT **a play**).

player /'pleɪə(r)/ *noun*
1 a person who plays a game: *football players*
2 a person who plays a musical instrument: *a trumpet player*

playground /'pleɪɡraʊnd/ *noun*
a piece of land where children can play

playing-cards /'pleɪɪŋ kɑ:dz/ *noun*
a set of 52 cards that you use for playing games ☞ Look at **card**.

playing-field /'pleɪɪŋ fi:ld/ *noun*
a field for sports like football and cricket

plea /pli:/ *noun*
asking for something with strong feeling: *He made a plea for help.*

plead /pli:d/ *verb* (**pleads**, **pleading**, **pleaded**)
ask for something in a very strong way: *He pleaded with his parents to buy him a guitar.*
plead guilty say in a court of law that you did something wrong: *She pleaded guilty to murder.*
plead not guilty say in a court of law that you did not do something wrong

pleasant /'pleznt/ *adjective*
nice, enjoyable or friendly: *The weather here is very pleasant.* ◇ *He's a very pleasant person.* ✪ opposite: **unpleasant**
pleasantly *adverb*
She smiled pleasantly.

please /pli:z/
a word that you use when you ask politely: *What's the time, please?* ◇ *Two cups of coffee, please.* ✪ You use **yes, please** to say that you will have something: *'Would you like a cake?' 'Yes, please.'*

please *verb* (**pleases, pleasing, pleased**) /pli:zd/
make somebody happy: *I wore my best clothes to please my mother.*

pleased /pli:zd/ *adjective*
happy: *He wasn't very pleased to see me.*
◇ *Are you pleased with your new watch?*

pleasure /'pleʒə(r)/ *noun*
1 (no plural) the feeling of being happy or enjoying something: *I go sailing for pleasure.*
2 (*plural* **pleasures**) something that makes you happy: *It was a pleasure to meet you.*
it's a pleasure You say 'it's a pleasure' as a polite way of answering somebody who thanks you: *'Thank you for your help.' 'It's a pleasure.'*
with pleasure You say 'with pleasure' to show in a polite way that you are happy to do something: *'Can you help me move these boxes?' 'Yes, with pleasure.'*

pleat /pli:t/ *noun*
a fold in a piece of cloth

pled /pled/ *American English for* **pleaded**

plenty /'plenti/ *pronoun*
as much or as many as you need; a lot: *Do you want to stay for dinner? There's plenty of food.*

pliers /'plaɪəz/ *noun* (plural)
a tool for holding things tightly or for cutting wire: *Have you got a pair of pliers?*

plod /plɒd/ *verb* (**plods, plodding, plodded**)
walk slowly in a heavy tired way: *We plodded up the hill in the rain.*

plot /plɒt/ *noun*
1 a secret plan to do something that is wrong: *a plot to kill the President*
2 what happens in a story, play or film: *This book has a very exciting plot.*
plot *verb* (**plots, plotting, plotted**)
make a secret plan to do something that is wrong: *They plotted to rob the bank.*

plough /plaʊ/ *noun*
a machine used on farms for digging and turning over the soil. Ploughs are usually pulled by tractors.
plough *verb* (**ploughs, ploughing, ploughed** /plaʊd/)
use a plough to dig and turn over the soil: *The farmer ploughed his fields.*

plow *American English for* **plough**

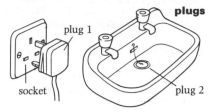

plug 1
plugs
socket
plug 2

plug /plʌg/ *noun*
1 a thing that joins a lamp, machine, etc to a place in the wall (called a **socket**) where there is electricity
2 a round thing that you put in the hole in a wash-basin or bath, to stop the water going out
plug *verb* (**plugs, plugging, plugged** /plʌgd/)
fill a hole with something: *I plugged the hole in the pipe with plastic.*
plug in put an electric plug into a place in the wall where there is electricity: *Can you plug the radio in, please?* ◇ *The lamp isn't plugged in.* **۞** opposite: **unplug**

plum /plʌm/ *noun*
a soft round fruit with a stone in the middle

plumber /'plʌmə(r)/ *noun*
a person whose job is to put in and repair things like water-pipes and baths

plump /plʌmp/ *adjective* (**plumper, plumpest**)
quite fat, in a nice way: *a plump baby*

plunge /plʌndʒ/ *verb* (**plunges, plunging, plunged** /plʌndʒd/)
1 jump or fall suddenly into something: *She plunged into the pool.*
2 push something suddenly and strongly into something else: *I plunged my hand into the water.*

plural /'plʊərəl/ *noun*
the form of a word that shows there is more than one: *The plural of 'child' is 'children'.*
plural *adjective*
Most plural nouns in English end in 's'.
☞ Look at **singular**.

plus /plʌs/ *preposition*
added to; and: *Two plus three is five (2 + 3 = 5).* ◇ *We have invited twelve friends to the party, plus my brother and his girlfriend.* ☞ Look at **minus**.

p	b	t	d	k	g	tʃ	dʒ	f	v	θ	ð
pen	**b**ad	**t**ea	**d**id	**c**at	**g**ot	**ch**ain	**j**am	**f**all	**v**an	**th**in	**th**is

p.m. /ˌpiː 'em/
You use 'p.m.' after a time to show that it is between midday and midnight: *The plane leaves at 3 p.m.* ✪ We use **a.m.** for times between midnight and midday.

pneumonia /njuːˈməʊniə/ *noun* (no plural)
a serious illness of the lungs

poach¹ /pəʊtʃ/ *verb* (**poaches, poaching, poached** /pəʊtʃt/)
cook food gently in or over water or milk: *a poached egg*

poach² /pəʊtʃ/ *verb* (**poaches, poaching, poached** /pəʊtʃt/)
kill and steal animals, birds or fish from another person's land
poacher *noun*
a person who poaches

PO Box /ˌpiː 'əʊ bɒks/ *noun* (*plural* **PO Boxes**)
a box in a post office for keeping the letters of a person or office: *The address is PO Box 63, Bristol BS7 1JN.*

pocket

pocket /ˈpɒkɪt/ *noun*
a small bag in your clothes for carrying things: *I put the key in my pocket.*
pick somebody's pocket steal money from somebody's pocket or bag

pocketbook /ˈpɒkɪtbʊk/ *American English for* **wallet**

pocket money /ˈpɒkɪt mʌni/ *noun* (no plural)
money that parents give to a child each week to buy things: *How much pocket money do you get?*

pod /pɒd/ *noun*
the long green part of some plants, that has seeds inside it. Peas grow in pods.

poem /ˈpəʊɪm/ *noun*
a piece of writing, usually with short lines that may rhyme. Poems try to show feelings or ideas: *I have written a poem.*

poet /ˈpəʊɪt/ *noun*
a person who writes poems: *Keats was a famous English poet.*

poetic /pəʊˈetɪk/ *adjective*
of or like poets or poetry: *poetic language*

poetry /ˈpəʊətri/ *noun* (no plural)
poems: *Wordsworth wrote beautiful poetry.*

point¹ /pɔɪnt/ *noun*
1 a small round mark (.) that shows part of a number: *2.5* (two point five)
2 a certain time or place: *It started to rain and at that point we decided to go home.*
3 the most important idea; the purpose or reason: *The point of going to school is to learn.* ◇ *What's the point of phoning her? She's not at home.*
4 the sharp end of something: *the point of a needle*
5 a mark that you win in a game or sport: *Our team scored six points.*
be on the point of If you are on the point of doing something, you are going to do it very soon: *I was on the point of going out when the phone rang.*
point of view your way of thinking about something: *I understand your point of view.*
there's no point in there is no good reason to do something: *There's no point in waiting for Julie – she isn't coming.*

point² /pɔɪnt/ *verb* (**points, pointing, pointed**)
show where something is using your finger, a stick, etc: *I asked him where the bank was and he pointed across the road.* ◇ *There was a sign pointing towards the city centre.*
point something at somebody or something hold something towards somebody or something: *She was pointing a gun at his head.*
point out tell or show something: *Eva pointed out that my bag was open.*

pointed /ˈpɔɪntɪd/ *adjective*
with a sharp end: *a long pointed nose*

pointless /ˈpɔɪntləs/ *adjective*
with no use or purpose: *It's pointless telling Paul anything – he never listens.*

poison /ˈpɔɪzn/ *noun* (no plural)
something that will kill you or make you very ill if you eat or drink it: *rat poison*
poison *verb* (**poisons, poisoning, poisoned** /ˈpɔɪznd/)
use poison to kill or hurt somebody or something

s	z	ʃ	ʒ	h	m	n	ŋ	l	r	j	w
so	**zoo**	**shoe**	vision	**hat**	**man**	**no**	sing	**leg**	**red**	**yes**	**wet**

poisonous /ˈpɔɪzənəs/ *adjective*
Something that is poisonous will kill you
or make you very ill if you eat or drink it:
Some berries are poisonous.

poke /pəʊk/ *verb* (**pokes, poking, poked**
/pəʊkt/)
1 push somebody or something hard with
your finger or another long thin thing: *She
poked me in the eye with a pencil.*
2 push something quickly somewhere:
Jeff poked his head out of the window.
poke *noun*
I gave her a poke to wake her up.

polar /ˈpəʊlə(r)/ *adjective*
of the North or South Pole
polar bear /ˌpəʊlə ˈbeə(r)/ *noun*
a white bear that lives near the North Pole

pole¹ /pəʊl/ *noun*
a long thin piece of wood or metal. Poles
are often used to hold something up: *a flagpole* ◇ *tent poles*

pole² /pəʊl/ *noun*
one of two places at the top and bottom of
the earth: *the North Pole* ◇ *the South
Pole*

police /pəˈliːs/ *noun* (plural)
a group of people whose job is to make sure
that people do not break the laws of a
country: *Have the police found the murderer?* ◇ *a police car*
police force /pəˈliːs fɔːs/ *noun*
all the police officers in a country or part of
a country
policeman /pəˈliːsmən/ *noun* (*plural*
policemen /pəˈliːsmən/)
a man who works in the police
police constable /pəˌliːs ˈkʌnstəbl/
noun
an ordinary police officer ◙ The short
form is **PC**.
police officer /pəˈliːs ɒfɪsə(r)/ *noun*
a policeman or policewoman
police station /pəˈliːs steɪʃn/ *noun*
an office where police officers work
policewoman /pəˈliːswʊmən/ *noun*
(*plural* **policewomen**)
a woman who works in the police

policy /ˈpɒləsi/ *noun* (*plural* **policies**)
the plans of a group of people: *What is the
government's policy on education?*

polish /ˈpɒlɪʃ/ *verb* (**polishes, polish-
ing, polished** /ˈpɒlɪʃt/)
rub something so that it shines: *Have you
polished your shoes?*

polish *noun* (no plural)
stuff that you put on something to make it
shine: *furniture polish*

polite /pəˈlaɪt/ *adjective*
If you are polite, you are helpful and kind
to other people and you do not do or say
things that make people sad or angry: *It is
polite to say 'please' when you ask for
something.* ◙ opposite: **impolite** or **rude**
politely *adverb*
He asked politely for a glass of water.
politeness /pəˈlaɪtnəs/ *noun* (no plural)
being polite

political /pəˈlɪtɪkl/ *adjective*
of or about the work of government: *A political party is a group of people who have
the same ideas about how to control their
country.* ◇ *political beliefs*
politically /pəˈlɪtɪkli/ *adverb*
a politically powerful country

politician /ˌpɒləˈtɪʃn/ *noun*
a person who works in the government or
who wants to work in the government:
Members of Parliament are politicians.

politics /ˈpɒlətɪks/ *noun* (no plural)
1 the work of government: *Are you interested in politics?*
2 the study of government: *She studied
Politics at university.*

pollen /ˈpɒlən/ *noun* (no plural)
the yellow powder in flowers

pollute /pəˈluːt/ *verb* (**pollutes, polluting, polluted**)
make air, rivers, etc dirty and dangerous:
*Many of Britain's rivers are polluted with
chemicals from factories.*
pollution /pəˈluːʃn/ *noun* (no plural)
1 polluting air, rivers, etc: *We must stop
the pollution of our beaches.*
2 dirty and dangerous stuff from cars, factories, etc

pond /pɒnd/ *noun*
a small area of water: *We have a fish-pond
in our garden.*

pony /ˈpəʊni/ *noun* (*plural* **ponies**)
a small horse

pony-tail /ˈpəʊniteɪl/ *noun*
long hair that you tie at the back of your
head so that it hangs down

pool /puːl/ *noun*
1 a little liquid or light on the ground:
After the rain there were pools of water on

i:	i	ɪ	e	æ	ɑ:	ɒ	ɔ:	ʊ	u	u:
see	happy	sit	ten	cat	father	got	saw	put	situation	too

poor

the road. ◇ *She was lying in a pool of blood.*
2 a place for swimming: *Karen dived into the pool.*

poor /pɔː(r)/ *adjective* (**poorer**, **poorest**)
1 with very little money: *She was too poor to buy clothes for her children.* ✪ opposite: **rich**. The noun is **poverty**.
2 a word that you use when you feel sad because somebody has problems: *Poor Tina! She's feeling ill.*
3 not good: *My grandfather is in very poor health.*

the poor *noun* (plural)
people who do not have much money

poorly /'pɔːli/ *adverb*
not well; badly: *The street is poorly lit.*

pop¹ /pɒp/ *noun* (no plural)
modern music that a lot of young people like: *What's your favourite pop group?* ◇ *pop music* ◇ *a pop singer*

pop² /pɒp/ *noun*
a short sharp sound: *The cork came out of the bottle with a loud pop.*

pop³ /pɒp/ *verb* (**pops**, **popping**, **popped** /pɒpt/)
1 make a short sharp sound; make something make a short sharp sound: *The balloon will pop if you put a pin in it.*
2 go somewhere quickly: *She has popped into the shop to buy a newspaper.*
3 put or take something somewhere quickly: *Katie popped a sweet into her mouth.* ◇ *He popped his head round the door to say goodbye.*

pop in go somewhere for a short time: *We were near Tim's house so we popped in for a cup of coffee.*

pop up appear suddenly: *Fast food restaurants are popping up everywhere.*

pope /pəʊp/ *noun*
the most important person in the Roman Catholic Church: *Pope John Paul*

popular /'pɒpjələ(r)/ *adjective*
liked by a lot of people: *Football is a popular sport in Britain.* ✪ opposite: **unpopular**

popularity /ˌpɒpjuˈlærəti/ *noun* (no plural)
being liked by a lot of people

population /ˌpɒpjuˈleɪʃn/ *noun*
the number of people who live in a place: *What is the population of your country?*

pork /pɔːk/ *noun* (no plural)
meat from a pig: *pork sausages* ☞ Note at **pig**

porridge /'pɒrɪdʒ/ *noun* (no plural)
soft food made from oats cooked with milk or water, that people eat for breakfast

port /pɔːt/ *noun*
a town or city by the sea, where ships arrive and leave: *Liverpool is a large port in the North of England.*

portable /'pɔːtəbl/ *adjective*
that you can move or carry easily: *a portable television*

porter /'pɔːtə(r)/ *noun*
1 a person whose job is to carry people's bags in places like railway stations and hotels
2 a person whose job is to look after the entrance of a hotel or other large building

portion /'pɔːʃn/ *noun*
a part of something that one person gets: *He gave a portion of the money to each of his children.* ◇ *a large portion of chips*

portrait /'pɔːtreɪt/ *noun*
a painting or picture of a person

position /pəˈzɪʃn/ *noun*
1 the place where somebody or something is: *Can you show me the position of your village on the map?*
2 the way a person is sitting or lying, or the way a thing is standing: *She was still sitting in the same position when I came back.*
3 how things are at a certain time: *He's in a difficult position – he hasn't got enough money to finish his studies.*

in position in the right place: *The dancers were in position, waiting for the music to start.*

positive /'pɒzətɪv/ *adjective*
1 completely certain: *Are you positive that you closed the door?*
2 that helps you or gives you hope: *The teacher was very positive about my work.*
positively *adverb*
really; certainly: *The idea is positively stupid.*

possess /pəˈzes/ *verb* (**possesses**, **possessing**, **possessed** /pəˈzest/)
have or own something: *He lost everything that he possessed in the fire.*
✪ **Have** and **own** are the words that we usually use.

ʌ	ɜː	ə	eɪ	əʊ	aɪ	aʊ	ɔɪ	ɪə	eə	ʊə
cup	bird	about	say	go	five	now	boy	near	hair	pure

possession /pə'zeʃn/ *noun*
1 (no plural) having or owning something: *The possession of drugs is a crime.*
2 possessions (plural) the things that you have or own

possibility /ˌpɒsə'bɪləti/ *noun* (*plural* **possibilities**)
something that might happen: *There's a possibility that it will rain, so take your umbrella.*

possible /'pɒsəbl/ *adjective*
If something is possible, it can happen or you can do it: *Is it possible to get to Birmingham by train?* ◇ *I'll phone you as soon as possible.* ✪ opposite: **impossible**

possibly /'pɒsəbli/ *adverb*
1 perhaps: *'Will you be free tomorrow?' 'Possibly.'*
2 in a way that can be done: *I'll come as soon as I possibly can.*

post¹ /pəʊst/ *noun*
a tall piece of wood or metal that stands in the ground to hold something or to show where something is: *Can you see a signpost anywhere?*

post² /pəʊst/ *noun* (no plural)
1 the way of sending and receiving letters, parcels, etc: *I sent your present by post.*
2 letters and parcels that you send or receive: *Did you get any post this morning?*

postage /'pəʊstɪdʒ/ *noun* (no plural)
money that you must pay when you send a letter or parcel

postal /'pəʊstl/ *adjective*
of the post: *postal collections*

postbox /'pəʊstbɒks/ *noun* (*plural* **postboxes**)
a box in the street where you put letters that you want to send

postcard

postcard /'pəʊstkɑːd/ *noun*
a card with a picture on one side, that you write on and send by post

postcode /'pəʊstkəʊd/ *noun*
a group of numbers and letters that you write at the end of an address ☞ picture on page 299

postman /'pəʊstmən/ *noun* (*plural* **postmen** /'pəʊstmən/)
a man who takes (**delivers**) letters and parcels to people

post office /'pəʊst ɒfɪs/ *noun*
a building where you go to send letters and parcels and to buy stamps

postwoman /'pəʊstwʊmən/ *noun* (*plural* **postwomen**)
a woman who takes (**delivers**) letters and parcels to people

post³ /pəʊst/ *verb* (**posts**, **posting**, **posted**)
1 send a letter or parcel: *Could you post this letter for me?*
2 send somebody to a place to do a job: *Sara's company have posted her to Japan for two years.*

poster /'pəʊstə(r)/ *noun*
a big piece of paper on a wall, with a picture or words on it

postpone /pə'spəʊn/ *verb* (**postpones**, **postponing**, **postponed** /pə'spəʊnd/)
say that something will happen at a later time, not now: *It's raining, so we will postpone the game until tomorrow.*

pot /pɒt/ *noun*
1 a deep round container for cooking: *a big pot of soup*
2 a container that you use for a special thing: *a teapot* ◇ *a pot of paint* ◇ *a plant pot*

potato /pə'teɪtəʊ/ *noun* (*plural* **potatoes**)
a round vegetable that grows under the ground, that is white on the inside and brown or yellow on the outside. You cook it before you eat it: *a baked potato*

pottery /'pɒtəri/ *noun* (no plural)
1 cups, plates and other things made from **clay** (heavy earth that becomes hard when it dries): *This shop sells beautiful pottery.*
2 making cups, plates and other things from clay: *Her hobby is pottery.*

poultry /'pəʊltri/ *noun* (plural)
birds that people keep on farms for their eggs or their meat. Hens, ducks and geese are poultry.

p	b	t	d	k	g	tʃ	dʒ	f	v	θ	ð
pen	**bad**	**tea**	**did**	**cat**	**got**	**chain**	**jam**	**fall**	**van**	**thin**	**this**

pounce /paʊns/ *verb* (**pounces, pouncing, pounced** /paʊnst/)
jump on somebody or something suddenly: *The cat pounced on the bird.*

pound /paʊnd/ *noun*
1 money that people use in Britain. There are 100 **pence** in a pound: *The computer cost six hundred pounds.* ◇ *a ten-pound note* ◇ *a pound coin* ✪ We write **£**: *I spent £40 today.*
2 a measure of weight (= 0.454 kilograms). There are 16 **ounces** in a pound: *Half a pound of mushrooms, please.* ◇ *two pounds of sugar* ◇ *These apples cost 40p a pound.* ✪ The short way of writing 'pound' is **lb**.

> ✪ In the past, people in Britain used **ounces**, **pounds** and **stones** to measure weight, not **grams** and **kilograms**. Now, many people use and understand both ways.

pour

pour /pɔː(r)/ *verb* (**pours, pouring, poured** /pɔːd/)
1 make liquid flow out of or into something: *She poured wine into my glass.* ◇ *She poured me a glass of wine.*
2 flow quickly: *Oil poured out of the damaged ship.*
it's pouring it is raining very hard

poverty /ˈpɒvəti/ *noun* (no plural)
being poor: *There are many people living in poverty in this city.*

powder /ˈpaʊdə(r)/ *noun*
dry stuff that is made of a lot of very small pieces: *washing-powder* (= for washing clothes) ◇ *face-powder* (= that you put on your face)

power /ˈpaʊə(r)/ *noun*
1 (no plural) being strong; being able to do something: *the power of the storm* ◇ *I did everything in my power* (= everything I could do) *to help her.*
2 (no plural) being able to make people do what you want: *The president has a lot of power.*

3 (no plural) what makes things work; energy: *nuclear power*
4 (*plural* **powers**) the right to do something: *Police officers have the power to arrest people.*
5 (*plural* **powers**) a strong person or country: *There is a meeting of world powers in Rome next week.*

power point /ˈpaʊə pɔɪnt/ *noun*
a set of holes in a wall where you can put an electric plug

power station /ˈpaʊə steɪʃn/ *noun*
a place where electricity is made

powerful /ˈpaʊəfl/ *adjective*
1 very strong; with a lot of power: *The car has a very powerful engine.* ◇ *The president is very powerful.*
2 that you can smell or hear clearly, or feel strongly: *a powerful drug*

practical /ˈpræktɪkl/ *adjective*
1 that is about doing or making things, not just about ideas: *Have you got any practical experience of teaching?*
2 able to do useful things: *I'm not a very practical person.*
3 possible to do easily: *Your plan isn't practical.*

practically /ˈpræktɪkli/ *adverb*
almost; nearly: *Don't go out – lunch is practically ready!* ◇ *It rained practically every day.*

practice /ˈpræktɪs/ *noun* (no plural)
1 doing something many times so that you will do it well: *You need lots of practice when you're learning to play a musical instrument.*
2 *American English for* **practise**
out of practice not good at something, because you have not done it for a long time

practise /ˈpræktɪs/ *verb* (**practises, practising, practised** /ˈpræktɪst/)
do something many times so that you will do it well: *If you want to play the piano well, you must practise every day.*

praise /preɪz/ *verb* (**praises, praising, praised** /preɪzd/)
say that somebody or something is good: *She was praised for her hard work.*
praise *noun* (no plural)
The book has received a lot of praise.

pram /præm/ *noun*
a thing that a baby lies in to go out. It has wheels so that you can push it.

prawn /prɔ:n/ *noun*
a small pink sea animal that you can eat

pray /preɪ/ *verb* (**prays, praying, prayed** /preɪd/)
speak to God or a god: *They prayed for help.*

prayer /preə(r)/ *noun*
words that you say when you speak to God or a god: *They said a prayer for peace.*

preach /pri:tʃ/ *verb* (**preaches, preaching, preached** /pri:tʃt/)
talk about God or a god to a group of people

precaution /prɪ'kɔ:ʃn/ *noun*
something that you do so that bad things will not happen: *I took the precaution of locking all the windows when I went out.*

precious /'preʃəs/ *adjective*
1 very valuable: *Diamonds are precious stones.*
2 that you love very much: *My family is very precious to me.*

precise /prɪ'saɪs/ *adjective*
exactly right: *I gave him precise instructions on how to get to my house.*
precisely *adverb*
exactly: *They arrived at two o'clock precisely.*

predict /prɪ'dɪkt/ *verb* (**predicts, predicting, predicted**)
say what you think will happen: *She predicted that it would rain, and she was right.*
prediction /prɪ'dɪkʃn/ *noun*
His predictions were not correct.

prefer /prɪ'fɜ:(r)/ *verb* (**prefers, preferring, preferred** /prɪ'fɜ:d/)
like one thing or person better than another: *Would you prefer tea or coffee?* ◇ *Jane wants to go to the cinema but I*
would prefer to stay at home. ◇ *He prefers going out to studying.*

preference /'prefrəns/ *noun*
liking one thing or person better than another: *We have lemonade and orange juice – do you have a preference?*

preferable /'prefrəbl/ *adjective*
better; that you like more: *I think living in the country is preferable to living in the city.*

preferably /'prefrəbli/ *adverb*
Phone me on Sunday morning, but preferably not too early!

prefix /'pri:fɪks/ *noun* (*plural* **prefixes**)
a group of letters that you add to the beginning of a word to make another word: *The prefix 'im-' means 'not', so 'impossible' means 'not possible'.* ☞ Look at **suffix**.

pregnant /'pregnənt/ *adjective*
If a woman is pregnant, she has a baby growing in her body.

prejudice /'predʒədɪs/ *noun*
a feeling of not liking somebody or something, before you know much about them: *She has a prejudice against foreigners.*

prejudiced /'predʒədɪst/ *adjective*
with strong and unfair ideas about somebody or something, before you know much about them: *He is prejudiced against me because I'm a woman.*

preparation /ˌprepə'reɪʃn/ *noun*
1 (no plural) making something ready: *the preparation of food*
2 preparations (plural) what you do to get ready for something: *wedding preparations*
in preparation for something to get ready for something: *I packed my bags in preparation for the journey.*

prepare /prɪ'peə(r)/ *verb* (**prepares, preparing, prepared** /prɪ'peəd/)
make somebody or something ready; make yourself ready: *Martin is in the kitchen preparing the dinner.* ◇ *I prepared well for the exam.*
prepared for something ready for something difficult or bad: *I wasn't prepared for all these problems.*
prepared to happy to do something: *I'm not prepared to give you any money.*

preposition /ˌprepə'zɪʃn/ *noun*
a word that you use before a noun or pronoun to show where, when, how, etc: *'In,'*

i:	i	ɪ	e	æ	ɑ:	ɒ	ɔ:	ʊ	u	u:
see	happy	sit	ten	cat	father	got	saw	put	situation	too

'for,' 'after' and *'above'* are all preposi-tions. ◇ *In the sentence 'He travelled from London to Munich', 'from'* and *'to'* are prepositions.

prescribe /prɪ'skraɪb/ *verb* (**prescribes, prescribing, prescribed** /prɪ'skraɪbd/)
say that somebody must take a medicine: *The doctor prescribed some tablets for her cough.*

prescription /prɪ'skrɪpʃn/ *noun*
a piece of paper where a doctor writes what medicine you need. You take it to a **chemist's** and get the medicine there.

presence /'prezns/ *noun* (no plural)
being in a place: *She was so quiet that I didn't notice her presence.*
in the presence of somebody with another person or other people there: *She signed the papers in the presence of a lawyer.*

present[1] /'preznt/ *adjective*
1 in a place: *There were 200 people pres-ent at the meeting.*
2 being or happening now: *What is your present job?*

present[2] /'preznt/ *noun* (no plural)
1 the time now: *I can't help you at present – I'm too busy.*
2 (*also* **present tense**) the form of a verb that you use to talk about now ☞ Look at **past** and **future**.

present[3] /'preznt/ *noun*
something that you give to or get from somebody: *a birthday present*

present[4] /prɪ'zent/ *verb* (**presents, pre-senting, presented**)
give something to somebody: *Who pre-sented the prizes to the winners?*
presentation /ˌprezn'teɪʃn/ *noun*
presenting something: *The presentation of the prizes will take place at 7.30.*

presently /'prezntli/ *adverb*
1 soon: *He will be here presently.*
2 now: *She's presently working in a café.*

preservation /ˌprezə'veɪʃn/ *noun* (no plural)
keeping something safe; making some-thing stay the same: *the preservation of rare birds*

preserve /prɪ'zɜːv/ *verb* (**preserves, preserving, preserved** /prɪ'zɜːvd/)
keep something safe; make something stay

the same: *Parts of the town are new, but they have preserved many of the old buildings.*

president /'prezɪdənt/ *noun*
1 the leader in many countries that do not have a king or queen: *the President of the United States of America*
2 the most important person in a big com-pany, club, etc
presidential /ˌprezɪ'denʃl/ *adjective*
of a president or his/her work: *the presid-ential elections*

press[1] /pres/ *verb* (**presses, pressing, pressed** /prest/)
1 push something: *If you press this but-ton, the door will open.* ◇ *She pressed her face against the window.*
2 make clothes flat and smooth using an iron: *This suit needs pressing.*

press[2] /pres/ *noun*
1 **the press** (no plural) newspapers and magazines and the people who write them: *She told her story to the press.*
2 (*plural* **presses**) pushing something: *Give the doorbell a press.*
3 (*plural* **presses**) a machine for printing things like books and newspapers

pressure /'preʃə(r)/ *noun*
1 the force that presses on something: *the air pressure in a car tyre*
2 a feeling of worry or unhappiness, for example because you have too many things to do: *the pressures of city life*

presume /prɪ'zjuːm/ *verb* (**presumes, presuming, presumed** /prɪ'zjuːmd/)
think that something is true but not be cer-tain: *She's not home yet so I presume she's still at work.*

pretend /prɪ'tend/ *verb* (**pretends, pre-tending, pretended**)
try to make somebody believe something that is not true: *He didn't want to talk, so he pretended to be asleep.*

pretty[1] /'prɪti/ *adjective* (**prettier, pretti-est**)
nice to look at: *a pretty little girl* ◇ *These flowers are very pretty.* ☞ Note at **beautiful**

pretty[2] /'prɪti/ *adverb*
quite; fairly: *It's pretty cold today.*

prevent /prɪ'vent/ *verb* (**prevents, pre-venting, prevented**)
stop somebody from doing something or

ʌ	ɜː	ə	eɪ	əʊ	aɪ	aʊ	ɔɪ	ɪə	eə	ʊə
cup	bird	about	say	go	five	now	boy	near	hair	pure

stop something happening: *Her parents want to prevent her from getting married.* ◇ *It is easier to prevent disease than to cure it.*

prevention /prɪ'venʃn/ *noun* (no plural)
preventing something: *the prevention of crime*

previous /'pri:viəs/ *adjective*
that happened or came before or earlier: *Who was the previous owner of the car?*
previously *adverb*
I work in a factory now, but previously I was a secretary.

prey /preɪ/ *noun* (no plural)
an animal or bird that another animal or bird kills for food: *Zebra are prey for lions.*

price /praɪs/ *noun*
how much money you pay to buy something: *The price is £15.* ◇ *Prices in this country are very high.*

prick /prɪk/ *verb* (**pricks**, **pricking**, **pricked** /prɪkt/)
make a very small hole in something, or hurt somebody, with a sharp point: *I pricked my finger on a needle.* ◇ *Prick the potatoes with a fork before you cook them.*
prick *noun*
a small sharp pain: *She felt the prick of a needle.*

prickle /'prɪkl/ *noun*
a sharp point on a plant or an animal: *A hedgehog has prickles.*
prickly /'prɪkli/ *adjective*
covered with prickles: *a prickly bush*

pride /praɪd/ *noun* (no plural)
1 being pleased about something that you or others have done or about something that you have; being proud: *She showed us her painting with great pride.*
2 the feeling that you are better than other people

priest /pri:st/ *noun*
a person who leads people in their religion: *a Buddhist priest*

primary /'praɪməri/ *adjective*
first; most important: *What is the primary cause of the illness?*
primary school /'praɪməri sku:l/ *noun*
a school for children between the ages of five and eleven

prime minister /,praɪm 'mɪnɪstə(r)/ *noun*
the leader of the government in some countries, for example in Britain

prince /prɪns/ *noun*
1 a man in a royal family, especially the son of a king or queen: *the Prince of Wales*
2 a man who is the ruler of a small country

princess /,prɪn'ses/ *noun* (*plural* **princesses**)
a woman in a royal family, especially the daughter of a king or queen or the wife of a prince

principal[1] /'prɪnsəpl/ *adjective*
most important: *My principal reason for going to Rome was to learn Italian.*

principal[2] /'prɪnsəpl/ *noun*
a person who is in charge of a school or college

principally /'prɪnsəpli/ *adverb*
mainly; mostly: *She sometimes travels to Europe, but she works principally in Africa.*

principle /'prɪnsəpl/ *noun*
1 a rule about how you should live: *He has very strong principles.*
2 a rule or fact about how something happens or works: *scientific principles*

print /prɪnt/ *verb* (**prints**, **printing**, **printed**)
1 put words or pictures onto paper using a machine. Books, newspapers and magazines are printed.
2 write with letters that are not joined together: *Please print your name and address clearly.*
print *noun*
1 (no plural) letters that a machine makes on paper: *The print is too small to read.*
2 (*plural* **prints**) a mark where something has pressed: *footprints in the snow*
3 (*plural* **prints**) a copy on paper of a painting or photograph

printer /'prɪntə(r)/ *noun*
1 a person or company that prints things like books or newspapers
2 a machine that prints words from a computer ☞ picture at **computer**

prison /'prɪzn/ *noun*
a place where people must stay when they have done something that is wrong: *He*

p	b	t	d	k	g	tʃ	dʒ	f	v	θ	ð
pen	**bad**	**tea**	**did**	**cat**	**got**	**chain**	**jam**	**fall**	**van**	**thin**	**this**

was sent to prison for robbing a bank.
◇ *She was in prison for 15 years.*

prisoner /ˈprɪznə(r)/ *noun*
a person who is in prison or any person
who is not free

private /ˈpraɪvət/ *adjective*
1 for one person or a small group of people
only, and not for anybody else: *The house
has a private swimming-pool* (= that only
the people who live in the house can use).
◇ *You shouldn't read his letters – they're
private.*
2 alone; without other people there: *I
would like a private meeting with the
manager.*
3 not of your job: *She never talks about
her private life with the people at work.*
4 not controlled by the government: *a private hospital* (= you must pay to go there)
◇ *private schools*
in private alone; without other people
there: *Can I speak to you in private?*
privately *adverb*
*Let's go into my office – we can talk more
privately there.*

privilege /ˈprɪvəlɪdʒ/ *noun*
something special that only one person or
a few people may do or have: *Prisoners
who behave well have special privileges.*
privileged /ˈprɪvəlɪdʒd/ *adjective*
*I felt very privileged when I was invited to
Buckingham Palace.*

prize /praɪz/ *noun*
something that you give to the person who
wins a game, race, etc: *I won first prize in
the painting competition.*

probable /ˈprɒbəbl/ *adjective*
If something is probable, it will almost certainly happen or it is almost certainly true:
It is probable that he will be late. ✪ opposite: **improbable**

probably /ˈprɒbəbli/ *adverb*
almost certainly: *I will probably see you
on Thursday.*

problem /ˈprɒbləm/ *noun*
1 something that is difficult; something
that makes you worry: *She has a lot of
problems. Her husband is ill and her son is
in prison.* ◇ *There is a problem with my
telephone – it doesn't work.*
2 a question that you must answer by
thinking about it: *I can't solve this
problem.*

proceed /prəˈsiːd/ *verb* (**proceeds, pro-
ceeding, proceeded**)
continue; go on: *If everyone is here, then
we can proceed with the meeting.* ✪ **Continue** and **go on** are the words that we
usually use.

process /ˈprəʊses/ *noun* (*plural* **pro-
cesses**)
a number of actions, one after the other,
for doing or making something: *He explained the process of building a boat.*
◇ *Learning a language is usually a slow
process.*

procession /prəˈseʃn/ *noun*
a line of people or cars that are moving
slowly along: *We watched the carnival
procession.*

produce¹ /prəˈdjuːs/ *verb* (**produces,
producing, produced** /prəˈdjuːst/)
1 make or grow something: *This factory
produces cars.* ◇ *What does the farm
produce?*
2 make something happen: *His hard work
produced good results.*
3 bring something out to show it: *She produced a ticket from her pocket.*
4 organize something like a play or film:
The play was produced by Peter Gordon.

produce² /ˈprɒdjuːs/ *noun* (no plural)
food that you grow on a farm or in a garden to sell: *fresh farm produce*

producer /prəˈdjuːsə(r)/ *noun*
1 a person who organizes something like a
play or film: *a television producer*
2 a company or country that makes or
grows something: *Brazil is an important
producer of coffee.*

product /ˈprɒdʌkt/ *noun*
something that people make or grow to
sell: *Coffee is Brazil's main product.*

production /prəˈdʌkʃn/ *noun*
1 (no plural) making or growing something: *the production of oil*
2 (*plural* **productions**) a play, film, etc

profession /prəˈfeʃn/ *noun*
a job that needs a lot of studying and special training: *She's a doctor by profession.*

professional /prəˈfeʃənl/ *adjective*
1 of or about somebody who has a profession: *I got professional advice from a
lawyer.*
2 who does something for money as a job:

s	z	ʃ	ʒ	h	m	n	ŋ	l	r	j	w
so	**zoo**	**shoe**	**vision**	**hat**	**man**	**no**	**sing**	**leg**	**red**	**yes**	**wet**

a professional footballer ☞ Look at **amateur**.

professionally /prə'feʃənəli/ *adverb*
He plays the piano professionally.

professor /prə'fesə(r)/ *noun*
an important teacher at a university:
Professor Hall

profile /'prəʊfaɪl/ *noun*
the shape of a person's face when you see it
from the side

profit /'prɒfɪt/ *noun*
money that you get when you sell something for more than it cost to buy or make:
*If you buy a bike for £70 and sell it for
£80, you make a profit of £10.*

profitable /'prɒfɪtəbl/ *adjective*
If something is profitable, it brings you
money: *a profitable business*

program /'prəʊgræm/ *noun*
1 a list of instructions that you give to a
computer
2 *American English for* **programme**
program *verb* (**programs, programming, programmed** /'prəʊgræmd/)
give instructions to a computer ✪ In
American English the spellings are **programing** and **programed**.
programmer *noun*
a person whose job is to write programs for
a computer

programme /'prəʊgræm/ *noun*
1 something on television or radio: *Did
you watch that programme about Japan
on TV last night?*
2 a piece of paper or a little book that tells
people at a play or concert what they are
going to see or hear: *There's a note about
the singer in the programme.*
3 a plan of things to do: *What is your
programme for tomorrow?*

progress¹ /'prəʊgres/ *noun* (no plural)
moving forward or becoming better: *Jo has
made good progress in maths this year.*
in progress happening: *Silence! Examination in progress.*

progress² /prə'gres/ *verb* (**progresses,
progressing, progressed** /prə'grest/)
move forward or become better: *I felt more
tired as the day progressed.*

prohibit /prə'hɪbɪt/ *verb* (**prohibits,
prohibiting, prohibited**)
say that people must not do something:
Smoking is prohibited in the theatre.

project /'prɒdʒekt/ *noun*
1 a big plan to do something: *a project to
build a new airport*
2 a piece of work that you do at school.
You find out a lot about something and
write about it: *We did a project on Africa.*

projector /prə'dʒektə(r)/ *noun*
a machine that shows films or pictures on
a wall or screen

prominent /'prɒmɪnənt/ *adjective*
1 easy to see, for example because it is
bigger than usual: *prominent teeth*
2 important and famous: *a prominent
writer*

promise¹ /'prɒmɪs/ *verb* (**promises,
promising, promised** /'prɒmɪst/)
say that you will certainly do or not do
something: *She promised to give me the
money today.* ◇ *I promise I'll come.*
◇ *Promise me that you won't be late!*

promise² /'prɒmɪs/ *noun*
saying that you will certainly do or not do
something
break a promise not do what you
promised
keep a promise do what you promised
make a promise say that you will
certainly do or not do something

promote /prə'məʊt/ *verb* (**promotes,
promoting, promoted**)
give somebody a more important job: *She
worked hard, and after a year she was
promoted to manager.*
promotion /prə'məʊʃn/ *noun*
The new job is a promotion for me.

prompt /prɒmpt/ *adjective*
quick: *She gave me a prompt answer.*
promptly *adverb*
quickly; not late: *We arrived promptly at
two o'clock.*

pronoun /'prəʊnaʊn/ *noun*
a word that you use in place of a noun:
'He', 'it', 'me' and 'them' are all pronouns.

pronounce /prə'naʊns/ *verb* (**pronounces, pronouncing, pronounced**
/prə'naʊnst/)
make the sound of a letter or word: *How do*

i:	i	ɪ	e	æ	ɑ:	ɒ	ɔ:	ʊ	u	u:
see	happy	sit	ten	cat	father	got	saw	put	situation	too

you pronounce your name? ◇ You don't pronounce the 'b' at the end of 'comb'.

pronunciation /prə,nʌnsi'eɪʃn/ *noun*
how you say a word or words: *There are two different pronunciations for this word. ◇ His pronunciation is very good.*

proof /pru:f/ *noun* (no plural)
something that shows that an idea is true: *Do you have any proof that you are the owner of this car?* ☻ The verb is **prove**.

propeller /prə'pelə(r)/ *noun*
a thing that is joined to the engine on a ship or an aeroplane. It turns round fast to make the ship or aeroplane move.

proper /'prɒpə(r)/ *adjective*
1 right or correct: *I haven't got the proper tools to mend the car.*
2 real: *He hasn't got any proper friends.*
properly *adverb*
well or correctly: *Close the door properly.*

property /'prɒpəti/ *noun*
1 (no plural) something that you have or own: *This book is the property of James Gray.*
2 (*plural* **properties**) a building and the land around it

prophet /'prɒfɪt/ *noun*
a person that God chooses to give his message to people

proportion /prə'pɔ:ʃn/ *noun*
1 a part of something: *A large proportion of people leave school when they are 16.*
2 the amount or size of one thing compared to another thing: *What is the proportion of men to women in the factory?*

proposal /prə'pəʊzl/ *noun*
1 a plan or idea about how to do something: *a proposal to build a new station*
2 asking somebody to marry you

propose /prə'pəʊz/ *verb* (**proposes, proposing, proposed** /prə'pəʊzd/)
1 say what you think should happen or be done: *I proposed that we should meet again on Monday.*
2 ask somebody to marry you: *Melissa proposed to Mike.*

protect /prə'tekt/ *verb* (**protects, protecting, protected**)
keep somebody or something safe: *Wear a*

hat to protect your head against the sun. ◇ Parents try to protect their children from danger.

protection /prə'tekʃn/ *noun* (no plural)
keeping somebody or something safe: *protection against disease*

protest /prə'test/ *verb* (**protests, protesting, protested**)
say or show strongly that you do not like something: *They protested against the government's plans.*
protest /'prəʊtest/ *noun*
They made a protest against the new tax.

Protestant /'prɒtɪstənt/ *noun*
a person who believes in the Christian God and who is not a Roman Catholic

proud /praʊd/ *adjective* (**prouder, proudest**)
1 If you feel proud, you are pleased about something that you or others have done or about something that you have: *They are very proud of their new house.*
2 A person who is proud thinks that he/she is better than other people: *She was too proud to say she was sorry.*
☻ The noun is **pride**.
proudly *adverb*
'I made this myself,' he said proudly.

prove /pru:v/ *verb* (**proves, proving, proved** /pru:vd/, **has proved** or **has proven** /'pru:vn/)
show that something is true: *The blood on his shirt proves that he is the murderer.*
☻ The noun is **proof**.

proverb /'prɒvɜ:b/ *noun*
a short sentence that people often say, that gives help or advice: *'The early bird catches the worm' is an English proverb.*

provide /prə'vaɪd/ *verb* (**provides, providing, provided**)
give something to somebody who needs it: *I'll provide the food for the party. ◇ The company have provided me with a car.*

provided /prə'vaɪdɪd/, **providing** /prə'vaɪdɪŋ/ *conjunction*
only if: *Phone me when you get home, providing it's not too late. ◇ I'll go provided that the children can come with me.*

province /'prɒvɪns/ *noun*
a part of a country: *Canada has ten provinces.*
provincial /prə'vɪnʃl/ *adjective*
of a province: *the provincial government*

ʌ	ɜ:	ə	eɪ	əʊ	aɪ	aʊ	ɔɪ	ɪə	eə	ʊə
c**u**p	b**ir**d	**a**bout	s**ay**	g**o**	f**i**ve	n**ow**	b**oy**	n**ea**r	h**air**	p**ure**

PS /ˌpiː ˈes/
You write 'PS' at the end of a letter, after your name, when you want to add something: ... *Love from Paul. PS I'll bring the car.*

psychiatrist /saɪˈkaɪətrɪst/ *noun*
a doctor who helps people who are ill in the mind

psychology /saɪˈkɒlədʒi/ *noun* (no plural)
the study of the mind and how it works
psychologist /saɪˈkɒlədʒɪst/ *noun*
a person who studies or knows a lot about psychology

pt *short way of writing* **pint**

PTO /ˌpiː tiː ˈəʊ/
please turn over; words at the bottom of a page that tell you to turn to the next page

pub /pʌb/ *noun*
a place where people go to have a drink and meet their friends

○ In Britain, you can buy **alcoholic** drinks like beer and wine in a pub if you are over the age of 18. In a lot of pubs you can also buy food.

public¹ /ˈpʌblɪk/ *adjective*
of or for everybody: *a public telephone* ◇ *Smoking is not allowed in public places.*
public convenience /ˌpʌblɪk kənˈviːniəns/ *noun*
a building or room with a toilet for everybody to use, for example in the street
public school /ˌpʌblɪk ˈskuːl/ *noun*
a school for pupils between the age of 13 and 18. Parents must pay to send their children to a public school.
public transport /ˌpʌblɪk ˈtrænspɔːt/ *noun*
buses and trains that everybody can use: *I usually travel by public transport.*
publicly *adverb*
to everybody; not secretly: *She spoke publicly about her friendship with the Prince.*

public² /ˈpʌblɪk/ *noun*
the public (no plural)
all people: *The palace is open to the public between 10 a.m. and 4 p.m.*
in public when other people are there: *I don't want to talk about it in public.*

publication /ˌpʌblɪˈkeɪʃn/ *noun*
1 (no plural) making and selling a book,

magazine, etc: *He became very rich after the publication of his first book.*
2 (*plural* **publications**) a book, magazine, etc

publicity /pʌbˈlɪsəti/ *noun* (no plural)
giving information about something so that people know about it: *There was a lot of publicity for the new film.*

publish /ˈpʌblɪʃ/ *verb* (**publishes, publishing, published** /ˈpʌblɪʃt/)
prepare and print a book, magazine or newspaper for selling: *This dictionary was published by Oxford University Press.*
publisher *noun*
a person or company that publishes books, magazines or newspapers

pudding /ˈpʊdɪŋ/ *noun*
1 something sweet that you eat at the end of a meal: *What's for pudding today?*
2 a kind of cake that you usually eat hot at the end of a meal

puddle /ˈpʌdl/ *noun*
a little water on the ground

puff /pʌf/ *noun*
a small amount of air, wind, smoke, etc that blows: *a puff of smoke*
puff *verb* (**puffs, puffing, puffed** /pʌft/)
1 come out in puffs: *Smoke was puffing out of the chimney.*
2 breathe quickly: *She was puffing as she ran up the hill.*

pull

pull¹ /pʊl/ *verb* (**pulls, pulling, pulled** /pʊld/)
1 move somebody or something strongly towards you: *She pulled the drawer open.*
2 go forward, moving something behind you: *The cart was pulled by two horses.*
3 move something somewhere: *He pulled up his trousers.*
pull down destroy a building: *The old school has been pulled down.*
pull in drive a car to the side of the road and stop: *I pulled in to look at the map.*

p	b	t	d	k	g	tʃ	dʒ	f	v	θ	ð
pen	**b**ad	**t**ea	**d**id	**c**at	**g**ot	**ch**ain	**j**am	**f**all	**v**an	**th**in	**th**is

pull yourself together control your feelings after being upset: *Pull yourself together and stop crying.*
pull up stop a car: *The driver pulled up at the traffic lights.*

pull² /pʊl/
pulling something: *Give the rope a pull.*

pullover /ˈpʊləʊvə(r)/ *noun*
a warm piece of clothing with sleeves, that you wear on the top part of your body. Pullovers are often made of wool.

pulse /pʌls/ *noun*
the beating of your heart that you feel in different parts of your body, especially in your wrist: *The nurse felt his pulse.*

pump /pʌmp/ *noun*
a machine that moves a liquid or gas into or out of something: *a bicycle-pump* ◇ *a petrol pump*
pump *verb* (**pumps, pumping, pumped** /pʌmpt/)
move a liquid or gas with a pump: *Your heart pumps blood around your body.*
pump up fill something with air, using a pump: *I pumped up my bicycle tyres.*

pumpkin /ˈpʌmpkɪn/ *noun*
a very large round vegetable with a thick orange skin

pun /pʌn/ *noun*
a funny use of a word that has two meanings, or that sounds the same as another word

punch /pʌntʃ/ *verb* (**punches, punching, punched** /pʌntʃt/)
1 hit somebody or something hard with your closed hand (your **fist**): *She punched me in the stomach.*
2 make a hole in something with a special tool: *He punched my ticket.*
punch *noun* (*plural* **punches**)
a punch on the chin

punctual /ˈpʌŋktʃuəl/ *adjective*
If you are punctual, you come or do something at the right time: *Please try to be punctual for your classes.*
punctually /ˈpʌŋktʃuəli/ *adverb*
They arrived punctually at seven o'clock.

punctuate /ˈpʌŋktʃueɪt/ *verb* (**punctuates, punctuating, punctuated**)
put marks like commas, full stops and question marks in writing

punctuation /ˌpʌŋktʃuˈeɪʃn/ *noun* (no plural)
using punctuation marks when you are writing
punctuation mark /pʌŋktʃuˈeɪʃn maːk/ *noun*
one of the signs that you use when you are writing. Commas (,), full stops (.) and colons (:) are all punctuation marks.

puncture /ˈpʌŋktʃə(r)/ *noun*
a hole in a tyre, that lets the air go out: *My bike has got a puncture.*
puncture *verb* (**punctures, puncturing, punctured** /ˈpʌŋktʃəd/)
make a puncture in something: *A piece of glass punctured the tyre.*

punish /ˈpʌnɪʃ/ *verb* (**punishes, punishing, punished** /ˈpʌnɪʃt/)
make somebody suffer because they have done something wrong: *The children were punished for telling lies.*
punishment /ˈpʌnɪʃmənt/ *noun*
What is the punishment for murder in your country? ◇ *The child was sent to bed as a punishment for being naughty.*

pupil /ˈpjuːpl/ *noun*
a person who is learning at school: *There are 30 pupils in the class.*

puppet /ˈpʌpɪt/ *noun*
a doll that you move by pulling strings or by putting your hand inside it and moving your fingers

puppy /ˈpʌpi/ *noun* (*plural* **puppies**)
a young dog

purchase /ˈpɜːtʃəs/ *verb* (**purchases, purchasing, purchased** /ˈpɜːtʃəst/)
buy something: *The company has purchased three new shops.* ✪ **Buy** is the word that we usually use.
purchase *noun*
buying something; something that you have bought: *She made several purchases and then left.*

pure /pjʊə(r)/ *adjective* (**purer, purest**)
1 not mixed with anything else; clean: *This shirt is pure cotton.* ◇ *pure mountain air*
2 complete or total: *What she said was pure nonsense.*
purely *adverb*
completely or only: *He doesn't like his job – he does it purely for the money.*

s	z	ʃ	ʒ	h	m	n	ŋ	l	r	j	w
so	**zoo**	**shoe**	vision	**hat**	**man**	**no**	sing	**leg**	**red**	**yes**	**wet**

purple /'pɜːpl/ *adjective*
with a colour between red and blue
purple *noun*
She often wears purple.

purpose /'pɜːpəs/ *noun*
the reason for doing something: *What is the purpose of your visit?*
on purpose because you want to; not by accident: *'You've broken my pen!' 'I'm sorry, I didn't do it on purpose.'*

purr /pɜː(r)/ *verb* (**purrs, purring, purred** /pɜːd/)
When a cat purrs, it makes a low sound that shows that it is happy.

purse

purse /pɜːs/ *noun*
1 a small bag that you keep money in
2 *American English for* **handbag**

pursue /pə'sjuː/ *verb* (**pursues, pursuing, pursued** /pə'sjuːd/)
follow somebody or something because you want to catch them: *The police pursued the stolen car for several kilometres.*
✪ **Chase** is the word that we usually use.

push

push /pʊʃ/ *verb* (**pushes, pushing, pushed** /pʊʃt/)
1 move somebody or something strongly away from you: *The car broke down so we had to push it to a garage.*
2 press something with your finger: *Push the red button to stop the bus.*
push *noun* (*plural* **pushes**)
She gave him a push and he fell.

pushchair /'pʊʃtʃeə(r)/ *noun*
a chair on wheels for a small child

pussy /'pʊsi/ *noun* (*plural* **pussies**)
a word for 'cat' that children use

pushchair

put /pʊt/ *verb* (**puts, putting, put, has put**)
move something to a place: *She put the book on the table.* ◇ *He put his hand in his pocket.* ◇ *Put* (= write) *your name at the top of the page.*
put away put something in its usual place: *She put the box away in the cupboard.*
put down put something on another thing, for example on the floor or a table
put somebody off make you feel that you do not like somebody or something, or that you do not want to do something: *The accident put me off driving.*
put something off not do something until a later time: *He put off his holiday because the children were ill.*
put on 1 take clothes and wear them: *Put on your coat.* ✪ opposite: **take off**
2 press or turn something to make an electrical thing start working: *I put on the TV.* ◇ *Put the lights on.* 3 make a record, cassette or compact disc start to play: *Let's put my new cassette on.*
put out stop a fire or stop a light shining: *She put out the fire with a bucket of water.*
put somebody through connect somebody on the telephone to the person that they want to speak to: *Can you put me through to the manager, please?*
put somebody up let somebody sleep in your home: *Can you put me up for the night?*
put up with somebody or **something** have pain or problems without complaining: *We can't change the bad weather, so we have to put up with it.*

puzzle[1] /'pʌzl/ *noun*
1 something that is difficult to understand or explain: *Janet's reason for leaving her job is a puzzle to me.*
2 a game that is difficult and makes you think a lot: *a crossword puzzle* ☞ Look also at **jigsaw puzzle**.

i:	i	ɪ	e	æ	ɑː	ɒ	ɔː	ʊ	u	uː
see	happy	sit	ten	cat	father	got	saw	put	situation	too

puzzle² /'pʌzl/ *verb* (**puzzles, puzzling, puzzled** /'pʌzld/)
make you think a lot because you cannot understand or explain it: *Tim's illness puzzled his doctors.*
puzzled *adjective*
If you are puzzled, you cannot understand or explain something: *She was puzzled when he didn't answer her letter.*
puzzling /'pʌzlɪŋ/ *adjective*
If something is puzzling, you cannot understand or explain it.

pyjamas /pə'dʒɑːməz/ *noun* (plural)
a loose jacket and trousers that you wear in bed

pyramid /'pɪrəmɪd/ *noun*
a shape with a flat bottom and three or four sides that come to a point at the top: *the pyramids of Egypt* ☞ picture on page 161

Qq

quack /kwæk/ *noun*
the sound that a duck makes
quack *verb* (**quacks, quacking, quacked** /kwækt/)
make this sound

qualification /ˌkwɒlɪfɪ'keɪʃn/ *noun*
an examination that you have passed, or training or knowledge that you need to do a special job: *He left school with no qualifications.*

qualify /'kwɒlɪfaɪ/ *verb* (**qualifies, qualifying, qualified** /'kwɒlɪfaɪd/, **has qualified**)
get the right knowledge and training and pass exams so that you can do a certain job: *Anna has qualified as a doctor.*
qualified *adjective*
a qualified nurse

quality /'kwɒləti/ *noun* (no plural)
how good or bad something is: *This furniture isn't very good quality.*

quantity /'kwɒntəti/ *noun* (*plural* **quantities**)
how much of something there is; amount: *I only bought a small quantity of cheese.*

quarrel /'kwɒrəl/ *verb* (**quarrels, quarrelling, quarrelled** /'kwɒrəld/)
talk angrily with somebody because you do not agree: *They quarrelled because they both wanted to use the car.* ✪ In American English the spellings are **quarreling** and **quarreled**.
quarrel *noun*
a fight with words; an argument: *He had a quarrel with his wife about who should do the housework.*

quarry /'kwɒri/ *noun* (*plural* **quarries**)
a place where people cut stone out of the ground to make things like buildings or roads

quarter /'kwɔːtə(r)/ *noun*
1 one of four equal parts of something; ¼: *a mile and a quarter* ◇ *The film starts in three-quarters of an hour.*
2 three months: *You get a telephone bill every quarter.*
3 a part of a town: *the student quarter*
(a) quarter past 15 minutes after the hour: *It's quarter past two.* ◇ *I'll meet you at a quarter past.* ✪ In American English you say **a quarter after**: *It's a quarter after seven.* ☞ Look at page 164.
(a) quarter to 15 minutes before the hour: *quarter to nine* ✪ In American English you say **a quarter of.** ☞ Look at page 164.
quarter-final /ˌkwɔːtə 'faɪnl/ *noun*
In a competition, a quarter-final is one of the four games that are played to choose who will play in the **semifinals**.

quay /kiː/ *noun* (*plural* **quays**)
a place in a harbour where ships go so that people can move things on and off them

queen /kwiːn/ *noun*
1 a woman who rules a country and who is from a royal family: *Queen Elizabeth II* (= the second), *the Queen of England*
2 the wife of a king

ʌ	ɜː	ə	eɪ	əʊ	aɪ	aʊ	ɔɪ	ɪə	eə	ʊə
cup	bird	about	say	go	five	now	boy	near	hair	pure

query /'kwɪəri/ noun (plural **queries**)
a question: Phone me if you have any queries.

query verb (**queries, querying, queried** /'kwɪərid/)
ask a question about something that you think is wrong: We queried the bill but the waitress said it was correct.

question¹ /'kwestʃən/ noun
1 something that you ask: They asked me a lot of questions. ◇ She didn't answer my question. ◇ What is the answer to question 3?
2 a problem that needs an answer: We need more money. The question is, where are we going to get it from?
in question that we are talking about: On the day in question I was in London.
out of the question not possible: No, I won't give you any more money. It's out of the question!

question mark /'kwestʃən mɑːk/ noun
the sign (?) that you write at the end of a question

question tag /'kwestʃən tæg/ noun
words that you put on the end of a sentence to make a question: In the sentence 'You are French, aren't you?', 'aren't you' is a question tag.

question² /'kwestʃən/ verb (**questions, questioning, questioned** /'kwestʃənd/)
ask somebody questions about something: The police questioned him about the stolen car.

questionnaire /ˌkwestʃə'neə(r)/ noun
a list of questions for people to answer: Please fill in (= write the answers on) the questionnaire.

queue /kjuː/ noun
a line of people who are waiting to do something: There's a long queue outside the cinema. ☞ picture on page 261
queue, queue up verb (**queues, queuing, queued** /kjuːd/)
stand in a queue: We queued for a bus.

quick /kwɪk/ adjective, adverb (**quicker, quickest**)
fast; that takes little time: It's quicker to travel by plane than by train. ◇ Can I make a quick telephone call? ☞ Look at **slow.**
quickly adverb
Come as quickly as you can!

quid /kwɪd/ noun (plural **quid**)
a pound in money: It costs five quid.
✪ This is an informal word.

quiet /'kwaɪət/ adjective (**quieter, quietest**)
1 with little sound or no sound: Be quiet – the baby's asleep. ◇ a quiet voice ✪ opposite: **loud** or **noisy** ☞ picture on page 263
2 without many people or without many things happening: London is very quiet on Sundays.
quiet noun (no plural)
being quiet: I need quiet when I'm working.
quietly adverb
Please close the door quietly.

quilt /kwɪlt/ noun
a soft thick cover for a bed. Quilts often have feathers inside.

quit /kwɪt/ American English for **leave¹ 1**

quite /kwaɪt/ adverb
1 not very; rather; fairly: It's quite warm today, but it's not hot. ◇ He plays the guitar quite well. ◇ We waited quite a long time.
2 completely: Dinner is not quite ready.
quite a few or **quite a lot of** a lot of something: There were quite a few people at the party. ◇ They drank quite a lot of wine.

quiz /kwɪz/ noun (plural **quizzes**)
a game where you try to answer questions: a quiz on television

quotation /kwəʊ'teɪʃn/, **quote** /kwəʊt/ noun
words that you say or write, that another person said or wrote before: That's a quotation from a poem by Keats.
quotation marks /kwəʊ'teɪʃn mɑːks/, **quotes** noun (plural)
the signs " " or ' ' that you use in writing before and after words that somebody said

quote /kwəʊt/ verb (**quotes, quoting, quoted**)
say or write something that another person said or wrote before: She quoted from the Bible.

p	b	t	d	k	g	tʃ	dʒ	f	v	θ	ð
pen	**bad**	**tea**	**did**	**cat**	**got**	**chain**	**jam**	**fall**	**van**	**thin**	**this**

Rr

rabbi /'ræbaɪ/ *noun* (*plural* **rabbis**)
a teacher or leader of the Jewish religion

rabbit /'ræbɪt/ *noun*
a small animal with
long ears. Rabbits
live in holes under
the ground.

rabbit

race¹ /reɪs/ *noun*
1 a competition to
see who can run,
drive, ride, etc fastest: *Who won the race?*
◇ *a horse-race*
2 the races (plural) a time when there
are a lot of horse-races in one place
racecourse /'reɪskɔ:s/, **racetrack**
/'reɪstræk/ *noun*
a place where you go to see horse-races

race² /reɪs/ *verb* (**races**, **racing**, **raced**
/reɪst/)
run, drive, ride, etc in a competition to see
who is the fastest: *The cars raced round the
track.*

race³ /reɪs/ *noun*
a group of people of the same kind, for example with the same colour of skin: *People
of many different races live together in
this country.*
racial /'reɪʃl/ *adjective*
of race: *racial differences*

racing /'reɪsɪŋ/ *noun* (no plural)
a sport where horses, cars, etc race against
each other: *a racing car*

racism /'reɪsɪzəm/ *noun* (no plural)
the belief that some groups (**races**) of
people are better than others
racist /'reɪsɪst/ *noun*
a person who believes that some races of
people are better than others
racist *adjective*
a racist comment

rack /ræk/ *noun*
a kind of shelf, made of bars, that you put
things in or on: *Put your bag in the luggage rack* (= on a bus or train).
racket, racquet /'rækɪt/ *noun*
a thing that you use for hitting the ball in
tennis, badminton and squash

racket

radar /'reɪdɑ:(r)/ *noun* (no plural) a way
of finding where a ship or an aircraft is
and how fast it is travelling by using radio
waves

radiation /ˌreɪdi'eɪʃn/ *noun* (no plural)
dangerous energy that some substances
send out

radiator /'reɪdieɪtə(r)/ *noun*
1 a metal thing with hot water inside that
you use to make a room warm
2 a part of a car that has water in it to keep
the engine cold

radio /'reɪdiəʊ/ *noun*
1 (no plural) sending or receiving sounds
that travel a long way through the air by
special waves: *The captain of the ship sent
a message by radio.*
2 (*plural* **radios**) an instrument that
brings voices or music from far away so
that you can hear them: *We listened to an
interesting programme on the radio.*

radius /'reɪdiəs/ *noun* (*plural* **radii**
/'reɪdiaɪ/)
the length of a straight line from the centre
of a circle to the outside ☞ picture on
page 161

raft /rɑ:ft/ *noun*
a flat boat with no sides and no engine

rag /ræg/ *noun*
1 a small piece of old cloth that you use for
cleaning
2 rags (plural) clothes that are very old
and torn: *She was dressed in rags.*

rage /reɪdʒ/ *noun*
strong anger

raid /reɪd/ *noun*
a sudden attack on a place: *a bank raid*
raid *verb* (**raids**, **raiding**, **raided**)
Police raided the house looking for drugs.

rail /reɪl/ *noun*
1 (*plural* **rails**) a long piece of wood or metal that is fixed to a wall or to something else: *There's a rail in the bathroom for hanging your towel on.*
2 rails (plural) the long pieces of metal that trains go on
3 (no plural) trains as a way of travelling: *British Rail* ◇ *I travelled from London to Leeds by rail* (= in a train).

railings /'reɪlɪŋz/ *noun* (plural)
a fence made of long pieces of metal

railroad /'reɪlrəʊd/ *American English for* **railway**

railway /'reɪlweɪ/ *noun*
1 (*also* **railway line**) the metal lines that trains go on from one place to another
2 a train service that carries people and things: *a railway timetable*
railway station /'reɪlweɪ steɪʃn/ *noun*
a place where trains stop so that people can get on and off

rain /reɪn/ *noun* (no plural)
the water that falls from the sky
rain *verb* (**rains**, **raining**, **rained** /reɪnd/)
When it rains, water falls from the sky: *It's raining.* ◇ *It rained all day.*

rainbow /'reɪnbəʊ/ *noun*
a half circle of bright colours that you sometimes see in the sky when rain and sun come together

raincoat /'reɪnkəʊt/ *noun*
a light coat that you wear when it rains

rain forest /'reɪn fɒrɪst/ *noun*
a forest in a hot part of the world where there is a lot of rain

rainy /'reɪni/ *adjective* (**rainier**, **rainiest**)
with a lot of rain: *a rainy day*

raise /reɪz/ *verb* (**raises**, **raising**, **raised** /reɪzd/)
1 move something or somebody up: *Raise your hand if you want to ask a question.*
♻ opposite: **lower**
2 make something bigger, higher, stronger, etc: *They've raised the price of petrol.* ◇ *She raised her voice* (= spoke louder).
3 get money from other people: *We raised £1 000 for the hospital.*
4 start to talk about something: *He raised an interesting question.*

raisin /'reɪzn/ *noun*
a dried grape

rake /reɪk/ *noun*
a tool with a long handle that you use in a garden for collecting leaves or for making the soil flat
rake *verb* (**rakes**, **raking**, **raked** /reɪkt/)
Rake up the dead leaves.

rally /'ræli/ *noun* (*plural* **rallies**)
1 a group of people walking or standing together to show that they feel strongly about something: *a peace rally*
2 a race for cars or motor cycles

ramp /ræmp/ *noun*
a path that goes to a higher or lower place: *I pushed the wheelchair up the ramp.*

ran *form of* **run**[1]

random /'rændəm/ *adjective*
at random without any special plan: *She chose a few books at random.*

rang *form of* **ring**[2]

range[1] /reɪndʒ/ *noun*
1 different things of the same kind: *This shop sells a range of bicycles.*
2 how far you can see, hear, shoot, travel, etc: *The gun has a range of five miles.*
3 the amount between the highest and the lowest: *The age range of the children is between eight and twelve.*
4 a line of mountains or hills

range[2] /reɪndʒ/ *verb* (**ranges**, **ranging**, **ranged** /reɪndʒd/)
be at different points between two things: *The ages of the students in the class range from 18 to 50.*

rank /ræŋk/ *noun*
how important somebody is in a group of people, for example in an army: *General is one of the highest ranks in the army.*

ransom /'rænsəm/ *noun*
money that you must pay so that a criminal will free a person that he/she has taken: *The kidnappers have demanded a ransom of a million pounds.*

rap /ræp/ *noun*
1 a quick knock: *I heard a rap at the door.*
2 a kind of music in which singers speak the words of a song very quickly
rap *verb* (**raps**, **rapping**, **rapped** /ræpt/)
1 hit something quickly and lightly: *She rapped on the door.*
2 speak the words of a song very quickly

rape /reɪp/ *verb* (**rapes, raping, raped**
/reɪpt/)
make somebody have sex when they do
not want to
rape *noun*
He was sent to prison for rape.

rapid /'ræpɪd/ *adjective*
quick; fast: *rapid changes*
rapidly *adverb*
The snow rapidly disappeared.

rare /reə(r)/ *adjective* (**rarer, rarest**)
1 If something is rare, you do not find or
see it often: *Pandas are rare animals.*
◇ *It's rare to see snow in April.*
2 Meat that is rare is only cooked a little.
rarely *adverb*
not often: *I rarely go to London.*

rash¹ /ræʃ/ *noun* (*plural* **rashes**)
a lot of small red spots on your skin

rash² /ræʃ/ *adjective* (**rasher, rashest**)
If you are rash, you do things too quickly,
without thinking: *You were rash to leave
your job before you had found a new one.*

raspberry /'rɑːzbəri/ *noun* (*plural* **raspberries**)
a small soft red fruit: *raspberry jam*

rat /ræt/ *noun*
an animal like a big mouse

rate /reɪt/ *noun*
1 the speed of something or how often
something happens: *The crime rate was
lower in 1993 than in 1992.*
2 the amount that something costs or that
somebody is paid: *My rate of pay is £5 an
hour.*
at any rate anyway; whatever happens:
*I hope to be back before ten o'clock – I
won't be late at any rate.*

rather /'rɑːðə(r)/ *adverb*
more than a little but not very; quite: *We
were rather tired after our long journey.*
◇ *It's rather a small room.*
rather than in the place of; instead of:
Could I have beer rather than wine?
would rather would prefer to do something: *I would rather go by train than by
bus.*

ration /'ræʃn/ *noun*
a small amount of something that you are
allowed to have when there is not enough
for everybody to have what they want:
food rations

rattle /'rætl/ *verb* (**rattles, rattling, rattled** /'rætld/)
1 make a lot of short sounds because it is
shaking: *The windows were rattling all
night in the wind.*
2 shake something so that it makes a lot of
small sounds: *She rattled the money in the
tin.*
rattle *noun*
1 the noise of things hitting each other:
the rattle of empty bottles
2 a toy that a baby can shake to make a
noise

raw /rɔː/ *adjective*
1 not cooked: *raw meat*
2 natural; as it comes from the soil, from
plants, etc: *raw sugar*

ray /reɪ/ *noun* (*plural* **rays**)
a line of light or heat: *the rays of the sun*

razor /'reɪzə(r)/ *noun*
a sharp thing that people use to cut hair off
their bodies (to **shave**): *an electric razor*
razor-blade /'reɪzə bleɪd/ *noun*
the thin metal part of a razor that cuts

Rd *short way of writing* **road**

---

re- *prefix*
You can add **re-** to the beginning of some
words to give them the meaning 'again',
for example:
rebuild = build again: *We rebuilt the
fence after the storm.*
redo = do again: *Your homework is all
wrong. Please redo it.*

---

reach /riːtʃ/ *verb* (**reaches, reaching,
reached** /riːtʃt/)
1 arrive somewhere: *It was dark when we
reached Paris.* ◇ *Have you reached the
end of the book yet?*
2 put out your hand to do or get something; be able to touch something: *I
reached for the telephone.* ◇ *Can you get
that book from the top shelf for me? I can't
reach.*
reach *noun* (no plural)
beyond reach, out of reach too far
away to touch: *Keep this medicine out of
the reach of children.*
within reach near enough to touch or
go to: *Is the beach within reach of the
hotel?*

ʌ	ɜː	ə	eɪ	əʊ	aɪ	aʊ	ɔɪ	ɪə	eə	ʊə
c**u**p	b**ir**d	**a**bout	s**ay**	g**o**	f**i**ve	n**ow**	b**oy**	n**ear**	h**air**	p**ure**

react /ri'ækt/ *verb* (**reacts, reacting, reacted**)
say or do something when another thing happens: *How did Jo react to the news?*

reaction /ri'ækʃn/ *noun*
what you say or do because of something that has happened: *What was her reaction when you told her about the accident?*

read /riːd/ *verb* (**reads, reading, read** /red/, **has read**)
1 look at words and understand them: *Have you read this book? It's very interesting.*
2 say words that you can see: *I read a story to the children.*
read out read something to other people: *The teacher read out the list of names.*
reading *noun* (no plural)
My interests are reading and football.

reader /'riːdə(r)/ *noun*
1 a person who reads something
2 a book for reading at school

ready /'redi/ *adjective*
1 prepared so that you can do something: *I'll be ready to leave in five minutes.*
2 prepared so that you can use it: *Dinner will be ready soon.*
3 happy to do something: *He's always ready to help.*
get ready make yourself ready for something: *I'm getting ready to go out.*
ready-made /,redi 'meɪd/ *adjective*
prepared and ready to use: *ready-made meals*

real /rɪəl/ *adverb*
1 not just in the mind; that really exists: *The film is about something that happened in real life.*
2 true: *The name he gave to the police wasn't his real name.*
3 natural; not a copy: *This ring is real gold.*
4 big or complete: *I've got a real problem.*

reality /ri'æləti/ *noun* (*plural* **realities**)
the way that something really is: *People think I have an interesting job, but in reality it's quite boring.*

realize /'rɪəlaɪz/ *verb* (**realizes, realizing, realized** /'rɪəlaɪzd/)
understand or know something: *When I got home, I realized that I had lost my*

key. ◇ *I didn't realize you were American.*

realization /,rɪəlaɪ'zeɪʃn/ *noun* (no plural)
understanding or knowing something

really /'rɪəli/ *adverb*
1 in fact; truly: *Do you really love him?*
2 very or very much: *I'm really hungry.*
◇ *'Do you like this music?' 'Not really.'*
3 a word that shows you are interested or surprised: *'I'm going to China next year.' 'Really?'*

rear /rɪə(r)/ *noun* (no plural)
the back part: *The kitchen is at the rear of the house.*
rear *adjective*
at the back: *the rear window of a car*

reason /'riːzn/ *noun*
why you do something or why something happens: *The reason I didn't come to the party was that I was ill.* ◇ *Is there any reason why you were late?*

reasonable /'riːznəbl/ *adjective*
1 fair and willing to listen to what other people say: *Be reasonable! You can't ask one person to do all the work!*
2 fair or right: *I think £20 is a reasonable price.*
○ opposite: **unreasonable**
reasonably /'riːznəbli/ *adverb*
1 quite, but not very: *The food was reasonably good.*
2 in a reasonable way: *Don't get angry – let's talk about this reasonably.*

reassure /,riːə'ʃʊə(r)/ *verb* (**reassures, reassuring, reassured** /,riːə'ʃʊəd/)
say or do something to make somebody feel safer or happier: *The doctor reassured her that she was not seriously ill.*
reassurance /,riːə'ʃʊərəns/ *noun*
what you say to make somebody feel safer or happier: *He needs reassurance that he is right.*

rebel¹ /'rebl/ *noun*
a person who fights against the people in control

rebel² /rɪ'bel/ *verb* (**rebels, rebelling, rebelled** /rɪ'beld/)
fight against the people in control: *She rebelled against her parents by refusing to go to university.*
rebellion /rɪ'beliən/ *noun*
a time when a lot of people fight against

p	b	t	d	k	g	tʃ	dʒ	f	v	θ	ð
pen	**bad**	**tea**	**did**	**cat**	**got**	**chain**	**jam**	**fall**	**van**	**thin**	**this**

the people in control: *Hundreds of people died in the rebellion.*

recall /rɪ'kɔːl/ *verb* (**recalls**, **recalling**, **recalled** /rɪ'kɔːld/)
remember something: *I can't recall the name of the hotel.* ✪ **Remember** is the word that we usually use.

receipt /rɪ'siːt/ *noun*
a piece of paper that shows you have paid for something: *Can I have a receipt?*

receive /rɪ'siːv/ *verb* (**receives**, **receiving**, **received** /rɪ'siːvd/)
get something that somebody has given or sent to you: *Did you receive my letter?* ✪ **Get** is the word that we usually use.

receiver /rɪ'siːvə(r)/ *noun*
the part of a telephone that you use for listening and speaking ☞ picture on page 300

recent /'riːsnt/ *adjective*
that happened a short time ago: *Is this a recent photo of your son?*
recently *adverb*
not long ago: *She's been on holiday recently – that's why she's so brown.*

reception /rɪ'sepʃn/ *noun*
1 (no plural) the place where you go first when you arrive at a hotel, company, etc: *Leave your key at reception if you go out.*
2 (plural **receptions**) a big important party: *a wedding reception*

receptionist /rɪ'sepʃənɪst/ *noun*
a person in a hotel, company, etc who helps you when you arrive and who may also answer the telephone

recipe /'resəpi/ *noun*
a piece of writing that tells you how to cook something

reckless /'rekləs/ *adjective*
A person who is reckless does dangerous things without thinking about what could happen: *reckless driving*

reckon /'rekən/ *verb* (**reckons**, **reckoning**, **reckoned** /'rekənd/)
believe something because you have thought about it: *I reckon the holiday will cost us £500.*

recognize /'rekəgnaɪz/ *verb*
(**recognizes**, **recognizing**, **recognized** /'rekəgnaɪzd/)
1 know again somebody or something

that you have seen or heard before: *I didn't recognize you without your glasses.*
2 know that something is true: *They recognize that there is a problem.*

recognition /ˌrekəg'nɪʃn/ *noun* (no plural)
recognizing somebody or something

recommend /ˌrekə'mend/ *verb* (**recommends**, **recommending**, **recommended**)
1 tell somebody that another person or thing is good or useful: *Can you recommend a hotel near the airport?*
2 tell somebody in a helpful way what you think they should do: *I recommend that you see a doctor.*

recommendation /ˌrekəmen'deɪʃn/ *noun*
We stayed at the Grand Hotel on Kurt's recommendation (= because he said it was good).

record¹ /'rekɔːd/ *noun*
1 notes about things that have happened: *Keep a record of all the money you spend.*
2 a round plastic thing that makes music when you play it on a **record-player**: *Put another record on.*
3 the best, fastest, highest, lowest, etc that has been done in a sport: *She holds the world record for long jump.* ◇ *He crossed the Atlantic in record time.*
break a record do better in a sport than anybody has done before

record² /rɪ'kɔːd/ *verb* (**records**, **recording**, **recorded**)
1 write notes about or make pictures of things that happen so you can remember them later: *In his diary he recorded everything that he did.*
2 put music or a film on a tape or record so that you can listen to or watch it later: *I recorded a concert from the radio.*

recorder /rɪ'kɔːdə(r)/ *noun*
a musical instrument that you blow. Children often play recorders. ☞ Look also at **tape recorder** and **video recorder**.

recording /rɪ'kɔːdɪŋ/ *noun*
sounds or pictures on a tape, record or film: *a new recording of Mozart's 'Don Giovanni'*

record-player /'rekɔːd pleɪə(r)/ *noun*
a machine that makes music come out of records

s	z	ʃ	ʒ	h	m	n	ŋ	l	r	j	w
so	**zoo**	**shoe**	vision	**hat**	**man**	**no**	sing	**leg**	**red**	**yes**	**wet**

recover /rɪˈkʌvə(r)/ verb (**recovers, recovering, recovered** /rɪˈkʌvəd/)
1 become well or happy again after you have been ill or sad: *She is slowly recovering from her illness.*
2 get back something that you have lost: *Police recovered the stolen car.*
recovery /rɪˈkʌvəri/ noun (no plural)
He made a quick recovery after his illness.

rectangle /ˈrektæŋgl/ noun
a shape with two long sides, two short sides and four angles of 90 degrees ☞ picture on page 161
rectangular /rekˈtæŋgjələ(r)/ adjective
with the shape of a rectangle: *This page is rectangular.*

recycle /ˌriːˈsaɪkl/ verb (**recycles, recycling, recycled** /ˌriːˈsaɪkld/)
do something to materials like paper and glass so that they can be used again: *Old newspapers can be recycled.*

red /red/ adjective (**redder, reddest**)
1 with the colour of blood: *She's wearing a bright red dress.* ◇ *red wine*
2 Red hair has a colour between red, orange and brown.
red noun
Lucy was dressed in red.

reduce /rɪˈdjuːs/ verb (**reduces, reducing, reduced** /rɪˈdjuːst/)
make something smaller or less: *I bought this shirt because the price was reduced from £20 to £12.* ◇ *Reduce speed now* (= words on a road sign).
reduction /rɪˈdʌkʃn/ noun
price reductions
✪ opposite: **increase**

redundant /rɪˈdʌndənt/ adjective
without a job because you are not needed any more: *When the factory closed, 300 people were made redundant.*

reed /riːd/ noun
a tall plant, like grass, that grows in or near water

reel /riːl/ noun
a thing with round sides that holds cotton for sewing, film for cameras, etc: *a reel of cotton*

reel

refer /rɪˈfɜː(r)/ verb (**refers, referring, referred** /rɪˈfɜːd/)
refer to somebody or **something**
1 talk about somebody or something:

When I said that some people are stupid, I wasn't referring to you! **2** be used to mean something: *The word 'child' refers here to anybody under the age of 16.*
3 look in a book or ask somebody for information: *If you don't understand a word, you may refer to your dictionaries.*

referee /ˌrefəˈriː/ noun
a person in a sport like football or boxing who controls the match

reference /ˈrefrəns/ noun
1 what somebody says or writes about something: *There are many references to Stratford in this book about Shakespeare.*
2 If somebody gives you a reference, they write about you to somebody who may give you a new job: *Did your boss give you a good reference?*
reference book /ˈrefrəns bʊk/ noun
a book where you look for information: *A dictionary is a reference book.*

reflect /rɪˈflekt/ verb (**reflects, reflecting, reflected**)
send back light, heat or sound: *A mirror reflects a picture of you when you look in it.*

reflection /rɪˈflekʃn/ noun
1 (plural **reflections**) a picture that you see in a mirror or in water: *He looked into the pool and saw a reflection of himself.*
2 (no plural) sending back light, heat or sound

reform /rɪˈfɔːm/ verb (**reforms, reforming, reformed** /rɪˈfɔːmd/)
change something to make it better: *The government wants to reform the education system in this country.*
reform noun
a change to make something better: *political reform*

refresh /rɪˈfreʃ/ verb (**refreshes, refreshing, refreshed** /rɪˈfreʃt/)
make somebody feel cooler, stronger or less tired: *A sleep will refresh you after your long journey.*
refreshing adjective
a cool, refreshing drink

refreshments /rɪˈfreʃmənts/ noun (plural)
food and drinks that you can buy in a place like a cinema or theatre: *Refreshments will be sold in the interval.*

refrigerator /rɪˈfrɪdʒəreɪtə(r)/ *noun*
a big metal box for keeping food and drink
cold and fresh ✪ **Fridge** is the word that
we usually use.

refuge /ˈrefjuːdʒ/ *noun*
a place where you are safe from somebody
or something
take refuge from something go to a
safe place to get away from something bad
or dangerous: *We took refuge from the hot
sun under a tree.*

refugee /ˌrefjuˈdʒiː/ *noun*
a person who must leave his/her country
because of danger

refund /rɪˈfʌnd/ *verb* (**refunds, refund-
ing, refunded**)
pay back money: *I took the camera back to
the shop and they refunded my money.*
refund /ˈriːfʌnd/ *noun*
money that is paid back to you: *The watch
I bought was broken so I asked for a
refund.*

refuse /rɪˈfjuːz/ *verb* (**refuses, refusing,
refused** /rɪˈfjuːzd/)
say 'no' when somebody asks you to do or
have something: *I asked Matthew to help,
but he refused.* ◇ *The shop assistant refused to give me my money back.*
refusal /rɪˈfjuːzl/ *noun*
saying 'no' when somebody asks you to do
or have something: *a refusal to pay*

regard[1] /rɪˈɡɑːd/ *verb* (**regards, regard-
ing, regarded**)
think of somebody or something in a certain way: *I regard her as my best friend.*

regard[2] /rɪˈɡɑːd/ *noun*
1 (no plural) what you think about somebody or something: *I have a high regard
for his work* (= I think it is very good).
2 (no plural) care: *She shows no regard
for other people's feelings.*
3 regards (plural) kind wishes: *Please
give my regards to your parents.*

reggae /ˈreɡeɪ/ *noun* (no plural)
a type of West Indian music

regiment /ˈredʒɪmənt/ *noun*
a group of soldiers in an army

region /ˈriːdʒən/ *noun*
a part of a country or of the world: *There
will be snow in northern regions today.*
regional /ˈriːdʒənl/ *adjective*
of a certain region

register[1] /ˈredʒɪstə(r)/ *noun*
a list of names: *The teacher keeps a register
of all the students in the class.*

register[2] /ˈredʒɪstə(r)/ *verb* (**registers,
registering, registered** /ˈredʒɪstəd/)
1 put a name on a list: *I would like to register for the English course.*
2 show a number or amount: *The thermometer registered 30°C.*

registration /ˌredʒɪˈstreɪʃn/ *noun* (no
plural)
putting a name on a list: *registration of
births, marriages and deaths*
registration number /redʒɪˈstreɪʃn
nʌmbə(r)/ *noun*
the numbers and letters on the front and
back of a car, etc

regret /rɪˈɡret/ *verb* (**regrets, regret-
ting, regretted**)
feel sorry about something that you did:
He regrets selling his car. ◇ *I don't regret
what I said to her.*
regret *noun*
*I don't have any regrets about leaving my
job.*

regular /ˈreɡjələ(r)/ *adjective*
1 that happens again and again with the
same amount of space or time in between:
*We have regular meetings every Monday
morning.* ◇ *regular breathing*
2 who goes somewhere or does something
often: *I've never seen him before – he's not
one of my regular customers.*
3 usual: *Who is your regular doctor?*
4 A word that is regular has the usual
verb forms or plural: *'Work' is a regular
verb.*
☞ Look at **irregular**.
regularly *adverb*
We meet regularly every Friday.

regulation /ˌreɡjuˈleɪʃn/ *noun*
something that controls what people do; a
rule or law: *You can't smoke here – it's
against fire regulations.*

rehearse /rɪˈhɜːs/ *verb* (**rehearses, rehearsing, rehearsed** /rɪˈhɜːst/)
do or say something again and again before you do it in front of other people: *We
are rehearsing for the concert.*
rehearsal /rɪˈhɜːsl/ *noun*
a time when you rehearse: *There's a rehearsal for the play tonight.*

reign /reɪn/ *noun*
a time when a king or queen rules a coun-

try: *The reign of Queen Elizabeth II began in 1952.*

reign *verb* (**reigns, reigning, reigned** /reɪnd/)
be king or queen of a country: *Queen Victoria reigned for a long time.*

rein /reɪn/ *noun*
a long thin piece of leather that a horse wears on its head so that a rider can control it

reindeer /'reɪndɪə(r)/ *noun* (*plural* **reindeer**)
a big animal that lives in very cold countries

reject /rɪ'dʒekt/ *verb* (**rejects, rejecting, rejected**)
say that you do not want somebody or something: *He rejected my offer of help.*

related /rɪ'leɪtɪd/ *adjective*
in the same family; connected: *'Are those two boys related?' 'Yes, they're brothers.'*

relation /rɪ'leɪʃn/ *noun*
1 a person in your family
2 a connection between two things: *There is no relation between the size of the countries and the number of people who live there.*

relationship /rɪ'leɪʃnʃɪp/ *noun*
how people, things or ideas are connected to each other; feelings between people: *I have a good relationship with my parents.* ◇ *The book is about the relationship between an Indian boy and an English girl.*

relative /'relətɪv/ *noun*
a person in your family

relatively /'relətɪvli/ *adverb*
quite: *This room is relatively small.*

relax /rɪ'læks/ *verb* (**relaxes, relaxing, relaxed** /rɪ'lækst/)
1 rest and be calm; become less worried or angry: *After a hard day at work I spent the evening relaxing in front of the television.*
2 become less tight or make something become less tight: *Let your body relax.*

relaxation /ˌriːlæk'seɪʃn/ *noun* (no plural)
You need more rest and relaxation.

relaxed *adjective*
She felt relaxed after her holiday.

release /rɪ'liːs/ *verb* (**release, releasing, released** /rɪ'liːst/)
let a person or an animal go free: *We opened the cage and released the bird.*

release *noun*
the release of the prisoners

relevant /'reləvənt/ *adjective*
connected with what you are talking or writing about; important: *We need somebody who can do the job well – your age is not relevant.* ◇ opposite: **irrelevant**

reliable /rɪ'laɪəbl/ *adjective*
that you can trust: *My car is very reliable.* ◇ *He is a reliable person.* ◇ opposite: **unreliable**

relied *form of* **rely**

relief /rɪ'liːf/ *noun* (no plural)
1 what you feel when pain or worry stops: *It was a great relief to know she was safe.*
2 food or money for people who need it: *Many countries sent relief to the people who had lost their homes in the floods.*

relies *form of* **rely**

relieved /rɪ'liːvd/ *adjective*
pleased because a problem or danger has gone away: *I was relieved to hear that you weren't hurt in the accident.*

religion /rɪ'lɪdʒən/ *noun*
1 (no plural) believing in a god
2 (*plural* **religions**) one of the ways of believing in a god, for example Christianity, Islam or Buddhism

religious /rɪ'lɪdʒəs/ *adjective*
1 of religion: *a religious leader*
2 with a strong belief in a religion: *I'm not very religious.*

reluctant /rɪ'lʌktənt/ *adjective*
If you are reluctant to do something, you do not want to do it: *Ian was reluctant to give me the money.*

reluctance /rɪ'lʌktəns/ *noun* (no plural)
being reluctant: *He agreed, but with great reluctance.*

reluctantly *adverb*
Ann reluctantly agreed to help with the washing-up.

rely /rɪ'laɪ/ *verb* (**relies, relying, relied** /rɪ'laɪd/, **has relied**)
rely on somebody or **something**
1 feel sure that somebody or something will do what they should do: *You can rely on him to help you.* 2 need somebody or

p	b	t	d	k	g	tʃ	dʒ	f	v	θ	ð
pen	**bad**	**tea**	**did**	**cat**	**got**	**chain**	**jam**	**fall**	**van**	**thin**	**this**

something: *I rely on my parents for money.* ✪ The adjective is **reliable**.

remain /rɪ'meɪn/ *verb* (**remains, remaining, remained** /rɪ'meɪnd/)
1 stay after other people or things have gone: *After the fire, very little remained of the house.*
2 stay in the same way; not change: *I asked her a question but she remained silent.*

remains /rɪ'meɪnz/ *noun* (plural)
what is left when most of something has gone: *the remains of an old church*

remark /rɪ'mɑːk/ *verb* (**remarks, remarking, remarked** /rɪ'mɑːkt/)
say something: *'It's cold today,' he remarked.*
remark *noun*
something that you say: *He made a remark about the food.*

remarkable /rɪ'mɑːkəbl/ *adjective*
unusual and surprising in a good way: *a remarkable discovery*
remarkably /rɪ'mɑːkəbli/ *adverb*
She speaks French remarkably well.

remedy /'remədi/ *noun* (*plural* **remedies**)
a way of making something better: *a remedy for toothache*

remember /rɪ'membə(r)/ *verb* (**remembers, remembering, remembered** /rɪ'membəd/)
keep something in your mind or bring something back into your mind; not forget something: *Can you remember his name?* ◇ *I remember posting the letter.* ◇ *Did you remember to go to the bank?*

remind /rɪ'maɪnd/ *verb* (**reminds, reminding, reminded**)
make somebody remember somebody or something: *This song reminds me of my holiday in France.* ◇ *I reminded her to buy some bread.*
reminder *noun*
something that makes you remember

remote /rɪ'məʊt/ *adjective* (**remoter, remotest**)
far from other places: *They live in a remote farmhouse in Scotland.*

remove /rɪ'muːv/ *verb* (**removes, removing, removed** /rɪ'muːvd/)
take somebody or something away or off:

The statue was removed from the museum. ◇ *Please remove your shoes before entering the temple.* ✪ It is more usual to use other words, for example **take out** or **take off**.

removal /rɪ'muːvl/ *noun*
removing something: *a removal van* (= a lorry that is used for moving furniture to a new house)

renew /ri'njuː/ *verb* (**renews, renewing, renewed** /ri'njuːd/)
get or give something new in the place of something old: *If you want to stay in America for another month you must renew your visa.*

rent /rent/ *verb* (**rents, renting, rented**)
1 pay to live in a place or to use something that belongs to another person: *I rent a flat in the centre of town.*
2 let somebody live in a place or use something that belongs to you, if they pay you: *Mr Hodges rents out rooms to students.*
rent *noun*
the money that you pay to live in a place or to use something that belongs to another person: *My rent is £300 a month.*

repair /rɪ'peə(r)/ *verb* (**repairs, repairing, repaired** /rɪ'peəd/)
make something that is broken good again; mend something: *Can you repair my bike?*
repair *noun*
The shop is closed for repairs to the roof.

repay /ri'peɪ/ *verb* (**repays, repaying, repaid** /ri'peɪd/, **has repaid**)
1 pay back money to somebody
2 do something for somebody to show your thanks: *How can I repay you for all your help?*
repayment /ri'peɪmənt/ *noun*
paying somebody back: *monthly repayments*

repeat /rɪ'piːt/ *verb* (**repeats, repeating, repeated**)
1 say or do something again: *He didn't hear my question, so I repeated it.*
2 say what another person has said: *Repeat this sentence after me.*
repeat *noun*
something that is done again: *There are a lot of repeats of old programmes on TV.*

repetition /ˌrepə'tɪʃn/ *noun*
saying or doing something again: *This book is boring – it's full of repetition.*

Dates

Saying dates

How do you say... ?:

APRIL   2002

M	1	8	15	22	29
T	2	9	16	23	30
W	3	10	17	24	
T	4	11	18	25	
S	7	14	21	28	

the twenty-fourth of April, two thousand and two

or   April the twenty-fourth, two thousand and two

1998   nineteen ninety-eight

1800   eighteen hundred

on, in or at?

on	5 August Monday Wednesday morning my birthday
in	August 2003 (the) summer the morning/afternoon/evening
at	the beginning of June the weekend Christmas night six o'clock

Writing dates

Here are some ways of writing the date:

24 April
April 24
24th April
April 24th

Sometimes we just write numbers:

24 April 2002

24/4/02
(in Britain)

4/24/02
(in the USA)

Months

January
February
March
April
May
June
July
August
September
October
November
December

Days

Sunday
Monday
Tuesday
Wednesday
Thursday
Friday
Saturday

Letter-writing

formal letters

the date

your address
(but NOT your name)

the name or title of the person you are writing to, and **their address**

18 St Lawrence Street
London
W10 5LX

12 May 1995

The Director
Tourist Information Centre
High St
Oxford
OX1 3SP

begin with:

Dear Sir
       Madam
       Sirs

Dear Mr Jones
       Mrs Jones
       Ms Jones
       Miss Jones

Dear Sir or Madam

I am writing to enquire about holiday accommodation in Oxford.

I would be grateful if you could send me details of cheap hotels or camp-sites near the city centre.

I look forward to hearing from you.

Yours faithfully

Julie Newton

Ms J Newton

end with:

Yours faithfully
(when you began with *Dear Sir*, etc)

Yours sincerely
(when you began with *Dear Mr Jones*, etc)

Yours truly (US)
Sincerely yours (US)

your signature

Letter-writing

informal letters

the date

your address
(but NOT your name)

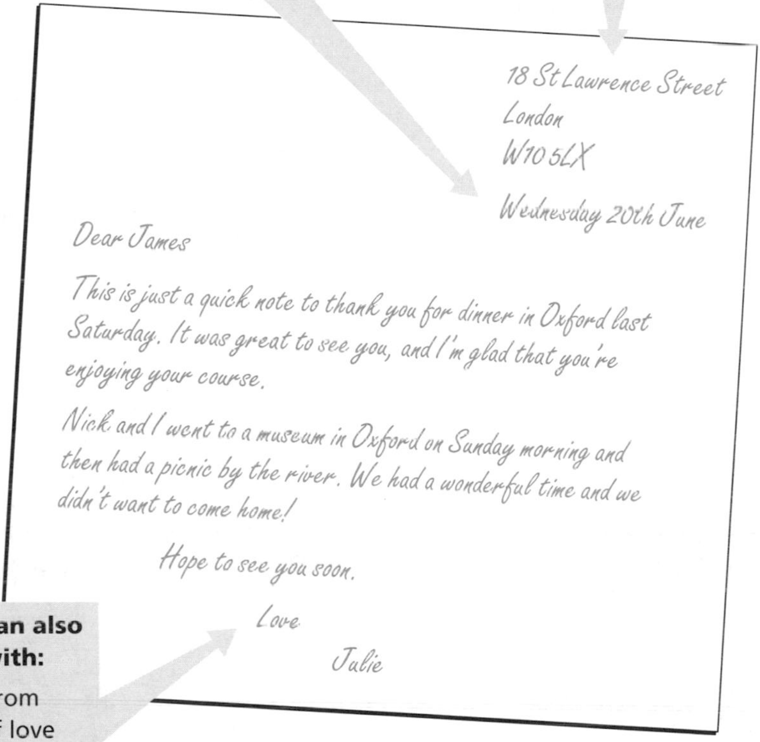

18 St Lawrence Street
London
W10 5LX

Wednesday 20th June

Dear James

This is just a quick note to thank you for dinner in Oxford last Saturday. It was great to see you, and I'm glad that you're enjoying your course.

Nick and I went to a museum in Oxford on Sunday morning and then had a picnic by the river. We had a wonderful time and we didn't want to come home!

Hope to see you soon.

Love

Julie

You can also end with:
Love from
Lots of love
Best wishes
Yours

stamp

Mr J Carter
14 North Road
Oxford
OX9 2LJ

envelope

address

postcode

Telephoning

Saying telephone numbers

36920   three six nine two o (You say it like **oh**.)
25844   two five eight double four

When you make a **telephone call**, you **pick up** the **receiver** and **dial** the number. The telephone **rings**, and the person you are telephoning **answers** it. If he/she is already using the telephone, it is **engaged**.

replace /rɪ'pleɪs/ *verb* (**replaces**, **replacing**, **replaced** /rɪ'pleɪst/)
1 put something back in the right place: *Please replace the books on the shelf when you have finished with them.*
2 take the place of somebody or something: *John Major replaced Margaret Thatcher as Prime Minister.*
3 put a new or different person or thing in the place of another: *The watch was broken so the shop replaced it with a new one.*

replacement /rɪ'pleɪsmənt/ *noun*
1 (*plural* **replacements**) a new or different person or thing that takes the place of another: *Sue is leaving the company next month so we need to find a replacement.*
2 (no plural) putting a new or different person or thing in the place of another

reply /rɪ'plaɪ/ *verb* (**replies**, **replying**, **replied** /rɪ'plaɪd/, **has replied**)
answer: *I have written to Jane but she hasn't replied.*
reply *noun* (*plural* **replies**)
an answer: *Have you had a reply to your letter?*
in reply as an answer: *What did you say in reply to his question?*

report¹ /rɪ'pɔːt/ *verb* (**reports**, **reporting**, **reported**)
tell or write about something that has happened: *We reported the accident to the police.*

report² /rɪ'pɔːt/ *noun*
1 something that somebody says or writes about something that has happened: *Did you read the newspaper reports about the earthquake?*
2 something that teachers write about a student's work

reporter /rɪ'pɔːtə(r)/ *noun*
a person who writes in a newspaper or speaks on the radio or television about things that have happened

represent /ˌreprɪ'zent/ *verb* (**represents**, **representing**, **represented**)
1 be a sign for something: *The yellow lines on the map represent roads.*
2 speak or do something for another person or other people: *Christie will represent Britain at the next Olympic Games.*

representative /ˌreprɪ'zentətɪv/ *noun*
a person who speaks or does something for a group of people: *There were representat-*

ives from every country in Europe at the meeting.

reproduce /ˌriːprə'djuːs/ *verb* (**reproduces**, **reproducing**, **reproduced** /ˌriːprə'djuːst/)
When animals or plants reproduce, they have young ones.
reproduction /ˌriːprə'dʌkʃn/ *noun* (no plural)
We are studying plant reproduction at school.

reptile /'reptaɪl/ *noun*
an animal with cold blood, that lays eggs. Snakes, lizards, crocodiles and tortoises are reptiles.

republic /rɪ'pʌblɪk/ *noun*
a country where people choose the government and the leader (the **president**): *the Republic of Ireland*
republican /rɪ'pʌblɪkən/ *noun*
1 a person who wants a republic
2 **Republican** a person in the Republican Party in the USA ☞ Look at **Democrat**.

reputation /ˌrepju'teɪʃn/ *noun*
what people think or say about somebody or something: *This restaurant has a good reputation.*

request /rɪ'kwest/ *verb* (**requests**, **requesting**, **requested**)
ask for something: *Passengers are requested not to smoke* (a notice in a bus).
♦ It is more usual to say **ask (for)**.
request *noun*
asking for something: *They made a request for money.*

require /rɪ'kwaɪə(r)/ *verb* (**requires**, **requiring**, **required** /rɪ'kwaɪəd/)
need something: *Do you require anything else?* ♦ **Need** is the word that we usually use.
requirement /rɪ'kwaɪəmənt/ *noun*
something that you need

rescue /'reskjuː/ *verb* (**rescues**, **rescuing**, **rescued**)
save somebody or something from danger: *She rescued the child when he fell in the river.*
rescue *noun*
come or **go to somebody's rescue**
try to help somebody: *The police came to his rescue.*

research /rɪ'sɜ:tʃ/ *noun* (no plural)
studying something carefully to find out more about it: *scientific research*
research *verb* (**researches, researching, researched** /rɪ'sɜ:tʃt/)
study something carefully to find out more about it: *Scientists are researching the causes of the disease.*

resemble /rɪ'zembl/ *verb* (**resembles, resembling, resembled** /rɪ'zembld/)
look like somebody or something: *Lisa resembles her mother.* ✪ It is more usual to say **look like**.
resemblance /rɪ'zembləns/ *noun*
There's no resemblance between my two brothers.

resent /rɪ'zent/ *verb* (**resents, resenting, resented**)
feel angry about something because it is not fair: *I resent Alan getting the job. He got it because he's the manager's son!*
resentment /rɪ'zentmənt/ *noun* (no plural)
a feeling of anger about something that is not fair

reserve[1] /rɪ'zɜ:v/ *verb* (**reserves, reserving, reserved** /rɪ'zɜ:vd/)
keep something for a special reason or to use later; ask somebody to keep something for you: *I would like to reserve a single room for tomorrow night, please.* ◇ *Those seats are reserved.*
reservation /,rezə'veɪʃn/ *noun*
a room, seat or another thing that you have reserved: *I made a reservation for a table for two.*

reserve[2] /rɪ'zɜ:v/ *noun*
1 something that you keep to use later: *reserves of food*
2 a person who will play in a game if another person cannot play
in reserve for using later: *Don't spend all the money – keep some in reserve.*

reservoir /'rezəvwɑ:(r)/ *noun*
a big lake where a town or city keeps water to use later

residence /'rezɪdəns/ *noun*
1 (no plural) living in a place: *a university hall of residence* (= a place where students live)
2 (*plural* **residences**) the place where an important or famous person lives: *the Prime Minister's residence*

resident /'rezɪdənt/ *noun*
a person who lives in a place

resign /rɪ'zaɪn/ *verb* (**resigns, resigning, resigned** /rɪ'zaɪnd/)
leave your job: *The director has resigned.*
resign yourself to something accept something that you do not like: *There were a lot of people at the doctor's so John resigned himself to a long wait.*

resignation /,rezɪg'neɪʃn/ *noun*
saying that you want to leave your job
hand in your resignation tell the person you work for that you are going to leave your job

resist /rɪ'zɪst/ *verb* (**resists, resisting, resisted**)
1 fight against somebody or something; try to stop somebody or something: *If he has a gun, don't try to resist.*
2 refuse to do or have something that you want to do or have: *I can't resist chocolate.*
resistance /rɪ'zɪstəns/ *noun* (no plural)
resisting somebody or something: *There was a lot of resistance to the plan to build a new motorway.*

resolution /,rezə'lu:ʃn/ *noun*
something that you decide to do: *Julie made a resolution to stop smoking.*

resort /rɪ'zɔ:t/ *noun*
a place where a lot of people go on holiday: *St Tropez is a seaside resort.*
a last resort the only person or thing left that can help: *Nobody else will lend me the money, so I am asking you as a last resort.*

resources /rɪ'sɔ:sɪz/ *noun* (plural)
things that a person or a country has and can use: *Oil is one of our most important natural resources.*

respect[1] /rɪ'spekt/ *noun* (no plural)
1 thinking that somebody is very good or clever: *I have a lot of respect for your father.*
2 being polite to somebody: *You should treat old people with more respect.*

respect[2] /rɪ'spekt/ *verb* (**respects, respecting, respected**)
think that somebody is good or clever: *The students respect their teacher.*

respectable /rɪ'spektəbl/ *adjective*
If a person or thing is respectable, people think he/she/it is good or correct: *She comes from a respectable family.*

ʌ	ɜ:	ə	eɪ	əʊ	aɪ	aʊ	ɔɪ	ɪə	eə	ʊə
c**u**p	b**ir**d	**a**bout	s**ay**	g**o**	f**i**ve	n**ow**	b**oy**	n**ear**	h**air**	p**ure**

respond /rɪˈspɒnd/ verb (**responds, responding, responded**)
do or say something to answer somebody or something: I said 'hello' and he responded by smiling.

response /rɪˈspɒns/ noun
an answer to somebody or something: I wrote to them but I've had no response.

responsible /rɪˈspɒnsəbl/ adjective
1 If you are responsible for somebody or something, you must look after them: The driver is responsible for the lives of the people on the bus.
2 A responsible person is somebody that you can trust: We need a responsible person to look after our son. **O** opposite: **irresponsible**
be responsible for something be the person who made something bad happen: Who was responsible for the accident?

responsibility /rɪˌspɒnsəˈbɪləti/ noun
1 (no plural) being responsible for somebody or something; having to look after somebody or something: She has responsibility for the whole department.
2 (plural **responsibilities**) something that you must do; somebody or something that you must look after: The dog is my brother's responsibility.

rest¹ /rest/ verb (**rests, resting, rested**)
1 sleep or be still and quiet: We worked all morning and then rested for an hour before starting work again.
2 be on something; put something on or against another thing: His arms were resting on the table.

rest² /rest/ noun
sleeping or being still and quiet: After walking for an hour, we stopped for a rest.

rest³ /rest/ noun (no plural)
the rest 1 what is there when a part has gone: If you don't want the rest, I'll eat it. ◇ I liked the beginning, but the rest of the film wasn't very good. 2 the other people or things: Jason watched TV and the rest of us went for a walk.

restaurant /ˈrestrɒnt/ noun
a place where you buy a meal and eat it

restless /ˈrestləs/ adjective
not able to be still: The children always get restless on long journeys.

restore /rɪˈstɔː(r)/ verb (**restores, restoring, restored** /rɪˈstɔːd/)
make something as good as it was before: The old palace was restored.

restrain /rɪˈstreɪn/ verb (**restrains, restraining, restrained** /rɪˈstreɪnd/)
stop somebody or something from doing something; control somebody or something: I couldn't restrain my anger.

restrict /rɪˈstrɪkt/ verb (**restricts, restricting, restricted**)
allow only a certain amount, size, sort, etc: Our house is very small, so we had to restrict the number of people we invited to the party.

restriction /rɪˈstrɪkʃn/ noun
a rule to control somebody or something: There are a lot of parking restrictions in the city centre.

rest room /ˈrest ruːm/ American English for **public convenience**

result¹ /rɪˈzʌlt/ noun
1 what happens because something else has happened: The accident was a result of bad driving.
2 the score or mark at the end of a game, competition or exam: When will you know your exam results? ◇ football results
as a result because of something: I got up late, and as a result I missed the train.

result² verb (**results, resulting, resulted**)
result in something make something happen: The accident resulted in the death of two drivers.

retire /rɪˈtaɪə(r)/ verb (**retires, retiring, retired** /rɪˈtaɪəd/)
stop working because you are a certain age: My grandfather retired when he was 65.
retired adjective
a retired teacher
retirement /rɪˈtaɪəmənt/ noun (no plural)
the time when a person stops working because he/she is a certain age: What is the age of retirement in your country?

retreat /rɪˈtriːt/ verb (**retreats, retreating, retreated**)
move back or away from somebody or

something, for example because you have lost a fight: *The enemy is retreating.*

retreat *noun*
retreating: *The army is now in retreat.*

return¹ /rɪ'tɜ:n/ *verb* (**returns, returning, returned** /rɪ'tɜ:nd/)
1 come or go back to a place: *They returned from Italy last week.*
2 give, put, send or take something back: *Will you return this book to the library?*

return² /rɪ'tɜ:n/ *noun*
1 (no plural) coming or going back to a place: *They met me at the airport on my return to Britain.*
2 (no plural) giving, putting, sending or taking something back: *the return of the stolen money*
3 (*plural* **returns**) (*also* **return ticket**) a ticket to travel to a place and back again: *A return to London, please.* ☞ Look at **single**.
in return If you do something in return for something else, you do it because somebody has helped you or given you something: *We have bought you a present in return for all your help.*

returns /rɪ'tɜ:nz/ *noun* (plural)
many happy returns words that you say on somebody's birthday

reunion /ri:'ju:niən/ *noun*
a meeting of people who have not seen each other for a long time: *We had a family reunion on my aunt's birthday.*

reveal /rɪ'vi:l/ *verb* (**reveals, revealing, revealed** /rɪ'vi:ld/)
tell something that was a secret or show something that was hidden: *She refused to reveal any names to the police.*

revenge /rɪ'vendʒ/ *noun* (no plural)
get, have or **take your revenge on somebody** do something bad to somebody who has done something bad to you: *He says he will take his revenge on the judge who sent him to prison.*

reverse¹ /rɪ'vɜ:s/ *verb* (**reverses, reversing, reversed** /rɪ'vɜ:st/)
1 make a car, etc go backwards: *I reversed the car into the garage.*
2 turn something the other way round: *Writing is reversed in a mirror.*
reverse the charges make a telephone call that the person you are telephoning will pay for

reverse² /rɪ'vɜ:s/ *noun* (no plural)
the opposite thing or way
in reverse in the opposite way; starting at the end and finishing at the beginning: *We ate our dinner in reverse – we started with the ice-cream and finished with the soup!*

review /rɪ'vju:/ *noun*
1 a piece of writing in a newspaper or magazine that says what somebody thinks about a book, film, play, etc: *The film got very good reviews.*
2 thinking again about something that happened before: *a review of all the important events of the year*
review *verb* (**reviews, reviewing, reviewed** /rɪ'vju:d/)
1 write a review about a book, film, play, etc
2 think again about something that happened before: *Let's review what we have learned in this lesson.*

revise /rɪ'vaɪz/ *verb* (**revises, revising, revised** /rɪ'vaɪzd/)
1 study again something that you have learnt, before an exam: *I'm revising for the Geography test.*
2 change something to make it better or more correct: *The book was revised.*

revision /rɪ'vɪʒn/ *noun* (no plural)
studying again something that you have learnt, before an exam: *I haven't done any revision for the maths exam.*

revive /rɪ'vaɪv/ *verb* (**revives, reviving, revived** /rɪ'vaɪvd/)
become or make somebody or something well or strong again: *They pulled the boy out of the river and tried to revive him, but he was already dead.*

revolt /rɪ'vəʊlt/ *verb* (**revolts, revolting, revolted**)
fight against the people in control: *The army is revolting against the government.*
revolt *noun*
when people fight against the people in control

revolting /rɪ'vəʊltɪŋ/ *adjective*
horrible; so bad that it makes you feel sick: *This meat tastes revolting.*

revolution /ˌrevə'lu:ʃn/ *noun*
1 a fight by people against their govern-

s	z	ʃ	ʒ	h	m	n	ŋ	l	r	j	w
so	**zoo**	**shoe**	vi**s**ion	**hat**	**man**	**no**	si**ng**	**leg**	**red**	**yes**	**wet**

ment, to put a new government in its place: *The French Revolution was in 1789.*
2 a big change in the way of doing things: *the Industrial Revolution*

reward /rɪ'wɔːd/ *noun*
a present or money that you give to thank somebody for something that they have done: *She is offering a £50 reward to anyone who finds her dog.*
reward *verb* (**rewards, rewarding, rewarded**)
give a reward to somebody: *Jason's parents bought him a bike to reward him for passing his exam.*

rewind /riː'waɪnd/ *verb* (**rewinds, rewinding, rewound** /riː'waʊnd/, **has rewound**)
make a tape (in a **tape recorder** or **video recorder**) go backwards: *Rewind the tape and play it again.*

rhinoceros

rhinoceros /raɪ'nɒsərəs/ *noun* (*plural* **rhinoceros** or **rhinoceroses**)
a big wild animal with thick skin and a horn on its nose. Rhinoceroses live in Africa and Asia. ✪ The short form is **rhino.**

rhyme¹ /raɪm/ *noun*
1 when two words have the same sound, for example 'bell' and 'well': *Her poetry is written in rhyme.*
2 a short piece of writing where the lines end with the same sounds

rhyme² /raɪm/ *verb* (**rhymes, rhyming, rhymed** /raɪmd/)
1 have the same sound as another word: *'Moon' rhymes with 'spoon' and 'chair' rhymes with 'bear'.*
2 have lines that end with the same sounds: *This poem doesn't rhyme.*

rhythm /'rɪðəm/ *noun*
a regular pattern of sounds that come again and again: *This music has a good rhythm.*

rib /rɪb/ *noun*
one of the bones around your chest
☞ picture on page 126

ribbon /'rɪbən/ *noun*
a long thin piece of pretty material for tying things: *She wore a ribbon in her hair.*

ribbon

rice /raɪs/ *noun* (no plural)
white or brown seeds from a plant that grows in hot countries, that we use as food: *Would you like rice or potatoes with your chicken?*

rich /rɪtʃ/ *adjective* (**richer, richest**)
1 with a lot of money: *a rich family* ✪ opposite: **poor**
2 with a lot of something: *This country is rich in oil.*
3 Food that is rich has a lot of fat or sugar in it: *a rich chocolate cake*
the rich *noun* (plural)
people who have a lot of money

rid /rɪd/ *verb*
get rid of somebody or **something**
throw something away or become free of somebody or something: *I got rid of my old coat and bought a new one.* ◇ *This dog is following me — I can't get rid of it.*

riddle /'rɪdl/ *noun*
a question that has a clever or funny answer: *Here's a riddle: What has four legs but can't walk? The answer is a chair!*

ride /raɪd/ *verb* (**rides, riding, rode** /rəʊd/, **has ridden** /'rɪdn/)
1 sit on a horse or bicycle and control it as it moves: *I'm learning to ride* (= a horse). ◇ *Don't ride your bike on the grass!* ✪ When you talk about spending time riding a horse, you say **go riding**: *I went riding today.*
2 travel in a car, bus or train: *We rode in the back of the car.* ✪ When you control a car, bus or train, you **drive** it.
ride *noun*
a journey on a horse or bicycle, or in a car, bus or train: *We went for a ride in the woods.* ◇ *I had a ride in his new car.*
rider *noun*
a person who rides a horse or bicycle
riding *noun* (no plural)
the sport of riding a horse

iː	i	ɪ	e	æ	ɑː	ɒ	ɔː	ʊ	u	uː
see	happy	sit	ten	cat	father	got	saw	put	situation	too

ridge /rɪdʒ/ *noun*
a long thin part of something that is higher than the rest, for example along the top of hills or mountains: *We walked along the ridge looking down at the valley below.*

ridiculous /rɪ'dɪkjələs/ *adjective*
so silly that it makes people laugh: *You can't play tennis with a football – that's ridiculous!*

rifle /'raɪfl/ *noun*
a long gun that you hold against your shoulder when you fire it

right¹ /raɪt/ *adjective, adverb*
opposite of left. Most people write with their right hand: *Turn right at the end of the street.*
right *noun* (no plural)
We live in the first house on the right.

right² /raɪt/ *adjective*
1 correct or true: *That's not the right answer.* ◊ *'Are you Mr Johnson?' 'Yes, that's right.'*
2 good; fair or what the law allows: *It's not right to leave young children alone in the house.*
3 best: *Is she the right person for the job?*
۞ opposite: **wrong**

right³ /raɪt/ *adverb*
1 correctly: *Have I spelt your name right?* **۞** opposite: **wrong**
2 exactly: *He was sitting right next to me.*
3 all the way: *Go right to the end of the road.*
4 immediately: *We left right after dinner.*
5 yes, I agree; yes, I will: *'I'll see you tomorrow.' 'Right.'*
6 You say 'right' to make somebody listen to you: *Are you ready? Right, let's go.*
right away immediately; now: *Phone the doctor right away.*

right⁴ /raɪt/ *noun*
1 (no plural) what is good or fair: *Young children have to learn the difference between right and wrong.*
2 (*plural* **rights**) what you are allowed to do, especially by law: *In Britain, everyone has the right to vote at 18.*

right angle /'raɪt æŋgl/ *noun*
an angle of 90 degrees. A square has four right angles. ☞ picture on page 161

right-hand /'raɪt hænd/ *adjective*
of or on the right: *The supermarket is on the right-hand side of the road.*
right-handed /,raɪt 'hændɪd/ *adjective*
If you are right-handed, you use your right hand more easily than your left hand.

rightly /'raɪtli/ *adverb*
correctly: *If I remember rightly, the party was on 15 June.*

rigid /'rɪdʒɪd/ *adjective*
1 hard and not easy to bend or move
2 not able to be changed; strict: *My school has very rigid rules.*

rim /rɪm/ *noun*
the edge of something round: *the rim of a cup*

rind /raɪnd/ *noun*
the thick hard skin of some fruits, or of bacon or cheese: *lemon rind*

ring

ring¹ /rɪŋ/ *noun*
1 a circle of metal that you wear on your finger
2 a circle: *Please stand in a ring.*
3 a space with seats around it, for a circus or boxing match

ring² /rɪŋ/ *verb* (**rings, ringing, rang** /ræŋ/, **has rung** /rʌŋ/)
1 make a sound like a bell: *The telephone is ringing.*
2 press or move a bell so that it makes a sound: *We rang the doorbell again but nobody answered.*
3 telephone somebody: *I'll ring you on Sunday.*
ring somebody back telephone somebody again: *I wasn't at home when Jo called, so I rang her back later.*
ring up telephone somebody: *Your brother rang up while you were out.*

ring³ /rɪŋ/ *noun*
the sound that a bell makes: *There was a ring at the door.*
give somebody a ring telephone somebody: *I'll give you a ring later.*

rinse /rɪns/ *verb* (**rinses, rinsing, rinsed** /rɪnst/)
wash something with water to take away

dirt or soap: *Wash your hair and rinse it well.*

riot /'raɪət/ *noun*
when a group of people fight and make a lot of noise and trouble: *There were riots in the streets after the football match.*
riot *verb* (**riots, rioting, rioted**)
The prisoners are rioting.

rip /rɪp/ *verb* (**rips, ripping, ripped** /rɪpt/)
pull or tear quickly and roughly: *I ripped my shirt on a nail.* ◇ *Joe ripped the letter open.*
rip up tear something into small pieces: *She ripped the photo up.*

ripe /raɪp/ *adjective* (**riper, ripest**)
Fruit that is ripe is ready to eat: *These bananas aren't ripe — they're still green.*

rise /raɪz/ *verb* (**rises, rising, rose** /rəʊz/, **has risen** /'rɪzn/)
go up; become higher or more: *The sun rises in the east and sets* (= goes down) *in the west.* ◇ *Prices are rising.*
rise *noun*
becoming higher or more: *a rise in the price of oil* ◇ *a pay rise*

risk /rɪsk/ *noun*
the possibility that something bad may happen; danger: *Do you think there's any risk of rain?*
at risk in danger: *Children are at risk from this disease.*
take a risk or **risks** do something when it is possible that something bad may happen because of it: *Don't take risks when you're driving.*
risk *verb* (**risks, risking, risked** /rɪskt/)
1 put somebody or something in danger: *He risked his life to save the child from the burning house.*
2 do something when there is a possibility that something bad may happen because of it: *If you don't work harder, you risk failing the exam.*

risky /'rɪski/ *adjective* (**riskier, riskiest**)
dangerous

rival /'raɪvl/ *noun*
a person who wants to do better than you or who is trying to take what you want: *John and Lucy are rivals for the job.*

river /'rɪvə(r)/ *noun*
a long wide line of water that flows into the sea: *the River Amazon*

road /rəʊd/ *noun*
the way from one place to another, where cars can go: *Is this the road to Brighton?* ◇ *My address is 47 Ridley Road, London NW10.* ○ The short way of writing 'Road' in addresses is **Rd**: *30 Welton Rd*
by road in a car, bus, etc: *It's a long journey by road — the train is faster.*

roam /rəʊm/ *verb* (**roams, roaming, roamed** /rəʊmd/)
walk or travel with no special plan: *Dogs were roaming the streets looking for food.*

roar /rɔː(r)/ *verb* (**roars, roaring, roared** /rɔːd/)
make a loud deep sound: *The lion roared.* ◇ *Everybody roared with laughter.*
roar *noun*
the roar of an aeroplane's engines

roast /rəʊst/ *verb* (**roasts, roasting, roasted**)
cook or be cooked in an oven or over a fire: *Roast the chicken in a hot oven.*
roast *adjective*
roast beef and roast potatoes

rob /rɒb/ *verb* (**robs, robbing, robbed** /rɒbd/)
take something that is not yours from a person or place: *They robbed a bank.*
☞ Note at **steal**
robber *noun*
a person who robs
robbery /'rɒbəri/ *noun* (*plural* **robberies**)
taking something that is not yours from a bank, etc: *What time did the robbery take place?*

robin /'rɒbɪn/ *noun*
a small brown bird with a red front

robot /'rəʊbɒt/ *noun*
a machine that can work like a person: *This car was built by robots.*

rock¹ /rɒk/ *noun*
1 (no plural) the very hard stuff that is in the ground and in mountains
2 (*plural* **rocks**) a big piece of this: *The ship hit the rocks.*

rock² /rɒk/, **rock music** /'rɒk mjuːzɪk/ *noun* (no plural)
a sort of modern music: *a rock concert*

rock³ /rɒk/ *verb* (**rocks, rocking, rocked** /rɒkt/)
move slowly backwards and forwards or

from side to side; make somebody or something do this: *The boat was rocking gently on the lake.* ◇ *I rocked the baby until she went to sleep.*

rocket /ˈrɒkɪt/ *noun*
1 an engine with long round sides that pushes a spacecraft up into space
2 a thing with long round sides that carries a bomb through the air
3 a **firework** that goes up into the air and then explodes

rocky /ˈrɒki/ *adjective* (**rockier, rockiest**)
with a lot of rocks: *a rocky path*

rod /rɒd/ *noun*
a thin straight piece of wood or metal: *a fishing-rod*

rode *form of* **ride**

role /rəʊl/ *noun*
1 the person you are in a play or film: *The role of the King was played by Bob Lewis.*
2 what a person does: *Your role is to tell other people what to do.*

roll[1] /rəʊl/ *verb* (**rolls, rolling, rolled** /rəʊld/)
1 move along, turning over and over; make something go over and over: *The pencil rolled off the table on to the floor.* ◇ *We rolled the rock down the path.*
2 move on wheels: *The car rolled down the hill.*
3 make something flat by moving something heavy on top of it: *Roll the pastry into a large circle.*
roll over turn your body a different way when you are lying down: *She rolled over.*
roll up make something into a long round shape or the shape of a ball: *Can you help me to roll up this carpet?*

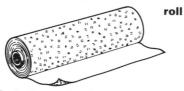
roll

roll[2] /rəʊl/ *noun*
1 something made into a long round shape by rolling it around itself many times: *a roll of material* ◇ *a roll of film*
2 a small round piece of bread made for one person: *a roll and butter*

roller-skate
/ˈrəʊlə skeɪt/ *noun*
a shoe with wheels on the bottom, for moving quickly on smooth ground
roller-skating
noun (no plural)
moving on roller-skates

roller-skate

Roman Catholic /ˌrəʊmən ˈkæθəlɪk/ *noun*
a member of the Christian church that follows the Pope

romance /rəʊˈmæns/ *noun*
1 a time when two people are in love: *a romance between a doctor and a nurse*
2 a story about love: *She writes romances.*

romantic /rəʊˈmæntɪk/ *adjective*
about love; full of feelings of love: *a romantic film*

roof /ruːf/ *noun* (*plural* **roofs**)
the top of a building or car, that covers it
☞ picture at **house**

room /ruːm/ *noun*
1 (*plural* **rooms**) one of the spaces with walls round it in a building: *How many rooms has your flat got?* ◇ *a classroom*

❂ A house or flat usually has a **living-room** (or **sitting-room** or **lounge**), **bedrooms**, a **bathroom**, a **toilet**, a **kitchen**, a **hall** and perhaps a **dining-room**.

2 (no plural) space; enough space: *There's no room for you in the car.*

root /ruːt/ *noun*
the part of a plant that is under the ground ☞ picture at **plant**

rope /rəʊp/ *noun*
very thick strong string

rose[1] *form of* **rise**

rose[2] /rəʊz/ *noun*
a flower with a sweet smell. It grows on a bush that has sharp points (called **thorns**) on it.

rope

rosy /ˈrəʊzi/ *adjective* (**rosier, rosiest**)
pink: *rosy cheeks*

rot /rɒt/ *verb* (**rots, rotting, rotted**)
become bad and soft, as things do when

they die: *Nobody picked the apples so they rotted.*

rotate /rəʊ'teɪt/ *verb* (**rotates, rotating, rotated**)
move in circles: *The earth rotates around the sun.*

rotten /'rɒtn/ *adjective*
1, old and not fresh; bad: *These eggs are rotten – they smell horrible!*
2 very bad; not nice or kind: *The weather was rotten all week.*

rough /rʌf/ *adjective* (**rougher, roughest**)
1 not smooth or flat: *It was difficult to walk on the rough ground*
2 not gentle or calm: *rough seas*
3 not exactly correct; made or done quickly: *Can you give me a rough idea how much it will cost?* ◇ *a rough drawing*

roughly /'rʌfli/ *adverb*
1 not gently: *He pushed me roughly away.*
2 about; not exactly: *The bike cost roughly £150.*

round¹ /raʊnd/ *adjective*
with the shape of a circle or a ball: *a round plate*

round² /raʊnd/ *adverb, preposition*
1 on or to all sides of something, often in a circle: *The earth moves round the sun.* ◇ *We sat round the table.* ◇ *He tied a scarf round his neck.* ☞ picture on page 128
2 in the opposite direction or in another direction: *I turned round and went home again.* ◇ *Turn your chair round.*
3 in or to different parts of a place: *We travelled round France last summer.*
4 from one person to another: *Pass these photos round the class.*
5 to somebody's house: *Come round* (= to my house) *at eight o'clock.*
6 to or on the other side of something: *There's a bank just round the corner.*
go round be enough for everybody: *Are there enough cakes to go round?*
round about nearly; not exactly: *It will cost round about £90.*
round and round round many times: *The bird flew round and round the room.*

round³ /raʊnd/ *noun*
1 a lot of visits, one after another, for ex-

ample as part of your job: *The postman starts his round at seven o'clock.*
2 one part of a game or competition: *the third round of the boxing match*
3 drinks for all the people in a group: *I'll buy this round. What would you like?*

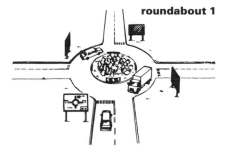

roundabout 1

roundabout /'raʊndəbaʊt/ *noun*
1 a place where roads meet, where cars must drive round in a circle
2 a big round machine at a fair. It has model animals or cars on it that children can ride on as it turns.

round trip /ˌraʊnd 'trɪp/ *noun*
a journey to a place and back again

route /ruːt/ *noun*
a way from one place to another: *What is the quickest route from London to Edinburgh?*

routine /ruː'tiːn/ *noun*
your usual way of doing things: *My morning routine is to get up at seven, have breakfast, then leave home at eight.*

row¹ /rəʊ/ *noun*
a line of people or things: *We sat in the front row of the theatre* (= the front line of seats). ◇ *a row of houses* ☞ picture on page 261

rowing

oar

rowing-boat

row² /rəʊ/ *verb* (**rows, rowing, rowed** /rəʊd/)
move a boat through water using long pieces of wood with flat ends (called **oars**): *We rowed across the lake.* ❸ When you

talk about spending time rowing as a sport, you say **go rowing**: *We went rowing on the river.*

rowing-boat /ˈrəʊɪŋ bəʊt/ *noun*
a small boat that you move through water using oars

row³ /raʊ/ *noun*
1 (*plural* **rows**) a noisy talk between people who do not agree about something: *She had a row with her boyfriend.*
2 (no plural) loud noise: *The children were making a terrible row.*

royal /ˈrɔɪəl/ *adjective*
of or about a king or queen: *the royal family*

royalty /ˈrɔɪəlti/ *noun* (no plural)
kings, queens and their families

rub /rʌb/ *verb* (**rubs**, **rubbing**, **rubbed** /rʌbd/)
move something backwards and forwards on another thing: *I rubbed my hands together to keep them warm.* ◊ *The cat rubbed its head against my leg.*
rub out take writing or marks off something by using a rubber or a cloth: *I rubbed the word out and wrote it again.*
rub *noun* (no plural)
Give your shoes a rub.

rubber /ˈrʌbə(r)/ *noun*
1 (no plural) material that we use to make things like car tyres
2 (*plural* **rubbers**) a small piece of rubber that you use for taking away marks that you have made with a pencil
rubber band /ˌrʌbə(r) ˈbænd/ *noun*
a thin circle of rubber that you use for holding things together

rubbish /ˈrʌbɪʃ/ *noun* (no plural)
1 things that you do not want any more: *old boxes, bottles and other rubbish* ◊ *Throw this rubbish in the bin.*
2 something that is bad, stupid or wrong: *You're talking rubbish!*

rucksack /ˈrʌksæk/ *noun*
a bag that you carry on your back, for example when you are walking or climbing

rudder /ˈrʌdə(r)/ *noun*
a flat piece of wood or metal at the back of a boat or an aeroplane. It moves to make the boat or aeroplane go left or right.

rude /ruːd/ *adjective* (**ruder**, **rudest**)
1 not polite: *It's rude to walk away when someone is talking to you.*
2 about things like sex or using the toilet: *rude words*
rudely *adverb*
'Shut up!' she said rudely.

rug

rug /rʌg/ *noun*
1 a small piece of thick material that you put on the floor
2 a thick piece of material that you put round your body to keep you warm

rugby /ˈrʌgbi/ *noun* (no plural)
a game like football for two teams of 13 or 15 players. In rugby, you can kick and carry the ball.

ruin /ˈruːɪn/ *verb* (**ruins**, **ruining**, **ruined** /ˈruːɪnd/)
damage something badly so that it is no longer good; destroy something completely: *I spilled coffee on my jacket and ruined it.* ◊ *The rain ruined our picnic.*
ruin *noun*
a building that has been badly damaged: *The old castle is now a ruin.*
in ruins badly damaged or destroyed: *The city was in ruins after the war.*

rule¹ /ruːl/ *noun*
1 (*plural* **rules**) something that tells you what you must or must not do: *It's against the school rules to smoke.* ◊ *break the rules* (= do something that you should not do)
2 (no plural) government: *India was once under British rule.*

rule² /ruːl/ *verb* (**rules**, **ruling**, **ruled** /ruːld/)
control a country: *Queen Victoria ruled for many years.*

ruler /ˈruːlə(r)/ *noun*
1 a long piece of plastic, metal or wood that you use for drawing straight lines or for measuring things
2 a person who rules a country

ruler

rum /rʌm/ *noun*
a strong alcoholic drink

rumble /'rʌmbl/ *verb* (**rumbles, rumbling, rumbled** /'rʌmbld/)
make a long deep sound: *I'm so hungry that my stomach is rumbling.*
rumble *noun* (no plural)
the rumble of thunder

rumor *American English for* **rumour**

rumour /'ru:mə(r)/ *noun*
something that a lot of people are talking about that is perhaps not true: *There's a rumour that our teacher is leaving.*

run[1] /rʌn/ *verb* (**runs, running, ran** /ræn/, **has run**)
1 move very quickly on your legs: *I was late so I ran to the bus-stop.*
2 go; make a journey: *The buses don't run on Sundays.*
3 control something and make it work: *Who runs the company?*
4 pass or go somewhere: *The road runs across the fields.*
5 flow: *The river runs into the North Sea.*
6 work: *The car had stopped but the engine was still running.*
7 move something somewhere: *He ran his fingers through his hair.*
run after somebody or **something** try to catch a person or an animal: *The dog ran after a rabbit.*
run away go quickly away from a place: *She ran away from home when she was 14.*
run out of something have no more of something: *We've run out of coffee. Will you go and buy some?*
run over somebody or **something** drive over somebody or something: *The dog was run over by a bus.*

run[2] /rʌn/ *noun*
moving very quickly on your legs: *I go for a run every morning.*

rung[1] *form of* **ring**[2]

rung[2] /rʌŋ/ *noun*
one of the steps of a ladder ☞ picture at **ladder**

runner /'rʌnə(r)/ *noun*
a person who runs

runner-up /ˌrʌnər 'ʌp/ *noun* (*plural* **runners-up** /ˌrʌnəz 'ʌp/)
a person or team that comes second in a race or competition

running[1] /'rʌnɪŋ/ *noun* (no plural)
the sport of running: *running shoes*

running[2] /'rʌnɪŋ/ *adjective*
one after another: *We won the competition for three years running.*

runway /'rʌnweɪ/ *noun* (*plural* **runways**)
a long piece of ground where aeroplanes take off and land

rural /'rʊərəl/ *adjective*
of the country, not the town: *The book is about life in rural France.*

rush /rʌʃ/ *verb* (**rushes, rushing, rushed** /rʌʃt/)
1 go or come very quickly: *The children rushed out of school.*
2 do something quickly or make somebody do something quickly: *We rushed to finish the work on time.*
3 take somebody or something quickly to a place: *She was rushed to hospital.*
rush *noun* (no plural)
1 a sudden quick movement: *At the end of the film there was a rush for the exits.*
2 a need to move or do something very quickly: *I can't stop now – I'm in a rush.*
the rush hour /ðə 'rʌʃ aʊə(r)/ *noun*
the time when a lot of people are going to or coming from work

rust /rʌst/ *noun* (no plural)
red-brown stuff that you sometimes see on metal that has been wet
rust *verb* (**rusts, rusting, rusted**)
become covered with rust: *My bike rusted because I left it out in the rain.*
rusty *adjective* (**rustier, rustiest**)
covered with rust: *a rusty nail*

rustle /'rʌsl/ *verb* (**rustles, rustling, rustled** /'rʌsld/)
make a sound like dry leaves moving together; make something make this sound: *Stop rustling your newspaper – I can't hear the film!*
rustle *noun* (no plural)
the rustle of leaves

iː	i	ɪ	e	æ	ɑː	ɒ	ɔː	ʊ	u	uː
see	happy	sit	ten	cat	father	got	saw	put	situation	too

Ss

sack¹ /sæk/ *noun*
a big strong bag for carrying heavy things:
a sack of potatoes

sack² /sæk/ *verb* (**sacks**, **sacking**,
sacked /sækt/)
say that somebody must leave their job:
*The manager sacked her because she was
always late.*
sack *noun* (no plural)
get the sack lose your job
give somebody the sack say that
somebody must leave their job

sacred /'seɪkrɪd/ *adjective*
with a special religious meaning: *A church
is a sacred building.*

sacrifice /'sækrɪfaɪs/ *verb* (**sacrifices**,
sacrificing, **sacrificed** /'sækrɪfaɪst/)
1 kill an animal as a present to a god: *They
sacrificed a lamb.*
2 stop doing or having something important so that you can help somebody or to
get something else: *During the war, many
people sacrificed their lives for their
country.*
sacrifice *noun*
*They made a lot of sacrifices to pay for
their son to go to university.*

sad /sæd/ *adjective* (**sadder**, **saddest**)
1 unhappy: *The children were very sad
when their dog died.* ☞ picture on page
262
2 that makes you feel unhappy: *a sad
story*
sadly *adverb*
She looked sadly at the empty house.
sadness /'sædnəs/ *noun* (no plural)
the feeling of being sad

saddle /'sædl/ *noun*
a seat on a horse or bicycle ☞ picture at
bicycle

safari /sə'fɑːri/ *noun* (*plural* **safaris**)
a journey to look at or hunt wild animals,
usually in Africa

safe¹ /seɪf/ *adjective* (**safer**, **safest**)
1 not in danger; not hurt: *Don't go out
alone at night – you won't be safe.*

2 not dangerous: *Is it safe to swim in this
river?* ◇ *Always keep medicines in a safe
place.*
safe and sound not hurt or broken: *The
child was found safe and sound.*
safely *adverb*
*Phone your parents to tell them you have
arrived safely.*

safe² /seɪf/ *noun*
a strong metal box with a lock where you
keep money or things like jewellery

safety /'seɪfti/ *noun* (no plural)
being safe: *He is worried about the safety
of his children.*

safety-belt /'seɪfti belt/ *noun*
a long thin piece of material that you put
round your body in a car or an aeroplane
to keep you safe in an accident

safety pin /'seɪfti
pin/ *noun*
a pin that you use
for joining things
together. It has a
cover over the point so that it is not
dangerous.

safety pin

sag /sæg/ *verb* (**sags**, **sagging**, **sagged**
/sægd/)
bend or hang down: *The bed is very old
and it sags in the middle.*

said *form of* **say¹**

sail

sail¹ /seɪl/ *noun*
a big piece of cloth on a boat. The wind
blows against the sail and moves the boat
along.

sail² /seɪl/ *verb* (**sails**, **sailing**, **sailed**
/seɪld/)
1 travel on water: *The ship sailed along
the coast.*
2 control a boat with sails: *We sailed the*

yacht down the river. ✪ When you talk about spending time sailing a boat, you say **go sailing**: *We often go sailing on the Thames at weekends.*

sailing *noun* (no plural)
the sport of controlling a boat with sails

sailor /'seɪlə(r)/ *noun*
a person who works on a ship

saint /seɪnt/ *noun*
a very good and holy person: *Saint Nicholas* ✪ You usually say /sənt/ before names. The short way of writing 'Saint' before names is **St**: *St George's church*

sake /seɪk/ *noun*
for the sake of somebody or **something, for somebody's** or **something's sake** to help somebody or something; because of somebody or something: *Chris and Jackie stayed together for the sake of their children.*
✪ You use expressions like **for goodness' sake**, **for God's sake** and **for Heaven's sake** to show that you are angry: *For goodness' sake, be quiet!*

salad /'sæləd/ *noun*
a dish of cold, usually raw vegetables: *Do you want chips or salad with your chicken?*

salary /'sæləri/ *noun* (*plural* **salaries**)
money that you receive every month for the work that you do

sale /seɪl/ *noun*
1 (no plural) selling something
2 (*plural* **sales**) a time when a shop sells things for less money than usual: *In the sale, everything was half-price.*
for sale If something is for sale, its owner wants to sell it: *Is this house for sale?*
on sale If something is on sale, you can buy it in shops: *The magazine is on sale at most newsagents.*

salesclerk /'seɪlzklɜːrk/ *American English for* **shop assistant**

salesman /'seɪlzmən/ *noun* (*plural* **salesmen** /'seɪlzmən/), **saleswoman** /'seɪlzwumən/ (*plural* **saleswomen**), **salesperson** /'seɪlzpɜːsn/ (*plural* **salespeople**)
a person whose job is selling things

salmon /'sæmən/ *noun* (*plural* **salmon**)
a big fish that lives in the sea and in rivers and that you can eat

salt /sɔːlt/ *noun* (no plural)
white stuff that comes from sea water and from the earth. We put it on food to make it taste better: *Add a little salt and pepper.*
salty *adjective* (**saltier**, **saltiest**)
with salt in it: *Sea water is salty.*

salute /sə'luːt/ *verb* (**salutes**, **saluting**, **saluted**)
make the special sign that soldiers make, by lifting your hand to your head: *The soldiers saluted as the Queen walked past.*
salute *noun*
The soldier gave a salute.

same /seɪm/ *adjective*
the same not different; not another: *Emma and I like the same kind of music.* ◇ *I've lived in the same town all my life.* ◇ *He went to the same school as me.*
same *pronoun*
all or **just the same** anyway: *I understand why you're angry. All the same, I think you should say sorry.*
same to you words that you use for saying to somebody what they have said to you: *'Have a good weekend.' 'Same to you.'*
the same not a different person or thing: *Do these two words mean the same?* ◇ *Your watch is the same as mine.*

sample /'sɑːmpl/ *noun*
a small amount of something that shows what the rest is like: *a free sample of perfume* ◇ *a blood sample*

sand /sænd/ *noun* (no plural)
powder made of very small pieces of rock, that you find next to the sea and in deserts
sandy *adjective* (**sandier**, **sandiest**)
with sand: *a sandy beach*

sandal /'sændl/ *noun*
a light open shoe that you wear in warm weather

sandals

sandwich /'sænwɪdʒ/ *noun* (*plural* **sandwiches**)
two pieces of bread with other food between them: *a cheese sandwich*

sane /seɪn/ *adjective* (**saner**, **sanest**)
with a normal healthy mind; not mad
✪ opposite: **insane**

sang *form of* **sing**

sank *form of* **sink**[2]

Santa Claus /ˈsæntə klɔːz/ *another word for* **Father Christmas**

sarcastic /sɑːˈkæstɪk/ *adjective*
If you are sarcastic, you say the opposite of what you mean, in an unkind way.

sardine /sɑːˈdiːn/ *noun*
a very small fish that you can eat. You often buy sardines in tins.

sari /ˈsɑːri/ *noun* (*plural* **saris**)
a long piece of material that Indian women wear around their bodies as a dress

sat *form of* **sit**

satchel /ˈsætʃəl/ *noun*
a bag that children use for carrying books to and from school

satellite /ˈsætəlaɪt/ *noun*
1 a thing in space that moves round a planet: *The moon is a satellite of the earth.*
2 a thing that people have sent into space. Satellites travel round the earth and send back pictures or television and radio signals: *satellite television*

satin /ˈsætɪn/ *noun* (no plural)
very shiny smooth cloth

satisfaction /ˌsætɪsˈfækʃn/ *noun* (no plural)
being pleased with what you or other people have done: *She finished painting the picture and looked at it with satisfaction.*

satisfactory /ˌsætɪsˈfæktəri/ *adjective*
good enough, but not very good: *Her work is not satisfactory.* **◯** opposite: **unsatisfactory**

satisfy /ˈsætɪsfaɪ/ *verb* (**satisfies, satisfying, satisfied** /ˈsætɪsfaɪd/, **has satisfied**)
give somebody what they want or need; be good enough to make somebody pleased: *Nothing he does satisfies his father.*
satisfied *adjective*
pleased because you have had or done what you wanted: *The teacher was not satisfied with my work.*
satisfying *adjective*
Something that is satisfying makes you pleased because it is what you want: *a satisfying result*

Saturday /ˈsætədeɪ/ *noun*
the seventh day of the week, next after Friday

sauce /sɔːs/ *noun*
a thick liquid that you eat on or with other food: *tomato sauce*

saucepan
/ˈsɔːspən/ *noun*
a round metal container for cooking

saucepan

saucer /ˈsɔːsə(r)/ *noun*
a small round plate that you put under a cup ☞ picture at **cup**

sausages

sausage /ˈsɒsɪdʒ/ *noun*
meat that is cut into very small pieces and made into a long, thin shape: *garlic sausage* ◇ *sausages and chips*

savage /ˈsævɪdʒ/ *adjective*
wild or fierce: *a savage attack by a large dog*

save /seɪv/ *verb* (**saves, saving, saved** /seɪvd/)
1 take somebody or something away from danger: *He saved me from the fire.* ◇ *The doctor saved her life.*
2 keep something, especially money, to use later: *I've saved enough money to buy a car.* ◇ *Save some of the meat for tomorrow.*
3 use less of something: *She saves money by making her own clothes.*
4 stop somebody from scoring a goal, for example in football
save up for something keep money to buy something later: *I'm saving up for a new bike.*

savings /ˈseɪvɪŋz/ *noun* (plural)
money that you are keeping to use later: *I keep my savings in the bank.*

saw[1] *form of* **see**

saw[2] /sɔː/ *noun*
a metal tool for cutting wood
saw *verb* (**saws, sawing, sawed** /sɔːd/, **has sawn** /sɔːn/)
She sawed a branch off the tree.

saw

sawdust /'sɔ:dʌst/ *noun* (no plural)
powder that falls when you saw wood

saxophone

saxophone /'sæksəfəʊn/ *noun*
a musical instrument made of metal that
you play by blowing into it

say¹ /seɪ/ *verb* (**says** /sez/, **saying**, **said**
/sed/, **has said**)
1 make words with your mouth: *You say
'please' when you ask for something.*
◇ *'This is my room,' he said.* ◇ *She said
that she was cold.*

say or **tell**?

Say and **tell** are not used in the same
way. Look at these sentences:

*Jo **said** 'I'm ready.'*

*Jo **said** (that) she was ready.*

*Jo **said** to me that she was ready.*

*Jo **told** me (that) she was ready.*

*Jo **told** me to close the door.*

2 give information: *The notice on the door
said 'Private'.* ◇ *The clock says half past
three.*
that is to say what I mean is . . .: *I'll see
you in a week, that's to say next Monday.*

say² /seɪ/ *noun*
have a say have the right to help decide
something: *I would like to have a say in
who we invite to the party.*

saying /'seɪɪŋ/ *noun*
a sentence that people often say, that gives
advice about something: *'Look before you
leap' is an old saying.*

scab /skæb/ *noun*
a hard covering that grows over your skin
where it is cut or broken

scaffolding /'skæfəldɪŋ/ *noun* (no
plural)
metal bars and pieces of wood joined together, where people like painters and
builders can stand when they are working
on high parts of a building

scald /skɔ:ld/ *verb* (**scalds**, **scalding**,
scalded)
burn somebody or something with very
hot liquid

scale /skeɪl/ *noun*
1 a set of marks on something for measuring: *This ruler has one scale in centimetres
and one scale in inches.*
2 how distances are shown on a map: *This
map has a scale of one centimetre to ten
kilometres.*
3 one of the flat hard things that cover the
body of animals like fish and snakes

scales /skeɪlz/
noun (plural)
a machine for
showing how heavy
people or things are

scalp /skælp/ *noun*
the skin on the top
of your head, under your hair

scales

scan /skæn/ *verb* (**scans**, **scanning**,
scanned /skænd/)
1 look carefully because you are trying to
find something: *They scanned the sea,
looking for a boat.*
2 read something quickly: *Jane scanned
the list until she found her name.*
scanner *noun*
a machine that gives a picture of the inside
of something. Doctors use one kind of
scanner to look inside people's bodies.

scandal /'skændl/ *noun*
1 (*plural* **scandals**) something that makes
a lot of people talk about it, perhaps in an
angry way: *There was a big scandal when
the Prince decided to get married again.*
2 (no plural) unkind talk about somebody
that gives you a bad idea of them

p	b	t	d	k	g	tʃ	dʒ	f	v	θ	ð
pen	**b**ad	**t**ea	**d**id	**c**at	**g**ot	**ch**ain	**j**am	**f**all	**v**an	**th**in	**th**is

scar /skɑ:(r)/ *noun*
a mark on your skin, that an old cut has
left
scar *verb* (**scars, scarring, scarred**
/skɑ:d/)
make a scar on skin: *His face was badly
scarred by the accident.*

scarce /skeəs/ *adjective* (**scarcer, scar-
cest**)
difficult to find; not enough: *Food for birds
and animals is scarce in the winter.*

scarcely /'skeəsli/ *adverb*
almost not; only just: *He was so frightened
that he could scarcely speak.*

scare /skeə(r)/ *verb* (**scares, scaring,
scared** /skeəd/)
make somebody frightened: *That noise
scared me!*
scare *noun*
a feeling of being frightened: *You gave me
a scare!*
scared *adjective*
frightened: *Claire is scared of the dark.*

scarecrow /'skeəkrəʊ/ *noun*
a thing that looks like a person, that
farmers put in their fields to frighten birds

scarves

scarf /skɑ:f/ *noun* (*plural* **scarves**
/skɑ:vz/)
a piece of material that you wear around
your neck or head

scarlet /'skɑ:lət/ *adjective*
with a bright red colour

scatter /'skætə(r)/ *verb* (**scatters, scat-
tering, scattered** /'skætəd/)
1 move quickly in different directions: *The
crowd scattered when it started to rain.*
2 throw things so that they fall in a lot of
different places: *She scattered the pieces of
bread on the grass for the birds.*

scene /si:n/ *noun*
1 a place where something happened: *The
police arrived at the scene of the crime.*
2 what you see in a place; a view: *He
painted scenes of life in the countryside.*
3 part of a play or film: *Act 1, Scene 2 of
'Hamlet'*

scenery /'si:nəri/ *noun* (no plural)
1 the things like mountains, rivers and
forests that you see around you in the
countryside: *What beautiful scenery!*
2 things on the stage of a theatre that
make it look like a real place

scent /sent/ *noun*
1 (*plural* **scents**) a smell: *This flower has
no scent.*
2 (no plural) a liquid with a nice smell,
that you put on your body: *a bottle of scent*
scented *adjective*
with a nice smell: *scented soap*

schedule /'ʃedju:l/ *noun*
a plan or list of times when things will happen or be done: *I've got a busy schedule
next week.*
behind schedule late: *We're behind
schedule with the work.*
on schedule with everything happening at the right time: *We are on schedule to
finish the work in May.*

scheme /ski:m/ *noun*
a plan: *a scheme to build more houses*

scholar /'skɒlə(r)/ *noun*
a person who has learned a lot about
something: *a famous history scholar*

scholarship /'skɒləʃɪp/ *noun*
money that is given to a good student to
help him/her to continue studying: *Adrian
won a scholarship to Cambridge.*

school /sku:l/ *noun*
1 (*plural* **schools**) a place where children
go to learn: *Lucy is at school.* ◇ *Which
school do you go to?*
2 (no plural) being at school: *I hate
school!* ◇ *He left school when he was
16.* ◇ *School starts at nine o'clock.*
3 (*plural* **schools**) a place where you go to
learn a special thing: *a language school*
schoolboy /'sku:lbɔɪ/, **schoolgirl**
/'sku:lgɜ:l/, **schoolchild** /'sku:ltʃaɪld/
(*plural* **schoolchildren**) *noun*
a boy or girl who goes to school
school-days /'sku:ldeɪz/ *noun* (plural)
the time in your life when you are at school

☞ Look at **nursery school, primary school, junior school, middle school, secondary school, grammar school** and **comprehensive school** to find out more about schools in Britain. You must pay to go to a **private school** or a **public school**. A **boarding-school** is a school where the pupils live. When you leave school, you may go to a **college** or **university**.

science /'saɪəns/
the study of natural things: *I'm interested in science.* ◇ *Biology, chemistry and physics are all sciences.*

science fiction /ˌsaɪəns 'fɪkʃn/ *noun* (no plural)
stories about things like travel in space, life on other planets or life in the future

scientific /ˌsaɪən'tɪfɪk/ *adjective*
of or about science: *a scientific experiment*

scientist /'saɪəntɪst/ *noun*
a person who studies science or works with science

scissors

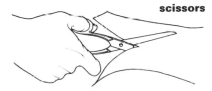

scissors /'sɪzəz/ *noun* (plural)
a tool for cutting that has two sharp parts that are joined together: *These scissors aren't very sharp.* ✪ Be careful! You cannot say 'a scissors'. You can say a **pair of scissors**: *I need a pair of scissors.* (or: *I need some scissors.*)

scoop /sku:p/ *verb* (**scoops, scooping, scooped** /sku:pt/)
use a spoon or your hands to take something up or out: *I scooped some ice-cream out of the bowl.*

scooter /'sku:tə(r)/ *noun*
a light motor cycle with a small engine

score /skɔ:(r)/ *noun*
the number of points, goals, etc that you win in a game or competition: *The winner got a score of 320.*

score *verb* (**scores, scoring, scored** /skɔ:d/)
win a point in a game or competition: *Italy scored three goals against France.*

scorn /skɔ:n/ *noun* (no plural)
the strong feeling you have when you think that somebody or something is not good enough: *He was full of scorn for my idea.*

Scout /skaʊt/ = Boy Scout

scramble /'skræmbl/ *verb* (**scrambles, scrambling, scrambled** /'skræmbld/)
move quickly up or over something, using your hands to help you: *They scrambled over the wall.*

scrambled eggs /ˌskræmbld 'egz/ *noun* (plural)
eggs that you mix together with milk and cook in a pan with butter

scrap /skræp/ *noun*
1 (plural **scraps**) a small piece of something: *a scrap of paper*
2 (no plural) something you do not want any more but that is made of material that can be used again: *scrap paper*

scrape /skreɪp/ *verb* (**scrapes, scraping, scraped** /skreɪpt/)
1 move a rough or sharp thing across something: *I scraped the mud off my shoes with a knife.*
2 hurt or damage something by moving it against a rough or sharp thing: *I fell and scraped my knee on the wall.*

scratch¹ /skrætʃ/ *verb* (**scratches, scratching, scratched** /skrætʃt/)
1 cut or make a mark on something with a sharp thing: *The cat scratched me!*
2 move your fingernails across your skin: *She scratched her head.*

scratch² /skrætʃ/ *noun* (plural **scratches**)
a cut or mark that a sharp thing makes: *Her hands were covered in scratches from the rose bush.*

from scratch from the beginning: *I threw away the letter I was writing and started again from scratch.*

scream /skri:m/ *verb* (**screams, screaming, screamed** /skri:md/)
make a loud high cry that shows you are afraid or hurt: *She saw the snake and screamed.* ◇ *He screamed for help.*

scream *noun*
a loud high cry: *a scream of pain*

screech /skri:tʃ/ *verb* (**screeches, screeching, screeched** /skri:tʃt/)
make a loud high sound: *The car's brakes screeched as it stopped suddenly.*

screen /skri:n/ *noun*
1 the flat square part of a television or computer where you see pictures or words ☞ picture at **computer**
2 the flat thing on the wall of a cinema, where you see films
3 a kind of thin wall that you can move around. Screens are used to keep away cold, light, etc or to stop people from seeing something: *The nurse put a screen around the bed.*

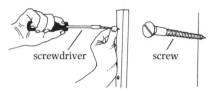

screwdriver   screw

screw /skru:/ *noun*
a small metal thing with a sharp end, that you use for fixing things together. You push it into something by turning it with a **screwdriver**.
screw *verb* (**screws, screwing, screwed** /skru:d/)
1 fix something to another thing using a screw
2 turn something to fix it to another thing: *Screw the lid on the jar.* ✪ opposite: **unscrew**
screw up make paper or material into a ball with your hand: *He screwed up the letter and threw it in the bin.*
screwdriver /'skru:draɪvə(r)/ *noun*
a tool for turning screws

scribble /'skrɪbl/ *verb* (**scribbles, scribbling, scribbled** /'skrɪbld/)
write something or make marks on paper quickly and without care: *The children scribbled in my book.*

script /skrɪpt/ *noun*
the written words that actors speak in a play or film

scrub /skrʌb/ *verb* (**scrubs, scrubbing, scrubbed** /skrʌbd/)
rub something hard to clean it, usually with a brush and soap and water: *He scrubbed the floor.*

scruffy /'skrʌfi/ *adjective* (**scruffier, scruffiest**)
untidy and perhaps dirty: *She was wearing scruffy jeans.*

sculptor /'skʌlptə(r)/ *noun*
a person who makes shapes from things like stone or wood

sculpture /'skʌlptʃə(r)/ *noun*
1 (no plural) making shapes from things like stone or wood
2 (*plural* **sculptures**) a shape made from things like stone or wood

sea /si:/ *noun*
1 (no plural) the salty water that covers large parts of the earth: *We went for a swim in the sea.* ◇ *The sea is very rough today.*
2 (*plural* **seas**) a big area of salty water: *the Black Sea*
at sea travelling on the sea: *We spent three weeks at sea.*

seafood /'si:fu:d/ *noun* (no plural)
fish and small animals from the sea that you can eat

seagull /'si:gʌl/ *noun*
a big grey or white bird with a loud cry, that lives near the sea

seal¹ /si:l/ *noun*
an animal with short fur that lives in and near the sea, and that eats fish

seal² /si:l/ *verb* (**seals, sealing, sealed** /si:ld/)
close something tightly by sticking two parts together: *She sealed the envelope.*

seam /si:m/ *noun*
a line where two pieces of cloth are joined together

search /sɜ:tʃ/ *verb* (**searches, searching, searched** /sɜ:tʃt/)
look carefully because you are trying to find somebody or something: *I searched everywhere for my pen.*
search *noun* (*plural* **searches**)
I found my key after a long search.
in search of somebody or **something** looking for somebody or something: *We drove round the town in search of a cheap hotel.*

sea shell /'si: ʃel/
noun
the hard outside
part of a small
animal that lives in
the sea

sea shells

seashore /'si:ʃɔ:(r)/
noun (no plural)
the land next to the sea; the beach

seasick /'si:sɪk/ adjective
If you are seasick, you feel ill in your stomach because the boat you are on is moving a lot.

seaside /'si:saɪd/ noun (no plural)
a place by the sea where people go on holiday: Let's go to the seaside.

season /'si:zn/ noun
1 one of the four parts of the year. The four seasons are **spring, summer, autumn** and **winter.**
2 a special time of the year for something: The football season starts in August.

seat /si:t/ noun
something that you sit on: the back seat of a car ◇ We had seats at the front of the theatre.
take a seat sit down: Please take a seat.

seat-belt /'si:t belt/ noun
a long thin piece of material that you put round your body in a car or an aeroplane to keep you safe in an accident

seaweed /'si:wi:d/ noun (no plural)
a plant that grows in the sea

second¹ /'sekənd/ adjective, adverb
next after first: February is the second month of the year.
secondly adverb
a word that you use when you are giving the second thing in a list: Firstly, it's too expensive and secondly, we don't really need it.

second² /'sekənd/ noun (no plural)
a person or thing that comes next after the first: Today is the second of April (April 2nd). ◇ I was the first to arrive, and Jim was the second.

second³ /'sekənd/ noun
1 a measure of time. There are 60 seconds in a **minute.**
2 a very short time: Wait a second! ◇ I'll be ready in a second.

secondary school /'sekəndri sku:l/
noun
a school for pupils between the ages of 11 and 18

second class /,sekənd 'klɑ:s/ noun (no plural)
1 the part of a train, plane, etc that it is cheaper to travel in: We sat in second class.
2 the cheapest but the slowest way of sending letters
second-class adjective, adverb
a second-class ticket ◇ I sent the letter second-class.
☞ Look at **first class** and at the Note at **stamp.**

second-hand /,sekənd 'hænd/ adjective, adverb
not new; used by another person before: second-hand books ◇ I bought this car second-hand.

secrecy /'si:krəsi/ noun (no plural)
not telling other people: They worked in secrecy.

secret¹ /'si:krət/ adjective
If something is secret, other people do not or must not know about it: They kept their wedding secret (= they did not tell anybody about it). ◇ a secret meeting
secretly adverb
without other people knowing: We are secretly planning a big party for her.

secret² /'si:krət/ noun
something that you do not or must not tell other people: I can't tell you where I'm going - it's a secret.
in secret without other people knowing: They met in secret.
keep a secret not tell other people a secret: Can you keep a secret?

secretary /'sekrətri/ noun (plural **secretaries**)
1 a person who types letters, answers the telephone and does other things in an office
2 an important person in the government: the Secretary of State for Education
3 American English for **minister 1**
secretarial /,sekrə'teəriəl/ adjective
of or about the work of a secretary: a secretarial college

secretive /'si:krətɪv/ adjective
If you are secretive, you do not like to tell

p	b	t	d	k	g	tʃ	dʒ	f	v	θ	ð
pen	**b**ad	**t**ea	**d**id	**c**at	**g**ot	**ch**ain	**j**am	**f**all	**v**an	**th**in	**th**is

other people about yourself or your plans: *Mark is very secretive about his job.*

section /'sekʃn/ *noun*
one of the parts of something: *This section of the road is closed.*

secure /sɪ'kjʊə(r)/ *adjective*
1 safe: *Don't climb that ladder – it's not very secure* (= it may fall). ◇ *Her job is secure* (= she will not lose it).
2 If you are secure, you feel safe and you are not worried: *Do you feel secure about the future?* ✪ opposite: **insecure**
3 well locked or protected so that nobody can go in or out: *This gate isn't very secure.*
securely *adverb*
Are all the windows securely closed?

security /sɪ'kjʊərəti/ *noun* (no plural)
1 the feeling of being safe: *Children need love and security.*
2 things that you do to keep a place safe: *We need better security at airports.*

see /si:/ *verb* (**sees, seeing, saw** /sɔ:/, **has seen** /si:n/)
1 know something using your eyes: *It was so dark that I couldn't see anything.* ◇ *Can you see that plane?* ◇ *I'm going to see a film tonight.*

see or look?

See and **look** are used in different ways. When you **see** something, you know about it with your eyes, without trying:

*Suddenly I **saw** a bird fly past the window.*

When you **look at** something, you turn your eyes towards it because you want to see it:

***Look at** this picture carefully. Can you **see** the bird?*

2 visit or meet somebody: *I'll see you outside the station at ten o'clock.*
3 understand something: *'You have to turn the key this way.' 'I see.'*
4 find out about something: *Look in the newspaper to see what time the film starts.*
5 make certain about something: *Please see that everybody is here.*
I'll see I will think about what you have

said and tell you what I have decided later: *'Will you lend me the money?' 'I'll see.'*
seeing that, seeing as because: *Seeing that you've got nothing to do, you can help me!*
see somebody off go to an airport or a station to say goodbye to somebody who is leaving
see to somebody or **something** do what you need to do for somebody or something: *Sit down – I'll see to the dinner.*
see you, see you later goodbye

seed /si:d/ *noun*
the small hard part of a plant from which a new plant grows

seek /si:k/ *verb* (**seeks, seeking, sought** /sɔ:t/, **has sought**)
try to find or get something: *You should seek help.*

seem /si:m/ *verb* (**seems, seeming, seemed** /si:md/)
make you think that something is true: *She seems tired.* ◇ *My mother seems to like you.* ◇ *Helen seems like* (= seems to be) *a nice girl.*

seen *form of* **see**

see-saw /'si: sɔ:/ *noun*
a special piece of wood that can move up and down when a child sits on each end

seize /si:z/ *verb* (**seizes, seizing, seized** /si:zd/)
take something quickly and strongly: *The thief seized my bag and ran away.*

seldom /'seldəm/ *adverb*
not often: *It seldom snows in Athens.*

select /sɪ'lekt/ *verb* (**selects, selecting, selected**)
take the person or thing that you like best; choose: *The manager has selected two new players for the team.* ✪ **Choose** is the word that we usually use.

selection /sɪ'lekʃn/ *noun*
1 (no plural) taking the person or thing you like best: *the selection of a new president*
2 (*plural* **selections**) a group of people or things that somebody has chosen, or a group of things that you can choose from: *This shop has a good selection of cassettes and compact discs.*

s	z	ʃ	ʒ	h	m	n	ŋ	l	r	j	w
so	**zoo**	**shoe**	**vision**	**hat**	**man**	**no**	**sing**	**leg**	**red**	**yes**	**wet**

self- /self/ *prefix*
by yourself; for yourself: *He is self-taught
– he never went to university.*

self-confident /ˌself ˈkɒnfɪdənt/ *adjective*
sure about yourself and what you can do

self-conscious /ˌself ˈkɒnʃəs/ *adjective*
worried about what other people think of you: *She walked into her new school feeling very self-conscious.*

self-employed /ˌself ɪmˈplɔɪd/ *adjective*
If you are self-employed, you work for yourself, not for somebody else's company: *He's a self-employed electrician.*

selfish /ˈselfɪʃ/ *adjective*
If you are selfish, you think too much about what you want and not about what other people want: *It was selfish of you to go out when your mother was ill.* ✪ opposite: **unselfish**
selfishly *adverb*
He behaved very selfishly.
selfishness /ˈselfɪʃnəs/ *noun* (no plural)
Her selfishness made me very angry.

self-service /ˌself ˈsɜːvɪs/ *adjective*
In a self-service shop or restaurant you take what you want and then pay for it.

sell /sel/ *verb* (**sells, selling, sold** /səʊld/, **has sold**)
give something to somebody who pays you money for it: *I sold my guitar for £200.* ◇ *He sold me a ticket.* ◇ *Newsagents usually sell chocolates and cigarettes.* ☞ Look at **buy**.
sell out be sold completely so that there are no more left: *I went to the shop to buy a newspaper, but they had all sold out.*
sell out of something sell all that you have of something: *We have oranges but we have sold out of apples.*

Sellotape /ˈseləʊteɪp/ *noun* (no plural)
clear paper or plastic that you buy in a narrow roll. You use it for sticking things like paper and cardboard together. ✪ **Sellotape** is a trade mark.

semi- /semi/ *prefix*
half: *A semicircle is a half circle.*

semicolon /ˌsemiˈkəʊlən/ *noun*
a mark (;) that you use in writing to separate parts of a sentence

semi-detached /ˌsemi dɪˈtætʃt/ *adjective*
A semi-detached house is joined to another house on one side.

semifinal /ˌsemiˈfaɪnl/ *noun*
In a competition, a semifinal is one of the two games that are played to find out who will play in the **final**.

senate /ˈsenət/ *noun*
1 one of the parts of the government in some countries
2 **the Senate** (no plural) the more important part of the government in the USA
senator /ˈsenətə(r)/ *noun*
a member of a senate

send /send/ *verb* (**sends, sending, sent** /sent/, **has sent**)
1 make something go somewhere: *I sent a letter to John.* ◇ *Have you sent your parents a postcard?*
2 make somebody go somewhere: *My company is sending me to New York.* ◇ *He was sent to prison for ten years.*
send for somebody or **something** ask for somebody or something to come to you: *Send for an ambulance!*
send off post something: *I'll send the letter off today.*

senior /ˈsiːniə(r)/ *adjective*
1 more important: *a senior officer in the army*
2 older: *a senior pupil*
✪ opposite: **junior**
senior citizen /ˌsiːniə ˈsɪtɪzn/ *noun*
an old person

sensation /senˈseɪʃn/ *noun*
1 a feeling: *I felt a burning sensation on my skin.*
2 great excitement or interest; something that makes people very excited: *The new film caused a sensation in Hollywood.*

sensational /senˈseɪʃənl/ *adjective*
very exciting or interesting: *sensational news*

sense¹ /sens/ *noun*
1 (*plural* **senses**) the power to see, hear, smell, taste or touch: *Dogs have a good sense of smell.*
2 (no plural) the ability to feel or understand something: *The boy had no sense of right and wrong.*
3 (no plural) the ability to think carefully about something and to do the right thing:

i:	i	ɪ	e	æ	ɑ:	ɒ	ɔ:	ʊ	u	u:
see	happy	sit	ten	cat	father	got	saw	put	situation	too

Did anybody have the sense to call the police?
4 (plural **senses**) a meaning: This word has four senses.
make sense be possible to understand: What does this sentence mean? It doesn't make sense to me.

sense² /sens/ verb (**senses, sensing, sensed** /senst/)
understand or feel something: I sensed that he was worried.

sensible /'sensəbl/ adjective
1 able to think carefully about something and to do the right thing: It was very sensible of you to call the police when you saw the accident.
2 right and good: We are going for a long walk, so wear some sensible shoes.
sensibly /'sensəbli/ adverb
She was sensibly dressed.

sensitive /'sensətɪv/ adjective
1 If you are sensitive about something, you easily become worried or unhappy about it: Don't say anything bad about her work — she's very sensitive about it.
○ opposite: **insensitive**
2 A person who is sensitive understands and is careful about other people's feelings: He's a very sensitive man. **○** opposite: **insensitive**
3 If something is sensitive, it is easy to hurt or damage: sensitive skin

sent form of **send**

sentence¹ /'sentəns/ noun
a group of words that tells you something or asks a question. When a sentence is written, it always begins with a capital letter and usually ends with a full stop.

sentence² /'sentəns/ noun
the punishment that a judge gives to somebody in a court of law
sentence verb (**sentences, sentencing, sentenced** /'sentənst/)
tell somebody in a court of law what their punishment will be: The judge sentenced the man to two years in prison.

separate¹ /'seprət/ adjective
1 away from something; not together or not joined: Cut the cake into eight separate pieces. ◇ In my school, the older children

are separate from the younger ones.
2 different; not the same: We stayed in separate rooms in the same hotel.
separately adverb
Shall we pay separately or together?

separate² /'sepəreɪt/ verb (**separates, separating, separated**)
1 stop being together: My parents separated when I was a baby.
2 divide people or things; keep people or things away from each other: The teacher separated the class into two groups.
3 be between two things: The Mediterranean separates Europe and Africa.
separation /ˌsepə'reɪʃn/ noun
The separation from my family and friends made me very unhappy.

September /sep'tembə(r)/ noun
the ninth month of the year

sergeant /'sɑːdʒənt/ noun
an officer in the army or the police

serial /'sɪəriəl/ noun
a story that is told in parts on television or radio, or in a magazine

series /'sɪəriːz/ noun (plural **series**)
1 a number of things of the same kind that come one after another: I heard a series of shots and then silence.
2 a number of television or radio programmes, often on the same subject, that come one after another: a TV series on dinosaurs

serious /'sɪəriəs/ adjective
1 very bad: That was a serious mistake.
◇ They had a serious accident.
2 important: a serious decision
3 not funny: a serious film
4 If you are serious, you are not joking or playing: Are you serious about going to live in Spain? ◇ You look very serious. Is something wrong?
seriously adverb
She's seriously ill.
take somebody or **something seriously** show that you know somebody or something is important: Don't take what he says too seriously — he is always joking.
seriousness /'sɪəriəsnəs/ noun (no plural)
The boy didn't understand the seriousness of his crime.

sermon /'sɜːmən/ noun
a talk that a priest gives in church

ʌ	ɜː	ə	eɪ	əʊ	aɪ	aʊ	ɔɪ	ɪə	eə	ʊə
cup	bird	about	say	go	five	now	boy	near	hair	pure

servant /'sɜːvənt/ noun
a person who works in another person's house, doing work like cooking and cleaning

serve /sɜːv/ verb (**serves**, **serving**, **served** /sɜːvd/)
1 do work for other people: *During the war he served in the army.*
2 give food or drink to somebody: *Breakfast is served from 7.30 to 9.00 a.m.*
3 help somebody in a shop to buy things: *Excuse me, Madam. Are you being served?*
it serves you right it is right that this bad thing has happened to you: *'I feel ill.' 'It serves you right for eating so much!'*

service /'sɜːvɪs/ noun
1 (plural **services**) a business that does useful work for all the people in a country or an area: *This town has a good bus service.* ◇ *the postal service*
2 (no plural) help or work that you do for somebody: *She left the company after ten years of service.*
3 (no plural) the work that somebody does for customers in a shop, restaurant or hotel: *The food was good but the service was very slow.*
4 (plural **services**) a meeting in a church with prayers and singing: *We went to the evening service.*
5 (plural **services**) the time when somebody looks at a car or machine to see that it is working well: *She takes her car to the garage for a service every six months.*
6 **services** (plural) a place by a motorway where you can stop to buy petrol and food and use the toilets
7 **the services** (plural) the army, navy and air force

service station /'sɜːvɪs steɪʃn/ noun
a place where you can buy petrol

serviette /ˌsɜːviˈet/ noun
a piece of cloth or paper that you use when you are eating to clean your mouth and hands and to keep your clothes clean

session /'seʃn/ noun
a time when people meet to do something: *The first swimming session is at nine o'clock.*

set¹ /set/ noun
a group of things of the same kind, or a group of things that you use together: *a set of six glasses* ◇ *a set of tools*

set² /set/ verb (**sets**, **setting**, **set**, **has set**)
1 put something somewhere: *Dad set the plate in front of me.*
2 make something ready to use or to start working: *I set my alarm clock for seven o'clock.* ◇ *I set the table* (= put knives, forks, etc on it).
3 make something happen: *They set the school on fire* (= made it start to burn).
4 When the sun sets, it goes down from the sky. ✿ opposite: **rise**
5 decide what something will be; fix something: *Let's set a date for the meeting.*
6 give somebody work to do: *Our teacher set us a lot of homework.*
7 become hard or solid: *Wait for the cement to set.*
set off, set out start a journey: *We set off for Oxford at two o'clock.*
set up start something: *The company was set up in 1981.*

settee /seˈtiː/ noun
a long soft seat for more than one person

setting /'setɪŋ/ noun
the place where something is or where something happens: *The house is in a beautiful setting on top of a hill.*

settle /'setl/ verb (**settles**, **settling**, **settled** /'setld/)
1 go to live in a new place and stay there: *Ruth left England and went to settle in America.*
2 decide something after talking with somebody; end a discussion or argument: *Have you settled your argument with Rajit?*
3 come down and rest somewhere: *The bird settled on a branch.*
4 pay something: *Have you settled your bill?*
settle down 1 sit down or lie down so that you are comfortable: *I settled down in front of the television.* **2** become calm and quiet: *The children settled down and went to sleep.* **3** begin to have a calm life in one place: *When are you going to get married and settle down?*
settle in start to feel happy in a new place: *We only moved to this flat last week and we haven't settled in yet.*

settlement /'setlmənt/ noun
1 an agreement about something after talking or arguing: *After long talks about*

p	b	t	d	k	g	tʃ	dʒ	f	v	θ	ð
pen	**b**ad	**t**ea	**d**id	**c**at	**g**ot	**ch**ain	**j**am	**f**all	**v**an	**th**in	**th**is

pay, the workers and their boss reached a settlement.
2 a group of homes in a place where no people have lived before: *a settlement in the forest*

seven /ˈsevn/ *number*
7
seventh /ˈsevnθ/ *adjective, adverb, noun*
1 7th
2 one of seven equal parts of something; 1/7

seventeen /ˌsevnˈtiːn/ *number*
17
seventeenth /ˌsevnˈtiːnθ/ *adjective, adverb, noun*
17th

seventy /ˈsevnti/ *number*
1 70
2 **the seventies** (plural) the numbers, years or temperature between 70 and 79
in your seventies between the ages of 70 and 79
seventieth /ˈsevntiəθ/ *adjective, adverb, noun*
70th

several /ˈsevrəl/ *adjective, pronoun*
more than two but not many: *I've read this book several times.* ◊ *Several letters arrived this morning.* ◊ *If you need a pen, there are several on the table.*

severe /sɪˈvɪə(r)/ *adjective* (**severer, severest**)
1 not kind or gentle: *severe punishment*
2 very bad: *a severe headache* ◊ *a severe* (= very cold) *winter*
severely *adverb*
They punished him severely. ◊ *She was severely injured in the accident.*

sew

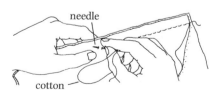

needle

cotton

sew /səʊ/ *verb* (**sews, sewing, sewed** /səʊd/, **has sewed** or **has sewn** /səʊn/)
use a needle and cotton to join pieces of material together or to join something to

material: *He sewed a button on his shirt.* ◊ *Can you sew?*
sewing *noun* (no plural)
something that you sew
sewing-machine /ˈsəʊɪŋ məʃiːn/ *noun*
a machine that you use for sewing

sex /seks/ *noun*
1 (*plural* **sexes**) being a male or a female: *What sex is your dog?* ◊ *the male sex*
2 (no plural) when two people put their bodies together, sometimes to make a baby: *She had sex with him.*

sh! /ʃ/
be quiet!: *Sh! You'll wake the baby up!*

shabby /ˈʃæbi/ *adjective* (**shabbier, shabbiest**)
old and untidy or dirty because you have used it a lot: *a shabby coat*
shabbily /ˈʃæbɪli/ *adverb*
She was shabbily dressed.

shade¹ /ʃeɪd/ *noun*
1 (no plural) a place where it is dark and cool because the sun doesn't shine there: *We sat in the shade of a big tree.*
2 (*plural* **shades**) a thing that keeps strong light from your eyes: *I bought a new shade for the lamp.*
3 (*plural* **shades**) how light or dark a colour is: *I'm looking for a shirt in a darker shade of green.*

shade² /ʃeɪd/ *verb* (**shades, shading, shaded**)
stop light from shining on something: *He shaded his eyes with his hand.*

— shadow

shadow /ˈʃædəʊ/ *noun*
a dark shape that you see near somebody or something that is in front of the light

shady /ˈʃeɪdi/ *adjective* (**shadier, shadiest**)
not in bright sunshine: *We sat in a shady part of the garden.*

shake /ʃeɪk/ *verb* (**shakes, shaking, shook** /ʃʊk/, **has shaken** /ˈʃeɪkən/)
1 move quickly from side to side or up and

down: *The house shakes when trains go past.* ◇ *He was shaking with fear.*

2 make something move quickly from side to side or up and down: *Shake the bottle before opening it.* ◇ *An explosion shook the windows.*

shake hands hold somebody's hand and move it up and down as a greeting

shake your head move your head from side to side to say 'no'

shaky /'ʃeɪki/ *adjective* (**shakier**, **shakiest**)

1 shaking because you are ill or frightened: *You've got shaky hands.*

2 not firm; not strong: *Don't sit in that chair – it's a bit shaky.*

shall /ʃəl/, /ʃæl/ *modal verb*

1 a word that you use instead of 'will' with 'I' and 'we' to show the future: *I shall see you tomorrow.*

2 a word that you use when you ask what is the right thing to do: *Shall I close the window?* ◇ *What shall we do tomorrow?*

> ✪ The negative form of 'shall' is **shall not** or the short form **shan't** /ʃɑːnt/:
>
> *I shan't be there.*
>
> The short form of 'shall' is **'ll**. We often use this:
>
> *I'll* (= I shall) *see you tomorrow.*
>
> ☞ Look at the Note on page 227 to find out more about **modal verbs**.

shallow /'ʃæləʊ/ *adjective* (**shallower**, **shallowest**)

not deep; with not much water: *This part of the river is shallow – we can walk across.* ☞ picture on page 262

shame /ʃeɪm/ *noun* (no plural)

the unhappy feeling that you have when you have done something wrong or stupid: *I was filled with* (= felt a lot of) *shame after I lied to my parents.* ✪ The adjective is **ashamed**.

it's a shame, **what a shame** it is sad; I am sorry: *It's a shame that you can't come to our party.*

shampoo /ʃæm'puː/ *noun* (*plural* **shampoos**)

a special liquid for washing your hair: *a bottle of shampoo*

shan't /ʃɑːnt/ = shall not

shape¹ /ʃeɪp/ *noun*

1 (*plural* **shapes**) what you see if you draw a line round something; the form of something: *What shape is the table – round or square?* ◇ *I bought a bowl in the shape of a fish.* ◇ *Circles, squares and triangles are all different shapes.*

2 (no plural) how good or bad something is; how healthy somebody is: *He was in bad shape after the accident.*

out of shape not in the right shape: *My jumper went out of shape when I washed it.*

shape² /ʃeɪp/ *verb* (**shapes**, **shaping**, **shaped** /ʃeɪpt/)

give a certain shape to something: *She shaped the clay into a pot.*

shaped *adjective*

with a certain shape: *He gave me a birthday card shaped like a cat.* ◇ *a heart-shaped box of chocolates*

share¹ /ʃeə(r)/ *verb* (**shares**, **sharing**, **shared** /ʃeəd/)

1 give parts of something to different people: *Share these sweets with your friends.* ◇ *We shared a large pizza between three of us.*

2 have or use something with another person: *I share a bedroom with my sister.*

share² /ʃeə(r)/ *noun*

a part of something bigger that each person has: *Here is your share of the money.* ◇ *I did my share of the work.*

shark

shark /ʃɑːk/ *noun*

a big fish that lives in the sea. Some sharks have sharp teeth and are dangerous.

sharp¹ /ʃɑːp/ *adjective* (**sharper**, **sharpest**)

1 with an edge or point that cuts or makes holes easily: *a sharp knife* ◇ *a sharp needle* ✪ opposite: **blunt**

2 strong and sudden: *a sharp bend in the road* ◇ *I felt a sharp pain in my leg.*

3 clear and easy to see: *We could see the sharp outline of the mountains against the sky.*

4 with a taste like lemons or vinegar: *If*

i:	i	ɪ	e	æ	ɑː	ɒ	ɔː	ʊ	u	u:
see	happy	sit	ten	cat	father	got	saw	put	situation	too

your drink tastes too sharp, add some sugar.

5 able to see, hear or learn well: *She's got a very sharp mind.* ◇ *sharp eyesight*
6 sudden and angry: *sharp words*
sharply *adverb*
The road bends sharply to the left. ◇ *'Go away!' he said sharply.*

sharp² /ʃɑːp/ *adverb*
1 exactly: *Be here at six o'clock sharp.*
2 with a big change of direction: *Turn sharp right at the next corner.*

sharpen /'ʃɑːpən/ *verb* (**sharpens**, **sharpening**, **sharpened** /'ʃɑːpənd/)
make something sharp or sharper: *sharpen a knife*
sharpener /'ʃɑːpnə(r)/ *noun*
a thing that you use for making something sharp: *a pencil-sharpener*

shatter /'ʃætə(r)/ *verb* (**shatters**, **shattering**, **shattered** /'ʃætəd/)
break into very small pieces; break something into very small pieces: *The glass hit the floor and shattered.* ◇ *The explosion shattered the windows.*

shave /ʃeɪv/ *verb* (**shaves**, **shaving**, **shaved** /ʃeɪvd/)
cut hair off your face or body by cutting it very close with a **razor**: *He shaves every morning.*
shave *noun*
I haven't had a shave today.
shaver *noun*
an electric tool that you use for shaving

shawl /ʃɔːl/ *noun*
a big piece of cloth that a woman wears round her shoulders, or that you put round a baby

she /ʃiː/ *pronoun* (*plural* **they**)
the woman or girl that the sentence is about: *'Where's your sister?' 'She's (= she is) at work.'*

shed¹ /ʃed/ *noun*
a small building where you keep things or animals: *There's a shed in the garden where we keep our tools.*

shed² /ʃed/ *verb* (**sheds**, **shedding**, **shed**, **has shed**)
let something fall off: *The snake shed its skin.*

she'd /ʃiːd/
1 = she had
2 = she would

sheep
sheep
lamb

sheep /ʃiːp/ (*plural* **sheep**)
an animal that people keep on farms for its meat and its wool

> ✪ A young sheep is called a **lamb**. Meat from a young sheep is also called **lamb**.

sheer /ʃɪə(r)/ *adjective*
1 complete: *sheer nonsense*
2 very steep: *a sheer drop to the sea*

sheet /ʃiːt/ *noun*
1 a big piece of thin material for a bed: *I put some clean sheets on the bed.*
2 a thin flat piece of something like paper, glass or metal: *a sheet of writing-paper*

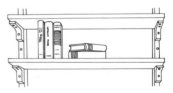
shelf

shelf /ʃelf/ *noun* (*plural* **shelves** /ʃelvz/)
a long flat piece of wood on a wall or in a cupboard, where things can stand: *Put the plates on the shelf.* ◇ *bookshelves*

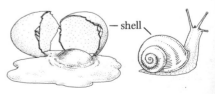
shells
shell

shell /ʃel/ *noun*
the hard outside part of birds' eggs and nuts and of some animals, for example snails and crabs ☞ Look also at **sea shell**.

she'll /ʃiːl/ = she will

shellfish /'ʃelfɪʃ/ noun (plural shell-fish)
a kind of animal that lives in water and that has a shell

shelter¹ /'ʃeltə(r)/ noun
1 (no plural) being safe from bad weather or danger: *We took shelter from the rain under a tree.* ◇ *People ran for shelter when the bombs started to fall.*
2 (plural **shelters**) a place where you are safe from bad weather or danger: *a bus shelter* (= for people who are waiting at a bus-stop)

shelter² /'ʃeltə(r)/ verb (**shelters, sheltering, sheltered** /'ʃeltəd/)
1 make somebody or something safe from bad weather or danger: *The trees shelter the house from the wind.*
2 go to a place where you will be safe from bad weather or danger: *Let's shelter from the rain under that tree.*

shelves plural of **shelf**

shepherd /'ʃepəd/ noun
a person who looks after sheep

she's /ʃiːz/
1 = she is
2 = she has

shield¹ /ʃiːld/ noun
a big piece of metal, wood or leather that soldiers carried in front of their bodies when they were fighting in wars long ago. Some police officers carry shields now.

shield² /ʃiːld/ verb (**shields, shielding, shielded**)
keep somebody or something safe from danger or from being hurt: *She shielded her eyes from the sun with her hand.*

shift¹ /ʃɪft/ verb (**shifts, shifting, shifted**)
move something to another place: *Can you help me to shift the bed? I want to sweep the floor.*

shift² /ʃɪft/ noun
a group of workers who begin work when another group finishes: *Each shift in the factory works for eight hours.* ◇ *the night shift*

shine /ʃaɪn/ verb (**shines, shining, shone** /ʃɒn/, has **shone**)
1 give out light: *The sun is shining.*
2 be bright: *I polished the silver until it shone.*

shine noun (no plural)
brightness: *This shampoo will give your hair a lovely shine.*

shiny adjective (**shinier, shiniest**)
a shiny new car

ship /ʃɪp/ noun
a big boat for long journeys on the sea: *We went to India by ship.*

ship verb (**ships, shipping, shipped** /ʃɪpt/)
send something in a ship: *New Zealand ships meat to Britain.*

shipping /'ʃɪpɪŋ/ noun (no plural)
ships: *The port is now open to shipping.*

shipwreck /'ʃɪprek/ noun
an accident at sea when a ship breaks in bad weather or on rocks
be shipwrecked be on a ship when it is in a shipwreck: *They were shipwrecked off the coast of Portugal.*

shirt /ʃɜːt/ noun
a thin piece of clothing that you wear on the top part of your body ☞ picture at **suit**

shiver /'ʃɪvə(r)/ verb (**shivers, shivering, shivered** /'ʃɪvəd/)
shake because you are cold, frightened or ill: *We were shivering with cold.*

shock¹ /ʃɒk/ noun
1 a very bad surprise: *The news of his death was a shock to all of us.*
2 a sudden pain when electricity goes through your body: *Don't touch that wire – you'll get an electric shock.*

shock² /ʃɒk/ verb (**shocks, shocking, shocked** /ʃɒkt/)
give somebody a very bad surprise; upset somebody: *She was shocked by his death.*

shocking /'ʃɒkɪŋ/ adjective
If something is shocking, it makes you feel upset, angry, or surprised in a very bad way: *a shocking crime*

shoe /ʃuː/ noun
a covering made of leather or plastic that you wear on your foot: *a pair of shoes* ◇ *What size are these shoes?* ◇ *a shoe shop* ☞ picture on next page

shoes

shoelace /ˈʃuːleɪs/ *noun*
a string that you tie to close a shoe: *Tie your shoelaces.*

shoestring /ˈʃuːstrɪŋ/ *American English for* **shoelace**

shone *form of* **shine**

shook *form of* **shake**

shoot¹ /ʃuːt/ *verb* (**shoots, shooting, shot** /ʃɒt/, **has shot**)
1 send a bullet from a gun or an arrow from a bow; hurt or kill a person or an animal with a gun: *She shot a bird.* ◇ *The police officer was shot in the arm.*
2 move quickly or suddenly: *The car shot past us.*
3 make a film: *They are shooting a film about the war.*

shoot² /ʃuːt/ *noun*
a new part of a plant: *The first shoots appear in spring.*

shop¹ *noun*
a building where you buy things: *a bookshop* ◇ *a clothes shop*
shop assistant /ˈʃɒp əsɪstənt/ *noun*
a person who works in a shop
shopkeeper /ˈʃɒpkiːpə(r)/ *noun*
a person who owns a small shop
shoplifter /ˈʃɒplɪftə(r)/ *noun*
a person who steals things from shops
shoplifting /ˈʃɒplɪftɪŋ/ *noun* (no plural)
stealing things from shops

shop² /ʃɒp/ *verb* (**shops, shopping, shopped** /ʃɒpt/)
go to buy things from shops: *I'm shopping for some new clothes.* ◐ *It is more usual to say* **go shopping**.
shopper *noun*
a person who is buying things: *The streets were full of shoppers.*

shopping /ˈʃɒpɪŋ/ *noun* (no plural)
1 buying things from shops: *She does her shopping after work.*
2 the things that you have bought in a shop: *Will you carry my shopping for me?*
go shopping go to buy things from shops
shopping centre /ˈʃɒpɪŋ sentə(r)/ *noun*
a place where there are a lot of shops together
shopping mall /ˈʃɒpɪŋ mɔːl/ *noun*
a big building where there are a lot of shops together

shore /ʃɔː(r)/ *noun*
the land next to the sea or a lake

short /ʃɔːt/ *adjective* (**shorter, shortest**)
1 very little from one end to the other: *Her hair is very short.* ◇ *We live a short distance from the beach.* ◐ opposite: **long** ☞ picture on page 262
2 very little from the bottom to the top: *I'm too short to reach the top shelf.* ◇ *a short fat man* ◐ opposite: **tall** ☞ picture on page 262
3 that only lasts for a little time: *The film was very short.* ◇ *a short holiday* ◐ opposite: **long**
be short of something not have enough of something: *I'm short of money this month.*
for short as a short way of saying or writing something: *My sister's name is Deborah, but we call her 'Deb' for short.*
short for something a short way of saying or writing something: *'Tom' is short for 'Thomas'.*

shortage /ˈʃɔːtɪdʒ/ *noun*
when there is not enough of something: *a water shortage* ◇ *There is a shortage of good teachers.*

short cut /ˌʃɔːt ˈkʌt/ *noun*
a shorter way to get somewhere: *We took a short cut to school across the field.*

shorten /ˈʃɔːtn/ *verb* (**shortens, shortening, shortened** /ˈʃɔːtnd/)
become shorter or make something shorter: *The trousers were too long, so I shortened them.*

shortly /ˈʃɔːtli/ *adverb*
soon: *The doctor will see you shortly, Mr Smith.* ◇ *We left shortly after six o'clock.*

s	z	ʃ	ʒ	h	m	n	ŋ	l	r	j	w
so	**zoo**	**shoe**	**vision**	**hat**	**man**	**no**	**sing**	**leg**	**red**	**yes**	**wet**

shorts /ʃɔːts/ *noun*
(plural)
1 short trousers that end above your knees: *a pair of shorts*
2 American English for **underpants**

shorts

shot¹ *form of* **shoot¹**

shot² /ʃɒt/ *noun*
1 firing a gun, or the noise that this makes: *He fired a shot.*
2 a photograph: *This is a good shot of you.*
3 kicking or hitting a ball in a sport like football

should /ʃʊd/ *modal verb*
1 a word that you use to tell or ask somebody what is the right thing to do: *If you feel ill, you should stay in bed.* ◇ *Should I invite him to the party?*
2 a word that you use to say what you think will happen or what you think is true: *They should arrive soon.*
3 the word for 'shall' in the past: *We asked if we should help her.*

○ The negative form of 'should' is **should not** or the short form **shouldn't** /ʃʊdnt/: *You shouldn't eat so much chocolate.*
☞ Look at the Note on page 227 to find out more about **modal verbs**.

shoulder /ˈʃəʊldə(r)/ *noun*
the part of your body between your neck and your arm ☞ picture on page 126

shouldn't /ˈʃʊdnt/ = **should not**

shout /ʃaʊt/ *verb* (**shouts, shouting, shouted**)
speak very loudly: *Don't shout at me!* ◇ *'Go back!' she shouted.*
shout *noun*
We heard a shout for help.

shove /ʃʌv/ *verb* (**shoves, shoving, shoved** /ʃʌvd/)
push somebody or something in a rough way: *They shoved him through the door.*

shovel /ˈʃʌvl/ *noun*
a tool like a **spade** with a short handle, that you use for moving earth or sand, for example
shovel *verb* (**shovels, shovelling, shovelled** /ˈʃʌvld/)
move something with a shovel: *We*

shovelled the snow off the path. ○ In American English the spellings are **shoveling** and **shoveled**.

show¹ /ʃəʊ/ *verb* (**shows, showing, showed** /ʃəʊd/, **has shown** /ʃəʊn/ or **has showed**)
1 let somebody see something: *She showed me her holiday photos.* ◇ *You have to show your ticket on the train.*
2 make something clear; explain something to somebody: *Can you show me how to use the computer?*
3 appear or be seen: *The anger showed in his face.*

show off talk loudly or do something silly to make people notice you: *Joyce drove her new car very fast to show off.*

show something off let people see something that is new or beautiful: *James wanted to show off his new jacket.*

show somebody round go with somebody and show them everything in a building: *David showed me round the school.*

show up arrive: *What time did they show up?*

show² /ʃəʊ/ *noun*
1 something that you watch at the theatre or on television: *a comedy show* ◇ *Did you enjoy the show?*
2 a group of things in one place that people go to see: *a flower show*
on show in a place where people can see it: *The paintings are on show at the National Gallery until 15 May.*

shower /ˈʃaʊə(r)/ *noun*
1 a place where you can wash by standing under water that falls from above you: *There's a shower in the bathroom.*
2 washing yourself in a shower: *I had a shower after the tennis match.*
3 rain that falls for a short time

shown *form of* **show¹**

shrank *form of* **shrink**

shred /ʃred/ *noun*
a small thin piece torn or cut off something: *shreds of paper*

shriek /ʃriːk/ *verb* (**shrieks, shrieking, shrieked** /ʃriːkt/)
make a loud high cry: *She shrieked in fear* (= because she was afraid).
shriek *noun*
He gave a shriek of pain.

iː	i	ɪ	e	æ	ɑː	ɒ	ɔː	ʊ	u	uː
see	happy	sit	ten	cat	father	got	saw	put	situation	too

shrill /ʃrɪl/ *adjective* (**shriller**, **shrillest**)
A shrill sound is high and loud: *a shrill whistle*

shrimp /ʃrɪmp/ *noun*
a small sea animal that you can eat

shrine /ʃraɪn/ *noun*
a special holy place: *the shrine at Lourdes*

shrink /ʃrɪŋk/ *verb* (**shrinks**, **shrinking**, **shrank** /ʃræŋk/ or **shrunk** /ʃrʌŋk/, **has shrunk**)
become smaller or make something smaller: *My jeans shrank when I washed them.*

shrub /ʃrʌb/ *noun*
a plant like a small low tree

shrug /ʃrʌg/ *verb* (**shrugs**, **shrugging**, **shrugged** /ʃrʌgd/)
move your shoulders to show that you do not know or do not care about something: *I asked her where Sam was but she just shrugged.*
shrug *noun* (no plural)
He answered my question with a shrug.

shrunk *form of* **shrink**

shudder /ˈʃʌdə(r)/ *verb* (**shudders**, **shuddering**, **shuddered** /ˈʃʌdəd/)
shake, for example because you are afraid: *He shuddered when he saw the snake.*
shudder *noun*
She felt a shudder of fear.

shuffle /ˈʃʌfl/ *verb* (**shuffles**, **shuffling**, **shuffled** /ˈʃʌfld/)
1 walk slowly, without taking your feet off the ground: *The old man shuffled along the road.*
2 mix playing-cards before a game

shut¹ /ʃʌt/ *verb* (**shuts**, **shutting**, **shut**, **has shut**)
1 move something so that it is not open: *Could you shut the door, please?*
2 move so that it is not open: *The door shut behind me.*
3 stop being open, so that people cannot go there: *The shops shut at 5.30.*
shut down close and stop working; make something close and stop working: *The factory shut down last year.*
shut up stop talking: *Shut up and listen!*
✪ This expression is quite rude.

shut² /ʃʌt/ *adjective*
closed; not open: *The restaurant is shut today.* ◇ *Is the door shut?* ☞ picture on page 263

shutter /ˈʃʌtə(r)/ *noun*
a wooden or metal thing that covers the outside of a window: *Close the shutters.*

shuttle /ˈʃʌtl/ *noun*
an aeroplane or a bus that goes to a place and then back again and again

shy /ʃaɪ/ *adjective* (**shyer**, **shyest**)
not able to talk easily to people you do not know: *He was too shy to speak to her.*
shyness /ˈʃaɪnəs/ *noun* (no plural)
being shy

sick /sɪk/ *adjective* (**sicker**, **sickest**)
not well; ill: *She's looking after her sick mother.*
be sick When you are sick, food comes up from your stomach and out of your mouth.
be sick of something have had or done too much of something, so that you do not want it any longer: *I'm sick of watching TV – let's go out.*
feel sick feel that food is going to come up from your stomach

sickness /ˈsɪknəs/ *noun* (no plural)
being ill: *He could not work for a long time because of sickness.*

side /saɪd/ *noun*
1 one of the flat outside parts of something: *A box has six sides.* ◇ *A piece of paper has two sides.*
2 the part of something that is not the front, back, top or bottom: *There is a door at the side of the house.* ☞ picture at **back**
3 the edge of something; the part that is away from the middle: *I stood at the side of the road.*
4 the right or left part of something: *He lay on his side.* ◇ *We drive on the left side of the road in Britain.*
5 one of two groups of people who fight or play a game against each other: *Which side won?*
be on somebody's side agree with or help somebody in a fight or argument: *Rose said I was wrong, but Andy was on my side.*
side by side next to each other: *They walked side by side.*
take sides show that you agree with one person, and not the other, in a fight or an argument

sidewalk /ˈsaɪdwɔːk/ *American English for* **pavement**

signs

sideways /ˈsaɪdweɪz/ *adjective, adverb*
1 to or from the side: *She looked sideways at the girl next to her.*
2 with one of the sides first: *We carried the table sideways through the door.*

siege /siːdʒ/ *noun*
1 when an army stays outside a town for a long time so that people and things cannot get in or out
2 when police stay outside a building for a long time to try to make a criminal come out

sigh /saɪ/ *verb* (**sighs, sighing, sighed** /saɪd/)
breathe once very deeply when you are sad, tired or pleased, for example
sigh *noun*
'I wish I had more money,' he said with a sigh.

sight /saɪt/ *noun*
1 (no plural) the power to see: *She has poor sight* (= she cannot see well).
2 (no plural) seeing somebody or something: *We had our first sight of London from the plane.*
2 (*plural* **sights**) something that you see: *The mountains were a beautiful sight.*
3 (*plural* **sights**) the interesting places to visit: *When you come to Paris I'll show you the sights.*
at first sight when you see somebody or something for the first time: *He fell in love with her at first sight.*
catch sight of somebody or **something** see somebody or something suddenly: *I caught sight of Fiona in the crowd.*
come into sight come where you can see it: *The train came into sight.*
in sight where you can see it: *Is the land in sight yet?*
lose sight of somebody or **something** no longer be able to see somebody or something: *After an hour at sea we lost sight of land.*
out of sight where you cannot see it: *We watched until the car was out of sight.*

sightseer /ˈsaɪtsiːə(r)/ *noun*
a person who is visiting interesting places: *The town was full of sightseers.*
sightseeing /ˈsaɪtsiːɪŋ/ *noun* (no plural)
visiting interesting places: *We did some sightseeing in Rome.*

sign¹ /saɪn/ *noun*
1 a mark, shape or movement that has a special meaning: *+ and – are signs that mean 'plus' and 'minus'.* ◊ *I put up my hand as a sign for him to stop.*
2 a thing with writing or a picture on it that tells you something: *The sign said 'No Smoking'.* ◊ *a road sign*
3 something that tells you about another thing: *Dark clouds are a sign of rain.*

sign² /saɪn/ *verb* (**signs, signing, signed** /saɪnd/)
write your name in your own way on something: *Sign here, please.* ◊ *I signed the cheque.* ✪ The noun is **signature**.

signal /ˈsɪɡnəl/ *noun*
a light, sound or movement that tells you something without words: *A red light is a signal for cars to stop.* ◊ *radio signals*
signal *verb* (**signals, signalling, signalled** /ˈsɪɡnəld/)
make a signal: *The policeman signalled to the children to cross the road.* ✪ In American English the spellings are **signaling** and **signaled**.

signature /ˈsɪɡnətʃə(r)/ *noun*
your name that you have written in your own way ☞ picture at **cheque**

significance /sɪɡˈnɪfɪkəns/ *noun* (no plural)
the importance or meaning of something: *What is the significance of this discovery?*

significant /sɪɡˈnɪfɪkənt/ *adjective*
important; with a special meaning: *The police say that the time of the robbery was very significant.*

signpost /ˈsaɪnpəʊst/ *noun*
a sign beside a road, that shows the way to a place and how far it is

Sikh /siːk/ *noun*
a person who follows one of the religions of India, called **Sikhism**

silence /ˈsaɪləns/ *noun*
1 (no plural) When there is silence, there

p	b	t	d	k	g	tʃ	dʒ	f	v	θ	ð
pen	**b**ad	**t**ea	**d**id	**c**at	**g**ot	**ch**ain	**j**am	**f**all	**v**an	**th**in	**th**is

is no sound: *I can only work in complete silence.*
2 (*plural* **silences**) a time when nobody speaks or makes a noise: *There was a long silence before she answered the question.*
in silence without speaking or making a noise: *We ate our dinner in silence.*

silent /'saɪlənt/ *adjective*
1 with no sound; completely quiet: *Everyone was asleep, and the house was silent.*
2 If you are silent, you are not speaking: *I asked him a question and he was silent for a moment before he answered.*
silently *adverb*
The cat moved silently towards the bird.

silk /sɪlk/ *noun* (no plural)
thin smooth cloth that is made from the threads that an insect (called a **silkworm**) makes: *This scarf is made of silk.* ◇ *a silk shirt*

silly /'sɪli/ *adjective* (**sillier, silliest**)
stupid; not clever: *Don't be so silly!* ◇ *It was silly of you to leave the door open when you went out.*

silver /'sɪlvə(r)/ *noun* (no plural)
1 a shiny grey metal that is very valuable: *a silver necklace*
2 things that are made of silver, for example knives, forks and plates
silver *adjective*
with the colour of silver: *silver paper*

similar /'sɪmələ(r)/ *adjective*
the same in some ways but not completely the same: *Rats are similar to mice, but they are bigger.* ◇ *Jane and her sister look very similar.*
similarity /ˌsɪmə'lærəti/ *noun* (*plural* **similarities**)
a way that people or things are the same: *There are a lot of similarities between the two countries.* ✪ opposite: **difference**

simple /'sɪmpl/ *adjective* (**simpler, simplest**)
1 easy to do or understand: *This dictionary is written in simple English.* ◇ *'How do you open this?' 'I'll show you – it's simple.'*
2 without a lot of different parts or extra things; plain: *She wore a simple black dress.* ◇ *a simple meal*

simplicity /sɪm'plɪsəti/ *noun* (no plural)
being simple: *I like the simplicity of these paintings.*

simplify /'sɪmplɪfaɪ/ *verb* (**simplifies, simplifying, simplified** /'sɪmplɪfaɪd/, **has simplified**)
make something easier to do or understand: *The story has been simplified so that children can understand it.*

simply /'sɪmpli/ *adverb*
1 in a simple way: *Please explain it more simply.*
2 only: *Don't get angry – I'm simply asking you to help.*
3 really: *The weather was simply terrible – it rained every day!*

sin /sɪn/ *noun*
something that your religion says you should not do, because it is very bad: *Stealing is a sin.*
sin *verb* (**sins, sinning, sinned** /sɪnd/)
do something that your religion says is very bad

since /sɪns/ *preposition*
in all the time after: *She has been ill since Sunday.* ◇ *I haven't seen him since 1987.*
since *conjunction*
1 from the time when: *She has lived here since she was a child.* ◇ *Jane hasn't phoned since she went to Berlin.*
2 because: *Since it's your birthday, I'll buy you a drink.*
since *adverb*
from then until now: *Andy left three years ago and we haven't seen him since.*
ever since in all the time from then until now: *George went to Canada in 1974 and he has lived there ever since.*

sincere /sɪn'sɪə(r)/ *adjective*
If you are sincere, you are honest and you mean what you say: *Were you being sincere when you said that you loved me?*
sincerely *adverb*
Yours sincerely words that you write at the end of a letter, before your name

sing /sɪŋ/ *verb* (**sings, singing, sang** /sæŋ/, **has sung** /sʌŋ/)
make music with your voice: *She sang a song.* ◇ *The birds were singing.*

s	z	ʃ	ʒ	h	m	n	ŋ	l	r	j	w
so	**zoo**	**sh**oe	vi**s**ion	**h**at	**m**an	**n**o	si**ng**	**l**eg	**r**ed	**y**es	**w**et

for or **since**?

We use **for** to say how long something has continued, for example in **hours**, **days** or **years**:

*She has been ill **for** three days.*

*I have lived in London **for** ten months.*

We have been married for **thirty** years.

We use **since** with points of time in the past, for example a **time** on the clock, a **date** or an **event**:

*I have been here **since** six o'clock.*

*She has been alone **since** her husband died.*

We have been married **since** 1965.

---

singer *noun*
a person who sings

single¹ /'sɪŋgl/ *adjective*
1 only one: *There wasn't a single cloud in the sky.*
2 not married: *Are you married or single?*
3 for one person: *I would like to book a single room, please.* ◇ *a single bed* ☞ Look at **double**.
4 for a journey to a place, but not back again: *How much is a single ticket to London, please?* ☞ Look at **return**.
every single each: *You answered every single question correctly.*

single² /'sɪŋgl/ *noun*
1 a ticket for a journey to a place, but not back again: *A single to Brighton, please.* ☞ Look at **return**.
2 a small record that has only one song on each side: *Have you heard Prince's new single?* ☞ Look at **album** and **LP**.

singular /'sɪŋgjələ(r)/ *noun* (no plural)
the form of a word that you use for one person or thing: *The singular of 'men' is 'man'.*
singular *adjective*
'Table' is a singular noun.
☞ Look at **plural**.

sink¹ /sɪŋk/ *noun*
the place in a kitchen where you wash dishes

sink² /sɪŋk/ *verb* (**sinks**, **sinking**, **sank** /sæŋk/, **has sunk** /sʌŋk/)
1 go down under water: *If you throw a stone into water, it sinks.* ◇ *The fishing boat sank to the bottom of the sea.* ☞ Look at **float**.
2 make a boat go down under water: *The ship was sunk by a bomb.*
3 go down: *The sun sank slowly behind the hills.*

---

sip /sɪp/ *verb* (**sips, sipping, sipped** /sɪpt/)
drink something slowly, taking only a little each time: *She sipped her coffee.*
sip *noun*
Can I have a sip of your Coke?

sir /sɜː(r)/ *noun*
1 (no plural) a polite way of speaking to a man, instead of using his name: *'Can I help you, sir?' asked the shop assistant.* ☞ Look at **madam**.
2 Sir (no plural) a word that you use at the beginning of a business letter to a man: *Dear Sir . . .* ☞ Look at **madam**.
3 Sir (no plural) the word that you use before the name of a **knight**: *Sir Winston Churchill*

siren /'saɪrən/ *noun*
a machine that makes a long loud sound to warn people about something. Police cars and fire-engines have sirens.

sister /'sɪstə(r)/ *noun*
1 Your sister is a girl or woman who has the same parents as you: *I've got two sisters and one brother.* ◇ *Jane and Anne are sisters.* ☞ picture on page 127
2 a nurse in a hospital

sister-in-law /'sɪstər ɪn lɔː/ *noun* (*plural* **sisters-in-law**)
1 the sister of your wife or husband
2 the wife of your brother ☞ picture on page 127

sit /sɪt/ *verb* (**sits, sitting, sat** /sæt/, **has sat**)
1 rest on your bottom: *We sat in the garden all afternoon.* ◇ *She was sitting on the sofa.*
2 (*also* **sit down**) put yourself down on your bottom: *Come and sit next to me.* ◇ *She came into the room and sat down.*
3 do an examination: *The students will sit their exams in June.*
sit up sit when you have been lying: *He sat up in bed and looked at the clock.*
sitting-room /'sɪtɪŋ ruːm/ *noun*
a room in a house where people sit and watch television or talk, for example

site /saɪt/ *noun*
a place where something is, was, or will be: *This house was built on the site of an old theatre.* ◇ *a camp-site*

situated /'sɪtʃueɪtɪd/ *adjective*
in a place: *The hotel is situated close to the beach.*

situation /ˌsɪtʃu'eɪʃn/ *noun*
the things that are happening in a certain place or at a certain time: *Sue is in a difficult situation – she can't decide what to do.*

six /sɪks/ *number* (*plural* **sixes**)
6
sixth /sɪksθ/ *adjective, adverb, noun*
1 6th
2 one of six equal parts of something; 1/6

sixteen /ˌsɪks'tiːn/ *number*
16
sixteenth /ˌsɪks'tiːnθ/ *adjective, adverb, noun*
16th

sixth form /'sɪksθ fɔːm/ *noun*
the classes in the last two years of secondary school in Britain. Pupils in the sixth form are usually aged between 16 and 18.

sixty /'sɪksti/ *number*
1 60
2 **the sixties** (plural) the numbers, years or temperature between 60 and 69
in your sixties between the ages of 60 and 69
sixtieth /'sɪkstiəθ/ *adjective, adverb, noun*
60th

size /saɪz/ *noun*
1 (no plural) how big or small something is: *My bedroom is the same size as yours.*
2 (*plural* **sizes**) an exact measurement: *Have you got these shoes in a bigger size?*

skate /skeɪt/ *noun*
1 an ice-skate; a boot with a long sharp piece of metal under it, that you wear for moving on ice: *a pair of skates*
2 a roller-skate; a shoe with wheels on the bottom, that you wear for moving quickly on smooth ground
skate *verb* (**skates, skating, skated**)
move on skates ✪ When you talk about spending time skating as a sport, you say **go skating**: *We go skating every weekend.*
skating-rink /'skeɪtɪŋ rɪŋk/ *noun*
a special place where you can skate on ice

ʌ	ɜː	ə	eɪ	əʊ	aɪ	aʊ	ɔɪ	ɪə	eə	ʊə
cup	bird	about	say	go	five	now	boy	near	hair	pure

skateboard /'skeɪtbɔːd/ *noun*
a long piece of wood or plastic on wheels.
You stand on it as it moves over the
ground.

skeleton

skeleton /'skelɪtn/ *noun*
the bones of a whole animal or person

sketch /sketʃ/ *verb* (**sketches, sketch-**
ing, sketched /sketʃt/)
draw something quickly: *I sketched the*
house.
sketch *noun* (*plural* **sketches**)
a picture that you draw quickly

skiing

skier

ski

ski /skiː/ *noun* (*plural* **skis**)
a long flat piece of wood, metal or plastic
that you fix to your boot so that you can
move over snow: *a pair of skis*
ski *verb* (**skis, skiing** /'skiːɪŋ/, **skied**
/skiːd/, **has skied**)
move over snow on skis: *Can you ski?*
❍ When you talk about spending time skiing as a sport, you say **go skiing**: *We went*
skiing in Austria.
skier *noun*
a person who skis
skiing *noun* (no plural)
the sport of moving over snow on skis
ski slope /'skiː sləʊp/ *noun*
a part of a mountain where you can ski

skid /skɪd/ *verb* (**skids, skidding,**
skidded)
If a car, lorry, etc skids, it moves suddenly

and dangerously to the side, for example
because the road is wet: *The lorry skidded*
on the icy road.

skies *plural of* **sky**

skilful /'skɪlfl/ *adjective*
very good at doing something: *a skilful*
tennis player
skilfully /'skɪlfəli/ *adverb*
The food was skilfully prepared.

skill /skɪl/ *noun*
1 (no plural) being able to do something
well: *You need great skill to fly a plane.*
2 (*plural* **skills**) a thing that you can do
well: *What skills do you need for this job?*

skilled /skɪld/ *adjective*
good at something because you have
learned about or done it for a long time:
skilled workers ❍ opposite: **unskilled**

skillful, skillfully American English
for **skilful, skillfully**

skin /skɪn/ *noun*
1 (no plural) what covers the outside of a
person or an animal's body: *She has dark*
skin.
2 (*plural* **skins**) the outside part of some
fruits and vegetables: *a banana skin*

skinny /'skɪni/ *adjective* (**skinnier, skin-**
niest)
too thin: *He's very skinny – he doesn't eat*
enough.

skip /skɪp/ *verb* (**skips, skipping,**
skipped /skɪpt/)
1 move along quickly with little jumps
from one foot to the other foot: *The child*
skipped along the road.
2 jump many times over a rope that is
turning
3 not do or have something that you
should do or have: *I skipped my class to-*
day and went swimming.
skip *noun*
a little jump
skipping-rope /'skɪpɪŋ rəʊp/ *noun*
a rope that you use for skipping

skirt /skɜːt/ *noun*
a piece of clothing for a woman or girl that
hangs from the middle of the body ☞ picture at **coat**

skull /skʌl/ *noun*
the bones in the head of a person or an
animal

p	b	t	d	k	g	tʃ	dʒ	f	v	θ	ð
pen	**b**ad	**t**ea	**d**id	**c**at	**g**ot	**ch**ain	**j**am	**f**all	**v**an	**th**in	**th**is

sky /skaɪ/ *noun* (*plural* **skies**)
the space above the earth where you can see the sun, moon and stars: *a beautiful blue sky* ◇ *There were no clouds in the sky.*

skyscraper /ˈskaɪskreɪpə(r)/ *noun*
a very tall building: *He works on the 49th floor of a skyscraper.*

slab /slæb/ *noun*
a thick flat piece of something: *slabs of stone* ◇ *a big slab of cheese*

slam /slæm/ *verb* (**slams, slamming, slammed** /slæmd/)
close something or put something down with a loud noise: *She slammed the door angrily.* ◇ *He slammed the book on the table and went out.*

slang /slæŋ/ *noun* (no plural)
words that a certain group of people use. You do not use slang when you need to be polite, and you do not usually use it in writing: *'Quid' is slang for 'pound'.*

slant /slɑ:nt/ *verb* (**slants, slanting, slanted**)
Something that slants has one side higher than the other or does not stand straight up: *My handwriting slants to the left.*

slap /slæp/ *verb* (**slaps, slapping, slapped** /slæpt/)
hit somebody with the flat inside part of your hand: *He slapped me in the face.*
slap *noun*
She gave me a slap across the face.

slaughter /ˈslɔ:tə(r)/ *verb* (**slaughters, slaughtering, slaughtered** /ˈslɔ:təd/)
1 kill an animal for food
2 kill a lot of people in a cruel way
slaughter *noun* (no plural)
killing animals or people

slave /sleɪv/ *noun*
a person who belongs to another person and must work for that person for no money

slavery /ˈsleɪvəri/ *noun* (no plural)
1 being a slave: *They lived in slavery.*
2 having slaves: *When did slavery end in America?*

sledge /sledʒ/ *noun*
a thing that you sit in to move over snow. A sledge has pieces of metal or wood instead of wheels. Large sledges are sometimes pulled by dogs.

sleep /sli:p/ *verb* (**sleeps, sleeping, slept** /slept/, **has slept**)
rest with your eyes closed, as you do at night: *I sleep for eight hours every night.* ◇ *Did you sleep well?*

○ Be careful! We usually say **be asleep**, not **be sleeping**:
I was asleep when you phoned.
We use **go to sleep** or **fall asleep** to talk about starting to sleep.

sleep *noun* (no plural)
I didn't get any sleep last night.
go to sleep start to sleep: *I got into bed and soon went to sleep.*

sleeping-bag /ˈsli:pɪŋ bæg/ *noun*
a big warm bag that you sleep in when you go camping

sleepless /ˈsli:pləs/ *adjective*
without sleep: *I had a sleepless night.*

sleepy /ˈsli:pi/ *adjective* (**sleepier, sleepiest**)
1 tired and ready to sleep: *I felt sleepy after that big meal.*
2 quiet, with not many things happening: *a sleepy little village*

sleet /sli:t/ *noun* (no plural)
snow and rain together

sleeve

sleeve /sli:v/ *noun*
the part of a coat, dress or shirt, for example, that covers your arm: *a shirt with short sleeves*

sleigh /sleɪ/ *noun*
a thing that you sit in to move over snow. A sleigh has pieces of metal or wood instead of wheels and is usually pulled by animals.

slender /ˈslendə(r)/ *adjective*
thin, in a nice way: *She has long, slender legs.*

slept *form of* **sleep**

slice /slaɪs/ *noun*
a thin piece that you cut off bread, meat or other food: *Would you like a slice of cake?*

◇ *slices of bread* ☞ picture at **bread** and on page 261

slice *verb* (**slices, slicing, sliced** /slaɪst/) cut something into slices: *Slice the onions.*

slide¹ /slaɪd/ *verb* (**slides, sliding, slid** /slɪd/, **has slid**) move smoothly or make something move smoothly across something: *She fell and slid along the ice.*

slide² /slaɪd/ *noun*
1 a long metal thing that children play on. They climb up steps, sit down, and then slide down the other side.
2 a small photograph that you show on a **screen**, using a **projector**

slight /slaɪt/ *adjective* (**slighter, slightest**)
small; not important or serious: *I've got a slight problem.* ◇ *a slight headache*

slightly /'slaɪtli/ *adverb*
a little: *I'm feeling slightly better today.*

slim /slɪm/ *adjective* (**slimmer, slimmest**)
thin, but not too thin: *a tall slim man*

sling¹ /slɪŋ/ *noun*
a piece of cloth that you wear to hold up an arm that is hurt: *She's got her arm in a sling.*

sling² /slɪŋ/ *verb* (**slings, slinging, slung** /slʌŋ/, **has slung**)
throw something without care: *He got angry and slung the book at me.*

slip¹ /slɪp/ *verb* (**slips, slipping, slipped** /slɪpt/)
1 move smoothly over something by mistake and fall or almost fall: *He slipped on the ice and broke his leg.*
2 go quickly and quietly so that nobody sees you: *Ann slipped out of the room when the children were asleep.*
3 put something in a place quickly and quietly: *He slipped the money into his pocket.*

slip² /slɪp/ *noun*
1 a small piece of paper: *Write your address on this slip of paper.*
2 a small mistake: *I made a slip.*

slipper /'slɪpə(r)/ *noun*
a light soft shoe that you wear in the house: *a pair of slippers*

slippery /'slɪpəri/ *adjective*
so smooth or wet that you cannot move on

it or hold it easily: *The skin of a fish is slippery.* ◇ *The road was wet and slippery.*

slit /slɪt/ *noun*
a long thin hole or cut

slit *verb* (**slits, slitting, slit, has slit**)
make a long thin cut in something: *I slit the envelope open with a knife.*

slither /'slɪðə(r)/ *verb* (**slithers, slithering, slithered** /'slɪðəd/)
move along like a snake: *The snake slithered across the floor.*

slogan /'sləʊgən/ *noun*
a short sentence or group of words that is easy to remember. Slogans are used to make people believe something or buy something: *'Faster than light' is the slogan for the new car.*

slope /sləʊp/ *noun*
a piece of ground that has one end higher than the other, like the side of a hill: *We walked down the mountain slope.*

slope *verb* (**slopes, sloping, sloped** /sləʊpt/)
have one end higher than the other: *The field slopes down to the river.* ◇ *a sloping roof*

slot /slɒt/ *noun*
a long thin hole that you push something through: *Put a coin in the slot and take your ticket.*

slot-machine /'slɒt məʃiːn/ *noun*
a machine that gives you things like drinks or sweets when you put money in a small hole

slow¹ /sləʊ/ *adjective* (**slower, slowest**)
1 A person or thing that is slow does not move or do something quickly: *a slow train* ◇ *She hasn't finished her work yet – she's very slow.*
2 If a clock or watch is slow, it shows a time that is earlier than the real time: *My watch is five minutes slow.*
☞ Look at **quick** and **fast**.
slow *adverb*
slowly: *Please drive slower.*
slowly *adverb*
The old lady walked slowly up the hill.

slow² /sləʊ/ *verb* (**slows, slowing, slowed** /sləʊd/)
slow down start to go more slowly; make somebody or something start to go more slowly: *The train slowed down as it*

i:	i	ɪ	e	æ	ɑ:	ɒ	ɔ:	ʊ	u	u:
see	happy	sit	ten	cat	father	got	saw	put	situation	too

came into the station. ◇ *Don't talk to me when I'm working – it slows me down.*

slug /slʌg/ *noun*
a small soft animal that moves slowly and eats plants

slum /slʌm/ *noun*
a poor part of a city where people live in old dirty buildings

slung *form of* **sling²**

sly /slaɪ/ *adjective*
A person who is sly tricks people or does things secretly.

smack /smæk/ *verb* (**smacks, smacking, smacked** /smækt/)
hit somebody with the inside part of your hand: *They never smack their children.*
smack *noun*
She gave her son a smack.

small /smɔːl/ *adjective* (**smaller, smallest**)
1 not big; little: *This dress is too small for me.* ◇ *My house is smaller than yours.*
2 young: *They have two small children.*
☞ picture on page 262

smart /smɑːt/ *adjective* (**smarter, smartest**)
1 right for a special or important time; clean and tidy: *She wore smart clothes for her job interview.* ◇ *He looks very smart in his new jacket.*
2 clever: *a smart businesswoman*
smartly *adverb*
She was very smartly dressed.

smash /smæʃ/ *verb* (**smashes, smashing, smashed** /smæʃt/)
1 break something into many pieces: *The boys smashed the window.*
2 break into many pieces: *I dropped the plate but it didn't smash.*
smash *noun*
the loud noise when something breaks into pieces: *The glass hit the floor with a smash.*

smashing /ˈsmæʃɪŋ/ *adjective*
very good; wonderful: *The food was smashing.*

smear /smɪə(r)/ *verb* (**smears, smearing, smeared** /smɪəd/)
spread soft stuff on something, making it dirty: *The child smeared chocolate over his clothes.*
smear *noun*
a dirty mark: *She had smears of paint on*

her dress.

smell /smel/ *verb* (**smells, smelling, smelt** /smelt/ or **smelled** /smeld/, **has smelt** or **has smelled**)
1 notice something with your nose: *Can you smell smoke?*
2 If something smells, you notice it with your nose: *This fish smells bad.* ◇ *The perfume smells of roses.*
3 have a bad smell: *Your feet smell!*
smell *noun*
something that you notice with your nose: *There's a smell of gas in this room.*

smelly /ˈsmeli/ *adjective* (**smellier, smelliest**)
with a bad smell: *smelly socks*

smile /smaɪl/ *verb* (**smiles, smiling, smiled** /smaɪld/)
move your mouth to show that you are happy or that you think something is funny: *He smiled at me.*
smile *noun*
She had a big smile on her face.

smile

smoke¹ /sməʊk/ *noun* (no plural)
the grey or black gas that you see in the air when something is burning: *The room was full of smoke.* ◇ *cigarette smoke*

smoke² /sməʊk/ *verb* (**smokes, smoking, smoked** /sməʊkt/)
have a cigarette, cigar or pipe in your mouth, and breathe the smoke in and out: *He was smoking a cigar.* ◇ *Do you smoke?*
smoking *noun* (no plural)
No smoking in the theatre.

smoked /sməʊkt/ *adjective*
prepared by putting it over a wood fire so that you can keep it for a long time: *smoked salmon*

smoker /ˈsməʊkə(r)/ *noun*
a person who smokes ✪ opposite: **non-smoker**

smoky /ˈsməʊki/ (**smokier, smokiest**) *adjective*
full of smoke: *a smoky room*

ʌ	ɜː	ə	eɪ	əʊ	aɪ	aʊ	ɔɪ	ɪə	eə	ʊə
cup	bird	about	say	go	five	now	boy	near	hair	pure

smooth /smuːð/ *adjective* (**smoother, smoothest**)
1 flat; not rough: *Babies have smooth skin.*
2 moving gently: *The weather was good so we had a very smooth flight.*
smoothly *adverb*
The plane landed smoothly.

smother /'smʌðə(r)/ *verb* (**smothers, smothering, smothered** /'smʌðəd/)
1 kill somebody by covering their face so that they cannot breathe
2 cover a thing with too much of something: *He smothered his cake with cream.*

smuggle /'smʌɡl/ *verb* (**smuggles, smuggling, smuggled** /'smʌɡld/)
take things secretly into or out of a country: *They were trying to smuggle drugs into France.*
smuggler /'smʌɡlə(r)/ *noun*
a person who smuggles: *drug smugglers*

snack /snæk/ *noun*
a small quick meal: *We had a snack on the train.*
snack bar /'snæk bɑː(r)/ *noun*
a place where you can buy and eat snacks

snag /snæɡ/ *noun*
a small problem: *The work will be finished tomorrow if there are no snags.*

snail

snail /sneɪl/ *noun*
a small soft animal with a hard shell on its back. Snails move very slowly.

snake

snake /sneɪk/ *noun*
an animal with a long thin body and no legs: *Do these snakes bite?*

snap¹ /snæp/ *verb* (**snaps, snapping, snapped** /snæpt/)
1 break suddenly with a sharp noise: *He snapped the pencil in two.*
2 say something in a quick angry way: *'Go away – I'm busy!' she snapped.*

3 try to bite somebody or something: *The dog snapped at my leg.*

snap² /snæp/, **snapshot** /'snæpʃɒt/ *noun*
a photograph: *She showed us her holiday snaps.*

snarl /snɑːl/ *verb* (**snarls, snarling, snarled** /snɑːld/)
When an animal snarls, it shows its teeth and makes a low angry sound: *The dog snarled at the stranger.*

snatch /snætʃ/ *verb* (**snatches, snatching, snatched** /snætʃt/)
take something quickly and roughly: *He snatched her handbag and ran away.*

sneak /sniːk/ *verb* (**sneaks, sneaking, sneaked** /sniːkt/)
go somewhere very quietly so that nobody sees or hears you: *She sneaked out of the classroom to smoke a cigarette.*

sneer /snɪə(r)/ *verb* (**sneers, sneering, sneered** /snɪəd/)
speak or smile in an unkind way to show that you do not like somebody or something or that you think they are not good enough: *I told her about my idea, but she just sneered at it.*
sneer *noun*
an unkind smile

sneeze /sniːz/ *verb* (**sneezes, sneezing, sneezed** /sniːzd/)
send air out of your nose and mouth with a sudden loud noise, for example because you have a cold: *Pepper makes you sneeze.*
sneeze *noun*
She gave a loud sneeze.

sniff /snɪf/ *verb* (**sniffs, sniffing, sniffed** /snɪft/)
1 make a noise by suddenly taking in air through your nose. People sometimes sniff when they have a cold or when they are crying.
2 smell something: *The dog was sniffing the meat.*
sniff *noun*
I heard a loud sniff.

snooze /snuːz/ *verb* (**snoozes, snoozing, snoozed** /snuːzd/)
sleep for a short time
snooze *noun*
I had a snooze after lunch.

p	b	t	d	k	ɡ	tʃ	dʒ	f	v	θ	ð
pen	**bad**	**tea**	**did**	**cat**	**got**	**chain**	**jam**	**fall**	**van**	**thin**	**this**

snore /snɔ:(r)/ verb (**snores, snoring, snored** /snɔ:d/)
make a noise in your nose and throat when you are asleep: *He was snoring loudly.*

snort /snɔ:t/ verb (**snorts, snorting, snorted**)
make a noise by blowing air through the nose: *The horse snorted.*

snow /snəʊ/ noun (no plural)
soft white stuff that falls from the sky when it is very cold
snow verb (**snows, snowing, snowed** /snəʊd/)
When it snows, snow falls from the sky: *It often snows in Scotland in winter.*
snowflake /'snəʊfleɪk/ noun
one piece of falling snow
snowy adjective (**snowier, snowiest**)
with a lot of snow: *snowy weather*

so¹ /səʊ/ adverb
1 a word that you use when you say how much, how big, etc something is: *This bag is so heavy that I can't carry it.* ☞ Look at **such**.
2 a word that makes another word stronger: *Why are you so late?*
3 also: *Julie is a teacher and so is her husband.* ◇ *'I like this music.' 'So do I.'* ✪ In negative sentences, we use **neither** or **nor**.
4 You use **so** instead of saying words again: *'Is John coming?' 'I think so.'* (= I think that he is coming)
and so on and other things like that: *The shop sells pens, paper and so on.*
not so ... as words that show how two people or things are different: *He's not so tall as his brother.*
or so words that you use to show that a number is not exactly right: *Forty or so people came to the party.*

so² /səʊ/ conjunction
1 because of this or that: *The shop is closed so I can't buy any bread.*
2 (also **so that**) in order that: *Speak louder so that everybody can hear you.* ◇ *I'll give you a map so you can find my house.*
so what? why is that important or interesting?: *'It's late.' 'So what? There's no school tomorrow.'*

soak /səʊk/ verb (**soaks, soaking, soaked** /səʊkt/)
1 make somebody or something very wet:

It was raining when I went out. I got soaked!
2 be in a liquid; let something stay in a liquid: *Leave the dishes to soak in hot water.*
soak up take in a liquid: *Soak the water up with a cloth.*
soaking adjective
very wet: *This towel is soaking.*

soap /səʊp/ noun (no plural)
stuff that you use with water for washing and cleaning: *a bar of soap*
soap opera /'səʊp ɒprə/ noun
a story about the lives of a group of people, that is on the TV or radio every day or several times each week
soap powder /'səʊp paʊdə(r)/ noun (no plural)
powder that you use for washing clothes
soapy adjective
with soap in it: *soapy water*

soar /sɔ:(r)/ verb (**soars, soaring, soared** /sɔ:d/)
1 fly high in the sky
2 go up very fast: *Prices are soaring.*

sob /sɒb/ verb (**sobs, sobbing, sobbed** /sɒbd/)
cry loudly, making short sounds
sob noun
'She's left me!' he said with a sob.

sober /'səʊbə(r)/ adjective
not drunk

so-called /,səʊ 'kɔ:ld/ adjective
a word that you use to show that you do not think another word is correct: *Her so-called friends did not help her* (= they are not really her friends).

soccer /'sɒkə(r)/ noun (no plural)
football

social /'səʊʃl/ adjective
of people together; of being with other people: *the social problems of big cities* ◇ *Anne has a busy social life* (= she goes out with friends a lot).
social security /,səʊʃl sɪ'kjʊərəti/ noun (no plural)
money that a government pays to somebody who is poor, for example because they have no job
social worker /'səʊʃl wɜ:kə(r)/ noun
a person whose job is to help people who have problems, for example because they are poor or ill

s	z	ʃ	ʒ	h	m	n	ŋ	l	r	j	w
so	**zoo**	**shoe**	vision	**hat**	**man**	**no**	sing	**leg**	**red**	**yes**	**wet**

society /sə'saɪəti/ *noun*
1 (no plural) a group of people living together, with the same ideas about how to live
2 (*plural* **societies**) a group of people who are interested in the same thing: *a music society*

sock /sɒk/ *noun*
a thing that you wear on your foot, inside your shoe: *a pair of socks*

socket /'sɒkɪt/ *noun*   **socks**
a place in a wall where you can push an electric plug
☞ picture at **plug**

sofa

sofa /'səʊfə/ *noun*
a long soft seat for more than one person: *Jane was sitting on the sofa.*

soft /sɒft/ *adjective* (**softer**, **softest**)
1 not hard or firm; that moves when you press it: *Warm butter is soft.* ◇ *a soft bed*
☞ picture on page 263
2 smooth and nice to touch; not rough: *soft skin* ◇ *My cat's fur is very soft.*
3 quiet or gentle; not loud: *soft music* ◇ *He has a very soft voice.*
4 not bright or strong: *the soft light of a candle*
5 kind and gentle; not strict: *She's too soft with her class and they don't do any work.*
soft drink /ˌsɒft 'drɪŋk/ *noun*
a cold drink with no alcohol in it, for example orange juice or lemonade
softly *adverb*
gently or quietly: *She spoke very softly.*

software /'sɒftweə(r)/ *noun* (no plural)
programs for a computer

soggy /'sɒgi/ *adjective* (**soggier**, **soggiest**)
very wet

soil /sɔɪl/ *noun* (no plural)
what plants and trees grow in; earth

solar /'səʊlə(r)/ *adjective*
of or using the sun: *solar energy*
the solar system /ðə 'səʊlə sɪstəm/ *noun* (no plural)
the sun and the planets that move around it

sold *form of* **sell**
be sold out When things are sold out, there are no more to sell: *I'm sorry – the bananas are sold out.*

soldier /'səʊldʒə(r)/ *noun*
a person in an army

sole[1] /səʊl/ *noun*
the bottom part of your foot or of a shoe: *These boots have leather soles.* ☞ picture on page 126   sole

sole[2] /səʊl/ *adjective*
only: *His sole interest is football.*

solemn /'sɒləm/ *adjective*
serious: *slow, solemn music*
solemnly *adverb*
'*I've got some bad news for you,*' he said solemnly.

solid /'sɒlɪd/ *adjective*
1 hard, not like a liquid or a gas: *Water becomes solid when it freezes.*
2 with no empty space inside; made of the same material inside and outside: *a solid rubber ball* ◇ *This ring is solid gold.*
solid *noun*
not a liquid or gas: *Milk is a liquid and cheese is a solid.*

solitary /'sɒlətri/ *adjective*
without others; alone: *She went for a long solitary walk.*

solo /'səʊləʊ/ *noun* (*plural* **solos**)
a piece of music for one person to sing or play: *a piano solo*
solo *adjective, adverb*
alone; without other people: *a solo performance* ◇ *She flew solo across the Atlantic.*

solution /sə'luːʃn/ *noun*
the answer to a question, problem or puzzle: *I can't find a solution to this problem.*

solve /sɒlv/ *verb* (**solves**, **solving**, **solved** /sɒlvd/)
find the answer to a question, problem or puzzle: *The police are still trying to solve the crime.*

i:	i	ɪ	e	æ	ɑ:	ɒ	ɔ:	ʊ	u	u:
see	happy	sit	ten	cat	father	got	saw	put	situation	too

some /sʌm/ *adjective, pronoun*
1 a number or amount of something: *I bought some tomatoes and some butter.*
◇ *This cake is nice. Do you want some?*
● In questions and after 'not' and 'if', we usually use **any**: *Did you buy any apples?*
◇ *I didn't buy any meat.*
2 part of a number or amount of something: *Some of the children can swim, but the others can't.*
3 I do not know which: *There's some man at the door who wants to see you.*
some more a little more or a few more: *Have some more coffee.* ◇ *Some more people arrived.*
some time quite a long time: *We waited for some time but she did not come.*

somebody /'sʌmbədi/, **someone** /'sʌmwʌn/ *pronoun*
a person; a person that you do not know: *There's somebody at the door.* ◇ *Someone has broken the window.* ◇ *Ask somebody else* (= another person) *to help you.*

somehow /'sʌmhaʊ/ *adverb*
in some way that you do not know: *We must find her somehow.*

someplace /'sʌmpleɪs/ *American English for* **somewhere**

somersault /'sʌməsɔːlt/ *noun*
a movement when you turn your body with your feet going over your head: *The children were doing somersaults on the carpet.*

something /'sʌmθɪŋ/ *pronoun*
a thing; a thing you cannot name: *There's something under the table. What is it?*
◇ *I want to tell you something.* ◇ *Would you like something else* (= another thing) *to eat?*
something like the same as somebody or something, but not in every way: *A rat is something like a mouse, but bigger.*

sometime /'sʌmtaɪm/ *adverb*
at a time that you do not know exactly: *I'll phone sometime tomorrow.*

sometimes /'sʌmtaɪmz/ *adverb*
not very often: *He sometimes writes to me.* ◇ *Sometimes I drive to work and sometimes I go by bus.*

somewhere /'sʌmweə(r)/ *adverb*
at, in or to a place that you do not know exactly: *They live somewhere near London.*

◇ *'Did she go to Spain last year?' 'No, I think she went somewhere else* (= to another place).'

son /sʌn/ *noun*
a boy or man who is somebody's child: *They have a son and two daughters.*
☞ picture on page 127

song /sɒŋ/ *noun*
1 (*plural* **songs**) a piece of music with words that you sing: *a pop song*
2 (no plural) singing; music that a person or bird makes

son-in-law /'sʌn ɪn lɔː/ *noun* (*plural* **sons-in-law**)
the husband of your daughter ☞ picture on page 127

soon /suːn/ *adverb*
not long after now, or not long after a certain time: *John will be home soon.* ◇ *She arrived soon after two o'clock.* ◇ *Goodbye! See you soon!*
as soon as at the same time that; when: *Phone me as soon as you get home.*
sooner or later at some time in the future: *Don't worry – I'm sure he will write to you sooner or later.*

soot /sʊt/ *noun* (no plural)
black powder that comes from smoke

soothe /suːð/ *verb* (**soothes**, **soothing**, **soothed** /suːðd/)
make somebody feel calmer and less unhappy: *The baby was crying, so I tried to soothe her by singing to her.*
soothing *adjective*
soothing music

sore /sɔː(r)/ *adjective*
If a part of your body is sore, it gives you pain: *My feet were sore after the long walk.* ◇ *I've got a sore throat.*

sorrow /'sɒrəʊ/ *noun*
sadness

sorry /'sɒri/ *adjective*
1 a word that you use when you feel bad about something you have done: *I'm sorry I didn't phone you.* ◇ *Sorry I'm late!* ◇ *I'm sorry for losing your pen.*
2 sad: *I'm sorry you can't come to the party.*
3 a word that you use to say 'no' politely: *I'm sorry – I can't help you.*
4 a word that you use when you did not hear what somebody said and you want

ʌ	ɜː	ə	eɪ	əʊ	aɪ	aʊ	ɔɪ	ɪə	eə	ʊə
cup	bird	about	say	go	five	now	boy	near	hair	pure

them to say it again: *'My name is Linda Willis.' 'Sorry? Linda who?'*
feel sorry for somebody feel sad because somebody has problems: *I felt sorry for her and gave her some money.*

sort[1] /sɔ:t/ *noun*
a group of things or people that are the same in some way; a type or kind: *What sort of music do you like best – pop or classical?* ◇ *We found all sorts of shells on the beach.*
sort of words that you use when you are not sure about something: *It's sort of long and thin, a bit like a sausage.*

sort[2] /sɔ:t/ *verb* (**sorts, sorting, sorted**)
put things into groups: *The machine sorts the eggs into large ones and small ones.*
sort out 1 make something tidy: *I sorted out my clothes and put the old ones in a bag.* 2 find an answer to a problem

SOS /ˌes əʊ 'es/ *noun*
a call for help from a ship or an aeroplane that is in danger

sought *form of* **seek**

soul /səʊl/ *noun*
1 (*plural* **souls**) the part of a person that some people believe does not die when the body dies
2 (*also* **soul music**) (no plural) a kind of Black American music: *a soul singer*
not a soul not one person: *I looked everywhere, but there wasn't a soul in the building.*

sound[1] /saʊnd/ *noun*
something that you hear: *I heard the sound of a baby crying.* ◇ *Light travels faster than sound.*

sound[2] /saʊnd/ *verb* (**sounds, sounding, sounded**)
seem a certain way when you hear it: *He sounded angry when I spoke to him on the phone.* ◇ *That sounds like a good idea.* ◇ *She told me about the book – it sounds interesting.*

sound[3] /saʊnd/ *adjective*
1 healthy or strong: *sound teeth*
2 right and good: *sound advice*
sound *adverb*
sound asleep sleeping very well: *The children are sound asleep.*

soup /su:p/ *noun* (no plural)
liquid food that you make by cooking things like vegetables or meat in water: *tomato soup*

sour /'saʊə(r)/ *adjective*
1 with a taste like lemons or vinegar: *If it's too sour, put some sugar in it.*
2 Sour milk tastes bad because it is not fresh: *This milk has gone sour.*

source /sɔ:s/ *noun*
a place where something comes from: *Our information comes from many sources.*

south /saʊθ/ *noun* (no plural)
the direction that is on your right when you watch the sun come up in the morning ☞ picture at **north**
south *adjective, adverb*
Brazil is in South America. ◇ *the south coast of England* ◇ *Birds fly south in the winter.*
southern /'sʌðən/ *adjective*
in or of the south part of a place: *Brighton is in southern England.*

souvenir /ˌsu:və'nɪə(r)/ *noun*
something that you keep to remember a place or something that happened: *I brought back this cowboy hat as a souvenir of America.*

sow /səʊ/ *verb* (**sows, sowing, sowed** /səʊd/, **has sown** /səʊn/ or **has sowed**)
put seeds in the ground: *The farmer sowed the field with corn.*

space /speɪs/ *noun*
1 (no plural) a place that is big enough for somebody or something to go into or onto it: *Is there space for me in your car?*
2 (*plural* **spaces**) an empty place between other things: *There is a space here for you to write your name.*
3 (no plural) the place far away outside the earth, where all the planets and stars are: *space travel*
spacecraft /'speɪskrɑːft/ *noun* (*plural* **spacecraft**)
a vehicle that travels in space
spaceman /'speɪsmæn/ (*plural* **spacemen**), **spacewoman** /'speɪswʊmən/ (*plural* **spacewomen**) *noun*
a person who travels in space
spaceship /'speɪsʃɪp/ *noun*
a vehicle that travels in space

spacious /'speɪʃəs/ *adjective*
with a lot of space inside: *a spacious kitchen*

p	b	t	d	k	g	tʃ	dʒ	f	v	θ	ð
pen	**b**ad	**t**ea	**d**id	**c**at	**g**ot	**ch**ain	**j**am	**f**all	**v**an	**th**in	**th**is

spade /speɪd/ *noun*
1 a tool that you use for digging ☞ picture at **dig**
2 **spades** (plural) the playing-cards that have the shape ♠ on them: *the queen of spades*

spaghetti /spə'geti/ *noun* (no plural)
a kind of food made from flour and water, that looks like long pieces of string

spanner
/'spænə(r)/ *noun*
a tool that you use
for turning **nuts** and
bolts

spanner

spare¹ /speə(r)/ *adjective*
1 extra; that you do not need now: *Have you got a spare tyre in your car?* ◇ *You can stay with us tonight. We've got a spare room.*
2 Spare time is time when you are not working: *What do you do in your spare time?*

spare² /speə(r)/ *verb* (**spares**, **sparing**, **spared** /speəd/)
be able to give something to somebody: *I can't spare the time to help you today.* ◇ *Can you spare any money?*

spark /spɑːk/ *noun*
a very small piece of fire

sparkle /'spɑːkl/ *verb* (**sparkles**, **sparkling**, **sparkled** /'spɑːkld/)
shine with a lot of very small points of light: *The sea sparkled in the sunlight.* ◇ *Her eyes sparkled with excitement.*
sparkle *noun* (no plural)
the sparkle of diamonds
sparkling *adjective*
1 that sparkles: *sparkling blue eyes*
2 Sparkling wine has a lot of small bubbles in it.

sparrow /'spærəʊ/ *noun*
a small brown bird

spat *form of* **spit**

speak /spiːk/ *verb* (**speaks**, **speaking**, **spoke** /spəʊk/, **has spoken** /'spəʊkən/)
1 say words; talk to somebody: *Please speak more slowly.* ◇ *Can I speak to John Smith, please?* (= words that you say on the telephone)

2 know and use a language: *I can speak French and Italian.*
3 talk to a group of people: *The chairwoman spoke for an hour at the meeting.*
speak up talk louder: *Can you speak up? I can't hear you!*

speaker /'spiːkə(r)/ *noun*
1 a person who is talking to a group of people
2 the part of a radio, cassette player, etc where the sound comes out

spear /spɪə(r)/ *noun*
a long stick with a sharp point at one end, used for hunting or fighting

special /'speʃl/ *adjective*
1 not usual or ordinary; important for a reason: *It's my birthday today so we are having a special dinner.*
2 for a particular person or thing: *He goes to a special school for deaf children.*
specially /'speʃəli/ *adverb*
1 for a particular person or thing: *I made this cake specially for you.*
2 very; more than usual or more than others: *The food was not specially good.*

specialist /'speʃəlɪst/ *noun*
a person who knows a lot about something: *She's a specialist in Chinese art.*

specialize /'speʃəlaɪz/ *verb* (**specializes**, **specializing**, **specialized** /'speʃəlaɪzd/)
specialize in something study or know a lot about one special thing: *This doctor specializes in natural medicine.*

species /'spiːʃiːz/ *noun* (*plural* **species**)
a group of animals or plants that are the same in some way: *a rare species of plant*

specific /spə'sɪfɪk/ *adjective*
1 particular: *Is there anything specific that you want to talk about?*
2 exact and clear: *He gave us specific instructions on how to get there.*
specifically /spə'sɪfɪkli/ *adverb*
I specifically asked you to buy butter, not margarine.

specimen /'spesɪmən/ *noun*
a small amount or part of something that shows what the rest is like; one example of a group of things: *a specimen of rock* ◇ *The doctor took a specimen of blood for testing.*

speck /spek/ *noun*
a very small bit of something: *specks of dust*

spectacles /'spektəklz/ *noun* (plural)
pieces of special glass that you wear over your eyes to help you see better: *a pair of spectacles* ✪ It is more usual to say **glasses**.

spectacular /spek'tækjələ(r)/ *adjective*
wonderful to see: *There was a spectacular view from the top of the mountain.*

spectator /spek'teitə(r)/ *noun*
a person who watches something that is happening: *There were 2 000 spectators at the football match.*

sped *form of* **speed²**

speech /spiːtʃ/ *noun*
1 (no plural) the power to speak, or the way that you speak
2 (*plural* **speeches**) a talk that you give to a group of people: *The President made a speech.*

speed¹ /spiːd/ *noun*
how fast something goes: *The car was travelling at a speed of 50 miles an hour.*
◇ *a high-speed train* (= that goes very fast)
speed limit /'spiːd limit/ *noun*
the fastest that you are allowed to travel on a road: *The speed limit on motorways is 100 kilometres an hour.*

speed² /spiːd/ *verb* (**speeds, speeding, sped** /sped/ or **speeded, has sped** or **has speeded**)
1 go or move very quickly: *He sped past me on his bike.*
2 drive too fast: *The police stopped me because I was speeding.*
speed up go faster; make something go faster

spell¹ /spel/ *verb* (**spells, spelling, spelt** /spelt/ or **spelled** /speld/, **has spelt** or **has spelled**)
use the right letters to make a word: '*How do you spell your name?*' '*A-Z-I-Z.*'
◇ *You have spelt this word wrong.*
spelling *noun*
the right way of writing a word: *Look in your dictionary to find the right spelling.*

spell² /spel/ *noun*
magic words
put a spell on somebody say magic words to somebody to change them or to make them do what you want: *The witch put a spell on the prince.*

spend /spend/ *verb* (**spends, spending, spent** /spent/, **has spent**)
1 pay money for something: *Louise spends a lot of money on clothes.*
2 use time for something: *I spent the summer in Italy.* ◇ *He spent a lot of time sleeping.*

sphere /sfɪə(r)/ *noun*
any round thing that is like a ball: *The earth is a sphere.* ☞ picture on page 161

spice /spaɪs/ *noun*
a powder or the seeds from a plant that you can put in food to give it a stronger taste. Pepper and ginger are spices.
spicy /'spaɪsi/ *adjective* (**spicier, spiciest**)
with spices in it: *Indian food is usually spicy.*

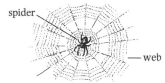

spider
— web

spider /'spaɪdə(r)/ *noun*
a small animal with eight legs, that catches and eats insects: *Spiders spin webs to catch flies.*

spied *form of* **spy**

spies
1 *plural of* **spy**
2 *form of* **spy**

spike /spaɪk/ *noun*
a piece of metal with a sharp point: *The fence has spikes along the top.*

spill /spɪl/ *verb* (**spills, spilling, spilt** /spɪlt/ or **spilled** /spɪld/, **has spilt** or **has spilled**)
If you spill a liquid, it flows out of something by accident: *I've spilt my wine!*
☞ picture on next page

spin /spɪn/ *verb* (**spins, spinning, spun** /spʌn/, **has spun**)
1 turn round quickly; turn something round quickly: *She spun a coin on the table.*

iː	i	ɪ	e	æ	ɑː	ɒ	ɔː	ʊ	u	uː
see	happy	sit	ten	cat	father	got	saw	put	situation	too

spill

2 make thread from wool or cotton
3 make a web: *The spider spun a web.*

spinach /'spɪnɪtʃ/ *noun* (no plural)
a vegetable with big green leaves

spine /spaɪn/ *noun*
the line of bones in your back ☞ picture
on page 126

spiral /'spaɪrəl/
noun
a long shape that
goes round and
round as it goes up:
A spring is a spiral.
spiral *adjective*
a spiral staircase

spiral

spirit /'spɪrɪt/
noun
1 the part of a
person that is not the body. Some people
think that your spirit does not die when
your body dies.
2 spirits (plural) strong alcoholic drinks.
Whisky and brandy are spirits.
3 spirits (plural) how you feel: *She's in
high spirits* (= happy) *today.*

spit /spɪt/ *verb* (**spits**, **spitting**, **spat**
/spæt/, **has spat**)
send liquid or food out from your mouth:
He spat on the ground. ◇ *The baby spat
her food out.*

spite /spaɪt/ *noun* (no plural)
wanting to hurt somebody: *She broke my
watch out of spite* (= because she wanted
to hurt me).
in spite of something although something is true; not noticing or not caring
about something: *I slept well in spite of the
noise.* ◇ *In spite of the bad weather, we
went out.*

splash /splæʃ/ *verb* (**splashes**, **splashing**, **splashed** /splæʃt/)
1 throw drops of liquid over somebody or

something and make them wet: *The car
splashed us as it drove past.*
2 move through water so that drops of it
fly in the air: *The children were splashing
around in the pool.*
splash *noun* (plural **splashes**)
1 the sound that a person or thing makes
when they fall into water: *Tom jumped
into the river with a big splash.*
2 a place where liquid has fallen: *There
were splashes of paint on the floor.*

splendid /'splendɪd/ *adjective*
very beautiful or very good: *a splendid palace* ◇ *What a splendid idea!*

splinter /'splɪntə(r)/ *noun*
a thin sharp piece of wood or glass that has
broken off a bigger piece: *I've got a splinter
in my finger.*

split /splɪt/ *verb* (**splits**, **splitting**, **split**,
has split)
1 break something into two parts: *I split
the wood with an axe.*
2 break open: *His jeans split when he sat
down.*
3 share something; give a part to each person: *We split the money between us.*
split up stop being together: *He has split
up with his wife.*
split *noun*
a long cut or hole in something

spoil /spɔɪl/ *verb* (**spoils**, **spoiling**, **spoilt**
/spɔɪlt/ or **spoiled** /spɔɪld/, **has spoilt** or
has spoiled)
1 make something less good than before:
The mud spoiled my shoes. ◇ *Did the bad
weather spoil your holiday?*
2 give a child too much so that they think
they can always have what they want: *She
spoils her grandchildren.* ◇ *a spoilt child*

spoke¹ *form of* **speak**

spoke² /spəʊk/ *noun*
one of the thin pieces of wire that join the
middle of a wheel to the outside, for example on a bicycle

spoken *form of* **speak**

spokesman /'spəʊksmən/ (*plural*
spokesmen /'spəʊksmən/), **spokes-
woman** /'spəʊkswʊmən/ (*plural*
spokeswomen) *noun*
a person who tells somebody what a group
of people has decided

ʌ	ɜː	ə	eɪ	əʊ	aɪ	aʊ	ɔɪ	ɪə	eə	ʊə
cup	bird	about	say	go	five	now	boy	near	hair	pure

sponge /spʌndʒ/ *noun*
1 a soft thing with a lot of small holes in it, that you use for washing yourself or cleaning things
2 a soft light cake

sponsor /'spɒnsə(r)/ *verb* (**sponsors**, **sponsoring**, **sponsored** /'spɒnsəd/)
give money so that something, for example a sports event, will happen: *The football match was sponsored by a large firm.*
sponsor *noun*
a person or company that sponsors

spoon /spu:n/
noun
a thing with a round
end that you use for
putting food in your   **spoon**
mouth or for mixing:

a wooden spoon ◇ *a teaspoon*
spoonful /'spu:nfʊl/ *noun*
the amount that you can put in one spoon:
Two spoonfuls of sugar in my tea, please.

sport /spɔ:t/ *noun*
a game that you do to keep your body strong and well and because you enjoy it: *Jane does a lot of sport.* ◇ *Football, swimming and tennis are all sports.*
sports centre /'spɔ:ts sentə(r)/ *noun*
a big building where you can play a lot of different sports
sportsman /'spɔ:tsmən/ *noun* (*plural* **sportsmen** /'spɔ:tsmən/), **sportswoman** /'spɔ:tswʊmən/ (*plural* **sportswomen**)
a person who plays sport

sports car /'spɔ:ts kɑ:(r)/ *noun*
a fast car, usually with a roof that you can open

spot¹ /spɒt/ *noun*
1 a small round
mark: *a red dress
with white spots*
2 a small red mark
on your skin: *A lot
of teenagers get*   **spotted**
spots on their face.

3 a place: *This is a good spot for a picnic.*
spotted *adjective*
with small round marks on it: *a spotted shirt*
spotty *adjective* (**spottier**, **spottiest**)
with small red marks on your skin: *a spotty face*

spot² /spɒt/ *verb* (**spots**, **spotting**, **spotted**)
see somebody or something suddenly: *She spotted her friend in the crowd.*

spout /spaʊt/ *noun*
the part of a container that is like a short tube, where liquid comes out. Teapots have spouts.

sprain /spreɪn/ *verb* (**sprains**, **spraining**, **sprained** /spreɪnd/)
hurt part of your body by turning it suddenly: *Scott fell and sprained his ankle.*

sprang *form of* **spring³**

spray /spreɪ/ *noun*
1 (no plural) liquid
in very small drops
that flies through
the air: *spray from
the sea*
2 (*plural* **sprays**)   **spray**
liquid in a can that

comes out in very small drops when you press a button: *hairspray*
spray *verb* (**sprays**, **spraying**, **sprayed** /spreɪd/)
make very small drops of liquid fall on something: *Somebody has sprayed paint on my car.*

spread /spred/ *verb* (**spreads**, **spreading**, **spread**, **has spread**)
1 open something so that you can see all of it: *The bird spread its wings and flew away.* ◇ *Spread out the map on the table.*
2 put soft stuff all over something: *I spread butter on the bread.*
3 move to other places or to other people; make something do this: *Fire quickly spread to other parts of the building.* ◇ *Rats spread disease.*
spread *noun* (no plural)
Doctors are trying to stop the spread of the disease.

                              spring

spring¹ /sprɪŋ/ *noun*
1 a thin piece of metal that is bent round and round. A spring will go back to the

same size and shape after you push or pull it.
2 a place where water comes out of the ground

spring² /sprɪŋ/ *noun*
the part of the year after winter, when plants start to grow

spring³ /sprɪŋ/ *verb* (**springs, springing, sprang** /spræŋ/, **has sprung** /sprʌŋ/)
jump or move suddenly: *The cat sprang on the mouse.*

sprinkle /'sprɪŋkl/ *verb* (**sprinkles, sprinkling, sprinkled** /'sprɪŋkld/)
throw drops or small pieces of something on another thing: *Sprinkle some sugar on the fruit.*

sprint /sprɪnt/ *verb* (**sprints, sprinting, sprinted**)
run a short distance very fast

sprout¹ /spraʊt/ *noun*
a Brussels sprout; a round green vegetable like a very small cabbage

sprout² /spraʊt/ *verb* (**sprouts, sprouting, sprouted**)
start to grow: *New leaves are sprouting on the trees.*

sprung *form of* **spring**³

spun *form of* **spin**

spy /spaɪ/ *noun* (*plural* **spies**)
a person who tries to learn secret things about another country, person or company
spy *verb* (**spies, spying, spied** /spaɪd/, **has spied**)
try to learn secret things about somebody or something
spy on somebody watch somebody or something secretly

squad /skwɒd/ *noun*
a small group of people who work together: *England's football squad* ◇ *a squad of police officers*

square /skweə(r)/ *noun*
1 a shape with four straight sides that are the same length and four right angles
☞ picture on page 161
2 an open space in a town with buildings around it: *Trafalgar Square* ◇ *the market square*
square *adjective*
with four straight sides that are the same

length: *a square table* ◇ A **square metre** is an area that is one metre long on each side.

squash¹ /skwɒʃ/ *verb* (**squashes, squashing, squashed** /skwɒʃt/)
1 press something hard and make it flat: *She sat on my hat and squashed it.*
2 push a lot of people or things into a small space: *We squashed five people into the back of the car.*

squash² /skwɒʃ/ *noun*
1 (no plural) a drink made from fruit juice and sugar. You add water before you drink it: *a glass of orange squash*
2 (*plural* **squashes**) a glass of this drink

squash³ /skwɒʃ/ *noun* (no plural)
a game where two players hit a small ball against a wall in a special room (called a **court**): *Have you ever played squash?*

squat /skwɒt/ *verb* (**squats, squatting, squatted**)
1 sit with your feet on the ground, your legs bent and your bottom just above the ground: *I squatted down to light the fire.*
2 live in an empty building that is not yours and that you do not pay for
squatter *noun*
a person who squats in an empty building

squeak /skwiːk/ *verb* (**squeaks, squeaking, squeaked** /skwiːkt/)
make a short high sound like a mouse: *The door was squeaking, so I put some oil on it.*
squeak *noun*
the squeak of a mouse
squeaky *adjective*
He's got a squeaky voice.

squeal /skwiːl/ *verb* (**squeals, squealing, squealed** /skwiːld/)
make a loud high sound like a pig: *The children squealed with excitement.*
squeal *noun*
the squeal of a pig

squeeze /skwiːz/ *verb* (**squeezes, squeezing, squeezed** /skwiːzd/)
1 press something hard between other things: *I squeezed an orange* (to make the juice come out).
2 go into a small space; push too much into a small space: *Can you squeeze another person into the back of your car?*

◇ *Fifty people squeezed into the small room.*
squeeze *noun*
She gave my arm a squeeze.

squirrel /'skwɪrəl/ *noun*
a small grey or brown animal with a big thick tail. Squirrels live in trees and eat nuts.

squirt /skwɜːt/ *verb* (**squirts**, **squirting**, **squirted**)
1 suddenly shoot out of something: *I opened the bottle and lemonade squirted everywhere.*
2 make liquid suddenly shoot out of something: *The elephant squirted the clown with water.*

St
1 *short way of writing* **saint**
2 *short way of writing* **street**

stab /stæb/ *verb* (**stabs**, **stabbing**, **stabbed** /stæbd/)
push a knife or another sharp thing into somebody or something: *He was stabbed in the back.*

stable¹ /'steɪbl/ *noun*
a building where you keep horses

stable² /'steɪbl/ *adjective*
Something that is stable will not move, fall or change: *Don't stand on that table – it's not very stable.* ○ *opposite:* **unstable**

stack /stæk/ *noun*
a lot of things on top of one another: *a stack of books*
stack *verb* (**stacks**, **stacking**, **stacked** /stækt/)
put things on top of one another: *I stacked the chairs after the concert.*

stadium /'steɪdɪəm/ *noun*
a place with seats around it where you can watch sports matches: *a football stadium*

staff /stɑːf/ *noun* (plural)
the group of people who work in a place: *The hotel staff were very friendly.*
staff room /'stɑːf ruːm/ *noun*
a room in a school where teachers can work and rest

stage¹ /steɪdʒ/ *noun*
the part of a theatre where actors, dancers, etc stand and move

stage² /steɪdʒ/ *noun*
a certain time in a longer set of things that

happen: *The first stage of the course lasts for two weeks.*
at this stage now: *At this stage I don't know what I'll do when I leave school.*

stagger /'stægə(r)/ *verb* (**staggers**, **staggering**, **staggered** /'stægəd/)
walk as if you are going to fall: *He staggered across the room with the heavy box.*

stain /steɪn/ *verb* (**stains**, **staining**, **stained** /steɪnd/)
make coloured or dirty marks on something: *The wine stained the carpet red.*
stain *noun*
She had blood stains on her shirt.

stairs /steəz/ *noun* (plural)
steps that lead up and down inside a building: *I ran up the stairs to the bedroom.* ☞ Look also at **downstairs** and **upstairs**.
staircase /'steəkeɪs/, **stairway** /'steəweɪ/ *noun*
a big group of stairs

stale /steɪl/ *adjective* (**staler**, **stalest**)
not fresh: *stale bread* ◇ *stale air*

stalk /stɔːk/ *noun*
one of the long thin parts of a plant that the flowers, leaves or fruit grow on

stall

stall /stɔːl/ *noun*
a big table with things on it that somebody wants to sell, for example in a street or market: *a fruit stall*

stammer /'stæmə(r)/ *verb* (**stammers**, **stammering**, **stammered** /'stæməd/)
say the same sound many times when you are trying to say a word: *'B-b-b-but wait for me,' she stammered.*

stamp¹ /stæmp/ *noun*
1 a small piece of paper that you put on a letter to show that you have paid to send it ☞ Note on next page and picture on page 299

❂ In Britain, you can buy stamps and send letters at a **post office**. Some shops also sell stamps. There are two kinds of stamp for sending letters to other parts of Britain: **first-class** stamps and **second-class** stamps. First-class stamps are more expensive and the letters arrive more quickly.

2 a small piece of wood or metal that you press on paper to make marks or words: *a date stamp*

stamp² /stæmp/ *verb* (**stamps**, **stamping**, **stamped** /stæmpt/)
1 put your foot down quickly and hard: *She stamped on the spider and killed it.*
2 walk by putting your feet down hard and loudly: *Mike stamped angrily out of the room.*
3 press a small piece of wood or metal on paper to make marks or words: *They stamped my passport at the airport.*

stand¹ /stænd/ *verb* (**stands**, **standing**, **stood** /stʊd/, **has stood**)
1 be on your feet: *She was standing by the door.*
2 (*also* **stand up**) get up on your feet: *The teacher asked us all to stand up.*
3 be in a place: *The castle stands on a hill.*
4 put something somewhere: *I stood the ladder against the wall.*
can't stand somebody or **something** hate somebody or something: *I can't stand this music.*
stand by 1 watch but not do anything: *How can you stand by while those boys kick the cat?* **2** be ready to do something: *Stand by until I call you!*
stand by somebody help somebody when they need it: *Julie's parents stood by her when she was in trouble.*
stand for something be a short way of saying or writing something: *USA stands for 'the United States of America'.*
stand out be easy to see: *Joe stands out in a crowd because he has got red hair.*
stand still not move: *Stand still while I take your photograph.*
stand up for somebody or **something** say that somebody or something is right; support somebody or something: *Everyone else said I was wrong, but my sister stood up for me.*
stand up to somebody show that you are not afraid of somebody

stand² /stænd/ *noun*
1 a table or small shop where you can buy things or get information: *a news-stand* (= where you can buy newspapers and magazines)
2 a piece of furniture that you can put things on: *an umbrella stand*

standard¹ /ˈstændəd/ *noun*
how good somebody or something is: *Her work is of a very high standard* (= very good).
standard of living /ˌstændəd əv ˈlɪvɪŋ/ *noun* (*plural* **standards of living**)
how rich or poor you are: *They have a low standard of living* (= they are poor).

standard² /ˈstændəd/ *adjective*
normal; not special: *Clothes are sold in standard sizes.*

stank *form of* **stink**

staple /ˈsteɪpl/ *noun*
a small, very thin piece of metal that you push through pieces of paper to join them together, using a special tool (called a **stapler**)
staple *verb* (**staples**, **stapling**, **stapled** /ˈsteɪpld/)
Staple the pieces of paper together.

star¹ /stɑː(r)/ *noun*
1 one of the small bright lights that you see in the sky at night
2 a shape with points ☞ picture on page 161

star² /stɑː(r)/ *noun*
a famous person, for example an actor or a singer: *a film star*
star *verb* (**stars**, **starring**, **starred** /stɑːd/)
1 be an important actor in a play or film: *He has starred in many films.*
2 have somebody as a star: *The film stars Julia Roberts and Patrick Swayze.*

stare /steə(r)/ *verb* (**stares**, **staring**, **stared** /steəd/)
look at somebody or something for a long time: *Everybody stared at her hat.* ◇ *He was staring out of the window.*

start¹ /stɑːt/ *verb* (**starts**, **starting**, **started**)
1 begin to do something: *I start work at nine o'clock.* ◇ *It started raining.* ◇ *She started to cry.*

2 begin to happen; make something begin to happen: *The film starts at 7.30.* ◇ *The police do not know who started the fire.*
3 begin to work or move; make something begin to work or move: *The engine won't start.* ◇ *I can't start the car.*
start off begin: *The teacher started off by asking us our names.*

start² /stɑːt/ *noun*
1 the beginning or first part of something: *She arrived after the start of the meeting.*
2 starting something: *We have got a lot of work to do, so let's make a start.*
for a start words that you use when you give your first reason for something: *'Why can't we go on holiday?' 'Well, for a start, we don't have any money.'*

starter /ˈstɑːtə(r)/ *noun*
a small amount of food that you eat as the first part of a meal: *What would you like as a starter: soup or melon?*

startle /ˈstɑːtl/ *verb* (**startles, startling, startled** /ˈstɑːtld/)
make somebody suddenly surprised or frightened: *You startled me when you knocked on the window.*

starve /stɑːv/ *verb* (**starves, starving, starved** /stɑːvd/)
die because you do not have enough to eat: *Millions of people are starving in some parts of the world.*
be starving be very hungry: *When will dinner be ready? I'm starving!*
starvation /stɑːˈveɪʃn/ *noun* (no plural)
The child died of starvation.

state¹ /steɪt/ *noun*
1 (no plural) how somebody or something is: *Your room is in a terrible state!* (= untidy or dirty)
2 (*plural* **states**) a country and its government: *Many schools are owned by the state.*
3 (*plural* **states**) a part of a country: *Texas is a state in the USA.*
state of mind how you feel: *What state of mind is he in?*

state² /steɪt/ *verb* (**states, stating, stated**)
say or write something: *I stated in my letter that I was looking for a job.*
statement /ˈsteɪtmənt/ *noun*
something that you say or write: *The driver made a statement to the police about the accident.*

station /ˈsteɪʃn/ *noun*
1 a railway station; a place where trains stop so that people can get on and off
2 a place where buses or coaches start and end their journeys: *a bus station*
3 a building for some special work: *a police station* ◇ *a fire station*
4 a television or radio company

stationery /ˈsteɪʃənri/ *noun* (no plural)
paper, pens and other things that you use for writing

statistics /stəˈtɪstɪks/ *noun* (plural)
numbers that give information about something: *Statistics show that women live longer than men.*

statue /ˈstætʃuː/ *noun*
the shape of a person or an animal that is made of stone or metal: *the Statue of Liberty in New York*

stay¹ /steɪ/ *verb* (**stays, staying, stayed** /steɪd/)
1 be in the same place and not go away: *Stay here until I come back.* ◇ *I stayed in bed until ten o'clock.*
2 continue in the same way and not change: *I tried to stay awake.*
3 live somewhere for a short time: *I stayed with my friend in Dublin.* ◇ *Which hotel are you staying at?*
stay behind be somewhere after other people have gone: *The teacher asked me to stay behind after the lesson.*
stay in be at home and not go out: *I'm staying in this evening because I am tired.*
stay up not go to bed: *We stayed up until after midnight.*

stay² /steɪ/ *noun* (*plural* **stays**)
a short time when you live somewhere: *Did you enjoy your stay in London?*

steady /ˈstedi/ *adjective* (**steadier, steadiest**)
1 if something is steady, it does not move or shake: *Hold the ladder steady while I stand on it.* ✪ opposite: **unsteady**
2 if something is steady, it stays the same: *We drove at a steady speed.* ◇ *steady rain*
steadily /ˈstedɪli/ *adverb*
Prices are falling steadily.

steak /steɪk/ *noun*
a thick flat piece of meat or fish: *steak and chips*

p	b	t	d	k	g	tʃ	dʒ	f	v	θ	ð
pen	**b**ad	**t**ea	**d**id	**c**at	**g**ot	**ch**ain	**j**am	**f**all	**v**an	**th**in	**th**is

steal /stiːl/ *verb* (**steals, stealing, stole** /stəʊl/, **has stolen** /ˈstəʊlən/)
secretly take something that is not yours: *Her money has been stolen.*

> ✪ You **steal** things, but you **rob** people and places (you steal things from them). A person who steals is called a **thief**.
>
> *They **stole** my camera.*
>
> *I've been **robbed**.*
>
> *They **robbed** a bank.*

steam /stiːm/ *noun* (no plural)
the gas that water becomes when it gets very hot: *There was steam coming from my cup of coffee.*
steam *verb* (**steams, steaming, steamed** /stiːmd/)
1 send out steam: *a steaming bowl of soup*
2 cook something in steam: *steamed vegetables*

steel /stiːl/ *noun* (no plural)
very strong metal that is used for making things like knives, tools or machines

steep /stiːp/ *adjective* (**steeper, steepest**)
A steep hill, mountain or road goes up quickly from a low place to a high place: *I can't cycle up the hill – it's too steep.*
steeply *adverb*
The path climbed steeply up the side of the mountain.

steer /stɪə(r)/ *verb* (**steers, steering, steered** /stɪəd/)
make a car, boat, bicycle, etc go the way that you want by turning a wheel or handle
steering-wheel /ˈstɪərɪŋ wiːl/ *noun*
the wheel that you turn to make a car go left or right ☞ picture at **car**

stem /stem/ *noun*
the long thin part of a plant that the flowers and leaves grow on ☞ picture at **plant**

step¹ /step/ *noun*
1 a movement when you move your foot up and then put it down in another place to walk, run or dance: *She took a step forward and then stopped.*
2 a place to put your foot when you go up or down: *These steps go down to the garden.*

steps

3 one thing in a list of things that you must do: *What is the first step in planning a holiday?*
step by step doing one thing after another; slowly: *This book shows you how to play the guitar, step by step.*

step² /step/ *verb* (**steps, stepping, stepped** /stept/)
move your foot up and put it down in another place when you walk: *You stepped on my foot!*

stepfather /ˈstepfɑːðə(r)/ *noun*
a man who has married your mother but who is not your father

stepladder /ˈsteplædə(r)/ *noun*
a short ladder

stepmother /ˈstepmʌðə(r)/ *noun*
a woman who has married your father but who is not your mother ✪ The child of your stepmother or stepfather is your **stepbrother** or **stepsister**.

stereo /ˈsteriəʊ/ *noun* (*plural* **stereos**)
a machine for playing records, cassettes or compact discs, with two parts (called **speakers**) that the sound comes from
stereo *adjective*
with the sound coming from two speakers: *a stereo cassette player*

sterling /ˈstɜːlɪŋ/ *noun* (no plural)
the money that is used in Britain: *You can pay in sterling or in American dollars.*

stern /stɜːn/ *adjective* (**sterner, sternest**)
serious and strict with people; not smiling: *Our teacher is very stern.*

stew /stjuː/ *noun*
food that you make by cooking meat or vegetables in liquid for a long time: *beef stew*
stew *verb* (**stews, stewing, stewed** /stjuːd/)
cook something slowly in liquid: *stewed fruit*

s	z	ʃ	ʒ	h	m	n	ŋ	l	r	j	w
so	**zoo**	**shoe**	vi**sio**n	**hat**	**man**	**no**	si**ng**	**leg**	**red**	**yes**	**wet**

steward /'stju:əd/ *noun*
a man whose job is to look after people on an aeroplane or a ship

stewardess /ˌstju:ə'des/ *noun (plural* **stewardesses)**
a woman whose job is to look after people on an aeroplane or a ship

stick¹ /stɪk/ *noun*
1 a long thin piece of wood: *We found some sticks and made a fire.* ◇ *The old man walked with a stick.*
2 a long thin piece of something: *a stick of chalk*

stick² /stɪk/ *verb* (**sticks, sticking, stuck** /stʌk/, **has stuck**)
1 push a pointed thing into something: *Stick a fork into the meat to see if it's cooked.*
2 join something to another thing with glue, for example; become joined in this way: *I stuck a stamp on the envelope.*
3 be fixed in one place so that it cannot move: *This door always sticks* (= it won't open).
4 put something somewhere: *Stick that box on the floor.* ✪ This is an informal use.

stick out come out of the side or top of something so you can see it easily: *The boy's head was sticking out of the window.*

stick something out push something out: *Don't stick your tongue out!*

stick to something continue with something and not change it: *We're sticking to Peter's plan.*

stick up for somebody or **something** say that somebody or something is right: *Everyone else said I was wrong, but Kim stuck up for me.*

sticker /'stɪkə(r)/ *noun*
a small piece of paper with a picture or words on it, that you can stick onto things: *She has a sticker on the window of her car.*

sticky /'stɪki/ *adjective* (**stickier, stickiest**)
Something that is sticky can stick to things or is covered with something that can stick to things: *Glue is sticky.* ◇ *sticky fingers*

stiff /stɪf/ *adjective* (**stiffer, stiffest**)
hard and not easy to bend or move: *stiff cardboard*

still¹ /stɪl/ *adverb*
1 a word that you use to show that some-

thing has not changed: *Do you still live in London?* ◇ *Is it still raining?*
2 although that is true: *She felt ill, but she still went to the party.*
3 a word that you use to make another word stronger: *It was cold yesterday, but today it's colder still.*

still² /stɪl/ *adjective, adverb*
without moving: *Please stand still while I take a photo.*

stillness /'stɪlnəs/ *noun* (no plural)
the stillness of the night

sting /stɪŋ/ *verb* (**stings, stinging, stung** /stʌŋ/, **has stung**)
1 If an insect or a plant stings you, it hurts you by pushing a small sharp part into your skin: *I've been stung by a bee!*
2 feel a sudden sharp pain: *The smoke made my eyes sting.*

sting *noun*
1 the sharp part of some insects that can hurt you: *A wasp's sting is in its tail.*
2 a hurt place on your skin where an insect or plant has stung you: *a bee sting*

stink /stɪŋk/ *verb* (**stinks, stinking, stank** /stæŋk/, **has stunk** /stʌŋk/)
have a very bad smell: *That fish stinks!*

stink *noun*
a very bad smell: *What a horrible stink!*

stir /stɜ:(r)/ *verb* (**stirs, stirring, stirred** /stɜ:d/)
1 move a spoon or another thing round and round to mix something: *He put sugar in his coffee and stirred it.*
2 move a little or make something move a little: *The wind stirred the leaves.*

stitch /stɪtʃ/ *noun* (plural **stitches**)
1 one movement in and out of a piece of material with a needle and thread when you are sewing
2 one of the small circles of wool that you put round a needle when you are knitting

stitch *verb* (**stitches, stitching, stitched** /stɪtʃt/)
make stitches in something; sew something: *I stitched a button on my skirt.*

stock /stɒk/ *noun*
things that a shop keeps ready to sell: *That bookshop has a big stock of dictionaries.*

in stock ready to sell

out of stock not there to sell: *I'm sorry, that cassette is out of stock at the moment.*

stock *verb* (**stocks, stocking, stocked** /stɒkt/)
keep something ready to sell: *We don't stock umbrellas.*

stocking /'stɒkɪŋ/ *noun*
a long thin thing that a woman wears over her leg and foot: *a pair of stockings*

stole, stolen *forms of* **steal**

stomach /'stʌmək/ *noun*
1 the part inside your body where food goes after you eat it
2 the front part of your body below your chest and above your legs
☞ picture on page 126
stomach-ache /'stʌmək eɪk/ *noun* (no plural)
a pain in your stomach: *I've got stomach-ache.*

stone /stəʊn/ *noun*
1 (no plural) the very hard stuff that is in the ground. Stone is sometimes used for building: *a stone wall*
2 (*plural* **stones**) a small piece of stone: *The children were throwing stones into the river.*
3 (*plural* **stones**) the hard part in the middle of some fruits, for example plums and peaches
stone
4 (*plural* **stones**) a small piece of beautiful rock that is very valuable: *A diamond is a precious stone.*
5 (*plural* **stone**) a measure of weight (= 6.3 kilograms). There are 14 **pounds** in a stone: *I weigh ten stone.*
☞ Note at **pound**

stony /'stəʊni/ *adjective* (**stonier, stoniest**)
with a lot of stones in or on it: *stony ground*

stood *form of* **stand**[1]

stool /stuːl/ *noun*
a small seat with no back

stoop /stuːp/ *verb* (**stoops, stooping, stooped** /stuːpt/)
If you stoop, you bend your body forward and down: *She stooped to pick up the baby.*

stool

stop[1] /stɒp/ *verb* (**stops, stopping, stopped** /stɒpt/)
1 finish moving or working; become still: *The train stopped at every station.* ◇ *The clock has stopped.* ◇ *I stopped to post a letter.*
2 not do something any more; finish: *Stop making that noise!*
3 make somebody or something finish moving or doing something: *Ring the bell to stop the bus.*
stop somebody (from) doing something not let somebody do something: *My dad stopped me from going out.*

stop[2] /stɒp/ *noun*
1 the moment when somebody or something finishes moving: *The train came to a stop.*
2 a place where buses or trains stop so that people can get on and off: *I'm getting off at the next stop.*
put a stop to something make something finish: *A teacher put a stop to the fight.*

store[1] /stɔː(r)/ *noun*
1 a big shop: *Harrods is a famous London store.*
2 things that you are keeping to use later: *a store of food*
3 *American English for* **shop**[1]

store[2] /stɔː(r)/ *verb* (**stores, storing, stored** /stɔːd/)
keep something to use later: *The information is stored on a computer.*

storey /'stɔːri/ *noun* (*plural* **storeys**)
one level in a building: *The building has four storeys.*

storm[1] /stɔːm/ *noun*
very bad weather with strong winds and rain: *a thunderstorm*

storm[2] /stɔːm/ *verb* (**storms, storming, stormed** /stɔːmd/)
move in a way that shows you are angry: *He stormed out of the room.*

stormy /'stɔːmi/ *adjective* (**stormier, stormiest**)
If the weather is stormy, there is strong wind and rain: *a stormy night*

story /'stɔːri/ *noun* (*plural* **stories**)
1 words that tell you about people and things that are not real: *Hans Christian Andersen wrote stories for children.* ◇ *a ghost story*
2 words that tell you about things that

really happened: *My grandmother told me stories about when she was a child.*

stove /stəʊv/ *noun*
a cooker or heater

straight¹ /streɪt/
adjective   **straight line**
(**straighter, straightest**)
1 with no curve or bend: *Use a ruler to draw a straight line.* ◊ *His hair is curly and mine is straight.* ☞ picture at **hair**
2 with one side as high as the other: *This picture isn't straight.*

straight   not straight

get something straight make sure that you understand something completely: *Let's get this straight. Are you sure you left your bike by the cinema?*

straight² /streɪt/ *adverb*
1 in a straight line: *Look straight in front of you.*
2 without stopping or doing anything else; directly: *Come straight home.* ◊ *She walked straight past me.*
straight away immediately; now: *I'll do it straight away.*
straight on without turning: *Go straight on until you come to the bank, then turn left.*

straighten /streɪtn/ *verb* (**straightens, straightening, straightened** /streɪtnd/)
become or make something straight

straightforward /ˌstreɪtˈfɔːwəd/ *adjective*
easy to understand or do: *The question was straightforward.*

strain /streɪn/ *verb* (**strains, straining, strained** /streɪnd/)
1 pour a liquid through something with small holes in it, to take away any other things in the liquid: *You haven't strained the tea – there are tea leaves in it.*
2 try very hard: *Her voice was so quiet that I had to strain to hear her.*
3 hurt a part of your body by making it

work too hard: *Don't read in the dark. You'll strain your eyes.*

strain *noun*
1 being pulled or made to work too hard: *The rope broke under* (= because of) *the strain.*
2 hurting a part of your body by making it work too hard: *back strain*

strand /strænd/ *noun*
one piece of thread or hair

stranded /ˈstrændɪd/ *adjective*
left in a place that you cannot get away from: *The car broke down and I was stranded on a lonely road.*

strange /streɪndʒ/ *adjective* (**stranger, strangest**)
1 unusual or surprising: *Did you hear that strange noise?*
2 that you do not know: *We were lost in a strange town.* ✪ Be careful! We use **foreign, not strange,** to talk about a person or thing that comes from another country.
strangely *adverb*
in a surprising or unusual way: *She usually talks a lot, but today she was strangely quiet.*

stranger /ˈstreɪndʒə(r)/ *noun*
1 a person who you do not know
2 a person who is in a place that he/she does not know: *I'm a stranger to this city.*
✪ Be careful! We use the word **foreigner** for a person who comes from another country.

strangle /ˈstræŋgl/ *verb* (**strangles, strangling, strangled** /ˈstræŋgld/)
kill somebody by pressing their neck very tightly

straps

strap

strap /stræp/ *noun*
a long flat piece of material that you use for carrying something or for keeping something in place: *a leather watch-strap*
strap *verb* (**straps, strapping, strapped** /stræpt/)
hold something in place with a strap: *I strapped the bag onto the back of my bike.*

p	b	t	d	k	g	tʃ	dʒ	f	v	θ	ð
pen	**b**ad	**t**ea	**d**id	**c**at	**g**ot	**ch**ain	**j**am	**f**all	**v**an	**th**in	**th**is

straw /strɔ:/ *noun*
1 (no plural) the dry stems of plants like wheat: *The rabbit sleeps on a bed of straw.* ◇ *a straw hat*
2 (*plural* **straws**) a thin paper or plastic tube that you can drink through
the last straw a bad thing that happens after many other bad things so that you lose hope

strawberry
/'strɔ:bəri/ *noun* (*plural* **strawberries**)
a small soft red fruit: *strawberry jam*

strawberry

stray /streɪ/ *adjective*
lost and away from home: *a stray dog*
stray *noun* (*plural* **strays**)
an animal that has no home

streak /stri:k/ *noun*
a long thin line: *She's got streaks of grey in her hair.* ◇ *a streak of lightning*

stream /stri:m/ *noun*
1 a small river
2 moving liquid, or moving things or people: *a stream of blood* ◇ *a stream of cars*
stream *verb* (**streams**, **streaming**, **streamed** /stri:md/)
move like water: *Tears were streaming down his face.*

streamline /'stri:mlaɪn/ *verb* (**streamlines**, **streamlining**, **streamlined** /'stri:mlaɪnd/)
give something like a car or boat a long smooth shape so that it can go fast through air or water

street /stri:t/ *noun*
a road in a city, town or village with buildings along the sides: *I saw Anna walking down the street.* ◇ *I live in Hertford Street.* ○ The short way of writing 'Street' in addresses is **St**: *91 Oxford St*

streetcar /'stri:tkɑ:(r)/ *American English for* **tram**

strength /streŋθ/ *noun* (no plural)
being strong: *I don't have the strength to lift this box – it's too heavy.*
strengthen /'streŋθn/ *verb* (**strengthens**, **strengthening**, **strengthened** /'streŋθnd/)
make something stronger

stress /stres/ *noun* (*plural* **stresses**)
1 saying one word or part of a word more strongly than another: *In the word 'dictionary', the stress is on the first part of the word.*
2 a feeling of worry because of problems in your life: *She's suffering from stress because she's got too much work to do.*
stressful /'stresfl/ *adjective*
a stressful job
stress *verb* (**stresses**, **stressing**, **stressed** /strest/)
1 say something strongly to show that it is important: *I must stress how important this meeting is.*
2 say one word or part of a word more strongly than another: *You should stress the first part of the word 'happy'.*

stretch¹ /stretʃ/ *verb* (**stretches**, **stretching**, **stretched** /stretʃt/)
1 pull something to make it longer or wider; become longer or wider: *The T-shirt stretched when I washed it.*
2 push your arms and legs out as far as you can: *Joe got out of bed and stretched.*
3 continue: *The beach stretches for miles.*
stretch out lie down with all your body flat: *The cat stretched out in front of the fire and went to sleep.*

stretch² /stretʃ/ *noun* (*plural* **stretches**)
a piece of land or water: *This is a beautiful stretch of countryside.*

stretcher /'stretʃə(r)/ *noun*
a kind of bed for carrying somebody who is ill or hurt: *They carried him to the ambulance on a stretcher.*

strict /strɪkt/ *adjective* (**stricter**, **strictest**)
If you are strict, you make people do what you want and do not allow them to behave badly: *Her parents are very strict – she always has to be home before ten o'clock.* ◇ *strict rules*
strictly *adverb*
1 definitely; in a strict way: *Smoking is strictly forbidden.*
2 exactly: *That is not strictly true.*

stride /straɪd/ *verb* (**strides**, **striding**, **strode** /strəʊd/, **has stridden** /'strɪdn/)
walk with long steps: *The police officer strode across the road.*
stride *noun*
a long step

strike[1] /straɪk/ *noun*
a time when people are not working because they want more money or are angry about something: *There are no trains today because the drivers are on strike.*

strike[2] /straɪk/ *verb* (**strikes**, **striking**, **struck** /strʌk/, **has struck**)
1 hit somebody or something: *A stone struck me on the back of the head.* ✪ **Hit** is the more usual word, but when you talk about **lightning**, you always use **strike**: *The tree was struck by lightning.*
2 stop working because you want more money or are angry about something: *The nurses are going to strike for better pay.*
3 ring a bell so that people know what time it is: *The clock struck nine.*
4 come suddenly into your mind: *It suddenly struck me that she looked like my sister.*
strike a match make fire with a match

striking /'straɪkɪŋ/ *adjective*
If something is striking, you notice it because it is very unusual or interesting: *That's a very striking hat.*

string /strɪŋ/ *noun*
1 very thin rope that you use for tying things: *I tied up the parcel with string.* ◊ *The little boy held a balloon on the end of a string.*
2 a line of things on a piece of thread: *She was wearing a string of blue beads.* ☞ picture on page 261
3 a piece of thin wire, etc on a musical instrument: *guitar strings*

strip[1] /strɪp/ *noun*
a long thin piece of something: *a strip of paper*

strip[2] /strɪp/ *verb* (**strips**, **stripping**, **stripped** /strɪpt/)
1 take off what is covering something: *I stripped the wallpaper off the walls.*
2 (*also* **strip off**) take off your clothes: *She stripped off and ran into the sea.*

stripe /straɪp/ *noun*
a long thin line of colour: *Zebras have black and white stripes.*

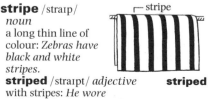
┌─ stripe

striped /straɪpt/ *adjective* **striped**
with stripes: *He wore a blue-and-white striped shirt.*

strode *form of* **stride**

stroke[1] /strəʊk/ *verb* (**strokes**, **stroking**, **stroked** /strəʊkt/)
move your hand gently over somebody or something to show love: *She stroked his hair.*

stroke[2] /strəʊk/ *noun*
1 a movement that you make with your arms when you are swimming, playing tennis, etc
2 a sudden serious illness when the brain stops working properly: *He had a stroke.*

stroll /strəʊl/ *verb* (**strolls**, **strolling**, **strolled** /strəʊld/)
walk slowly: *We strolled along the beach.*
stroll *noun*
We went for a stroll by the river.

stroller /'strəʊlə(r)/ *American English for* **pushchair**

strong /strɒŋ/ *adjective* (**stronger**, **strongest**)
1 with a powerful body, so that you can carry heavy things: *I need somebody strong to help me move this piano.* ☞ picture on page 263
2 that you cannot break easily: *Don't stand on that chair – it's not very strong.* ◊ *a strong belief*
3 that you can see, taste, smell, hear or feel clearly: *I like strong tea* (= with not much milk in it). ◊ *a strong smell of oranges* ◊ *strong winds*
strongly *adverb*
I strongly believe that he is wrong.

struck *form of* **strike**[2]

structure /'strʌktʃə(r)/ *noun*
1 (no plural) the way that something is made: *We are studying the structure of a bird's wing.*
2 (*plural* **structures**) a building or another thing that people have made with many parts: *The new post office is a tall glass and brick structure.*

struggle /'strʌgl/ *verb* (**struggles**, **struggling**, **struggled** /'strʌgld/)
1 try very hard to do something that is not easy: *We struggled to lift the heavy box.*
2 move your arms and legs a lot when you are fighting or trying to get free: *She struggled to get away from her attacker.*
struggle *noun*
In 1862 the American slaves won their struggle for freedom.

i:	i	ɪ	e	æ	ɑ:	ɒ	ɔ:	ʊ	u	u:
see	happy	sit	ten	cat	father	got	saw	put	situation	too

stubborn /'stʌbən/ *adjective*
A stubborn person does not change his/her ideas easily or do what other people want him/her to do: *She's too stubborn to say sorry.*

stuck[1] *form of* **stick**[2]

stuck[2] /stʌk/ *adjective*
1 not able to move: *This drawer is stuck – I can't open it.* ◇ *I was stuck in Italy with no money.*
2 not able to do something because it is difficult: *If you get stuck, ask your teacher for help.*

student /'stjuːdnt/ *noun*
a person who is studying at a university or college: *Tim is a student of history.*

studio /'stjuːdiəʊ/ *noun* (*plural* **studios**)
1 a room where an artist works
2 a room where people make films, radio and television programmes, or records: *a television studio*

study[1] /'stʌdi/ *verb* (**studies**, **studying**, **studied** /'stʌdid/, **has studied**)
1 spend time learning about something: *He studied French at university.*
2 look at something carefully: *We must study the map before we leave.*

study[2] /'stʌdi/ *noun* (*plural* **studies**)
1 learning: *He's doing a course in Business Studies.*
2 a room in a house where you go to study, read or write

stuff[1] /stʌf/ *noun* (no plural)
any material, substance or group of things: *What's this blue stuff on the carpet?* ◇ *Put your stuff in this bag.*

stuff[2] /stʌf/ *verb* (**stuffs**, **stuffing**, **stuffed** /stʌft/)
1 fill something with something: *The pillow was stuffed with feathers.*
2 push something quickly into another thing: *He took the money quickly and stuffed it into his pocket.*

stuffy /'stʌfi/ *adjective* (**stuffier**, **stuffiest**)
If a room is stuffy, it has no fresh air in it: *Open the window – it's very stuffy in here.*

stumble /'stʌmbl/ *verb* (**stumbles**, **stumbling**, **stumbled** /'stʌmbld/)
hit your foot against something when you are walking or running, and almost fall: *The old lady stumbled and fell as she was going upstairs.*

stump /stʌmp/ *noun*
the small part that is left when something is cut off or broken: *a tree stump*

stun /stʌn/ *verb* (**stuns**, **stunning**, **stunned** /stʌnd/)
1 hit a person or animal on the head so hard that he/she/it cannot see, think or make a sound for a short time
2 make somebody very surprised: *His sudden death stunned his family and friends.*

stung *form of* **sting**

stunk *form of* **stink**

stunning /'stʌnɪŋ/ *adjective*
very beautiful; wonderful: *a stunning dress*

stunt /stʌnt/ *noun*
something dangerous or difficult that you do to make people look at you: *James Bond films have a lot of exciting stunts.*

stupid /'stjuːpɪd/ *adjective*
not intelligent; silly: *Don't be so stupid!* ◇ *What a stupid question!*
stupidity /stjuː'pɪdəti/ *noun* (no plural)
being stupid
stupidly *adverb*
I stupidly forgot to close the door.

stutter /'stʌtə(r)/ *verb* (**stutters**, **stuttering**, **stuttered** /'stʌtəd/)
say the same sound many times when you are trying to say a word: *'I d-d-don't understand,' he stuttered.*

style /staɪl/ *noun*
1 a way of doing, making or saying something: *I don't like his style of writing.*
2 the shape or kind of something: *This shop sells jumpers in lots of different colours and styles.* ◇ *a hairstyle*

subject /'sʌbdʒɪkt/ *noun*
1 the person or thing that you are talking or writing about: *What is the subject of the talk?*
2 something you study at school, university or college: *I'm studying three subjects: Maths, Physics and Chemistry.*
3 the word in a sentence that does the action of the verb: *In the sentence 'Sue ate the cake', 'Sue' is the subject.* ☞ Look at **object**.
4 a person who belongs to a certain country: *British subjects*

submarine /ˌsʌbmə'riːn/ *noun*
a boat that can travel under the sea

subscription /səb'skrɪpʃn/ *noun*
money that you pay, for example to get the
same magazine each month or to join a
club: *I've got a subscription to 'Vogue'
magazine.*

substance /'sʌbstəns/ *noun*
anything that you can see, touch or use for
making things; a material: *Stone is a hard
substance.*   ◇ *chemical substances*

substitute /'sʌbstɪtjuːt/ *noun*
a person or thing that you put in the place
of another: *Our goalkeeper was ill, so we
found a substitute.*
substitute *verb* (**substitutes, substi-
tuting, substituted**)
put somebody or something in the place of
another: *You can substitute margarine for
butter.*

subtitles /'sʌbtaɪtlz/ *noun* (plural)
words at the bottom of a film that help you
to understand it: *It was a French film with
English subtitles.*

subtract /səb'trækt/ *verb* (**subtracts,
subtracting, subtracted**)
take a number away from another num
ber: *If you subtract 6 from 9, you get 3.*
◎ opposite: **add**
subtraction /səb'trækʃn/ *noun* (no
plural)
taking a number away from another number   ☞ Look at **addition**.

suburb /'sʌbɜːb/ *noun*
one of the parts of a town or city outside
the centre: *Wimbledon is a suburb of London.*   ◇ *We live in the suburbs.*

subway /'sʌbweɪ/ *noun* (plural **sub-
ways**)
1 a path that goes under a busy road, so
that people can cross safely
2 *American English for* **underground**²

succeed /sək'siːd/ *verb* (**succeeds, suc-
ceeding, succeeded**)
do or get what you wanted to do or get: *She
finally succeeded in getting a job.*   ◇ *I
tried to get a ticket for the concert but I
didn't succeed.*   ☞ Look at **fail**.

success /sək'ses/ *noun*
1 (no plural) doing or getting what you
wanted; doing well: *I wish you success
with your studies.*
2 (plural **successes**) somebody or some-

thing that does well or that people like a
lot: *The film 'Ghost' was a great success.*
◎ opposite: **failure**
successful /sək'sesfl/ *adjective*
a successful actor   ◇ *The party was very
successful.*   ◎ opposite: **unsuccessful**
successfully /sək'sesfəli/ *adverb*
He completed his studies successfully.

such /sʌtʃ/ *adjective*
1 a word that you use when you say how
much, how big, etc something is: *It was
such a nice day that we decided to go to the
beach.*   ☞ Look at **so**.
2 a word that makes another word
stronger: *He wears such strange clothes.*
3 like this or that: *'Can I speak to Mrs
Graham?' 'I'm sorry. There's no such person here.'*
such as like something; for example:
*Sweet foods such as chocolate can make
you fat.*

suck /sʌk/ *verb* (**sucks, sucking, sucked**
/sʌkt/)
1 pull something into your mouth, using
your lips: *The baby sucked milk from its
bottle.*
2 hold something in your mouth and
touch it a lot with your tongue: *She was
sucking a sweet.*

sudden /'sʌdn/ *adjective*
If something is sudden, it happens quickly
when you do not expect it: *His death was
very sudden.*
all of a sudden suddenly: *We were
watching TV when all of a sudden the door
opened.*
suddenly *adverb*
He left very suddenly.   ◇ *Suddenly there
was a loud noise.*

suffer /'sʌfə(r)/ *verb* (**suffers, suffering,
suffered** /'sʌfəd/)
feel pain, sadness or something else that is
not pleasant: *I'm suffering from toothache.*

sufficient /sə'fɪʃnt/ *adjective*
as much or as many as you need or want;
enough: *There was sufficient food to last
two weeks.*   ◎ **Enough** is the word that
we usually use.
◎ opposite: **insufficient**

suffix /'sʌfɪks/ *noun* (plural **suffixes**)
letters that you add to the end of a word to
make another word: *If you add the suffix*

p	b	t	d	k	g	tʃ	dʒ	f	v	θ	ð
pen	**b**ad	**t**ea	**d**id	**c**at	**g**ot	**ch**ain	**j**am	**f**all	**v**an	**th**in	**th**is

'-ly' to the adjective 'quick', you make the adverb 'quickly'. ☞ Look at **prefix**.

suffocate /'sʌfəkeɪt/ *verb* (**suffocates, suffocating, suffocated**)
die or make somebody die because there is no air to breathe

sugar /'ʃʊɡə(r)/ *noun*
1 (no plural) sweet stuff that comes from some sorts of plant: *Do you take sugar in your coffee?*
2 (*plural* **sugars**) a spoonful of sugar: *Two sugars, please.*

suggest /sə'dʒest/ *verb* (**suggests, suggesting, suggested**)
say what you think somebody should do or what should happen: *I suggest that you stay here tonight.* ◇ *Simon suggested going for a walk.* ◇ *What do you suggest?*
suggestion /sə'dʒestʃən/ *noun*
I don't know what to buy for her birthday. Have you got any suggestions? ◇ *I would like to make a suggestion.*

suicide /'suːɪsaɪd/ *noun*
killing yourself
commit suicide kill yourself

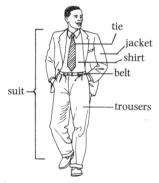

tie
jacket
shirt
belt
suit
trousers

suit¹ /suːt/ *noun*
a jacket and trousers, or a jacket and skirt, that you wear together and that are made from the same material

suit² /suːt/ *verb* (**suits, suiting, suited**)
1 If something suits you, it looks good on you: *Does this hat suit me?*
2 be right for you; be what you want or need: *Would it suit you if I came at five o'clock?*

suitable /'suːtəbl/ *adjective*
right for somebody or something: *This film*

isn't suitable for children. ✪ opposite: **unsuitable**
suitably /'suːtəbli/ *adverb*
Tony wasn't suitably dressed for a party.

suitcase
/'suːtkeɪs/ *noun*
a large bag with flat sides that you carry your clothes in when you travel

suitcase

sulk /sʌlk/ *verb*
(**sulks, sulking, sulked** /sʌlkt/)
not speak because you are angry about something: *She's been sulking in her room all day because her mum wouldn't let her go to the party.*

sum /sʌm/ *noun*
1 a simple piece of work with numbers, for example adding or dividing: *Children learn how to do sums.*
2 an amount of money: *£200 000 is a large sum of money.*
3 the answer that you have when you add numbers together: *The sum of two and five is seven.*

summary /'sʌməri/ *noun* (*plural* **summaries**)
a short way of telling something by giving only the most important facts: *Here is a summary of the news . . .*

summer /'sʌmə(r)/ *noun*
the warmest time of the year: *I am going to Spain in the summer.* ◇ *the summer holidays*

summit /'sʌmɪt/ *noun*
the top of a mountain

sun /sʌn/ *noun* (no plural)
1 the sun the big round thing in the sky that gives us light in the day, and heat: *The sun is shining.*
2 light and heat from the sun: *We sat in the sun all morning.*

sunbathe /'sʌnbeɪð/ *verb* (**sunbathes, sunbathing, sunbathed** /'sʌnbeɪðd/)
lie in the sun so that your skin becomes darker: *We sunbathed on the beach.*

sunburn /'sʌnbɜːn/ *noun* (no plural)
red painful skin that you get when you have been in the hot sun for too long
sunburned /'sʌnbɜːnd/, **sunburnt** /'sʌnbɜːnt/ *adjective*
sunburned shoulders

s	z	ʃ	ʒ	h	m	n	ŋ	l	r	j	w
so	**zoo**	**shoe**	**vision**	**hat**	**man**	**no**	**sing**	**leg**	**red**	**yes**	**wet**

Sunday /'sʌndeɪ/ *noun*
the first day of the week; the day before
Monday

sung *form of* **sing**

sun-glasses /'sʌnglɑːsɪz/ *noun*
(plural)
glasses with dark glass in them that you
wear in strong light: *a pair of sun-glasses*

sunk *form of* **sink²**

sunlight /'sʌnlaɪt/ *noun* (no plural)
the light from the sun

sunny /'sʌni/ *adjective* (**sunnier, sun-
niest**)
bright with light from the sun: *a sunny
day*

sunrise /'sʌnraɪz/ *noun* (no plural)
the time in the morning when the sun
comes up

sunset /'sʌnset/ *noun*
the time in the evening when the sun goes
down: *The park closes at sunset.*

sunshine /'sʌnʃaɪn/ *noun* (no plural)
the light and heat from the sun: *We sat
outside in the sunshine.*

suntan /'sʌntæn/ *noun*
When you have a suntan, your skin is
brown because you have been in the hot
sun: *I'm trying to get a suntan.*
suntanned /'sʌntænd/ *adjective*
suntanned arms

super /'suːpə(r)/ *adjective*
very good; wonderful: *That was a super
meal.* ◇ *His new car is super.*

superb /suː'pɜːb/ *adjective*
very good or beautiful: *a superb holiday*
◇ *The view from the window is superb.*

superior /suː'pɪəriə(r)/ *adjective*
better or more important than another
person or thing: *I think fresh coffee is superior to instant coffee.* ❂ opposite:
inferior

superlative /suː'pɜːlətɪv/ *noun*
the form of an adjective or adverb that
shows the most of something: *'Most intelligent', 'best' and 'fastest' are all super-
latives.*
superlative *adjective*
*'Youngest' is the superlative form of
'young'.*

supermarket /'suːpəmɑːkɪt/ *noun*
a big shop where you can buy food and

other things. You choose what you want
and then pay for everything when you
leave.

❂ In a supermarket you put the things
you want to buy in a **basket** or a **trolley**
and pay for them at the **checkout**.

supersonic /ˌsuːpə'sɒnɪk/ *adjective*
faster than the speed of sound: *Concorde is
a supersonic aeroplane.*

superstition /ˌsuːpə'stɪʃn/ *noun*
a belief in good and bad luck and other
things that cannot be explained: *People
say that walking under a ladder brings bad
luck, but it's just a superstition.*
superstitious /ˌsuːpə'stɪʃəs/ *adjective*
If you are superstitious, you believe in
good and bad luck and other things that
cannot be explained.

superstore /'suːpəstɔː(r)/ *noun*
a very big shop: *There's a new superstore
on the edge of town.*

supervise /'suːpəvaɪz/ *verb*
(**supervises, supervising, supervised**
/'suːpəvaɪzd/)
watch to see that people are working correctly: *I supervised the builders.*
supervision /ˌsuːpə'vɪʒn/ *noun* (no
plural)
supervising or being supervised: *Children
must not play here without supervision.*
supervisor /'suːpəvaɪzə(r)/ *noun*
a person who supervises

supper /'sʌpə(r)/ *noun*
the last meal of the day: *We had supper
and then went to bed.*

supply /sə'plaɪ/ *verb* (**supplies, sup-
plying, supplied** /sə'plaɪd/, **has supplied**)
give or sell something that somebody
needs: *The school supplies us with books.*
◇ *The lake supplies water to thousands of
homes.*
supply *noun* (*plural* **supplies**)
an amount of something that you need:
supplies of food

support /sə'pɔːt/ *verb* (**supports, sup-
porting, supported**)
1 hold somebody or something up, so that
they do not fall: *The bridge isn't strong
enough to support heavy lorries.*
2 help somebody to live by giving things
like money, a home or food: *She has three
children to support.*
3 say that you think that somebody or

something is right or the best: *Everybody else said I was wrong but Paul supported me.* ◇ *Which football team do you support?*

support *noun*
1 (no plural) help: *Thank you for all your support.*
2 (*plural* **supports**) something that holds up another thing: *a roof support*

supporter /sə'pɔːtə(r)/ *noun*
a person who helps somebody or something by giving money, or by showing interest, for example: *football supporters*

suppose /sə'pəʊz/ *verb* (**supposes**, **supposing**, **supposed** /sə'pəʊzd/)
1 think that something is true or will happen but not be sure: *'Where's Jenny?' 'I don't know – I suppose she's still at work.'*
2 a word that you use when you agree with something but are not happy about it: *'Can I borrow your pen?' 'Yes, I suppose so – but don't lose it.'*

supposed /sə'pəʊzd/ *adjective*
be supposed to 1 If you are supposed to do something, you should do it: *They were supposed to meet us here.* ◇ *You're not supposed to smoke in this room.* **2** If something is supposed to be true, people say it is true: *This is supposed to be a good restaurant.*

supposing /sə'pəʊzɪŋ/ *conjunction*
if: *Supposing we miss the bus, how will we get to the airport?*

supreme /su:'pri:m/ *adjective*
highest or most important: *the Supreme Court*

sure /ʃɔː(r)/ *adjective* (**surer, surest**), *adverb*
If you are sure, you know that something is true or right: *I'm sure I've seen that man before.* ◇ *If you're not sure how to do it, ask your teacher.*
be sure to If you are sure to do something, you will certainly do it: *If you work hard, you're sure to pass the exam.*
for sure without any doubt: *I think he's coming to the party but I don't know for sure.*
make sure check something so that you are certain about it: *I think the party starts at eight, but I'll phone to make*

sure. ◇ *Make sure you don't leave your bag on the bus.*
sure enough as I thought: *I said they would be late, and sure enough they were.*

surely /'ʃɔːli/ *adverb*
a word that you use when you think that something must be true, or when you are surprised: *Surely you know where your brother works!*

surfing
surf
surfer
surfboard

surf /sɜːf/ *noun* (no plural)
the white part on the top of waves in the sea

surfing *noun* (no plural)
the sport of riding over waves on a long piece of wood or plastic (called a **surfboard**) ✪ You can say **go surfing**: *We went surfing.*

surfer *noun*
a person who surfs

surface /'sɜːfɪs/ *noun*
1 the outside part of something: *A tomato has a shiny red surface.*
2 the top of water: *She dived below the surface.*

surgeon /'sɜːdʒən/ *noun*
a doctor who does **operations**. A surgeon cuts your body to take out or mend a part inside: *a brain surgeon*

surgery /'sɜːdʒəri/ *noun*
1 (no plural) cutting somebody's body to take out or mend a part inside: *He needed surgery after the accident.*
2 (*plural* **surgeries**) a place where you go to see a doctor or dentist

surname /'sɜːneɪm/ *noun*
the name that a family has. Your surname is usually your last name: *Her name is Ann Jones. Jones is her surname.* ☞ Note at **name**

surprise¹ /sə'praɪz/ *noun*
1 (no plural) the feeling that you have when something happens suddenly that

you did not expect: *She looked at me in surprise when I told her the news.*
2 (*plural* **surprises**) something that happens when you do not expect it: *Don't tell him about the birthday party – it's a surprise!*
take somebody by surprise happen when somebody does not expect it: *Your phone call took me by surprise – I thought you were on holiday.*
to my surprise I was surprised that: *I thought she would be angry but, to my surprise, she smiled.*

surprise² /sə'praɪz/ *verb* (**surprises, surprising, surprised** /sə'praɪzd/)
do something that somebody does not expect: *I arrived early to surprise her.*
surprised *adjective*
If you are surprised, you feel or show surprise: *I was surprised to see Tim yesterday – I thought he was in Canada.*
surprising *adjective*
If something is surprising, it makes you feel surprise: *The news was surprising.*
surprisingly *adverb*
The exam was surprisingly easy.

surrender /sə'rendə(r)/ *verb* (**surrenders, surrendering, surrendered** /sə'rendəd/)
stop fighting because you cannot win: *After six hours on the roof, the man surrendered to the police.*

surround /sə'raʊnd/ *verb* (**surrounds, surrounding, surrounded**)
be or go all around something: *The lake is surrounded by trees.*

surroundings /sə'raʊndɪŋz/ *noun* (plural)
everything around you, or the place where you live: *The farm is in beautiful surroundings.* ◊ *I don't like seeing animals in a zoo – I prefer to see them in their natural surroundings.*

survey /'sɜːveɪ/ *noun* (*plural* **surveys**)
asking questions about what people think or do, or what is happening: *We did a survey of people's favourite TV programmes.*

survive /sə'vaɪv/ *verb* (**survives, surviving, survived** /sə'vaɪvd/)
continue to live after a difficult or dangerous time: *Camels can survive for many*

days without water. ◊ *Only one person survived the plane crash.*

survival /sə'vaɪvl/ *noun* (no plural)
surviving: *Food and water are necessary for survival.*

survivor /sə'vaɪvə(r)/ *noun*
a person who survives: *The government sent help to the survivors of the earthquake.*

suspect /sə'spekt/ *verb* (**suspects, suspecting, suspected**)
1 think that something is true, but not be certain: *John wasn't at college today – I suspect that he's ill.*
2 think that somebody has done something wrong but not be certain: *They suspect Helen of stealing the money.*
suspect /'sʌspekt/ *noun*
a person who you think has done something wrong. *The police have arrested two suspects.*

suspicion /sə'spɪʃn/ *noun*
1 an idea that is not totally certain: *We have a suspicion that he is unhappy.*
2 a feeling that somebody has done something wrong: *When she saw the £100 note in his wallet she was filled with suspicion.*

suspicious /sə'spɪʃəs/ *adjective*
1 If you are suspicious, you do not believe somebody or something, or you feel that something is wrong: *The police are suspicious of her story.*
2 A person or thing that is suspicious makes you feel that something is wrong: *There was a man waiting outside the school. He looked very suspicious.*
suspiciously *adverb*
'What are you doing here?' the woman asked suspiciously.

swallow¹ /'swɒləʊ/ *verb* (**swallows, swallowing, swallowed** /'swɒləʊd/)
make food or drink move down your throat from your mouth: *I can't swallow these tablets without water.*

swallow² /'swɒləʊ/ *noun*
a small bird

swam *form of* **swim**

swamp /swɒmp/ *noun*
soft wet ground

swan

swan /swɒn/ *noun*
a big white bird with a very long neck.
Swans live on rivers and lakes.

swap /swɒp/ *verb*
(**swaps, swapping, swapped** /swɒpt/)
change one thing for another thing; give
one thing and get another thing for it: *Do
you want to swap chairs with me?* (= you
have my chair and I'll have yours) ◇ *I
swapped my T-shirt for Tom's cassette.*

swarm /swɔːm/ *noun*
a big group of flying insects: *a swarm of
bees*
swarm *verb* (**swarms, swarming,
swarmed** /swɔːmd/)
fly or move quickly in a big group: *The fans
swarmed into the stadium.*

sway /sweɪ/ *verb* (**sways, swaying,
swayed** /sweɪd/)
move slowly from side to side: *The trees
were swaying in the wind.*

swear /sweə(r)/ *verb* (**swears, swear-
ing, swore** /swɔː(r)/, **has sworn** /swɔːn/)
1 say bad words: *Don't swear at your
mother!*
2 make a serious promise: *He swears that
he is telling the truth.*
swear-word /'sweə wɜːd/ *noun*
a bad word

sweat /swet/ *noun* (no plural)
water that comes out of your skin when
you are hot or afraid
sweat *verb* (**sweats, sweating,
sweated**)
have sweat coming out of your skin: *The
room was so hot that everyone was
sweating.*
sweaty *adjective* (**sweatier, sweatiest**)
covered with sweat: *sweaty socks*

sweater /'swetə(r)/ *noun*
a warm piece of clothing with sleeves, that
you wear on the top part of your body.
Sweaters are often made of wool.

sweatshirt /'swetʃɜːt/ *noun*
a piece of clothing like a sweater, made of
thick cotton

sweep /swiːp/ *verb* (**sweeps, sweeping,
swept** /swept/, **has swept**)

1 clean something by moving dirt or other
things away with a brush: *I swept the
floor.*
2 push something along or away quickly
and strongly: *The bridge was swept away
by the floods.*
sweep up move something away with a
brush: *I swept up the broken glass.*

sweet¹ /swiːt/ *adjective* (**sweeter,
sweetest**)
1 with the taste of sugar: *Honey is sweet.*
2 pretty: *What a sweet little girl!*
3 kind and gentle: *It was sweet of you to
help me.*
4 with a good smell: *the sweet smell of
roses*
sweetly *adverb*
in a pretty, kind or nice way: *She smiled
sweetly.*

sweet² /swiːt/ *noun*
1 a small piece of sweet food. Chocolates
and toffees are sweets: *He bought a packet
of sweets for the children.*
2 sweet food that you eat at the end of a
meal: *Do you want any sweet?*

swell /swel/ *verb* (**swells, swelling,
swelled** /sweld/, **has swollen** /'swəʊlən/
or **has swelled**)
swell up become bigger or thicker than it
usually is: *After he hurt his ankle it began
to swell up.*

swelling /'swelɪŋ/ *noun*
a place on the body that is bigger or fatter
than it usually is: *She has got a swelling on
her head where she fell and hit it.*

swept *form of* **sweep**

swerve /swɜːv/ *verb* (**swerves, swer-
ving, swerved** /swɜːvd/)
turn suddenly so that you do not hit something: *The driver swerved when she saw
the child in the road.*

swift /swɪft/ *adjective* (**swifter, swift-
est**)
quick or fast: *We made a swift decision.*
swiftly *adverb*
She ran swiftly up the stairs.

swim /swɪm/ *verb* (**swims, swimming,
swam** /swæm/, **has swum** /swʌm/)
move your body through water: *Can you
swim?* ◇ *I swam across the lake.*
❂ When you talk about spending time
swimming as a sport, you usually say **go
swimming**: *I go swimming every day.*

swim *noun* (no plural)
Let's go for a swim.
swimmer *noun*
a person who swims: *He's a good swimmer.*
swimming *noun* (no plural)
Swimming is my favourite sport.
swimming-costume /ˈswɪmɪŋ kɒstjuːm/, **swimsuit** /ˈswɪmsuːt/ *noun*
a piece of clothing that a woman or girl wears for swimming
swimming-pool /ˈswɪmɪŋ puːl/ *noun*
a special place where you can swim
swimming-trunks /ˈswɪmɪŋ trʌŋks/ *noun* (plural)
short trousers that a man or boy wears for swimming

swing¹ /swɪŋ/ *verb* (**swings, swinging, swung** /swʌŋ/, **has swung**)
1 hang from something and move backwards and forwards or from side to side through the air: *The monkey was swinging from a tree.*
2 make somebody or something move in this way: *He swung his arms as he walked.*
3 move in a curve: *The door swung open.*

swing

swing² /swɪŋ/ *noun*
a seat that hangs down. Children sit on it to move backwards and forwards through the air.

switch¹ /swɪtʃ/ *noun* (plural **switches**)
a small thing that you press to stop or start electricity: *Where is the light switch?*

switch

switch² /swɪtʃ/ *verb* (**switches, switching, switched** /swɪtʃt/)
change to something different: *I switched to another seat because I couldn't see the film.*
switch off press something to stop electricity: *I switched the TV off.* ◇ *Don't forget to switch off the lights!*

switch on press something to start electricity: *Switch the radio on.*

switchboard /ˈswɪtʃbɔːd/ *noun*
the place in a large office where somebody answers telephone calls and sends them to the right people

swollen *form of* **swell**
swollen /ˈswəʊlən/ *adjective*
thicker or fatter than it usually is: *a swollen ankle*

swoop /swuːp/ *verb* (**swoops, swooping, swooped** /swuːpt/)
fly down quickly: *The bird swooped down to catch a fish.*

swop /swɒp/ = **swap**

sword /sɔːd/ *noun*
a long sharp knife for fighting

swore, sworn *forms of* **swear**

swot /swɒt/ *verb* (**swots, swotting, swotted**)
study hard before an exam: *Debbie is swotting for her test next week.*

swum *form of* **swim**

swung *form of* **swing¹**

syllable /ˈsɪləbl/ *noun*
a part of a word that has one **vowel** sound when you say it. 'Swim' has one syllable and 'system' has two syllables.

syllabus /ˈsɪləbəs/ *noun* (plural **syllabuses**)
a list of all the things that you must study on a course

symbol /ˈsɪmbl/ *noun*
a mark, sign or picture that shows something: *+ and − are symbols for plus and minus in mathematics* ◇ *A dove is the symbol of peace.*

sympathetic /ˌsɪmpəˈθetɪk/ *adjective*
If you are sympathetic, you show that you understand other people's feelings when they have problems: *Everyone was very sympathetic when I was ill.* ☺ opposite: **unsympathetic**
sympathetically /ˌsɪmpəˈθetɪkli/ *adverb*
He smiled sympathetically.

sympathize /ˈsɪmpəθaɪz/ *verb* (**sympathizes, sympathizing, sympathized** /ˈsɪmpəθaɪzd/)
sympathize with somebody show

that you understand somebody's feelings when they have problems: *I sympathize with you – I've got a lot of work too.*

sympathy /'sɪmpəθi/ *noun* (no plural)
understanding another person's feelings and problems: *She wrote me a letter of sympathy when my father died.*

symphony /'sɪmfəni/ *noun* (*plural* **symphonies**)
a long piece of music for a large orchestra: *Beethoven's fifth symphony*

symptom /'sɪmptəm/ *noun*
something that shows that you have an illness: *A sore throat is often a symptom of a cold.*

synagogue /'sɪnəgɒg/ *noun*
a building where Jewish people go to pray

synthetic /sɪn'θetɪk/ *adjective*
made by people, not natural: *Nylon is a synthetic material, but wool is natural.*

syrup /'sɪrəp/ *noun* (no plural)
thick sweet liquid made with sugar and water or fruit juice: *peaches in syrup*

system /'sɪstəm/ *noun*
1 a group of things or parts that work together: *the railway system* ◇ *We have a new computer system at work.*
2 a group of ideas or ways of doing something: *What system of government do you have in your country?*

Tt

tablecloth

table

table /'teɪbl/ *noun*
1 a piece of furniture with a flat top on legs
2 a list of facts or numbers: *There is a table of irregular verbs at the back of this dictionary.*
set or **lay the table** put knives, forks, plates and other things on the table before you eat

tablecloth /'teɪblklɒθ/ *noun*
a cloth that you put over a table when you have a meal

tablespoon /'teɪblspu:n/ *noun*
a big spoon that you use for putting food on plates

tablet /'tæblət/ *noun*
a small hard piece of medicine that you swallow: *Take two of these tablets before every meal.*

table tennis /'teɪbl tenɪs/ *noun* (no plural)
a game where players use a round bat to hit a small light ball over a net on a big table

tackle /'tækl/ *verb* (**tackles**, **tackling**, **tackled** /'tækld/)
1 start to do a difficult job: *I'm going to tackle my homework now.* ◇ *How shall we tackle this problem?*
2 try to take the ball from somebody in a game like football
3 try to catch and hold somebody: *I tackled the thief but he ran away.*

tact /tækt/ *noun* (no plural)
knowing how and when to say things so that you do not hurt people: *She told him the meal was horrible – she's got no tact.*

tactful /'tæktfl/ *adjective*
careful not to say or do things that may make people unhappy or angry: *He wrote me a tactful letter about the money I owe him.*

tactfully /'tæktfəli/ *adverb*
in a tactful way

tactless /'tæktləs/ *adjective*
not careful about people's feelings: *It was tactless of you to ask how old she was.*

tag /tæg/ *noun*
a small piece of paper or material fixed to something, that tells you about it; a label: *I looked at the price tag to see how much the dress cost.*

tail /teɪl/ *noun*
1 the long thin part at the end of an an-

ʌ	ɜ:	ə	eɪ	əʊ	aɪ	aʊ	ɔɪ	ɪə	eə	ʊə
cup	**bird**	**about**	**say**	**go**	**five**	**now**	**boy**	**near**	**hair**	**pure**

imal's body: *The dog wagged its tail.*
☞ pictures at **cat** and **fish**
2 the part at the back of something: *the tail of an aeroplane*
3 tails (plural) the side of a coin that does not have the head of a person on it
☞ Note at **heads**

tailor /'teɪlə(r)/ *noun*
a person whose job is to make clothes for men

take /teɪk/ *verb* (**takes**, **taking**, **took** /tʊk/, **has taken** /'teɪkn/)
1 move something or go with somebody to another place: *Take your coat with you – it's cold.* ◇ *Mark took me to the station.*
☞ picture at **bring**
2 put your hand round something and hold it: *She took the baby in her arms.* ◇ *Take this money – it's yours.*
3 steal something: *Somebody has taken my bike.*
4 need an amount of time: *The journey took four hours.*
5 travel in a bus, train, etc: *I took a taxi to the hospital.*
6 eat or drink something: *I took the medicine.*
7 agree to have something: *This restaurant doesn't take cheques.*
it takes you need something: *It takes a long time to learn a language.*
take after somebody be or look like somebody in your family: *She takes after her mother.*
take away remove something: *I took the knife away from the child.*
take down write something that somebody says: *He took down my address.*
take off When an aeroplane takes off, it leaves the ground.
take something off 1 remove clothes: *Take your coat off.* ○ opposite: **put on**
2 have time as a holiday, not working: *I am taking a week off in June.*
take over look after a business, etc when another person stops: *Robert took over the farm when his father died.*
take up use or fill time or space: *The bed takes up half the room.* ◇ *The new baby takes up all her time.*

take-away /'teɪk əweɪ/ *noun* (*plural* **take-aways**)
1 a restaurant that sells hot food that you take out with you to eat somewhere else: *a*

Chinese *take-away*
2 food that you buy at this kind of restaurant: *Let's get a take-away.*
take-away *adjective*
a take-away pizza

take-off /'teɪk ɒf/ *noun*
the time when an aeroplane leaves the ground

tale /teɪl/ *noun*
a story: *fairy tales*

talent /'tælənt/ *noun*
the natural ability to do something very well: *Fiona has a talent for drawing.*
talented *adjective*
with a talent: *a talented musician*

talk¹ /tɔːk/ *verb* (**talks**, **talking**, **talked** /tɔːkt/)
speak to somebody; say words: *She is talking to her boyfriend on the telephone.*
◇ *We talked about our holiday.*

talk² /tɔːk/ *noun*
1 when two or more people talk about something: *Dave and I had a long talk about the problem.* ◇ *The two countries are holding talks to try and end the war.*
2 when a person speaks to a group of people: *Professor Wilson gave an interesting talk on Chinese art.*

talkative /'tɔːkətɪv/ *adjective*
A person who is talkative talks a lot.

tall /tɔːl/ *adjective* (**taller**, **tallest**)
1 A person or thing that is tall goes up a long way: *a tall tree* ◇ *Richard is taller than his brother.* ○ opposite: **short**
☞ picture on page 262
2 You use 'tall' to say or ask how far it is from the bottom to the top of somebody or something: *How tall are you?* ◇ *She's 1.62 metres tall.* ☞ Note at **high**

tame /teɪm/ *adjective* (**tamer**, **tamest**)
A tame animal is not wild and is not afraid of people: *a tame squirrel*
tame *verb* (**tames**, **taming**, **tamed** /teɪmd/)
make a wild animal tame

tan /tæn/ *noun*
When you have a tan, your skin is brown because you have been in the hot sun.
tanned /tænd/ *adjective*
with a brown skin because you have been in the hot sun

tangerine /ˌtændʒəˈriːn/ *noun*
a fruit like a small sweet orange, with a
skin that is easy to take off

tangle /ˈtæŋgl/ *verb* (**tangles**, **tangling**,
tangled /ˈtæŋgld/)
mix or twist something like string or hair
so that it is difficult to separate ✪ opposite: **untangle**
tangle *noun*
This string is in a tangle.
tangled *adjective*
*The cat has been playing with my wool
and now it's all tangled.*

tank /tæŋk/ *noun*
1 a container for liquids or gas: *a petrol
tank* (in a car)
2 a strong heavy vehicle with big guns.
Tanks are used by armies in wars.

tanker /ˈtæŋkə(r)/ *noun*
a ship that carries petrol or oil: *an
oil-tanker*

tap¹ /tæp/ *noun*
a thing that you
turn to make
something like
water or gas come
out of a pipe: *Turn
the tap off.*

tap

tap² /tæp/ *verb* (**taps**, **tapping**, **tapped**
/tæpt/)
hit or touch somebody or something
quickly and lightly: *She tapped me on the
shoulder.* ◇ *I tapped on the window.*
tap *noun*
They heard a tap at the door.

tape /teɪp/ *noun*
1 a long thin piece of special plastic in a
plastic box, that stores (**records**) sound,
music or moving pictures so that you can
listen to or watch it later. You use it in a
tape recorder or a **video recorder**: *I have
got the concert on tape.* ◇ *Will you play
your new Michael Jackson tape?*
2 a long thin piece of material or paper
tape *verb* (**tapes**, **taping**, **taped** /teɪpt/)
put (**record**) sound, music or moving pictures on tape so that you can listen to or
watch it later: *I taped the film that was on
TV last night.*

tape-measure /ˈteɪp meʒə(r)/ *noun*
a long thin piece of metal, plastic or cloth
for measuring things

tape recorder /ˈteɪp rɪˌkɔːdə(r)/ *noun*
a machine that can put (**record**) sound or
music on tape and play it again later

tapestry /ˈtæpəstri/ *noun* (*plural* **tap-
estries**)
a piece of cloth with pictures on it made
from coloured thread

tar /tɑː(r)/ *noun* (no plural)
black stuff that is thick and sticky when it
is hot, and hard when it is cold. Tar is used
for making roads.

target /ˈtɑːgɪt/ *noun*
a thing that you try to hit with a bullet or
an arrow, for example: *The bomb hit its
target.*

tart /tɑːt/ *noun*
a piece of pastry with fruit or jam on it:
Would you like a piece of apple tart?

tartan /ˈtɑːtn/ *noun*
a special pattern on material that comes
from Scotland: *a tartan skirt*

task /tɑːsk/ *noun*
a piece of work that you must do; a job: *I
had the task of cleaning the floors.*

taste¹ /teɪst/ *noun*
1 (no plural) the power to know about
food and drink with your mouth: *When
you have a cold, you often lose your sense
of taste.*
2 (*plural* **tastes**) the feeling that a certain
food or drink gives in your mouth: *Sugar
has a sweet taste and lemons have a sour
taste.* ◇ *I don't like the taste of this
cheese.*
3 (*plural* **tastes**) a little bit of food or
drink: *Have a taste of the wine to see if you
like it.*
4 (no plural) being able to choose nice
things: *She has good taste in clothes.*

taste² /teɪst/ *verb* (**tastes**, **tasting**,
tasted)
1 feel or know a certain food or drink in
your mouth: *Can you taste onions in this
soup?*
2 eat or drink a little of something: *Taste
this cheese to see if you like it.*
3 give a certain feeling when you put it in
your mouth: *Honey tastes sweet.*

tasty /ˈteɪsti/ *adjective* (**tastier**, **tastiest**)
good to eat: *The soup was very tasty.*

tattoo /təˈtuː/ *noun* (*plural* **tattoos**)
a picture on somebody's skin, made with a

needle and coloured liquid: *He had a tattoo of a snake on his arm.*

taught *form of* **teach**

tax /tæks/ *noun* (*plural* **taxes**)
money that you have to pay to the government. You pay tax from the money you earn or when you buy things: *There is a tax on cigarettes in this country.*
tax *verb* (**taxes**, **taxing**, **taxed** /tækst/)
make somebody pay tax

taxi /'tæksi/ *noun*
a car that you can travel in if you pay the driver: *I took a taxi to the airport.* ◇ *I came by taxi.*

tea /ti:/ *noun*
1 (no plural) a brown drink that you make with hot water and the dry leaves of a special plant: *Would you like a cup of tea?*
2 (*plural* **teas**) a cup of this drink: *Two teas, please.*
3 (no plural) the dry leaves that you use to make tea
4 (*plural* **teas**) a small afternoon meal of sandwiches, cakes and cups of tea
❍ Some people call their evening meal **tea**.

tea bag /'ti: bæg/ *noun*
a small paper bag with tea leaves inside. You use it to make tea.

teapot /'ti:pɒt/ *noun*
a special pot for making and pouring tea

teapot

teach /ti:tʃ/ *verb* (**teaches**, **teaching**, **taught** /tɔ:t/, **has taught**)
give somebody lessons; tell or show somebody how to do something: *My mother taught me to drive.* ◇ *Marco is teaching me Italian.* ☞ Look at **learn**.

teaching *noun* (no plural)
the job of a teacher

teacher /'ti:tʃə(r)/ *noun*
a person whose job is to teach: *He's my English teacher.*

team /ti:m/ *noun*
1 a group of people who play a sport or a game together against another group: *Which team do you play for?* ◇ *a football team*
2 a group of people who work together: *a team of doctors*

tear¹ /tɪə(r)/ *noun*
a drop of water that comes from your eye when you cry
be in tears be crying: *I was in tears at the end of the film.*
burst into tears suddenly start to cry: *He read the letter and burst into tears.*

tear² /teə(r)/ *verb*
(**tears**, **tearing**, **tore** /tɔ:(r)/, **has torn** /tɔ:n/)
1 pull something apart or make an untidy hole in something: *She tore her dress on a nail.*

tear

◇ *I tore the piece of paper in half.* ◇ *I can't use this bag – it's torn.*
2 pull something roughly and quickly away from somebody or something: *I tore a page out of the book.*
3 come apart; break: *Paper tears easily.*
4 move very fast: *He tore down the street.*
tear up pull something into small pieces: *I tore the letter up and threw it away.*

tear³ /teə(r)/ *noun*
an untidy hole in something like paper or material: *You've got a tear in your jeans.*

tease /ti:z/ *verb* (**teases**, **teasing**, **teased** /ti:zd/)
say unkind things to somebody because you think it is funny: *People often tease me because I'm short.*

teaspoon /'ti:spu:n/ *noun*
a small spoon that you use for putting sugar into tea or coffee

tea towel /'ti: taʊəl/ *noun*
a small cloth that you use for drying things like plates and cups after you wash them

technical /'teknɪkl/ *adjective*
of or about the machines and materials used in science and in making things: *technical knowledge*

technician /tek'nɪʃn/ *noun*
a person who works with machines or instruments: *a laboratory technician*

technique /tek'ni:k/ *noun*
a special way of doing something: *new techniques for learning languages*

technology /tek'nɒlədʒi/ *noun* (no plural)
studying science and ideas about how

things work, and using this to build and make things: *Technology is very important for the future.* ◊ *computer technology*

teddy bear /'tedi beə(r)/, **teddy** (*plural* **teddies**) *noun*
a toy for children that looks like a bear

teddy bear

tedious /'ti:diəs/ *adjective*
very long and not interesting: *a tedious journey*

teenager /'ti:neidʒə(r)/ *noun*
a person who is between the ages of 13 and 19

teenage /'ti:neidʒ/ *adjective*
a teenage boy

teens /ti:nz/ *noun* (plural)
the time when you are between the ages of 13 and 19: *She is in her teens.*

teeth *plural of* **tooth**

telegram /'teligræm/ *noun*
a message that you send very quickly by radio or by electric wires

telephone¹ /'telifəun/ *noun*
an instrument that you use for talking to somebody who is in another place: *What's your telephone number?* ◊ *Can I make a telephone call?* ◊ *The telephone's ringing – can you answer it?*
on the telephone using a telephone to speak to somebody: *He's on the telephone to his wife.*
○ **Phone** is the more usual word.

telephone² /'telifəun/ *verb* (**telephones, telephoning, telephoned** /'telifəund/)
use a telephone to speak to somebody: *I must telephone my parents.* ○ **Phone** is the more usual word.

telephone box /'telifəun bɒks/ (*plural* **telephone boxes**), **telephone kiosk** *noun*
a kind of small building in the street or in a public place that has a telephone in it

telephone directory /'telifəun dɪrektəri/ *noun* (*plural* **telephone directories**)
a book of people's names, addresses and telephone numbers

telescope /'teliskəup/ *noun*
a long round instrument with special glass inside it. You use it to look at things that are a long way from you.

television /'telivɪʒn/ *noun*
1 (*plural* **televisions**) (*also* **television set**) a machine like a box that shows moving pictures with sound
2 (no plural) things that you watch on a television: *I watched television last night.* ◊ *What's on television?* ◊ *a television programme*
3 a way of sending pictures and sounds so that people can watch them on television: *satellite television*
○ The short forms are **TV** and **telly**.

telex /'teleks/ *noun*
1 (no plural) a way of sending messages. You type the message on a special machine that sends it very quickly to another place by telephone.
2 (*plural* **telexes**) a message that you send or receive in this way

tell /tel/ *verb* (**tells, telling, told** /təuld/, **has told**)
1 give information to somebody by speaking or writing: *I told her my new address.* ◊ *This book tells you how to make bread.* ◊ *He told me that he was tired.*
2 say what somebody must do: *Our teacher told us to read this book.*
☞ Note at **say**
can tell know, guess or understand something: *I can tell that he's been crying because his eyes are red.* ◊ *I can't tell the difference between James and his brother. They look exactly the same!*
tell somebody off speak to somebody in an angry way because they have done something wrong: *I told the children off for making so much noise.*

telly /'teli/ *short for* **television**

temper /'tempə(r)/ *noun*
how you feel: *She's in a bad temper this morning.*
have a temper If you have a temper, you often get angry and cannot control what you do or say: *He has a terrible temper.*
in a temper angry: *She's in a temper because she's tired.*
lose your temper suddenly become angry

ʌ	ɜː	ə	eɪ	əu	aɪ	au	ɔɪ	ɪə	eə	uə
cup	**bird**	**about**	**say**	**go**	**five**	**now**	**boy**	**near**	**hair**	**pure**

temperature /'temprətʃə(r)/ *noun*
how hot or cold somebody or something is:
*On a very hot day, the temperature
reaches 35° C.* ◇ *a high/low temperature*
have a temperature feel very hot because you are ill
take somebody's temperature see
how hot somebody is, using a special instrument called a **thermometer**

temple /'templ/ *noun*
a building where people go to pray and
worship God or a god

temporary /'temprəri/ *adjective*
Something that is temporary lasts for a
short time: *I had a temporary job in the
summer holidays.* ◇ opposite: **permanent**
temporarily /'temprərəli/ *adverb*
*The road is temporarily closed for re-
pairs.*

tempt /tempt/ *verb* (**tempts, tempting,
tempted**)
make somebody want to do something, especially something that is wrong: *He saw
the money on the table, and he was
tempted to steal it.*
temptation /temp'teɪʃn/ *noun*
1 (*plural* **temptations**) a thing that
makes you want to do something wrong:
*Don't leave the money on your desk – it's
a temptation to thieves.*
2 (no plural) a feeling that you want to do
something that you know is wrong: *the
temptation to eat another chocolate*
tempting *adjective*
Something that is tempting makes you
want to do or have it: *That cake looks very
tempting!*

ten /ten/ *number*
10

tenant /'tenənt/ *noun*
a person who pays money to live in or use a
place

tend /tend/ *verb* (**tends, tending,
tended**)
usually do or be something: *Men tend to be
taller than women.*
tendency /'tendənsi/ *noun* (*plural* **tend-
encies**)
something that a person or thing often
does: *He has a tendency to be late.*

tender /'tendə(r)/ *adjective*
1 kind and gentle: *a tender look*
2 Tender meat is soft and easy to cut or
bite. ◇ opposite: **tough**
3 If a part of your body is tender, it hurts
when you touch it.
tenderly *adverb*
in a kind and gentle way: *He touched her
arm tenderly.*
tenderness /'tendənəs/ *noun* (no
plural)
a feeling of tenderness

tennis /'tenɪs/ *noun* (no plural)
a game for two or four players who hold
rackets and hit a small ball over a net:
Let's play tennis.
tennis court /'tenɪs kɔːt/ *noun*
a special place where you play tennis

tense¹ /tens/ *adjective* (**tenser, tensest**)
1 worried because you are waiting for
something to happen: *I always feel very
tense before exams.*
2 pulled tightly: *tense muscles*
tension /'tenʃn/ *noun*
being tense: *Tension can give you
headaches.*

tense² /tens/ *noun*
the form of a verb that shows if something
happens in the past, present or future

tent

tent /tent/ *noun*
a kind of a house made of cloth. You sleep
in a tent when you go camping: *We put up
our tent.*

tenth /tenθ/ *adjective, adverb, noun*
1 10th
2 one of ten equal parts of something; ¹/₁₀

term /tɜːm/ *noun*
1 the time between holidays when schools
and colleges are open: *The summer term is
from April to July.*
2 a word or group of words connected
with a special subject: *a computing term*

terminal /'tɜːmɪnl/ *noun*
a building where people begin and end
their journeys by bus, train, aeroplane or

p	b	t	d	k	g	tʃ	dʒ	f	v	θ	ð
pen	**bad**	**tea**	**did**	**cat**	**got**	**chain**	**jam**	**fall**	**van**	**thin**	**this**

ship: *Passengers for Nairobi should go to Terminal 2.*

terrace /'terəs/ *noun*
1 a flat place outside a house or restaurant: *We had our lunch on the terrace.*
2 a line of houses that are joined together
terraced house /,terəst 'haʊs/ *noun*
a house that is part of a line of houses that are all joined together

terrible /'terəbl/ *adjective*
very bad: *She had a terrible accident.*
◇ *The food in that restaurant is terrible!*

terribly /'terəbli/ *adverb*
1 very: *I'm terribly sorry!*
2 very badly: *He played terribly.*

terrific /tə'rɪfɪk/ *adjective*
1 very good; wonderful: *What a terrific idea!*
2 very great: *a terrific storm*

terrify /'terɪfaɪ/ *verb* (**terrifies**, **terrifying**, **terrified** /'terɪfaɪd/, **has terrified**)
make somebody very frightened: *Spiders terrify me!*
terrified *adjective*
very frightened: *Di is terrified of dogs.*

territory /'terətri/ *noun* (*plural* **territories**)
the land that belongs to one country: *This island was once French territory.*

terror /'terə(r)/ *noun* (no plural)
very great fear: *He screamed in terror.*

terrorist /'terərɪst/ *noun*
a person who frightens, hurts or kills people so that the government, etc will do what he/she wants: *The terrorists put a bomb in the station.*
terrorism /'terərɪzəm/ *noun* (no plural)
an act of terrorism

test /test/ *verb* (**tests**, **testing**, **tested**)
1 use or look at something carefully to find out how good it is or if it works well: *The doctor tested my eyes.* ◇ *I don't think drugs should be tested on animals.*
2 ask somebody questions to find out what they know or what they can do: *The teacher tested us on our spelling.*
test *noun*
a blood test ◇ *a maths test* ◇ *Did you pass your driving test?*

test-tube /'test tju:b/ *noun*
a long thin glass tube that you use in chemistry

text /tekst/ *noun*
1 (no plural) the words in a book, newspaper or magazine: *This book has a lot of pictures but not much text.*
2 (*plural* **texts**) a book or a short piece of writing that you study: *Read the text and answer the questions.*

textbook /'tekstbʊk/ *noun*
a book that teaches you about something: *a biology textbook*

texture /'tekstʃə(r)/ *noun*
the way that something feels when you touch it: *Silk has a smooth texture.*

than /ðən/, /ðæn/ *conjunction, preposition*
You use 'than' when you compare people or things: *I'm older than him.* ◇ *You speak Spanish much better than she does.*
◇ *We live less than a kilometre from the beach.*

thank /θæŋk/ *verb* (**thanks**, **thanking**, **thanked** /θæŋkt/)
tell somebody that you are pleased because they gave you something or helped you: *I thanked Tina for the present.*
no, thank you You use 'no, thank you' to say that you do not want something: *'Would you like some more tea?' 'No, thank you.'* ✪ You can also say **no, thanks**.
thank you, thanks You use 'thank you' or 'thanks' to tell somebody that you are pleased because they gave you something or helped you: *Thank you very much for the flowers.* ◇ *'How are you?' 'I'm fine, thanks.'*
thanks *noun* (plural)
words that show you are pleased because somebody gave you something or helped you: *Please give my thanks to your sister for her help.*
thanks to somebody or **something** because of somebody or something: *We're late, thanks to you!*

thankful /'θæŋkfl/ *adjective*
happy that something good has happened: *I was thankful for a rest after the long walk.*
thankfully /'θæŋkfəli/ *adverb*
You say 'thankfully' when you are pleased about something: *There was an accident, but thankfully nobody was hurt.*

s	z	ʃ	ʒ	h	m	n	ŋ	l	r	j	w
so	**zoo**	**shoe**	vision	**hat**	**man**	**no**	sing	**leg**	**red**	**yes**	**wet**

Thanksgiving /ˌθæŋksˈgɪvɪŋ/ *noun*
(no plural)
a special holiday in October or November
for people in Canada and the USA

that¹ /ðæt/ *adjective, pronoun* (*plural*
those)
a word that you use to talk about a person
or thing that is there or then: *'Who is that
boy in the garden?' 'That's my brother.'*
◇ *She got married in 1989. At that time,
she was a teacher.* ☞ picture at **this**

that² /ðæt/ *adverb*
so: *The next village is ten kilometres from
here. I can't walk that far.*

that³ /ðət/ *pronoun*
which, who or whom: *A lion is an animal
that lives in Africa.* ◇ *The people (that) I
met were very nice.* ◇ *I'm reading the
book (that) you gave me.*

that⁴ /ðət/, /ðæt/ *conjunction*
a word that you use to join two parts of a
sentence: *Jo said (that) she was unhappy.*
◇ *I'm sure (that) he will come.* ◇ *I was
so hungry (that) I ate all the food.*

thaw /θɔː/ *verb* (**thaws, thawing**
/ˈθɔːɪŋ/, **thawed** /θɔːd/)
warm something that is frozen so that it
becomes soft or liquid; get warmer so that
it becomes soft or liquid: *The ice is
thawing.*

the¹ /ðə/, /ði/, /ðiː/ *article*
1 a word that you use before the name of
somebody or something when it is clear
what person or thing you mean: *I bought a
shirt and some trousers. The shirt is blue.*
◇ *The sun is shining.*
2 a word that you use before numbers and
dates: *Monday the sixth of May*
3 a word that you use to talk about a
group of people or things of the same kind:
the French (= all French people) ◇ *Do
you play the piano?*
4 a word that you use before the names of
rivers, seas, etc and some countries: *the
Seine* ◇ *the Atlantic* ◇ *the United States
of America* ✪ Before the names of most
countries, we do not use 'the ': *I went to
France.* (NOT: *I went to the France.*)

the² /ðə/, /ði/ *adverb*
a word that you use to talk about two
things happening together: *The more you
eat, the fatter you get.*

theater *American English for* **theatre**

theatre /ˈθɪətə(r)/ *noun*
a building where you go to see plays: *I'm
going to the theatre this evening.*

theft /θeft/ *noun*
taking something that is not yours; stealing: *She was sent to prison for theft.* ◇ *I
told the police about the theft of my car.*

their /ðeə(r)/ *adjective*
of them: *What is their phone number?*

theirs /ðeəz/ *pronoun*
something that belongs to them: *Our flat
is smaller than theirs.*

them /ðəm/, /ðem/ *pronoun* (plural)
1 a word that shows more than one person, animal or thing: *I wrote them a letter
and then I phoned them.* ◇ *I'm looking
for my keys. Have you seen them?*
2 him or her: *If anybody phones, tell them
I'm busy.*

theme /θiːm/ *noun*
something that you talk or write about:
*The theme of his speech was 'Europe in the
1990s'.*

themselves /ðəmˈselvz/ *pronoun*
(plural)
1 a word that shows the same people, animals or things that you have just talked
about: *They bought themselves a new car.*
2 a word that makes 'they' stronger: *Did
they build the house themselves?*
by themselves 1 alone; without other
people: *The children went out by themselves.* **2** without help: *They cooked dinner by themselves.*

then /ðen/ *adverb*
1 at that time: *I became a teacher in
1989. I lived in Bristol then, but now I
live in London.* ◇ *I can't come next week.
I will be on holiday then.*
2 next; after that: *We had dinner and then
did the washing-up.*
3 if that is true: *'I don't feel well.' 'Then
why don't you go to the doctor's?'*

theory /ˈθɪəri/ *noun* (*plural* **theories**)
an idea that tries to explain something:
*There are a lot of different theories about
how life began.*

therapy /ˈθerəpi/ *noun* (no plural)
a way of helping people who are ill in their
body or mind, usually without drugs:
speech therapy

there¹ /ðeə(r)/ *adverb*
in, at or to that place: *Don't put the box*

iː	i	ɪ	e	æ	ɑː	ɒ	ɔː	ʊ	u	uː
see	happy	sit	ten	cat	father	got	saw	put	situation	too

there – put it here. ◇ *Have you been to Bonn? I'm going there next week.*
there you are words that you say when you give something to somebody: *'There you are,' she said, giving me a cake.*

there² /ðeə(r)/ *pronoun*
1 a word that you use with verbs like 'be', 'seem' and 'appear' to show that something is true or that something is happening: *There is a man at the door.* ◇ *Is there a film on TV tonight?* ◇ *There aren't any shops in this village.*
2 a word that makes people look or listen: *There's the bell for my class! I must go.*

therefore /'ðeəfɔ:(r)/ *adverb*
for that reason: *Simon was busy and therefore could not come to the meeting.*

thermometer
/θə'mɒmɪtə(r)/
noun
an instrument that
shows how hot or
cold something is

thermometer

these /ði:z/
adjective, pronoun
(plural)
a word that you use
to talk about people
or things that are
here or now: *These
books are mine.*
◇ *Do you want these?* ☞ picture at **this**

they /ðeɪ/ *pronoun* (plural)
1 the people, animals or things that the sentence is about: *Jo and David came at two o'clock and they left at six o'clock.* ◇ *'Where are my keys?' 'They're (= they are) on the table.'*
2 a word that you use instead of 'he' or 'she': *Someone phoned for you – they said they would phone again later.*
3 people: *They say it will be cold this winter.*

they'd /ðeɪd/
1 = they had
2 = they would

they'll /ðeɪl/ = they will

they're /ðeə(r)/ = they are

they've /ðeɪv/ = they have

thick /θɪk/ *adjective* (**thicker, thickest**)
1 far from one side to the other: *The walls*

are very thick.* ◇ *It's cold outside, so wear a thick coat.* ✪ opposite: **thin**
☞ picture on page 262
2 You use 'thick' to say or ask how far something is from one side to the other: *The ice is six centimetres thick.*
3 with a lot of people or things close together: *a thick forest*
4 If a liquid is thick, it does not flow easily: *This paint is too thick.* ✪ opposite: **thin**
5 difficult to see through: *thick smoke*
thickness /'θɪknəs/ *noun* (no plural)
The wood is 3 cm in thickness.

thief /θi:f/ *noun* (*plural* **thieves** /θi:vz/)
a person who steals something: *A thief stole my car.*

thigh /θaɪ/ *noun*
the part of your leg above your knee
☞ picture on page 126

thin /θɪn/ *adjective* (**thinner, thinnest**)
1 not far from one side to the other; not thick: *The walls in this house are very thin.* ◇ *I cut the bread into thin slices.*
☞ picture on page 262
2 not fat: *He's tall and thin.* ☞ picture on page 262
3 If a liquid is thin, it flows easily like water: *The soup was very thin.* ✪ opposite: **thick**
4 not close together: *My father's hair is getting thin.*

thing /θɪŋ/ *noun*
1 an object: *What's that red thing?*
2 what happens or what you do: *A strange thing happened to me yesterday.* ◇ *That was a difficult thing to do.*
3 an idea or subject: *We talked about a lot of things.*
4 **things** (plural) what you own: *Have you packed your things for the journey?*

think /θɪŋk/ *verb* (**thinks, thinking, thought** /θɔ:t/, **has thought**)
1 use your mind: *Think before you answer the question.*
2 believe something: *I think it's going to rain.* ◇ *'Do you think Sara will come tomorrow?' 'Yes, I think so.' (= I think that she will come)* ◇ *I think they live in Rome but I'm not sure.*
think about somebody or **something 1** have somebody or something in your mind: *I often think about that day.*
2 try to decide whether to do something: *Paul is thinking about leaving his job.*

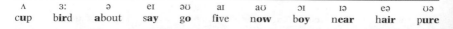

ʌ	ɜ:	ə	eɪ	əʊ	aɪ	aʊ	ɔɪ	ɪə	eə	ʊə
cup	bird	about	say	go	five	now	boy	near	hair	pure

think of somebody or **something**
1 have something in your mind: *I can't think of her name.* **2** have an opinion about somebody or something: *What do you think of this music?* **3** try to decide whether to do something: *We're thinking of going to America.*

third /θɜ:d/ *adjective, adverb, noun*
1 3rd
2 one of three equal parts of something; 1/3

thirst /θɜ:st/ *noun* (no plural)
the feeling you have when you want to drink something ❂ Be careful! You cannot say 'I have thirst' in English. You must say 'I am thirsty'.

thirsty /ˈθɜ:sti/ *adjective* (**thirstier, thirstiest**)
If you are thirsty, you want to drink something: *Salty food makes you thirsty.*

thirteen /ˌθɜ:ˈti:n/ *number*
13
thirteenth /ˌθɜ:ˈti:nθ/ *adjective, adverb, noun*
13th

thirty /ˈθɜ:ti/ *number*
1 30
2 **the thirties** (plural) the numbers, years or temperature between 30 and 39
in your thirties between the ages of 30 and 39
thirtieth /ˈθɜ:tiəθ/ *adjective, adverb, noun*
30th

this¹ /ðɪs/ *adjective, pronoun* (*plural* **these**)
a word that you use to talk about a person or thing that is here or now: *Come and look at this photo.* ◇ *This is my sister.* ◇ *I am on holiday this week.* ◇ *How much does this cost?* ☞ picture on next page

this² /ðɪs/ *adverb*
so: *The other film was not this good* (= not as good as this film).

thistle /ˈθɪsl/ *noun*
a plant with purple flowers and leaves that have sharp points

thorn /θɔ:n/ *noun*
a sharp point that grows on a plant: *Rose bushes have thorns.*

thorough /ˈθʌrə/ *adjective*
careful and complete: *We gave the room a thorough clean.*

thoroughly /ˈθʌrəli/ *adverb*
1 carefully and completely: *He cleaned the room thoroughly.*
2 completely; very or very much: *I thoroughly enjoyed the film.*

those /ðəʊz/ *adjective, pronoun* (plural)
a word that you use to talk about people or things that are there or then: *I don't know those boys.* ◇ *Her grandfather was born in 1850. In those days, there were no cars.* ◇ *Can I have those?* ☞ picture on next page

though¹ /ðəʊ/ *conjunction*
1 in spite of something; although: *I was very cold, though I was wearing my coat.* ◇ *Though she was in a hurry, she stopped to talk.*
2 but: *I thought it was right though I wasn't sure.*
as though in a way that makes you think something: *The house looks as though nobody lives there.* ◇ *I'm so hungry – I feel as though I haven't eaten for days!*

though² /ðəʊ/ *adverb*
however: *I like him very much. I don't like his wife, though.*

thought¹ *form of* **think**

thought² /θɔ:t/ *noun*
1 (no plural) thinking: *After a lot of thought, I decided not to take the job.*
2 (*plural* **thoughts**) an idea: *Have you had any thoughts about what you want to do when you leave school?*

thoughtful /ˈθɔ:tfl/ *adjective*
1 If you are thoughtful, you are thinking carefully: *She listened with a thoughtful look on her face.*
2 A person who is thoughtful is kind, and thinks and cares about other people: *It was very thoughtful of you to cook us dinner.*

thousand /ˈθaʊznd/ *number*
1 000: *a thousand people* ◇ *two thousand and fifteen* ◇ *There were thousands of birds on the lake.*
thousandth /ˈθaʊznθ/ *adjective, adverb, noun*
1 000th

thread /θred/ *noun*
a long thin piece of cotton, wool, etc that you use with a **needle** for sewing

p	b	t	d	k	g	tʃ	dʒ	f	v	θ	ð
pen	**bad**	**tea**	**did**	**cat**	**got**	**chain**	**jam**	**fall**	**van**	**thin**	**this**

this, these, that and those

He caught **this** fish.
He didn't catch **that** fish.

thread *verb* (**threads, threading, threaded**)
put thread through the hole in a needle

threat /θret/ *noun*
1 a promise that you will hurt somebody if they do not do what you want
2 a person or thing that may damage or hurt somebody or something: *Pollution is a threat to the lives of animals and people.*

threaten /'θretn/ *verb* (**threatens, threatening, threatened** /'θretnd/)
1 say that you will hurt somebody if they do not do what you want: *They threatened to kill everyone on the plane.* ◇ *She threatened him with a knife.*
2 seem ready to do something bad: *The dark clouds threatened rain.*

three /θri:/ *number*
3

threw *form of* **throw**

thrill /θrɪl/ *noun*
a sudden strong feeling of excitement

thrill *verb* (**thrills, thrilling, thrilled** /θrɪld/)
make somebody feel strong excitement

thrilled *adjective*
very happy and excited: *We are all thrilled that you have won the prize.*

thrilling *adjective*
very exciting: *a thrilling adventure*

thriller /'θrɪlə(r)/ *noun*
an exciting book, film or play about a crime

throat /θrəʊt/ *noun*
1 the front part of your neck ☞ picture on page 126
2 the part inside your neck that takes food and air down from your mouth into your body: *I've got a sore throat (= my throat hurts).*

throb /θrɒb/ *verb* (**throbs, throbbing, throbbed** /θrɒbd/)
beat quickly and strongly: *His heart was throbbing with excitement.*

throne /θrəʊn/ *noun*
a special chair where a king or queen sits

through /θruː/ *preposition, adverb*
1 from one side or end of something to the other side or end: *We drove through the tunnel.* ◇ *What can you see through the window?* ◇ *She opened the gate and we walked through.* ☞ picture on page 128
2 from the beginning to the end of something: *We travelled through the night.*
3 connected by telephone: *Can you put me through to Jill Knight, please?* ◇ *I tried to phone you but I couldn't get through.*
4 because of somebody or something: *She got the job through her father.*

throughout /θruː'aʊt/ *preposition, adverb*
1 in every part of something: *We painted the house throughout.* ◇ *She is famous throughout the world.*
2 from the beginning to the end of something: *They talked throughout the film.*

throw /θrəʊ/ *verb* (**throws, throwing, threw** /θruː/, **has thrown** /θrəʊn/)
1 move your arm quickly to send something through the air: *Throw the ball to Alex.* ◇ *The boys were throwing stones at people.*
2 do something quickly and without care: *She threw on her coat* (= put it on quickly) *and ran out of the house.*
3 move your body or part of it quickly: *He threw his arms up.*
throw something away or **out** put something in the dustbin because you do not want it: *Don't throw that box away.*
throw *noun*
What a good throw!

thrust /θrʌst/ *verb* (**thrusts, thrusting, thrust, has thrust**)
push somebody or something suddenly and strongly: *She thrust the money into my hand.*
thrust *noun*
a strong push

thud /θʌd/ *noun*
the sound that a heavy thing makes when it hits something: *The book hit the floor with a thud.*

thumb /θʌm/ *noun*
the short thick finger at the side of your hand ☞ picture on page 126

thumbtack /'θʌmtæk/ *American English for* **drawing-pin**

thump /θʌmp/ *verb* (**thumps, thumping, thumped** /θʌmpt/)
1 hit something hard with your hand or a heavy thing: *He thumped on the door.*
2 make a loud sound by hitting or beating hard: *Her heart was thumping with fear.*

thunder /'θʌndə(r)/ *noun* (no plural)
a loud noise in the sky when there is a storm ✪ The light that you see in the sky in a storm is called **lightning**.
thunder *verb* (**thunders, thundering, thundered** /'θʌndəd/)
1 make the sound of thunder: *It thundered all night.*
2 make a sound like thunder: *The lorries thundered along the road.*

thunderstorm /'θʌndəstɔːm/ *noun*
a storm with a lot of rain, thunder and lightning

Thursday /'θɜːzdeɪ/ *noun*
the fifth day of the week, next after Wednesday

thus /ðʌs/ *adverb*
1 in this way: *Hold the wheel in both hands, thus.*
2 because of this: *He was very busy and was thus unable to come to the meeting.*

tick¹ /tɪk/ *noun*
the sound that a clock or watch makes
tick *verb* (**ticks, ticking, ticked** /tɪkt/)
make this sound: *I could hear a clock ticking.*

tick² /tɪk/ *noun*
a small mark like this ✓, that shows that something is correct, for example: *Put a tick by the correct answer.*
tick *verb* (**ticks, ticking, ticked** /tɪkt/)
make a mark like this ✓ by something: *Tick the right answer.*

ticket /'tɪkɪt/ *noun*
a small piece of paper or card that you must buy to travel or to go into a cinema, theatre or museum, for example: *Do you want a single or a return ticket?* ◇ *a theatre ticket* ◇ *a ticket collector* (= a person who takes tickets from people on a train or at a station)
ticket office /'tɪkɪt ɒfɪs/ *noun*
a place where you buy tickets

iː	i	ɪ	e	æ	ɑː	ɒ	ɔː	ʊ	u	uː
see	happy	sit	ten	cat	father	got	saw	put	situation	too

tickle /'tɪkl/ *verb* (**tickles, tickling, tick-led** /'tɪkld/)
1 touch somebody lightly with your fingers to make them laugh: *She tickled the baby's feet.*
2 have the feeling that something is touching you lightly: *My nose tickles.*

tide /taɪd/ *noun*
the movement of the sea towards the land and away from the land: *The tide is coming in.* ◇ *The tide is going out.* ✪ **High tide** is when the sea is nearest the land, and **low tide** is when the sea is furthest from the land.

tidy /'taɪdi/ *adjective* (**tidier, tidiest**)
1 with everything in the right place: *Her room is very tidy.*
2 If you are tidy, you like to have everything in the right place: *a tidy boy*
✪ opposite: **untidy**
tidily /'taɪdɪli/ *adverb*
Put the books back tidily when you've finished with them.
tidiness /'taɪdɪnəs/ *noun* (no plural)
being tidy
tidy, tidy up *verb* (**tidies, tidying, tidied** /'taɪdid/, **has tidied**)
make something tidy: *I tidied the house before my parents arrived.* ◇ *Can you help me to tidy up?*

tie[1] /taɪ/ *noun*
1 a long thin piece of cloth that you wear round your neck with a shirt ☞ picture at **suit**
2 when two teams or players have the same number of points at the end of a game or competition: *The match ended in a tie.*
3 something that holds people together: *Our school has ties with a school in France.*

tie[2] /taɪ/ *verb* (**ties, tying, tied** /taɪd/, **has tied**)
1 fasten two ends of string, rope, etc together to hold somebody or something in place: *The prisoner was tied to a chair.* ◇ *I tied a scarf round my neck.*
2 end a game or competition with the same number of points for both teams or players: *France tied with Spain for second place.*
tie somebody up put a piece of rope around somebody so that they cannot

move: *The robbers tied up the owner of the shop.*
tie something up put a piece of string or rope around something to hold it in place: *I tied up the parcel with string.*

tiger /'taɪgə(r)/ *noun*
a wild animal like a big cat, with yellow fur and black stripes. Tigers live in Asia.

tight /taɪt/ *adjective* (**tighter, tightest**)
1 fixed firmly so that you cannot move it easily: *a tight knot* ◇ *I can't open this jar of jam – the lid is too tight.*
2 small, so that there is no space between it and your body: *These shoes are too tight.* ◇ *tight trousers*
✪ opposite: **loose** ☞ picture on page 263
tight, tightly *adverb*
Hold tight! ◇ *I tied the string tightly around the box.*

tighten /'taɪtn/ *verb* (**tightens, tightening, tightened** /'taɪtnd/)
become tighter or make something tighter: *Can you tighten this screw?* ✪ opposite: **loosen**

tightrope /'taɪtrəʊp/ *noun*
a rope or wire high above the ground. **Acrobats** walk along tightropes in a **circus**.

tights /taɪts/ *noun* (plural)
a thin piece of clothing that a woman or girl wears over her feet and legs: *a pair of tights* ☞ picture at **dress**

tile /taɪl/ *noun*
a flat square thing. We use tiles for covering roofs, walls and floors.

till[1] /tɪl/ *conjunction*
up to the time when: *Let's wait till the rain stops.*
till *preposition*
1 up to a certain time: *I'll be here till Monday.*
2 before: *I didn't arrive till six o'clock.*

till[2] /tɪl/ *noun*
a drawer or box for money in a shop

tilt /tɪlt/ *verb* (**tilts, tilting, tilted**)
have one side higher than the other; move something so that it has one side higher than the other: *She tilted the tray and all the glasses fell off.*

timber /'tɪmbə(r)/ *noun* (no plural)
wood that we use for building and making things

ʌ	ɜː	ə	eɪ	əʊ	aɪ	aʊ	ɔɪ	ɪə	eə	ʊə
cup	bird	about	say	go	five	now	boy	near	hair	pure

time¹ /taɪm/ noun
1 (plural **times**) a certain point in the day or night, that you say in hours and minutes: 'What time is it?' 'It's twenty past six.' ◇ What's the time? ◇ Can you tell me the times of trains to Brighton, please?
2 (no plural) all the seconds, minutes, hours, days, weeks, months and years: Time passes quickly when you're busy.
3 (no plural) an amount of minutes, days, etc: They have lived here for a long time. ◇ I haven't got time to help you now – I'm late for school. ◇ It takes a long time to learn a language.
4 (plural **times**) a certain moment or occasion: I've seen this film four times. ◇ Come and visit us next time you're in England.
5 (plural **times**) experience; something that you do: We had a great time on holiday.
6 (plural **times**) certain years in history: In Shakespeare's times, not many people could read.

at a time together; on one occasion: The lift can carry six people at a time.

at one time in the past, but not now: We were in the same class at one time.

at the time then: My family moved to London in 1986 – I was four at the time.

at times sometimes: A teacher's job can be very difficult at times.

by the time when: By the time we arrived they had eaten all the food.

for the time being now, but not for long: You can stay here for the time being, until you find a flat.

from time to time sometimes; not often: I see my cousin from time to time.

have a good time enjoy yourself: Have a good time at the party!

in a week's, etc time after a week, etc: I'll see you in a month's time.

in good time at the right time or early: I want to get to the station in good time.

in time **1** not late: If you hurry, you'll arrive in time for the film. **2** at some time in the future: You will find speaking English easier in time.

it's about time words that you use to say that something should be done now: It's about time you started studying if you want to pass the exam.

it's time to it is the right time to do something: It's time to go home.

on time not late or early: My train was on time.

spend time use time to do something: I spend a lot of time playing tennis.

take your time do something slowly

tell the time read the time from a clock or watch: Can your children tell the time?

time after time, time and time again many times

time² /taɪm/ verb (**times, timing, timed** /taɪmd/)
1 plan something so that it will happen when you want: The bomb was timed to explode at six o'clock.
2 measure how much time it takes to do something: We timed the journey – it took half an hour.

times /taɪmz/ noun (plural)
a word that you use to show how much bigger, smaller, more expensive, etc one thing is than another thing: Edinburgh is five times bigger than Oxford.

times preposition
multiplied by: Three times four is twelve.

timetable /'taɪmteɪbl/ noun
a list of times when something happens: A train timetable shows when trains arrive and leave. ◇ A school timetable shows when lessons start.

timid /'tɪmɪd/ adjective
shy and easily frightened
timidly adverb
She opened the door timidly and came in.

tin /tɪn/ noun
1 (no plural) a soft white metal
2 (plural **tins**) a metal container for food and drink that keeps it fresh: I opened a tin of beans. ☞ picture at **container**
tinned /tɪnd/ adjective
in a tin so that it will stay fresh: tinned peaches
tin-opener /'tɪn əʊpənə(r)/ noun
a tool for opening tins

tiny /'taɪni/ adjective (**tinier, tiniest**)
very small: Ants are tiny insects.

tip¹ /tɪp/ noun
the pointed or thin end of something: the tips of your fingers

tip² /tɪp/ verb (**tips, tipping, tipped** /tɪpt/)
give a small, extra amount of money to somebody who has done a job for you, for

p	b	t	d	k	g	tʃ	dʒ	f	v	θ	ð
pen	bad	tea	did	cat	got	chain	jam	fall	van	thin	this

example a waiter or a taxi-driver: *Do you tip hairdressers in your country?*
tip *noun*
I left a tip on the table.

tip[3] /tɪp/ *noun*
a small piece of advice: *She gave me some useful tips on how to pass the exam.*

tip[4] /tɪp/ *verb* (**tips**, **tipping**, **tipped** /tɪpt/)
1 move so that one side goes up or down; move something so that one side goes up or down: *Don't tip your chair back.*
2 turn something so that the things inside fall out: *She opened a tin of beans and tipped them into a bowl.*
tip over turn over; make something turn over: *The boat tipped over and we all fell in the water.* ◇ *Don't tip your drink over!*

tiptoe /'tɪptəʊ/ *verb* (**tiptoes**, **tiptoeing**, **tiptoed** /'tɪptəʊd/)
walk quietly on your toes: *He tiptoed into the bedroom.*
on tiptoe on your toes: *She walked on tiptoe.*

tire *American English for* **tyre**

tired /'taɪəd/ *adjective*
If you are tired, you need to rest or sleep: *I've been working all day and I'm really tired.* ◇ *He's feeling tired.*
be tired of something have had or done too much of something, so that you do not want it any longer: *I'm tired of watching TV – let's go out.*
tiring /'taɪərɪŋ/ *adjective*
If something is tiring, it makes you tired: *a tiring journey*

tissue /'tɪʃuː/ *noun*
a thin piece of soft paper that you use as a handkerchief: *a box of tissues*
tissue-paper /'tɪʃuː peɪpə(r)/ *noun* (no plural)
thin paper that you use for wrapping things

title /'taɪtl/ *noun*
1 the name of something, for example a book, film or picture: *What is the title of this poem?*
2 a word like 'Mr', 'Mrs' or 'Doctor' that you put in front of a person's name

to[1] /tə/, /tu/, /tuː/ *preposition*
1 a word that shows where somebody or something is going, etc: *She went to Italy.*

◇ *James has gone to school.* ◇ *I gave the book to Paula.* ◇ *He sent a letter to his parents.* ◇ *Be kind to animals.*
2 a word that shows how many minutes before the hour: *It's two minutes to six.* ☞ Look at page 164.
3 a word that shows the last or the highest time, price, etc: *The museum is open from 9.30 to 5.30.* ◇ *Jeans cost from £20 to £45.*
4 on or against something: *He put his hands to his ears.*
5 a word that shows how something changes: *The sky changed from blue to grey.*
6 a word that shows why: *I came to help.*
7 a word that you use for comparing things: *I prefer football to tennis.*

to[2] /tə/, /tu/
a word that you use before verbs to make the **infinitive**: *I want to go home.* ◇ *Don't forget to write.* ◇ *She asked me to go but I didn't want to* (= to go).

toad /təʊd/ *noun*
an animal like a big frog, with a rough skin

toast[1] /təʊst/ *noun* (no plural)
a thin piece of bread that you have cooked so that it is brown: *I had a slice of toast and jam for breakfast.*
toast *verb* (**toasts**, **toasting**, **toasted**)
cook bread to make it brown: *toasted sandwiches*
toaster *noun*
a machine for making toast

toast[2] /təʊst/ *verb* (**toasts**, **toasting**, **toasted**)
hold up a glass of wine and wish somebody happiness or success before you drink: *We all toasted the bride and groom* (at a wedding).
toast *noun*
They drank a toast to the Queen.

tobacco /tə'bækəʊ/ *noun* (no plural)
special dried leaves that people smoke in cigarettes, cigars and pipes

today /tə'deɪ/ *adverb, noun* (no plural)
1 (on) this day: *What shall we do today?* ◇ *Today is Friday.*
2 (at) the present time; now: *Most families in Britain today have a car.*

s	z	ʃ	ʒ	h	m	n	ŋ	l	r	j	w
so	**zoo**	**sh**oe	vi**s**ion	**h**at	**m**an	**no**	si**ng**	**l**eg	**r**ed	**y**es	**w**et

toe /təʊ/ *noun*
1 one of the five parts at the end of your
foot ☞ picture on page 126
2 the part of a shoe or sock that covers the
end of your foot
toenail /'təʊneɪl/ *noun*
the hard part at the end of your toe ☞ picture on page 126

toffee /'tɒfi/ *noun*
hard brown sweet food made from sugar,
butter and water

together /tə'geðə(r)/ *adverb*
1 with each other or close to each other:
*John and Lisa usually walk home to-
gether.* ◇ *Stand with your feet together.*
◇ *They live together.*
2 so that they are joined to or mixed with
each other: *Tie the ends of the rope together.* ◇ *Add these numbers together.*
◇ *Mix the eggs and sugar together.*

toilet /'tɔɪlət/ *noun*
a large bowl with a seat, that you use
when you need to empty waste from your
body. The room that it is in is also called a
toilet: *I'm going to the toilet.*
toilet paper /'tɔɪlət peɪpə(r)/ *noun* (no
plural)
paper that you use in the toilet
toilet roll /'tɔɪlət rəʊl/ *noun*
a roll of paper that you use in the toilet

token /'təʊkən/ *noun*
1 a small thing that you use to show
something else: *This gift is a token of our
friendship.*
2 a piece of paper, plastic or metal that
you use instead of money to pay for something: *a book token*

told *form of* **tell**

tolerant /'tɒlərənt/ *adjective*
If you are tolerant, you let people do things
although you may not like or understand
them: *You need to be very tolerant with
young children.* ❍ opposite: **intolerant**
tolerance /'tɒlərəns/ *noun* (no plural)
tolerance of other religions ❍ opposite:
intolerance

tolerate /'tɒləreɪt/ *verb* (**tolerates, tol-
erating, tolerated**)
let people do something that you may not
like or understand: *He won't tolerate
rudeness.*

tomato
/tə'mɑːtəʊ/ *noun*
(*plural* **tomatoes**)
a soft red fruit that
you cook or eat in
salads: *tomato soup*

tomato

tomb /tuːm/ *noun*
a thing made of
stone where a dead person's body is buried

tomorrow /tə'mɒrəʊ/ *adverb, noun*
(no plural)
(on) the day after today: *Let's go swimming tomorrow.* ◇ *I'll see you tomorrow
morning.* ◇ *We are going home the day
after tomorrow.*

ton /tʌn/ *noun*
1 a measure of weight (= 1.016 kilograms). There are 2 240 **pounds** in a ton.
❍ In the USA, a ton is 2 000 pounds.
2 **tons** (plural) a lot: *He's got tons of
money.*

tone /təʊn/ *noun*
how something sounds: *I knew he was
angry by the tone of his voice.*

tongue /tʌŋ/ *noun*
the soft part inside your mouth that moves
when you talk or eat
tongue-twister /'tʌŋ ˌtwɪstə(r)/ *noun*
words that are difficult to say together
quickly: *'Red lorry, yellow lorry' is a
tongue-twister.*

tonight /tə'naɪt/ *adverb, noun* (no
plural)
(on) the evening or night of today: *I'm going to a party tonight.*

tonne /tʌn/ *noun*
a measure of weight. There are 1 000 **kilograms** in a tonne.

too /tuː/ *adverb*
1 also; as well: *Green is my favourite colour but I like blue too.*
2 more than you want or need: *These
shoes are too big.* ◇ *She put too much
milk in my coffee.*

took *form of* **take**

tool /tuːl/ *noun*
a thing that you hold in your hand and use
to do a special job: *Hammers and saws are
tools.*

tooth /tuːθ/ *noun* (*plural* **teeth** /tiːθ/)
1 one of the hard white things in your

mouth that you use for eating: *I brush my teeth after every meal.*

⊕ A **dentist** is a person whose job is to look after teeth. If a tooth is bad, the dentist may **fill** it or **take** it **out**. People who have lost their own teeth can wear **false teeth**.

2 one of the long sharp parts of a comb or saw

toothache /'tu:θeɪk/ *noun* (no plural)
a pain in your tooth: *I've got toothache.*

toothbrush /'tu:θbrʌʃ/ *noun* (*plural* **toothbrushes**)
a small brush for cleaning your teeth

toothpaste /'tu:θpeɪst/ *noun* (no plural)
stuff that you put on your toothbrush and use for cleaning your teeth

top¹ /tɒp/ *noun*
1 the highest part of something: *There's a church at the top of the hill.*
2 a cover that you put on something to close it: *Where's the top of this jar?*
3 a piece of clothing that you wear on the top part of your body
on top on its highest part: *The cake had cream on top.*
on top of something on or over something: *A tree fell on top of my car.*

top² /tɒp/ *adjective*
highest: *Put this book on the top shelf.*

topic /'tɒpɪk/ *noun*
something that you talk, learn or write about; a subject: *The topic of the discussion was war.*

torch /tɔ:tʃ/ *noun*
(*plural* **torches**)
a small electric light
that you can carry

torch

tore, **torn** *forms of* **tear²**

tortoise

tortoise /'tɔ:təs/ *noun*
an animal with a hard shell on its back, that moves very slowly

torture /'tɔ:tʃə(r)/ *verb* (**tortures**, **torturing**, **tortured** /'tɔ:tʃəd/)
make somebody feel great pain, often to make them give information: *They tortured her until she told them her name.*

torture *noun* (no plural)
the torture of prisoners

the Tory Party /ðə 'tɔ:ri pɑ:ti/ *another word for* **the Conservative Party**

toss /tɒs/ *verb* (**tosses**, **tossing**, **tossed** /tɒst/)
1 throw something quickly and without care: *I tossed the paper into the bin.*
2 move quickly up and down or from side to side; make something do this: *The boat tossed around on the big waves.*
3 decide something by throwing a coin in the air and seeing which side shows when it falls: *We tossed a coin to see who would pay for the meal.*

total¹ /'təʊtl/ *adjective*
complete; if you count everything or everybody: *There was total silence in the classroom.* ◇ *What was the total number of people at the meeting?*

totally /'təʊtəli/ *adverb*
completely: *I totally agree.*

total² /'təʊtl/ *noun*
the number you have when you add everything together

touch¹ /tʌtʃ/ *verb* (**touches**, **touching**, **touched** /tʌtʃt/)
1 put your hand or finger on somebody or something: *Don't touch the paint – it's still wet.* ◇ *He touched me on the arm.*
2 be so close to another thing or person that there is no space in between: *The two wires were touching.* ◇ *Her coat was so long that it touched the ground.*

touch² /tʌtʃ/ *noun*
1 (*plural* **touches**) when a hand or finger is put on somebody or something: *I felt the touch of his hand on my arm.*
2 (no plural) the feeling in your hands and skin that tells you about something: *He can't see, but he can read by touch.*
be or **keep in touch with somebody** meet, telephone or write to somebody often: *Are you still in touch with Kevin?* ◇ *Let's keep in touch.*
get in touch with somebody write to, or telephone somebody: *I'm trying to get in touch with my cousin.*
lose touch with somebody stop meeting, telephoning or writing to somebody: *I've lost touch with all my old friends from school.*

tough /tʌf/ adjective (**tougher, toughest**)
1 difficult to tear or break; strong: Leather is tougher than paper.
2 difficult: This is a tough job.
3 If meat is tough, it is difficult to cut and eat. ✪ opposite: **tender**
4 very strong in your body: You need to be tough to go climbing in winter.
5 strict or firm: a tough leader

tour /tʊə(r)/ noun
1 a short visit to see a building or city: They gave us a tour of the house.
2 a journey to see a lot of different places: We went on a tour of Scotland.
tour verb (**tours, touring, toured** /tʊəd/)
We toured France for three weeks.

tourism /'tʊərɪzəm/ noun (no plural)
arranging holidays for people: This country earns a lot of money from tourism.

tourist /'tʊərɪst/ noun
a person who visits a place on holiday

tournament /'tɔːnəmənt/ noun
a sports competition with a lot of players or teams: a tennis tournament

tow /təʊ/ verb (**tows, towing, towed** /təʊd/)
pull a car, etc using a rope or chain: My car was towed to a garage.

towards /tə'wɔːdz/, **toward** /tə'wɔːd/ preposition
1 in the direction of somebody or something: We walked towards the river. ◊ I couldn't see her face – she had her back towards me. ☞ picture on page 128
2 to somebody or something: The people in the village are always very friendly towards tourists.
3 at a time near: Let's meet towards the end of the week.
4 to help pay for something: I bought Sam's birthday present and Tom gave me £5 towards it.

towel /'taʊəl/ noun
a piece of cloth that you use for drying yourself: I washed my hands and dried them on a towel.

tower /'taʊə(r)/ noun
a tall narrow building or a tall part of a building: the Eiffel Tower ◊ a church tower

tower block /'taʊə(r) blɒk/ noun
a very tall building with a lot of flats or offices inside

town /taʊn/ noun
a place where there are a lot of houses and other buildings: Banbury is a town near Oxford. ◊ I'm going into town to do some shopping.
✪ A town is bigger than a **village** but smaller than a **city**.

town hall /ˌtaʊn 'hɔːl/ noun
a building with offices for people who control a town

toy /tɔɪ/ noun
a thing for a child to play with

trace¹ /treɪs/ noun
a mark or sign that shows that somebody or something has been in a place: The police could not find any trace of the missing child.

trace² /treɪs/ verb (**traces, tracing, traced** /treɪst/)
1 look for and find somebody or something: The police have traced the stolen car.
2 put thin paper over a picture and draw over the lines to make a copy

track¹ /træk/ noun
1 a rough path or road: We drove along a track through the woods.
2 **tracks** (plural) a line of marks that an animal, a person or a vehicle makes on the ground: We saw his tracks in the snow.
3 the metal lines that a train runs on
4 a special road for races
5 one song or piece of music on a cassette, compact disc or record

track² /træk/ verb (**tracks, tracking, tracked** /trækt/)
follow signs or marks to find somebody or something
track down find somebody or something after looking: I finally tracked her down.

track suit /'træk suːt/ noun
a special jacket and trousers that you wear for sport

tractor /'træktə(r)/ noun
a big strong vehicle that people use on farms to pull heavy things

p	b	t	d	k	g	tʃ	dʒ	f	v	θ	ð
pen	**bad**	**tea**	**did**	**cat**	**got**	**chain**	**jam**	**fall**	**van**	**thin**	**this**

tractor

trade¹ /treɪd/ *noun*
1 (no plural) the buying and selling of things: *trade between Britain and the USA*
2 (*plural* **trades**) a job: *Dave is a plumber by trade.*

trade² /treɪd/ *verb* (**trades, trading, traded**)
buy and sell things: *Japan trades with many different countries.*

trade mark /'treɪd mɑːk/ *noun*
a special mark or name that a company puts on the things it makes and that other companies must not use

trade union /ˌtreɪd 'juːnɪən/ *noun*
a group of workers who have joined together to talk to their managers about things like pay and the way they work

tradition /trə'dɪʃn/ *noun*
something that people in a certain place have done or believed for a long time: *In Britain it's a tradition to give chocolate eggs at Easter.*
traditional /trə'dɪʃənl/ *adjective*
traditional English food
traditionally /trə'dɪʃənəli/ *adverb*
Driving trains was traditionally a man's job.

traffic /'træfɪk/ *noun* (no plural)
all the cars, etc that are on a road: *There was a lot of traffic on the way to work this morning.*
traffic jam /'træfɪk dʒæm/ *noun*
a long line of cars, etc that cannot move very fast
traffic-lights /'træfɪk laɪts/ *noun* (plural)
lights that change from red to orange to green to tell cars, etc when to stop and start
traffic warden /'træfɪk wɔːdn/ *noun*
a person who checks that cars park in the right places and for the right time

tragedy /'trædʒədi/ *noun* (*plural* **tragedies**)
1 a very sad thing that happens: *The child's death was a tragedy.*
2 a serious and sad play: *Shakespeare's 'King Lear' is a tragedy.*

tragic /'trædʒɪk/ *adjective*
very sad: *a tragic accident*
tragically /'trædʒɪkli/ *adverb*
He died tragically at the age of 25.

trail¹ /treɪl/ *noun*
1 a line of marks that show which way a person or thing has gone: *There was a trail of blood from the cut in her leg.*
2 a path in the country: *We followed the trail through the forest.*

trail² /treɪl/ *verb* (**trails, trailing, trailed** /treɪld/)
pull something along behind you; be pulled along behind somebody or something: *Her long hair trailed behind her in the wind.*

trailer /'treɪlə(r)/ *noun*
1 a vehicle with no engine that a car or lorry pulls along
2 a short piece from a film that shows you what it is like

train

train¹ /treɪn/ *noun*
carriages or wagons that are pulled by an engine along a railway line: *I'm going to Bristol by train.*
catch a train get on a train to go somewhere: *We caught the 7.15 train to Leeds.*
change trains go from one train to another: *You have to change trains at Reading.*

✪ You get **on** and **off** trains at a **station**. A **goods train** or a **freight train** carries things and a **passenger train** carries people.

train² /treɪn/ *verb* (**trains, training, trained** /treɪnd/)
1 teach a person or an animal to do something: *He was trained as a pilot.*
2 make yourself ready for something by

studying or doing something a lot: *Ann is training to be a doctor.* ◇ *He goes running every morning – he's training for the race.*

trainers

trainer /'treɪnə(r)/ *noun*
1 a person who teaches other people to do a sport
2 a person who teaches animals to do something
3 a soft shoe that you wear for running

training /'treɪnɪŋ/ *noun* (no plural)
getting ready for a sport or job: *She is in training for the Olympic Games.*

traitor /'treɪtə(r)/ *noun*
a person who harms his/her country or friends to help another person or country

tram /træm/ *noun*
an electric bus that goes along rails in a town

tramp /træmp/ *noun*
a person with no home or job, who goes from place to place

trample /'træmpl/ *verb* (**tramples, trampling, trampled** /'træmpld/)
walk on something and push it down with your feet: *Don't trample on the flowers!*

transfer /træns'fɜ:(r)/ *verb* (**transfers, transferring, transferred** /træns'fɜ:d/)
move somebody or something to a different place: *I want to transfer £500 to my bank account in Spain.*
transfer /'trænsfɜ:(r)/ *noun*
Keiko wants a transfer to another class.

transform /træns'fɔ:m/ *verb* (**transforms, transforming, transformed** /træns'fɔ:md/)
change somebody or something so that they are or look completely different: *Electricity has transformed people's lives.*
transformation /,trænsfə'meɪʃn/ *noun*
a complete change

transistor /træn'zɪstə(r)/ *noun*
a small part inside something electrical, for example a radio or television

translate /træns'leɪt/ *verb* (**translates, translating, translated**)
say or write in one language what somebody has said or written in another language: *This letter is in German – can you translate it into English for me?*
translation /træns'leɪʃn/ *noun*
1 (no plural) translating: *translation from English into French*
2 (*plural* **translations**) something that somebody has translated
translator /træns'leɪtə(r)/ *noun*
a person who translates

transparent /træns'pærənt/ *adjective*
If something is transparent, you can see through it: *Glass is transparent.*

transport /'trænspɔ:t/ *noun* (no plural)
a way of carrying people or things from one place to another: *road transport* ◇ *I travel to school by public transport* (= bus or train).
transport /træn'spɔ:t/ *verb* (**transports, transporting, transported**)
carry people or things from one place to another: *The goods were transported by air.*

trap /træp/ *noun*
1 a thing that you use for catching animals: *The rabbit's leg was caught in a trap.*
2 a plan to trick somebody: *I knew the question was a trap, so I didn't answer it.*
trap *verb* (**traps, trapping, trapped** /træpt/)
1 keep somebody in a place that they cannot escape from: *They were trapped in the burning building.*
2 catch or trick somebody or something

trash /træʃ/ *American English for* **rubbish**
trash can /'træʃ kæn/ *American English for* **dustbin**

travel /'trævl/ *verb* (**travels**, **travelling, travelled** /'trævld/)
go from one place to another: *I would like to travel round the world.* ◇ *I travel to school by bus.* ◇ *She travelled 800 km in one day.* ○ In American English the spellings are **traveling** and **traveled**.
travel *noun* (no plural)
travelling: *My hobbies are music and travel.*
travel agency /'trævl eɪdʒənsi/ *noun* (*plural* **travel agencies**)

a company that plans holidays and journeys for people

travel agent /'trævl eɪdʒənt/ *noun*
a person who works in a travel agency

traveler *American English for* **traveller**

traveller /'trævələ(r)/ *noun*
a person who is travelling
traveller's cheque /'trævələz tʃek/ *noun*
a special cheque that you can use when you go to other countries

tray /treɪ/ *noun*
a flat thing that you use for carrying food or drinks

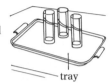
tray

tread /tred/ *verb*
(**treads, treading, trod** /trɒd/, **has trodden** /'trɒdn/)
put your foot down: *He trod on my foot.*

treasure /'treʒə(r)/ *noun*
gold, silver, jewels or other things that are worth a lot of money

treasurer /'treʒərə(r)/ *noun*
a person who looks after the money of a club or a group of people

treat¹ /triːt/ *verb* (**treats, treating, treated**)
1 behave towards somebody or something: *How does your boss treat you?* ◇ *Treat these glasses with care.*
2 try to make a sick person well again: *The doctor is treating him for cancer.*
treat something as something
think about something in a certain way: *They treated my idea as a joke.*

treat² /triːt/ *noun*
something very special that makes somebody happy: *My parents took me to the theatre as a treat for my birthday.*

treatment /'triːtmənt/ *noun*
1 (no plural) the way that you behave towards somebody or something: *Their treatment of the animals was very cruel.*
2 (*plural* **treatments**) the things that a doctor does to try to make a sick person well again: *a treatment for cancer*

treaty /'triːti/ *noun* (*plural* **treaties**)
an agreement between countries: *The two countries signed a peace treaty.*

tree /triː/ *noun*
a big tall plant with a trunk, branches and

tree
leaf
trunk — branch — twig

leaves: *an oak tree* ◇ *Apples grow on trees.*

tremble /'trembl/ *verb* (**trembles, trembling, trembled** /'trembld/)
shake, for example because you are cold, afraid or ill: *She was trembling with fear.*

tremendous /trə'mendəs/ *adjective*
1 very big or very great: *The new trains travel at a tremendous speed.*
2 very good: *The match was tremendous.*
tremendously *adverb*
very or very much: *The film was tremendously exciting.*

trench /trentʃ/ *noun* (*plural* **trenches**)
a long narrow hole that you make in the ground

trend /trend/ *noun*
a change to something different: *new trends in science*

trespass /'trespəs/ *verb* (**trespasses, trespassing, trespassed** /'trespəst/)
go on somebody's land without asking them if you can: *A sign on the gate of the big house said 'No Trespassing'.*
trespasser *noun*
a person who trespasses

trial /'traɪəl/ *noun*
1 the time when a person is in a **court of law** so that people (the **judge** and **jury**) can decide if he/she has done something wrong and what the punishment will be
2 using something to see if it is good or bad: *trials of a new drug*
on trial 1 in a court of law so that people can decide if you have done something wrong: *She was on trial for murder.* **2** If you have something on trial, you are using it to decide if you like it, before you buy it: *We've got the car on trial for a week.*

triangle /'traɪæŋgl/ noun
a shape with three straight sides ☞ picture on page 161
triangular /traɪ'æŋgjələ(r)/ adjective
with the shape of a triangle

tribe /traɪb/ noun
a small group of people who have the same language and customs: the Zulu tribes of Africa
tribal /'traɪbl/ adjective
tribal dances

tribute /'trɪbjuːt/ noun
something that you do, say or give to show that you respect or admire somebody: They built a statue in London as a tribute to Nelson Mandela.

trick¹ /trɪk/ noun
1 a clever plan that makes somebody believe something that is not true: He got the money from me by a trick.
2 something that you do to make somebody seem stupid: The children hid their teacher's books to play a trick on her.
3 something clever that you have learned to do: card tricks

trick² /trɪk/ verb (tricks, tricking, tricked /trɪkt/)
do something that is not honest to get what you want from somebody: He tricked the old lady so that she gave him all her money.

trickle /'trɪkl/ verb (trickles, trickling, trickled /'trɪkld/)
move slowly like a thin line of water: Tears trickled down her cheeks.
trickle noun
a trickle of blood

tricky /'trɪki/ adjective (trickier, trickiest)
difficult; hard to do: a tricky question

tricycle /'traɪsɪkl/ noun
a thing like a bicycle with three wheels

tried form of try

tries
1 form of try
2 plural of try

trigger /'trɪgə(r)/ noun
the part of a gun that you pull with your finger to fire it

trim /trɪm/ verb (trims, trimming, trimmed /trɪmd/)
cut something to make it tidy: He trimmed my hair.
trim noun
My hair needs a trim.

trip¹ /trɪp/ noun
a short journey to a place and back again: We went on a trip to the mountains.

trip² /trɪp/ verb (trips, tripping, tripped /trɪpt/)
hit your foot against something so that you fall or nearly fall: She tripped over the step.
trip up make somebody fall or nearly fall: Gary put out his foot and tripped me up.

triple /'trɪpl/ adjective
with three parts: the triple jump
triple verb (triples, tripling, tripled /'trɪpld/)
become or make something three times bigger: Sales have tripled this year.

triumph /'traɪʌmf/ noun
great success; winning: The race ended in triumph for the German team.

trivial /'trɪviəl/ adjective
not important: She gets angry about trivial things.

trod, trodden forms of tread

trolleys

trolley /'trɒli/ noun (plural trolleys)
a thing on wheels that you use for carrying things: a supermarket trolley

trombone /trɒm'bəʊn/ noun
a large musical instrument. You play it by blowing and moving a long tube up and down.

troops /truːps/ noun (plural)
soldiers

trophy /'trəʊfi/ noun (plural trophies)
a thing, for example a silver cup, that you get when you win a competition: a tennis trophy

p	b	t	d	k	g	tʃ	dʒ	f	v	θ	ð
pen	**b**ad	**t**ea	**d**id	**c**at	**g**ot	**ch**ain	**j**am	**f**all	**v**an	**th**in	**th**is

the tropics /ðə ˈtrɒpɪks/ *noun* (plural)
the very hot part of the world
tropical /ˈtrɒpɪkl/ *adjective*
of or from the tropics: *tropical fruit*

trot /trɒt/ *verb* (**trots, trotting, trotted**)
run with short quick steps: *The horse trotted along the road.*

trouble¹ /ˈtrʌbl/ *noun*
1 (*plural* **troubles**) difficulty, problems or worry: *We had a lot of trouble finding the book you wanted.* ◇ *She told me all her troubles.*
2 (no plural) extra work: *'Thanks for your help!' 'Oh, it was no trouble.'*
3 (*plural* **troubles**) when people are fighting or arguing: *There was a lot of trouble after the football match last Saturday.*
4 (no plural) pain or illness: *He's got heart trouble.*
be in trouble have problems, for example because you have done something wrong: *I'll be in trouble if I get home late.* ◇ *He's in trouble with the police.*
get into trouble do something that brings problems because it is wrong: *You'll get into trouble if you park your car here.*
go to a lot of trouble do extra work: *They went to a lot of trouble to help me.*

trouble² /ˈtrʌbl/ *verb* (**troubles, troubling, troubled** /ˈtrʌbld/)
worry somebody; bring somebody problems or pain: *I was troubled by the news.* ◇ *I'm sorry to trouble you, but you're sitting in my seat.*

trough /trɒf/ *noun*
a long open box that holds food or water for animals

trousers /ˈtraʊzəz/ *noun* (plural)
a piece of clothing for your legs and the lower part of your body: *Your trousers are on the chair.* ☞ picture at **suit**
❸ Be careful! You cannot say 'a trousers'. You can say **a pair of trousers**: *I bought a new pair of trousers.* (or: *I bought some new trousers.*)

trout /traʊt/ *noun* (*plural* **trout**)
a fish that lives in rivers and that you can eat

truant /ˈtruːənt/ *noun*
a child who stays away from school when he/she should be there
play truant stay away from school

truce /truːs/ *noun*
when people or groups agree to stop fighting for a short time

truck /trʌk/ *noun*
1 a big vehicle for carrying heavy things: *a truck driver*
2 an open part of a train where heavy things are carried

true /truː/ *adjective*
1 right or correct: *Is it true that you are leaving?* ◇ *Glasgow is in England: true or false?*
2 that really happened: *It's a true story.*
3 real: *A true friend will always help you.*
❸ The noun is **truth**.
come true happen in the way that you hoped: *Her dream came true.*

truly /ˈtruːli/ *adverb*
really: *I'm truly sorry.*
Yours truly words that you can use at the end of a formal letter

trumpet

trumpet /ˈtrʌmpɪt/ *noun*
a musical instrument that you blow

trunk /trʌŋk/ *noun*
1 the thick part of a tree, that grows up from the ground ☞ picture at **tree**
2 a big strong box for carrying things when you travel
3 an elephant's long nose ☞ picture at **elephant**
4 *American English for* **boot 2**

trunks /trʌŋks/ *noun* (plural)
short trousers that a man or boy wears for swimming

trust¹ /trʌst/ *noun* (no plural)
feeling sure that somebody or something will do what they should do; feeling that somebody is honest and good: *Put your trust in God.*

trust² /trʌst/ *verb* (**trusts, trusting, trusted**)
feel sure that somebody or something will

do what they should do; believe that somebody is honest and good: *You can't trust him with money.* ◇ *You can trust Penny to do the job well.*

trustworthy /'trʌstwɜ:ði/ *adjective*
A trustworthy person is somebody that you can trust.

truth /tru:θ/ *noun* (no plural)
being true; what is true: *There is no truth in what he says – he is lying.* ◇ *We need to find out the truth about what happened.*
tell the truth say what is true: *Are you telling me the truth?*

truthful /'tru:θfl/ *adjective*
1 true: *a truthful answer*
2 A person who is truthful tells the truth.
truthfully /'tru:θfəli/ *adverb*
You must answer me truthfully.

try /traɪ/ *verb* (**tries, trying, tried** /traɪd/, **has tried**)
1 work hard to do something: *I tried to remember her name but I couldn't.* ◇ *I'm not sure if I can help you but I'll try.*
2 use or do something to find out if you like it: *Have you ever tried Japanese food?*
3 ask somebody questions in a court of law to decide if they have done something wrong: *He was tried for murder.*
try and do something try to do something: *I'll try and come early tomorrow.*
try on put on a piece of clothing to see if you like it and if it is big enough: *I tried the jeans on but they were too small.*
try *noun* (*plural* **tries**)
I can't open this door – will you have a try?

T-shirt

T-shirt /'ti: ʃɜ:t/ *noun*
a kind of shirt with short sleeves and no collar

tub /tʌb/ *noun*
a round container: *a tub of ice-cream*
☞ picture at **container**

tube /tju:b/ *noun*
1 a long thin pipe for liquid or gas
2 a long thin soft container with a hole

and a cap at one end: *a tube of toothpaste*
☞ picture at **container**
3 the underground railway in London: *Shall we go by bus or by tube?*

tuck /tʌk/ *verb* (**tucks, tucking, tucked** /tʌkt/)
put or push the edges of something inside or under something else: *He tucked his shirt into his trousers.*

Tuesday /'tju:zdeɪ/ *noun*
the third day of the week, next after Monday

tuft /tʌft/ *noun*
a group of hairs, grass, etc growing together

tug /tʌg/ *verb* (**tugs, tugging, tugged** /tʌgd/)
pull something hard and quickly: *I tugged at the rope and it broke.*
tug *noun*
1 a sudden hard pull: *The little girl gave my hand a tug.*
2 a small strong boat that pulls big ships

tuition /tju'ɪʃn/ *noun* (no plural)
teaching: *A lot of students have extra tuition before their exams.*

tulip /'tju:lɪp/ *noun*
a flower that comes in spring

tumble /'tʌmbl/ *verb* (**tumbles, tumbling, tumbled** /'tʌmbld/)
fall suddenly: *He tumbled down the steps.*

tummy /'tʌmi/ *noun* (*plural* **tummies**)
the part of your body between your chest and your legs; your stomach

tuna /'tju:nə/ *noun* (*plural* **tuna**)
a large fish that lives in the sea and that you can eat

tune /tju:n/ *noun*
a group of musical notes that make a nice sound when you play or sing them together: *I know the tune but I don't know the words.*
tune *verb* (**tunes, tuning, tuned** /tju:nd/)
do something to a musical instrument so that it makes the right sounds: *She tuned the piano.*

tunnel /'tʌnl/ *noun*
a long hole under the ground or sea for a road or railway ☞ picture on next page

turban /'tɜ:bən/ *noun*
a long piece of material that you put round and round your head

i:	i	ɪ	e	æ	ɑ:	ɒ	ɔ:	ʊ	u	u:
see	happy	sit	ten	cat	father	got	saw	put	situation	too

tunnel

turkey /'tɜːki/ *noun* (*plural* **turkeys**)
a big bird that people keep on farms and that you can eat. In Britain, people often eat turkeys at Christmas.

turn¹ /tɜːn/ *verb* (**turns**, **turning**, **turned** /tɜːnd/)
1 move round, or move something round: *The wheels are turning.* ◊ *Turn the key.* ◊ *She turned round and walked towards the door.*
2 move in a different direction: *Turn left at the traffic-lights.*
3 become different: *The weather has turned cold.*
4 make somebody or something change: *The sun turned her hair blond.*
5 find a certain page in a book: *Turn to page 97.*
turn down 1 say no to what somebody wants to do or to give you: *They offered me the job but I turned it down.* **2** move the switch that controls something like a radio or a heater so that it makes less sound, heat, etc: *I'm too hot – can you turn the heating down?*
turn into something become different; change somebody or something into something different: *Water turns into ice when it gets very cold.*
turn off move the handle, switch, etc that controls something, so that it stops: *Turn the tap off.* ◊ *Turn off the television.*
turn on move the handle, switch, etc that controls something, so that it starts: *Could you turn the light on?*
turn out be something in the end: *It rained this morning, but it has turned out to be a lovely day.*
turn out a light switch off a light
turn over move so that the other side is on top: *If you turn over the page you'll find the answers on the other side.*
turn up 1 arrive: *Has David turned up yet?* **2** move the switch that controls something like a radio or a heater so that it

makes more sound, heat, etc: *Turn up the television – I can't hear it properly.*

turn² /tɜːn/ *noun*
1 turning something round: *Give the screw a few turns.*
2 a change of direction: *Take a left turn at the end of this road.*
3 the time when you can or should do something: *It's your turn to do the washing-up!*
in turn one after the other: *I spoke to each of the students in turn.*
take turns at something, take it in turns to do something do something one after the other: *You can't both use the computer at the same time. Why don't you take it in turns?*

turning /'tɜːnɪŋ/ *noun*
a place where one road joins another road: *Take the first turning on the right.*

turnip /'tɜːnɪp/ *noun*
a round white vegetable that grows under the ground

turquoise /'tɜːkwɔɪz/ *adjective*
with a colour between blue and green

turtle /'tɜːtl/ *noun*
an animal that lives in the sea and has a hard shell on its back

tusk /tʌsk/ *noun*
a long pointed tooth that grows beside the mouth of an elephant ☞ picture at **elephant**

tutor /'tjuːtə(r)/ *noun*
a teacher who teaches one person or a small group

TV /ˌtiː 'viː/ *short for* **television**

tweezers /'twiːzəz/ *noun* (plural)
a small tool made of two pieces of metal joined at one end. You use tweezers for holding or pulling out very small things: *She pulled the splinter out of her finger with a pair of tweezers.*

twelve /twelv/ *number*
12
twelfth /twelfθ/ *adjective, adverb, noun*
12th

twenty /'twenti/ *number*
1 20
2 **the twenties** (plural) the numbers, years or temperature between 20 and 29
in your twenties between the ages of 20 and 29

ʌ	ɜː	ə	eɪ	əʊ	aɪ	aʊ	ɔɪ	ɪə	eə	ʊə
cup	bird	about	say	go	five	now	boy	near	hair	pure

twentieth /'twentiəθ/ *adjective, adverb, noun*
20th

twice /twaɪs/ *adverb*
two times: *I have been to Japan twice.* ◇ *He ate twice as much as I did.*

twig /twɪg/ *noun*
a small thin branch of a tree ☞ picture at **tree**

twilight /'twaɪlaɪt/ *noun* (no plural)
the time after the sun has gone down and before it gets completely dark

twin /twɪn/ *noun*
1 Twins are two people who have the same mother and who were born on the same day: *David and John are twins.* ◇ *I have got a twin sister.*
2 one of two things that are the same: *twin beds*

twinkle /'twɪŋkl/ *verb* (**twinkles, twinkling, twinkled** /'twɪŋkld/)
shine with a small bright light that comes and goes. *Stars twinkle.*

twist /twɪst/ *verb* (**twists, twisting, twisted**)
1 turn strongly: *Twist the lid off the jar.*
2 change the shape of something by turning it in different directions; turn in many different directions: *She twisted the metal into strange shapes.* ◇ *The path twists and turns through the forest.*
3 wind threads, etc round and round each other: *They twisted the sheets into a rope and escaped through the window.*

twitch /twɪtʃ/ *verb* (**twitches, twitching, twitched** /twɪtʃt/)
make a sudden quick movement with a part of your body: *Rabbits twitch their noses.*

two /tu:/ *number*
2
in two into two pieces: *The cup fell on the floor and broke in two.*

type[1] /taɪp/ *noun*
a group of things that are the same in some way; a sort or kind: *An almond is a type of nut.* ◇ *What type of music do you like?*

type[2] /taɪp/ *verb* (**types, typing, typed** /taɪpt/)
make words on paper with a **typewriter** or **word processor**: *Her secretary types all her letters.* ◇ *Can you type?*
type *noun* (no plural)
the letters that a machine makes on paper: *The type is too small – I can't read it.*

typewriter /'taɪpraɪtə(r)/ *noun*
a machine with keys that you use to make words on paper: *an electric typewriter*

typical /'tɪpɪkl/ *adjective*
Something that is typical is a good example of its kind: *We had a typical English breakfast - bacon, eggs, toast and tea.*
typically /'tɪpɪkli/ *adverb*
in a typical way: *She is typically British.*

tyrant /'taɪrənt/ *noun*
a person with a lot of power who rules a country in a cruel way
tyrannical /tɪ'rænɪkl/ *adjective*
a tyrannical ruler

tyre /'taɪə(r)/ *noun*
a circle of rubber around the outside of a wheel, for example on a car or bicycle: *I think we've got a flat tyre* (= a tyre without enough air inside). ☞ picture at **car** and **bicycle**

Uu

UFO /ˌju: ef 'əʊ/ *noun* (*plural* **UFOs**)
a strange object that some people think they have seen in the sky and that may come from another planet. UFO is short for 'unidentified flying object'.

ugly /'ʌgli/ *adjective* (**uglier, ugliest**)
not beautiful to look at: *an ugly face*

umbrella /ʌm'brelə/ *noun*
a thing that you hold over your head to keep you dry when it rains: *It started to rain, so I put my umbrella up.* ☞ picture on next page

umpire /'ʌmpaɪə(r)/ *noun*
a person who controls a tennis or cricket match

p	b	t	d	k	g	tʃ	dʒ	f	v	θ	ð
pen	**b**ad	**t**ea	**d**id	**c**at	**g**ot	**ch**ain	**j**am	**f**all	**v**an	**th**in	**th**is

umbrella

un- *prefix*
You can add **un-** to the beginning of some words to give them the opposite meaning, for example:
unhappy = not happy
untrue = not true
undress = take clothes off (the opposite of **dress**)

unable /ʌn'eɪbl/ *adjective*
not able to do something: *John is unable to come to the meeting because he is ill.*

unanimous /ju'nænɪməs/ *adjective*
with the agreement of every person: *The decision was unanimous.*

unarmed /ˌʌn'ɑ:md/ *adjective*
If you are unarmed, you do not have a gun or any weapon: *an unarmed police officer*

unavoidable /ˌʌnə'vɔɪdəbl/ *adjective*
If something is unavoidable, you cannot stop it or get away from it: *He had no money, so selling his car was unavoidable.*

unaware /ˌʌnə'weə(r)/ *adjective*
If you are unaware of something, you do not know about it: *I was unaware of the danger.*

unbearable /ʌn'beərəbl/ *adjective*
If something is unbearable, you cannot accept it because it is so bad: *Everyone left the room because the noise was unbearable.*
unbearably /ʌn'beərəbli/ *adverb*
It was unbearably hot.

unbelievable /ˌʌnbɪ'li:vəbl/ *adjective*
very surprising or difficult to believe

unborn /ˌʌn'bɔ:n/ *adjective*
not yet born: *an unborn child*

uncertain /ʌn'sɜ:tn/ *adjective*
not sure; not decided: *I'm uncertain about what to do.*
uncertainty /ʌn'sɜ:tnti/ *noun* (plural **uncertainties**)
not being sure: *There is uncertainty about who will be the next prime minister.*

uncle /'ʌŋkl/ *noun*
the brother of your mother or father, or the husband of your aunt: *Uncle Paul* ☞ picture on page 127

uncomfortable /ʌn'kʌmftəbl/ *adjective*
not comfortable: *The chair was hard and uncomfortable.*
uncomfortably /ʌn'kʌmftəbli/ *adverb*
The room was uncomfortably hot.

uncommon /ʌn'kɒmən/ *adjective*
not common; that you do not see, hear, etc often: *This tree is uncommon in Britain.*

unconscious /ʌn'kɒnʃəs/ *adjective*
1 If you are unconscious, you are in a kind of sleep and you do not know what is happening: *She fell and hit her head and she was unconscious for three days.*
2 If you are unconscious of something, you do not know about it: *Mike seemed unconscious that I was watching him.*
unconsciousness /ʌn'kɒnʃəsnəs/ *noun* (no plural)
being unconscious

uncover /ʌn'kʌvə(r)/ *verb* (**uncovers**, **uncovering**, **uncovered** /ʌn'kʌvəd/)
take something from on top of another thing: *Uncover the pan and cook the soup for 30 minutes.*

under /'ʌndə(r)/ *preposition, adverb*
1 in or to a place that is lower than or below something: *The cat is under the table.*
◇ *The boat sailed under the bridge.* ◇ *The boat filled with water, then went under.*
☞ picture on page 125
2 less than something: *If you are under 17 you are not allowed to drive a car.*
3 covered by something: *I'm wearing a vest under my shirt.*
4 controlled by somebody or something: *The team are playing well under their new captain.*

undergo /ˌʌndə'gəʊ/ *verb* (**undergoes**, **undergoing**, **underwent** /ˌʌndə'went/, **has undergone** /ˌʌndə'gɒn/)
If you undergo something, it happens to

s	z	ʃ	ʒ	h	m	n	ŋ	l	r	j	w
so	**zoo**	**shoe**	vision	**hat**	**man**	**no**	sing	**leg**	**red**	**yes**	**wet**

you: *Laura is in hospital undergoing an operation.*

undergraduate /ˌʌndəˈgrædʒuət/ *noun*
a student at a university

underground¹ /ˈʌndəgraʊnd/ *adjective, adverb*
under the ground: *an underground car park*

underground² /ˈʌndəgraʊnd/ *noun* (no plural)
an underground railway: *I go to work by underground.* ◇ *We took the Underground to Piccadilly Circus.*

undergrowth /ˈʌndəgrəʊθ/ *noun* (no plural)
bushes and other plants that grow under trees: *There was a path through the undergrowth.*

underline /ˌʌndəˈlaɪn/ *verb* (**underlines, underlining, underlined** /ˌʌndəˈlaɪnd/)
draw a line under a word or words: This sentence is underlined.

underneath /ˌʌndəˈniːθ/ *preposition, adverb*
under or below something: *The dog sat underneath the table.* ◇ *She wore a black jacket with a red jumper underneath.*

underpants /ˈʌndəpænts/ *noun* (plural)
a piece of clothing that a man or boy wears under his trousers: *a pair of underpants*

undershirt /ˈʌndəʃɜːt/ *American English for* **vest**

understand /ˌʌndəˈstænd/ *verb* (**understands, understanding, understood** /ˌʌndəˈstʊd/, **has understood**)
1 know what something means or why something happens: *I didn't understand what the teacher said.* ◇ *He doesn't understand Spanish.* ◇ *I don't understand why you're so angry.*
2 know something because somebody has told you about it: *I understand that the plane from Geneva will be late.*
make yourself understood make people understand you: *My German isn't very good but I can usually make myself understood.*

understanding¹ /ˌʌndəˈstændɪŋ/ *adjective*
If you are understanding, you listen to

other people's problems and you try to understand them: *My parents are very understanding.*

understanding² /ˌʌndəˈstændɪŋ/ *noun* (no plural)
knowing about something, or knowing how somebody feels: *He's got a good understanding of computers.*

understood *form of* **understand**

undertaker /ˈʌndəteɪkə(r)/ *noun*
a person whose job is to organize **funerals** (the time when dead people are buried or burned)

underwater /ˌʌndəˈwɔːtə(r)/ *adjective, adverb*
below the top of water: *Can you swim underwater?*

underwear /ˈʌndəweə(r)/ *noun* (no plural)
clothes that you wear next to your body, under your other clothes

underwent *form of* **undergo**

undo /ʌnˈduː/ *verb* (**undoes** /ʌnˈdʌz/, **undoing, undid** /ʌnˈdɪd/, **has undone** /ʌnˈdʌn/)
open something that was tied or fixed: *I undid the string and opened the parcel.* ◇ *I can't undo these buttons.*
undone *adjective*
not tied or fixed: *Your shoelaces are undone.*

undoubtedly /ʌnˈdaʊtɪdli/ *adverb*
certainly; without doubt: *She is undoubtedly very intelligent.*

undress /ˌʌnˈdres/ *verb* (**undresses, undressing, undressed** /ʌnˈdrest/)
take clothes off yourself or another person: *He undressed and got into bed.* ◇ *She undressed her baby.*
get undressed take off your clothes: *I got undressed and had a shower.*

uneasy /ʌnˈiːzi/ *adjective*
worried that something is wrong: *I started to feel uneasy when the children didn't come home.*
uneasily /ʌnˈiːzɪli/ *adverb*
She looked uneasily around the room.

unemployed /ˌʌnɪmˈplɔɪd/ *adjective*
If you are unemployed, you want a job but

you do not have one: *I was unemployed for a year after leaving school.*

unemployment /ˌʌnɪm'plɔɪmənt/ *noun* (no plural)
when there are not enough jobs for the people who want to work: *If the factory closes, unemployment in the town will increase.*

uneven /ˌʌn'i:vn/ *adjective*
not smooth or flat: *We had to drive slowly because the road was so uneven.*

unexpected /ˌʌnɪk'spektɪd/ *adjective*
surprising because you did not expect it: *an unexpected visit*
unexpectedly *adverb*
She arrived unexpectedly.

unfair /ˌʌn'feə(r)/ *adjective*
Something that is unfair does not treat people in the same way or in the right way: *It was unfair to give chocolates to some of the children and not to the others.*
unfairly *adverb*
He left his job because the boss was treating him unfairly.

unfamiliar /ˌʌnfə'mɪliə(r)/ *adjective*
that you do not know; strange: *I woke up in an unfamiliar room.*

unfashionable /ʌn'fæʃnəbl/ *adjective*
not fashionable: *unfashionable clothes*

unfit /ˌʌn'fɪt/ *adjective*
1 not healthy or strong: *She never takes any exercise – that's why she's so unfit.*
2 not good enough for something: *This house is unfit for people to live in.*

unfold /ʌn'fəʊld/ *verb* (**unfolds**, **unfolding**, **unfolded**)
open something to make it flat; open out and become flat: *Marie unfolded the newspaper and started to read.* ◇ *The sofa unfolds to make a bed.*

unfortunate /ʌn'fɔ:tʃənət/ *adjective*
not lucky: *It's unfortunate that you were ill on your birthday.*
unfortunately *adverb*
it is unfortunate that: *I would like to give you some money, but unfortunately I haven't got any.*

unfriendly /ˌʌn'frendli/ *adjective*
not friendly; not kind or helpful to other people

ungrateful /ʌn'greɪtfl/ *adjective*
If you are ungrateful, you do not show thanks when somebody helps you or gives you something: *Don't be so ungrateful! I spent all morning looking for this present.*

unhappy /ʌn'hæpi/ *adjective* (**unhappier**, **unhappiest**)
not happy; sad: *He was very unhappy when his wife left him.*
unhappily /ʌn'hæpɪli/ *adverb*
'I failed the exam,' she said unhappily.
unhappiness /ʌn'hæpɪnəs/ *noun* (no plural)
John has had a lot of unhappiness in his life.

unhealthy /ʌn'helθi/ *adjective* (**unhealthier**, **unhealthiest**)
1 not well; often ill: *an unhealthy child*
2 that can make you ill: *unhealthy food*

uniform /'ju:nɪfɔ:m/ *noun*
the special clothes that everybody in the same job, school, etc wears: *Police officers wear blue uniforms.*

uninhabited /ˌʌnɪn'hæbɪtɪd/ *adjective*
where nobody lives: *an uninhabited island*

union /'ju:niən/ *noun*
1 (*plural* **unions**) a group of workers who have joined together to talk to their managers about things like pay and the way they work: *the National Union of Teachers*
2 (*plural* **unions**) a group of people or countries that have joined together
3 (no plural) coming together: *The union of England and Scotland was in 1707.*
the Union Jack /ðə ˌju:niən 'dʒæk/ *noun*
the flag of the United Kingdom

unique /ju'ni:k/ *adjective*
not like anybody or anything else: *Everybody in the world is unique.*

unit /'ju:nɪt/ *noun*
1 one complete thing or group that may be part of something larger: *The book has twelve units.*
2 a measurement: *A metre is a unit of length and a kilogram is a unit of weight.*

unite /ju'naɪt/ *verb* (**unites**, **uniting**, **united**)
join together to become one; put two things together: *East and West Germany united in 1990.*
united *adjective*
joined together: *the United States of America*

ʌ	ɜ:	ə	eɪ	əʊ	aɪ	aʊ	ɔɪ	ɪə	eə	ʊə
cup	bird	about	say	go	five	now	boy	near	hair	pure

universal /ˌjuːnɪˈvɜːsl/ adjective
of, by or for everybody: This subject is of
universal interest.

the universe /ðə ˈjuːnɪvɜːs/ noun (no
plural)
the earth and all the stars, planets and
everything else in space

university /ˌjuːnɪˈvɜːsəti/ noun (plural
universities)
a place where people go to study more difficult subjects after they have left school:
I'm hoping to go to university next year.
◇ My sister is at university studying
Chemistry. ✪ If you pass special courses
at a university, you get a **degree**.

unjust /ˌʌnˈdʒʌst/ adjective
not just; not fair or right: This tax is unjust
because poor people pay as much as rich
people.

unkind /ˌʌnˈkaɪnd/ adjective
not kind; cruel: It was unkind of you to
laugh at her hat.

unknown /ˌʌnˈnəʊn/ adjective
1 that you do not know: an unknown face
2 not famous: an unknown actor

unless /ənˈles/ conjunction
if not; except if: You will be late unless you
leave now. ◇ Unless you work harder
you'll fail the exam.

unlike /ˌʌnˈlaɪk/ preposition
not like; different from: She is thin, unlike
her sister who is quite fat.

unlikely /ʌnˈlaɪkli/ adjective (unlike-
lier, unlikeliest)
If something is unlikely, it will probably
not happen: It is unlikely that it will rain.
◇ He is unlikely to pass the exam.

unload /ˌʌnˈləʊd/ verb (unloads, un-
loading, unloaded)
take off or out the things that a car, lorry,
ship or plane is carrying: I unloaded the
shopping from the car. ◇ They unloaded
the ship at the dock.

unlock /ˌʌnˈlɒk/ verb (unlocks, unlock-
ing, unlocked /ˌʌnˈlɒkt/)
open something with a key: I unlocked the
door and went in.

unlucky /ʌnˈlʌki/ adjective (unluckier,
unluckiest)
1 If you are unlucky, good things do not
happen to you: She's unlucky – she plays
very well but she never wins a game.
2 Something that is unlucky brings bad

luck: Some people think that the number
13 is unlucky.

unluckily /ʌnˈlʌkɪli/ adverb
it is unlucky that: Unluckily, I missed the
bus.

unmarried /ˌʌnˈmærɪd/ adjective
not married; without a husband or wife

unnecessary /ʌnˈnesəsri/ adjective
not necessary; not needed

unpack /ˌʌnˈpæk/ verb (unpacks, un-
packing, unpacked /ˌʌnˈpækt/)
take all the things out of a bag, suitcase,
etc: Have you unpacked your suitcase?
◇ We arrived at the hotel, unpacked, and
then went to the beach.

unpaid /ˌʌnˈpeɪd/ adjective
not paid: an unpaid bill

unpleasant /ʌnˈpleznt/ adjective
not pleasant; not nice: There was an unpleasant smell of bad fish.

unpleasantly adverb
It was unpleasantly hot in that room.

unplug /ˌʌnˈplʌg/ verb (unplugs, un-
plugging, unplugged /ˌʌnˈplʌgd/)
take the electric plug of a machine out of a
place in a wall (called a **socket**) where
there is electricity: Could you unplug the
TV?

unpopular /ˌʌnˈpɒpjələ(r)/ adjective
not popular; not liked by many people:
He's unpopular at work because he's lazy.

unreliable /ˌʌnrɪˈlaɪəbl/ adjective
not reliable; that you cannot trust: Don't
lend her any money – she's very unreliable. ◇ an unreliable car

unsafe /ˌʌnˈseɪf/ adjective
not safe; dangerous: Don't climb on that
wall – it's unsafe.

unsatisfactory /ˌʌnsætɪsˈfæktri/ adjective
not satisfactory; not good enough: Tina's
work was unsatisfactory so I asked her to
do it again.

unstable /ˌʌnˈsteɪbl/ adjective
Something that is unstable may fall, move
or change: This bridge is unstable. ◇ unstable government

unsuccessful /ˌʌnsəkˈsesfl/ adjective
If you are unsuccessful, you have not done
what you wanted and tried to do: I tried to
repair the bike but I was unsuccessful.

unsuccessfully /ˌʌnsəkˈsesfəli/ adverb
Gary tried unsuccessfully to lift the box.

p	b	t	d	k	g	tʃ	dʒ	f	v	θ	ð
pen	**b**ad	**t**ea	**d**id	**c**at	**g**ot	**ch**ain	**j**am	**f**ull	**v**an	**th**in	**th**is

unsuitable /ˌʌn'suːtəbl/ adjective
not suitable; not right for somebody or
something: This film is unsuitable for
children.

unsure /ˌʌn'ʃʊə(r)/ adjective
not sure: We were unsure what to do.

untidy /ʌn'taɪdi/ adjective (**untidier**,
untidiest)
not tidy; not with everything in the right
place: Your room is always so untidy!
untidiness /ʌn'taɪdinəs/ noun (no
plural)
I hate untidiness!

untie /ʌn'taɪ/ verb (**unties**, **untying**,
untied /ʌn'taɪd/, **has untied**)
1 take off the string or rope that is holding
something or somebody: I untied the
parcel.
2 make a knot or bow loose: Can you
untie this knot?

until /ən'tɪl/ conjunction
up to the time when: Stay in bed until you
feel better.
until preposition
1 up to a certain time: The shop is open
until 6.30.
2 before: I can't come until tomorrow.

untrue /ˌʌn'truː/ adjective
not true or correct: What you said was
completely untrue.

unusual /ʌn'juːʒuəl/ adjective
If something is unusual, it does not often
happen or you do not often see it: It's unusual to see a cat without a tail. ◇ What
an unusual name!
unusually /ʌn'juːʒuəli/ adverb
It was an unusually hot summer.

unwanted /ˌʌn'wɒntɪd/ adjective
not wanted: unwanted children

unwelcome /ˌʌn'welkəm/ adjective
If somebody or something is unwelcome,
you are not happy to have or see them: an
unwelcome visitor

unwell /ʌn'wel/ adjective
not well; ill

unwilling /ˌʌn'wɪlɪŋ/ adjective
If you are unwilling to do something, you
are not ready or happy to do it: He was unwilling to lend me any money.

unwrap /ˌʌn'ræp/ verb (**unwraps**, **un-
wrapping**, **unwrapped** /ˌʌn'ræpt/)
take off the paper or cloth that is around
something: I unwrapped the parcel.

up /ʌp/ preposition, adverb
1 in or to a higher place: We climbed up
the mountain. ◇ Put your hand up if you
know the answer. ☞ picture on page 128
2 from sitting or lying to standing: Stand
up, please. ◇ What time do you get up?
(= out of bed)
3 in a way that is bigger, stronger, etc: The
price of petrol is going up. ◇ Please turn
the radio up – I can't hear it.
4 so that it is finished: Who used all the
coffee up?
5 along: We walked up the road.
6 towards and near somebody or something: She came up to me and asked me the
time.
7 into pieces: Cut the meat up.
be up be out of bed: 'Is Joe up?' 'No, he's
still asleep.'
it's up to you you are the person who
should do or decide something: 'What
shall we do this evening?' 'I don't mind.
It's up to you.'
up to 1 as far as; until: Up to now, she
has worked very hard. **2** as much or as
many as: Up to 300 people came to the
meeting. **3** doing something: What is that
man up to?

update /ˌʌp'deɪt/ verb (**updates**, **updat-
ing**, **updated**)
make something more modern or add new
things to it: The information on the computer is updated every week.

uphill /ˌʌp'hɪl/ adverb
up, towards the top of a hill: It's difficult to
ride a bicycle uphill.

upon /ə'pɒn/ preposition
on ◐ **On** is the word that we usually use.
once upon a time a long time ago
(words that sometimes begin children's
stories): Once upon a time there was a
beautiful princess . . .

upper /'ʌpə(r)/ adjective
higher than another; top: the upper lip
◐ opposite: **lower**

upright /'ʌpraɪt/ adjective, adverb
standing straight up, not lying down: Put
the ladder upright against the wall.

upset /ˌʌp'set/ verb (**upsets**, **upsetting**,
upset, **has upset**)
1 make somebody feel unhappy or wor-

ried: *You upset Tom when you said he was fat.*
2 make something go wrong: *The bad weather upset our plans for the weekend.*
3 knock something so that it turns over and things fall out: *I upset a glass of wine all over the table.*

upset /ˈʌpset/ *noun*
an illness in your stomach: *Sara has got a stomach upset.*

upset /ˌʌpˈset/ *adjective*
1 unhappy or worried: *The children were very upset when their dog died.*
2 ill: *I've got an upset stomach.*

upside down
/ˌʌpsaɪd ˈdaʊn/
adverb
with the top part at the bottom: *The picture is upside down.*

upside down

upstairs
/ˌʌpˈsteəz/ *adverb*
to or on a higher floor of a building: *I went upstairs to bed.*

upstairs *adjective*
An upstairs window was open.
✪ opposite: **downstairs**

upwards /ˈʌpwədz/, **upward**
/ˈʌpwəd/ *adverb*
up; towards a higher place: *We climbed upwards, towards the top of the mountain.* ✪ opposite: **downwards**

urban /ˈɜːbən/ *adjective*
of a town or city: *urban areas*

urge /ɜːdʒ/ *verb* (**urges, urging, urged**
/ɜːdʒd/)
try to make somebody do something: *I urged him to stay for dinner.*

urge *noun*
a strong feeling that you want to do something: *I had a sudden urge to laugh.*

urgency /ˈɜːdʒənsi/ *noun* (no plural)
the need to do something quickly because it is very important

urgent /ˈɜːdʒənt/ *adjective*
so important that you must do it or answer it quickly: *The doctor received an urgent telephone call.*

urgently *adverb*
I must see you urgently.

us /əs/, /ʌs/ *pronoun* (plural)
me and another person or other people; me

and you: *We were pleased when she invited us to dinner.* ◇ *John wrote to us.*

use[1] /juːz/ *verb* (**uses, using, used**
/juːzd/)
1 do a job with something: *Could I use your telephone?* ◇ *Do you know how to use this machine?* ◇ *Wood is used to make paper.*
2 take something: *Don't use all the milk.*

use up use something until you have no more: *I've used up all the coffee, so I need to buy some more.*

use[2] /juːs/ *noun*
1 (no plural) using: *This pool is for the use of hotel guests only.*
2 (plural **uses**) what you can do with something: *This tool has many uses.*

have the use of something have the right to use something: *I've got the use of Jim's car while he's on holiday.*

it's no use it will not help to do something: *It's no use telling her anything – she never listens.*

make use of something find a way of using something: *If you don't want that box, I can make use of it.*

used[1] /juːzd/ *adjective*
not new: *The garage sells used cars.*

used[2] /juːst/ *adjective*
be used to something know something well because you have seen, heard, tasted, done, etc it a lot: *I'm used to walking because I haven't got a car.*

get used to something begin to know something well after a time: *I'm getting used to my new job.*

used[3] /juːst/ *verb*
used to words that tell us about something that happened often or that was true in the past: *She used to smoke when she was young.* ◇ *I used to be afraid of dogs, but now I like them.* ◇ *I didn't use to like fish, but I do now.*

useful /ˈjuːsfl/ *adjective*
good and helpful for doing something: *This bag will be useful for carrying my books.*

useless /ˈjuːsləs/ *adjective*
1 not good for anything: *A car is useless without petrol.*
2 that does not do what you hoped: *It was useless asking my brother for money – he didn't have any.*

iː	i	ɪ	e	æ	ɑː	ɒ	ɔː	ʊ	u	uː
see	**happy**	**sit**	**ten**	**cat**	**father**	**got**	**saw**	**put**	sit**u**ation	**too**

user /'juːzə(r)/ *noun*
a person who uses something: *computer users*

usual /'juːʒuəl/ *adjective*
that happens most often: *It's not usual for children in Britain to go to school on Saturdays.*
as usual as happens most often: *Julie was late, as usual.*
usually /'juːʒuəli/ *adverb*
We usually go to Spain for our holidays, but this year we are staying at home.

utter[1] /'ʌtə(r)/ *adjective*
complete: *The room was in utter darkness and I couldn't see anything.*
utterly *adverb*
completely or very: *That's utterly impossible!*

utter[2] /'ʌtə(r)/ *verb* (**utters, uttering, uttered** /'ʌtəd/)
say something or make a sound with your mouth: *He uttered a cry of pain.*

Vv

V *short way of writing* **volt**

v /viː/ *short for* **versus**: *Liverpool v Manchester United*

vacancy /'veɪkənsi/ *noun* (*plural* **vacancies**)
1 a job that nobody is doing: *We have a vacancy for a secretary in our office.*
2 a room in a hotel that nobody is using: *The sign outside the hotel said 'no vacancies'* (= the hotel is full).

vacant /'veɪkənt/ *adjective*
empty; with nobody in it: *a vacant room*

vacation /və'keɪʃn/ *noun*
1 a holiday time when a university is not open: *the summer vacation*
2 *American English for* **holiday**

vacuum /'vækjuəm/ *noun*
a space with no air, gas or anything else in it

vacuum cleaner /'vækjuəm ˌkliːnə(r)/ *noun*
a machine that cleans carpets by sucking up dirt

vague /veɪg/ *adjective* (**vaguer, vaguest**)
not clear or not exact: *I couldn't find the house because he gave me very vague directions.*
vaguely *adverb*
I vaguely remember what happened.

vacuum cleaner

vain /veɪn/ *adjective* (**vainer, vainest**)
1 too proud of what you can do or how you look ○ The noun is **vanity**.
2 with no success; useless: *They made a vain attempt to save his life.*
in vain with no success: *I tried in vain to sleep.*

valid /'vælɪd/ *adjective*
If something like a ticket or a cheque is valid, you can use it and other people will accept it: *Your bus ticket is valid for one week.*

valley /'væli/ *noun* (*plural* **valleys**)
low land, usually with a river, between hills or mountains: *the Loire Valley*

valuable /'væljuəbl/ *adjective*
1 worth a lot of money: *Is this ring valuable?*
2 very useful: *valuable information*

value[1] /'væljuː/ *noun*
1 (*plural* **values**) how much money you

can sell something for: *What is the value of this painting?*

2 (no plural) how useful or important something is: *Their help was of great value.*

3 (no plural) how much something is worth compared with its price: *The meal was good value at only £4.50.*

value² /'vælju:/ *verb* (**values, valuing, valued** /'vælju:d/)
1 think that something is very important: *I value my freedom.*
2 say how much money something is worth: *The house was valued at £80 000.*

vampire /'væmpaɪə(r)/ *noun*
a dead person in stories who comes to life at night and drinks people's blood

van

van /væn/ *noun*
a kind of big car or small lorry for carrying things

vandal /'vændl/ *noun*
a person who damages and breaks things that belong to other people: *Vandals have damaged the telephone box by our house.*

vandalism /'vændəlɪzəm/ *noun* (no plural)
damage by vandals: *Vandalism is a problem in this part of the city.*

vanilla /və'nɪlə/ *noun* (no plural)
a plant that gives a taste to some sweet foods, for example white ice-cream

vanish /'vænɪʃ/ *verb* (**vanishes, vanishing, vanished** /'vænɪʃt/)
go away suddenly; disappear: *The thief ran into the crowd and vanished.*

vanity /'vænəti/ *noun* (no plural)
being too proud of what you can do or how you look ○ The adjective is **vain**.

varied, varies *forms of* **vary**

variety /və'raɪəti/ *noun*
1 (no plural) If something has variety, it is full of different things and changes often: *There's a lot of variety in my new job.*
2 (no plural) a lot of different things:

There's a large variety of dishes on the menu.
3 (*plural* **varieties**) a kind of something: *This variety of apple is very sweet.*

various /'veəriəs/ *adjective*
many different: *We sell this shirt in various colours and sizes.*

varnish /'vɑːnɪʃ/ *noun* (no plural)
a clear paint with no colour, that you put on something to make it shine

vary /'veəri/ *verb* (**varies, varying, varied** /'veərid/, **has varied**)
be or become different from each other: *These tapes vary in price from £6 to £9.*

vase /vɑːz/ *noun*
a pot that you put cut flowers in

vast /vɑːst/ *adjective*
very big: *Australia is a vast country.*

vase

veal /viːl/ *noun* (no plural)
meat from a young cow (a **calf**) ☞ Note at **cow**

vegetable /'vedʒtəbl/ *noun*
a plant that we eat. Potatoes, carrots and beans are vegetables: *vegetable soup*

vegetarian /ˌvedʒɪ'teəriən/ *noun*
a person who does not eat meat

vehicle /'viːəkl/ *noun*
any thing that carries people or things from one place to another. Cars, buses and bicycles are all vehicles.

veil /veɪl/ *noun*
a piece of thin material that a woman puts over her head and face: *Women wear veils in a lot of Muslim countries.*

vein /veɪn/ *noun*
one of the small tubes in your body that carry blood to the heart

velvet /'velvɪt/ *noun* (no plural)
cloth that is soft and thick on one side: *red velvet curtains*

verb /vɜːb/ *noun*
a word that tells you what somebody or something is or does. 'Go', 'sing', 'happen' and 'be' are all verbs.

verdict /'vɜːdɪkt/ *noun*
what the **jury** in a court of law decides at the end of a **trial**

p	b	t	d	k	g	tʃ	dʒ	f	v	θ	ð
pen	**bad**	**tea**	**did**	**cat**	**got**	**chain**	**jam**	**fall**	**van**	**thin**	**this**

verse /vɜːs/ *noun*
1 (no plural) poetry; writing in lines that has a **rhythm**: *The play is written in verse.*
2 (*plural* **verses**) a group of lines in a song or poem: *This song has five verses.*

version /'vɜːʃn/ *noun*
1 a form of something that is different in some way: *a new version of a Beatles song*
2 what one person says or writes about something that happened: *His version of the accident is different from mine.*

versus /'vɜːsəs/ *preposition*
on the other side in a sport; against: *There's a good football match on TV tonight – England versus Brazil.* ✪ The short way of writing 'versus' is **v** or **vs.**

vertical /'vɜːtɪkl/ *adjective*
Something that is vertical goes straight up, not from side to side: *a vertical line* ☞ picture on page 161

very[1] /'veri/ *adverb*
You use 'very' before another word to make it stronger: *London is a very big town.* ◇ *She speaks very quietly.* ◇ *I like chocolate very much.* ◇ *I'm not very hungry.*

very[2] /'veri/ *adjective*
same; exact: *You are the very person I wanted to see!* ◇ *We climbed to the very top of the mountain.*

vest /vest/ *noun*
1 a piece of clothing that you wear under your other clothes on the top part of your body
2 *American English for* **waistcoat**

vet /vet/, **veterinary surgeon**
/ˌvetrənri 'sɜːdʒən/ *noun*
a doctor for animals

via /'vaɪə/ *preposition*
going through a place: *We flew from London to Sydney via Bangkok.*

vibrate /vaɪ'breɪt/ *verb* (**vibrates**, **vibrating**, **vibrated**)
move very quickly from side to side or up and down: *The house vibrates every time a train goes past.*
vibration /vaɪ'breɪʃn/ *noun*
You can feel the vibrations from the engine when you are in the car.

vicar /'vɪkə(r)/ *noun*
a priest in the Church of England

vice- /vaɪs/ *prefix*
a word that you use before another word, to show somebody who is next to the leader in importance: *The vice-captain leads the team when the captain is ill.* ◇ *the Vice-President*

vicious /'vɪʃəs/ *adjective*
cruel; wanting to hurt somebody or something: *a vicious attack*

victim /'vɪktɪm/ *noun*
a person or animal that is hurt or killed by somebody or something: *The victims of the car accident were taken to hospital.*

victory /'vɪktəri/ *noun* (*plural* **victories**)
winning a fight, game or war

video /'vɪdiəʊ/ *noun* (*plural* **videos**)
1 (*also* **video recorder**) a machine that puts television programmes on tape, so that you can watch them later: *Have you got a video?*
2 tape in a box (called a **cassette**) that you put into a video recorder to show films, for example: *We stayed at home and watched a video.* ◇ *Can you get this film on video?*

view /vjuː/ *noun*
1 what you can see from a certain place: *There is a beautiful view of the mountains from our window.*
2 what you believe or think about something: *What are your views on marriage?*
in view of something because of something: *In view of the bad weather we decided to cancel the match.*
on view in a place for people to see: *Her paintings are on view at the museum.*

viewer /'vjuːə(r)/ *noun*
a person who watches television

vigorous /'vɪgərəs/ *adjective*
strong and active: *vigorous exercise*
vigorously *adverb*
She shook my hand vigorously.

vile /vaɪl/ *adjective* (**viler**, **vilest**)
very bad; horrible: *What a vile smell!*

villa /'vɪlə/ *noun*
a house with a garden, often where people stay on holiday

village /'vɪlɪdʒ/ *noun*
a small place where people live. A village is smaller than a town: *a village in the mountains*
villager *noun*
a person who lives in a village

villain /'vɪlən/ *noun*
a bad person, usually in a book, play or film

vine /vaɪn/ *noun*
a plant that grapes grow on

vinegar /'vɪnɪgə(r)/ *noun* (no plural)
a liquid with a strong sharp taste. You put it on food and use it for cooking: *I mixed some oil and vinegar to put on the salad.*

vineyard /'vɪnjəd/ *noun*
a piece of land where vines grow

viola /vi'əʊlə/ *noun*
a musical instrument with strings that is a little bigger than a violin

violent /'vaɪələnt/ *adjective*
A person or thing that is violent is very strong and dangerous and hurts people: *a violent man* ◇ *a violent storm*
violence /'vaɪələns/ *noun* (no plural)
being violent: *Do you think there's too much violence on TV?*
violently *adverb*
Did she behave violently towards you?

violet /'vaɪələt/ *noun*
a small purple flower
violet *adjective*
with a purple colour

bow
violin

violin /ˌvaɪə'lɪn/ *noun*
a musical instrument made of wood, with strings across it. You play a violin with a **bow**: *I play the violin.*

VIP /ˌviː aɪ 'piː/ *noun*
a person who is famous or important. 'VIP' is short for **very important person**: *The Prime Minister is a VIP.*

virtually /'vɜːtʃuəli/ *adverb*
almost: *The two boys look virtually the same.*

virus /'vaɪrəs/ *noun* (*plural* **viruses**)
a very small living thing that can make you ill: *a flu virus*

visa /'viːzə/ *noun*
a special piece of paper or mark in your passport to show that you can go into a country

visible /'vɪzəbl/ *adjective*
If something is visible, you can see it: *Stars are only visible at night.* ◇ opposite: **invisible**

vision /'vɪʒn/ *noun*
1 (no plural) the power to see; sight: *He wears glasses because he has poor vision.*
2 (*plural* **visions**) a picture in your mind; a dream: *They have a vision of a world without war.*

visit /'vɪzɪt/ *verb* (**visits**, **visiting**, **visited**)
go to see a person or place for a short time: *Have you ever visited Westminster Abbey?* ◇ *She visited me in hospital.*
visit *noun*
This is my first visit to New York.
pay somebody a visit go to see somebody

visitor /'vɪzɪtə(r)/ *noun*
a person who goes to see another person or a place for a short time: *The old lady never has any visitors.* ◇ *Millions of visitors come to Rome every year.*

visual /'vɪʒuəl/ *adjective*
of or about seeing: *Painting and cinema are visual arts.*

vital /'vaɪtl/ *adjective*
very important; that you must do or have: *It's vital that she sees a doctor – she's very ill.*

vitamin /'vɪtəmɪn/ *noun*
one of the things in food that you need to be healthy: *Oranges are full of vitamin C.*

vivid /'vɪvɪd/ *adjective*
1 with a strong bright colour: *vivid yellow*
2 that makes a very clear picture in your mind: *I had a very vivid dream last night.*
vividly *adverb*
I remember my first day at school vividly.

vocabulary /və'kæbjələri/ *noun* (*plural* **vocabularies**)
1 all the words in a language
2 a list of words in a lesson or book: *We have to learn this new vocabulary for homework.*
3 all the words that somebody knows

voice /vɔɪs/ *noun*
the sounds that you make when you speak or sing: *Steve has a very deep voice.*
at the top of your voice very loudly: *'Come here!' she shouted at the top of her voice.*
raise your voice speak very loudly

volcano /vɒl'keɪnəʊ/ *noun* (*plural* **volcanoes**)
a mountain with a hole in the top where fire, gas and hot liquid rock (called **lava**) sometimes come out
volcanic /vɒl'kænɪk/ *adjective*
volcanic rocks

volleyball /'vɒlibɔːl/ *noun* (no plural)
a game where two teams try to hit a ball over a high net with their hands

volt /vəʊlt/ *noun*
a measure of electricity ✪ The short way of writing 'volt' is **V**.

volume /'vɒljuːm/ *noun*
1 (no plural) the amount of space that something fills, or the amount of space inside something: *What is the volume of this box?*
2 (no plural) the amount of sound that something makes: *I can't hear the radio. Can you turn the volume up?*
3 (*plural* **volumes**) a book, especially one of a set: *The dictionary is in two volumes.*

voluntary /'vɒləntri/ *adjective*
1 If something is voluntary, you do it because you want to, not because you must: *She made a voluntary decision to leave the job.*
2 If work is voluntary, you are not paid to do it: *He does voluntary work at a children's hospital.*
voluntarily /'vɒləntrəli/ *adverb*
because you want to, not because you must: *She left the job voluntarily.*

volunteer /ˌvɒlən'tɪə(r)/ *verb* (**volunteers, volunteering, volunteered** /ˌvɒlən'tɪəd/)
say that you will do something that you do not have to do: *I volunteered to do the washing-up.*
volunteer *noun*
a person who volunteers to do a job: *They're asking for volunteers to help at the Christmas party.*

vomit /'vɒmɪt/ *verb* (**vomits, vomiting, vomited**)
When you vomit, food comes up from your stomach and out of your mouth. ✪ It is more usual to say **be sick**.

vote /vəʊt/ *verb* (**votes, voting, voted**)
choose somebody or something by putting up your hand or writing on a piece of paper: *Who did you vote for in the election?*
vote *noun*
There were 96 votes for the plan, and 25 against.
voter *noun*
a person who votes in a political election

voucher /'vaʊtʃə(r)/ *noun*
a piece of paper that you can use instead of money to pay for something

vowel /'vaʊəl/ *noun*
one of the letters *a, e, i, o* or *u* , or the sound that you make when you say it ☞ Look at **consonant**.

voyage /'vɔɪɪdʒ/ *noun*
a long journey by boat or in space: *a voyage from London to New York*

vs short way of writing **versus**

Ww

wade /weɪd/ *verb* (**wades, wading, waded**)
walk through water: *Can we wade across the river, or is it too deep?*

wag /wæg/ *verb* (**wags, wagging, wagged** /wægd/)
move or make something move from side to side or up and down: *She wagged her*

ʌ	ɜː	ə	eɪ	əʊ	aɪ	aʊ	ɔɪ	ɪə	eə	ʊə
cup	bird	about	say	go	five	now	boy	near	hair	pure

finger at me. ◇ *My dog's tail wags when he's happy.*

wages /'weɪdʒɪz/ *noun* (plural)
the money that you receive every week for the work that you do: *Our wages are paid every Friday.* ◇ *low wages*

wagon /'wægən/ *noun*
1 a vehicle with four wheels that a horse pulls
2 a part of a train where things like coal are carried

wail /weɪl/ *verb* (**wails, wailing, wailed** /weɪld/)
make a long sad cry or noise: *The little boy started wailing for his mother.*

waist /weɪst/ *noun*
the part around the middle of your body
☞ picture on page 126

waistcoat /'weɪskəʊt/ *noun*
a piece of clothing like a jacket with no sleeves

wait¹ /weɪt/ *verb* (**waits, waiting, waited**)
stay in one place until something happens or until somebody or something comes: *If I'm late, please wait for me.* ◇ *We've been waiting a long time.*
I can't wait words that you use when you are very excited about something that is going to happen: *I can't wait to see you again!*
keep somebody waiting make somebody wait because you are late or busy: *The doctor kept me waiting for half an hour.*
wait and see wait and find out later: *'What are we having for dinner?' 'Wait and see!'*
wait up not go to bed until somebody comes home: *I will be home late tonight so don't wait up for me.*

wait² /weɪt/ *noun*
a time when you wait: *We had a long wait for the bus.*

waiter /'weɪtə(r)/ *noun*
a man who brings food and drink to your table in a restaurant

waiting-room /'weɪtɪŋ ruːm/ *noun*
a room where people can sit and wait, for example to see a doctor or to catch a train

waitress /'weɪtrəs/ *noun* (plural **waitresses**)
a woman who brings food and drink to your table in a restaurant

wake /weɪk/, **wake up** *verb* (**wakes, waking, woke** /wəʊk/, **has woken** /'wəʊkən/)
1 stop sleeping: *What time did you wake up this morning?*
2 make somebody stop sleeping: *The noise woke me up.* ◇ *Don't wake the baby.*
○ It is more usual to say **wake up** than **wake**.

walk¹ /wɔːk/ *verb* (**walks, walking, walked** /wɔːkt/)
move on your legs, but not run: *I usually walk to work.* ◇ *We walked 20 kilometres today.*
walk out leave suddenly because you are angry: *He walked out of the meeting.*

walk² /wɔːk/ *noun*
a journey on foot: *The beach is a short walk from our house.* ◇ *I took the dog for a walk.*
go for a walk walk somewhere because you enjoy it: *It was a lovely day so we went for a walk in the park.*

walker /'wɔːkə(r)/ *noun*
a person who is walking

Walkman /'wɔːkmən/ *noun* (plural **Walkmans**)
a small cassette player or radio with **headphones**, that is easy to carry ○ **Walkman** is a trade mark.

wall /wɔːl/ *noun*
1 a side of a building or room: *There's a picture on the wall.* ☞ picture at **house**
2 a thing made of stones or bricks around a garden, field or town, for example: *There's a high wall around the prison.*

wallet

wallet /'wɒlɪt/ *noun*
a small flat case for paper money, that you can carry in your pocket

wallpaper /'wɔːlpeɪpə(r)/ *noun* (no plural)
special paper that you use for covering the walls of a room

p	b	t	d	k	g	tʃ	dʒ	f	v	θ	ð
pen	**bad**	**tea**	**did**	**cat**	**got**	**chain**	**jam**	**fall**	**van**	**thin**	**this**

walnut /'wɔːlnʌt/ *noun*
a nut that you can eat

wander /'wɒndə(r)/ *verb* (**wanders**, **wandering**, **wandered** /'wɒndəd/)
walk slowly with no special plan: *We wandered around the town until the shops opened.*

want /wɒnt/ *verb* (**wants**, **wanting**, **wanted**)
1 wish to have or do something: *Do you want a chocolate?* ◇ *I want to go to Italy.* ◇ *She wanted me to give her some money.* ✪ **Would like** is more polite than **want**: *Would you like a cup of tea?*
2 need something: *Your car wants a wash!*

war /wɔː(r)/ *noun*
fighting between countries or between groups of people: *the First World War*
at war fighting: *The two countries have been at war for five years.*
declare war start a war: *In 1812 Napoleon declared war on Russia.*

ward /wɔːd/ *noun*
a big room in a hospital that has beds for the patients

warden /'wɔːdn/ *noun*
a person whose job is to look after a place and the people in it: *the warden of a youth hostel* ☞ Look also at **traffic warden**.

wardrobe /'wɔːdrəub/ *noun*
a cupboard where you hang your clothes

warehouse /'weəhaus/ *noun* (*plural* **warehouses** /'weəhauzɪz/)
a big building where people keep things before they sell them: *a furniture warehouse*

warm¹ /wɔːm/ *adjective* (**warmer**, **warmest**)
1 a little hot: *It's warm by the fire.*
2 Warm clothes are clothes that stop you feeling cold: *It's cold in Scotland, so take some warm clothes with you.*
3 friendly and kind: *Martha is a very warm person.* ✪ opposite: **cold**
warmly *adverb*
The children were warmly dressed. ◇ *He thanked me warmly.*

warm² /wɔːm/ *verb* (**warms**, **warming**, **warmed** /wɔːmd/)
warm up become warmer, or make somebody or something warmer: *I warmed up some soup for lunch.* ◇ *It was*

cold this morning, but it's warming up now.

warmth /wɔːmθ/ *noun* (no plural)
1 heat: *the warmth of the sun*
2 friendliness and kindness: *the warmth of his smile*

warn /wɔːn/ *verb* (**warns**, **warning**, **warned** /wɔːnd/)
tell somebody about danger or about something bad that may happen: *I warned him not to go too close to the fire.*
warning *noun*
something that warns you: *There is a warning on every packet of cigarettes.*

was form of **be**

wash¹ /wɒʃ/ *verb* (**washes**, **washing**, **washed** /wɒʃt/)
1 clean somebody, something or yourself with water: *Have you washed the car?* ◇ *Wash your hands before you eat.* ◇ *I washed and dressed quickly.*
2 flow somewhere many times: *The sea washed over my feet.*
3 move something with water: *The house was washed away by the river.*
wash up clean the plates, knives, forks, etc after a meal: *I washed up after dinner.*

wash² /wɒʃ/ *noun* (no plural)
cleaning something with water: *I gave the car a wash.*
have a wash wash yourself: *I had a quick wash.*
in the wash being washed: *All my socks are in the wash!*

wash-basin /'wɒʃ beɪsn/ *noun*
the place in a bathroom where you wash your hands and face

washing /'wɒʃɪŋ/ *noun* (no plural)
clothes that you need to wash or that you have washed: *Shall I hang the washing outside to dry?* ◇ *I've done the washing.*
washing-machine /'wɒʃɪŋ məʃiːn/ *noun*
a machine that washes clothes
washing-powder /'wɒʃɪŋ paudə(r)/ *noun* (no plural)
soap powder for washing clothes
washing-up /ˌwɒʃɪŋ 'ʌp/ *noun* (no plural)
cleaning the plates, knives, forks, etc after a meal: *I'll do the washing-up.*
washing-up liquid /ˌwɒʃɪŋ 'ʌp lɪkwɪd/ *noun* (no plural)
a liquid that you use for washing plates, etc

s	z	ʃ	3	h	m	n	ŋ	l	r	j	w
so	**zoo**	**sh**oe	vision	**h**at	**m**an	**no**	si**ng**	**l**eg	**r**ed	**y**es	**w**et

washroom /'wɒʃruːm/
a room with a toilet in it ✪ This word is
only used in American English.

wasn't /'wɒznt/ = was not

wasp /wɒsp/ *noun*
a yellow and black insect that flies and can
sting people

waste¹ /weɪst/ *verb* (**wastes, wasting,
wasted**)
use too much of something or not use
something in a good way: *She wastes a lot
of money on cigarettes.* ◇ *He wasted his
time at university – he didn't do any
work.*

waste² /weɪst/ *noun* (no plural)
1 not using something in a good way: *It's
a waste to throw away all this food!*
◇ *This watch was a waste of money – it's
broken already!*
2 things that people throw away because
they are not useful: *A lot of waste from the
factories goes into this river.*

waste³ /weɪst/ *adjective*
that you do not want because it is not
useful

waste-paper basket /,weɪst 'peɪpə
bɑːskɪt/ *noun*
a container where you put things like
paper that you do not want

watch

watch¹ /wɒtʃ/ *noun* (*plural* **watches**)
a thing that shows what time it is. You
wear a watch on your wrist. ☞ Note at
clock

watch² /wɒtʃ/ *verb* (**watches, watching, watched** /wɒtʃt/)
1 look at somebody or something for some
time: *We watched television all evening.*
◇ *Watch how I do this.*
2 look after something or somebody:
*Could you watch my suitcase while I buy
a ticket?*
watch out be careful because of somebody or something dangerous: *Watch out!
There's a car coming.*
watch out for somebody or **something** look carefully and be ready for

somebody or something dangerous:
Watch out for ice on the roads.

watch³ /wɒtʃ/ *noun* (no plural)
keep watch look out for danger: *The
soldier kept watch at the gate.*

water¹ /'wɔːtə(r)/ *noun* (no plural)
the liquid in rivers, lakes and seas that
people and animals drink

water² /'wɔːtə(r)/ *verb* (**waters, watering, watered** /'wɔːtəd/)
1 give water to plants: *Have you watered
the plants?*
2 When your eyes water, they fill with
tears: *The smoke made my eyes water.*

watering-can /'wɔːtərɪŋ kæn/ *noun*
a container that you use for watering
plants

water-colour /'wɔːtə kʌlə(r)/ *noun*
a picture that you make with paint and
water

waterfall /'wɔːtəfɔːl/ *noun*
a place where water falls from a high place
to a low place

water melon /'wɔːtə melən/ *noun*
a big round fruit with a thick green skin. It
is pink inside with a lot of black seeds.

waterproof /'wɔːtəpruːf/ *adjective*
If something is waterproof, it does not let
water go through it: *a waterproof jacket*

water-skiing /'wɔːtə skiːɪŋ/ *noun* (no
plural)
the sport of moving fast over water on long
boards (called **water-skis**), pulled by a
boat

wave¹ /weɪv/ *verb* (**waves, waving,
waved** /weɪvd/)
1 move your hand from side to side in the
air to say hello or goodbye or to make a
sign to somebody: *She waved to me as the
train left the station.* ◇ *Who are you
waving at?*
2 move something quickly from side to
side in the air: *The children were waving
flags as the President's car drove past.*
3 move up and down or from side to side:
The flags were waving in the wind.

wave² /weɪv/ *noun*
1 one of the lines of water that moves
across the top of the sea
2 moving your hand from side to side in

iː	i	ɪ	e	æ	ɑː	ɒ	ɔː	ʊ	u	uː
see	happy	sit	ten	cat	father	got	saw	put	situation	too

the air, to say hello or goodbye or to make a sign to somebody

3 a gentle curve in hair

4 a movement like a wave on the sea, that carries heat, light, sound, etc: *radio waves*

wavy /'weɪvi/ *adjective* (**wavier, waviest**)
Something that is wavy has gentle curves in it: *She has wavy black hair.* ☞ picture at **hair**

wavy line

wax /wæks/ *noun* (no plural)
the stuff that is used for making candles

way /weɪ/ *noun*

1 (*plural* **ways**) a road or path that you must follow to go to a place: *Can you tell me the way to the station, please?* ◇ *I lost my way and I had to look at the map.*

2 (*plural* **ways**) a direction; where somebody or something is going or looking: *Come this way.* ◇ *She was looking the other way.*

3 (no plural) distance: *It's a long way from Glasgow to London.*

4 (*plural* **ways**) how you do something: *What is the best way to learn a language?* ◇ *He smiled in a friendly way.*

by the way words that you say when you are going to talk about something different: *By the way, I had a letter from Ann yesterday.*

give way **1** stop and let somebody or something go before you: *You must give way to traffic coming from the right.* **2** agree with somebody when you did not agree before: *After a long argument, my parents finally gave way and said I could go on holiday with my friends.* **3** break: *The ladder gave way and Ben fell to the ground.*

in the way in front of somebody so that you stop them from seeing something or moving: *I couldn't see the television because Jane was in the way.*

no way a way of saying 'no' more strongly: *'Can I borrow your bike?' 'No way!'*

on the way when you are going somewhere: *I stopped to have a drink on the way to Bristol.*

out of the way not in a place where you stop somebody from moving or doing something: *Get out of the way! There's a car coming!*

the right way up or **round** with the correct part at the top or at the front: *Is this picture the right way up?*

the wrong way up or **round** with the wrong part at the top or at the front: *Those two words are the wrong way round.*

way in where you go into a building: *Here's the museum. Where's the way in?*

way of life how people live: *Is the way of life in Europe different from America?*

way out where you go out of a place: *I can't find the way out.*

WC /ˌdʌblju: 'si:/ *noun*
a toilet

we /wi:/ *pronoun* (plural)
I and another person or other people; you and I: *John and I went out last night – we went to the theatre.* ◇ *Are we late?*

weak /wi:k/ *adjective* (**weaker, weakest**)

1 not powerful or strong: *She felt very weak after her long illness.* ◇ *a weak government* ☞ picture on page 263

2 that can break easily: *The bridge was too weak to carry the heavy lorry.*

2 that you cannot see, taste, smell, hear or feel clearly: *weak tea*

✪ opposite: **strong**

weaken /'wi:kən/ *verb* (**weakens, weakening, weakened** /'wi:kənd/)
become less strong or make somebody or something less strong: *He was weakened by the illness.*

weakness /'wi:knəs/ *noun*

1 (no plural) not being strong: *I have a feeling of weakness in my legs.*

2 (*plural* **weaknesses**) something that is wrong or bad in a person or thing

wealth /welθ/ *noun* (no plural)
having a lot of money, land, etc: *He is a man of great wealth.*

wealthy *adjective* (**wealthier, wealthiest**)
rich: *a wealthy family*

weapon /'wepən/ *noun*
a thing that you use for fighting. Guns and swords are weapons.

wear¹ /weə(r)/ *verb* (**wears, wearing, wore** /wɔ:(r)/, **has worn** /wɔ:n/)
have clothes, etc on your body: *She was wearing a red dress.* ◇ *I wear glasses.*

wear off become less strong: *The pain is wearing off.*

wear out become thin or damaged be-

cause you have used it a lot; make something do this: *Children's shoes usually wear out very quickly.*
wear somebody out make somebody very tired: *She wore herself out by working too hard.*

wear² /weə(r)/ *noun* (no plural)
1 clothes: *sportswear*
2 using something and making it old: *This carpet is showing signs of wear – we will need to buy a new one soon.*

weather /'weðə(r)/ *noun* (no plural)
how much sunshine, rain, wind, etc there is at a certain time, or how hot or cold it is: *What was the weather like in Spain?* ◇ *bad weather*
weather forecast /'weðə fɔːkɑːst/ *noun*
words on television, radio or in a newspaper that tell you what the weather will be like: *The weather forecast says it will be sunny and dry tomorrow.*

weave /wiːv/ *verb* (**weaves, weaving, wove** /wəʊv/, **has woven** /'wəʊvn/)
make cloth by putting threads over and under one other: *These scarves are woven in Scotland.*

web /web/ *noun*
a thin net that a spider makes to catch flies
☞ picture at **spider**

wedding /'wedɪŋ/ *noun*
a time when a man and a woman get married: *Jane and Phil invited me to their wedding.* ◇ *a wedding dress*

we'd /wiːd/
1 = we had
2 = we would

Wednesday /'wenzdeɪ/ *noun*
the fourth day of the week, next after Tuesday

weed /wiːd/ *noun*
a wild plant that grows where you do not want it: *The garden of the old house was full of weeds.*
weed *verb* (**weeds, weeding, weeded**)
pull weeds out of the ground

week /wiːk/ *noun*
1 a time of seven days, usually from Sunday to the next Saturday: *I'm going on holiday next week.* ◇ *I play tennis twice a week.* ◇ *I saw him two weeks ago.* ○ A **fortnight** is the same as two weeks.
2 Monday to Friday or Monday to Satur-

day: *I work during the week but not at weekends.*
weekday /'wiːkdeɪ/ *noun*
any day except Saturday or Sunday: *I only work on weekdays.*
weekend /ˌwiːk'end/ *noun*
Saturday and Sunday: *What are you doing at the weekend?*
weekly /'wiːkli/ *adjective, adverb*
that happens or comes every week or once a week: *a weekly magazine* ◇ *I am paid weekly.*
weep /wiːp/ *verb* (**weeps, weeping, wept** /wept/, **has wept**)
cry ○ **Cry** is the word that we usually use.
weigh /weɪ/ *verb* (**weighs, weighing, weighed** /weɪd/)
1 measure how heavy somebody or something is using a machine called **scales**: *The shop assistant weighed the tomatoes.*
2 have a certain number of kilos, etc: *'How much do you weigh?' 'I weigh 55 kilos.'*
weight /weɪt/ *noun*
1 (no plural) how heavy somebody or something is: *Do you know the weight of the parcel?*
2 (*plural* **weights**) a piece of metal that you use on **scales** for measuring how heavy something is
lose weight become thinner and less heavy: *I'm getting fat – I need to lose weight!*
put on weight become fatter and heavier
weird /wɪəd/ *adjective* (**weirder, weirdest**)
very strange: *a weird dream*
welcome¹ /'welkəm/ *adjective*
If somebody or something is welcome, you are happy to have or see them: *The cool drink was welcome on such a hot day.* ◇ *Welcome to Oxford!*
be welcome to be allowed to do or have something: *If you come to England again, you're welcome to stay with us.*
make somebody welcome show a visitor that you are happy to see him/her
you're welcome polite words that you say when somebody has said 'thank you': *'Thank you.' 'You're welcome.'*
welcome² /'welkəm/ *verb* (**welcome, welcoming, welcomed** /'welkəmd/)
show that you are happy to have or see

p	b	t	d	k	g	tʃ	dʒ	f	v	θ	ð
pen	**b**ad	**t**ea	**d**id	**c**at	**g**ot	**ch**ain	**j**am	**f**all	**v**an	**th**in	**th**is

somebody or something: *He came to the door to welcome us.*

welcome *noun*
They gave us a great welcome when we arrived.

welfare /'welfeə(r)/ *noun* (no plural)
the health and happiness of a person: *The school looks after the welfare of its students.*

well¹ /wel/ *adjective* (**better, best**)
healthy; not ill: *'How are you?' 'I'm very well, thanks.'*

well² /wel/ *adverb* (**better, best**)
1 in a good or right way: *You speak English very well.* ◇ *These shoes are very well-made.* ✿ opposite: **badly**
2 completely or very much: *I don't know Cathy very well.* ◇ *Shake the bottle well before you open it.*
as well also: *'I'm going out.' 'Can I come as well?'*
as well as something and also: *She has a flat in London as well as a house in Edinburgh.*
do well be successful: *He did well in his exams.*
may or **might as well** words that you use to say that you will do something, often because there is nothing else to do: *If you've finished the work, you may as well go home.*
well done! words that you say to somebody who has done something good: *'I got the job!' 'Well done!'*

well³ /wel/
1 a word that you often say when you are starting to speak: *'Do you like it?' 'Well, I'm not really sure.'*
2 a word that you use to show surprise: *Well, that's strange!*

well⁴ /wel/ *noun*
a deep hole for getting water or oil from under the ground: *an oil well*

we'll /wi:l/
1 = we will
2 = we shall

wellingtons /'welɪŋtənz/, **wellington boots** /ˌwelɪŋtən 'bu:ts/ *noun* (plural)
long rubber boots that you wear to keep your feet and part of your legs dry

well-known /ˌwel 'nəʊn/ *adjective*
famous: *a well-known writer*

well off /ˌwel 'ɒf/ *adjective*
rich: *They are very well off and they live in a big house.*

went *form of* **go**¹

wept *form of* **weep**

were *form of* **be**

we're /wɪə(r)/ = we are

weren't /wɜ:nt/ = were not

west /west/ *noun* (no plural)
1 where the sun goes down in the evening: *Which way is west?* ◇ *They live in the west of England.* ☞ picture at **north**
2 **the West** (no plural) the countries of North America and Western Europe
west *adjective, adverb*
West London ◇ *The town is five miles west of here.*

western /'westən/ *adjective*
in or of the west of a place: *Western parts of the country will be very cold.*

western /'westən/ *noun*
a film or book about cowboys in the west of the United States of America

wet /wet/ *adjective* (**wetter, wettest**)
1 covered in water or another liquid; not dry: *This towel is wet – can I have a dry one?* ◇ *wet paint* ☞ picture on page 263
2 with a lot of rain: *a wet day*
✿ opposite: **dry**

we've /wiv/ = we have

whale

whale /weɪl/ *noun*
a very big animal that lives in the sea and looks like a fish

what /wɒt/ *pronoun, adjective*
1 a word that you use when you ask about somebody or something: *What's your*

name? ◇ What are you reading? ◇ What time is it? ◇ What kind of music do you like?
2 the thing that: I don't know what this word means. ◇ Tell me what to do.
3 a word that you use to show surprise or other strong feelings: What a terrible day! ◇ What a beautiful picture!
what about ...? words that you use when you suggest something: What about going to the cinema tonight?
what ... for? why?; for what use?: What did you say that for? ◇ What's this machine for?
what is ... like? words that you use when you want to know more about somebody or something: 'What's her brother like?' 'He's very nice.'
what's on? what television programme, film, etc is being shown?: What's on TV tonight?
what's up? what is wrong?: You look sad. What's up?

whatever /wɒt'evə(r)/ adjective
of any kind; any or every: These animals eat whatever food they can find.
whatever pronoun
1 anything or everything: I'll do whatever I can to help you.
2 it does not matter what: Whatever you do, don't be late.

what's /wɒts/
1 = what is
2 = what has

wheat /wiːt/ noun (no plural)
a plant with seeds (called **grain**) that we can make into flour

wheel /wiːl/ noun
a thing like a circle that turns round to move something. Cars and bicycles have wheels. ☞ picture at **car**
wheel verb (**wheels, wheeling, wheeled** /wiːld/)
push along something that has wheels: I wheeled my bicycle up the hill.

wheelchair /'wiːltʃeə(r)/ noun
a chair with wheels for somebody who cannot walk

when /wen/ adverb
1 at what time: When did she arrive? ◇ I don't know when his birthday is.

2 at the time that: I saw her in May, when she was in London.
when conjunction
at the time that: It was raining when we left school. ◇ He came when I called him.

wheelchair

whenever /wen'evə(r)/ conjunction
1 at any time: Come and see us whenever you want.
2 every time that: Whenever I see her, she talks about her boyfriend.

where /weə(r)/ adverb, conjunction
1 in or to what place: Where do you live? ◇ I asked her where she lived. ◇ Where is she going?
2 in which; at which: This is the street where I live.

whereas /ˌweər'æz/ conjunction
a word that you use between two different ideas: John likes travelling, whereas I don't.

wherever /weər'eve(r)/ adverb, conjunction
1 at, in or to any place: Sit wherever you like.
2 a way of saying 'where' more strongly: Wherever did I put my keys?

whether /'weðə(r)/ conjunction
if: She asked me whether I was Spanish. ◇ I don't know whether to go or not.

which /wɪtʃ/ adjective, pronoun
1 what person or thing: Which colour do you like best – blue or green? ◇ Which flat do you live in?
2 a word that shows what person or thing: Did you read the poem (which) Louise wrote?
3 a word that you use before you say more about something: Her new dress, which she bought in London, is beautiful.

iː	i	ɪ	e	æ	ɑː	ɒ	ɔː	ʊ	u	uː
see	happy	sit	ten	cat	father	got	saw	put	situation	too

whichever /wɪtʃ'evə(r)/ *adjective, pronoun*
any person or thing: *Here are two books – take whichever you want.*

while[1] /waɪl/ *conjunction*
1 during the time that; when: *The telephone rang while I was having a shower.*
2 at the same time as: *I listen to the radio while I'm eating my breakfast.*

while[2] /waɪl/ *noun* (no plural)
some time: *Let's sit here for a while.*
◇ *I'm going home in a while.*

whilst /waɪlst/ *conjunction*
while: *He waited whilst I looked for my keys.*

whine /waɪn/ *verb* (**whines, whining, whined** /waɪnd/)
make a long high sad sound: *The dog was whining outside the door.*

whip /wɪp/ *noun*
a long piece of leather or rope with a handle, for hitting animals or people
whip *verb* (**whips, whipping, whipped** /wɪpt/)
1 hit an animal or a person with a whip: *The rider whipped the horse to make it go faster.*
2 mix food very quickly with a fork, for example, until it is light and thick: *whipped cream*

whirl /wɜ:l/ *verb* (**whirls, whirling, whirled** /wɜ:ld/)
move round and round very quickly: *The dancers whirled round the room.*

whisk /wɪsk/ *verb* (**whisks, whisking, whisked** /wɪskt/)
1 mix eggs or cream very quickly
2 move somebody or something very quickly: *The President was whisked away in a helicopter.*
whisk *noun*
a tool that you use for mixing eggs or cream

whisker /'wɪskə(r)/ *noun*
one of the long hairs that grow near the mouth of cats, mice and other animals
☞ picture at **cat**

whisky /'wɪski/ *noun*
1 (no plural) a strong alcoholic drink
2 (*plural* **whiskies**) a glass of whisky

whisper /'wɪspə(r)/ *verb* (**whispers, whispering, whispered** /'wɪspəd/)
speak very quietly: *He whispered so that he would not wake the baby up.*
whisper *noun*
She spoke in a whisper.

whistle /'wɪsl/ *noun*
1 a small musical instrument that makes a long high sound when you blow it: *The referee blew his whistle to end the match.*
2 the long high sound that you make when you blow air out between your lips
whistle *verb* (**whistles, whistling, whistled** /'wɪsld/)
make a long high sound by blowing air out between your lips or through a whistle: *She whistled to her dog.*

white /waɪt/ *adjective* (**whiter, whitest**)
1 with the colour of snow or milk
2 with light-coloured skin
3 with milk: *a white coffee*
white wine /ˌwaɪt 'waɪn/ *noun*
wine with a light colour
white *noun*
1 (no plural) the colour of snow or milk: *She was dressed in white.*
2 (*plural* **whites**) a person with white skin
3 (*plural* **whites**) the part inside an egg that is round the yellow middle

whiz /wɪz/ *verb* (**whizzes, whizzing, whizzed** /wɪzd/)
move very quickly: *The bullet whizzed past his head.*

who /hu:/ *pronoun*
1 what person or people: *Who is that girl?* ◇ *I don't know who did it.*
2 a word that shows what person or people: *He's the boy who invited me to his party.* ◇ *The people (who) I met on holiday were very nice.*

who'd /hu:d/
1 = who had
2 = who would

whoever /hu'evə(r)/ *pronoun*
1 the person who; any person who: *Whoever broke the glass must pay for it.*
2 a way of saying 'who' more strongly: *Whoever gave you those flowers?*

whole /həʊl/ *adjective*
complete; with no parts missing: *He ate the whole cake!* ◇ *We are going to Spain*

for a whole month.
whole *noun* (no plural)
1 all of something: *I spent the whole of the weekend in bed.*
2 a thing that is complete: *Two halves make a whole.*
on the whole in general: *On the whole, I think it's a good idea.*

who'll /huːl/ = who will

whom /huːm/ *pronoun*
1 what person or people: *To whom did you give the money?*
2 a word that you use to say what person or people: *She's the woman (whom) I met in Greece.*
○ **Who** is the word that we usually use.

who're /ˈhuːə(r)/ = who are

who's /huːz/
1 = who is
2 = who has

whose /huːz/ *adjective, pronoun*
of which person: *Whose car is this?*
◇ *That's the boy whose sister is a singer.*

who've /huːv/ = who have

why /waɪ/ *adverb*
for what reason: *Why are you late?* ◇ *I don't know why she's angry.*
why not words that you use to say that something is a good idea: *Why not ask Kate to go with you?*

wicked /ˈwɪkɪd/ *adjective*
very bad: *a wicked witch*

wide /waɪd/ *adjective* (**wider, widest**)
1 far from one side to the other: *a wide road* ○ opposite: **narrow** ☞ picture on page 262
2 You use 'wide' to say or ask how far something is from one side to the other: *The table was 2 m wide.* ◇ *How wide is the river?* ☞ picture on page 161
3 completely open: *wide eyes*
wide *adverb*
completely; as far or as much as possible: *Open your mouth wide.* ◇ *I'm wide awake!*
wide apart a long way from each other: *She stood with her feet wide apart.*

widen /ˈwaɪdn/ *verb* (**widens, widening, widened** /ˈwaɪdnd/)
become wider; make something wider: *They are widening the road.*

widespread /ˈwaɪdspred/ *adjective*
If something is widespread, it is happening in many places: *The disease is becoming more widespread.*

widow /ˈwɪdəʊ/ *noun*
a woman whose husband is dead

widower /ˈwɪdəʊə(r)/ *noun*
a man whose wife is dead

width /wɪdθ/ *noun*
how far it is from one side of something to the other; how wide something is: *The room is five metres in width.* ☞ picture on page 161

wife /waɪf/ *noun* (*plural* **wives** /waɪvz/)
the woman that a man is married to ☞ picture on page 127

wig /wɪg/ *noun*
a covering for your head made of hair that is not your own

wild /waɪld/ *adjective* (**wilder, wildest**)
1 Wild plants and animals live or grow in nature, not with people: *wild flowers*
2 excited; not controlled: *She was wild with anger.*

wildlife /ˈwaɪldlaɪf/ *noun* (no plural)
animals and plants in nature

will¹ /wɪl/ *modal verb*
1 a word that shows the future: *Do you think she will come tomorrow?*
2 a word that you use when you agree or promise to do something: *I'll (= I will) carry your bag.*
3 a word that you use when you ask somebody to do something: *Will you open the window, please?*

○ The negative form of 'will' is **will not** or the short form **won't** /wəʊnt/:
They won't be there.
The short form of 'will' is **'ll**. We often use this:
You'll (= you will) be late.
He'll (= he will) drive you to the station.
☞ Look at the Note on page 227 to find out more about **modal verbs.**

will² /wɪl/ *noun*
1 (no plural) the power of your mind that makes you choose, decide and do things: *She has a very strong will and nobody can stop her doing what she wants to do.*

2 (no plural) what somebody wants: *The man made him get into the car against his will* (= when he did not want to).

3 (*plural* **wills**) a piece of paper that says who will have your money, house, etc when you die: *My grandmother left me £2 000 in her will.*

willing /'wɪlɪŋ/ *adjective*
ready and happy to do something: *I'm willing to lend you some money.*
willingly *adverb*
I'll willingly help you.
willingness /'wɪlɪŋnəs/ *noun* (no plural)
willingness to help

win /wɪn/ *verb* (**wins, winning, won** /wʌn/, **has won**)
1 be the best or the first in a game, race or competition: *Who won the race?* ◇ *Tom won and I was second.* ✪ opposite: **lose**
2 receive something because you did well or tried hard: *I won a prize in the competition.* ◇ *Who won the gold medal?*
✪ Be careful! You **earn** (not **win**) money by working.
win *noun*
Our team has had five wins this year.

wind¹ /wɪnd/ *noun*
air that moves: *The wind blew his hat off.* ◇ *strong winds*
windy *adjective* (**windier, windiest**)
with a lot of wind: *It's very windy today!*

wind² /waɪnd/ *verb* (**winds, winding, wound** /waʊnd/, **has wound**)
1 make something long go round and round another thing: *The nurse wound the bandage around my finger.*
2 turn a key or handle to make something work or move: *The clock will stop if you don't wind it up.* ◇ *The driver wound her car window down.*
3 A road or river that winds has a lot of bends and turns: *The path winds through the forest.*

windmill

windmill /'wɪndmɪl/ *noun*
a tall building with long flat parts that turn in the wind

window /'wɪndəʊ/ *noun*
an opening in a wall or in a car, for example, with glass in it: *It was cold, so I closed the window.* ◇ *She looked out of the window.* ☞ picture at **house**
window-pane /'wɪndəʊ peɪn/ *noun*
a piece of glass in a window
window-sill /'wɪndəʊ sɪl/, **window-ledge** /'wɪndəʊ ledʒ/ *noun*
a shelf under a window

windscreen /'wɪndskriːn/ *noun*
the big window at the front of a car
☞ picture at **car**
windscreen wiper /'wɪndskriːn ˌwaɪpə(r)/ *noun*
a thing that cleans rain and dirt off the windscreen while you are driving

windshield /'wɪndʃiːld/ *American English for* **windscreen**

windsurfing

windsurfing /'wɪndsɜːfɪŋ/ *noun* (no plural)
the sport of moving over water on a special board with a sail ✪ You can say **go windsurfing**: *Have you been windsurfing?*
windsurfer *noun*
1 a special board with a sail. You stand on it as it moves over the water.
2 a person who rides on a board like this

wine /waɪn/ *noun*
an alcoholic drink made from grapes: *red wine* ◇ *white wine* ◇ *Do you like sweet or dry wine?*

wing /wɪŋ/ *noun*
the part of a bird, an insect or an aeroplane that helps it to fly ☞ picture at **bird**

wink /wɪŋk/ *verb* (**winks, winking, winked** /wɪŋkt/)
close and open one eye quickly to make a

friendly or secret sign: *She winked at me.*
wink *noun*
He gave me a wink.

winner /'wɪnə(r)/ *noun*
a person or animal that wins a game, race or competition: *The winner was given a prize.* ✪ opposite: **loser**

winning /'wɪnɪŋ/ *adjective*
that wins a game, race or competition: *the winning team*

winter /'wɪntə(r)/ *noun*
the coldest part of the year: *It often snows in winter.*

wipe /waɪp/ *verb* (**wipes, wiping, wiped** /waɪpt/)
make something clean or dry with a cloth: *The waitress wiped the table.* ◊ *I washed my hands and wiped them on a towel.*
wipe off take away something by wiping: *She wiped the writing off the blackboard.*
wipe out destroy a place completely, or kill a lot of people: *The bombs wiped out many villages.*
wipe up take away liquid by wiping with a cloth: *I wiped up the milk on the floor.*
wipe *noun*
He gave the table a quick wipe.

wire /'waɪə(r)/ *noun*
a long piece of very thin metal: *electrical wires* ◊ *a piece of wire.*

wisdom /'wɪzdəm/ *noun* (no plural)
knowing and understanding a lot about many things; being wise: *Some people think that old age brings wisdom.*

wise /waɪz/ *adjective* (**wiser, wisest**)
A person who is wise knows and understands a lot about many things: *a wise old man* ◊ *You made a wise choice.*
wisely *adverb*
Many people wisely stayed at home in the bad weather.

wish¹ /wɪʃ/ *verb* (**wishes, wishing, wished** /wɪʃt/)
1 want something that is not possible or that probably will not happen: *I wish I could fly!* ◊ *I wish I had passed the exam!* ◊ *I wish I were rich.*
2 say that you hope somebody will have something: *I wished her a happy birthday.*
3 want to do or have something: *I wish to*

see the manager. ✪ It is more usual to say **want** or **would like.**
wish for something say to yourself that you want something and hope that it will happen: *You can't have everything you wish for.*

wish² /wɪʃ/ *noun* (*plural* **wishes**)
a feeling that you want something: *I have no wish to go.*
best wishes words that you write at the end of a letter, before your name, to show that you hope somebody is well and happy: *See you soon. Best wishes, Lucy.*
make a wish say to yourself that you want something and hope that it will happen: *Close your eyes and make a wish!*

wit /wɪt/ *noun* (no plural)
speaking or writing in a clever and funny way

witch /wɪtʃ/ *noun* (*plural* **witches**)
a woman in stories who uses magic to do bad things

with /wɪð/ *preposition*
1 having or carrying: *a man with grey hair* ◊ *a house with a garden* ◊ *a woman with a suitcase*
2 a word that shows people or things are together: *I live with my parents.* ◊ *Mix the flour with milk.* ◊ *I agree with you.*
3 using: *I cut it with a knife.* ◊ *Fill the bottle with water.*
4 against: *I played tennis with my sister.*
5 because of: *Her hands were blue with cold.*

withdraw /wɪð'drɔː/ *verb* (**withdraws, withdrawing, withdrew** /wɪð'druː/, **has withdrawn** /wɪð'drɔːn/)
1 take something out or away: *I withdrew £100 from my bank account.*
2 move back or away: *The army withdrew from the town.*
3 say that you will not take part in something: *Rob has withdrawn from the race.*

wither /'wɪðə(r)/ *verb* (**withers, withering, withered** /'wɪðəd/)
If a plant withers, it becomes dry and dies: *The plants withered in the hot sun.*

within /wɪ'ðɪn/ *preposition*
1 inside: *There are 400 prisoners within the prison walls.*
2 before the end of: *I will be back within an hour.*
3 not further than: *We live within a mile of the station.*

without /wɪ'ðaʊt/ *preposition*
1 not having, showing or using something: *It's cold – don't go out without your coat.* ◇ *coffee without milk*
2 not being with somebody or something: *He left without me.*
do without manage when something is not there: *There isn't any tea so we will have to do without.*
without doing something not doing something: *They left without saying goodbye.*

witness /'wɪtnəs/ *noun* (*plural* **witnesses**)
1 a person who sees something happen and can tell other people about it later: *There were two witnesses to the accident.*
2 a person in a court of law who tells what he/she saw
witness *verb* (**witnesses, witnessing, witnessed** /'wɪtnəst/)
see something happen: *She witnessed a murder.*

witty /'wɪti/ *adjective* (**wittier, wittiest**)
clever and funny: *a witty answer*

wives *plural of* **wife**

wizard /'wɪzəd/ *noun*
a man in stories who has magic powers

wobble /'wɒbl/ *verb* (**wobbles, wobbling, wobbled** /'wɒbld/)
move a little from side to side: *That chair wobbles when you sit on it.*
wobbly *adjective*
If something is wobbly, it moves a little from side to side: *My legs feel wobbly.*

woke, woken *forms of* **wake**

wolf /wʊlf/ *noun* (*plural* **wolves** /wʊlvz/)
a wild animal like a big dog

woman /'wʊmən/ *noun* (*plural* **women** /'wɪmɪn/)
a grown-up female person: *men, women and children*

won *form of* **win**

wonder[1] /'wʌndə(r)/ *verb* (**wonders, wondering, wondered** /'wʌndəd/)
ask yourself something; want to know something: *I wonder what that noise is.*
◇ *I wonder why he didn't come.*
I wonder if words that you use to ask a question politely: *I wonder if I could use your phone.*

wonder[2] /'wʌndə(r)/ *noun*
1 (no plural) a feeling that you have when you see or hear something very strange, surprising or beautiful: *The children looked up in wonder at the big elephant.*
2 (*plural* **wonders**) something that gives you this feeling: *the wonders of modern medicine*
it's a wonder it is surprising that: *It's a wonder you weren't killed in the accident.*
no wonder it is not surprising: *She didn't sleep last night – no wonder she's tired.*

wonderful /'wʌndəfl/ *adjective*
very good; excellent: *What a wonderful present!* ◇ *This food is wonderful.*

won't /wəʊnt/ = **will not**

wood /wʊd/ *noun*
1 (no plural) the hard part of a tree: *Put some more wood on the fire.* ◇ *The table is made of wood.*
2 (*also* **woods**) a big group of trees, smaller than a forest: *a walk in the woods*
wooden /'wʊdn/ *adjective*
made of wood: *a wooden box*

wool /wʊl/ *noun* (no plural)
1 the soft thick hair of sheep
2 thread or cloth that is made from the hair of sheep: *a ball of wool* ◇ *This jumper is made of wool.*
☞ picture at **knit**
woollen /'wʊlən/ *adjective*
made of wool: *woollen socks*
woolly *adjective*
made of wool, or like wool: *a woolly hat*

woolen, wooly *American English for* **woollen, woolly**

word /wɜːd/ *noun*
1 (*plural* **words**) a sound that you make or a letter or group of letters that you write, that has a meaning: *What's the French word for 'dog'?* ◇ *Do you know the words of this song?*
2 (no plural) a promise: *She gave me her word that she wouldn't tell anyone.*
have a word with somebody speak to somebody: *Can I have a word with you?*
in other words saying the same thing in a different way: *Joe doesn't like hard work – in other words, he's lazy!*
keep your word do what you promised:

Claire said she would come, and she kept her word.

take somebody's word for it believe what somebody says

word for word using exactly the same words: *Ian repeated word for word what you told him.*

word processor /'wɜːd ˌprəʊsesə(r)/ *noun*
a small computer that you can use for writing

wore *form of* **wear**[1]

work[1] /wɜːk/ *noun*
1 (no plural) doing or making something: *Digging the garden is hard work.* ◇ *She's lazy – she never does any work.*
2 (no plural) what you do to earn money; a job: *I'm looking for work.* ◇ *What time do you start work?*
3 (no plural) the place where you have a job: *I phoned him at work.* ◇ *I'm not going to work today.*
4 (no plural) something that you make or do: *The teacher marked our work.*
5 (*plural* **works**) a book, painting or piece of music: *the works of Shakespeare* ◇ *a work of art*
6 works (plural) a place where people make things with machines: *the steelworks*

at work doing some work: *The group are at work on* (= making) *a new album.*

get to work start doing something: *Let's get to work on this washing-up.*

out of work If you are out of work, you do not have a job that you are paid to do: *How long have you been out of work?*

work[2] /wɜːk/ *verb* (**works, working, worked** /wɜːkt/)
1 do or make something; be busy: *You will need to work harder if you want to pass the exam.*
2 do something as a job and get money for it: *Susy works for the BBC.* ◇ *I work at the car factory.*
3 go correctly or do something correctly: *We can't watch the TV – it isn't working.* ◇ *How does this computer work?*
4 make something do something: *Can you show me how to work this machine?*
5 have the result you wanted: *I don't think your plan will work.*

work out 1 have the result you wanted: *I hope your plans work out.* **2** do exercises

to keep your body strong and well: *I work out every day.*

work something out find the answer to something: *We worked out the cost of the holiday.* ◇ *Why did she do it? I can't work it out.*

workbook /'wɜːkbʊk/ *noun*
a book where you write answers to questions, that you use when you are studying something

worker /'wɜːkə(r)/ *noun*
a person who works: *factory workers* ◇ *an office worker*

workman /'wɜːkmən/ *noun* (*plural* **workmen** /'wɜːkmən/)
a man who works with his hands to build or repair something

worksheet /'wɜːkʃiːt/ *noun*
a piece of paper where you write answers to questions, that you use when you are studying something

workshop /'wɜːkʃɒp/ *noun*
1 a place where people make or repair things
2 a time when people meet and work together to learn about something

world /wɜːld/ *noun*
1 (no plural) the earth with all its countries and people: *a map of the world* ◇ *Which is the biggest city in the world?*
2 (*plural* **worlds**) all the people who do the same kind of thing: *the world of politics*

think the world of somebody or **something** like somebody or something very much: *She thinks the world of her grandchildren.*

world-famous /ˌwɜːld 'feɪməs/ *adjective*
known everywhere in the world: *a world-famous writer*

worldwide /ˌwɜːld'waɪd/ *adjective*
that you find everywhere in the world: *Pollution is a worldwide problem.*

worm /wɜːm/ *noun*
a small animal with a long thin body and no legs. Worms live in the ground or in other animals.

worn *form of* **wear**[1]

worn-out /ˌwɔːn 'aʊt/ *adjective*
1 old and completely finished because you

p	b	t	d	k	g	tʃ	dʒ	f	v	θ	ð
pen	**b**ad	**t**ea	**d**id	**c**at	**g**ot	**ch**ain	**j**am	**f**all	**v**an	**th**in	**th**is

have used it a lot: *I threw the shoes away because they were worn-out.*
2 very tired: *He's worn-out after his long journey.*

worried /'wʌrid/ *adjective*
unhappy because you think that something bad will happen or has happened: *Fiona is worried that she's going to fail the exam.* ◇ *I'm worried about my brother – he looks ill.*

worry¹ /'wʌri/ *verb* (**worries, worrying, worried** /'wʌrid/, **has worried**)
1 feel that something bad will happen or has happened: *I worried when Mark didn't come home at the usual time.* ◇ *Don't worry if you don't know the answer.* ◇ *There's nothing to worry about.*
2 make somebody feel that something bad will happen or has happened: *Philip's illness is worrying his parents.*

worry² /'wʌri/ *noun*
1 (no plural) a feeling that something bad will happen or has happened: *Her face showed signs of worry.*
2 (*plural* **worries**) a problem; something that makes you feel worried: *I have a lot of worries.*

worse /wɜːs/ *adjective* (**bad, worse, worst**)
1 more bad; less good: *The weather today is worse than yesterday.* ◇ *Her Spanish is bad but her Italian is even worse.*
2 more ill: *If you get worse, you must go to the doctor's.*
worse *adverb*
more badly

worship /'wɜːʃɪp/ *verb* (**worships, worshipping, worshipped** /'wɜːʃɪpt/)
1 show that you believe in God or a god by praying: *Christians worship in a church.*
2 love somebody very much or think that somebody is wonderful: *She worships her grandchildren.*
worship *noun* (no plural)
A mosque is a place of worship.

worst /wɜːst/ *adjective* (**bad, worse, worst**)
most bad: *He's the worst player in the team!* ◇ *the worst day of my life*
worst *adverb*
most badly: *Jane played badly, but I played worst of all.*
worst *noun* (no plural)
the most bad thing or person: *I'm the worst in the class at grammar.*

if the worst comes to the worst if something very bad happens: *If the worst comes to the worst and I fail the exam, I'll take it again next year.*

worth¹ /wɜːθ/ *adjective*
1 with a value of: *This house is worth £70 000.*
2 good or useful enough to do or have: *Is this film worth seeing?* ◇ *It's not worth asking Lyn for money – she never has any.*

worth² /wɜːθ/ *noun* (no plural)
value: *This painting is of little worth.*
worth of how much of something an amount of money will buy: *I'd like ten pounds' worth of petrol, please.*

worthless /'wɜːθləs/ *adjective*
with no value or use: *A cheque is worthless if you don't sign it.*

worthwhile /ˌwɜːθ'waɪl/ *adjective*
good or useful enough for the time that you spend or the work that you do: *The hard work was worthwhile because I passed the exam.*

would /wʊd/ *modal verb*
1 the word for 'will' in the past: *He said he would come.*
2 a word that you use to talk about a situation that is not real: *If I had a million pounds, I would buy a big house.*
3 a word that you use to ask something in a polite way: *Would you close the door, please?*
4 a word that you use to talk about something that happened many times in the past: *When I was young, my grandparents would visit us every Sunday.*
would like want; words that you use when you ask or say something in a polite way: *Would you like a cup of tea?* ◇ *I would like to go to Africa.*

○ The negative form of 'would' is **would not** or the short form **wouldn't** /wʊdnt/:

He wouldn't help me.

The short form of 'would' is **'d**. We often use this:

I'd (= I would) *like to meet her.*

They'd (= they would) *help if they had the time.*

☞ Look at the Note on page 227 to find out more about **modal verbs.**

s	z	ʃ	ʒ	h	m	n	ŋ	l	r	j	w
so	**zoo**	**sh**oe	vi**si**on	**h**at	**m**an	**n**o	si**ng**	**l**eg	**r**ed	**y**es	**w**et

would've /'wʊdəv/ = would have

wound[1] *form of* **wind**[2]

wound[2] /wuːnd/ *verb* (**wounds, wounding, wounded**)
hurt somebody: *The bullet wounded him in the leg.*
wound *noun*
a hurt place in your body made by something like a gun or a knife: *a knife wound*

wove, woven *forms of* **weave**

wow /waʊ/
a word that shows surprise and pleasure: *Wow! What a lovely car!*

wrap /ræp/ *verb* (**wraps, wrapping, wrapped** /ræpt/)
put paper or cloth around somebody or something: *The baby was wrapped in a blanket.* ◇ *She wrapped the glass up in paper.* ○ opposite: **unwrap**

wrapper /'ræpə(r)/ *noun*
a piece of paper or plastic that covers something like a sweet or a packet of cigarettes: *Don't throw your wrappers on the floor!*

wrapping /'ræpɪŋ/ *noun*
a piece of paper or plastic that covers a present or something that you buy: *I took the new shirt out of its wrapping.*
wrapping paper /'ræpɪŋ peɪpə(r)/ *noun* (no plural)
special paper that you use to wrap presents

wreath /riːθ/ *noun* (*plural* **wreaths**) /riːðz/
a circle of flowers or leaves: *She put a wreath on the grave.*

wreck /rek/ *noun*
a ship, car or plane that has been very badly damaged in an accident: *a shipwreck at sea*
wreck *verb* (**wrecks, wrecking, wrecked** /rekt/)
break or destroy something completely: *The fire wrecked the hotel.*

wreckage /'rekɪdʒ/ *noun* (no plural)
the broken parts of something that has been badly damaged: *They found a child in the wreckage of the plane.*

wrench /rentʃ/ *American English for* **spanner**

wrestle /'resl/ *verb* (**wrestles, wrestling, wrestled** /'resld/)
fight by trying to throw somebody to the ground. People often wrestle as a sport.
wrestler *noun*
a person who wrestles as a sport
wrestling *noun* (no plural)
the sport where two people fight and try to throw each other to the ground: *a wrestling match*

wriggle /'rɪgl/ *verb* (**wriggles, wriggling, wriggled** /'rɪgld/)
turn your body quickly from side to side, like a worm: *The teacher told the children to stop wriggling.*

wring /rɪŋ/ *verb* (**wrings, wringing, wrung** /rʌŋ/, **has wrung**)
press and twist something with your hands to make water come out: *He wrung the towel out and put it outside to dry.*

wrinkle /'rɪŋkl/ *noun*
a small line in something, for example in the skin of your face: *My grandmother has a lot of wrinkles.*
wrinkled /'rɪŋkld/ *adjective*
with a lot of wrinkles

wrist /rɪst/ *noun*
the part of your body where your arm joins your hand ☞ picture on page 126

write /raɪt/ *verb* (**writes, writing, wrote** /rəʊt/, **has written** /'rɪtn/)
1 make letters or words on paper using a pen or pencil: *Write your name at the top of the page.* ◇ *He can't read or write.*
2 write and send a letter to somebody: *My mother writes to me every week.* ◇ *I wrote her a postcard.*
3 make a story, book, etc: *Shakespeare wrote plays.*
write down write something on paper, so that you can remember it: *I wrote down his telephone number.*

writer /'raɪtə(r)/ *noun*
a person who writes books, stories, etc: *Charles Dickens was a famous writer.*

writing /'raɪtɪŋ/ *noun* (no plural)
1 words that somebody puts on paper: *I can't read your writing – it's so small.*
2 putting words on paper: *Writing is slower than telephoning.*
in writing written on paper: *They have*

i:	i	ɪ	e	æ	ɑː	ɒ	ɔː	ʊ	u	uː
see	happy	sit	ten	cat	father	got	saw	put	situation	too

offered me the job on the telephone but not in writing.

writing-paper /'raɪtɪŋ peɪpə(r)/ *noun* (no plural)
paper for writing letters on

written *form of* **write**

wrong[1] /rɒŋ/ *adjective*
1 not true or not correct: *She gave me the wrong key, so I couldn't open the door.* ◇ *This clock is wrong.* ✪ opposite: **right**
2 bad, or not what the law allows: *Stealing is wrong.* ◇ *I haven't done anything wrong.* ✪ opposite: **right**
3 not the best: *We're late because we took the wrong road.* ✪ opposite: **right**
4 not as it should be, or not working well: *There's something wrong with my car – it won't start.* ◇ *'What's wrong with Mrs Snow?' 'She's got a cold.'*

wrong *adverb*
not correctly; not right: *You've spelt my name wrong.*

go wrong 1 stop working well: *The video has gone wrong – can you mend it?*
2 not happen as you hoped or wanted: *All our plans went wrong.*

wrong[2] /rɒŋ/ *noun* (no plural)
what is bad or not right: *Babies don't know the difference between right and wrong.*

wrongly /'rɒŋli/ *adverb*
not correctly: *The letter didn't arrive because it was wrongly addressed.*

wrote *form of* **write**

wrung *form of* **wring**

Xx

Xmas /'eksməs/ *short for* **Christmas**
✪ **Xmas** is used mainly in writing.

X-ray /'eksreɪ/ *noun*
a photograph of the inside of your body that is made by using a special light that you cannot see: *The doctor took an X-ray of my arm to see if it was broken.*

X-ray *verb* (**X-rays, X-raying, X-rayed** /'eksreɪd/)
take a photograph using an X-ray machine: *She had her leg X-rayed.*

xylophone /'zaɪləfəʊn/ *noun*
a musical instrument with metal or wooden bars that you hit with small hammers

Yy

yacht /jɒt/ *noun*
1 a boat with **sails** that is used for racing
2 a big boat with a motor: *a millionaire's yacht*

yard[1] /jɑːd/ *noun*
a measure of length (= 91 centimetres). There are three **feet** or thirty-six **inches** in a yard. ✪ The short way of writing 'yard' is **yd**. ☞ Note at **foot**

yard[2] /jɑːd/ *noun*
a piece of hard ground next to a building,

with a fence or wall around it: *The children were playing in the school yard.* ◇ *a farmyard*

yawn /jɔːn/ *verb* (**yawns, yawning, yawned** /jɔːnd/)
open your mouth wide because you are tired

yawn *noun*
'I'm going to bed now,' she said with a yawn.

yd *short way of writing* **yard**[1]

ʌ	ɜː	ə	eɪ	əʊ	aɪ	aʊ	ɔɪ	ɪə	eə	ʊə
cup	**bird**	**about**	**say**	**go**	**five**	**now**	**boy**	**near**	**hair**	**pure**

yeah /jeə/
yes ○ This is an informal word.

year /jɪə(r)/ *noun*
1 a time of 365 or 366 days from 1 January to 31 December. A year has twelve **months**: *Where are you going on holiday this year?* ◇ *'In which year were you born?' 'In 1976.'* ◇ *I left school last year.*
2 any time of twelve months: *I have known Chris for three years.* ◇ *My son is five years old.* ◇ *I have a five-year-old son.* ◇ *a two-year-old* ○ Be careful! You can say: *She's ten.* or: *She's ten years old.* (BUT NOT: *She's ten years.*)
all year round through all the year: *The swimming-pool is open all year round.*

yearly /'jɪəli/ *adjective, adverb*
that happens or comes every year or once a year: *a yearly visit* ◇ *We meet twice yearly.*

yeast /ji:st/ *noun* (no plural)
stuff that you use for making bread rise

yell /jel/ *verb* (**yells, yelling, yelled** /jeld/)
shout loudly: *'Look out!' she yelled as the car came towards them.*
yell *noun*
He gave a yell of pain.

yellow /'jeləʊ/ *adjective*
with the colour of a lemon or of butter: *She was wearing a yellow shirt.* ◇ *bright yellow flowers*
yellow *noun*
Yellow is my favourite colour.

yes /jes/
a word that you use for answering a question. You use 'yes' to agree, to say that something is true, or to say that you would like something: *'Have you got the key?' 'Yes, here it is.'* ◇ *'Would you like some coffee?' 'Yes, please.'*

yesterday /'jestədeɪ/ *adverb, noun* (no plural)
(on) the day before today: *I saw Tom yesterday.* ◇ *I phoned you yesterday afternoon but you were out.* ◇ *I sent the letter the day before yesterday.*

yet¹ /jet/ *adverb*
1 until now: *I haven't finished the book yet.* ◇ *Have you seen that film yet?*
☞ Note at **already**

2 now; as early as this: *You don't need to go yet – it's only seven o'clock.*
3 in the future: *They may win yet.*
as yet until now: *As yet, I haven't met her.*
yet again once more: *John is late yet again!*

yet² /jet/ *conjunction*
but; however: *We arrived home tired yet happy.*

yoghurt /'jɒgət/ *noun*
thick liquid food made from milk: *strawberry yoghurt* ◇ *Do you want a yoghurt?*

yolk /jəʊk/ *noun*
the yellow part in an egg

you /ju:/, /ju/ *pronoun*
1 the person or people that I am speaking to: *You are late.* ◇ *I phoned you yesterday.*
2 any person; a person: *You can buy stamps at a post office.*

you'd /ju:d/
1 = you had
2 = you would

you'll /ju:l/ = you will

young¹ /jʌŋ/ *adjective* (**younger** /'jʌŋgə(r)/, **youngest** /'jʌŋgɪst/)
in the early part of life; not old: *They have two young children.* ◇ *You're younger than me.* ☞ picture on page 262

young² /jʌŋ/ *noun* (plural)
1 baby animals: *Birds build nests for their young.*
2 **the young** (plural) children and young people: *a television programme for the young*

your /jɔ:(r)/ *adjective*
of you: *Where is your car?* ◇ *Do you all have your books?* ◇ *Show me your hands.*

you're /jɔ:(r)/ = you are

yours /jɔ:z/ *pronoun*
1 something that belongs to you: *Is this pen yours or mine?*
2 **Yours** a word that you write at the end of a letter: *Yours sincerely ...* ◇ *Yours faithfully ...*

yourself /jɔ:'self/ *pronoun* (plural **yourselves** /jɔ:'selvz/)
1 a word that shows 'you' when I have

p	b	t	d	k	g	tʃ	dʒ	f	v	θ	ð
pen	**b**ad	**t**ea	**d**id	**c**at	**g**ot	**ch**ain	**j**am	**f**all	**v**an	**th**in	**th**is

just talked about you: *Did you hurt your-self?* ◇ *Buy yourselves a drink.*
2 a word that makes 'you' stronger: *Did you make this cake yourself?* ◇ *'Who told you?' 'You told me yourself!'*
by yourself, by yourselves **1** alone; without other people: *Do you live by your-self?* **2** without help: *You can't carry all those bags by yourself.*

youth / juːθ/ *noun*
1 (no plural) the part of your life when you are young: *He spent his youth in Ger-*

many. ◇ *She was very poor in her youth.*
2 (*plural* **youths** /juːðz/) a boy or young man
3 **the youth** (plural) young people: *the youth of this country*
youth club /ˈjuːθ klʌb/ *noun*
a club for young people
youth hostel /ˈjuːθ hɒstl/ *noun*
a cheap place where young people can stay when they are travelling or on holiday

you've /juːv/ = **you have**

Zz

zebra

zebra /ˈzebrə/ *noun*
an African wild animal like a horse, with black and white lines on its body
zebra crossing /ˌzebrə ˈkrɒsɪŋ/ *noun*
a black and white path across a road. Cars must stop there to let people cross the road safely.

zero /ˈzɪərəʊ/ *noun*
1 the number 0
2 the point between + and – on a thermo-meter: *The temperature is five degrees be-low zero.*

zigzag

zigzag /ˈzɪgzæg/ *noun*
a line that goes sharply up and down

zip /zɪp/ *noun*
a long metal or plastic thing with a small part that you pull to close and open things like clothes and bags
zip *verb* (**zips, zipping, zipped** /zɪpt/)

zip

zip up close something with a zip: *She zipped up her dress.*

zip code /ˈzɪp kəʊd/ *American English for* **postcode**

zipper /ˈzɪpə(r)/ *American English for* **zip**

zone /zəʊn/ *noun*
a place where something special happens: *Do not enter the danger zone!*

zoo /zuː/ *noun* (*plural* **zoos**)
a place where you can see wild animals in cages or behind fences

zoom /zuːm/ *verb* (**zooms, zooming, zoomed** /zuːmd/)
move very fast: *Mark zoomed past in his car.*

s	z	ʃ	ʒ	h	m	n	ŋ	l	r	j	w
so	**zoo**	**shoe**	vision	**hat**	**man**	**no**	sing	**leg**	**red**	**yes**	**wet**

Irregular verbs

Infinitive	Past tense	Past participle
be	was, were	been
bear	bore	borne
beat	beat	beaten
become	became	become
begin	began	begun
bend	bent	bent
bet	bet, betted	bet, betted
bind	bound	bound
bite	bit	bitten
bleed	bled	bled
blow	blew	blown
break	broke	broken
breed	bred	bred
bring	brought	brought
broadcast	broadcast	broadcast
build	built	built
burn	burnt, burned	burnt, burned
burst	burst	burst
buy	bought	bought
catch	caught	caught
choose	chose	chosen
cling	clung	clung
come	came	come
cost	cost	cost
creep	crept	crept
cut	cut	cut
deal	dealt	dealt
dig	dug	dug
do	did	done
draw	drew	drawn
dream	dreamt, dreamed	dreamt, dreamed
drink	drank	drunk
drive	drove	driven
eat	ate	eaten
fall	fell	fallen
feed	fed	fed
feel	felt	felt
fight	fought	fought
find	found	found
flee	fled	fled
fling	flung	flung
fly	flew	flown
forbid	forbade	forbidden
forget	forgot	forgotten
forgive	forgave	forgiven
freeze	froze	frozen
get	got	got
give	gave	given
go	went	gone

Infinitive	Past tense	Past participle
grind	ground	ground
grow	grew	grown
hang	hung, hanged	hung, hanged
have	had	had
hear	heard	heard
hide	hid	hidden
hit	hit	hit
hold	held	held
hurt	hurt	hurt
keep	kept	kept
kneel	knelt, kneeled	knelt, kneeled
know	knew	known
lay	laid	laid
lead	led	led
lean	leant, leaned	leant, leaned
leap	leapt, leaped	leapt, leaped
learn	learnt, learned	learnt, learned
leave	left	left
lend	lent	lent
let	let	let
lie	lay	lain
light	lit, lighted	lit, lighted
lose	lost	lost
make	made	made
mean	meant	meant
meet	met	met
mislead	misled	misled
mistake	mistook	mistaken
misunderstand	misunderstood	misunderstood
mow	mowed	mown
overhear	overheard	overheard
oversleep	overslept	overslept
overtake	overtook	overtaken
pay	paid	paid
prove	proved	proved, proven
put	put	put
read	read	read
repay	repaid	repaid
ride	rode	ridden
ring	rang	rung
rise	rose	risen
run	ran	run
saw	sawed	sawn
say	said	said
see	saw	seen
seek	sought	sought
sell	sold	sold
send	sent	sent
set	set	set
sew	sewed	sewed, sewn
shake	shook	shaken
shed	shed	shed
shine	shone	shone
shoot	shot	shot

Infinitive	Past tense	Past participle
show	showed	shown, showed
shrink	shrank	shrunk
shut	shut	shut
sing	sang	sung
sink	sank	sunk
sit	sat	sat
sleep	slept	slept
slide	slid	slid
sling	slung	slung
slit	slit	slit
smell	smelt, smelled	smelt, smelled
sow	sowed	sown, sowed
speak	spoke	spoken
speed	sped, speeded	sped, speeded
spell	spelt, spelled	spelt, spelled
spend	spent	spent
spill	spilt, spilled	spilt, spilled
spin	spun	spun
spit	spat	spat
split	split	split
spoil	spoilt, spoiled	spoilt, spoiled
spread	spread	spread
spring	sprang	sprung
stand	stood	stood
steal	stole	stolen
stick	stuck	stuck
sting	stung	stung
stink	stank	stunk
stride	strode	stridden
strike	struck	struck
swear	swore	sworn
sweep	swept	swept
swell	swelled	swollen, swelled
swim	swam	swum
swing	swung	swung
take	took	taken
teach	taught	taught
tear	tore	torn
tell	told	told
think	thought	thought
throw	threw	thrown
thrust	thrust	thrust
tread	trod	trodden
understand	understood	understood
undo	undid	undone
upset	upset	upset
wake	woke	woken
wear	wore	worn
weave	wove	woven
weep	wept	wept
win	won	won
wind	wound	wound
wring	wrung	wrung
write	wrote	written

424

Geographical names

If there are different words for the adjective and the person who comes from a particular place, we also give the word for the person, for example **Finland; Finnish** (person: **Finn**).

	noun	adjective	
/æfˈgænɪstɑːn/	Afghanistan	Afghan	/ˈæfgæn/
/ˈæfrɪkə/	Africa	African	/ˈæfrɪkən/
/ælˈbeɪniə/	Albania	Albanian	/ælˈbeɪniən/
/ælˈdʒɪəriə/	Algeria	Algerian	/ælˈdʒɪəriən/
/əˈmerɪkə/	America	American	/əˈmerɪkən/
/æŋˈgəʊlə/	Angola	Angolan	/æŋˈgəʊlən/
/ænˈtɑːktɪk/	the Antarctic	Antarctic	/ænˈtɑːktɪk/
/ˈɑːktɪk/	the Arctic	Arctic	/ˈɑːktɪk/
/ˌɑːdʒənˈtiːnə/	Argentina	Argentinian,	/ˌɑːdʒənˈtɪniən/
		Argentine	/ˈɑːdʒəntaɪn/
/ɑːˈmiːniə/	Armenia	Armenian	/ɑːˈmiːniən/
/ˈeɪʃə/	Asia	Asian	/ˈeɪʃən/
/ətˈlæntɪk/	the Atlantic	the Atlantic	/ətˈlæntɪk/
/ɒˈstreɪliə/	Australia	Australian	/ɒˈstreɪliən/
/ˈɒstriə/	Austria	Austrian	/ˈɒstriən/
/ˌæzəbaɪˈdʒɑːn/	Azerbaijan	Azerbaijani	/ˌæzəbaɪˈdʒɑːni/
/ˌbæŋgləˈdeʃ/	Bangladesh	Bangladeshi	/ˌbæŋgləˈdeʃi/
/biˌeləˈruːs/	Belarus	Belorussian	/biˌeləˈrʌʃn/
/ˈbeldʒəm/	Belgium	Belgian	/ˈbeldʒən/
/beˈniːn/	Benin	Beninese	/ˌbenɪˈniːz/
/bəˈlɪviə/	Bolivia	Bolivian	/bəˈlɪviən/
/ˌbɒzniə ˌhɜːtsəgəˈviːnə/	Bosnia-Herzegovina	Bosnian	/ˈbɒzniən/
/bɒtˈswɑːnə/	Botswana	Botswanan	/bɒˈtswɑːnən/
/brəˈzɪl/	Brazil	Brazilian	/brəˈzɪliən/
/ˈbrɪtn/	Britain	British	/ˈbrɪtɪʃ/
		(person: Briton)	/ˈbrɪtn/
/bʌlˈgeəriə/	Bulgaria	Bulgarian	/bʌlˈgeəriən/
/bɜːˈkiːnə/	Burkina	Burkinese	/ˌbɜːkɪˈniːz/
/buˈrʊndi/	Burundi	Burundian	/buˈrʊndiən/
/kæmˈbəʊdiə/	Cambodia	Cambodian	/kæmˈbəʊdiən/
/ˌkæməˈruːn/	Cameroon	Cameroonian	/ˌkæməˈruːniən/
/ˈkænədə/	Canada	Canadian	/kəˈneɪdiən/
/ˌkærəˈbiːən/	the Caribbean	Caribbean	/ˌkærəˈbiːən/
/ˌsentrəl ˌæfrɪkən rɪˈpʌblɪk/	Central African Republic		
/tʃæd/	Chad	Chadian	/ˈtʃædiən/
/ˈtʃɪli/	Chile	Chilean	/ˈtʃɪliən/
/ˈtʃaɪnə/	China	Chinese	/ˌtʃaɪˈniːz/
/kəˈlɒmbiə/	Colombia	Colombian	/kəˈlɒmbiən/
/ˈkɒŋgəʊ/	Congo	Congolese	/ˌkɒŋgəˈliːz/

	noun	**adjective**	
/ˌkɒstə ˈriːkə/	Costa Rica	Costa Rican	/ˌkɒstə ˈriːkən/
/krəʊˈeɪʃə/	Croatia	Croatian	/krəʊˈeɪʃən/
/ˈkjuːbə/	Cuba	Cuban	/ˈkjuːbən/
/ˈsaɪprəs/	Cyprus	Cypriot	/ˈsɪpriət/
/ˌtʃek rɪˈpʌblɪk/	Czech Republic	Czech	/tʃek/
/ˈdenmɑːk/	Denmark	Danish	/ˈdeɪnɪʃ/
		(person: Dane)	/deɪn/
/ˈekwədɔː(r)/	Ecuador	Ecuadorian	/ˌekwəˈdɔːriən/
/ˈiːdʒɪpt/	Egypt	Egyptian	/iˈdʒɪpʃn/
/el ˈsælvədɔː(r)/	El Salvador	Salvadorean	/ˌsælvəˈdɔːriən/
/ˈɪŋglənd/	England	English	/ˈɪŋglɪʃ/
		(person: Englishman,	/ˈɪŋglɪʃmən/
		Englishwoman)	/ˈɪŋglɪʃwʊmən/
/eˈstəʊniə/	Estonia	Estonian	/eˈstəʊniən/
/ˌiːθiˈəʊpiə/	Ethiopia	Ethiopian	/ˌiːθiˈəʊpiən/
/ˈjʊərəp/	Europe	European	/ˌjʊərəˈpiən/
/ˈfɪnlənd/	Finland	Finnish	/ˈfɪnɪʃ/
		(person: Finn)	/fɪn/
/frɑːns/	France	French	/frentʃ/
		(person: Frenchman,	/ˈfrentʃmən/
		Frenchwoman)	/ˈfrentʃwʊmən/
/ˈgæmbiə/	Gambia	Gambian	/ˈgæmbiən/
/ˈdʒɔːdʒə/	Georgia	Georgian	/ˈdʒɔːdʒən/
/ˈdʒɜːməni/	Germany	German	/ˈdʒɜːmən/
/ˈgɑːnə/	Ghana	Ghanaian	/gɑːˈneɪən/
/ˌgreɪt ˈbrɪtn/	Great Britain	British	/ˈbrɪtɪʃ/
		(person: Briton)	/ˈbrɪtn/
/griːs/	Greece	Greek	/griːk/
/ˌgwɑːtəˈmɑːlə/	Guatemala	Guatemalan	/ˌgwɑːtəˈmɑːlən/
/ˈgɪni/	Guinea	Guinean	/ˈgɪniən/
/ˈheɪti/	Haiti	Haitian	/ˈheɪʃn/
/ˈhɒlənd/	Holland	Dutch	/dʌtʃ/
/hɒnˈdʒʊərəs/	Honduras	Honduran	/hɒnˈdʒʊərən/
/ˈhʌŋgəri/	Hungary	Hungarian	/hʌŋˈgeəriən/
/ˈaɪslənd/	Iceland	Icelandic	/aɪsˈlændɪk/
		(person: Icelander)	/ˈaɪsləndə(r)/
/ˈɪndiə/	India	Indian	/ˈɪndiən/
/ˌɪndəˈniːziə/	Indonesia	Indonesian	/ˌɪndəˈniːziən/
/ɪˈrɑːn/	Iran	Iranian	/ɪˈreɪniən/
/ɪˈrɑːk/	Iraq	Iraqi	/ɪˈrɑːki/
/ˈaɪələnd/	Ireland	Irish	/ˈaɪrɪʃ/
		(person: Irishman,	/ˈaɪərɪʃmən/
		Irishwoman)	/ˈaɪərɪʃwʊmən/
/ˈɪzreɪl/	Israel	Israeli	/ɪzˈreɪli/
/ˈɪtəli/	Italy	Italian	/ɪˈtæliən/
/ˌaɪvəri ˈkəʊst/	Ivory Coast	Ivorian	/aɪˈvɔːriən/
/dʒəˈmeɪkə/	Jamaica	Jamaican	/dʒəˈmeɪkən/
/dʒəˈpæn/	Japan	Japanese	/ˌdʒæpəˈniːz/
/ˈdʒɔːdn/	Jordan	Jordanian	/dʒɔːˈdeɪniən/
/ˌkæzækˈstɑːn/	Kazakhstan	Kazakh	/kəˈzæk/

	noun	**adjective**	
/'kenjə/	Kenya	Kenyan	/'kenjən/
/ˌkɪəgɪz'stɑːn/	Kirgyzstan	Kirgyz	/kɪə'gɪːz/
/kə'rɪə/	Korea	Korean	/kə'rɪən/
/ku'weɪt/	Kuwait	Kuwaiti	/ku'weɪti/
/laʊs/	Laos	Laotian	/'laʊʃn/
/'lætviə/	Latvia	Latvian	/'lætviən/
/'lebənən/	Lebanon	Lebanese	/ˌlebə'niːz/
/'lɪbiə/	Libya	Libyan	/'lɪbiən/
/ˌlɪθju'eɪniə/	Lithuania	Lithuanian	/ˌlɪθju'eɪniən/
/ˌmæsə'dəʊniə/	Macedonia (former Yugoslav republic)	Macedonian	/ˌmæsə'dəʊniən/
/ˌmædə'gæskə(r)/	Madagascar	Madagascan (person: Malagasy)	/ˌmædə'gæskən/ /ˌmælə'gæsɪ/
/mə'lɑːwi/	Malawi	Malawian	/mə'lɑːwiən/
/mə'leɪziə/	Malaysia	Malaysian	/mə'leɪziən/
/'mɑːli/	Mali	Malian	/'mɑːliən/
/ˌmedɪtə'reɪniən/	the Mediterranean	Mediterranean	/ˌmedɪtə'reɪniən/
/'meksɪkəʊ/	Mexico	Mexican	/'meksɪkən/
/mɒl'dəʊvə/	Moldova	Moldovan	/mɒl'dəʊvən/
/mə'rɒkəʊ/	Morocco	Moroccan	/mə'rɒkən/
/ˌməʊzæm'biːk/	Mozambique	Mozambiquean	/ˌməʊzæm'biːkən/
/ˌmiːæn'mɑː(r)/	Myanmar	Myanmar	/ˌmiːæn'mɑː(r)/
/nɪ'pɔːl/	Nepal	Nepalese	/ˌnepə'liːz/
/'neðələndz/	the Netherlands	Dutch (person: Dutchman, Dutchwoman)	/dʌtʃ/ /'dʌtʃmən/ /'dʌtʃwʊmən/
/ˌnjuː 'ziːlənd/	New Zealand	New Zealand (person: New Zealander)	/ˌnjuː 'ziːlənd/ /ˌnjuː 'ziːləndə(r)/
/ˌnɪkə'rægjuə/	Nicaragua	Nicaraguan	/ˌnɪkə'rægjuən/
/niː'ʒeə(r)/	Niger	Nigerien	/niː'ʒeəriən/
/naɪ'dʒɪəriə/	Nigeria	Nigerian	/naɪ'dʒɪəriən/
/ˌnɔːðən 'aɪələnd/	Northern Ireland	Northern Irish	/ˌnɔːðen 'aɪərɪʃ/
/'nɔːweɪ/	Norway	Norwegian	/nɔː'wiːdʒən/
/pə'sɪfɪk/	the Pacific	Pacific	/pə'sɪfɪk/
/ˌpɑːkɪ'stɑːn/	Pakistan	Pakistani	/ˌpɑːkɪ'stɑːni/
/'pæləstaɪn/	Palestine	Palestinian	/ˌpælə'stɪniən/
/'pænəmɑː/	Panama	Panamanian	/ˌpænə'meɪniən/
/ˌpæpuə ˌnjuː 'gɪni/	Papua New Guinea	Papuan	/'pæpuən/
/'pærəgwaɪ/	Paraguay	Paraguayan	/ˌpærə'gwaiən/
/pə'ruː/	Peru	Peruvian	/pə'ruːviən/
/'fɪlɪpiːnz/	the Philippines	Philippine (person: Filipino)	/'fɪlɪpiːn/ /ˌfɪlɪ'piːnəʊ/
/'pəʊlənd/	Poland	Polish (person: Pole)	/'pəʊlɪʃ/ /pəʊl/
/'pɔːtʃʊgl/	Portugal	Portuguese	/ˌpɔːtʃʊ'giːz/
/ˌpwɜːtəʊ 'riːkəʊ/	Puerto Rico	Puerto Rican	/ˌpwɜːtəʊ 'riːkən/
/ru'meɪniə/	Romania	Romanian	/ru'meɪniən/
/'rʌʃə/	Russia	Russian	/rʌʃn/
/ru'ændə/	Rwanda	Rwandan	/ru'ændən/
/ˌsaʊdi ə'reɪbiə/	Saudi Arabia	Saudi	/'saʊdi/

	noun	adjective	
/'skɒtlənd/	Scotland	Scottish	/'skɒtɪʃ/
		(person: Scot,	/skɒt/
		Scotsman,	/'skɒtsmən/
		Scotswoman)	/'skɒtswʊmən/
/ˌsenɪ'gɔ:l/	Senegal	Senegalese	/ˌsenɪgə'li:z/
/siˌerə li'əʊn/	Sierra Leone	Sierra Leonean	/siˌerə li'əʊniən/
/ˌsɪŋgə'pɔ:(r)/	Singapore	Singaporean	/ˌsɪŋgə'pɔ:riən/
/sləʊ'vækiə/	Slovakia	Slovak	/'sləʊvæk/
/sləʊ'vi:niə/	Slovenia	Slovenian	/sləʊ'vi:niən/
/sə'mɑ:liə/	Somalia	Somali	/sə'mɑ:li/
/ˌsaʊθ 'æfrɪkə/	South Africa	South African	/ˌsaʊθ 'æfrɪkən/
/speɪn/	Spain	Spanish	/'spænɪʃ/
		(person: Spaniard)	/'spænɪəd/
/ˌsri: 'læŋkə/	Sri Lanka	Sri Lankan	/ˌsri: 'læŋkən/
/su'dɑ:n/	Sudan	Sudanese	/ˌsu:də'ni:z/
/'swi:dn/	Sweden	Swedish	/'swi:dɪʃ/
		(person: Swede)	/swi:d/
/'swɪtsələnd/	Switzerland	Swiss	/swɪs/
/'sɪriə/	Syria	Syrian	/'sɪriən/
/taɪ'wɑ:n/	Taiwan	Taiwanese	/ˌtaɪwə'ni:z/
/tæˌdʒi:kɪ'stɑ:n/	Tajikistan	Tajik	/tə'dʒi:k/
/ˌtænzə'ni:ə/	Tanzania	Tanzanian	/ˌtænzə'ni:ən/
/'taɪlænd/	Thailand	Thai	/taɪ/
/tɪ'bet/	Tibet	Tibetan	/tɪ'betn/
/'təʊgəʊ/	Togo	Togolese	/ˌtəʊgə'li:z/
/tju'nɪziə/	Tunisia	Tunisian	/tju'nɪziən/
/'tɜ:ki/	Turkey	Turkish	/'tɜ:kɪʃ/
		(person: Turk)	/tɜ:k/
/tɜ:kˌmenɪ'stɑ:n/	Turkmenistan	Turkmen	/'tɜ:kmen/
/ju:'gændə/	Uganda	Ugandan	/ju:'gændən/
/ju:'kreɪn/	Ukraine	Ukrainian	/ju:'kreɪniən/
/juˌnaɪtɪd 'kɪŋdəm/	the United Kingdom	British	/'brɪtɪʃ/
/ˌju: 'keɪ/	(also UK)		
/juˌnaɪtɪd ˌsteɪts əv ə'merɪkə/	the United States of America	American	/ə'merɪkən/
/ˌju: es 'eɪ/ /ˌju: 'es/	(also USA and US)		
/'jʊərəgwaɪ/	Uruguay	Uruguayan	/ˌjʊərə'gwaɪən/
/ʊzˌbekɪ'stɑ:n/	Uzbekistan	Uzbek	/'ʊzbek/
/ˌvenə'zweɪlə/	Venezuela	Venezuelan	/ˌvenə'zweɪlən/
/ˌvjet'næm/	Vietnam	Vietnamese	/ˌvjetnə'mi:z/
/weɪlz/	Wales	Welsh	/welʃ/
		(person: Welshman,	/'welʃmən/
		Welshwoman)	/'welʃwʊmən/
/ˌwest 'ɪndiz/	the West Indies	West Indian	/ˌwest 'ɪndiən/
	(the Republic of)		
/'jemən/	Yemen	Yemeni	/'jeməni/
/ˌju:gəʊ'slɑ:viə/	Yugoslavia	Yugoslavian	/ˌju:gəʊ'slɑ:viən/
		(person: Yugoslav)	/'ju:gəʊslɑ:v/
/zɑ:'ɪə(r)/	Zaire	Zairean	/zɑ:'ɪəriən/
/'zæmbɪə/	Zambia	Zambian	/'zæmbiən/
/zɪm'bɑ:bwi/	Zimbabwe	Zimbabwean	/zɪm'bɑ:bwiən/

Phonetic symbols

Vowels

iː	see	/siː/	ʌ	cup	/kʌp/
i	happy	/ˈhæpi/	ɜː	bird	/bɜːd/
ɪ	sit	/sɪt/	ə	about	/əˈbaʊt/
e	ten	/ten/	eɪ	say	/seɪ/
æ	cat	/kæt/	əʊ	go	/gəʊ/
ɑː	father	/ˈfɑːðə(r)/	aɪ	five	/faɪv/
ɒ	got	/gɒt/	aʊ	now	/naʊ/
ɔː	saw	/sɔː/	ɔɪ	boy	/bɔɪ/
ʊ	put	/pʊt/	ɪə	near	/nɪə(r)/
u	situation	/ˌsɪtʃuˈeɪʃn/	eə	hair	/heə(r)/
uː	too	/tuː/	ʊə	pure	/pjʊə(r)/

Consonants

p	pen	/pen/	s	so	/səʊ/
b	bad	/bæd/	z	zoo	/zuː/
t	tea	/tiː/	ʃ	shoe	/ʃuː/
d	did	/dɪd/	ʒ	vision	/ˈvɪʒn/
k	cat	/kæt/	h	hat	/hæt/
g	got	/gɒt/	m	man	/mæn/
tʃ	chain	/tʃeɪn/	n	no	/nəʊ/
dʒ	jam	/dʒæm/	ŋ	sing	/sɪŋ/
f	fall	/fɔːl/	l	leg	/leg/
v	van	/væn/	r	red	/red/
θ	thin	/θɪn/	j	yes	/jes/
ð	this	/ðɪs/	w	wet	/wet/

(ˈ) shows the strong stress: it is in front of the part of the word that you say most strongly, for example **because** /bɪˈkɒz/.

(ˌ) shows a weaker stress. Some words have a part that is said with a weaker stress as well as a strong stress, for example **OK** /ˌəʊ ˈkeɪ/.

(r) at the end of a word means that in British English you say this sound only when the next word begins with a vowel sound. In American English, you always pronounce this 'r'.

Some words, for example **at** and **must**, have two pronunciations. We give the usual pronunciation first. The second pronunciation must be used when the word is stressed, and is also often used when the word is at the end of a sentence. For example:

This book is for /fə(r)/ *Lisa.*
Who is this book for? /fɔː(r)/